SONAR™ X2 Power!:
The Comprehensive Guide

Scott R. Garrigus

CENGAGE
Learning®

Professional • Technical • Reference

Australia • Brazil • Japan • Korea • Mexico • Singapore • Spain • United Kingdom • United States

CENGAGE
Learning

Professional • Technical • Reference

SONAR™ X2 Power!: The Comprehensive Guide
Scott R. Garrigus

Publisher and General Manager, Cengage Learning PTR:
Stacy L. Hiquet

Associate Director of Marketing:
Sarah Panella

Manager of Editorial Services:
Heather Talbot

Marketing Manager: Mark Hughes

Acquisition Editor: Orren Merton

Project and Copy Editor: Marta Justak

Technical Reviewer: Steve Thomas

Interior Layout Tech: MPS Limited

Cover Designer: Mike Tanamachi

Indexer: Sharon Shock

Proofreader: Megan Belanger

Library of Congress Control Number: 2013930066

ISBN-13: 978-1-285-19894-1

ISBN-10: 1-285-19894-8

Cengage Learning PTR

20 Channel Center Street

Boston, MA 02210

USA

Cengage Learning is a leading provider of customized learning solutions with office locations around the globe, including Singapore, the United Kingdom, Australia, Mexico, Brazil, and Japan. Locate your local office at: **international.cengage.com/region**

Cengage Learning products are represented in Canada by Nelson Education, Ltd.

For your lifelong learning solutions, visit **cengageptr.com**

Visit our corporate website at **cengage.com**

Printed in the United States of America
1 2 3 4 5 6 7 15 14 13

Acknowledgments

First and foremost, I want to thank everyone who purchased this book. For technical writers and those of us who write for niche markets, every sale counts, so I truly appreciate your support.

I also want to thank my long-time fans and all the people who take the time to visit my website, in addition to reading my ramblings in the DigiFreq pro audio and music technology newsletter. Also, special thanks to those of you who took the time to inform me about your thoughts regarding past editions of the book, as well as any errata that were found. I appreciate your help.

Thanks to Tara Zanett, Marcus Dandurand, Jimmy Landry, Andrew Rossa, Joshua Langberg, Seth Kellogg, Zyler Vega, Ben Blanchard, Noel Borthwick, and the rest of the Cakewalk team.

Thanks to Steve Thomas for all his great work on the tech edit and helping me find any errors in the material that I missed.

Thanks to Orren Merton, Stacy Hiquet and the rest of the Cengage Learning team.

Special thanks to Marta Justak for all her hard work in keeping this project together. Without her help, this book would not have been possible.

And finally, thanks to my family, friends, and to God for all that I have.

About the Author

Scott R. Garrigus is a professional musician, artist, and multimedia developer. He has a B.A. in music performance with an emphasis in sound recording technology from UMass, Lowell. His current endeavors include the following:

▷ Garrigus.com (**garrigus.com**): Official website of Scott R. Garrigus.

▷ Power Books (**garrigus.com?PowerBooks**): Author of the Cakewalk SONAR Power! book series and the Sony Sound Forge Power book series.

▷ ProAudioTutor (**garrigus.com?ProAudioTutor**): Author of the ProAudioTutor music technology tutorial series.

▷ DigiFreq (**garrigus.com?DigiFreq**): Publisher of the DigiFreq music technology newsletter and website, a free resource for professional musicians and home recording users.

▷ NewTechReview (**garrigus.com?NewTechReview**): Publisher of the NewTechReview consumer technology newsletter and website, a free resource for consumers and technology enthusiasts.

Contents

Introduction   xv

Chapter 1 Getting to Know SONAR X2   1

The Way SONAR Works 1

   Skylight and the Views 1

SONAR Producer vs. Studio vs. Essential 3

A Basic Studio Setup 3

   Computer 4

   Audio Interface (Sound Card) 4

   MIDI Interface 6

   MIDI Keyboard Controller 6

   Control Surface 6

   Microphone 6

   Speakers (Monitors) 7

Finding Help When You Need It 7

Chapter 2 SONAR X2 Customization   9

Organizing Files 9

Changing File Locations 9

   Customizing Audio Folders 10

   Per-Project Audio Folders 10

   The Picture Folder 10

Customizing the Workspace 11

   Colors 11

   The Control Bar 11

   Program and Plug-In Menus 12

   Working with Screensets 15

   X-Ray Windows 17

   Using Key Bindings 18

   Transforming the Track View 19

Customizing MIDI Settings 21

   Working with MIDI Devices 21

   Setting Global MIDI Options 22

   Understanding Instrument Definitions 22

Optimal Audio Settings 27

   Adjusting the Buffer Size Slider 27

   Setting Driver Mode 27

ASIO Drivers 28
Setting Queue Buffers and I/O Buffer Sizes 28
Read and Write Caching 29
Panning Laws 29

Chapter 3 Creating and Working with Projects — 31

Opening Projects 31
Opening in Recovery Mode 32
Finding Missing Audio Files 32
Creating a New Project 34
What's a Template? 35
Creating Your Own Template 35
Saving Your Project 40
Project File Types 40
Additional Saving Features 42

Chapter 4 Finding Your Way Around the SONAR Workspace — 45

The Now Time 45
Show Me the Now Time 45
Setting the Now Time 47
The Go Functions 49
Go-Time (G) 49
Go-From and Go-Thru (Shift+G) 49
Go-Beginning and Go-End (Ctrl+Home and Ctrl+End) 49
Go-Previous Measure and Go-Next Measure
(Ctrl+PgUp and Ctrl+PgDn) 50
Go-Previous Marker and Go-Next Marker (Ctrl+Shift+PgUp
and Ctrl+Shift+PgDn) 50
Markers, Oh My! 50
Make Your Mark(ers) 50
Editing the Markers 51
Navigating with Markers 52
Searching for Data 53

Chapter 5 Recording Audio and MIDI — 55

Preliminary Parameters 55
The Inspector 55
Metronome 55
MIDI Echo 57
MIDI Input Quantize 59
Sampling Rate and Bit Depth 60
Input Monitoring 60
Record Mode 61

Recording and Playback 62
Multiple Track Recording and Playback 64
Loop Recording 64
Punch Recording 66
Step Recording 67
Importing 70
    The Media Browser 70
    Importing from SONAR Project Files 72
    Importing MIDI Files, Project5, and Step Sequencer Patterns 73
    Importing Audio Files 73
    CD Ripping 74
Synchronization 74
    Synchronization Basics 74
    MIDI Sync 75
    SMPTE/MIDI Time Code 75

Chapter 6 The Basics of Editing

                                                                                                          79
The Global Editing Tools 79
    The Smart Tool and Other Tools 79
    The Edit Filter 80
    Snap to Grid Settings 81
Arranging with the Track View 82
    Dealing with Tracks 83
    Dealing with Clips 92
Using the Piano Roll View 107
    Working with Multiple Tracks 109
    Dealing with Notes 110
    Dealing with Drum Tracks 115
    Dealing with Controllers 120
    The Inline Piano Roll View 122
Using the Step Sequencer View 123
    Opening the Step Sequencer View 124
    Setting Up the Step Sequencer View 124
    Working with Notes 125
    Working with Controllers 128
    Step Recording Patterns 128
    Working with Step Sequencer Clips 129
Using the Event List View 130
    Opening the View 130
    Filtering Events 130
    Editing Events 131

Using the Tempo View 133

    Opening the View 133

    Editing Tempo Changes 133

    Using the Tempo Commands 134

Chapter 7 Advanced Audio and MIDI Editing   137

Advanced Data Selection 137

    Selecting a Range of Data by Time 137

    Selecting a Range of Data by Filter 138

    Some Selection Applications 138

Advanced Audio Editing 139

    Removing DC Offset 139

    Adjusting Audio Volume 140

    Getting Rid of Silence 144

    Playing It Backward 145

The Process Menu 146

    Deglitch 146

    Slide 146

    Nudge 147

    Quantize 147

    The Groove Quantize Feature 149

    Saving Groove Patterns 150

    The Find/Change Feature 151

    The Length Feature 153

    The Retrograde Feature 153

    The Transpose Feature 154

    The Scale Velocity Feature 154

    Fit to Time 154

    Fit Improvisation 155

Audio Snap 155

    AudioSnap Preparation 156

    Fix and Regroove (Quantize) 158

    Extract a Groove and MIDI 159

    Multitrack AudioSnap Alignment 160

Chapter 8 Using Soft Synths in Your Projects   163

Using Soft Synths 163

    The Insert Soft Synth Function and the Browser 165

    The Synth Rack 168

The Cakewalk TTS-1 173

    TTS-1 Basics 173

The Roland GrooveSynth 176
    Working with Synth Sounds. 176
    Working with Drum Kits 177
The Pentagon I 178
    Loading and Saving Programs 178
The PSYN II 179
    Loading and Saving Programs 180
The Cyclone. 181
    Cyclone Basics. 181
RXP REX Player. 185
    RXP Basics 186
TruePianos (Amber Module) 188
    Basic Interface. 188
    Global Options 189
    Advanced Interface 189
ReWire 190
SoundFonts 190
    Using the sfz SoundFont Player 190
Session Drummer 3 192
    Session Drummer 3 Basics 192
Dimension Pro 196
    Working with Programs 196
    Using Elements to Create Programs 197
    Using the Modulators Section 198
Rapture 199
    Working with Programs 200
    Using Elements to Create Programs 201
DropZone 205
    DropZone Basics 205
    Using Elements to Create Programs 206
z3ta+ 209
    Loading and Saving Programs 209
    Using z3ta+ as an Effects Processor 210
Cakewalk Sound Center 211
Studio Instruments 211
    Interface Basics 212
    SI-Bass Guitar 213
    SI-Drum Kit 213
    SI-Electric Piano 214
    SI-String Section 215

Chapter 9 Creating Music with Beats and Loops   217

Groove Clips 217
    Creating Groove Clips 217
    The Loop Construction View 219
    Saving Groove Clips 222
    Exporting MIDI Groove Clips 222
Working with Groove Clips 222
    Controlling Project Pitch 222
    Pitch Markers 223
The Matrix View 224
    Grabbing Files for the Grid 225
    Configuring Columns and Rows 226
    Controlling Cells and Columns 227
    Record a Matrix View Performance 228

Chapter 10 Mixing Music in SONAR   231

The Console View 231
    The MIDI Track Strips 232
    The Audio Track Strips 235
    The Buses 238
    The Mains 241
Configuring the Console and Track Views 242
    Strip Arrangement and Selection 242
    Number of Buses 242
    The Track Managers 242
    Show/Hide Console Components 243
    Changing the Meters 243

Chapter 11 Exploring Effects Plug-Ins   247

Offline or Real Time? 247
    Offline Processing 247
    Real-Time Processing 248
Audio Effects 253
    Equalization 254
    Delay 259
    Chorus 261
    Flanging and Phasing 262
    Reverberation 264
    Dynamics 271
    Changing Time and Pitch 280

Amplifier Simulation 287
Analog Tape Simulation – Cakewalk FX2 Tape Sim. 289
Analog Vacuum-Tube Simulation – TL-64 Tube Leveler 289
Other Effects 291
Sidechaining Effects 318
External Hardware Effects 320
MIDI Effects 321
Automatic Arpeggios 321
Chord Analysis 322
Echo Delay 322
MIDI Event Filter 323
Quantize 323
Transpose 324
Velocity 324

Chapter 12 Automation and Control Surfaces

    327

Taking Snapshots 327
Automating the Mix 328
Automation Write Modes 328
Automation Time Base 329
Recording Automation 330
Grouping 330
Quick Groups 331
Creating Permanent Groups 331
Ungrouping and Deleting Groups 332
Group Properties 332
Remote Control 333
Global Remote Control Support 334
Control Surface Setup 334
Edirol PCR-800 MIDI Controller 335
The Active Controller Technology (ACT) MIDI Controller 335
Where Am I? 339
Working with Envelopes 340
Automation Lanes 340
Creating and Editing Envelopes 341
Additional Envelope Editing 345
Automating Effects and Soft Synths 347
Automating Effects Parameters 347
Automating Soft Synth Parameters 347
The Next Steps 348

Chapter 13 Export Audio and Burn CDs   349

Preparing a Project for CD Audio 349
   Converting Your MIDI Tracks 349
   Exporting Your Audio Tracks 352
Burning CDs with SONAR 354

Chapter 14 Surround Sound with SONAR   357

Setting Up Your Studio 357
   Surround Sound Cards 357
   Surround Sound Monitors 358
Setting Up SONAR for Surround 360
   Surround Project Option 361
   Surround Sound Bussing 364
Surround Sound Mixing 365
   Surround Sound Panning 366
Surround Sound Effects 370
   Dedicated Surround Effects 370
   Using Stereo Effects in Surround 372
Exporting Your Surround Project 374
   Downmixing 375
   Exporting to Multichannel WAV or WMA 375
   Encoding and Burning 376

Chapter 15 Standard Music Notation via the Staff View   377

The Staff View 377
Changing the Layout 379
   Percussion Tracks 380
   Showing Pedal Events and Chord Grids 381
   Changing Text Fonts 381
   Rhythmic Appearance 382
Dealing with Notes 383
   Selecting 383
   Editing 384
   Drawing (or Adding) 385
   Erasing 385
   Scrub and Step Play 385
Dealing with Symbols and Lyrics 386
   Chord Symbols and Grids 386
   Expression Marks 389
   Hairpin Symbols 391

Pedal Marks 392

Lyrics 393

The Fretboard and Tablature 394

The Fret Pane 394

Tablature 395

Printing Your Music 398

Chapter 16 Studio Control with StudioWare and Sysx 401

System Exclusive 401

The Sysx View 401

Receiving System Exclusive Data 402

Sending System Exclusive Data 404

Editing Bank Data 406

Sharing with Friends 407

Introducing Studio Ware 407

The StudioWare View 408

Opening a StudioWare Panel 408

Taking a Snapshot 409

Recording Control Movements 411

Chapter 17 The Cakewalk Application Language (CAL)   413

What Is CAL? 413

Running a CAL Program 414

The CAL Files 414

Dominant 7th Chord.CAL 414

Other Chord.CAL Programs 415

Random Time.CAL 415

Scale Velocity.CAL 416

Split Channel to Tracks.CAL 416

Split Note to Tracks.CAL 417

Thin Controller Data.CAL 418

Other Thin.CAL Programs 419

Viewing CAL Programs 419

Introduction to CAL Programming 420

The `include` Function 421

Variables 422

User Input 422

The `forEachEvent` Function 422

Conditions 422

Arithmetic 423

Master Presets 423
CAL Conclusion 425

Chapter 18 Audio for Video with SONAR 427
Importing Video Files 427
Exporting Video Files 430
Exporting Audio Files 431
    Audio File Formats 431
    Exporting to Windows Media 434
    Exporting to MP3 435

Index   **439**

Introduction

This is the first book on the market that deals exclusively with Cakewalk's SONAR X2. You can find other Cakewalk-related and generic books about using computers to create and record music that might provide a small amount of information about SONAR X2, but none of them provides complete coverage of the product. Of course, SONAR X2 comes with an excellent manual, but like most other manuals, it is meant only as a feature guide.

Instead of simply describing the features of the program and how they work, I'm going to dig deep down into the software and show you exactly how to use the product with step-by-step examples and exercises that will help make your composing and recording sessions run more smoothly. I'll explain the available features, and I'll do it in a manner you can understand and use right away.

With SONAR X1, Cakewalk redesigned the user interface and created an entirely new workflow. In SONAR X2, Cakewalk has built upon the foundation of X1 by adding new features and refining the workflow even more. With these changes, will it be difficult to get up and running with the new version? No. This *SONAR X2 Power!* book provides the information you need to get comfortable with SONAR X2. If you are a new SONAR user, I'll show you each of the features with information on what they are, why you need them, and how to use them. If you are a seasoned SONAR user, I'll let you know the differences between version X1 and X2. I will also cover what you need to know about the refined workflow. And since SONAR X2 comes in three different flavors (Producer, Studio, and Essential), I will also include information about what features are found in each.

What You Need to Begin

I'm going to assume that SONAR is installed on your computer and that you know how to start the program. In addition, you should have at least skimmed through the user's guide that comes with the software, and you should have all your external audio and MIDI gear set up already. I'm also going to assume that you know how to use your mouse for clicking, dragging, double-clicking, right-clicking, and so on. You also should know how to work with basic Windows features (such as Windows Explorer), and you should have access to the Internet.

In addition, a basic knowledge of music, MIDI, and digital audio concepts is required to use SONAR. Before going any further, I would recommend that you look at some of the following resources if you are just getting started with computer-based music creation:

> ▷ *Desktop Music Handbook:* **garrigus.com?DesktopMusic**
> ▷ *MIDI Power!:* **garrigus.com?MIDIPower**
> ▷ *The MIDI Manual:* **garrigus.com?MIDIManual**
> ▷ *Audio Made Easy:* **garrigus.com?AudioMadeEasy**

Conventions Used in This Book

Throughout this book, you'll find a sort of shorthand to describe the various actions you need to take in order to perform tasks. Here is what you need to know before reading any further:

▷ **Clicking:** Whenever I say to click [*item*], it means to use the left mouse button to click the mentioned item. I may also tell you to Ctrl+click, Shift+click, or Alt+click an item, which means you need to hold the specific PC keyboard key while left-clicking the item. Right-clicking will be mentioned explicitly.

▷ **Choosing:** Whenever I say to choose *item > item*, it means to left-click on the specified SONAR menus. Most of the time, I will be talking about SONAR's main menu, but each view also has its own menu, so I will mention a specific menu when necessary.

▷ **Pressing:** Whenever I say to press *item* or press *item+item*, it means to press the specified key or key+key on your keyboard.

▷ **Preferences:** Whenever I mention SONAR's Preferences dialog box, I'm going to assume that you have the Advanced option activated. To do this, start SONAR and choose Edit > Preferences from the main menu. In the dialog box, choose the Advanced option, which is located at the bottom left. Click OK.

▷ **Website Links:** Whenever I provide a website link, type in exactly what is shown in **bold** and don't include any punctuation that may surround the link, such as a link to my website (**garrigus.com?Sonar EventInspector**). For that link, you would type **garrigus.com?SonarEventInspector** without including the parentheses or period.

Lastly, be sure to sign up for my free pro audio and home recording newsletter (**garrigus.com?DigiFreq**) for additional SONAR articles, book updates, and free video tutorials. Thanks, and I hope you enjoy the book!

Getting to Know SONAR X2

B ECAUSE SONAR X2 IS SUCH A POWERFUL APPLICATION, you can use it for a variety of different tasks, including composing music, developing computer game music and sounds, producing compact discs, creating audio for the Web, and even scoring films and videos. SONAR provides a number of features to support all these endeavors and more. As a matter of fact, you can use SONAR as the central piece of software in your studio because it controls all your music gear from your computer via on-screen control panels. No matter which way you decide to use SONAR, you'll find plenty of flexibility and power in the tools provided.

The Way SONAR Works

In SONAR, all your music data for a single body of work is organized as a project. A project can be anything from a Top 40 song or a 30-second radio spot to a full-length symphonic score, such as a movie soundtrack. Along with the music data, all of SONAR's settings for a single work are stored in the project. A project is saved on disk as a single file with a .CWP or .CWB file extension. The difference between the two file types is that a work (.CWP) file stores only MIDI data and project settings, and it references external audio files. A bundle (.CWB) file includes any audio data within the file itself so that all project data is stored in a single file.

The music data within a project is organized into units called *tracks*, *clips*, and *events*. *Events*, which are the smallest units, consist of single pieces of data, such as one note played on a MIDI keyboard. *Clips* are groups of events. They can be anything from a simple MIDI melody to an entire vocal performance recorded as audio. *Tracks* are used to store clips. For example, a pop song project might contain seven tracks of music data—six for the instruments and one for the vocal performance. Each track can contain any number of clips that might represent one long performance or different parts of a performance. SONAR Producer and SONAR Studio give you unlimited tracks. The only limitations are the speed of your CPU and hard drive and the amount of memory (RAM) you have in your computer.

Skylight and the Views

Dubbed *Skylight*, SONAR's GUI (graphical user interface) is comprised of a number of different components that allow you to work with the data in a project. The most prominent components are the Track view, the MultiDock, the Inspector, the Browser, and the Control Bar (see Figure 1.1).

Track View

Control Bar

Inspector

Browser

MultiDock

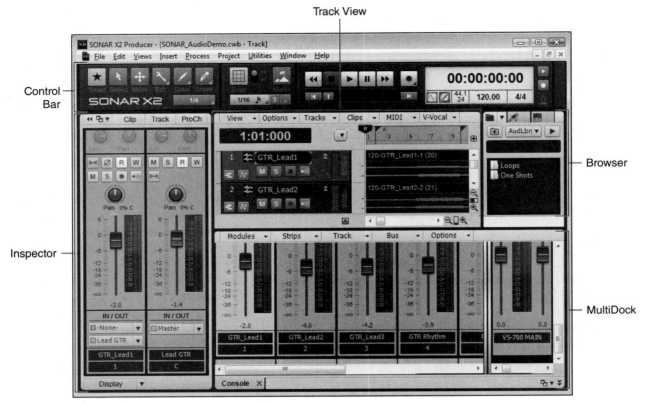

Figure 1.1 SONAR's Skylight interface streamlines your project work.
Source: Cakewalk®, Inc.

The Track View and the Secondary Views

To record, edit, and mix music in a SONAR project, you need to use views—windows that allow you to see and manipulate your music in a variety of ways. The most important is the Track view. In this window, you can see all the tracks that are available in a project. You also can view and edit all the basic track settings, as well as all the clips contained in each track. I'll talk about the Track view extensively in a number of different chapters.

In addition to the Track view, there are a number of secondary views that provide specialized functions:

▷ **Staff.** The Staff view lets you edit your music as standard notation. By selecting one or more MIDI tracks in the Track view and opening the Staff view, you can see your music just as if it were notes on a printed page. See Chapter 15.

▷ **Piano Roll.** Although the Staff view is great for traditional music editing, it doesn't access expressive MIDI data, such as note velocity or pitch bend controller messages. For that data, you can use the Piano Roll view. This view displays notes as they might appear on a player-piano roll. See Chapter 6.

▷ **Event List.** The Event List view shows individual events in a track (or the entire project) as special keywords and numbers in a list. Using this view is similar to looking at the raw MIDI data that is recorded from your MIDI keyboard or controller. You can edit the characteristics of single notes and MIDI controller messages by typing in data. See Chapter 6.

▷ **Loop Construction.** The Loop Construction view gives you an easy way to create your own sample loops and beats. You can use these loops, which are digital audio clips designed to be played over and over, to construct entire songs. See Chapter 9.

▷ **Console.** When you're ready to mix all your MIDI and audio tracks down to a single stereo file, you can use the Console view. This tool is made to look and function like a real recording studio mixing console. And just like a real mixing console, you can monitor volume levels via on-screen meters, as well as mute and solo individual tracks or groups of tracks. See Chapter 10.

The MultiDock

To keep all the views from cluttering up your workspace, SONAR provides the MultiDock. In this single window, you can dock multiple views and then access the views via the MultiDock's tabbed interface. In addition, you can float the MultiDock for even more flexible positioning, such as on a second PC screen. For previous SONAR users, the MultiDock takes the place of the tabbed interface in the Track view. See Chapter 2.

The Inspector

A smooth session workflow requires that you have easy access to the most frequently used parameters—that is the purpose of SONAR's Inspector. Divided into the Properties Inspector and Track Inspector, SONAR's Inspector lets you quickly view and edit parameters for selected clips and tracks. It also gives you access to the ProChannel effects for each track. For previous SONAR users, the Inspector replaces the Clip Properties and Track Properties dialog boxes. See Chapters 3, 5, 6, and 11.

The Browser

When working on a project, you also need organized access to content such as audio, MIDI, and video files. All content files supported by SONAR can be retrieved via the Browser. Plus, with drag-and-drop support, you can import almost anything into a project just by dragging—even entire projects. In addition, the Browser lets you organize the plug-ins installed on your system and manage all the software synths in a project. For previous SONAR users, the Browser takes the place of the Loop Explorer and the Synth Rack. See Chapters 5, 6, 8, and 11.

The Control Bar

Acting as a main control area, SONAR's Control Bar accesses all of the global parameters and tools pertaining to the entire application. The Control Bar is divided into various modules that group together like parameters, including those for transport control, global tool selection, performance indication, and more. For previous SONAR users, the Control Bar replaces all the toolbars that are no longer available. As with the Track view, I'll talk about the Control Bar extensively in a number of different chapters.

SONAR Producer vs. Studio vs. Essential

SONAR comes in three editions: Producer, Studio, and Essential. Producer gives you everything you need to compose, record, edit, produce, mix, and master your music. Studio comes in a close second, providing most of the features in Producer, but some of the more professional options, such as the ProChannel, mastering effects, various software synths (and more), are not included. Essential is the least expensive of the three, but also the most limited. In addition to only running as a 32-bit application (although it can still be used under Windows 64-bit), Essential lacks many of the main features of SONAR and even has restrictions. Go to **www.cakewalk.com/products/sonar/ versions.aspx** for a comparison of the three SONAR editions. I will also be providing indications as to which features are available in which versions throughout the book.

A Basic Studio Setup

Over the years, I've built up quite an arsenal of tools that currently reside in my home studio. But you don't need a ton of gizmos and gadgets to produce great music. If I were to scale down my setup to include only the basics, I'd be left with everything I need to compose and record my tunes with SONAR.

Computer

Other than SONAR itself, a basic studio revolves around one main component—your PC. If you already have a PC, be sure to check it against Cakewalk's system requirements for SONAR (**www.cakewalk.com/products/SONAR/X2-Producer**).

If your system matches (or exceeds) the minimum system requirements, you should be all set to run SONAR. If not, then you should consider either upgrading or purchasing a new system. If you decide to go with a new system, you might want to think about building it yourself or picking out the components and having it built for you. It's not that a generic Gateway or Dell PC won't do, but they are not really optimized for audio work.

For my current DAW (Digital Audio Workstation), I decided to get a system that was purposely built for audio—a Sweetwater Creation Station rackXT.

CREATION STATION DETAILS: To learn more about my Creation Station DAW, go to **garrigus.com?rackXT** to read information, watch videos, and ask any questions you may have.

OPTIMIZE YOUR AUDIO PC: One of the reasons that many people can get away with using a less powerful system is that they have optimized it for audio work. There are a number of things you can do to your PC that will make it run more efficiently for the purposes of making music. These include making adjustments to the system itself, as well as to the Windows OS. If you'd like more information about how to optimize your audio PC, go to **www.digifreq.com/digifreq/article.asp?ID=14** to check out my feature article entitled "Optimize Your Audio PC." Also, go to **www.digifreq.com/digifreq/articles.asp** for more great articles.

Audio Interface (Sound Card)

The most important thing to consider when purchasing an audio interface for use with SONAR is whether there are WDM or ASIO drivers available for the card. You'll need to get in touch with the manufacturer of the card to verify this. Why is it so important? Because SONAR supports a Microsoft technology called *Windows Driver Model* (WDM) and a Steinberg technology called *Audio Stream Input Output* (ASIO). If you have a sound card that has WDM or ASIO drivers, SONAR will give you much better performance in terms of audio latency. Basically, latency is a form of audio delay that occurs when a software program such as SONAR can't communicate with your audio interface fast enough while processing audio data, which results in an audible delay. This is usually noticeable only with features that use real-time processing. In SONAR, these include input monitoring and real-time soft synth performance.

THE CAKEWALK AUDIO HARDWARE GUIDE: Go to **www.cakewalk.com/support/kb/reader.aspx/2007013101** for a list of audio interfaces recommended by Cakewalk.

Of course, there are many other things to consider when choosing a particular card. Common opinion is that a PCI-based interface provides the best performance, but today's FireWire and USB interfaces usually perform just as well. It really depends on the interface and how well the drivers are written. You should also be aware of the types of connections that audio interfaces supply. The typical audio interface provides a number of different audio inputs and outputs, including line level, microphone level, and speaker. Line-level inputs and outputs are used to transfer sound from CD players, radios, electronic keyboards, or any other standard audio device. Microphones generate a very low audio level by themselves, so they need a special input of their own, which is connected to an internal preamplifier on the interface. Speakers also need their own special connector with a built-in amplifier to produce a decent amount of volume.

Many audio interfaces also offer digital inputs and outputs. These special connectors let you attach the interface directly to compatible devices such as some CD players and DAT (*Digital Audio Tape*) decks. Using these connections gives you the best possible sound because audio signals stay in the digital domain and don't need to be converted into analog signals. In addition, connectors come in a variety of forms. Low-cost interfaces usually provide the same 1/8-inch jacks used for headphones on boom boxes. For better quality, there are 1/4-inch, RCA, or XLR jacks. Connections can also be balanced or unbalanced. Balanced connections provide shielding to protect the audio signal against RFI (*Radio Frequency Interference*). Unbalanced connections don't provide any type of protection.

If you want to be able to record more than one audio track at once, you'll need an interface with multiple audio connections. Most average interfaces internally mix all of their audio sources down to one stereo signal, but higher-end interfaces let you record each device separately on its own discrete stereo channel. This capability is much more desirable in a music recording studio, but not everyone needs it.

A good quality audio signal is something that everybody desires. During recording, the sampling rate plays a big part in the quality of the audio signal. Suffice it to say, the higher the sampling rate that an audio interface can handle, the better the sound quality. The sampling rate of a CD is 44.1kHz (44,100 samples per second); all interfaces on the market support this. Professional interfaces can hit 96kHz or higher.

Bit resolution is also a factor in determining digital sound quality. The more bits you have to represent your signal, the better it will sound. The CD standard is 16 bits, which is supported by all interfaces. Most cards also go up to 24 bits.

Two other measurements you need to look for are signal-to-noise ratio and frequency response. As with the other measurements mentioned earlier, the higher, the better. Since all electronic devices produce some amount of noise, the signal-to-noise ratio of an audio interface tells you how much higher the signal strength is compared to the amount of internal noise made by the interface. The greater the number, the quieter the interface will be. A good signal-to-noise measurement is about 90dB or higher. Frequency response is actually a range of numbers, which is based on the capabilities of human hearing. The frequency response of human hearing is approximately 20Hz to 20kHz. A good sound card will encompass at least that range, maybe even more.

What do I use? I actually have a number of different interfaces. In the studio, I use the Cakewalk V-Studio 700 System. This system is a combination control surface and audio/MIDI interface, which basically provides a professional studio setup in one package (not including the computer).

SCOTT'S V-STUDIO 700 SETUP: Go to **garrigus.com?VStudio700** for more information about the V-Studio 700 and about how I'm using it in my home studio. Also, check out **garrigus.com? VStudio700eBook** to download a free copy of my *Cakewalk V-Studio 700: A Closer Look eBook*.

I also use the Saffire PRO 40 from Focusrite (**digifreq.com?SaffirePRO40**). This is a FireWire-based interface that provides eight built-in mic/instrument pre-amps, digital I/O, a built-in MIDI interface, and more. I really like this box a lot because I can use it anywhere and not have to fuss with a PCI card installation. You can monitor it from either software or hardware, and it provides a stand-alone mode so that it can be used without a computer. It also works nicely with SONAR. I mainly use the PRO 40 with my laptop PC for a mobile studio setup.

MIDI Interface

If you have any external MIDI devices (like a MIDI keyboard), then you'll need a MIDI interface for your computer. If you have a simple setup with only one MIDI keyboard, then you can easily get away with a simple single- or double-port MIDI interface. The best way to go here is to get a USB-based interface. It will be easy to install (just plug it in), and it won't take up an IRQ or PCI slot inside your computer. Also, be sure that the interface has compatible drivers (depending on what Windows OS you are using). Bad drivers can cause problems. Other than that, the only major difference between interfaces is the number of ports they provide. If you have many external MIDI devices, it's best to connect each device to its own dedicated MIDI port. I'm currently using the MIDI interface(s) built into the Cakewalk V-Studio 700 and the Focusrite Saffire PRO 40. This is nice because I don't need two separate devices for audio and MIDI. Many audio interfaces now double as a MIDI interface and include at least one MIDI port.

MIDI Keyboard Controller

If you plan to record some of your musical tracks as MIDI data (using either external MIDI synths or software synths), you'll need some type of MIDI controller for your performance. Most people opt for a MIDI keyboard since it is the most popular type of controller and almost anyone can learn to play keyboard. I currently use a number of different keyboards—one with weighted keys (for piano performances) and one with nonweighted keys (for synth, organ, and other performances). The weighted keyboard is the VX8 from CME (**digifreq.com?CMEVX8**). The nonweighted keyboard is the Edirol PCR-800. Unfortunately, Roland no longer makes the PCR keyboards, but they have a new line of A-PRO MIDI Keyboard Controllers (**digifreq.com?CakewalkKeyboard**). Cakewalk has made sure that the A-PRO keyboards work especially well with SONAR. In addition, the A-PRO keyboards can be used as control surfaces to control SONAR via built-in buttons, knobs, and sliders; however, you may still need an additional control surface for other tasks.

Control Surface

While not an absolute necessity, a control surface can save you a lot of time and mouse maneuvers. A control surface is a MIDI device that provides real buttons, knobs, and sliders that can be used to control the different software-based parameters that you normally adjust with your mouse on your computer screen. A control surface can be used for record/playback transport control, editing, and even mixing. As I mentioned earlier, I'm using the Cakewalk V-Studio 700 System (**garrigus.com?VStudio700**), which includes a professional control surface that is specifically made to be integrated with SONAR. In addition, I use the AlphaTrack from Frontier Design Group with my laptop PC. It provides a touch-sensitive, high-resolution, motorized fader and three touch-sensitive encoder knobs along with a number of other controls that make mixing in SONAR so much easier when working in a mobile studio situation. Unfortunately, the AlphaTrack is no longer available, but the PreSonus FaderPort is a nice alternative (**digifreq.com?FaderPort**).

Microphone

If you plan to do any acoustic recording (vocals, acoustic guitar, and so on), you'll need a good microphone. There are literally hundreds of microphones on the market, and entire books have been written on the subject, so I won't go into great detail here. Basically, the microphone you choose depends on the application. I needed a good vocal mic, but not something that was going to put me in the poor house. While I would have loved to get a Neumann U87 (one of the best), there was no way I could afford one. So luckily, Shure came to my rescue with their KSM27. It's a great vocal mic that isn't too expensive. I like the fact that it can also be used for other applications in a pinch.

Unfortunately, the KSM27 is no longer available, but Shure still provides an entire line of KSM model microphones. However, what's right for me might not be right for you, so I've rounded up a number of online resources for you to educate yourself on the subject of microphones:

> ▷ Music Technology Article Index: **www.digifreq.com/digifreq/articles.asp**
> ▷ Microphone University: **www.dpamicrophones.com/en/Mic-University.aspx**
> ▷ A Brief Guide to Microphones: **www.audio-technica.com/cms/site/9904525cd25e0d8d/index.html**
> ▷ A Brief Guide to Microphone Selection: **www.audio-technica.com/cms/site/7cadf671dea2c9e0/index.html**

Speakers (Monitors)

You also need to be able to hear the music you're recording, so you'll need a good set of speakers (or *monitors*, as they're called in the professional audio world). Like microphones, there are literally hundreds of different monitors on the market. For home studio purposes, you'll probably want to get yourself a good pair of active nearfield monitors. They're called *active* because they come with a built-in amplifier, which saves you from having to buy an external amp and match it to your monitors. They're called *nearfield* because you listen to them at a fairly close distance (about four feet). This lets you set up your home studio in just about any space you can find because you don't have to acoustically treat the room, at least not professionally.

> **CREATING THE RIGHT RECORDING ENVIRONMENT:** For some tips about how to set up your home studio space for better recording, go to **www.digifreq.com/digifreq/article.asp?ID=36** to check out my feature article entitled "Creating the Right Recording Environment."

You'll find a wide variety of monitors available, but I'm currently having fun with the VXT8 monitors from KRK Systems (**digifreq.com?KRK**). These are a pair of active nearfield monitors that really deliver great sound. However, what I like might not be what you like, so I've included a couple of online resources to help you choose the right monitors for you.

> ▷ Music Technology Article Index: **www.digifreq.com/digifreq/articles.asp**
> ▷ eCoustics.com Speaker Articles: **www.ecoustics.com/Home/Home_Audio/Speakers/Speaker_Articles/**

Finding Help When You Need It

Cakewalk provides a number of ways for you to find help when you're having a problem with SONAR. The two most obvious places to look are the user's guide and the SONAR Help file. Actually, these two sources contain basically the same information, but with the Help file, you can perform a search to find something really specific. At the first sign of trouble, you should go through the troubleshooting information. If you can't find an answer to your problem there, you can pay a visit to the Cakewalk website.

> **SONAR OFFLINE HELP:** By default, SONAR uses an online version of its Help file. This means that when you choose SONAR's Help menu, your Web browser will automatically launch and display help via the Cakewalk website. However, an offline version of help still exists. If you would rather use that, choose Edit > Preferences (P) and choose File – Advanced. Then activate the Always Use Offline Help option.

The SONAR X2 support site (**www.cakewalk.com/Support/product.aspx/SONAR-X2**) contains a ton of helpful information, including FAQs and technical documents that provide details on a number of Cakewalk-related topics. You can also find great information at the DigiFreq forums (**www.digifreq.com/digifreq/discuss/default.asp**). I have a special section set up where you can trade tips, advice, and information with other Cakewalk users. Many times, you'll find that someone has had the same problem you're having and has already found a solution. Isn't sharing great?

FREE MUSIC TECHNOLOGY NEWSLETTER: Be sure to sign up for a free subscription to my DigiFreq music technology newsletter. DigiFreq is a monthly email newsletter that teaches you more about music technology. It provides free news, articles, reviews, tips, and tutorials for home recording and professional musicians. By applying for your own free subscription, you can learn all about the latest music product releases, read straightforward reviews, explore related Web resources, and have a chance to win free products from brand-name manufacturers. Go to **digifreq.com?DigiFreq** to get your free subscription.

You can also contact Cakewalk Technical Support directly. You can either email your questions or call them on the phone. Contact information can be found at: **www.cakewalk.com/support/contact/default.aspx**. But remember, in order to receive technical support, you have to be a registered user. If you call or send email, you'll be asked for your serial number.

PROAUDIOTUTOR: In addition to all those resources, you can find pro audio and music technology training in the form of books, software, and video tutorials at my ProAudioTutor website (**garrigus.com/?ProAudioTutor**). You can also contact me directly by going to **www.garrigus.com** and using the **Contact** link to get in touch via email or the postal service.

SONAR X2 Customization

A LTHOUGH WE ALL MAY BE SONAR users, that doesn't mean we like to work with the product in exactly the same way. I have my way of doing things, and you probably have your own way. Luckily, SONAR provides a number of settings so you can make the program conform to your way of working.

Organizing Files

As you work with SONAR, you'll deal with many different types of files. These include project files, audio files, StudioWare files, CAL files, and so on. To keep things organized, SONAR specifies different disk locations for storing each file type. Initially, SONAR stores most of the files in its Cakewalk Content folder on your hard drive, but that doesn't mean they have to stay there.

If you want to get the best performance from your DAW PC, I suggest you have a basic three–hard drive configuration. Use one drive (the system or C drive) to store SONAR and all your other software and plug-ins. Also, keep SONAR's Picture Cache folder on the C drive (more on this later). Use a second drive to store all your project files, audio files, and content files. And use a third drive for streaming software synth sample libraries (see Chapter 8).

Changing File Locations

During installation, SONAR asks where you would like to put the Cakewalk Content folder. I recommend putting it on your second drive. However, if you didn't do that, you can still specify your own content file locations. Press P and choose File – Folder Locations in the Preferences dialog box. Shown there is a list of all the different content file types, along with their default folder locations. Personally, I recommend putting all of these on a second hard drive in a main folder called *Cakewalk Content* with subfolders for each different type of file. By default, SONAR installs these files in C:\Cakewalk Content on your system. You can do this by simply cutting and pasting (or dragging and dropping the files) with Windows Explorer. The file types that correspond to each of the locations shown in the dialog box are as follows:

> Project Files—.CWP (Work), .CWB (Bundle), and .MID (MIDI) files.
> Templates—.CWT files.
> Track Templates—.CWX files.
> Track Icons—.BMP files.
> CAL Files—.CAL files.
> Wave Files—All audio file types supported by SONAR. See a list by clicking the Files of Type menu in the File > Import > Audio dialog box.
> Video Files—.AVI, .MPG, and .MOV files.
> Sysx Files—MIDI System Exclusive (.SYX) files.
> Play List—SONAR Play List (.SET) files.

▷ Groove Quantize—SONAR Groove Quantize (.GRV) files.
▷ StudioWare—SONAR StudioWare (.CakewalkStudioWare) files.
▷ Drum Maps—SONAR Drum Map (.MAP) files.
▷ Plug-in Layouts—SONAR Plug-in Layout (.PGL) files.
▷ Step Sequences—SONAR Step Sequencer Pattern (.SST) files.
▷ FX Chain Presets—SONAR FX Chain Preset (.FXC) files.

After you've finished moving the files to their new locations, simply type the new locations into the fields in the dialog box. You can also browse for the locations using the ellipsis buttons at the end of each field.

Customizing Audio Folders

Although I've already talked about sample loops and audio files that you can import into your projects, SONAR has to deal with additional audio files that represent the audio tracks that you record directly into SONAR. SONAR stores the data for these audio tracks in a special folder on your hard drive. By default, this folder is located at C:\Cakewalk Projects\Audio Data. As I mentioned earlier, for better performance, it's best to keep audio files on a dedicated hard drive. To change the location of your audio data folder, follow these steps:

1. Press P and choose File – Audio Data in the Preferences dialog box.
2. In the Global Audio Folder parameter, type the new location for your audio data folder. You can also click the ellipsis button to the right of the parameter to browse for a new location.
3. By default, whenever you import an audio file into a project, SONAR will automatically make a copy of that file and place it in your audio data folder. If you don't want SONAR to do this, then deactivate the Always Copy Imported Audio Files option. Click OK.

> **ALWAYS COPY IMPORTED AUDIO FILES:** If your audio folder is located on the same hard drive as the audio you are importing, you can save drive space by deactivating the Always Copy Imported Audio Files option. But if your audio folder is located on a different drive, you should keep this option activated. I recommend this because if you are using a second hard drive to store your audio data, you don't want SONAR to have to look for your imported audio in a different location on a different drive. This will decrease playback and recording efficiency.

Per-Project Audio Folders

Instead of storing all the audio data from all your projects in the same folder, you can use a different folder for each project, if you'd like. These folders are called *per-project audio folders*. I recommend using this option because all the data for each project is then stored in its own separate location, which makes it easy to find if you want to access the audio files associated with a project (perhaps for editing in a different software application). To set up SONAR for per-project audio folders, activate the Use Per-Project Audio Folders option in the File – Audio Data section of the Preferences dialog box. Now when you create a new project, you will be able to specify a folder name for it.

The Picture Folder

Whenever you record audio data using SONAR, the program creates temporary picture files for the audio data in your project. These files hold "drawings" of the audio waveforms. Initially, these picture files are stored in the C:\Cakewalk Picture Cache folder on your hard drive. I recommend leaving it there, but you can change this location by editing the Picture Folder field in the File – Audio Data section of the Preferences dialog box.

Customizing the Workspace

Not only can you change the way SONAR handles files, but you also can change the way SONAR looks and responds to your commands. By customizing the SONAR workspace, you can increase your efficiency with the program and make it more comfortable to use. You can adjust the colors, Control Bar, plug-in menus, window locations, keyboard shortcuts, and Track view controls.

Colors

You can change the colors of many of the elements in the SONAR workspace, but not all. Some of the colors are permanently set. As usual, SONAR ships with a default set of colors. However, you might find a different set of colors more pleasant to work with, or maybe you can see some colors better than others. Changing the colors SONAR uses is simple—just follow these steps:

1. Press P and choose Customization – Colors in the Preferences dialog box.
2. Using the Color Category list, choose the work area in SONAR for which you would like to change colors.
3. In the Screen Element list, select the element(s) you want to change. Ctrl-click to select multiple elements.
4. Next, select how you want the element(s) to look by choosing a color from the right side of the dialog box. You can have the color of the element follow the color of some of the default Windows element colors, or you can use a specific color.
5. You also can change the background wallpaper of the SONAR workspace by choosing one of the options at the bottom of the dialog box. If you choose the Custom option, you can even load your own Windows bitmap (.BMP) file for display. Loading your own file is not particularly useful, but it can be fun.
6. If you want SONAR to use the same color settings every time you run the program, make sure the Save Changes for Next Session option is activated.
7. If you'd like to set up a number of different color schemes, you can save your settings as a Preset. Just type a name for the current color settings in the Presets field (at the top of the dialog) and click the Save button (the button with the picture of a floppy disk). Then you can change color schemes quickly by simply choosing a Preset.
8. When you've finished making your changes, click OK.
9. Some color changes won't take effect immediately, so if it looks like the element(s) didn't change to your selected colors, save your project and exit SONAR. Then restart SONAR.

You can also share your color sets with others using the Import Colors and Export Colors buttons at the bottom of the dialog box.

The Control Bar

Instead of having multiple toolbars, SONAR has one global toolbar called the *Control Bar*. Located, by default, at the top of the SONAR workspace, the Control Bar gives you quick access to many of SONAR's major functions. These functions are grouped into individual modules, which represent all of the different aspects of SONAR's use, such as transport control, data selection/editing, recording/playback, and more. I will be talking more about the individual modules and their functions throughout the book.

Changing Control Bar Position

You can dock the Control Bar at the top or bottom of the workspace by dragging and dropping it. If you drop the Control Bar anywhere within the workspace, it will become a floating window. This is useful if you have more than one PC screen in your studio and you'd like to keep the Control Bar on one screen while putting parts of the interface on the other. You can also right-click on the Control Bar background to use a menu for docking and floating. If the Control Bar is too big to fit all the modules on your screen, you'll need to hide some modules. You cannot resize the Control Bar even when it is a floating window.

Changing Control Bar Appearance

To show/hide the Control Bar, choose Views > Control Bar or press C. In addition, you can change the Control Bar configuration by moving, showing, or hiding its individual modules. To show/hide modules, right-click the Control Bar background and add/remove check marks next to the modules listed in the menu. To move a module within the Control Bar, drag the module's gripper (see Figure 2.1) left or right. Also, in case you're wondering, you cannot move individual modules outside of the Control Bar.

Figure 2.1 Drag the left side (gripper) of a module to move it within the Control Bar.
Source: Cakewalk®, Inc.

Program and Plug-In Menus

In SONAR versions 1 through 8.5, the main menu remained basically the same, and you could also customize those menus—but no longer.

Main Menu and View Menus

Beginning with SONAR X1, not only has the main menu changed, but also many of the menu items have been moved and now reside as menus in each of the individual views. The individual view menus are located at the top of each view and are accessed like any other Windows application menu. I'll be talking more about the menus throughout the book, but here are some of the major main menu modifications:

> ▷ File—This menu has remained the same.
> ▷ Edit—Many of the edit functions have been moved to the Track view menu.
> ▷ Views—New program components have been added here, but all previous views are still listed here as well.
> ▷ Insert—Most functions are still here, but some have been moved to a new Project menu.
> ▷ Process—Any processing functions related specifically to clips and tracks have been moved to the Track view menu.
> ▷ Project—This is a new menu that contains global project-related functions.
> ▷ Utilities—Renamed from the previous Tools menu but otherwise the same.
> ▷ Window and Help—Both of these menus are basically the same.
> ▷ Transport and Go (Removed)—The functions from the previous Transport and Go menus are now accessed via the Transport and Markers modules of the Control Bar.
> ▷ Tracks (Removed)—The functions from this menu have been moved to the Track view menu.

Lastly, you can no longer customize the main menu, and the view menus cannot be customized, either. You can, however, customize SONAR's plug-in menus.

Customizing Plug-In Menus

Instead of having long, confusing menus listing all your effects and soft synth plug-ins, you can now have organized menus that provide quicker and easier access. You can create and edit menu layouts for MIDI effects, audio effects, and soft synths. The procedure for editing these menus is the same, but the menus are accessed via different areas of SONAR. One way is to right-click a clip in the Track view and use either the Insert Effect or Process Effect menu to access the Plug-in Layouts menu located at the top of the last submenu. In addition, you can click the PlugIns tab of SONAR's Browser. Just below the PlugIns tab are buttons to display audio, MIDI, synth, and ReWire plug-in menus. To change the current menu layout, click the down-arrow next to the PlugIns tab and choose a new layout (see Figure 2.2). Choosing Manage Layouts opens the Cakewalk Plug-in Manager.

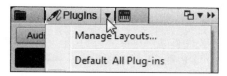

Figure 2.2 Access plug-in menus via the PlugIns tab of SONAR's Browser.
Source: Cakewalk®, Inc.

To show you how to edit plug-in menu layouts, let me walk you through an example of how I like to organize the audio effects plug-ins that come with SONAR. Instead of one long list of audio effects, I like to organize my plug-ins by category. Here's how:

1. In addition to the Browser, you can choose Utilities > Cakewalk Plug-in Manager to customize plug-in layouts.
2. In the upper-right corner of the window (where it says Plug-in Menu Layouts), click the New button (the first one from left to right) to create a blank layout. Then type a new name for the layout. For this example, let's call it AudioFX Categories.
3. Use the New Folder button to create the following folders: Chorus, EQ, Delay, Flanger, Compressor, Reverb, Spectrum Analysis, Mastering, Simulation, Pitch, MultiFX, and Surround.
4. To put the folders in alphabetical order, click Sort All.
5. In the Plug-in Categories list, select the DirectX Audio Effects (DX) option.
6. In the Registered Plug-ins list, select the following effects (hold down Ctrl on your computer keyboard to make multiple selections): Cakewalk Multivoice Chorus/Flanger and Sonitus:fx Modulator. Select the Chorus folder you created earlier and click Add Plug-in to add these effects to the folder.

> **DEFAULT PLUG-IN PRESETS:** After adding effects to a folder, you can also specify default presets for each effect. Right-click an effect in the folder and choose Properties. In the Item Properties dialog box, choose a preset from the Default Preset menu. Click OK. Now when you insert the effect into a project, it will automatically default to the preset you selected.

7. Select the following effects and add them to the Compressor folder: Cakewalk Compressor/Gate, Sonitus:fx Compressor, Sonitus:fx Gate, and Sonitus:fx Multiband. Also, from the VST Audio Effects (VST) plug-in category, add the following effect: LP64_Multiband.
8. Back in the DirectX Audio Effects (DX) category, select the following effects and add them to the Delay folder: Cakewalk Tempo Delay and Sonitus:fx Delay.
9. Select the following effects and add them to the EQ folder: Cakewalk HF Exciter, Cakewalk Modfilter, Cakewalk Para-Q, and Sonitus:fx Equalizer. Also from the VST Audio Effects (VST) plug-in category, add the following effects: LP64_EQ.
10. Back in the DirectX Audio Effects (DX) category, select the following effects and add them to the Flanger folder: Cakewalk Classic Phaser, Cakewalk Multivoice Chorus/Flanger, Sonitus:fx Modulator, Sonitus:fx Phase, and Sonitus:fx Wahwah.
11. Select the following effects and add them to the Mastering folder: Cakewalk Analyst, Sonitus:fx Compressor, Sonitus:fx Equalizer, and Sonitus:fx Multiband. Also, from the VST Audio Effects (VST) plug-in category, add the following effects: Boost11, LP64_EQ, LP64_Multiband, and Vintage_Channel_VC64.

> **MULTIPLE CATEGORIES:** You may have noticed that I added the LP64_EQ, LP64_Multiband, and Sonitus:fx Multiband effects to the EQ, Compressor, and Mastering folders. Those effects can also be used for mastering, so I like to have them in multiple categories, making them easier to find, depending on what I'm doing. You can do this with any of the effects you have installed—add them to multiple folders for easier access and better organization.

12. Back in the DirectX Audio Effects (DX) plug-in category, select the following effects and add them to the MultiFX folder: Sonitus:fx Modulator. Also from the VST Audio Effects (VST) plug-in category, add the following effects: PX64_PercussionStrip, VX64_VocalStrip, z3ta+fx, and z3ta+_fx2.
13. Back in the DirectX Audio Effects (DX) plug-in category, select the following effects and add them to the Pitch folder: Cakewalk Pitch Shifter and Cakewalk Time/Pitch Stretch 2.
14. Select the following effects and add them to the Reverb folder: Cakewalk Studioverb2 and Sonitus:fx Reverb. Also from the VST Audio Effects (VST) plug-in category, add the following effects: BREVERB 2 Cakewalk and PerfectSpace.
15. Back in the DirectX Audio Effects (DX) plug-in category, select the following effects and add them to the Simulation folder: Cakewalk AliasFactor and Sonitus:fx Wahwah. Also, from the VST Audio Effects (VST) plug-in category, add the following effect: TH2 Producer.
16. Back in the DirectX Audio Effects (DX) plug-in category, select the following effect and add it to the Spectrum Analysis folder: Cakewalk Analyst.
17. Select the following effects and add them to the Surround folder: Sonitus:fx Surround and Sonitus:fx SurroundComp.
18. Click Collapse All to close all the folders in the menu layout. You can also use the Expand All button to open all folders when working on a layout.
19. Select the Surround folder and click Add Separator to add a separator to the layout.
20. Select the Sonitus:fx Phase effect and add it to the layout below the separator. Also from the VST Audio Effects (VST) plug-in category, add the following effect: Channel Tools.
21. If you ever want to remove an item or folder, select it and click Remove.
22. If you want to move items or folders up or down in the list, either drag and drop them or select them and use the Move Up, Move Down, or Promote button. Promote moves an item outside of a folder if it resides in one.
23. In the upper-right corner of the window, click the Save button (the one with the floppy disk on it) to save the new menu layout.
24. If you ever want to delete a layout, select it from the Layout File list and click the Delete button (the one with the big red X shown on it). Click Close to finish.

Now you can quickly access all your audio effects by category, and you can add other third-party plug-ins to this layout (see Figure 2.3) in addition to the ones that come with SONAR.

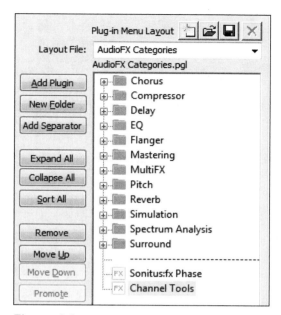

Figure 2.3 Use the Cakewalk Plug-in Manager to configure SONAR's plug-in menus to your liking.
Source: Cakewalk®, Inc.

Working with Screensets

When you're working on a project in SONAR, you need to use many of the views described in Chapter 1. When you save the project, the size, position, and state of the views (and any other windows) are saved along with it. This capability is nice because you can pick up exactly where you left off the next time you open the project. As you get more experienced with SONAR, you'll probably find that having the views set up in certain configurations helps your recording sessions go more smoothly. For instance, you might like having the Track view positioned at the top of the workspace and the Staff view and the Piano Roll view positioned underneath it.

What if you come up with a few favorite configurations that you'd like to use during different stages of the same project? Or what if you want to use those configurations in a different project? That's where *screensets* come in handy. Using screensets, you can easily save and recall different workspace configurations.

Window Positioning and the MultiDock

Just like in the Windows OS, any window in SONAR can be positioned anywhere inside the SONAR workspace. Windows can also be positioned outside of SONAR by floating them; click the upper-left corner of the window's title bar and choose Enable Floating from the menu. To make different views visible, use the Views menu or the keyboard shortcuts listed in that menu. In addition, the main interface elements (the Control Bar, Browser, Inspector, and MultiDock) can be docked to various parts of the workspace. Docking option icons for each element are located as follows: Browser (top-right corner), Inspector (top-left corner), and MultiDock (bottom-right corner), similar to Figure 2.4. Right-click the Control Bar background for docking options.

Figure 2.4 Use these icons to access docking options for the Browser, Inspector, and MultiDock.
Source: Cakewalk®, Inc.

While other windows in the interface cannot be docked individually, they *can* be docked using the MultiDock (see Figure 2.5).

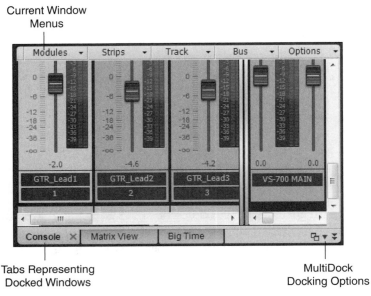

Figure 2.5 Use the MultiDock to dock any view, fx, or synth window.
Source: Cakewalk®, Inc.

The MultiDock is a single window into which multiple other windows (views, fx, synths) can be docked. To dock a window, just drag it by its title bar into the MultiDock, which will turn blue to indicate that the window can be docked. If you want to keep a window from docking, press and hold Ctrl while dragging. All windows docked in the MultiDock become tabbed and can be accessed via the tabs located at the bottom (when the MultiDock is docked below the Track view) or at the top (when floated or docked above) of the MultiDock window. Click the tab name to access the window or press Ctrl+Shift+Left/Right Arrow to cycle through the tabs. Click the X button on the tab to close the window. Right-click the tab (or click and drag the tab) to undock the window. The advantages of this are that the MultiDock can be positioned anywhere, and any docked windows are positioned along with it, thus reducing screen clutter and giving you quick access to multiple windows. For example, you can click and drag in the blank tab area of the MultiDock to move it to a second screen for full-screen access to all your views.

LOCK CONTENTS: Some views (Piano Roll, Staff, Event List, Step Sequencer) allow you to have multiple instances open. For example, you can have a separate Piano Roll window for each MIDI track. After you've opened a view in the MultiDock, right-click the view's tab and choose Lock Contents. This will lock the view to the specific track and allow you to open more instances of the same view.

Creating and Selecting Screensets

SONAR allows the creation of up to 10 screensets per project. They are saved in the project file. These screensets can be accessed in three different ways: via the Screenset module in the Control Bar, using the Views > Screensets menu, or by pressing 1 through 0 on your PC keyboard. SONAR ships with 10 default screensets, but you can create your own. To make workflow as intuitive as possible, SONAR automatically saves the current window configuration as the current screenset whenever you save a project or change to a different screenset. If you inadvertently change a screenset and want to go back to its previous configuration, you can use the Views > Screensets > Revert Current Screenset to do so. However, you can also lock screensets to prevent changes by choosing Views > Screensets > Lock/Unlock Current Screenset. The basic procedure for creating permanent screensets is as follows:

1. Choose a screenset to change or choose Views > Screensets > Duplicate Current Screenset To in order to base the new screenset on an existing one.
2. Configure the visibility, position, size, and zoom levels of windows in the workspace.
3. Choose Views > Screensets > Rename Current Screenset to give the screenset a meaningful name.
4. Choose Views > Screensets > Lock/Unlock Current Screenset to lock the screenset.
5. Choose File > Save (or press Ctrl+S) to save the project.

Importing Screensets

Since screensets are stored along with a project, they can't be stored and accessed globally. But you can import screensets from other projects by opening two projects in SONAR simultaneously. With both projects open, use the Windows menu to choose the project into which you want to import the screensets. Then choose Views > Screensets > Import Screensets from [*name of second project*]. Keep in mind that any locked screensets in the current project will not be changed.

> **FULL SCREEN SCREENSET:** An additional option that affects the entire SONAR application window (and is saved in screensets) is Full Screen mode. What this option does is resize the SONAR window to fill the current screen and also remove the title bar to provide a small amount of additional vertical workspace. To toggle the option, choose Window > Full Screen (or press F11).
>
> One of my favorite screenset configurations is having the Track view showing and nothing else. To achieve this, I press C, B, D, I to hide the Control Bar, Browser, MultiDock, and Inspector. Then I press F11 to activate Full Screen mode and save the screenset.

X-Ray Windows

Even with screensets, working with windows that are not docked in SONAR can become cumbersome when you have a lot of them open at once and they are overlapping each other. To help with this situation, SONAR provides an X-Ray Windows feature, which makes the current top window transparent so you can see the windows underneath. This feature works on the AudioSnap palette, the Piano Roll view, plug-in effects and soft synths, and controller/surface plug-ins. To X-Ray a window, hover your mouse over the window and press Shift+X. The exception is the Piano Roll view. You may first need to click the upper-left corner of the view's title bar and choose Enable Floating from the menu for the X-Ray feature to work.

You can also adjust how the X-Ray Windows feature works by pressing P and choosing Customization – Display in the Preferences dialog box. In the Enable X-Ray section, use the Enable X-Ray option to enable/disable the feature. Adjust the Opacity parameter to determine how transparent a window will become when you X-Ray it. You can also adjust the speed of the X-Ray using the Fade Out Time and Fade In Time parameters. I like to set these both to 10 (the lowest value you can enter) because it saves time. In addition, you can create a keyboard shortcut (via Key Bindings) to X-Ray all open windows at once. Look for X-Ray All FX/Synths in the Global Bindings list of the Bind Context section of the Key Bindings dialog box.

Using Key Bindings

Key bindings are one of the most useful customization features that SONAR provides. They give you quick access to most of SONAR's features. Instead of having to click through a series of menus, you can simply press a key combination on your computer's keyboard. Initially, SONAR ships with a collection of default key bindings, such as for opening and saving a project. These bindings are displayed next to their assigned menu functions, as in SONAR's main menu.

Creating Your Own Key Bindings

The wonderful thing about key bindings is that if you don't like them, you can change them. You can also create new ones for functions that don't already have default key bindings. You can assign more than 600 different key bindings using just about any key combination. Here's how to do it:

1. Press P and choose Customization – Keyboard Shortcuts in the Preferences dialog box.
2. Using the Area drop-down list, choose the work area in SONAR that contains the function you want to bind. For example, if you want to bind one of the Track view functions, choose Track view from the list.
3. In the Key list, select the key combination that you want to bind to a function.

> **QUICK KEY FINDING:** Since SONAR provides a very long list of key combinations from which to choose, it can be difficult to find the exact key combination you want by scrolling through the list. To find a key combination quickly, click the Locate Key button. Then press the key combination on your computer keyboard, and the combination will be automatically highlighted in the Key list.

4. In the Function list, select the SONAR function that you want to bind to the selected key combination.
5. Click the Bind button. You will see a connection created.
6. As I mentioned before, you can create more than 600 key bindings. You can also remove single key bindings using the Unbind button. If you want to get rid of all key bindings, just click the Zap All button. To remove all bindings from a single SONAR view, click the Zap View button.

> **UNBIND DEFAULT KEY BINDINGS:** You can assign different key bindings to take the place of the default bindings that SONAR provides. However, if you want to just remove a binding from a key combination, you can assign it to the Do Nothing function. Now when you press the keyboard combination, nothing will happen.

7. If you would like to share your key bindings with another SONAR user, you can export them by clicking the Export button. Likewise, you can use key bindings from someone else by clicking the Import button.
8. When you're done, click the OK button.

> **SAVE CHANGES FOR NEXT SESSION:** When you activate the Save Changes for Next Session option, any key bindings you created will be saved so you can use them every time you run SONAR. If this option is not activated, you will lose any changes you've made when you exit the program. This option is activated by default. I suggest you keep it that way, unless for some reason you just need a few temporary key bindings during a recording session.

After you've created (or changed) some key bindings, you'll notice the changes displayed next to the functions in SONAR's menus.

Using MIDI Key Bindings

In addition to creating key bindings using your computer keyboard, you can assign the keys on your MIDI keyboard synthesizer or controller as key bindings to execute functions within SONAR. For example, you could assign the File > New function in SONAR to the Middle C key on your keyboard. Then, when you press Middle C, SONAR would open the New Project File dialog box.

> **REMOTE MIDI KEY BINDINGS:** If your studio is set up so that your computer isn't located next to your MIDI keyboard or controller, using MIDI key bindings is a great way to still have access to SONAR. For example, if you want to be able to start and stop SONAR recording via your MIDI keyboard, you can just assign one MIDI key binding along with the Shift key or controller to the Play/Stop function and another MIDI key binding along with the Shift key or controller to the Record function.

You create MIDI key bindings the same way you create computer keyboard bindings. The only difference is that you have to select MIDI as the Type of Keys option in the dialog box and make sure to activate MIDI key bindings by selecting the Enabled option (see Figure 2.6). Also, when you select a key combination in the Key list, you select musical keys rather than computer keyboard keys.

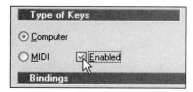

Figure 2.6 You select MIDI as the Type of Keys option and select Enabled to active MIDI key bindings. *Source:* Cakewalk®, Inc.

In addition, in order to prevent the MIDI key bindings from activating while you're performing, you need to set up a Shift key or controller to turn on and off the MIDI key bindings. Under MIDI Shift Options, you can assign a MIDI key or controller message to act as an on/off switch. When you want to use a MIDI key binding, activate the Shift key or controller first to tell SONAR you're about to use a MIDI key binding.

Transforming the Track View

Even though I'll be talking a lot more about the Track view throughout the book, I want to cover a few of the Track view attributes that SONAR allows you to configure. These include the Track pane controls and the Time Ruler.

Located near the top of the Track pane of the Track view is the Track Control menu (see Figure 2.7), which can be used to hide/show controls for MIDI, audio, instrument tracks, and buses.

Figure 2.7 Use the Track Control menu to access different track control configurations.
Source: Cakewalk®, Inc.

SONAR comes with a number of predefined control configurations. For example, choosing Mix from the menu displays controls that are relevant for mixing a project. However, you can customize these configurations (and even create new ones) to your liking. To customize the visibility of the controls, do the following:

1. Choose Track Control Manager from the Track Control menu. The Track Control Manager replaces the Widget Tab Manager from SONAR 8.5 and earlier.
2. Choose an existing configuration from the Preset Name menu or create a new configuration by clicking New.
3. To delete an existing configuration, click Delete.
4. In the table, you'll see six columns. The first column (Widget Section) displays a list of all available track controls. In the second column (Audio Strip), put check marks next to the controls that you want to be visible in all audio tracks.
5. In the third column (MIDI Strip), put check marks next to the widgets that you want to be visible in all MIDI tracks.
6. In the fourth column (Instrument Strip), put check marks next to the widgets that you want to be visible in all instrument tracks.
7. In the fifth column (Bus Strip), put check marks next to the widgets that you want to be visible in all buses.
8. In the sixth column (Surround Bus Strip), put check marks next to the widgets that you want to be visible in all surround buses.
9. To set the configuration back to its default, click Restore Preset Defaults.
10. To put check marks next to all controls in all columns, click Select All Controls. Click OK.

Customizing the Track Controls

Other than the track number, name, peak meter indicator, and size button located in the top row of each track, all other track controls can be moved to different locations. Simply hold down the Alt key and drag a control to a new location. As you drag a control, you'll see a red outline around the control, and your mouse will change to reflect the current operation, as shown in Figure 2.8.

Figure 2.8 Alt+click and drag controls to change their location in the Track pane.
Source: Cakewalk®, Inc.

Altering controls in one track type alters all tracks of that type. For example, if you change the positions of controls on an audio track, it affects all audio tracks. To restore the original positions of all controls, right-click any track of the type you want to restore and choose Restore Default Control Order.

Customizing the Time Ruler

By default, the Time Ruler displays the measure numbers in the current project. The Time Ruler format can also be changed (in the Track and Piano Roll views) to display Hours:Minutes:Seconds:Frames, Samples, or Milliseconds. In addition, rather than showing just one time format, you can set up the Time Ruler to display multiple formats simultaneously. To do this, click the Add Ruler button (located at the right end of the Time Ruler) and choose a format to add. After you've added multiple formats, you can use the Remove Ruler button to remove any formats currently displayed (see Figure 2.9).

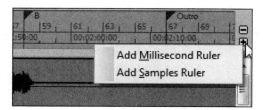

Figure 2.9 Customize the Time Ruler to display multiple formats.
Source: Cakewalk®, Inc.

Customizing MIDI Settings

Even though SONAR does a good job of setting up all its MIDI options during installation, it's still a good idea to go through them to make sure that everything is the way you want it to be. You might be surprised at how much control you have over how SONAR handles MIDI data. Not only can you designate which MIDI devices the program will use, but you can also determine what types of MIDI data will be recorded and optimize MIDI playback.

Working with MIDI Devices

The first time you run SONAR, it scans your computer system to see whether you have a MIDI interface installed. SONAR prompts you to select the available MIDI ports that you want to use, but you can always change your selections later.

MIDI PORTS: A *MIDI interface* is a device that is plugged into your computer, allowing it to understand the MIDI language. Every MIDI interface has at least two connections on it, called *MIDI ports*. One is the MIDI In port, which is used to receive MIDI data; the other is the MIDI Out port, which is used to send MIDI data. Some of the more sophisticated MIDI interfaces on the market have multiple pairs of MIDI ports, which allow you to connect more than one MIDI instrument to your computer.

To see which MIDI ports SONAR is using and to designate the ports you want to use, follow these steps:

1. Press P and choose MIDI – Devices in the Preferences dialog box.
2. Put a check mark next to the input and output ports that you want to be able to access for use within SONAR.

3. You can also use your own names for the ports by double-clicking the name and typing in something new. Then activate the Use Friendly Name to Represent MIDI Devices option. When you do this, SONAR will use your names wherever MIDI ports are displayed in the software.

All the ports selected here will be available via the Input and Output controls of each MIDI track.

Setting Global MIDI Options

SONAR provides a number of different MIDI options, some of which are global and some of which are project oriented. The project-oriented options are saved and loaded along with project files. The global options remain the same, no matter which project is currently open.

Filtering Out MIDI Messages

The global MIDI options enable you to select the types of MIDI messages you want to record in SONAR. Sometimes, you might not want certain MIDI data to be included in your recordings. For example, if your MIDI keyboard sends channel aftertouch messages or key aftertouch messages, you might want to filter them out. These types of messages are very resource-intensive and can sometimes bog down your synthesizer with too much data.

> **MIDI MESSAGES:** For details on MIDI messages, be sure to check out the MIDI documentation references I provided in the Introduction.

By default, SONAR has notes, controllers, program (patch) changes, pitch bend, and system exclusive messages activated, and it has key aftertouch and channel aftertouch deactivated. If you want to change these settings, press P and choose MIDI – Playback and Recording in the Preferences dialog box. Then, in the Record section, put check marks next to the types of MIDI messages you want SONAR to record.

Optimizing MIDI Playback

To get smooth and consistent playback of MIDI data, SONAR uses a buffer (a temporary storage area) to hold the data before it gets sent out through the MIDI interface. This buffer keeps the data from getting backed up, which can cause erratic playback or even stop playback altogether. The buffer also helps to control playback latency. Whenever you change a parameter in SONAR while a project is playing, a slight delay occurs between the time you make the adjustment and when you hear the results. That's called *latency*.

To control that latency, SONAR provides a MIDI playback buffer. If the buffer is set too low, it can cause erratic playback, and if it is set too high, it can cause noticeable latency. By default, the buffer size is set to 250 milliseconds. This setting should be fine in most cases. However, you might want to experiment to find an even better setting. The trick is to find the lowest setting that doesn't affect playback. I've been able to get away with a setting of 100 most of the time unless I have a lot of MIDI data being played in a project. You can change the buffer size by pressing P and choosing MIDI – Playback and Recording in the Preferences dialog box. Then type in a new value for the Prepare Using parameter in the Playback section.

Understanding Instrument Definitions

Most MIDI instruments today provide a bank of sounds compatible with the General MIDI standard. At the same time, most instruments provide additional sounds, as well as other features that aren't defined by General MIDI. Some older MIDI instruments don't support General MIDI at all. To let you work more efficiently with these instruments, SONAR provides instrument definitions.

GENERAL MIDI: Sounds in a MIDI instrument are stored as groups of parameter settings called *patches*, and patches are stored in groups called *banks*. A MIDI instrument can have up to 16,384 banks of 128 patches each. This means that a MIDI instrument can theoretically contain up to 2,097,152 different sounds, although most don't.

With such a great potential for diversity, MIDI instruments from one manufacturer usually don't provide the same functionality as instruments from another manufacturer. This point is important because MIDI data is ambiguous. The same data can be played back using any MIDI instrument, but that doesn't mean it will sound the same. Different instruments contain different sounds, and they interpret MIDI differently as well.

To remedy the problem, *General MIDI* (GM) was created. GM is a set of rules applied to the MIDI language that standardizes the types of sounds contained in a MIDI instrument (along with their patch numbers) and how different MIDI controller messages are interpreted. Most modern MIDI instruments provide a special bank of GM sounds and a GM operating mode. When you are running in GM mode, different MIDI instruments respond to the same MIDI data in the same way. MIDI data played back on one instrument is guaranteed to sound the same when played on any other instrument.

Using instrument definitions, you can "tell" SONAR all about the features and capabilities provided by each of the MIDI instruments in your studio. This information includes the name of each patch, the range of notes supported by each patch, the supported MIDI controller messages, the supported registered parameter numbers (RPNs) and nonregistered parameter numbers (NRPNs), and the bank select method used. Basically, instrument definitions refer to the patches in your MIDI instruments by name rather than number when you're assigning sounds to tracks in SONAR. The same applies for musical note names and MIDI controller message names.

Setting Up Your Instruments

SONAR includes a number of predefined instrument definitions so that you can assign them without having to go through the process of creating your own. You can assign instrument definitions to each of the MIDI ports on your MIDI interface. You can also assign them to the individual MIDI channels (1 through 16).

MIDI CHANNELS: The MIDI language provides 16 different channels of performance data over a single MIDI port connection. MIDI instruments can be set to receive MIDI data on a single channel if necessary. This means you can control up to 16 different MIDI instruments (each with its own unique sound), even if they are all connected to the same MIDI port on your MIDI interface. In addition, most MIDI instruments are capable of playing more than one sound at a time. This means the instrument is *multitimbral*. If you assign a different sound to each of the 16 MIDI channels, a single MIDI instrument can play 16 different sounds simultaneously.

To assign instrument definitions to each of the MIDI ports and channels in your setup, follow these steps:

1. Press P and choose MIDI – Instruments in the Preferences dialog box.
2. From the Output/Channel list, select the MIDI port(s) or MIDI channel(s) to which you want to assign definitions. Ctrl+click or Shift+click to select more than one simultaneously.
3. From the Uses Instrument list, select the instrument definition you want to use. For example, if you're going to use the MIDI instrument that's connected to the selected port in General MIDI mode, choose the General MIDI instrument definition.

> **SAVE CHANGES FOR NEXT SESSION:** Under the Output/Channel list is the Save Changes for Next Session option. When you select it, any assignments you create will be saved so that you can use them every time you run SONAR. If this option is not selected, you will lose any changes you make when you exit the program. I suggest you select this option, unless for some reason you change the configuration of your studio for each new recording session.

After you click OK, SONAR will know the capabilities of your MIDI instrument(s) and will act appropriately when you access different features, such as editing MIDI controller messages.

Predefined Instrument Definitions

If you don't see a specific instrument definition for your MIDI instrument listed in the Preferences dialog box, SONAR imports more definitions. The program ships with a large collection of additional instrument definitions that cover many of the MIDI instruments on the market from manufacturers such as Alesis, E-mu, Ensoniq, General Music, Korg, Kurzweil, Roland, and Yamaha. The instrument definitions are stored in files with .INS extensions. For example, the Yamaha instrument definitions are stored in the file YAMAHA.INS. Importing these files is simple; just follow these steps:

1. Press P and choose MIDI – Instruments in the Preferences dialog box.
2. Click the Define button to open the Define Instruments and Names dialog box.
3. Click the Import button to open the Import Instrument Definitions dialog box and select the .INS file you want to import. For example, if Yamaha manufactures your MIDI instrument, select the YAMAHA.INS file; then click Open. The .INS files are usually located at C:\Cakewalk Content\SONAR X2 Producer\instruments by default.
4. When SONAR displays a list of the instrument definitions contained in that file, select the one(s) you want and click the OK button. Your selections will be listed under Instruments in the Define Instruments and Names dialog box.
5. Click the Close button, and you will see your selections listed under Uses Instrument in the Preferences dialog box. From here, you can assign the instrument definitions as described earlier and then click OK.

Creating Your Own Instrument Definitions

More than likely, you'll find instrument definitions for all your MIDI equipment either included with SONAR or available for download from the Internet. On the off chance that you don't, SONAR allows you to create your own definitions. This can be a bit complicated because you must have a good knowledge of the MIDI language, and you need to be able to read the MIDI implementation charts that came with your instruments.

> **MIDI IMPLEMENTATION CHARTS:** The MIDI language contains more than 100 different messages to convey musical information, and a MIDI instrument isn't required to send or recognize all of them. A MIDI instrument needs to transmit and receive only the messages that are relevant to the features it provides; it can ignore all the other messages. Therefore, manufacturers include MIDI implementation charts with all their products.
>
> A MIDI implementation chart lists all the types of MIDI messages that are transmitted and recognized by its accompanying MIDI instrument. The chart includes the note range of the instrument, the MIDI controller messages it supports, whether it supports system exclusive messages, and more.

To give you an idea of how to read a simple MIDI implementation chart and how to create a basic instrument definition, I want to go through the process step by step:

1. Press P and choose MIDI – Instruments in the Preferences dialog box.
2. Click the Define button to open the Define Instruments and Names dialog box.

3. Take a look at Table 2.1, which shows the MIDI implementation chart for an E-mu PROformance Plus Stereo Piano MIDI instrument.

Table 2.1 E-mu PROformance Plus MIDI Implementation Chart

MIDI	Receive	Transmit	Values
Note On	Y	N	
Note Off	Y	N	
Pitch Bend	Y	N	
Program Change	Y	N	
Overflow Mode	Y	Y	
Channel Pressure	N	N	
Polyphonic Pressure	N	N	
Control Change	Y	N	PWH, 1, 7
Sustain Pedal	Y	N	64
Sostenuto Pedal	Y	N	66
Soft Pedal	Y	N	67
Split Pedal	Y	N	70
All Notes Off	Y	N	
Omni Mode	N	N	Ignored
Poly Mode	N	N	Ignored
Mono Mode	N	N	Ignored
System Exclusive	N	N	

4. Right-click Instruments on the left side of the Define Instruments and Names dialog box; select Add Instrument from the menu that appears.
5. Type a name for the new instrument. For this example, type **E-mu PROformance Plus**.
6. Open the new instrument by double-clicking it to display its data.
7. Take a look at what the new instrument contains. SONAR automatically creates the standard settings needed. Because the E-mu PROformance Plus doesn't support bank select messages, RPNs, or NRPNs, you don't need to change them. The PROformance supports the standard MIDI controllers, too, so you don't have to change them, either. You do need to change the patch names, though.

8. Open the Patch Names for Banks folder in the E-mu PROformance Plus instrument by double-clicking it. You should see General MIDI listed there. Because this instrument doesn't support GM, you need to change that name.

9. To change the General MIDI patch names list, you need to create a new patch names list first, specifically for the PROformance, by right-clicking on the Patch Names folder on the right side of the Define Instruments and Names dialog box.

10. Select Add Patch Names List from the menu that appears and type a name for the new list. In this case, type **E-mu PROformance Plus**.

11. The PROformance manual shows all the patch names for the instrument (numbers 0 to 31). To add those names to the new patch name list, right-click the list and select Add Patch Name from the menu that appears.

12. Type a name for the first patch (in this case, **Dark Grand**) and press the Enter key on your computer keyboard. Because this is just an example, you can leave the list as-is, but if you were to add more names to the list, it would look something like Figure 2.10.

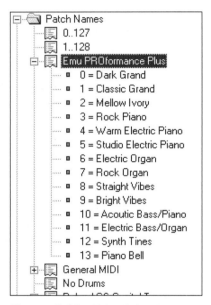

Figure 2.10 This dialog box shows a patch name list for the E-mu PROformance Plus.
Source: Cakewalk®, Inc.

13. Drag and drop the E-mu PROformance Plus patch names list into the General MIDI list in the E-mu PROformance Plus instrument definition.

14. In the Bank Number dialog box, enter the number of the bank that you want to use for this set of patch names. Click OK. The patch names list for the instrument will be changed. Click Close.

This set of steps was actually a very simplified demonstration of how to create your own instrument definition. If the controller names need to be changed or if the instrument supports RPNs or NRPNs, you can create and edit those lists in the same way you do a patch name list. It's doubtful that you'll ever need to create your own instrument definitions because SONAR comes with a large number of them, and you can download even more from the Internet, but just in case, you can find more details in the SONAR user's guide.

Optimal Audio Settings

When SONAR plays back digital audio on your computer, it puts a lot of stress on the system. A CD-quality digital audio recording requires 44,100 numbers (samples) to be processed every second. During playback, much of your computer's processing power is used solely for that purpose. Depending on the power of your system, this processing can make the response of some of SONAR's controls a bit sluggish, particularly the Console view controls. For example, if you adjust the volume of a digital audio track in the Console view during playback, you might experience a slight delay between the time you make the adjustment and the time you hear the results. As I mentioned earlier, this period is called *latency,* and you'll want as little of it as possible to occur during your sessions.

SONAR provides a number of different advanced settings that enable you to reduce latency. The first time you start the program, it attempts to make some educated guesses about what these settings should be, and although these settings usually work just fine, you still might be able to squeeze better performance out of your computer system. However, adjusting these settings can be tricky, and unfortunately, there are no set rules. But there are some general guidelines you can follow to optimize your audio settings for the best possible performance.

Adjusting the Buffer Size Slider

One of the most important adjustments you can make is to the Buffer Size slider, and it's pretty simple to do. The lower you set the slider, the lower the latency will be; the higher you set it, the higher the latency will be. It can't be that simple, can it? No, I'm afraid not. By lowering the Buffer Size slider, you also run the risk of making your playback unstable. If you set the Buffer Size slider too low, you might hear dropouts or glitches, or playback might even stop altogether. And the lower you set the Buffer Size slider, the fewer digital audio tracks you can play at the same time.

To find the right setting, you have to experiment with a number of different projects. For projects with only a few digital audio tracks, you might be able to get away with a very low Buffer Size slider setting. For projects with many digital audio tracks, you might have to raise the Buffer Size slider and put up with a bit of latency while you work. The amount of latency also depends on the driver mode you are using (see Setting Driver Mode below). The Buffer Size slider works for all modes except ASIO (see ASIO Drivers below). To set the Buffer Size slider, press P and choose Audio – Driver Settings in the Preferences dialog box. Then adjust the Buffer Size slider (located in the Mixing Latency section). Drag the slider left to lower latency and drag it right to increase latency.

> **PRACTICAL BUFFER SIZE SLIDER SETTINGS:** A good rule of thumb for setting the Buffer Size slider is this: If you are recording using Input Monitoring or playing soft synths live via your MIDI keyboard, set your latency to a low value—maybe as low as 4 to 6 milliseconds when using ASIO or WDM sound card drivers. If you are playing many audio tracks and using a lot of real-time effects while mixing down, then set your latency to a higher value to relieve the strain on your computer system—perhaps a value of around 50 milliseconds (or higher if needed) when you are using ASIO or WDM sound card drivers.

Setting Driver Mode

As with MIDI settings, the first time you run SONAR, it scans your computer system to see whether you have a sound card installed. SONAR then automatically chooses the drivers that will be used with your card, but you might get better performance by using different drivers. To choose the type of drivers you want to use with SONAR, press P and choose Audio – Playback and Recording in the Preferences dialog box. Then use the Driver Mode menu to choose a mode.

> **SOUND CARD DRIVERS:** MME drivers are an older variety of Windows sound card drivers and are provided for the support of older sound cards that might still be in existence. If at all possible, do not choose the MME option for your sound card output because it will provide very poor playback performance. Instead, you will want to choose WDM or ASIO, depending on the type of drivers you have available. You also have a third choice (WASAPI) if you are using Windows Vista. As to which driver is better, that's a tough call. It really depends on the quality of the driver and how well it was programmed, so you'll have to try them all to see which provides you with better performance. Cakewalk recommends ASIO drivers in most cases.

ASIO Drivers

With ASIO drivers, instead of using the Buffer Size slider to adjust latency, you have to use the ASIO control panel for your sound card. I'm using the Cakewalk V-Studio 700 system in my studio, and its ASIO control panel looks like Figure 2.11.

Figure 2.11 Use the ASIO control panel to adjust latency when you are using ASIO drivers.
Source: Cakewalk®, Inc.

To access the panel for your sound card, press P and choose Audio – Driver Settings in the Preferences dialog box. Then click the ASIO Panel button to adjust the audio buffer size. The lower the buffer size, the lower the latency; the higher the buffer size, the higher the latency. It works just like the Buffer Size slider, mentioned previously.

Setting Queue Buffers and I/O Buffer Sizes

Two other settings that affect latency and audio performance are the number of buffers in the playback queue and the I/O (input/output) buffer sizes. Like the Buffer Size slider, if they are set too low, you can experience dropouts or glitches during playback/recording. Higher settings mean more latency. Again, you need to experiment with the settings. I've found that values between 2 and 4 for the number of buffers in the playback queue and between 128 and 256 for the I/O buffer sizes work quite well. If you want to change them, you can follow these steps:

1. Press P and choose Audio – Driver Settings in the Preferences dialog box.
2. The Buffers in Playback Queue setting is located in the Mixing Latency section. Type in a new value.

3. With the Preferences dialog box still open, choose Audio – Sync and Caching.

4. The Playback and Record I/O Buffer Size settings are located in the File System section. Type in new values.

Read and Write Caching

When your computer sets aside a part of its memory to hold recently read or written information from a disk drive, the process is known as *disk caching*. Windows uses disk caching to help speed up read-and-write operations to your disk drives. When data is read or written to a disk as a continuous stream (as with digital audio), disk caching can actually slow things down.

SONAR has two options that let you enable or disable disk caching while the program is running. By default, SONAR keeps disk caching disabled, and I recommend you keep them disabled. If you have a large amount of memory in your computer, disk caching may actually improve performance. If you want to see whether enabling this option makes any difference with your computer system, press P. Then choose Audio – Sync and Caching in the Preferences dialog box. In the File System section, add/remove check marks next to the Enable Read Caching and Enable Write Caching options.

IMPROVING AUDIO PERFORMANCE: For more information about optimizing SONAR, be sure to read the SONAR help file section entitled *Improving Audio Performance*.

Also, if you'd like more information about how to optimize your audio PC, go to **www.digifreq.com/digifreq/article.asp?ID=14** to check out my feature article entitled "Optimizing Your Music & Audio PC." In addition, go to **www.digifreq.com/digifreq/articles.asp** for more great articles, and go to **www.digifreq.com/digifreq** to sign up for my free music technology newsletter.

Panning Laws

Don't worry, we're not talking legal issues here, but if you ignore the laws of panning, your music could very well suffer. Panning determines where the sound of a track will be heard in the sound field between two stereo speakers. Unfortunately, it's not as straightforward as that because there are different kinds of panning to which SONAR provides you access via the Stereo Panning Law parameter. Press P and choose Audio – Driver Settings in the Preferences dialog box. You'll see the parameter located in the top section of the box, and you can set it by simply choosing a value from the drop-down menu.

Each panning law will affect the sound of your audio tracks in a different way as you pan the tracks around the stereo field. For example, if you create a project with one panning law and then you change the panning law after the project is finished, the playback will sound different (and probably worse because some panning laws will raise the volume of tracks when panned and some will lower the volume, which can wreak havoc on a stereo mix). As such, you should probably use the same law for all your projects.

Which law should you choose? Well, without getting overly complicated—even though SONAR's default panning law is 0dB center, sin/cos taper, constant power, you may want to consider the –3dB center, sin/cos taper, constant power panning law. This law is supported by most multitrack recording software and is used when designing analog mixing boards, which makes it somewhat of a standard.

The Stereo Panning Law parameter is saved along with your project, but it's still a good idea to make a note of what law you used by adding it to the Project > Info window. Plus, if you are working with other musicians on the same project, and they have something other than SONAR, you will definitely need to tell them to change their panning law appropriately.

Creating and Working with Projects

A PROJECT IS SONAR'S WAY OF REPRESENTING a song or any other musical body of work. A project holds all your music data, including MIDI and audio, along with a number of program settings. You can't do anything in SONAR without first creating a new project or opening an existing one.

Opening Projects

Every time you start SONAR, it presents you with the Quick Start dialog box. In this dialog box, you can open an existing project or a project you recently worked with, or you can create a new one.

If you choose to open an existing project, SONAR displays a standard file selection dialog box so that you can select the project you want to load. If you changed the disk location of your project files (as described in Chapter 2), the dialog box will initially display the contents of the folder you specified. Of course, you can examine other disk locations just as you would when you are loading a file in any other Windows application.

By choosing the Open a Recent Project option, you can open a project you've worked with previously. You simply select the project from the list and then click the folder button next to the list. SONAR keeps track of the last eight projects you've used. When you open a ninth, the project on the bottom of the list is bumped off—not killed or deleted, just removed from the list.

You can also open an existing or recent project using SONAR's standard menu functions. To open an existing project, just choose File > Open. To open a recent project, select the File menu and click the name of the project you want to open in the list on the bottom half of the menu (see Figure 3.1).

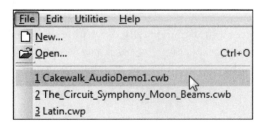

Figure 3.1 You can use the File menu to open an existing or recent project.
Source: Cakewalk®, Inc.

> **SHOW THIS AT STARTUP:** Personally, I find it easier to use the standard menu functions to open a project. To keep the Quick Start dialog box from appearing every time you start SONAR, remove the check mark next to the Show This at Startup option at the bottom of the box.

Opening in Recovery Mode

If you've used Microsoft Windows for any length of time, you've no doubt come across its notorious Safe Mode, which allows you to start the OS in a somewhat crippled state if you're having trouble booting up your PC. Basically, Safe Mode lets you start Windows with only the bare essentials needed to run the OS. For instance, all unnecessary device drivers are disabled, which enables you to troubleshoot Windows and attempt to find the source of your faulty start-up.

SONAR provides a similar feature (called *File Recovery Mode* or *Safe Mode* in previous versions) for use when opening project files. Like any computer data, project files can become corrupt occasionally, preventing you from opening them. This corruption can be caused by computer resource limitations or bad audio effects, MIDI effects, or soft synth plug-ins. Using File Recovery Mode, SONAR loads a project file with only the Track view (in its default layout) open and attempts to recover as much viable data from the file as possible. If you had any other open views in the project, they will not open. You are also prompted for each and every plug-in that you have assigned to your tracks in the project. This feature lets you determine whether a particular plug-in is preventing you from opening your project. Here is how File Recovery Mode works:

1. When opening a project using one of the methods described earlier, hold down the Shift key on your PC keyboard. This tells SONAR to open the project in File Recovery Mode and displays the File Open – Safe Mode dialog box.
2. If your project contains any plug-ins assigned to your tracks, the dialog box will ask you whether you want to load the plug-ins. You have four choices: Yes, Yes to All, No, and No to All. Choosing Yes will load the currently displayed plug-in. Choosing No will not load the currently displayed plug-in. Choosing Yes to All will close the dialog box and load all plug-ins. Choosing No to All will close the dialog box and open the project without any plug-ins.
3. If you don't choose either Yes to All or No to All, the Safe Mode dialog box will ask you about each individual plug-in contained in the project, and you will have to answer either Yes or No to each one. This method allows you to determine whether a certain plug-in is causing trouble and which plug-in it is.

> **SAFE SAVING:** If you load a project in File Recovery Mode with some or all of the plug-ins disabled, be careful when you save the project to disk. You should save the project with a different name so the original file remains intact. If you save the file using the same name, the original file will be overwritten, and all your plug-in assignments will be lost.

Personally, I've found the best way to use File Recovery Mode is to load a project and individually determine whether or not each plug-in should be loaded. This lets me narrow down the problem to a specific plug-in. I may lose the settings for that troublesome plug-in, but I can keep all the settings for any other plug-ins I have assigned to my tracks in the project.

Finding Missing Audio Files

Another problem that can occur when you are opening projects that contain audio data is that SONAR might be unable to determine the location of the data for that project on your disk. This can happen if you move the location of your Audio Data folder and you forget to specify the new location in the SONAR folder settings. You can also run into this problem if you use individual folders for each project. But if your data gets misplaced, you can use SONAR's Find Missing Audio function.

1. When you open a project in which SONAR cannot find the associated audio data for the audio tracks, the Find Missing Audio dialog box is displayed (see Figure 3.2).

Figure 3.2 Use the Find Missing Audio function to locate misplaced audio data.
Source: Cakewalk®, Inc.

2. To locate the missing audio data, you can navigate manually through the folders on your hard drive using the Look In drop-down menu, or you can use the Search feature. The Look In drop-down menu is self-explanatory. To use Search, click the Search button. SONAR will automatically search your entire hard drive for the audio file currently displayed in the File Name field of the Find Missing Audio dialog box. During the search, the Search for Missing Audio dialog box is shown (see Figure 3.3). If the file is found, select it and click OK. If the file isn't found, click Cancel and search for it manually.

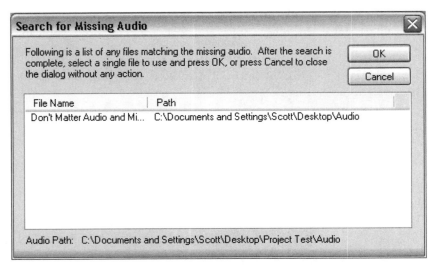

Figure 3.3 Use Search for Missing Audio to automatically locate audio files.
Source: Cakewalk®, Inc.

3. After you've found the missing file, you can move it to your project's audio data folder, copy it to your project's audio data folder (which also leaves a copy of the file in its current location), or have the project point to the file in its current location. You accomplish these tasks by choosing one of the options in the After Locating the Missing Audio section of the Find Missing Audio dialog box (Move File to Project Audio Folder, Copy File to Project Audio Folder, or Reference File from Present Location, respectively).

4. To finish the operation, click the Open button. If you no longer want to use the file in your project, you can click the Skip button. To discard all audio data for a project, click Skip All.

5. If your project contains data from more than one audio file, you need to repeat Steps 2 through 4 for each missing file.

Any files that you couldn't find or just skipped over will be replaced with silence in your project. The clips will still appear in the tracks, but the clips will be empty.

Creating a New Project

To create a new project, you can select the appropriate option in the Quick Start dialog box, or you can choose File > New from SONAR's menu. Whichever method you use, SONAR displays the New Project File dialog box. To utilize the dialog box, do the following:

1. By default, SONAR has the Per-Project Audio Folders option activated (see Chapter 2). Per-project audio folders allow you to create a separate disk drive folder for each of your projects. To disable the Per-Project Audio Folders option for the current new project you are creating, remove the check mark next to the Store Project Audio in Its Own Folder option.

2. If you decide to keep the Per-Project Audio Folders option activated, type in a name for your new project in the Name field. This name will also be used as the project's folder name.

3. If you want to use a different folder name and location for your project, type a new disk path in the Location field. You can also browse for a new location by clicking the ellipsis button located at the right side of the field.

4. The audio for your project is automatically stored in a folder called *Audio* inside the project folder. If you want to use a different folder name and location for the project audio, type a new disk path in the Audio Path field or browse for a new location via the ellipsis button.

5. Whether or not you use per-project audio folders, you need to choose a template upon which to base your new project. Do this by making a selection in the Template list. Click OK.

After you make your selection, SONAR creates a new project complete with predefined settings that reflect the template you selected.

What's a Template?

A *template* is a special type of file upon which new projects are based. You can think of templates as predefined projects. Templates contain the settings for all the parameters in a project. They enable you to set up a new project quickly and easily for a particular type of musical session. You can use a template called *Normal* to start a new project totally from scratch. And if you don't find what you need in the templates included with SONAR, you can always create your own.

Creating Your Own Template

Any parameters that are saved in a project can also be saved as a template. To create your own template, you simply follow these steps:

1. Choose File > New and then choose the Normal template. Choosing this template creates a new, blank project, ready to be filled.
2. Set SONAR's parameters to reflect the type of template you want to create. This includes track configurations.
3. Choose File > Save As to display the Save As dialog box.
4. Choose Template from the Save as Type menu.
5. If you've created a special folder for storing templates, you can save your new template in that folder by choosing the Template Files option for the Go to Folder parameter.
6. Enter a name for your new template in the File Name field and click Save.

The next time you want to create a new project, your template will be listed along with the other templates in the New Project File dialog box.

AUTOMATIC TEMPLATE: If you want to have SONAR configured in a particular way every time you run the program, simply create a new template and save it as the NORMAL.CWT file. You also need to make sure the On Startup Load Normal Template option is activated. To do so, press P. Then choose File – Advanced in the Preferences dialog box and put a check mark next to the option.

But what parameters do you need to set when you're creating a new template? I'll go through them one at a time.

Track Configuration and Parameters

Before you start recording any MIDI or audio data in SONAR, you have to set up your tracks in the Track view. You need to add tracks and tell SONAR their types (MIDI or audio) by right-clicking in the Track pane of the Track view and choosing either Insert Audio Track or Insert MIDI Track from the menu. You can also use SONAR's Insert menu. Continue doing this until you have all the tracks you need for your template. You can add Track Folders to your template as well; they enable you to group different audio and MIDI tracks together. Software synth instrument tracks can be added, too, but I'll talk about those in Chapter 8.

In addition to adding new tracks, you need to set up the accompanying parameters for each track. These parameters include the name, channel, bank, patch, volume, pan, input, and output.

> **ADDITIONAL PARAMETERS:** When you look in the Track view, you'll notice there are some additional parameters available for adjustment. These parameters are not usually set up when you create a template, so I will cover them later in the book.

You can change all of these parameters directly in the Track view (see Figure 3.4). You can also use the Inspector to change track parameters (and properties), but I'll talk more about that in Chapter 5.

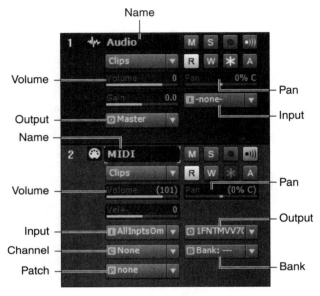

Figure 3.4 You can change all track parameters in the Track view.
Source: Cakewalk®, Inc.

NAME

To name a track, double-click in its Name field in the Track view and then type the name. Press the Enter key on your computer keyboard when you're done; that's all there is to it. A track name can be anything from a short, simple word like *Drums* to a longer, descriptive phrase such as *Background Vocals (Left Channel)*.

MIDI CHANNEL

This parameter is for MIDI tracks only. It tells SONAR what MIDI channel you want it to use to play back the data in a track. To change this parameter, just click the MIDI Channel control and choose a channel.

BANK

Also for MIDI tracks only, the Bank parameter tells SONAR which bank of sounds you want to use in your MIDI instrument. To change this parameter, just click the Bank control and choose a bank.

PATCH

Also for MIDI tracks only, the Patch parameter tells SONAR which patch (or sound) you want to use from the bank in your MIDI instrument. To choose a patch, click the Patch control. If you set up your instrument definitions as described in Chapter 2, you should see the names of the patches for your MIDI instrument in the Patch list.

VOLUME

The Volume parameter sets the initial loudness of a track. That's basically all there is to it. You can set the volume by clicking and dragging in the Volume control. Drag to the left to lower the volume; drag to the right to increase the volume. You can also change the volume numerically by clicking the Volume parameter to highlight it, pressing F2, typing in a new value, and pressing Enter. The value can range from 0 (off) to 127 (maximum) for MIDI tracks and -INF to +6dB for audio tracks. To set the volume to its default value (0dB), double-click it.

PAN

The Pan parameter determines where the sound of a track will be heard in the sound field between two stereo speakers. You can make the sound play out of the left speaker, the right speaker, or anywhere in between. That is called *panning*. You can set the pan by clicking and dragging in the Pan control. Drag to the left to pan the track to the left; drag to the right to pan the track to the right. You can also change the pan numerically as described earlier for Volume. The pan value can range from 100% L (100 percent left) to 100% R (100 percent right). A value of 0% C is dead center. To set the panning to its default value (0% C), double-click it. Pan works on both MIDI and audio tracks.

INPUT

The Input parameter lets SONAR know where the data for that track will be recorded from—an audio track or a MIDI track. To set the Input for an audio track, choose one of the inputs from your sound card from the Input menu. For example, if you have a Cakewalk V-Studio 700, some of your choices might be Left 1-2 (VS-700), Right 1-2 (VS-700), or Stereo 1-2 (VS-700). If you pick either the left or right choice, the track will record audio from either the left or right input on your sound card. If you pick the stereo choice, the track will record audio from both inputs at the same time, making it a stereo audio track.

Setting the Input parameter for a MIDI track is a bit different. Because MIDI can have multiple ports, and each port has 16 different channels, you can choose to record data using any one of those ports/channels. Just make sure your MIDI instrument is set to the same port/channel that you choose as your input, or your performance won't be recorded. You can also use the MIDI Omni setting, which allows SONAR to record data on all 16 channels at the same time. This way, the data from your MIDI instrument will be recorded, regardless of the channel to which it is set. But if you're using multiple instruments, each one set to a different channel, you're better off just setting the correct channel in each of the tracks from the start (also see MIDI Input Presets on the next page.).

OUTPUT (OUTPUT TO)

The Output parameter tells SONAR which MIDI port or sound card output you want to use to play back the data in a track. If the track is MIDI, you can select a MIDI port from the Output menu. If the track is audio, you can select a sound card output or an audio bus from the Output menu.

CHANGING MULTIPLE PROPERTIES: You can also change the properties for multiple tracks simultaneously. Just select the tracks you want to adjust by Ctrl+clicking or Shift+clicking on the appropriate track numbers in the Track view. Then press and hold Ctrl while adjusting the control for the property you would like to change. This is known as the Quick Groups feature.

MIDI Input Presets

When you choose an input for a MIDI track, you might notice a couple of selections in the menu that I didn't mention earlier—the Preset and Manage Presets selections. Normally, when you choose an input for a MIDI track, you are limited to a single port and single channel selection. Using MIDI input presets, you can set up a MIDI track so that it records data from multiple ports and specific multiple channels of your choice. This type of flexibility can come in handy if you have a number of outboard MIDI devices sending MIDI data to SONAR that you would like to have recorded on the same MIDI track.

To set up a MIDI input preset, follow these steps:

1. Click the Input control of the MIDI track and choose Manage Presets to open the MIDI Input Presets dialog box.
2. You'll see two lists in the box. In the left list, you will see all the MIDI ports provided by your MIDI interface. In the right list, you will see all the MIDI channels available for each port. To allow MIDI input on a port/channel, put a check mark under that port/channel. You can activate as many port/channel combinations as you'd like.
3. If you want to allow MIDI input on all the channels of a port, click the OMNI button at the end of the Channel list for that port.
4. When you're finished activating ports and channels, type a name for your new preset in the Preset field at the top of the dialog box.
5. Click the Save button (the floppy disk icon) to save your preset. Click OK.

After you have created your preset(s), they will be listed under the Preset selection in the Input menu for your MIDI track(s).

Timebase

Just like all sequencing software, SONAR uses clock ticks to keep track of the timing of your MIDI performance. Most of the time, you see the clock ticks as measures and beats because the program translates them automatically. Hundreds of clock ticks occur for each measure or beat.

The number of clock ticks that happen within a beat are called *pulses per quarter note* (PPQ) or the *timebase*. The timebase determines the resolution or accuracy of your MIDI timing data. For example, if you want to use eighth-note septuplets (seven eighth notes per quarter note) in your performance, you have to use a timebase that is divisible by seven (such as 168 PPQ); otherwise, SONAR cannot record the septuplets accurately. By default, SONAR uses a timebase of 960 PPQ, which means every quarter note is represented by 960 clock ticks. You can set the timebase anywhere from 48 to 960 PPQ. To set the timebase, press P and choose Project – Clock in the Preferences dialog box. In the Ticks per Quarter-Note section, choose the timebase you want to use.

System Exclusive Banks

SONAR includes a System Exclusive (Sysx) view, which lets you store MIDI System Exclusive messages in up to 256 banks (or storage areas). All the data in the view is saved along with a project, which means that each project can hold its own unique library of Sysx data. This capability can be very useful when you're putting together templates for special MIDI recording situations. Because the Sysx view is a significant part of SONAR, I will talk about it in more detail in Chapter 16. I just wanted to mention it here so that you know that data contained in the view is saved along with your template.

File Information and Comments

SONAR enables you to save description information in a project, including title, subtitle, instructions, author, copyright, keywords, and comments. This information can be useful to remind yourself exactly what the file contains, especially when you're creating a template. To add information to a project, choose Project > Info to open the File Info window. Type the information you want to save with the project file or template.

> **AUTOMATIC FILE INFO:** If you plan to share your project or template files with others, and you want them to follow special instructions you've included in the File Info window (or you just want to be sure they see your copyright notice), you can display the File Info window automatically when the file is opened. Just save the project or template while the File Info window is still open. The only caveat is that the window opens behind the Track view, so it may not be seen right away. Use the Window menu to bring the File Info window to the front.

Tempo, Meter, and Key

Every piece of music needs to have a tempo, meter (time signature), and key, so SONAR sets and saves these parameters within a project or template.

SETTING THE TEMPO

You can set the tempo for your piece by following these steps:

1. Make sure the Transport module is visible in the Control Bar (see Figure 3.5).

Figure 3.5 To set the tempo for a project, you can use the Transport module in the Control Bar.
Source: Cakewalk®, Inc.

2. Click the Tempo display. The Tempo will be highlighted.
3. Type a new value between 8.00 and 1000.00 for the tempo. You can also use the + and − spin controls to adjust the tempo with your mouse.
4. Press Enter to set the tempo.

SETTING THE METER (TIME SIGNATURE) AND KEY (KEY SIGNATURE)

Because a piece of music can have multiple time signatures and key signatures, SONAR will add multiple meters and keys to a project. For the purpose of creating a template, you'll probably want to set only the initial meter and key. To do so, follow these steps:

1. Choose Views > Meter/Key (or press Alt+Shift+6) to open the Meter/Key view.
2. Double-click the first meter/key change in the list to open the Meter/Key Signature dialog box. (For this example, there should be only one meter/key change listed.)
3. Enter the Beats per Measure and the Beat Value you want to use. For example, if your song were in 6/8 time, you would change the Beats per Measure to 6 and the Beat Value to 8.
4. Choose a key from the Key Signature menu. For example, if your song is in the key of A, choose 3 Sharps (A). Click OK.

Other Parameters

A few other parameters are saved along with projects and templates, including synchronization settings, MIDI echo, metronome, record mode, and punch in/out times. You'll usually set these parameters while you're working on a project (not beforehand), so I'll talk more about them in Chapter 5. For the purpose of creating a template, you can just let these parameters be saved at their default values.

ADDITIONAL TEMPLATE MATERIAL: A template can also contain MIDI and audio data, which can be useful if you have some favorite drum grooves or melodic phrases that you like to use frequently in your projects. Simply store these tidbits as clips in one of the tracks, and the MIDI and audio data will be saved along with it when you save the template. Then, whenever you create a new project with that template, the MIDI and audio data will be ready and waiting for you to use.

THE ULTIMATE TEMPLATE: When inspiration hits, you don't want to waste your time fiddling with sequencer setup parameters; you want to be able to start your software and get right to work. If you create a template file that contains everything set just the way you like it, you'll have a much better chance of getting that cool lick down before you forget it. For instructions on how to set up the ultimate template, check out my "MIDI & Digital Audio Music Sequencer Techniques (Part 2)" article (**www.digifreq.com/digifreq/article.asp?ID=13**) at DigiFreq.

Saving Your Project

When it comes time to save your SONAR project, follow these steps:

1. Choose File > Save As to open the Save As dialog box.
2. Choose the type of project file you want to save from the Save as Type menu.
3. Enter a name for the file in the File Name field.
4. By default, SONAR has the Per-Project Audio Folders option activated. Per-project audio folders allow you to create a separate disk drive folder for each of your projects. To disable the Per-Project Audio Folders option when saving your project, remove the check mark next to the Copy All Audio with Project option.
5. If you decide to keep the Per-Project Audio Folders option activated, type a disk path in the Project Path field to be the storage location for your project. You can also browse for a location by clicking the ellipsis button located at the right side of the field.
6. The audio for your project is automatically stored in a folder called *Audio* inside the project folder. If you want to use a different folder name and location for the project audio, type a new disk path in the Audio Path field.
7. If you would like SONAR to create a separate audio file for each unique clip in your project, activate the Create One File per Clip option. This can be useful if you want to keep things organized and keep track of all the clips in your project outside of SONAR. It is also useful for editing audio clips outside of SONAR with another audio application. Click Save.

Project File Types

You can save projects as four different types of files: MIDI (.MID), Open Media Format (.OMF), project (.CWP), and bundle (.CWB).

MIDI Files

If you ever need to collaborate on a MIDI project with someone who owns a sequencing application other than SONAR, you should save your project as a MIDI (.MID) file. A MIDI file is a standard type of file that you can use to transfer musical data between different music software applications. Most music programs on the market today can load and save MIDI files. The problem with MIDI files, however, is that they can store only MIDI data; they can't hold audio data. None of SONAR's settings is saved within a MIDI file, either, so if you're working on a project alone or everyone else in your songwriting group uses SONAR, you don't need to deal with MIDI files. Of course, MIDI files can be useful in other circumstances, such as when you're composing music for multimedia or sharing your music with others via the Internet.

Open Media Format

As with MIDI files, if you collaborate with someone who doesn't own SONAR, you can save your file in Open Media Format (.OMF). Instead of MIDI data, the Open Media Format only saves the audio data from a project. Why would you need this format? Well, you might want to bring your project into another studio where they don't have SONAR available and hire a recording engineer to mix or master your project. To export your project to OMF, follow these steps:

1. Choose File > Export > OMF to open the Export OMF dialog box.
2. From the Save In menu (at the top), select the folder to which you want to save your OMF file. Then type a name for the file in the File Name field.
3. Choose a file type from the Save as Type menu. Choose OMF Version 1 or 2, depending on the application being used to import the OMF file. Usually, newer applications support Version 2.
4. In the Audio Format section, choose whether you want the audio data from your project saved in Wave format or AIFC format. Usually, if you are using a Windows-based PC, you should use Wave format. For Macs, AIFC format is the norm.
5. In the Audio Packaging section, choose whether you want to embed the audio data from your project into the OMF file or whether you want the audio data saved as separate audio files. Choose the Embed Audio within OMF or Reference Audio Externally option, respectively.
6. If you want the stereo tracks in your project to be converted into two separate mono tracks, activate the Split Stereo Tracks into Dual Mono option. This option can come in handy if the application you'll use to open the OMF file only supports stereo tracks as two separate mono tracks.
7. If you have any archived tracks in your SONAR project, you can include them in the exported OMF file by activating the Include Archived Tracks option.
8. In SONAR, Groove clips contain multiple repetitions of the same audio data over a number of different measures in a track. Normally, when you export a project, the Groove clips are simply exported as one clip that contains the Groove clip information. However, some applications might not support this type of clip, so you might need to save each repetition of each Groove clip as a separate audio clip. To do so, activate the Mix Each Groove Clip as a Separate Clip option. This process can take a long time, depending on the size of your project. Click Save.

If you choose to embed the audio data in the OMF file, you will export only one file. If you choose to reference the audio data externally, you will have one OMF file, along with all the audio files representing the tracks from your original project.

Project Files

If you're working on a project that contains only MIDI data and no audio data, you should save the project as a project (.CWP) file. Project files store all the MIDI data in a project, plus all the parameter settings for the project. Project files do not store audio data, but they can reference it.

> **MANAGING PROJECTS MANUALLY:** If you decide to manage your project audio files manually using the Per-Project Audio Folders option, you should save your audio projects as project files. In this case, the audio data is stored separately from the project file.

Bundle Files

You can save projects that contain both MIDI and audio data as bundle (.CWB) files, although I recommend saving them as work (.CWP) files and using the Per-Project Audio Folders option. If you use a bundle file, you can store all the data in a project (MIDI data, audio data, and project parameter settings) in a single file, but this format is best used for archiving completed projects. A single file makes it very easy to keep track of all the data in a project and make a backup of the project for easy recovery in case something goes wrong.

> **BEWARE OF BUNDLES:** Unfortunately, bundle files have been known to be unstable at times. Since I started writing SONAR books, I've heard from quite a few users who have had trouble with bundle files becoming corrupt. There hasn't been any explanation as to why this happens (and it doesn't happen often), but the best way to avoid the situation is not to use bundle files at all. Instead, use the Per-Project Audio Folders option and save your project as a project file in its own folder. Then, to save disk space when archiving your projects, you can use a compression utility to save the folder to a compressed file format, such as a ZIP file. Windows XP, Vista, and 7 have built-in support for ZIP files.

Additional Saving Features

SONAR provides some extra save-related features that can help you recover past project versions.

Auto-Save Feature

SONAR has an Auto-Save feature that automatically saves your data to a special backup file at fixed time intervals or every time a certain number of changes have been made to the project. Using this feature is a great way to keep your data safe in case a power outage occurs or if you make a huge mistake that you can't undo. To activate Auto-Save, follow these steps:

1. Press P and choose File – Advanced in the Preferences dialog box.
2. For the option Auto-Save Every 0 Minutes or 0 Changes, set either the number of minutes or the number of changes to occur for SONAR to automatically save your project.
3. If you want to disable Auto-Save, set both the minutes and changes values back to 0. Click OK.

During an automatic save, SONAR saves your project in a special file with a different name. If your project is named myproject.cwp, for example, SONAR automatically saves to a file named "auto save version of myproject.cwp." If you ever need to recover your project, you can just open the special Auto-Save file and then save it under the original filename.

File Versioning

As you work on a project, you will save it many different times so that you don't lose your changes during each recording session. There may be times, however, when you wish you could go back to a different version of the same project. One of the most common reasons for this is that you made some major changes to the project that can no longer be undone. In this type of situation, SONAR's File Versioning feature can come in very handy.

When using File Versioning, SONAR will automatically save multiple, successive versions of your project—each with its own date and timestamp. If you ever want to revert to an earlier version of the project, you simply choose the file with the appropriate date/time, and your project is instantly returned to a previous state. To activate File Versioning, do the following:

1. Press P and choose File – Advanced in the Preferences dialog box.
2. Activate the Enable versioning of project (.CWP) files option.

3. For the Number of Versions to Keep parameter, enter the number of file versions you want SONAR to keep track of while File Versioning is active. You can enter a number as high as 999, but remember that each file version is an actual project file that is saved to disk and takes up space on your hard drive. For a small project, something like 5 is a reasonable number, but for larger projects that require many changes, you may want to use 20 or more. It depends on how far back you may want to revert the project. Click OK.

Now when you edit your project and save it, the current version of the project is saved under the original project name, and a previous version (without the edits you made) is saved using the project name plus a timestamp in the filename. Once SONAR reaches the Number of Versions to Keep limit, one of the versions is bumped off the list and deleted.

If you ever want to revert the current project back to a previous state, you need to choose File > Revert. The Revert dialog box shows a list of all the dates and times related to the previous versions of the project. Simply select a date/time and click OK. SONAR loads the data from the timestamped project file, and you are instantly returned to the previous version of the project, which now becomes the current version.

Finding Your Way Around the SONAR Workspace

T O RECORD, PLAY, AND EDIT YOUR MUSIC IN SONAR, you have to know how to navigate through the data in your project. SONAR includes a number of tools that examine and manipulate your data: the Track, Piano Roll, Staff, and Event views. Although each of these views provides a different way to edit your data, they all share some common means of control. In other words, even though your data appears (and is edited) differently in each view, you access the data in a similar manner, no matter which view you use. A little confused? Don't worry, you'll understand exactly what I mean after you finish reading this chapter.

The Now Time

In addition to the musical data itself, the timing of your performance is stored during recording. This means that SONAR keeps track of exactly when you play each note on your MIDI keyboard during a performance, and it stores those notes along with a *timestamp* (a timing value) containing the measure, beat, and clock tick when each note occurred.

To give you access to your data in a project, SONAR provides a feature known as the *Now time*. The Now time is essentially a pointer that indicates your current time location within a project. For example, the beginning of a project has a Now time of 1:01:000 (designating measure, beat, and tick), which is the first beat of the first measure. If you want to view the data at the second beat of the tenth measure, for example, you have to set the Now time to 10:02:000. Of course, you can get more precise by specifying clock ticks, such as a Now time of 5:03:045, which would be the forty-fifth clock tick of the third beat in the fifth measure.

The Now time is also updated in real time, which means it changes constantly during recording or playback of a project. For example, when you play your project, the Now time counts along and shows you the current measure, beat, and tick while you listen to your music.

Show Me the Now Time

You can view the Now time in several different ways. The Now time is displayed numerically in the Transport module of the Control Bar (see Figure 4.1) and the upper-left corner of the Track view.

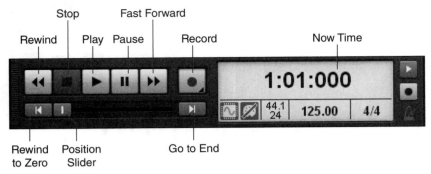

Figure 4.1 You can view the Now time via the Control Bar and Track view.
Source: Cakewalk®, Inc.

You'll notice that the Now time is shown as measures, beats, and ticks. But it can be displayed in a variety of formats, including: hours, minutes, seconds, and frames (known as *SMPTE*), milliseconds, and samples. Left-click either display to cycle through the formats or right-click to choose specifically. Both displays can be set independently.

WHAT IS SMPTE? SMPTE (which is derived from the Society of Motion Picture and Television Engineers) is a special timing code used for synchronizing audio and video data, although it can be used for other purposes, too. NASA originally developed the technology because it needed an accurate way to keep track of space mission data. In SONAR, you can use SMPTE to keep track of the timing of your project. SONAR automatically converts the measures, beats, and ticks in a project to the hours, minutes, seconds, and frames format used by SMPTE. The Frames parameter comes from the fact that SMPTE is used extensively with video, film, and television.

Video is created by recording a series of still picture frames very quickly. When these frames are played back, you see them as a moving picture. You can use SMPTE to time video data accurately, down to a single frame. Every second of video data usually has 30 frames, but the number depends on the data format. You'll learn more details about using SMPTE in Chapter 5.

THE BIG TIME VIEW: If you have some of your MIDI instruments set up in your home studio a fair distance away from your computer, you might have trouble reading the very tiny Now time display on the Transport module of the Control Bar. To remedy this situation, Cakewalk has included the Big Time view, which displays the Now time in large numbers on your computer screen.

To access the Big Time view, choose Views > Big Time (or press Alt+Shift+3). The Big Time view has its own window, so you can position it anywhere within the SONAR workspace. You can toggle the time format and the beat marker by clicking them. You can also change the font, color, and size of the text display by right-clicking in the window and then making your selections in the standard Windows Font dialog box.

In addition to being displayed numerically, the Now time is displayed graphically in any of SONAR's view windows. In the Track, Piano Roll, and Staff views, the Now time is displayed as a vertical line cursor that extends from the top to the bottom of the view. As the Now time changes (from being set manually or in real time during playback or recording), the cursor in each of the views follows along in perfect sync and indicates graphically the place in the project at which the Now time is pointing currently. To see what I mean, try the following steps:

1. Open a project in SONAR that contains MIDI data.
2. Click the Play button (or press the spacebar) to start playing the project.
3. Look at the Track view. See the Now time cursor moving across the track display as the music plays?
4. Choose Views > Piano Roll View (or press Alt+3) and look at the Piano Roll view. The same thing is happening, right? Notice the row of numbers just above the place where the Now time cursor is moving. This is the Time Ruler, and every view has one (except the Event view, which I'll talk about shortly). The Time Ruler displays the measure numbers in the current project. By lining up the top of the Now time cursor with the Time Ruler in any of the views, you can get a quick estimate of the current Now time.

TIME RULER FORMAT: If you right-click the Time Ruler in the Track view and choose Time Ruler Format, you can change the format of the measurements shown. So instead of keeping track of the Now time in measures, beats, and ticks, you can use hours, minutes, seconds, and frames. The sample's measurement setting comes in handy when you are editing audio data, which I'll discuss in Chapters 6 and 7. You can also display multiple Time Rulers as discussed in Chapter 3.

---

5. Choose Views > Staff View (or press Alt+6) and look at the Staff view. Like the Piano Roll view, the Staff view has a scrolling Now time cursor and a Time Ruler.
6. Choose Views > Event List (or press Alt+8) and look at the Event List view. It's different from all the other views because it shows the data as one long list instead of displaying it from left to right. And instead of a vertical line, it shows the Now time cursor as a small red box. While a project plays, the Now time cursor in the Event List view moves down the list, and it marks the same place in the project that all the other view cursors do. Everything is synchronized to the Now time.
7. To control playback, you can use the Transport module in the Control Bar (see Figure 4.1) or your PC keyboard: Play/Stop = spacebar; Rewind to Zero = W; and Go to End = Ctrl+End. If you'd like to control Rewind, Fast Forward, and Pause via your keyboard, you can set up shortcuts for the following functions in the Key Bindings dialog box (as explained in Chapter 2): Start/Stop Rewind, Start/Stop Fast Forward, and Play/Pause.

PLAYBACK AUTOMATIC STOP: You'll notice that once the Now time reaches the end of the longest track, SONAR keeps playing. If you would rather have SONAR stop playback automatically, choose Options > Stop at Project End from the Track view menu.

Setting the Now Time

As you just saw, the Now time changes automatically as a project is played, but you can also set it manually. SONAR gives you this capability so you can access different parts of your project for editing.

Numerically

If you want to set the Now time to a precise numerical value, use the Go dialog box, as follows:

1. If you want to set the Now time using measures, beats, and ticks, press G to open the Go dialog box.
2. Type the measures, beats, and ticks value you want to use and press Enter (or click OK). You can also click the spin controls to change the value.

> **NOW TIME SHORTCUTS:** If you want to set the Now time quickly to a particular measure or beat, you don't have to enter all the numerical values. For example, to set the Now time to measure 2, type **2**. That's it. Or to set the Now time to measure 5, beat 3, type **5:3** or **5 spacebar 3**. To specify ticks, you must enter something for all the values.

3. If you want to set the Now time using hours, minutes, seconds, and frames, press P. Then choose Customization – Display in the Preferences dialog box and put a check mark next to the Display All Times as SMPTE option. Click OK. Keep in mind that this option changes all time entry in SONAR to the SMPTE format, so you'll need to uncheck it to go back to measures, beats, and ticks.

4. Press G and type the hours, minutes, seconds, and frames values you want to use.

> **SMPTE SHORTCUTS:** Just as with the measures, beats, and ticks, if you want to set the Now time quickly to a particular hour, minute, or second, you don't have to enter all the numerical values. For example, to set the Now time to 2 minutes, type **0:2**. To set the Now time to 5 minutes, 3 seconds, type **0:5:3**. To specify frames, you must enter something for all the values.

Graphically

Remember when I described the Time Rulers in each of the views? Well, you can change the Now time quickly by simply clicking in the bottom area of any of the Time Rulers.

1. With a project open, click on or below the numbers in the Time Ruler of the Track view. See how the Now time changes?

2. Open the Piano Roll view. Then click the Time Ruler in the Piano Roll view. Same result, right? Depending on where you click the Time Ruler, the Now time changes to the appropriate value within the measure that you click.

> **SNAP TO GRID:** You might notice that when you click the Time Ruler in any of the views, the Now time is automatically set to a value close to where you clicked but not at the exact location. This is due to SONAR's Snap to Grid feature. I'll talk more about this in Chapter 6, but for now, you can press N to toggle the feature on/off.

3. As before, the Event List view works a little differently. Here, you can click any event in the list, and the Now time will change to the exact timing value of that event.

The Position Slider

Another quick way to set the Now time graphically is to use the Position slider in the Transport module of the Control Bar (see Figure 4.1). To use the slider, just click and drag it. As you drag the slider, the Now time will update one measure at a time. Double-click the slider to quickly rewind to the beginning of a project.

The Now Time Marker

As you were clicking around in the Time Rulers of the various views, you might have noticed the flag attached to the top of the Now time cursor. This flag is the Now time marker. It adds a special functionality to the Now time cursor. By clicking and dragging the Now time marker, you can set a place in your project to which the Now time cursor will return every time you stop playback.

In earlier versions of SONAR, the Now time cursor would always return to the beginning of a project when playback was stopped. Now you can have it return to the Now time marker instead. Why is this useful? Well, suppose that you're editing data in a certain section of a project, and you want to hear how your changes sound. Just set the Now time marker to the edit spot and start playback. When you stop playback, you'll be returned to the edit spot you designated with the marker. In addition, you can drag the Now time marker during playback (but not recording) to change the Now time on the fly.

> **REWIND TO NOW MARKER:** If you would rather not have the Now time cursor return to the Now time marker when you stop playback, choose Options > On Stop, Rewind to Now Marker in the Track view menu. You can also temporarily toggle this setting by holding down Ctrl while you press the spacebar to start/stop playback. For example, if you have the option activated, SONAR will automatically rewind to the Now time marker when you press the spacebar to stop playback. If you press Ctrl+Space instead, SONAR will temporarily deactivate the option and stop playback at the current Now time cursor position and move the Now time marker to the stop point. If you want to stop playback without rewinding or moving the Now time marker, you can click the Pause button in the Transport module of the Control Bar. To access Pause via the keyboard, you can set up a key binding for the Play/Pause function, as described in Chapter 2.

The Go Functions

In addition to allowing you to set the Now time numerically and graphically, SONAR provides a few special functions that let you quickly change the Now time to some musically related points in a project. To activate them, press the appropriate key(s) (shown in parentheses). The following sections provide explanations for the functions.

Go-Time (G)

Go-Time changes the Now time numerically by entering measure, beat, and tick values. It works as described earlier in this chapter in Setting the Now Time – Numerically.

Go-From and Go-Thru (Shift+G)

When you're editing data in SONAR, you need to select the data that you want to use. This process is the same as in any computer program that lets you work with data. For instance, if you want to delete some text in a word processor, first you select the data to highlight it, and then you delete it.

If you have some data currently selected in your project, you can set the Now time to the time that corresponds to the beginning (called the *From time*) or the end (called the *Thru time*) of the selection using the Go-From and Go-Thru functions, respectively. But while Shift+G is set up by default for Go-From, there is no default shortcut for Go-Thru. However, you can set up your own key binding for the Go-Thru function, as described in Chapter 2.

Go-Beginning and Go-End (Ctrl+Home and Ctrl+End)

The Go-Beginning and Go-End functions are pretty self-explanatory. Simply put, they set the Now time to correspond to the beginning or the end of a project, respectively.

Go-Previous Measure and Go-Next Measure (Ctrl+PgUp and Ctrl+PgDn)

As with Go-Beginning and Go-End, Go-Previous Measure and Go-Next Measure are self-explanatory. They let you set the Now time to correspond to the first beat of the previous measure or the first beat of the next measure relative to the current Now time, respectively. In other words, if the Now time is set at 5:01:000 (beat 1 of measure 5), selecting Go-Previous Measure changes it to 4:01:000 (beat 1 of measure 4), and selecting Go-Next Measure changes it to 6:01:000 (beat 1 of measure 6).

If, however, the Now time is set to something like 5:01:050, Go-Previous Measure actually changes it to the first beat of the current measure, which, in this case, would be 5:01:000.

Go-Previous Marker and Go-Next Marker (Ctrl+Shift+PgUp and Ctrl+Shift+PgDn)

The Go-Previous Marker and Go-Next Marker functions work in a similar manner to the Go-Previous Measure and Go-Next Measure functions. Go-Previous Marker and Go-Next Marker set the Now time to correspond to the closest previous marker or next marker relative to the current Now time. Of course, because I haven't told you about markers yet, you're probably wondering what I mean. So let's talk about markers, shall we?

Markers, Oh My!

All the methods for setting the Now time that I've described so far have been based on numbers or predefined musical designations, such as measures, beats, or the beginning and ending of a project. These methods are all fine when you already have the music for your project written out so you know exactly where everything occurs ahead of time, but what if you're creating a song from scratch simply by recording the parts on the fly? In a case like that, being able to put names on certain locations within a project would be very helpful, and that's exactly what markers do.

Using markers, you can assign a name to any exact point in time (in either measures, beats, and ticks or SMPTE) in a project. They are great for designating the places where the verses and choruses start and end within a song. And they make it easy for you to jump to any point in a project that you specify by name.

Make Your Mark(ers)

Creating markers is a simple process. Essentially, you just need to set the Now time to the measure, beat, and tick at which you want to place the marker in the project, activate the Marker dialog box, and type in a name. Activating the Marker dialog box is the key here because you can do so in a number of different ways. To create a marker, just follow these steps:

1. Set the Now time to the measure, beat, and tick or the SMPTE time at which you want to place the marker in the project.
2. Choose Project > Insert Marker to open the Marker dialog box. You can also open the Marker dialog box by pressing M; holding the Ctrl key and clicking just above the Time Ruler (the Marker section) in the Track, Staff, or Piano Roll view; right-clicking on a Time Ruler; clicking on the Insert Marker button in the Markers module of the Control Bar; or clicking on the Insert Marker button in the Markers view.
3. Type a name for the marker in the Name field.
4. If you want the marker to be assigned to a measure/beat/tick value, you don't need to do anything more. The measure/beat/tick time of the marker is shown in the Time field in the middle of the Marker dialog box.
5. If you want the marker to be assigned to a SMPTE time, activate the Lock to SMPTE (Real World) Time option.

LOCK TO SMPTE TIME: If you use the Lock to SMPTE (Real World) Time value, your marker will be assigned an exact hour/minute/second/frame value. It will retain that value, no matter what. Even if you change the tempo of the project, the marker will keep the same time value, although its measure/beat/tick location might change because of the tempo. This feature is especially handy when you're putting music and sound to video because you need to have cues that always happen at an exact moment in the project.

By leaving a marker assigned to a measure/beat/tick value, you can be sure that it will always occur at that measure, beat, and tick, even if you change the tempo of the project.

When you click OK, your marker (with its name) will be added to the Marker section, just above the Time Ruler in the Track, Staff, and Piano Roll views.

REAL-TIME MARKERS: Usually, you add markers to a project while no real-time activity is going on, but you can also add them while a project is playing. Simply press M, and SONAR will create a marker at the current Now time. The new marker will be assigned a temporary name automatically; you can change this name later.

Editing the Markers

Editing existing markers is just as easy as creating new ones. You can change their names and times, make copies of them, and delete them.

Changing Marker Names

To change the name of a marker, follow these steps:

1. Right-click the marker in the Marker section of the Time Ruler in one of the views to open the Marker dialog box. Alternatively, choose Views > Markers (or press Alt+Shift+4) to open the Markers view and double-click the marker in the list to open the Marker dialog box.
2. Type a new name for the marker. Click OK.

Changing Marker Time

Follow these steps to change the time value of a marker numerically:

1. Right-click the marker in one of the Time Rulers or double-click it in the Markers view.
2. Type a new measure/beat/tick value for the marker. If you want to use a SMPTE value, activate the Lock to SMPTE (Real World) Time option and then type a new hour/minute/second/frame value for the marker. Click OK.

You can also change the time value of a marker graphically by simply dragging the marker within the Marker section of the Time Ruler in one of the views. Drag the marker to the left to decrease its time value or drag it to the right to increase its time value.

Making a Copy of a Marker

To make a copy of a marker, follow these steps:

1. Hold down the Ctrl key.
2. Click and drag a marker in the Marker section of the Time Ruler in one of the views to a new time location.
3. Release the mouse button and then the Ctrl key. SONAR will display the Marker dialog box.
4. Enter a name for the marker. You can also change the time by typing a new value, if you want. The time value is initially set to the time for the location on the Time Ruler to which you dragged the marker. Click OK.

Deleting a Marker

You can delete a marker in one of two ways—either directly in the Track, Staff, or Piano Roll view or via the Markers view. Here's the exact procedure:

    1a. If you want to use the Track, Staff, or Piano Roll view, click and hold the left mouse button on the marker you want to delete.

    or

    1b. If you want to use the Markers view, choose Views > Markers (or press Alt+Shift+4) to open the Markers view. Then select the marker you want to delete from the list.

    2. Press the Delete key.

Navigating with Markers

Of course, what good would creating markers do if you couldn't use them to navigate through the data in your project? What's more, all you need to do is select the name of a marker, and the Now time will be set automatically to the exact time of that marker. You can jump to a specific marker in a project in two different ways—by using either the Markers view or the Markers module in the Control Bar.

Using the Markers View

To jump to a specific marker using the Markers view, follow these steps:

    1. Choose Views > Markers (or press Alt+Shift+4) to open the Markers view.

    2. Select the marker to which you want to jump from the list. SONAR will set the Now time to correspond to that marker, and the Track, Staff, Piano Roll, and Event List views will jump to that time.

Using the Markers Module

To jump to a specific marker using the Markers module, just select the marker from the menu (see Figure 4.2).

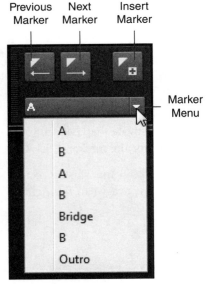

Figure 4.2 Using the Markers module, you can set the Now time to any marker by simply selecting a name from the menu.
Source: Cakewalk®, Inc.

SONAR will set the Now time to correspond to that marker, and the Track, Staff, Piano Roll, and Event List views will jump to that time.

QUICK MARKER LIST: Another quick way to jump to a specific marker is to press G to access the Go dialog box. Then press F5 to bring up a list of all the markers in the current project. Select a marker from the list and click OK twice. The Now time will be set to the time corresponding to that marker.

Searching for Data

Until now, I have been describing how to navigate through the data in a project by somehow specifying the Now time, with the result being that you go to a specific point in the project. Well, what happens when you don't know the exact position to which you want to move in a project? For instance, out of all the data in all the tracks in your project, suppose that you need to set the Now time to the first occurrence of the note Middle C? Instead of playing the project and trying to listen for the note or looking through each and every track manually, you can use SONAR's Go-Search function.

Go-Search examines all the data in your project automatically and finds any MIDI events that have certain attributes that you specify. Upon finding the first event of the specified type, Go-Search sets the Now time to correspond to that event. This function is very useful for finding significant points within a project and placing markers there or for doing precision editing tasks. To use the Go-Search function, follow these steps:

1. Set the Now time to the beginning of the project. If you don't take this step, Go-Search will start looking at your data at the current Now time, not at the beginning of the project. This means, for example, that if the Now time is currently set to 10:01:000, Go-Search does not look at any of the data contained in the first nine measures.
2. Select a track in the project by clicking on its track number.
3. Choose Process > Find/Change to open the Event Filter – Search dialog box.
4. Select the criteria for your search. Don't let all the settings in the Event Filter – Search dialog box intimidate you; they aren't very complicated to use. Basically, all you need to do is select the types of MIDI events you want to include in your search. For instance, if you want to look for MIDI note and pitch wheel events (but nothing else), deselect all the event types, except for Note and Wheel.

DESELECT ALL EVENT TYPES: By the way, whenever you open the Event Filter – Search dialog box, it automatically has all event types selected. To deselect all event types quickly, click the None button. The All button performs the exact opposite operation.

After you select all your event types, you need to set the ranges for each of the parameters. For example, suppose that you want to look for any MIDI note events between the pitches of C5 and G7 and with a velocity between 50 and 80. To do so, simply set the Note Key Minimum parameter to C5, the Note Key Maximum parameter to G7, the Note Velocity Minimum parameter to 50, and the Note Velocity Maximum parameter to 80. You can also specify a range of durations (note length) if you want. Each event type has its own unique set of parameter ranges: Key Aftertouch has key and pressure parameters, Patch Change has bank and patch number parameters, and so on. You can also set up searches that are a little more complicated by excluding ranges of parameters. If you select the Exclude (exc) option next to any of the parameter range settings, the search excludes event types with that specific parameter range. For example, if you want to search for MIDI note events that do not fall within the range of C5 and G7, you set up the Minimum and Maximum parameters, as in the earlier example, and you activate the Key Exclude option. Using the Event Filter – Search dialog box, you can specify special events, too, such as Audio, SysxData, Text, and Chord events. These special events don't include any additional parameter settings, though, so Go-Search simply finds any events of that kind within the data of your project. Finally, you can choose to set a range of MIDI channels, beats, or ticks to search. These are called *non-special events*.

SAVING PRESETS: Because setting these search criteria every time you need to find specific data in a project can be tedious, it would be nice if you could save the settings for future use. Well, you can. Just type a name in the Preset field at the top of the Event Filter – Search dialog box and click the Save button (the button with the little disk icon on it). All your current search criteria settings will be saved under that name. The next time you use Go-Search, you can simply select the name from the Preset drop-down list, and all your previous settings will be loaded. You can save as many Presets as you want, and if you ever want to delete one, just select it from the list and click the Delete button (the button with the red X on it).

---

5. Click OK. Then click Cancel twice to close both the Event – Filter Replace and Event Filter – Search dialog boxes. The reasoning for this is that the Go-Search function uses the criteria in the Event Filter – Search dialog, but that dialog is actually part of another function called Process > Find/Replace, which I'll be talking more about in Chapter 7.
6. Choose Edit > Select > None (or press Ctrl+Shift+A) to get rid of the track selection you made earlier, unless you only want to search in the selected track. If you select some data in the project, the search will be conducted only on that selected data.
7. Press Ctrl+G to find the first instance of the search criteria in the project.

SONAR will search through the data in your project, find the first event that falls under the search parameters that you specified, and then set the Now time to correspond to that event. If you want to apply that same search again to find the next event with the same criteria, press Ctrl+G again. SONAR will continue the search (beginning at the current Now time), find the next event that falls under the search parameters you specified, set the Now time to correspond to that event, and so on.

5

Recording Audio and MIDI

B EING ABLE TO RECORD AND PLAY YOUR MUSIC WITH SONAR turns your computer into a full-fledged recording studio. You'll probably use the recording and playback features of SONAR most often. Therefore, I'm going to devote separate sections of the chapter to the various ways you can possibly record data in SONAR.

Preliminary Parameters

In Chapter 3, you learned about a number of parameters you could save to define a project template. Some of those parameters were related to recording, including track parameters, timebase, tempo, meter, and key. I'll mention those parameters throughout this chapter, but I won't go into detail about how to change them.

The Inspector

Setting the parameters for individual tracks can be cumbersome sometimes because you have to widen the track parameter display before you can access the parameters for a track. To make setting track parameters easier, SONAR provides the Inspector. You can use the Inspector for audio, MIDI, and Instrument tracks, as well as buses. To expand/collapse the Inspector, press I. By default, the Inspector is docked on the left side of the SONAR workspace, but you can dock it to the right or undock (float) it as explained in Chapter 2.

When you click on a track icon to make the track active, the Inspector displays the relevant parameters for that track, plus the parameters for the bus to which the track is being routed for output. This means that you can keep the track parameters in the Track pane hidden, but still have easy access to them simply by making the appropriate track active. The Inspector also allows you to access current track and clip properties by clicking the Clip (Shift+I) and Track (Ctrl+Shift+I) buttons at the top, respectively. I'll talk more about these in detail throughout the book, along with the SONAR Producer exclusive ProChannel (see Chapter 11).

In addition to the track parameters, you need to be aware of a few other parameters before you do any recording in SONAR. I didn't describe them in Chapter 3 because you usually set the following parameters while you're working on a project, not beforehand.

Metronome

If you've ever taken music lessons, you know what a *metronome* is. It's a device that makes a sound for each beat in each measure of a piece of music. You simply set the tempo you want, and the metronome sounds each beat accurately and precisely. You use this device to help you play in time with the correct rhythm. In SONAR, the metronome feature helps you keep the right time so that your music data is stored at the right measure and beat within the project.

The metronome feature in SONAR is electronic, and it's a bit more sophisticated than what you might find in a handheld unit. First, the tempo for the metronome is the same as the tempo setting for the project, so when you set the project tempo, you're also setting the metronome tempo. Metronome functions are accessed via the Transport module in the Control Bar (see Figure 5.1). You can toggle the metronome on/off for playback/recording using the Metronome During Playback (Ctrl+F3) and Metronome During Record (F3) buttons, respectively.

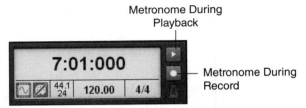

Figure 5.1 Use the Metronome buttons to turn it on/off and access its other parameters.
Source: Cakewalk®, Inc.

Normally, you would just have to turn the metronome on and off, but in SONAR, you need to set several other parameters before you use the metronome feature. You can access these parameters by right-clicking either of the Metronome buttons to open the Project – Metronome pane of the Preferences dialog box.

Metronome Settings

Using the metronome settings, you can determine whether the metronome will sound during playback, recording, or both by activating the Playback and Recording options. You also can select whether the metronome will use your computer's sound card or one of your MIDI instruments to make its sound by activating the Use Audio Metronome or Use MIDI Note option. In addition, you can set a Beat Subdivision. This parameter controls how many times the metronome will sound between measures on the unaccented beats. For example, if you have a project in 4/4 time and you set the Beat Subdivision to 1, then the metronome will sound one accented beat at the start of each measure and three unaccented beats in-between to designate each quarter note. If you set the Beat Subdivision to 1/2, then the metronome will sound one accented beat at the start of each measure and seven unaccented beats in-between to designate each eighth note, and so on.

Count-In

Using the Record Count-In option, you can get the feel of the tempo before SONAR starts recording your performance. Depending on how you set it, the metronome will sound a number of beats or measures before recording begins. For example, if your project is set for a 4/4 meter, and you set the Count-In option to 1 Measure, the metronome will sound four beats before SONAR begins recording.

Audio Metronome

If you choose the Use Audio Metronome option, the settings in the Audio Metronome section determine which sound card output will be used for the metronome sound, as well as the type of sound the metronome will use when it plays. To choose a sound for the first beat of every metronome tick, use the First Beat menu. There is also a dB setting located to the right of the list that determines how loud each first beat will be. To choose a sound for all other metronome ticks, use the Other Beats menu. There is also a dB setting for this parameter. Normally, you'll want to have the First Beat parameter set a little louder than the Other Beats parameter so that the first metronome tick is accented.

> **METRONOME SOUNDS:** SONAR ships with 38 different sounds that you can use for the audio metronome. If you would like to use some of your own sounds for the audio metronome, you can do so by adding audio files to SONAR's metronome folder: C:\Cakewalk Content\SONAR X2 Producer\Metronome (substitute Producer with Studio or Essential, depending on your version).
>
> Just copy the audio file representing your sound to this folder. The file must be a WAV file, using the PCM (no compression) format, 16-bit, 44.1 kHz sample rate. The name that you give to the file is what will show up in the First Beat and Other Beats lists.

After choosing metronome sounds, use the Output list to choose the bus or sound card output you would like to use for the audio metronome.

MIDI Note

If you select the Use MIDI Note option, the settings in the MIDI Note section determine which MIDI instrument is used to make the metronome sound and which note is used for the first beat and remaining beats of each measure. In the Port and Channel fields, you can set the MIDI port and channel that your MIDI instrument uses. Duration determines how long each metronome "beep" will sound. The duration is measured in ticks, so if you use a timebase of 120 ticks per quarter note, a duration of 15 would be equivalent to a thirty-second note.

You can set the pitch (Key) and loudness (Velocity) of the first beat and remaining beats in each measure by using the First Beat and Other Beats options. If you want the first beat of each measure to be accented, you should set the velocity a little higher in the First Beat Velocity parameter. For example, you could set it to 127 and set the Other Beats Velocity to 110. Also, if your MIDI instrument is General MIDI–compatible, and you set the Channel option to 10, you can use a percussion instrument for the metronome sound. I like to use a rimshot sound.

MIDI Echo

Some MIDI instruments do not provide any way for you to play them except by sending them MIDI messages. These instruments are called *modules*. To play a module, you need to trigger the module's sounds by playing another instrument, such as a MIDI keyboard. If you connect the MIDI output from the MIDI keyboard to the MIDI input of the module, you can play the sounds in the module by performing on the keyboard.

But what if you want to record your performance using SONAR? In that case, you would have to connect the MIDI output from the keyboard to the MIDI input on your computer. This means that you would no longer be sending MIDI messages from the keyboard to the module, so how would you hear your performance? You could connect the MIDI output from your computer to the MIDI input of the module, but the MIDI messages from the keyboard would still go directly to the computer and not the module. To remedy this situation, SONAR includes a feature called *MIDI echo*.

Basically, MIDI echo takes the MIDI messages from your computer's MIDI input(s) and sends them back out to your computer's MIDI output(s). You can control the MIDI channels *from* which the data is echoed and the ports and channels *to* which it is echoed.

The Input Echo Button

Each MIDI track in a project provides an Input Echo button. This button is located right next to the Mute, Solo, and Record controls in a track (see Figure 5.2).

Figure 5.2 The Input Echo button controls MIDI echo for a MIDI track.
Source: Cakewalk®, Inc.

The Input Echo button provides three states: On, Off, and Auto Thru. By default, the Input Echo button is set to Off. When Input Echo is set to Off, MIDI data coming into a MIDI track (via the MIDI port/channel that is set using its Input parameter) is not echoed to the MIDI port that is set using its Output parameter. However, if you make a MIDI track as the active track (by clicking its icon), Input Echo is set automatically to Auto Thru, which means that any MIDI data coming into the MIDI port/channel set in that track's Input parameter is echoed automatically to the MIDI port set in that track's Output parameter.

> **DISABLE AUTO THRU:** If you would rather not have Auto Thru active so your MIDI track doesn't enable MIDI echo automatically when the track is activated, you can disable the Auto Thru feature by pressing P. Then choose MIDI – Playback and Recording and remove the check mark next to the Always Echo Current MIDI Track option.

By clicking the Input Echo button, you can change its state. If you click the button to turn it on, it will become highlighted. When the Input Echo for a MIDI track is turned on, it means that any MIDI data coming into the MIDI port/channel set in that track's Input parameter is echoed to the MIDI port set in that track's Output parameter.

Echo Applications

So what can you do with MIDI input echoing? The most basic application allows you to hear the sounds you are playing on your MIDI module or software synth, as I described earlier. But you can also use input echoing for some more sophisticated applications, such as recording multiple MIDI performances at the same time or layering sounds of multiple synths from one MIDI performance.

RECORDING MULTIPLE PERFORMANCES

Suppose that you're in a situation where you need to record the performances of more than one MIDI musician at the same time, and each musician is using a different synth. This means that each one will want to hear his individual performance during recording. Accomplishing this is actually quite easy with SONAR's Input Echo feature.

Depending on the number of musicians you need to record, you would create a MIDI track in your project to represent each musician. Then set the Input parameter for each MIDI track to correspond to the MIDI port/channel each musician is using for his MIDI device. Next, you would set the Output parameter for each MIDI track to the MIDI port that is being used for each musician's synthesizer. Finally, you would set the Input Echo button to On for each of the MIDI tracks. Each musician's individual performance would be recorded to a separate MIDI track, and during recording, each musician would be able to hear his performance in real time.

LAYERING MULTIPLE SYNTHS

Creating new synthesizer sounds requires knowledge of synth programming, and not everyone has the time or patience to try programming his own sounds. But there's an easier way to experiment with new synth sounds. You can combine (or layer) the sounds from multiple synths to create an entirely new sound. SONAR's Input Echo feature makes this very easy to do. Here's an example of how you can accomplish it:

1. Choose File > New to create a new project.
2. Choose Insert > Soft Synth > Dimension LE (or Dimension Pro, depending on your version of SONAR).
3. In the Insert Soft Synth Options dialog box, activate the Simple Instrument Track and Synth Property Page options. Leave all the other options deactivated.
4. Assign a sound to the Dimension LE (Pro) synth by clicking the area labeled Empty Program and choosing a preset from the Program Browser by double-clicking it.
5. Repeat Steps 2, 3, and 4 to set up one more software synth.
6. Set the Input parameters for both of the Instrument tracks you just created to the same MIDI port and channel that you are using for your MIDI keyboard.
7. Set the Input Echo buttons on both Instrument tracks to On.
8. Play your MIDI keyboard.

Isn't that cool? When you play on your MIDI keyboard, you should hear the sounds from both of the software synths playing at the same time. They are effectively layered together, creating a new sound from the combination of both. Of course, you can take this even further and continue to layer more synths, creating a huge ensemble of sound.

MIDI Input Quantize

If you're not especially proficient at playing your musical instrument, you might find that your recorded notes end up a little ahead or behind the beat. If you're going for a live feel and your playing isn't overly sloppy, then using the raw track may be fine. However, if you're going for a more exact sound (such as the type used in electronic or techno-style music), you might want to apply quantizing. When you apply quantizing to MIDI data, the function will automatically move your notes to the closest specified note value, thus correcting the timing of your performance. Normally, quantizing is done after data is recorded because this gives you the flexibility to go back to your original performance if you don't like the quantized result. But some people like to have their data quantized as it's being recorded, which can be done with SONAR's MIDI Input Quantize function.

Each MIDI track in a project has its own independent MIDI Input Quantize controls, which can be accessed in the Input Quantize section of the Inspector when the MIDI track is active (see Figure 5.3). To toggle the function for a MIDI track, click the Input Quantize button.

Input Quantize Resolution

Figure 5.3 Correct timing mistakes during recording with MIDI Input Quantize.
Source: Cakewalk®, Inc.

Click the Input Quantize Resolution control and choose a note value from the list. This note value should represent the shortest note duration that you will be recording. For example, if your performance will contain sixteenth notes but nothing smaller, then choose 1/16. You can also customize the Input Quantize function by choosing Quantize Settings. This will open the Input Quantize dialog box, which is discussed in detail in Chapter 7 (along with all of SONAR's other quantize functions).

Sampling Rate and Bit Depth

SONAR lets you set the sampling rate and bit depth used for the audio data that you record. Depending on the sophistication of your sound card, you can set the sampling rate up to 384,000Hz and the bit depth up to 64-bit.

So what settings should you use? Well, the higher the sampling rate and bit depth, the better the quality of your recorded audio. Higher settings do put more strain on your computer system, however, and the data takes up more memory and hard disk space. Plus, if your input signal is already bad (if you use a low-end microphone to record your vocals, for instance), higher settings won't make it sound any better.

Personally, I find using 24-bit, 48kHz audio works nicely. These settings provide a good balance between audio quality and computer resources. The only problem to watch out for is if you plan to put your music on CD. In that case, the audio needs to have a sampling rate of 44,100Hz and a bit depth of 16-bit. However, I recommend using 24-bit, 48kHz during all phases of a project and then exporting to 16-bit, 44.1kHz at the end when you need to put the audio on CD.

DVD AUDIO: If you plan to put your music onto either the DVD-A (DVD Audio) or DVD-V (DVD Video) format, you should be sure to use high settings for the bit depth and sampling rate of your project. If you plan to use DVD-A, then you should use a bit depth of 24 and a sampling rate of up to 192,000Hz. If you plan to use DVD-V, then you should use a bit depth of 24 and a sampling rate of 48,000Hz but up to 96,000Hz. It's also a good idea to use these settings if you plan to create a surround sound project, since that's what publishing to DVD is all about.

To access the sampling rate for a project, press P and then choose Audio – Driver Settings in the Preferences dialog box. In the Default Settings for New Projects section, you can make your selection from the Sampling Rate list. While you're there, also make sure to set the appropriate Audio Driver Bit Depth (for example, 24-bit) so that your sound card is set to record properly.

Also, in the Preferences dialog box, you'll need to set the bit depth for the current project by choosing File – Audio Data. Then in the File bit depths section, set the Record Bit Depth parameter (again, 24-bit is a good choice).

Input Monitoring

When you record an audio track, you usually want to listen to your performance while it's being recorded. In the past, due to the limitations of sound card drivers, you could listen only to the "dry" version of your performance. This meant that you would have to listen to your performance without any effects applied. With the input monitoring feature in SONAR, however, you can listen to your performance with effects applied as it is being recorded. This can be especially useful, for example, when you are recording vocals, when it's customary to let the singer hear a little echo or reverberation during his performance. If you're not sure what I'm talking about, don't worry.

Similar to MIDI tracks, audio tracks provide an Input Echo button located to the right of Mute, Solo, and Record buttons. This button can be turned on or off, and it activates or deactivates the input-monitoring feature.

MONITOR ON ALL TRACKS: You can easily activate or deactivate input monitoring on all audio tracks at once using the Mix module in the Control Bar. In the module, use the Input Echo [On/Off] All Tracks button (see Figure 5.4).

Figure 5.4 Monitor on all tracks using the Input Echo [On/Off] All Tracks option.
Source: Cakewalk®, Inc.

WATCH OUT FOR FEEDBACK: Input monitoring might cause a feedback loop between your sound card inputs and outputs. For example, this happens when the signal coming out of a speaker is fed back into a microphone and the sound keeps looping and building up into a very loud signal. This feedback looping can damage your speakers. To be safe, you might want to turn down the volume on your speaker system before you activate input monitoring. If you hear feedback, deactivate input monitoring. For a possible solution to your feedback problem, check the mixer settings for your sound card. Some sound cards have a monitoring feature that should be turned off when you are using input monitoring. However, the best thing is to use headphones to monitor playback during recording. Go back to using monitors during the mixing stage of your project, which is explained in Chapter 10.

Record Mode

When you record MIDI or audio data into an empty track, SONAR simply places that data into the track within a new clip. When you record data in a track that already contains data, what happens to that existing data?

SONAR provides two different recording modes. (Actually there are three, but I'll talk about Auto Punch in the "Punch Recording" section of this chapter.) Both of these modes provide a different means of dealing with existing data. The Sound on Sound mode mixes the new data with the existing data so that you have overlapping clips on a track. For example, if you record a vocal part into a track that already contains music, the vocal part will be recorded on top of the music. The Overwrite mode replaces the existing data with the new data. So in this example, the music is erased, and the vocal takes its place. When you try to play the track, you hear only the vocal.

Keep in mind that you need to deal with recording modes only when you're recording data into a track that already contains data. More than likely, you won't be doing that very often because SONAR records an unlimited number of tracks, and you can easily place each part of your song on a separate track. If you do need to set the recording mode, press P and choose Project – Record in the Preferences dialog box (or right-click the Record button in the Transport module of the Control Bar). In the Recording Mode section of the dialog box, choose either Sound on Sound or Overwrite and click OK.

TRACK LANES AND CLIP GROUPS: If you choose the Sound on Sound recording mode, SONAR will place each recording that you do on the same track in separate clips. This means that if you record to the same track more than once, each recording will be put in a different clip, even if those recordings overlap. In order to work with overlapping clips in the same track, you can activate the Create New Lanes on Overlap option so that each overlapping clip will be put on a separate Take lane. Then to access those lanes, you can right-click the track number and choose Lanes > Show/Hide Takes from the menu (or press Shift+T). There is also a Take Lanes button in the bottom left of the track header (see Figure 5.5). The Show/Hide Takes option easily accesses and edits overlapping clips in the same track. I'll talk more about Take lanes in Chapter 6.

In addition to Take Lanes, SONAR lets you create clip groups during recording. This feature automatically links recorded clips for easy, simultaneous editing. This is very useful, for example, when recording multi-track drums. Each drum instrument can be recorded separately, but then later edited simultaneously and remain synchronized. If you activate the Group Clips Across Tracks option, any recorded clips will be auto-matically grouped after recording is finished. Also note that when loop recording, each time the project loops, a separate group of clips is created.

Figure 5.5 Click the Take Lanes button to show/hide a track's Take lanes.
Source: Cakewalk®, Inc.

Recording and Playback

Believe it or not, you now have the knowledge you need to start recording in SONAR. Nothing is very complicated about the process, but you should follow a number of steps to make sure everything occurs smoothly. Here and in the following sections, I'll give you step-by-step instructions how to record MIDI tracks, audio tracks, and multiple tracks. To get started, follow these steps:

1. Create a new project or open an existing one. If you use a template to create a new project, you might be able to skip some of the following steps, but you should run through them anyway, just in case.
2. Set the meter and key signature for the project. The default settings are 4/4 and the key of C Major.
3. Set the metronome and tempo parameters. The default tempo for a new project is 120 beats per minute.
4. Set the timebase for the project. The default setting is 960 PPQ (pulses per quarter note). More often than not, you won't have to change this setting.
5. Set the recording mode. Unless you plan to record data to a track that already contains data, you can skip this step. The default recording mode is Sound on Sound.
6. Set the sampling rate and file bit depth for the project when recording audio.
7. Add a new audio or MIDI track to the Track view and adjust the track's properties.
8. If you want to hear effects added to your performance while recording audio, activate input monitoring. Then add effects to your track by right-clicking the Fx bin and choosing Audio FX > [*the effect you would like to add*]. You can also drag and drop effects from the Browser (see Chapter 11).
9. Arm the track for recording to let SONAR know that you want to record data on the track. To the right of (or underneath) the Name parameter in the Track view, you'll see three buttons labeled M, S, and one button with a red dot shown on it. Click the button with the red dot to arm the track for recording.

10. If you're recording MIDI, skip to Step 13. If you arm an audio track, you'll notice the meter (shown to the right of or underneath the Fx bin) light up. This meter displays the level of the audio input for your sound card in decibels.

THE DECIBEL: *Decibel* is a very complicated term to describe. The most basic explanation would be that a decibel is a unit of measurement used to determine the loudness of sound. In SONAR, the audio meters can range from –90dB (soft) to 0dB (loud). To change the display range of a meter, right-click it and choose a new setting from the menu. For a more detailed explanation, see the following topic in the SONAR Help file: Editing Audio > Digital Audio Fundamentals > The Decibel Scale.

---

11. Set the audio input level for your sound card so that it's not too loud or too soft. To do so, you have to use the software mixer that came with your sound card (or the hardware controls provided by your sound card breakout box). You will need to read the documentation for your sound card to find out how to use it correctly.

12. When you have access to the input level controls for your sound card, begin your performance, playing at the loudest level at which you plan to record. As you play, the meter for the track will light up, displaying the sound level of your performance. You should adjust the input level so that when you play the loudest part of your performance, the meter does *not* turn red. If it turns red, the input level is too high. When you play the loudest part of your performance, if the meter lights up anywhere between –12dB and –6dB (for 16-bit depth) or –18dB and –12dB (for 24-bit depth), then you have a good input level setting. The reason you don't want the level to be too high is so you have enough room for doing edits, adding effects, and mixing. You also don't want the level to be too low because then you'll have more noise in the audio.

13. Set the Now time to the point in the project where you would like the recording to begin. Most of the time, it will be at the very beginning of the project, but SONAR provides flexibility to let you record data to a track starting at any measure, beat, or tick within a project.

14. To start recording, click the Record button in the Transport module of the Control Bar (or press R). If you set a Count-In, the metronome will first count the number of beats you entered, and then SONAR will begin recording.

15. Perform the material you want to record.

16. After you finish performing, click the Stop button (or press the spacebar). SONAR will create a new clip in the track containing the data you just recorded.

17. Listen to your performance by setting the Now time back to its original position and clicking the Play button (or pressing the spacebar). If you don't like the performance, you can erase it by selecting Edit > Undo Recording (or pressing Ctrl+Z). Then go back to Step 13 and try recording again.

UNDO HISTORY: SONAR provides an Undo feature that reverses any action you take while working on a project. You're probably familiar with this feature because it is included in most applications that manipulate data, such as word processing software. SONAR goes a bit further by providing an Undo History feature. This feature logs every step you take while working on a project and undoes each step all the way back to the beginning of your current session. The Undo History is not saved, though, so as soon as you close a project, you lose the ability to undo any changes.

To access the Undo History feature, select Edit > History to open the Undo History dialog box. You will see a list of all the tasks you've done during the current session. To go back to a certain point in the session, select a task in the list and click OK. SONAR will undo any tasks performed after the task you selected. The Maximum Undo Levels parameter determines how many tasks SONAR will log in the Undo History list. You can set this parameter higher if you'd like. Remember, though, that the more tasks SONAR keeps track of, the more memory and hard disk space it needs.

> **EDIT MIDI DATA:** If you find that your performance is good for the most part, except for a few trouble spots, you might want to try fixing the mistakes by editing the MIDI notes, rather than using Undo and then performing the entire thing all over again.

18. After you've recorded a performance you like, disarm the track by clicking its Record (red dot) button again. By disarming the track, you won't accidentally record over the data while you're recording any additional tracks.

19. Go back to Step 7 and record any additional tracks you want to add to the project. While you're recording the new tracks, you will hear the previously recorded tracks being played back. Because you can hear these tracks, you might want to turn off the metronome and just follow the music of the previous tracks as you perform the material for the new ones.

> **SAVE YOUR PROJECT:** Be sure to save your project after each successful track recording. This step isn't mandatory, but it's a good precautionary measure because you never know when your computer might crash on you. Rather than lose that really great performance you just recorded, quickly select File > Save (or press Ctrl+S), so that you can rest easy knowing that your data is safe. You can also use the Auto-Save feature discussed in Chapter 3.

Multiple Track Recording and Playback

If you have more than one MIDI input on your MIDI interface or more than one audio input on your sound card, you can record to multiple tracks simultaneously. Recording multiple tracks works well when you need to record an entire band of musicians. Instead of having each musician play individually (which can sometimes ruin the "groove"), you can record everyone's part at once (which usually makes the song flow much better).

To record multiple tracks, just follow the same instructions I outlined earlier for recording MIDI and audio tracks. The only difference is that you must set up and arm more than one track. Also, make sure you set each track to a different MIDI or sound card input. In addition, if you want to group the recorded clips for synchronized editing (such as when recording multitrack drums), then be sure to activate the Group Clips Across Tracks option. When you start recording, the MIDI or audio data for each musician will be recorded to separate tracks simultaneously.

Loop Recording

If you plan to add a vocal track or an instrumental track (such as a guitar solo) to your project—something that might require more than one try to get right—you might want to use loop recording instead of recording and undoing a single track over and over again manually. Loop recording records several tracks (or takes), one right after the other, without having to stop between each one. Here's how it works:

1. Follow Steps 1 through 12 in the previous "Recording and Playback" section.
2. Click and drag your mouse over the measure numbers in the Track view Time Ruler to select the portion of the project you would like to loop.
3. Press Shift+L to set the loop points and turn looping on. You can also use the Loop module in the Control Bar to do these things. Then set the Now time to somewhere before the loop start time (if you're not looping from the beginning of the project).

4. Right-click the Record button in the Control Bar – Transport. In the Loop Recording section of the Preferences dialog box, select either Store Takes in a Single Track or Store Takes in Separate Tracks. The first option stores each performance in the same track but in different clips stacked on top of each other. The second option stores each performance in a different track but automatically sets the same track parameters as the one you began with. The option I like to use depends on the amount of flexibility I need. For example, if I'm trying to record the perfect vocal track and want to piece it together from a number of different takes, then I'll choose the Store Takes in a Single Track option and use the Take lanes and comping features after I'm done recording. If I want to record multiple takes but use each take separately and apply different effects, then I'll choose the Store Takes in Separate Tracks option.

TAKE LANES: If you choose the Store Takes in a Single Track option, SONAR will place each recording that you do on the same track in separate clips. This means that if you record to the same track more than once, each recording will be put in a different clip, even if those recordings overlap. In order to work with overlapping clips in the same track, you can activate the Create New Lanes on Overlap option in the Lanes section of the dialog box, so that each overlapping clip will be put on a separate Take lane. Then to access those lanes, you can right-click the track icon and choose Lanes > Show/Hide Takes from the menu (or press Shift+T). The Take lanes feature easily accesses and edits overlapping clips in the same track (see Chapter 6 for more information).

MULTITRACK LOOP RECORDING: If you plan to record multiple tracks at once while looping and you want to do synchronized editing later on those tracks (such as in the case of mulitrack drums), be sure to activate the Group Clips Across Tracks option in the Clip Groups section of the dialog box.

---

5. Click the Record button in the Control Bar – Transport (or press R) to start recording. If you set a Count-In, the metronome will count the number of beats you entered, and SONAR will begin recording.
6. Perform the material you want to record until you get a good take.
7. After you finish performing, click the Stop button (or press the spacebar) to stop recording. SONAR will create one track with multiple takes or a new track containing the data you just recorded for every loop you cycled through.
8. To listen to one of the recorded tracks, solo it by clicking the S button next to its Name parameter in the Track view. If you're working with Take lanes, you'll notice M and S buttons to the right of the name of each lane, which stand for Mute and Solo, respectively. Click one of the S buttons to solo and listen to a lane.
9. After you've found a performance that you like and want to keep, you can delete the others by right-clicking the appropriate track number and choosing Delete Track from the menu. For lanes, you can click the Delete Lane button (shown with an X on it) for the lane you want to delete (see Figure 5.6).

Figure 5.6 Click the Delete Lane button to delete a Take lane.
Source: Cakewalk®, Inc.

ARCHIVE TRACKS: Instead of deleting all the extra tracks you created during looping, you might want to keep them for later use. You can do so by using SONAR's Archive feature. By archiving tracks, you store them within the current project, but they become invisible to SONAR. This means that when you play your project, the archived tracks will not play. As a matter of fact, archiving tracks helps increase SONAR's performance because it doesn't process the tracks at all when they are archived. To archive a track, right-click its number and choose MSR > Archive. You can also just click the track's A button. You can still make changes to the track (and the data in it), but SONAR will not play it.

Punch Recording

When you make a mistake while recording MIDI data, it's usually no big deal because you can make corrections easily (such as changing the pitch of a note) with SONAR's various editing tools. But what about when you're recording audio? Sure, you can edit the data by cutting and pasting sections or processing it with effects, but usually, to get a smooth-sounding performance, you have to record your performance all over again. Using SONAR's punch recording feature, you can re-record only the part of the performance you messed up, leaving the good parts alone.

Using punch recording, you can set up SONAR to start and stop recording automatically at precise times during a project. You therefore can record over certain parts of your performance without having to redo the entire thing. Punching is very similar to regular audio track recording, but with a few differences. Here is the step-by-step procedure:

1. Suppose that you want to correct some mistakes on an audio track you just recorded. To get started, make sure the track is still armed for recording (its Record (red dot) button is red).
2. Right-click the Record button in the Control Bar – Transport. In the Recording Mode section of the dialog box, select Auto Punch. You can also choose whether you want the punch to overwrite the existing data or be blended with the existing data by choosing the Overwrite or Sound on Sound mode, respectively. Then, in the Punch In Time field, type the measure, beat, and tick at which you want SONAR to begin recording. In the Punch Out Time field, type the measure, beat, and tick at which you want SONAR to stop recording. The section of the track that falls between the Punch In Time and the Punch Out Time should contain the part of your performance in which you made the mistakes. In addition, if you use the Sound on Sound recording mode, you can decide whether or not you want to hear previous takes by using the Mute Previous Takes option. You can also use the Punch module in the Control Bar to adjust punch settings.

SET PUNCH POINTS QUICKLY: For a quick way to set the Punch In and Out Times, just click and drag in the Time Ruler of the Track view to make a data selection; then right-click the Time Ruler and choose Set Punch Points from the menu.

3. Set the Now time to the point in the project before the Punch In Time where you want playback to begin. You might want to start from the very beginning of the project or just a few measures before the Punch In Time. However long it takes you to get into the groove of the performance is how far ahead of the Punch In Time you should set the Now time.
4. Click the Record button (or press R) to start recording. If you set a Count-In, the metronome will count the number of beats you entered, and then SONAR will begin playback.
5. Play along with the existing material, exactly as you did before when you first recorded the track. When SONAR reaches the Punch In Time, it will automatically start recording the new part of your performance.

6. When the Now time has passed the Punch Out Time, SONAR will stop recording, and you can click the Stop button (or press the spacebar) to stop SONAR. SONAR will replace any existing material between the Punch In Time and the Punch Out Time with the new material you just played. As long as you didn't make any mistakes this time, your track will be fixed.

7. Listen to your performance by setting the Now time back to its original position and clicking the Play button (or pressing the spacebar) to start playback. If you don't like the performance, you can erase it by choosing Edit > Undo Recording (or pressing Ctrl+Z). Then go back to Step 3 and try recording again.

ANYTIME RECORDING (MANUAL PUNCH RECORDING): In addition to automatic punch recording, you can punch in and out manually by simply arming and disarming a track during recording. You can also change track inputs during recording. By default, SONAR doesn't allow you to do these things. To enable these features, activate the Allow Arm Changes During Playback/Record option in the Project – Record pane of the Preferences dialog box. One thing to keep in mind, however, is that with this option activated, SONAR has to keep all sound card devices open at all times. This can put additional strain on your PC. To reduce some of that strain, you can keep the option deactivated when you don't need it, or you can disable some of the sound card devices listed in the Audio – Devices pane of the dialog box. For example, you may only use one or two inputs/outputs on your sound card, although it may offer more. You can disable the extra inputs/outputs to reduce PC strain while using the Allow Arm option. You can also reduce the number of inputs available by keeping the check mark next to the Only For Inputs In Project option located just below the Allow Arm option.

Step Recording

Even though you might be an accomplished musician, more than likely you have one main instrument you're good at playing. If that instrument is the keyboard, that skill puts you ahead of some other musicians because the keyboard is one of the easiest instruments to use to record a MIDI performance. You can use other MIDI instruments, such as MIDI woodwind instruments, MIDI drums, and MIDI guitars, but those instruments tend to be very expensive. And if you learn to play a wind instrument or the drums or a guitar, you probably have a real instrument of that kind, not a MIDI one. This puts you at a bit of a disadvantage when you're trying to record MIDI tracks. However, SONAR provides a feature called *step recording* that records a MIDI track one note at a time without having to worry about the timing of your performance.

In other words, you select the type of note you want to enter (such as a quarter note or a sixteenth note), and then you press one or more keys on your MIDI keyboard. SONAR records those notes into the track with the timing you selected. You can also enter the measure, beat, and tick at which you want the notes to occur. Here's how the step recording feature works:

1. Create a new project or open an existing one. If you use a template to create a new project, you might be able to skip some of the following steps, but you probably should run through them anyway, just in case.

2. Set the meter and key signature for the project. The default settings are 4/4 and the key of C Major.

3. Set the Tempo parameter. The default tempo for a new project is 120 beats per minute.

4. Set the timebase for the project. The default setting is 960 PPQ. More often than not, you won't have to change this setting.

5. Step Recording always uses the Sound on Sound (Blend) record mode, so you do not need to set this parameter.

6. Add a new MIDI track to the Track view and adjust the track's properties. You can also just use an existing MIDI track by clicking its icon to make it the active track. You do not need to arm the MIDI track for recording. Step recording adds data to the track whether the track is armed or not.

7. Press Shift+R to open the Step Record window (see Figure 5.7). There is a Basic/Advanced button, which allows you to switch between the Basic and Advanced modes of the Step Record window. The Basic mode simply provides fewer parameters and a smaller window. It might come in handy when you don't need access to all the parameters and would like the window to take up less space on the screen. I'll be talking about the Advanced mode here, which covers the parameters for both modes.

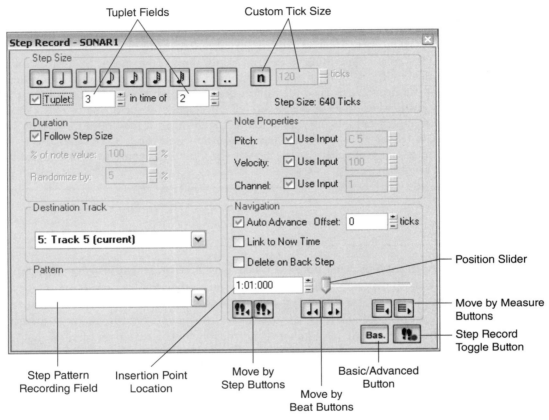

Figure 5.7 Using the Step Record window, you can record MIDI data to a track without having to worry about the timing of your performance.
Source: Cakewalk®, Inc.

8. In the Step Size section, choose the size of the note you want to record by clicking the appropriate button. For example, if you want to record a quarter note, click the button with the picture of a quarter note on it. You can also record dotted notes by activating one of the dotted buttons. And you can record tuplets by activating the Tuplet option and entering values for the type of tuplet you want to record. In addition, you can set a custom step size by activating the Custom Ticks Step Value button and entering the number of ticks you want to use.

NUMBER KEYPAD SHORTCUTS: You can use the Num Pad on your computer keyboard to activate most of the features in the Step Record window. Just hover your mouse over a button or parameter to see what Num Pad key to press. Also, be sure that your Num Lock button on your Num Pad is activated.

9. In the Duration section, you can set the length of the note, independent of the step size. More often than not, you'll want the duration to be the same as the step size. To make things easier, you can activate the Follow Step Size option, so that both values will be the same, and you won't have to bother selecting a duration. If you don't activate the Follow Step Size option, you can have the duration be a percentage of the step size. For example, if you have a step size of a quarter note and you'd like the duration to be half of that (or an eighth note duration), set the % of Note Value parameter to 50%. In addition, you can randomize the duration by entering a value for the Randomize By parameter. This can be useful if you want to keep your step-recorded music from sounding too "robotic" in nature.

10. In the Destination Track section, you can choose the track to which you want to record your MIDI data. This should already be set to the track you chose earlier in Step 6, but you can switch to another track at any time.

11. In the Note Properties section, you can set how the pitch, velocity, and channel of each note will be recorded. If you want any of the parameters to use the data values that are received from your MIDI keyboard, just activate the Use Input option for each parameter. If you want to set any of the parameters to a permanent value, no matter what you play on your MIDI keyboard, deactivate the Use Input option and enter a value for the parameter. All recorded notes will then use the exact values that you enter.

12. In the Navigation section, set the Insertion Point location (the point in the track to which you'd like to record notes) by entering a value into the Insertion Point field or moving the Position slider. If you want the Now time to correspond to the Insertion Point location, activate the Link to Now time option. I like to use this option most of the time because I usually use the Now time to keep track of where I am in a project, whether it is recording or editing data. But the Insertion Point location gives you the flexibility to record data independently of the Now time, so that it's really up to you about how you like to work in SONAR.

13. To record a note, press a key on your MIDI instrument. For example, if you want to record a Middle C to the track, press Middle C on your MIDI instrument. You can press more than one key at a time if you want to record a chord. For example, if you want to record a C Major chord, press the C, E, and G keys on your MIDI instrument at the same time.

14. SONAR will record the data to the track (as well as display it in the Track, Staff, Piano Roll, and Event List views) and (if the Auto Advance option in the Navigation section is activated, which it is by default) will move the Insertion Point location forward by the step size amount (which is a quarter note in this example). If the Auto Advance option isn't activated, you have to click one of the Move buttons to move the Insertion Point location manually. Also, if you want to record a rest instead of a note, you have to click one of the Move buttons. This way, SONAR will move the Insertion Point location ahead by the step size amount without recording anything. You can also use the Move buttons to move the Insertion Point location backward, in case you want to record more data at a previous point in the track. If you want previous data to be deleted automatically when you move backward, activate the Delete on Back Step option.

RECORD PATTERNS: If you need to record many repeating patterns, you might want to use the Pattern option in the Step Record dialog box. In the Pattern box, you can enter a pattern of beats that SONAR will follow automatically, so that you don't have to click the Move buttons at all, even for rests. For example, if you need to record a pattern with notes on the first two beats, a rest on the third beat, and another note on the fourth beat, you enter 12.4 (the period represents a rest) in the Pattern box. Now when you start to record the pattern, you simply press keys on your MIDI instrument for beats 1 and 2, SONAR advances past beat 3 because it is a rest, and then you press another key for beat 4. Then you keep repeating the same routine over and over again until you get to the point in your music where you no longer need to repeat the same rhythmic pattern. I know this process sounds a bit complicated, but if you play with it for a while, you'll get the hang of it. To stop using the Pattern option, just select the text in the Pattern box and delete it. The Pattern drop-down list will store 10 of your previously entered patterns for quick selection.

15. You can keep the Step Record dialog box open while you tend to other tasks. If you'd like to do something else before you finish using the Step Record feature, just click the Activate Step Record button (or press Shift+R) to turn off step recording. Then click the button or press the keys again when you're ready to do some more step recording.

16. When you're finished recording, click the Activate Step Record button (or press Shift+R) to turn off step recording. Alternatively, you can just close the Step Record window.

17. Listen to your performance by setting the Now time back to its original position and clicking the Play button in the Control Bar – Transport (or pressing the spacebar) to start playback. If you don't like the performance, you can erase it by selecting Edit > Undo Recording. Then go back to Step 8 and try recording again.

STEP RECORDING ALTERNATIVES: As an alternative to the Step Record feature, you might want to try using the Staff view (see Chapter 15). With the Staff view, you still can enter your MIDI data one note at a time without worrying about performance timing. Plus, the Staff view allows you to enter and edit your data using standard music notation. You might also want to try the Step Sequencer feature (see Chapter 6), which allows you to create your own MIDI patterns using a note grid interface.

Importing

One other way you can get MIDI and audio data into a project is to import it rather than record it. SONAR imports data from audio files, MIDI files, and other project files. Why would you want to import files? Well, you might have a great drum track in a project or a MIDI file that you want to use in another project. You also might want to use sample loops for some of the material in your audio tracks. Importing material is actually very easy.

The Media Browser

The easiest way to import various forms of content into SONAR is via the Media pane of the Browser. Using the Media Browser, you can import files stored on disk by dragging and dropping them. These include audio files, MIDI files, and even entire project files. To use the Media Browser, follow these steps:

1. Press B to open the Browser and then click the Media tab to access the Media Browser (see Figure 5.8).

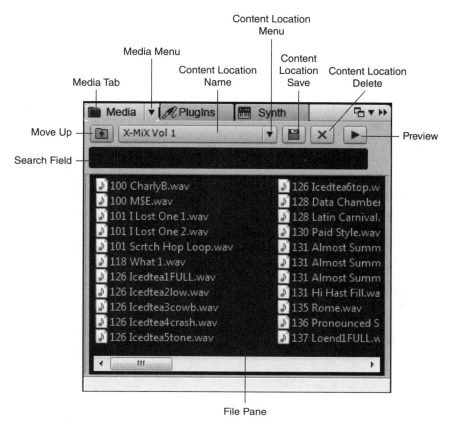

Figure 5.8 Use the Media pane of the Browser to drag and drop files into a project.
Source: Cakewalk®, Inc.

2. Initially, you'll see the File pane in which you can double-click folders or use the Move Up button to navigate folders on your disks. If you click the Media Menu button and choose Views > Folders, you can have a Folders pane for navigation as well. When you select a folder, its contents are displayed in the File pane. You can display files as icons, a list, or a detailed list by using the same Views choice in the Media menu.

3. Additional navigation options are provided by the Content Location controls. These controls allow you to create and use favorite file locations for quick access. Click the Content Location Menu button to choose a location. Folders and files in that location are instantly displayed.

4. To save a favorite location, navigate to it using the Folders/File panes. Then click the Content Location Name field to enter a new name or just leave the current folder name. Press Enter. Then click the Content Location Save button. If you want to remove a favorite location, choose it and then click the Content Location Delete button.

5. To preview an audio file, select it and then click the Preview button. Click the button again to stop playback. You can also listen to multiple files simultaneously by Ctrl+clicking to select them. If you want files to play back automatically, choose the Auto-Preview option in the Media Menu. SONAR will play all selected files repeatedly until you click stop. If you don't want file previewing to be looped, choose Loop Preview in the Media Menu. Also, by default, SONAR plays loop-based files (like Groove clips, see Chapter 9) at the project tempo. If you want regular audio files to play at the project tempo as well, choose the Preview at Host Tempo option in the Media Menu. In addition, you can choose which bus or sound card output the Browser uses for playback by choosing Audio Preview Bus in the Media Menu.

> **PERSONAL PREVIEW SETTINGS:** For previewing audio files, I like to have the Auto-Preview and Preview at Host Tempo options activated, but the Loop Preview option deactivated. I also like to set up a special preview bus for playback so I can have individual control over the Browser output. Also, I hardly ever use the Preview button. Instead, I click files to start playback and then click anywhere in the blank background of the File pane to stop.

6. To preview MIDI files, you need to use a soft synth. If you already have one in your project, you can choose it via the Synth Preview Output option in the Media Menu. If not, you can use SONAR's Insert > Soft Synth menu. You can also add synths via the Browser, but I'll talk more about this in Chapter 8. With a soft synth added and chosen in the Media Menu, you can preview MIDI files the same way you preview audio files.
7. To add a file to a project, just drag and drop it into the Track view. If you drag the file onto an existing track, the clip will be added to that track. If you drag the file onto a blank area of the Clips pane, a new track containing the file will be created. Also, depending on the horizontal position to which you drag and drop, the file will be added at the mouse location in the track.

> **ADDITIONAL FILE FUNCTIONS:** The Media Browser also provides some basic features for file management. First, you can drag and drop clips into the Browser to store them in content locations for future use. This feature comes in very handy, especially if you like to create your own loops inside of SONAR. In addition, you can right-click a file in the Browser to rename it, delete it, and insert it into the project at the current Now Time.

In addition to media files, the Browser can be used to add track icons, track templates, and more. I'll talk about those features later in the book. In the meantime, some of the older methods of importing are discussed in the following sections.

Importing from SONAR Project Files

Importing data from a project or a MIDI file into another project is just a matter of copying and pasting, as shown in the following steps. To get started, just follow these steps:

1. Open the project file from which you want to copy data.
2. In the Track view, select the clips you want to copy. You also can select an entire track or a number of whole tracks to copy.
3. Select Edit > Copy to open the Copy dialog box. Make sure the Events in Tracks option is activated (as well as any other data types you want to copy) and then click OK.
4. Open the project into which you want to paste the data.
5. In the Track view, select the track where you want to start pasting the data. If you copied more than one track, the first copied track will be pasted to the selected track, and the other copied tracks will be pasted to consecutive tracks after the selected one.
6. Set the Now time to the point in the track at which you want the data to be pasted.
7. Select Edit > Paste to open the Paste dialog box. You don't have to change any of the parameters here. Click OK.

SONAR will copy the data you selected from the first project and place a copy of it into the second project in the tracks and at the Now time you specify.

> **IMPORT PROJECT FROM BROWSER:** You can also use the Browser to copy an entire project file into another. Under the Media tab, find the project you want to import; then drag and drop the project file into an existing project to import the entire project.

Importing MIDI Files, Project5, and Step Sequencer Patterns

SONAR also imports data directly from a MIDI file, Project5 pattern, or Step Sequencer pattern. (See Chapter 6 for more information about the Step Sequencer.) For those of you who own Cakewalk's other sequencing software called *Project5*, you can now use your Project5 patterns (which are basically MIDI files in a special format) within SONAR. To import a MIDI file, Project5 pattern, or Step Sequencer pattern into your existing SONAR project, do the following:

1. Select the MIDI track into which you want to import the file.
2. Set the Now time to the point in the track that the file should be placed.
3. Choose File > Import > MIDI (or you can just click in the track to move the Now time and then right-click and choose Import MIDI from the menu) to open the Import MIDI dialog box.
4. Select the type of file you want to import using the Files of Type parameter.
5. Choose a file you want to import.
6. If you want to listen to the file before you import it, click the Play button. Click Open.

Importing Audio Files

SONAR imports a variety of audio file formats about which you can find more information in Chapter 18. This is important because at some time you might want to record some audio using another program, and you might want to use that data in one of your SONAR projects. Doing so is really simple; just follow these steps:

1. Select the track into which you want to import the audio file.
2. Set the Now time to the point in the track that the file should be placed.
3. Select File > Import > Audio (or you can just right-click in the track and choose Import Audio from the menu) to open the Import Audio dialog box.
4. Choose the audio file(s) you want to import. Hold down the Ctrl key to select more than one audio file.
5. If you want to listen to the file before you import it, choose a bus or sound card output in the Preview Bus menu and then click the Play button. This function will not work if you select multiple files.
6. If the file is a stereo audio file, either you can have the left and right channels merged into one track, or you can split between two different tracks (starting with the one you selected). To have the file split, activate the Import as Mono Tracks option.
7. If you want the audio file to be copied to the same location as all the other audio files in your project, keep the Copy Audio to Project Folder option activated. Most of the time, you will want to have this option activated because it keeps things more organized. Also, if you have your audio located on a second hard drive, this will increase SONAR's performance because it doesn't have to look on a different drive when playing the imported audio in your project.
8. If you want to convert the bit depth of the audio file during import, use the Bit Depth parameter to choose a value. If you set the parameter to Original, the audio file will be imported using its original bit depth. Click Open.

> **SAMPLE RATE CONVERSION:** If the sampling rate of the audio file you are importing is different from your project's sampling rate, SONAR will automatically convert the sampling rate of the audio file to match the sampling rate of the project.

CD Ripping

In addition to audio files, SONAR allows you to import audio directly from an audio CD. This process is called *ripping*. You can rip audio from a CD into SONAR by doing the following:

1. If you want to rip one CD track into a specific audio track and location in SONAR, click an audio track to make it active and set the Now time to designate the import point. If you rip more than one track, SONAR will automatically create a new audio track for each imported CD track.
2. Put an audio CD into your drive.
3. Choose File > Import > Audio CD to open the Import Audio CD Tracks dialog box.
4. Choose your drive from the Source Drive list. The tracks on your CD will then be shown in the Track list.
5. To audition a track, select it and click Play.
6. If you want to change the bit depth of the imported track, choose a new setting in the Import Bit Depth menu. By default, SONAR mixes audio internally using 32-bit and can also be set to use 64-bit, so changing the import bit depth really doesn't make a difference and just adds another unnecessary conversion process. Personally, I import audio at the original bit depth.
7. To import a single track, select it and click OK.
8. To import multiple tracks, select them using Ctrl+click or Shift+click and click OK.

STEREO TO MONO: CD audio is always in stereo. This means that when ripping a CD track, the resulting audio track will be stereo. If you would rather have two mono tracks (one containing the left channel audio and one containing the right channel audio), select the stereo audio track and choose Tracks > Bounce to Track(s) from the Track view menu. Choose Tracks for the Source Category, choose Split Mono for the Channel Format, and set Dithering to None. When you click OK, SONAR will automatically create two new mono audio tracks from the original stereo track.

Synchronization

One other aspect related to recording that you should know about is synchronization. This subject is fairly complicated and a bit beyond the scope of this book, but you might need to utilize synchronization in two somewhat popular situations. I'll cover a few of the basics and explain how to use synchronization in those two particular situations.

Synchronization Basics

All music is based on time. Without time, there is no music. To record and play music data, SONAR needs a timing reference. It uses this reference to determine the exact measure, beat, and tick at which an event should be stored during recording or at which it should be played. When you work with SONAR alone, it uses one of two different clock sources as its reference—either the clock built into your computer (internal) or the clock built into your sound card (audio). By default, SONAR uses the internal clock as its timing reference. Because the internal clock cannot be used if you have audio data in your project, SONAR automatically changes the clock to audio when a track's source is set to an audio input or when an audio file is inserted into the project. So the built-in clock on your sound card provides the timing for all the data you record into a project, and SONAR keeps all the tracks synchronized during playback. This is called *internal synchronization*.

Sometimes, though, you might need to synchronize SONAR externally with another piece of equipment. For example, if you have a drum machine (a special type of MIDI instrument that plays only drum sounds) containing some special songs that you programmed into it, you might want to have the data in your current SONAR project play along with the data contained in the drum machine. You would have to synchronize SONAR to the drum machine. In this situation, the drum machine would be known as the *master device*, and SONAR would be the *slave device*. The master would send messages to the slave, telling it when to start and stop playback and what tempo to use so that they could stay in sync with one another. To accomplish this, you need to use what is called *MIDI Sync*.

MIDI Sync

MIDI Sync is a special set of MIDI messages that synchronizes MIDI devices to one another. These messages include Start (which tells a slave device to start playback at the beginning of the song), Stop (which tells a slave device to stop playback), Continue (which tells a slave device to continue playback from the current location in the song—the Now time in SONAR), Song Position Pointer or SPP (which tells a slave device to jump to a specific time position in the song—the Now time in SONAR), and Clock (a steady pulse of ticks sent to the slave device, telling it the speed of the current tempo of the song).

To synchronize SONAR with an external MIDI device using MIDI Sync, follow these steps:

1. Configure your drum machine (or other MIDI device you want to use as the master) to transmit MIDI Sync messages. You'll have to refer to the user guide for your device for information on how to do so.
2. In SONAR, open the project you want to synchronize. Press P and then choose Project – Clock in the Preferences dialog box.
3. In the Source section, click the MIDI Sync option and then click OK.
4. Follow the steps outlined earlier for recording or playing MIDI tracks. However, when you activate recording or playback, SONAR won't respond right away. Instead, it will display a message that says "Waiting for MIDI Sync" in the Transport module of the Control Bar.
5. After you see this message, start playback on your master device. It will send a Start message to SONAR, and both the device and SONAR will play through the song in sync with one another. In the case of the drum machine, you will hear it play its sounds in time with the music being played by SONAR.
6. To stop playback, don't use the commands in SONAR; instead, stop playback from the master device. It will send SONAR a Stop message, and SONAR will stop at the same time automatically.

While working with SONAR via MIDI Sync, just remember to start, stop, and navigate through the project using the master device instead of SONAR. Otherwise, all the other steps for recording and playback are the same.

SMPTE/MIDI Time Code

You might need to use synchronization when you're composing music to video. Here, though, the synchronization method is different because a VCR is not a MIDI device, so MIDI Sync won't work. Instead, you have to use SMPTE/MIDI Time Code. You learned a little about SMPTE in Chapter 4, so you know it is a timing reference that counts hours, minutes, seconds, and frames (as in video frames). But you really didn't learn how it works.

> **SYNC TO A TAPE DECK:** In addition to video, SMPTE/MIDI Time Code is used often to synchronize a sequencer to an external multitrack tape recorder or DAT (*Digital Audio Tape*) deck. The procedure for doing so is the same.

SMPTE is a complex audio signal that is recorded onto a tape track (or, in the case of video, onto one of the stereo audio tracks) using a time code generator. This signal represents the absolute amount of time over the length of the tape in hours, minutes, seconds, and frames. A sequencer (such as SONAR) reading the code can be synchronized to any exact moment along the length of the entire tape recording. In this case, the VCR would be the master, and

SONAR would be the slave. When you play the tape in the VCR, SONAR will play the current project in sync to the exact hour, minute, second, and frame.

Reading the time code from tape requires a SMPTE converter, which translates the SMPTE code into MTC (*MIDI Time Code*). The MIDI Time Code is read by the MIDI interface and sent to the sequencer (SONAR). MIDI Time Code is the equivalent of SMPTE, except it exists as special MIDI messages rather than an audio signal. As SONAR receives MTC, it calculates the exact measure, beat, and tick that correspond to the exact time reading. This means you can start playback anywhere along the tape, and SONAR will begin playing or recording MIDI or audio data at precisely the right point in the current project in perfect sync.

As an example, suppose that you need to compose some music to video. This video could be your own or a video from a client. To synchronize SONAR to the video, you need to follow these steps:

1. If the video is your own, you need to add SMPTE Time Code to it using a SMPTE generator. This process is called *striping*. I won't go into the details of doing that here. You'll need to purchase a SMPTE generator and read the instructions in the included manual on how to stripe SMPTE to tape. If the video is from a client, he will probably stripe the tape before sending it to you.

SMPTE CONVERTER: You also need a SMPTE converter to read the time code from the tape. If you have a professional MIDI interface attached to your computer, it might provide SMPTE generating and converting capabilities. Check the user manual to make sure. You might be able to save yourself some money.

---

2. In SONAR, open the project you want to synchronize. Press P and then choose Project – Clock in the Preferences dialog box.
3. In the Timecode Format section, you need to select a frame rate for the time code. If you're composing music to your own video, just use the default selection, 30 FPS ndf (Frames Per Second – Non-Drop Frame). If you're composing music for a client, he should let you know the frame rate you need to use.

FRAME RATES: Different types of video material use different tape speeds for recording. The frame rate corresponds to the number of frames per second used to record the video to tape. For film, 24 frames per second is commonly used. For video, several different rates are used, depending on whether the video is recorded in color or black and white, and so on. For more information about frame rates, you should consult the user guide for your SMPTE generating/reading device.

---

4. You might also need to enter a SMPTE/MTC Offset in hours, minutes, seconds, and frames. Whether you need to enter an offset depends on whether the video material starts at the very beginning of the time code stripe, which is a value of 00:00:00:00.

SMPTE OFFSET: When you stripe a tape with SMPTE, the time code always starts with a value of 00 hours, 00 minutes, 00 seconds, and 00 frames. However, the actual video material on the tape may start a bit later, say at 00 hours, 01 minutes, 20 seconds, 00 frames. If that's the case (your client should let you know this fact), you need to enter an offset of 00:01:20:00 into SONAR, so SONAR will begin playing the project at that time rather than at the initial time code value.

---

5. After you finish entering the settings, click OK.

6. Now you can follow the steps outlined earlier for recording or playing MIDI or audio tracks. However, when you activate recording or playback, SONAR won't respond right away. Instead, it will display a message saying "Waiting for 30 Frame" (or whatever frame rate you selected) in the Transport module of the Control Bar.

7. After you see this message, start playback on your master device. (In this case, start the tape playing in the VCR.) It will then send SMPTE code to SONAR, and both the device and SONAR will play through the song in sync. In the case of the VCR, you will see it play the video in time with the music that is being played by SONAR.

8. To stop playback, don't use the commands in SONAR; instead, stop playback from the master device.

A little confused? Well, as I said, synchronization is a complicated subject. You'll find a little more information in the SONAR Help files, but it isn't any easier to understand than the information I've provided here. Your best bet is to experiment as much as possible with synchronization and get a good beginner book on audio recording. Knowing how to utilize synchronization is worthwhile, in case a situation that requires it ever arises.

The Basics of Editing

A FTER YOU'VE FINISHED RECORDING ALL YOUR TRACKS, it's time to do some editing. Actually, if you're like me, you might end up doing some editing during the recording process. This is especially true for MIDI tracks because it's so easy to fix the pitch or timing of a note quickly if you happen to make a mistake or two. You'll do most of your editing after the fact, though, and SONAR provides a number of different tools to get the job done.

> **BACK UP YOUR PROJECT:** Before you do any kind of editing to your recently recorded material, I suggest you make a backup of your project file. That way, if you totally mess things up during the editing process, you'll still have your raw recorded tracks. Choose File > Save As and save your project under a new name into the same folder. I usually use the original project name and append _orig to it to designate that it contains the original unedited tracks.

The Global Editing Tools

There are three main features provided by SONAR that are used to edit data: the tools, the Edit Filter, and the Snap to Grid settings. One important thing to remember is that the tools and the Snap to Grid settings are global in nature, meaning that they apply to the entire SONAR application (with one exception being the Piano Roll view, which I'll talk about later in this chapter). So, for example, you can use the Smart tool to arrange tracks and edit clips in the Track view, as well as edit MIDI notes in the Piano Roll view, etc. In addition, the same Snap to Grid settings are used for all views (although the Piano Roll view also has alternate settings available).

The Smart Tool and Other Tools

You can access the tools in a variety of ways including the Tools module in the Control Bar, the Tools HUD (Heads Up Display), and your PC keyboard. As you can see in Figure 6.1, there are six main tools (Smart, Select, Move, Edit, Draw, and Erase), which can be activated by clicking on them. Additional tools exist under the Edit, Draw, and Erase tools, which can be accessed by right-clicking those buttons.

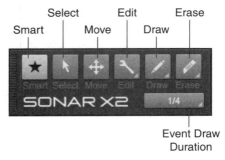

Figure 6.1 The Tools module in the Control Bar houses SONAR's global editing tools.
Source: Cakewalk®, Inc.

Of course, when editing data, you won't want to keep moving your mouse back and forth between editing and tool selection. To remedy this, SONAR provides the Tools HUD. While your mouse is inside the editing area of any view, you can either press T or click your middle mouse button to reveal the Tools HUD. As you'll notice, it looks and functions exactly like the Control Bar Tools module. One exception is that in the Track view, the HUD includes the Edit Filter, which I'll talk about shortly.

Finally, for even quicker tool access, you can use the function keys on your PC keyboard: Smart (F5), Select (F6), Move (F7), Edit (F8), Draw (F9), and Erase (F10). Also note that to access (and cycle through) the secondary tools under Edit, Draw, and Erase, you simply press the appropriate key multiple times.

> **SMARTER WORKFLOW WITH THE SMART TOOL:** As you may have noticed from its name, the Smart tool is not like the others. Instead of being dedicated to a particular editing function, the Smart tool can be used to perform the same functions as most of the other tools, depending on the situation. For example, you can use the Smart tool to select, edit, and move clips in the Track view. Normally, those procedures would require three different tools. The Smart tool, however, automatically switches to the other tools depending on where you place it (I'll talk more about how this works later in the chapter).
>
> As such, learning to work with the Smart tool will help to keep your editing tasks as efficient as possible. Because of this, I'll be emphasizing the Smart tool in most situations, except where another tool is explicitly required.

The Edit Filter

Because the Clips pane of the Track view allows you to edit a number of different types of data (including clips, transients, automation, and MIDI notes), and that data can sometimes overlap, editing tasks can be cumbersome to say the least. SONAR's Edit Filter solves this problem by allowing you to choose the type of active data for editing. Each track in SONAR provides its own individual Edit Filter (see Figure 6.2).

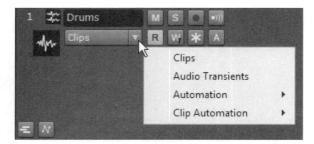

Figure 6.2 Choose a data type for editing via a track's Edit Filter.
Source: Cakewalk®, Inc.

To choose a track's editing data type, click its Edit Filter control and choose a type from the menu. You can also hover your mouse over the track and open the Tools HUD to access the Edit Filter from there. Once chosen, the data type becomes active, and all other data types become inaccessible so that you don't make accidental changes. For example, choosing Automation allows you to edit automation envelopes (see Chapter 12), but it doesn't allow clip or audio transient (see Chapter 7) editing.

> **QUICK EDIT FILTER SELECTION AND GHOSTED DATA:** Instead of using the track or Tools HUD to access the Edit Filter, you can Shift+click on a data type to quickly switch to that type for editing. For example, Shift+click on the background of a clip to choose Clip for the Edit Filter.
>
> You should also be aware that inactive data can be displayed as either "ghosted" or not shown at all by choosing View > Display > Display Ghosted Data from the Track view menu.

Snap to Grid Settings

You might notice that when you click the Time Ruler in any of the views, the Now time is automatically set to a value close to where you clicked but not at the exact location. This is due to SONAR's Snap to Grid feature. Snap to Grid automatically snaps the Now time cursor and any data edits to the nearest predefined value. This feature makes it easy to specify quick and precise settings for editing. For example, you can use it to align the start of a clip in the Track view to the beginning of a measure, or you can move a note in the Piano Roll view to the nearest sixteenth note. The Snap to Grid feature ensures that edits are perfectly aligned to the snap grid of a project as represented by the Time Ruler.

The Snap Module

With the exception of the Piano Roll view (which provides additional alternate settings), all of the views in SONAR share the same Snap to Grid settings, which are accessed via the Snap module of the Control Bar (see Figure 6.3).

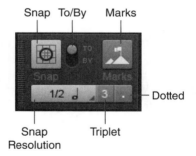

Figure 6.3 Use the Snap module in the Control Bar to access the Snap to Grid settings.
Source: Cakewalk®, Inc.

To toggle Snap to Grid on/off, click the Snap button or press N. Set a snap value by right-clicking the Snap Resolution button and choosing a value from the menu. If you choose a musical note value, you can also set it to triplet or dotted by clicking the Triplet and Dotted buttons, respectively. You can also have your edits snap to the beginning of measures by choosing Measure or to exact ticks, samples, frames, or seconds by choosing the appropriate option and typing in an exact value.

In addition, you can have your edits snap "to" a value or snap "by" a value by clicking the To/By switch. When the switch is set to TO, your edits will snap to the nearest snap value. For example, with a snap value of Measure, moving a clip in the Track view will snap the beginning of that clip to the nearest measure line along the Time Ruler. When the switch is set to BY, your edits will snap by the current snap value. For example, with a snap value of Measure, moving a clip in the Track view will snap the beginning of that clip to one measure away from its current location. If the beginning of the clip was located at measure 2, beat 2, and it was moved toward the beginning of the project, it would be snapped to measure 1, beat 2 (exactly one measure away).

Smart Grid

The zooming functions of SONAR (which I'll talk about later in this chapter) allow you to magnify data and do precise editing. More often than not, you'll probably want to use different snap values, depending on the zoom level. SONAR's Smart Grid feature handles this situation automatically. By default, the Smart Grid feature is activated, and you'll notice the value shown on the Snap Resolution button changes as you zoom in/out. If you don't want to use this feature, you can deactivate it by right-clicking the Snap Resolution button and choosing Smart Grid from the menu.

Landmarks and Snap Intensity

In addition to using notes and numeric values for the snap value, you can activate Landmarks, which can be toggled on/off by clicking the Marks button. Landmarks in SONAR are markers, audio transients, MIDI notes, clips, automation nodes, and the Now time. You can set the Landmarks you want to use (which are active in addition to the snap value) by right-clicking the Marks button (or pressing Shift+N) and putting check marks next to the appropriate options in the Landmarks section of the Preferences dialog box. Also, activating the Snap to Nearest Audio Zero Crossings option will snap data to the nearest silent point in an audio waveform. (I'll talk more about zero crossings in the "Audio Editing" section later in this chapter.)

Of course, there may be times when you want to move data freely without having it snap to a value or Landmark. While you could just turn snap off every time you want to do this, an easier method is to use the Snap Intensity feature (previously known as *Magnetic Strength* in earlier versions of SONAR). In the same dialog box that appears when you right-click the Marks button, you'll see the Snap Intensity slider at the top. Move the slider left (toward Light) for less "pull" toward a snap value or Landmark, and move it right (toward Extreme) for more "pull" toward a snap value or Landmark. If you keep the Snap Intensity slider somewhere in the middle, you can still snap edits but also move them freely between snap values and Landmarks in case you don't want to have the edits snapped to an exact value. Use the Magnetic Test slider to test the Snap Intensity before clicking OK.

ALTERNATE SNAP SETTINGS: There may be times when you want to temporarily change the Snap to Grid settings, perhaps for very precise editing, such as when dealing with ticks or samples. SONAR allows you to set up an alternate snap value, which you can access by pressing and holding N. While holding N, the snap value is temporarily changed to the alternate value of your choice. You can do your edits and then let go of N to automatically switch back to the normal snap value. You can set up the alternate value while holding N.

The Piano Roll view also provides its own Snap to Grid settings, which I'll talk about later in the "Using the Piano Roll View" section of this chapter.

Arranging with the Track View

Since the first part of the editing process deals with arranging the material in your project, it's logical to start with arranging. Basically, this step involves rearranging the tracks and clips in your project so they provide a better representation of the song you're trying to create. For example, after listening to the project a few times, you might find that the guitar part in the second verse sounds better in the first verse, or you might want the vocal to come in a little earlier during the chorus. You can accomplish these feats by manipulating your tracks and clips.

Dealing with Tracks

You already learned how to work with the Track view in terms of setting up track parameters, navigating within SONAR, and recording new tracks. Manipulating includes selecting, sorting, inserting, and otherwise changing your original data.

Scrolling

The Track view consists of two areas: the Track pane (on the left) shows the track parameters, and the Clips pane (on the right) shows the track data. The Clips pane contains scroll bars (see Figure 6.4). These scroll bars work the same as scroll bars in any standard Windows application. Either you click the arrows to move the display, or you click and drag the scroll bars to move the display.

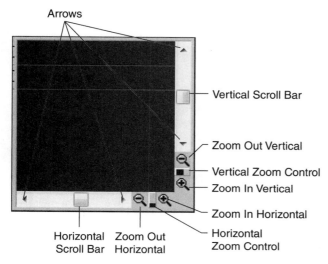

Figure 6.4 Using the scroll bars, you can access additional information that doesn't fit on the screen.
Source: Cakewalk®, Inc.

The horizontal scroll bar displays all the data in all the tracks. As you scroll to the right, the measure numbers on the Time Ruler increase. Scrolling doesn't change the Now time, though. The vertical scroll bar affects both the Track and Clips pane areas. As you move the bar up or down, the different tracks in the project are displayed, starting from 1 (at the top of the list).

In addition to the Track view, scroll bars are available in all the other views. In the Piano Roll view, you can scroll horizontally to display the data in a track similar to the clips in the Track view. You also can scroll vertically to display different MIDI note ranges. The Event List view is the oddball because it only lets you scroll vertically to display all the events in a track as one long list.

> **SCROLL LOCK:** During playback, SONAR automatically scrolls the display so that you can see the portion of the project currently playing. However, you can temporarily stop SONAR from scrolling while playback continues by using the Scroll Lock feature. This can be useful when you want to edit some data but continue to listen to the rest of the project. Clicking on some data in the Clips pane (or Note pane of the Piano Roll view) will activate the Scroll Lock feature. You can also press the Scroll Lock key on your PC keyboard. Click anywhere in the background of the Clips pane or right-click in the Time Ruler (or press Scroll Lock again) to deactivate Scroll Lock and resume scrolling. If you don't like this feature, choose Options > Click Behavior > Left Click Locks Scroll to toggle it. Even with this feature disabled, the Scroll Lock key will work.

Zooming

The Track view (as well as other views, except the Event List view) also provides zooming functions. Using these functions, you can magnify the data in a track, in case you want to do some really precise editing. If you take a look at the bottom-right corner of the Track view (refer to Figure 6.4), you'll notice two sets of buttons.

Using the buttons along the bottom, you can magnify the track data horizontally. When you click the Zoom In button, the clips will grow larger horizontally and give you a more detailed look at the data they contain. Clicking the Zoom Out button does the opposite. The same buttons along the side of the Track view perform the same functions, except they affect the display vertically. You'll also notice that as you zoom in vertically, the track parameters will be shown beneath each track in the Track pane. In addition, you'll notice a little control button between each set of zoom buttons. These control buttons show you the current level of magnification. Click and hold the mouse on any Zoom control button, and a Zoom meter will appear. You can use the meter to change the Zoom level by dragging your mouse (see Figure 6.5).

Figure 6.5 You can also change the Zoom level via the Zoom meters.
Source: Cakewalk®, Inc.

THE ZOOM TOOL

In addition to the aforementioned zoom features, SONAR provides the Zoom tool. You can use this tool to select a range of data and zoom in on that selection. To use it, follow these steps:

1. Press and hold Z while using any of SONAR's other tools. This is the only way to access the Zoom tool because it's sort of a hidden feature.
2. Move your mouse pointer within the Clips pane, and it will turn into a magnifying glass.
3. Click and drag anywhere within the area to select some data.
4. Release the mouse button and the Z key. SONAR will zoom in on the selection (both horizontally and vertically, depending on how you drag the mouse), and your mouse pointer will return to your previously chosen tool.

> **QUICKLY UN-ZOOM:** To quickly undo the view change you made by using the Zoom tool, press Alt+Z. You can also redo the same zoom action by pressing Alt+Shift+Z. If you'd rather use mouse buttons to access these features, press and hold the right mouse button and click the left mouse button to undo the view change (same as Alt+Z). Press and hold the left mouse button and click the right mouse button to redo the same zoom action (same as Alt+Shift+Z).

THE FAST ZOOM FEATURE

If you have a mouse wheel, SONAR also provides the Fast Zoom feature. Normally, if you use the mouse wheel, it scrolls the current view vertically up or down. But using certain keyboard shortcuts, you can use the mouse wheel for quick and easy zooming, as follows:

▷ **1x Zoom In or Out.** To zoom in or out normally using the mouse wheel, hold down the Alt key and move the mouse wheel forward (zoom in) or backward (zoom out).

▷ **2x Zoom In or Out.** To zoom in or out with increased magnification, hold down the Alt+Shift keys.

▷ **Track Scale Zoom.** To adjust the track scale (zoom in or out of the data inside of clips), hover your mouse over the track you want to adjust and hold down the Alt+Ctrl keys. This feature only works in the Track view.

You can also adjust the behavior of the Fast Zoom feature by doing the following:

1. Choose Options > Mouse Wheel Zoom Options in the Track view menu to open the Mouse Wheel Zoom Options dialog box.
2. In the Zoom Factor section, you can set the magnification for horizontal and vertical zooming. A setting of 1 will magnify the data by a factor of 1 every time you move the mouse wheel. A setting of 2 will magnify by a factor of 2, and so on.
3. In the Zoom In section, you can specify where the zoom will be centered. So, as you zoom in, the center of the zoomed display will be located according to these settings. The most intuitive settings are At Cursor, which will center the zoom at the position of your mouse cursor. You can, however, change this so that horizontally, the zoom will be centered at the current Now time, and vertically at the currently active track.
4. The Zoom Out section options work the same as the Zoom In section options, except the Zoom Out options specify where the zoom will be centered when zooming out.
5. Set the Simultaneous Horizontal and Vertical Zoom option. Activating this option will zoom the data both horizontally and vertically at the same time. You'll probably want to keep this option activated most of the time. If you turn it off, the Alt and Alt+Shift shortcuts will only zoom vertically, and the Alt+Ctrl will zoom horizontally. The Track Scale Zoom feature is not available when this option is turned off.

TIME RULER ZOOM AND SCROLL

You can also zoom and scroll in the Track view (and Piano Roll view) using the Time Ruler. Position your mouse in the upper part of the Time Ruler (until it looks like a magnifying glass with a downward arrow) and then do one of the following:

▷ **Horizontal zoom.** Click/drag up/down to zoom out/in horizontally. Hold Shift while dragging for smaller zoom increments.
▷ **Vertical zoom.** Right-click/drag up/down to zoom out/in vertically.
▷ **Horizontal scroll.** Click/drag left/right to scroll horizontally.
▷ **Fit to Project.** Double-click to fit the entire project into the current size of the Clips pane in the Track view.

AUTO ZOOM

When working on large projects, it is sometimes beneficial to have all the tracks minimized so that you can get an overview of all (or most of the tracks) in a project (depending on your screen size). But when you want to edit a track, you'll have to zoom in because minimized tracks are usually too small to do any kind of precision editing. Zooming in/out every time you want to edit a track can become time consuming, so SONAR provides Auto Zoom for this situation.

To use Auto Zoom, first resize all tracks vertically by pressing the Ctrl+Up Arrow key multiple times to set the initial size for all tracks. Then click on a track to make it the active track. Vertically resize that track to the zoom size you want to use by clicking/dragging the bottom of the track down (see Figure 6.6).

Figure 6.6 Resize a track vertically to set the zoom size for Auto Zoom.
Source: Cakewalk®, Inc.

Now activate Auto Zoom by choosing View > Auto Track Zoom from the Track view menu or by pressing Shift+Z. Clicking on a different track will automatically resize that track to the zoom size and resize the previous track to the same size as all other tracks.

The Project Navigator

In addition to scrolling and zooming using the various features previously described, SONAR provides the Project Navigator. This is the pane located at the top of the Track view (below the menu, but above the Time Ruler). If you don't see this pane, that means the Project Navigator is not activated. To toggle the Project Navigator, press Alt+N. To make the pane larger/smaller, click and drag the bottom of the pane.

> **PROJECT NAVIGATOR VIEW:** You can also display the Project Navigator as a separate view by choosing Views > Navigator (or pressing Alt+Shift+8).

The Project Navigator provides a bird's-eye view of all the data in a project. You'll notice many rectangular shapes shown in the Navigator. These shapes represent the tracks and clips in the current project. The green rectangle represents the data that is currently visible in the Track view.

SCROLLING

To scroll through a project (either horizontally or vertically), position your mouse anywhere inside the green rectangle and click/drag your mouse horizontally or vertically. If you drag horizontally past the left or right side of the Track view, the Navigator will continue to scroll until you reach the beginning or end of the project. If you drag vertically past the top of the Track view or the bottom of the Navigator, scrolling will continue until you are displaying track 1 or the last track in the project.

> **LEFT-CLICK SCROLLING:** To move quickly through a project, just left-click anywhere within the Project Navigator pane (outside of the rectangle). You can also deactivate the left-click option by right-clicking in the Project Navigator pane and choosing Left Click Positions Rectangle.

ZOOMING

In addition to clicking inside the green rectangle, you can click any of its nodes (small squares around its perimeter) to change the current zoom level. Click and drag the top and bottom nodes to zoom in or out vertically. Click and drag the left or right nodes to zoom in or out horizontally. Click and drag any of the corner nodes to zoom vertically and horizontally at the same time.

> **PROJECT NAVIGATOR OPTIONS:** To quickly set one of six horizontal zoom levels, right-click anywhere within the Project Navigator pane and choose Horz Zoom Level 1 through 5. The sixth option (Horz Zoom to Project) will fit all the data in the current project into the current size of the pane.
>
> In addition, you can set the vertical size of the data shown in the pane by choosing one of three Track Height options: Short, Medium, or Tall. Track Height just changes the displayed size of the data, not the zoom level.

Zooming Keyboard Shortcuts

I talked about scrolling via keyboard shortcuts in Chapter 4, but SONAR also allows you to perform quick zoom procedures with your PC keyboard, as follows:

▷ **Fit Tracks to Window (F).** Resizes all tracks vertically so they fit the current Track view size.
▷ **Fit Project to Window (Shift+F).** Resizes entire project so it fits the current Track view size.
▷ **Zoom In/Out Horizontally (Ctrl+Right or Left Arrow).** Zoom the Track view in/out horizontally around the Now time position.
▷ **Zoom In/Out Vertically (Ctrl+Down or Up Arrow).** Zoom the Track view in/out vertically.
▷ **Zoom In/Out Track Vertically (Ctrl+Shift+Down or Up Arrow).** Zoom the currently active track in/out vertically.
▷ **Zoom In/Out Track Waveform (Ctrl+Alt+Up or Down Arrow).** Zoom in/out the currently active audio track waveform (see "Audio Editing" later in this chapter) or MIDI track notes.
▷ **Zoom In/Out All Track Waveforms (Alt+Up or Down Arrow).** Zoom in/out all audio track waveforms and MIDI track notes.

Selecting

To manipulate your tracks for editing, you have to select them first. To select a single track, click the number of the track you want to select. To select multiple tracks, use the following procedures:

▷ To select more than one track, hold down the Ctrl key as you click the track numbers.
▷ To select a range of tracks, click the number of the first track and then hold down the Shift key and click the number of the last track.
▷ To select all tracks in a project, choose Edit > Select > All or press Ctrl+A.
▷ To deselect all tracks in a project, choose Edit > Select > None or press Ctrl+Shift+A.
▷ To deselect a track while keeping others selected, hold down the Ctrl key as you click the track number.

By the way, all these procedures also work in the other views; the only difference is the items being selected. Some special selection features are also available, but I'll talk about them later in this chapter and in Chapter 7.

Sorting Tracks

You can change the order in which the tracks appear in a couple of different ways. Being able to sort the tracks can be useful if you want to keep related tracks together in the track list. For instance, you might want to keep all the percussion tracks or all the vocal tracks together. It's easier to work on your song when the tracks are grouped together in this way.

CLICKING AND DRAGGING

The easiest way to move a track within a list is to drag it to a new location. Just position your mouse over the little icon next to the name of the track you want to move (see Figure 6.7); then click and drag it up or down anywhere in the list. When you release your mouse button, the track will move to the new location and take on a new track number.

Figure 6.7 Click and drag a track icon to move the track within the track list.
Source: Cakewalk®, Inc.

USING THE TRACK SORT FUNCTION

You also can use the Track Sort function to sort tracks in the list, based on the track properties. You use this function as follows:

1. Choose Tracks > Sort Tracks from the Track view menu to open the Sort Tracks dialog box.
2. In the Sort By section, select the track property by which you want to sort the tracks.
3. In the Order section, select whether you want the tracks to be sorted in ascending or descending order. Click OK.

Remember, the track numbers for the tracks will also be changed because the tracks have moved to new locations in the list. However, each track maintains its parameter settings and data.

Track Folders

In addition to sorting tracks, you can organize them into groups called *Track Folders*. A Track Folder acts like a container that can hold any number of other tracks—MIDI, audio, and so on.

CREATING TRACK FOLDERS

To create a Track Folder, use one of the following methods:

▷ Right-click in the Tracks pane and choose Insert Track Folder.
▷ Choose Insert > Track Folder from SONAR's main menu.
▷ Right-click an existing track and choose Move to Folder > New Track Folder.

ADDING/REMOVING TRACKS TO/FROM TRACK FOLDERS

To add or remove tracks to/from a Track Folder, use one of the following methods:

▷ To add a track to a Track Folder, drag-and-drop the track onto the Track Folder. You can also right-click the track and choose Move to Folder > [*name of the existing Track Folder*].
▷ To remove a track from a Track Folder, drag-and-drop the track outside the Track Folder. You can also right-click the track and choose Remove from Folder.

EDITING TRACK FOLDERS

In addition to their organizational power, Track Folders provide composite editing power, which means that you can apply global changes to all the tracks in a Track Folder by applying the editing to the Track Folder itself. Just remember that when I talk about editing single tracks, those editing features can also be used on Track Folders. In the meantime, here are some of the things you can do to control Track Folders, along with all the tracks within them:

▷ To select a Track Folder and all the tracks it contains, click the Track Folder number area (the empty space to the left of the folder icon).
▷ To show or hide all the tracks in a Track Folder, click the Track Folder's plus/minus icon.
▷ To archive all the tracks in a Track Folder, click the Track Folder's A button.

▷ To mute all the tracks in a Track Folder, click the Track Folder's M button.

▷ To solo all the tracks in a Track Folder, click the Track Folder's S button.

▷ To enable recording for all the tracks in a Track Folder, click the Track Folder's R button.

▷ To enable input monitoring for all the tracks in a Track Folder, click the Track Folder's Input Echo button.

TRACK FOLDER NOTES: You can add text notes to a Track Folder to label it with information about what is in the folder, what edits you've done to the folder, and so on. To do this, first widen the folder by clicking and dragging the bottom of the folder down. Then double-click the Track Folder note area (located below the Track Folder's name) and type in your text. Press Enter to finish. You can also double-click the folder icon to open the Folder Properties dialog box and type notes into the Description field.

USING QUICK GROUPS: Using the Quick Groups feature, you can group track parameters in a Track Folder and then make parameter changes to all tracks in the folder simultaneously. For example, all track volume parameters can be grouped. Then by changing one track volume, they all change. To do this, first select the Track Folder to select all tracks in it; then press and hold Ctrl while clicking and dragging on a track parameter. Check out the Quick Groups section of Chapter 12 for more information.

Track Icons

In addition to Track Folders, SONAR provides the Track Icons feature to help with the organization of tracks. Track Icons identifies the contents of a track. Basically, this feature assigns a picture to each track in a project. This picture can be of anything you like, but SONAR provides a number of helpful Track Icons, such as pictures of musical instruments and other musical symbols. For example, you could assign a guitar picture to all your guitar tracks so that with a quick glance at the screen, you would know what type of data is contained in those tracks. By the way, when I discuss Track Icons, I'm talking about the icons located beneath the track header, not the small icon located to the right of the track number. If your tracks are minimized, you'll need to widen them first to see the Track Icons. Press Ctrl+Down Arrow repeatedly to widen tracks.

SHOWING/HIDING TRACK ICONS

You have the option to show or hide Track Icons with a quick click of the mouse. Icons are displayed in the Track view, Console view, and Inspector. Icons are also shown in the Synth Rack, which I'll talk about in Chapter 8. You can control whether icons are shown in each individual area or in all the areas at once.

To show/hide Track Icons in all the areas, choose Views > Icons > Show Icons. To show/hide Track Icons in each area, choose Views > Icons > [*name of the area*] > Show Icons.

TRACK ICON SETTINGS

You can also control the size of Track Icons in each area by choosing Views > Icons > [*name of the area*] > Large Icons or Small Icons.

The Track view provides some additional settings that determine whether or not standard or custom icons are shown and where they are shown. Choose Views > Icons > Track View > and one of the following: Show in Header, Show Custom in Header, or Show in Strip.

LOADING TRACK ICONS

If you want to change a Track Icon for a specific track, right-click the Track Icon and choose Load Track Icon from the menu to display the Open dialog box.

Select a Track Icon and click Open to assign that icon to the track. If you decide you don't like that icon, you can load another one or go back to using the default icon by right-clicking the icon and choosing Reset Track Icon from the menu.

CREATING TRACK ICONS

If you have some artistic talent, SONAR allows you to create your own Track Icons. It doesn't provide any tools for this purpose, so you'll need to get your hands on some graphics software. Simply create a graphic image that is 128 by 128 pixels square in size and save it as a BMP file (the standard Windows graphic file format). Put the file in your Track Icons folder (the location of which can be found in the File – Folder Locations section of the Preferences dialog box), and the icon will be available for you to use within SONAR.

Inserting Tracks

If you ever need to insert a new track between two existing tracks in the list, you can do so by following these steps:

1. Right-click the track number of the track above which you want to insert a new track.
2. From the menu, select Insert Audio Track or Insert MIDI Track, depending on the type of track you need.

SONAR will move the current track down one location in the list and insert a new track at the location on which you clicked. For example, if you right-click track 2 and select Insert MIDI Track, SONAR will move track 2 (and all the tracks below it) down by one and insert a new MIDI track at number 2 in the list.

INSERTING MULTIPLE TRACKS

To save time, you can also insert more than one track simultaneously by doing the following:

1. Choose Insert > Multiple Tracks to open the Insert Tracks dialog box.
2. In the Audio section, set the Track Count parameter to the number of audio tracks you would like to insert. Set the parameter to zero if you don't want to insert any audio tracks.
3. Set the Main Destination parameter. This parameter determines the Output setting for the new tracks.
4. If you want all new tracks that you insert in your project to use the same Output setting (as designated by the Main Destination parameter), activate the Set as Default Bus option.
5. To add a send to the new tracks, select an output for that send (see Chapter 10) using the Send list.
6. In the MIDI section, set the Track Count parameter to the number of MIDI tracks you would like to insert. Set the parameter to zero if you don't want to insert any MIDI tracks.
7. Set the Port and Channel parameters. These parameters determine the Port and Channel parameter settings for the new MIDI tracks. Click OK.

SONAR inserts the new tracks to the end of the track list, so if you want them positioned differently in the list, you will need to move them manually.

TRACK TEMPLATES

In addition to the previous track inserting methods, SONAR provides Track Templates. The Track Templates feature allows you to insert a group of tracks along with their corresponding settings. This feature makes it easy for you to create and reuse your favorite track configurations.

To create your own Track Template, simply insert some tracks into your project. Then set their parameters—this includes all track parameters, as well as inserted effects and their settings, along with the Mute, Solo, and Record button settings. Select the tracks and choose File > Export > Track Template to open the Export Track Template dialog box. Type in a name for the template and click Save.

To use an existing Track Template, choose Insert > Track Template and choose a template from the Import Track Template dialog box. You can also right-click in the Tracks pane of the Track view and choose Insert from Track Template > [*name of the Track Template*] from the menu. SONAR ships with a number of predefined Track Templates to give you an idea of how to use this feature.

> **DRAG-AND-DROP TRACK TEMPLATES:** The easiest method for inserting Track Templates is by dragging and dropping them from the Browser. They are located under the Media tab in the Content Location called *Track Templates*. As an added bonus, you can drag templates to any location in the track list, and they will be inserted at that location.

Cloning Tracks

If you ever need to make an exact copy of any tracks in your project (including events, properties, effects, and sends), you can do the following:

1. Select the track(s) you want to copy.
2. Choose Tracks > Clone Track(s) from the Track view menu to open the Clone Track(s) dialog box.

> **CLONE A TRACK:** For a quicker method, just right-click the track(s) you want to copy and choose Clone Track to open the Clone Track(s) dialog box.

3. You can choose to copy the events within the track(s), the track properties, the effects assigned to the track(s), the bus sends, or all of the above. Simply activate the appropriate options. There is also an option for preserving linked clips (see "Linked Clips" later in this chapter).
4. You can also choose how many copies of the track(s) you want to make by entering a number in the Repetitions field.
5. To designate the number of the first copied track, enter a number in the Starting Track field. Your first copied track will use this number, and all other copies will be numbered consecutively after this one. Click OK.

Erasing Tracks

Getting rid of tracks you no longer need is very easy. Simply select the track(s) and choose Tracks > Delete Track(s) from the Track view menu. Alternatively, you can right-click the selected track(s) and choose Delete Track from the menu. But SONAR also provides another erasing function that's a little more flexible. Instead of erasing the track entirely, it allows you to delete all the data in the track while keeping the track properties intact. To do so, just select the track(s) and then choose Tracks > Wipe Track(s) from the Track view menu.

Hiding Tracks

Using the Track Manager, you can hide tracks in the Track view. To hide or unhide tracks, follow these steps:

1. Press H to open the Track Manager. You will see a list of all the tracks in the Track view.
2. To hide an individual track, click to remove the check mark next to that track in the list and then click OK.
3. To hide a group of tracks (such as all the audio tracks, MIDI tracks, muted tracks, or archived tracks), click the appropriate button—Audio, MIDI, Muted, Archived—to select the appropriate group. Then press the spacebar to remove the check marks.
4. The Console view (see Chapter 10) also has a Track Manager. The two Track Managers can work independently from one another. However, by default, they are synchronized via the Keep track/console visibility states

in sync option. This means that if you hide a track in the Track view, it will also be hidden in the Console view. I normally keep this option activated because it helps to keep things consistent when switching back and forth between the Console view and Track view. Click OK.

You can make tracks reappear by adding check marks in the Track Manager. These changes to the Track view are in appearance only; they don't affect what you hear during playback. For example, if you hide an audio track that outputs data during playback, you'll hear that data, even if you hide the track. Hiding tracks can come in handy when you want to work only on a certain group of tracks, and you don't want to be distracted or overwhelmed by the number of controls being displayed.

> **HIDE TRACK AND TRACK FOLDERS:** You can hide a single track by right-clicking its track number and choosing Hide Track. To make the track visible again, you need to use the Track Manager.
>
> You might also want to use Track Folders to keep the track list organized. Tracks in folders can easily be hidden and made visible with a simple click to the +/− button (located to the left of a folder's name).
>
> In addition, some useful keyboard shortcuts include: Hide Selected Tracks (Ctrl+H), Show Only Selected Tracks (Ctrl+Shift+H), Show and Fit Selection (Ctrl+Alt+H), and Show All Tracks (Shift+H). Remember that you can undo/redo any view change by pressing Alt+Z and Alt+Shift+Z.

Dealing with Clips

Unless you insert, copy, or erase tracks in your project, you're not actually doing any kind of data manipulation. If you move a track in the track list or sort the tracks, that doesn't change the data within them. To make changes to the data in your project, you have to manipulate the clips within the tracks.

Clip Properties

For organizational purposes, SONAR allows you to change the way clips are displayed. To change the properties, you can click inside of a clip to select it. Then click the Clip button at the top of the Inspector (I) to open the Clip Properties (or press Shift+I). Here, you can assign a name to the clip (which doesn't have to be the same name as the track in which the clip resides) and also set the color of the clip.

> **DOUBLE-CLICK CLIP PROPERTIES:** For another way to access clip properties, choose Options > Click Behavior > Double-Click in the Track view menu to change the double-click behavior for MIDI/audio clips to Clip Properties. Then you can simply double-click a clip to quickly open the Clip Properties section of the Inspector.

The name and the color of a clip don't affect the data within your project, but you also can change the start time of the clip (using the Start field). The start time is the position within the project at which the clip begins. If you enter a new start time for the clip, the clip is moved to the new time within the track, and during playback SONAR will play the clip at the new time. This move *does* change the data in your project. If you decide later that you want to move the clip back to its original location (shown in the Original Time field), click inside the field and choose Revert to original time stamp. You can also mute the clip so that it will not produce any sound during playback by activating the Mute option.

In addition, Clip Properties allows you to lock clip positions and data within a clip. To lock a clip, choose the clip attributes you would like to lock from the Lock menu. If you choose Pos/Data, then both the position of the clip in the project and the data within the clip cannot be changed until you unlock the clip. The Lock option can help you keep from making accidental changes to your data.

You may have also noticed the Groove Clip, AudioSnap, and Clip Effects sections. These will be discussed in Chapters 9, 7, and 11, respectively. Two more things to note are that you can keep the Clip Properties open while you work with different clips, and you can select multiple clips to change their properties simultaneously.

View Options

You can change whether the names you assign to clips will be displayed and whether clips will be displayed with a graphical representation of the data they contain. In other words, if a clip contains audio data, it shows a drawing of what the sound wave for the audio data might look like. For MIDI data, the clip shows a mini piano roll display.

To change these options, use the View > Display menu in the Track view menu and choose the appropriate options (Display Clip Names and Display Clip Contents). You can also choose whether to display vertical rule lines for the Time Ruler (using the Vertical Grid Lines option), whether to display track separators (using the Display Track Separators option), and whether to display the Audio Scale (using the Show Audio Scale option).

You'll also notice that at the top of each clip is a small section, which is called the *clip header*. You can click a clip header to select a clip, and you can drag a clip header to move a clip. If you don't want to display clip headers, choose View > Display > Maximize Waveform Height in the Track view menu. Selecting and moving are then performed using the top half of the clip, which I'll talk more about later in "Selecting Clips" and "Moving and Copying Clips."

In addition, you'll sometimes see a clip header indicator located inside the clip header at the end of a clip (see Figure 6.8). On audio clips, the clip header indicator can be clicked to access clip FX or V-Vocal (see Chapter 11), or it can indicate various AudioSnap processing, such as stretching (see Chapter 7). On MIDI clips, the clip header indicator can be clicked to open that clip in the various views (Piano Roll, Staff, Event List, and Step Sequencer). Once you choose a view from the menu, double-clicking that clip anytime will then automatically open it in the chosen view. I'll talk more about the Piano Roll, Event List, and Step Sequencer views later in this chapter. See Chapter 15 for more information about the Staff view.

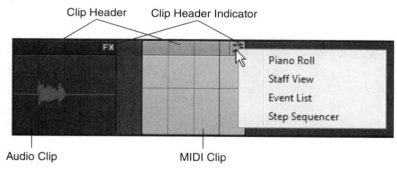

Figure 6.8 Use the Clip Header Indicator to access various clip-specific features.
Source: Cakewalk®, Inc.

A number of other options involving clips can be adjusted via the Options > Click Behavior menu in the Track view. You can determine whether a left-click, right-click, or both will set the Now time. You can also determine what default view will open automatically when you double-click audio and MIDI clips. Finally, the Left Click Locks Scroll option automatically stops the Track view from scrolling if you decide to do some editing during playback. To resume scrolling, just click anywhere in the background of the Clips pane or right-click in the top half of the Time Ruler. Playback scrolling can also be toggled via the Scroll Lock key on your PC keyboard.

Selecting Clips

SONAR provides a variety of ways to select the data within clips. Selecting data is performed using the Smart or Select tool, along with Aim Assist (depending on the situation).

THE SMART AND SELECT TOOLS

Activate the Smart (F5) or Select (F6) tool. Click inside a clip (or a clip header) to select the clip. Ctrl+click to select/deselect multiple clips. You can also right-click and drag over multiple clips to select them (also called *lassoing*). To get rid of any selection, click once in the gray workspace (or press Ctrl+Shift+A).

Another selection method involves selecting only a portion of a clip or multiple clips. This procedure is called *working with partial clips*. This capability is useful when you want to split a clip into smaller clips or when you want to only process part of a clip or multiple clips. To make a partial clip selection, position your mouse inside a clip (not the clip header). Then click and drag your mouse. Drag across several clips (even if they reside in different tracks) to make a partial selection of multiple clips. If you drag beyond the edge of the view, SONAR will scroll so you can even select clips not currently displayed. In addition, once a selection is made, you can extend the selection by holding Shift and then clicking to the left or right of the selection (clicking above or below will also adjust the selection). If there is no selection, Shift+click will create a selection starting at the Now time and ending at the mouse location.

You may have noticed that the partial selection was automatically snapped to a specific time interval. That's because partial selections are affected by the Snap to Grid function. To do a freeform selection, you need to turn off Snap to Grid (press N to toggle).

AIM ASSIST

Another function that makes selecting data easy is Aim Assist, which is accessed by pressing X. Aim Assist provides a vertical white line marking the exact position of the mouse cursor in the Clips pane of the Track view or the Notes pane of the Piano Roll view. (See "Using the Piano Roll View" later in this chapter.) As you move your mouse in the Clips pane, you'll notice the line following the cursor. Aim Assist makes it easier when you're trying to line up the mouse with a specific location in the project for precise editing or marker alignment. This is especially true when your mouse is located in the lower portion of the Clips pane with the Time Ruler being located at the very top.

You'll also notice that Aim Assist displays the mouse location as a numerical value in the Time Ruler. This shows you the exact time location of your mouse cursor. In addition, you can change the time format by right-clicking the Time Ruler and choosing Time Ruler Format from the menu. Or you can add additional Time Rulers to the pane using the Add Ruler button (shown as a + button at the right of the Time Ruler). In addition, Aim Assist follows the Snap to Grid settings, making it even easier to line up clips and other data.

SELECTION AUDITION

After you've made a data selection, you can audition it by pressing Shift+spacebar. What is nice about this feature is that it allows you to quickly preview your data selection and keep the Now time cursor at its original location. You can also cancel the preview before it's finished by pressing just the spacebar again. If you press Shift+spacebar to cancel the preview, the Now time is repositioned to the point at which playback stopped.

Clip Groups

Even though you can make multiple clip selections, once you click to create a new selection, the previous selection is lost. To overcome this limitation, SONAR provides clip groups. This feature treats multiple selected clips as a single unit so if you edit/process one clip in a group, you do the same for all other clips in the same group. A group can be comprised of both MIDI and audio clips residing in any track(s). However, partial clip selections are not supported.

Groups can only contain whole clips. But you can get around this by first splitting the clip(s) (see the section "Splitting and Combining Clips" later in this chapter) into the data segments you want to edit and then grouping those clips.

CREATING AND REMOVING CLIP GROUPS

You create a clip group in two ways, one of which is to have SONAR create one automatically during recording. As I mentioned in Chapter 5, when recording multiple tracks simultaneously, you can have the clips in those tracks automatically grouped by activating the Group Clips Across Tracks option. SONAR will even create different groups for each take if you are doing loop recording.

For existing clips, you can create a clip group by first selecting more than one clip. Then right-click one of the selected clips and choose Create Selection Group From Selected Clips. SONAR will add a number to the top-left corner of each clip in the group, which represents the group number.

Keep in mind that a clip can only belong to one group, so if you select any clips that already belong to a different group, those clips will become part of the new group. Incidentally, that is how you would add clips to an existing group. Select any clip in the existing group (by clicking its clip header) and Ctrl+click any clips you would like to add. Then use the Create Selection Group From Selected Clips function, and all the clips will become part of a new group.

To remove clips from a group, first click the clip header of one of the clips to select the group. Then Ctrl+click the clip header(s) of the clip(s) you want to keep in the group—this removes them from the selection. Finally, right-click one of the remaining selected clips and choose Remove Selected Clips From Groups. You can also remove all clips from all groups by choosing Edit > Select > All (or pressing Ctrl+A) to select all clips in the project. Then right-click one of the selected clips and choose Remove Selected Clips From Groups.

EDITING CLIP SELECTION GROUPS

Before I go any further, keep in mind that the editing, processing, and effects functions mentioned here will be explained in detail later in this chapter, as well as in Chapters 7 and 11. To edit all the clips in a group, click the clip header of one of the clips to select the entire group and then apply your edits. You can also edit a single clip in a group by clicking inside the clip to select only that clip and then applying your edits. The edits will only be applied to the single clip rather than the whole group.

SPLITTING CREATES NEW GROUPS: By default, if you split clips in a group, SONAR automatically creates new groups. If you'd rather it didn't, press P and choose Customization – Editing in the Preferences dialog box. Then in the Clips section, remove the check mark next to the option: When splitting clips in groups, create new groups. See "Splitting and Combining Clips" later in this chapter.

BEWARE HIDDEN CLIPS: Earlier in this chapter, I told you how to hide and unhide tracks. When selecting and editing clips in a group, keep in mind that any hidden clips that belong to the group are affected as well. Hidden clips in a group are only hidden from sight; they are not exempt from any editing or processing that you apply to the entire group.

After you've selected the clips in a group, any edits you apply to one clip in the group will affect all the other clips in the group. However, there are some exceptions to this rule, depending on the functions you use to edit the clips. For example, if you apply any of the functions from SONAR's Process menu, all clips will be affected. This is also true when adding effects to a clip FX bin by right-clicking a clip and choosing Insert Effect.

Other types of edits, however, will only affect clips that fall in the same time range along the Time Ruler. For example, as you can see in Figure 6.9, I am slip-editing (see "Slip-Editing" later in this chapter) the end of a clip that belongs to clip group 7. But only two clips in the group are being affected because those are the only two clips in the group that reside in the same time range. Basically, if you are using a function that affects an entire clip, all selected clips in a group are affected. If you are using a function that affects only part of a clip, changes only occur to clips that are in the same time range.

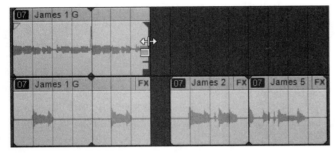

Figure 6.9 Some editing functions only work with groups when the clips are within the same time range.
Source: Cakewalk®, Inc.

Splitting and Combining Clips

Using partial selections, you can combine and split clips into new smaller or larger clips. Combining clips is very easy. Just select the clips you want to combine and choose Clips > Bounce to Clip(s) in the Track view menu. SONAR will create one new clip from the old selected ones.

THE BOUNCE TO TRACK(S) FUNCTION

The problem with the Bounce to Clip(s) function is that it works only on clips that are on the same track. If you want to combine clips from different tracks, you have to use the Bounce to Track(s) function as follows:

> **ONLY AUDIO TRACKS:** The Bounce to Track(s) function also has a limitation: it works only with audio tracks, unless you are using software synthesizers. In that case, it will also work with MIDI tracks.

1. Select the clips you want to combine.
2. Choose Tracks > Bounce to Track(s) in the Track view menu to open the Bounce to Track(s) dialog box.
3. Because you are combining clips from multiple tracks into one clip, the new clip has to reside on a single track. In the Destination list, choose the track on which you want your new combined clip to reside.
4. The Bounce to Track(s) function lets you determine the format of your new clip. In the Channel Format list, choose the format you want to use. Choose Stereo to create a single stereo track from your combined clips. Choose Split Mono to create two new tracks; one holds the left stereo channel of your new audio data, and the other holds the right channel. Choose Mono to create a single mono track from your combined clips.
5. In the Source Category field, choose how you want SONAR to deal with the output from each bus. Select the Buses option for situations in which you have each track assigned to a different output bus, and you want the combined clips from each track to be put on a separate new track. Choose the Main Outputs option for situations in which you have each track assigned to a different physical sound card output, and you want the combined clips from each track to be put on a separate new track. Choose the Entire Mix option to combine all

the clips from the selected tracks onto one new track. Choose the Tracks option to create a new track for each selected track in the Source Buses/Track section. More often than not, you'll want to choose Entire Mix so that all selected clips are combined into one clip on one new track.

6. In the Source Buses/Tracks section, select the buses that you want SONAR to use when combining your clips.

7. In the Dithering field, choose None. Dithering is used to smooth out bit depth conversions and is normally used when you are converting audio data from a higher bit depth to a lower bit depth.

8. In the Mix Enables section, activate the automation and effects options you want to include in the new clip from the clips being combined. Usually, you should keep all these options activated so that any automation and effects will be applied to the bounce. If you want a higher quality bounce, activate the 64-bit Engine option, but just keep in mind that this consumes more processing power, and the bounce will take longer. If you have trouble with the bounce procedure, you can try removing the check mark next to the Fast Bounce option. The bounce will then be done in real time, and you can also listen to it being performed by activating the Audible Bounce option.

9. If you choose to do a real-time bounce, you can also include any live performance input by activating the Live Input option. For example, you can record the output of a software synth (see Chapter 8) during the bounce by playing your MIDI keyboard as SONAR bounces the audio. Any selected data and live input will be bounced to the new track as a combined audio clip.

10. If you want to save your settings as a preset for quicker bouncing the next time you use this feature, type in a name for the preset in the Preset field. Then click the Save button (the button with the floppy disk shown on it).

11. Click OK. During the bounce, you can press Esc to stop the bounce before it is completed. When you do this, SONAR will ask if you would like to keep the partial bounce. If you choose yes, then a new track is created; otherwise, SONAR simply disregards the bounced data.

THE SPLIT FUNCTION

SONAR enables you to split clips using its Split function. It works like this:

1. Set the Now time at the point where you want the split to occur.
2. Select the clip(s) or track(s) that you want to split.
3. Right-click inside the selection and choose Split to open the Split Clips dialog box.
4. Choose the split option you want to use. The Split at Time option splits a clip at a certain measure, beat, or tick. The Split at Selection option splits a clip at both ends of a selected data area. The Split Repeatedly option splits a clip into a bunch of smaller clips instead of just two new smaller ones. Just enter the measure at which you want the first split to occur and the number of measures at which you want each consecutive split to occur after that. For example, if you have a clip that begins at measure 2 and ends at measure 7, and you want to create three two-bar clips out of it, enter 2 for the starting measure and 2 for the split interval. The Split at Each Marker option lets you split clips according to the markers you set up in the Track view. Finally, the Split When Silent for at Least option lets you split clips at any place within them where silence occurs. You can set the interval of silence that SONAR has to look for by entering a number of measures.
5. If you are splitting MIDI clips, you have the option of having them split nondestructively, which means that any data (such as note durations) that extends beyond the split point isn't deleted; only the appearance of the clips is changed. To do this, activate the Use Non-Destructive Cropping When Splitting MIDI Clips option. More than likely, you usually will want to have this option activated. Click OK.

QUICK SPLIT: If you don't need the added functionality of the Split Clips dialog box and you just want to do a quick split of selected data at the Now time position, press S.

SPLITTING ON THE BEAT

Although the Split function allows you to do multiple splits automatically, it only does so at the beginning of each measure. For more flexibility, SONAR allows you to do splits using the snap grid as follows:

1. Select the tracks in which you want to split the clips.
2. Change the Edit Filter of one of the tracks to Audio Transients.
3. Change the Snap Resolution to the split value you want to use. For example, if you want to create a split at every half note along the Time Ruler, choose 1/2.
4. Right-click in one of the clips of the track that's showing audio transients and choose Pool > Add MBT to Pool.
5. Right-click the clip header of one of the selected tracks and choose Split Clip(s) at AudioSnap Pool.
6. Right-click in one of the clips of the track that's showing audio transients and choose Pool > Add MBT to Pool.
7. Change the Edit Filter of the track back to Clips, and you now have splits at every interval of the Snap Resolution.

THE SMART AND SPLIT TOOLS

In addition to the Split function, SONAR lets you split clips with either the Smart or Split tool, as follows:

1. Press F5 for the Smart tool or press F8 repeatedly until the Split tool is selected (shown as a pair of scissors).
2. To split a single clip at a single location, Alt+click with the Smart tool or just click with the Split tool.
3. To split a selection, Alt+click (Smart tool) or just click (Split tool) and drag anywhere within the Clips pane to select some data. You can make a selection over multiple clips and multiple tracks simultaneously (see Figure 6.10).
4. Release the mouse button. SONAR will split all the selected clips according to the boundaries of the selection.

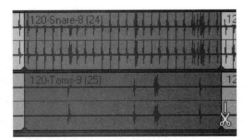

Figure 6.10 Use the Smart or Split tool to split clips.
Source: Cakewalk®, Inc.

Moving and Copying Clips

You can change the arrangement of your data by moving and copying clips to new locations, either within the same tracks or into other tracks. One way to move a clip is to change its start time via the Inspector. You also can move a clip by clicking in the clip header of the clip with the Smart tool (F5) or anywhere in the clip with the Move tool (F7) and dragging it to a new location with your mouse. As long as the track you're dragging the clip into doesn't contain any other existing clips, you don't have to worry because SONAR will move the clip to its new location.

However, if the track contains existing data, SONAR will ask how you want the data to be handled by displaying the Drag and Drop Options dialog box. If the box doesn't appear, you can access it by choosing Options > Drag and Drop Options from the Track view menu. In the dialog, you have to choose one of three options: Blend Old and New, Replace Old with New, or Slide Over Old to Make Room.

> **ASK THIS EVERY TIME:** If you have the Ask This Every Time option activated in the Drag and Drop Options dialog box, SONAR will open the box every time you drag data, even if there is no existing data in the track to which you're dragging. If you don't want this to happen, deactivate the Ask This Every Time option.

If you choose the Blend Old and New option, the clip you're moving will overlap any existing clips. This means that the clips remain separate, but they overlap so that during playback the data in the overlapping sections will play simultaneously. If you chose the Replace Old with New option, the overlapping portion of the clip you are moving will replace (which means it will erase and take the place of) the portion of the clip being overlapped. If you chose the Slide Over Old to Make Room option, the start times of any existing clips will be changed to make room for the new clip. During playback, the new clip will play at the time it was placed, and the existing clips will play a little later, depending on how much their start times had to be changed.

If you would rather copy a clip instead of moving it, you can use SONAR's Copy, Cut, and Paste functions. Actually, using the Cut function is the same as moving a clip. If you use the Copy function, you can keep the original clip in its place and put a copy of it in the new location. This procedure works as follows:

1. Select the clip(s) you want to copy.
2. Choose Edit > Copy (Ctrl+C) to immediately copy the clip(s) or choose Edit > Copy Special (Ctrl+Alt+C) to open the Copy dialog box.
3. If you open the Copy dialog box, choose the type(s) of data you want to copy. Usually, you should choose the Events in Tracks option.
4. Click OK.
5. Click the number of the track into which you want to copy the clips.
6. Set the Now time to the point in the track at which you want to place the clips.
7. Choose Edit > Paste (Ctrl+V) to immediately paste the clips or choose Edit > Paste Special (Ctrl+Alt+V) to open the Paste dialog box and then click the Advanced button to open the advanced Paste dialog box.
8. Choose the options you want to use. Most of these options are self-explanatory. Setting the Starting at Time option is the same as setting the Now time in Step 6. Setting the Destination: Starting Track option is the same as setting the track in Step 5. The Repetitions option lets you create more than one copy of the clip if you want. I've already talked about the What to Do with Existing Material options. The Paste as New Clips option creates a new clip and then follows the overlapping rules that you chose with the What to Do with Existing Material options. The Paste into Existing Clips option merges the clip that you are copying with any existing clips that it overlaps. Material from both clips is merged into one. Click OK.

If some of these options sound a little confusing, just experiment with them a bit. Make an extra backup of your project and then use it to go wild with the copying and pasting functions. Try every possible combination, and soon you'll get the hang of using them.

> **QUICK CLIP COPY:** You can copy a clip quickly by holding down the Ctrl key and clicking and dragging the clip header of the clip to a new location. If you hold Ctrl+Shift, the clip will be locked (either horizontally or vertically, depending on which way you move first) so that you don't accidentally move it to a new track or start time. A copy of the clip will be made and placed at the new location.

Linked Clips

You might have noticed a few other options in the Paste dialog, namely the Linked Repetitions and Link to Original Clip(s) options. These options deal with a special feature in SONAR called *linked clips*. Using this feature, you can link copies of a clip to each other so that any changes you make to one clip will affect the other clips that are linked to it. This way, you can create repeating patterns easily and later make changes to the patterns. Keep in mind that linked clips are not the same as clip groups. Linked clips all contain the same data, whereas clips in a group can contain any data.

For example, you might have a cool drum pattern in a clip that takes up one measure, and you want to repeat that pattern through the first eight measures of your song. You can copy the clip and then paste it (setting the Repetitions to 7 and activating the Linked Repetitions and Link to Original Clips options). SONAR will copy your clip and paste seven identical, linked copies of it. If you make any changes to one of the clips, these changes affect them all. For instance, you can change the snare drum from sounding on beat 2 to sounding on beat 3 in one of the clips, and the change will happen in all of them.

If you ever want to unlink linked clips, just follow these steps:

1. Select the clips you want to unlink. You don't have to unlink all linked clips in a group. For example, if you have four linked clips, you can select two of them to unlink, and the two that you leave unselected will remain linked.
2. Right-click one of the selected clips and choose Unlink to open the Unlink Clips dialog box.
3. Choose an unlink option. The New Linked Group option unlinks the selected clips from the original group but keeps the selected clips linked to each other. The Independent, Not Linked at All option totally unlinks the clips from any others. Click OK.

Linked clips are shown with dotted outlines in the Clips pane of the Track view. When you unlink them, they appear as normal clips again.

Erasing Clips

Deleting any clips that you no longer need is an easy process. Simply follow these steps:

1. Select the clip(s) you want to delete.
2. Choose Edit > Delete (or press Delete) to immediately delete the clip(s) or choose Edit > Delete Special to open the Delete dialog box for more options.
3. Make sure that the Events in Tracks option is activated.
4. If you want SONAR to remove the space that's created when you delete the clips, activate the Delete Hole option. SONAR will move any other existing clips in the track backward (toward the beginning of the project) by the amount of time opened when you delete the clips.
5. If you activate the Shift by Whole Measures option as well, the existing clips will be moved back only to the nearest whole measure. Click OK.

Inserting Space

Instead of manipulating existing data, you might need to introduce silent parts into your project. You can do so by using SONAR's Insert Time/Measures feature. This feature inserts blank space in the form of measures, ticks, seconds, or frames. You can insert the space either into the whole project or into selected tracks. It works like this:

1. Choose Edit > Select > None (Ctrl+Shift+A) to clear any currently selected data in the project.
2. If you want to insert space into the whole project, skip to Step 3. Otherwise, select the tracks into which you want to insert space.
3. Set the Now time to the point in the tracks or project at which you want the space inserted.
4. Choose Project > Insert Time/Measures to open the Insert Time/Measures dialog box.
5. The At Time field reflects the current Now time, which can be changed by typing a new value or pressing F5 and choosing a marker.
6. For the Insert field, type the number of units of blank space you want inserted.
7. Select the type of unit you want inserted: measures, ticks, seconds, or frames.
8. In the Slide section, choose the types of data that will be affected by the insert process. The types of data you select will be moved to make room for the new blank space. Of course, you'll almost always want to have the

Events in Tracks option activated. When you're inserting space into selected tracks, the Events in Tracks option is usually the only one you want to have activated. However, when you're inserting space into the entire project, more than likely you'll want to have all the options activated.

After you click OK, SONAR will insert the number of measures, ticks, seconds, or frames you typed into the Insert parameter at the Now time you specified. It also will move the types of data you selected by sliding the data forward in time (toward the end of the project). For instance, if you inserted a measure of blank space into the entire project at measure 2, then all the data in all the tracks starting at measure 2 will be shifted forward by one measure. Whatever data was in measure 2 will be in measure 3, any data that was in measure 3 will be in measure 4, and so on.

Slip-Editing

Up until now, all of the editing functions I've described in this chapter work by making permanent changes to the MIDI and audio data in your clips and tracks. This is called *destructive processing* because it "destroys" the original data by modifying (or overwriting) it according to any editing you apply.

UNDO FUNCTION: As you know, you can remove any destructive processing done to your data by using SONAR's Undo function. You also can load a saved copy of your project containing the original data. However, neither of these restoration methods is as convenient as using nondestructive processing.

In contrast to destructive processing, SONAR also includes some editing functions (called *slip-editing* functions) that provide *nondestructive* processing. The slip-editing functions are nondestructive because they don't apply any permanent changes to your data. Instead, they are applied only during playback and let you hear the results while leaving your original data intact.

You can use the slip-editing functions to crop the beginning or end of a clip, shift the contents of a clip, or shift-crop the beginning or end of a clip. Slip-editing can be done on multiple clips at once by selecting the clips first.

CROPPING A CLIP

To crop the beginning or end of a clip, follow these steps:

1. Choose the Smart (F5) or Edit (F8) tool. If you want to crop the beginning of a clip, position your mouse over the middle or bottom-left end of the clip until the cursor changes as shown in Figure 6.11.

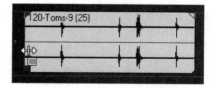

Figure 6.11 Position your mouse over the middle or bottom-left end of the clip to crop the beginning.
Source: Cakewalk®, Inc.

2. Click and drag your mouse to the right so that the clip changes length.
3. If you want to crop the end of a clip, follow Steps 1 and 2 but drag the middle or bottom-right end of the clip to the left.

When you crop a clip, the data that is cropped is not deleted. Instead, the data is hidden from view and masked so you will not hear it during playback.

> **REPOSITION YOUR CLIPS:** When you crop a clip, the length of the clip is altered. The space where the cropped data used to be will be filled with silence during playback. You might need to make some adjustments to the positions of your clips within your tracks.

> **PERMANENT CHANGES:** If you ever want to apply your cropping changes to a clip permanently, choose Clips > Apply Trimming in the Track view menu. This will also reduce the size of your project because it deletes the cropped data.

Shifting a Clip

Instead of cropping a clip (and thus changing its length), you can shift the data inside the clip without changing the clip's length. To shift a clip, follow these steps:

1. Using the Smart tool (F5), press and hold the Alt+Shift keys.
2. Position your mouse over the clip until the cursor looks as it appears in Figure 6.12.

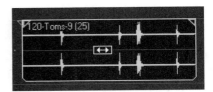

Figure 6.12 To shift a clip, use Alt+Shift with the Smart tool.
Source: Cakewalk®, Inc.

3. Click and drag to the left to shift the data in the clip toward the beginning of the clip.
4. Click and drag to the right to shift the data toward the end of the clip.

When you shift a clip, the data in the beginning or the end of the clip is cropped, but the length of the clip is not altered.

Shift-Cropping a Clip

Shift-cropping is a combination of the aforementioned functions. When you shift-crop a clip, the data in the clip is shifted, and the length of the clip is altered. To shift-crop a clip, follow these steps:

1. Using the Smart tool (F5) or Edit tool (F8), press and hold the Alt+Shift keys.
2. Position your mouse over the left or right end of the clip (depending on whether you want to shift-crop the beginning or end of the clip).
3. Click and drag to the left or right to alter the length of the clip and shift the data inside the clip at the same time.

The slip-editing functions can be very powerful alternatives to cutting and pasting. Since the data from the clips isn't deleted, you can edit the clips at any time to specify the portions of their data that will sound during playback. For example, if you have a clip that contains a vocal phrase, and the first word in the phrase isn't quite right, you can crop it. But later on, if you decide that the word actually sounded good, just uncrop it, and your data will be restored. SONAR also provides additional nondestructive editing with envelopes (see Chapter 12).

Audio Editing

Although SONAR provides separate views for precise editing of MIDI data, it doesn't provide a dedicated view for editing audio data. Instead, the Track view doubles as an audio editor. To edit audio in the Track view, you use all of the functions described previously in this chapter to edit any audio clips in your tracks. There are some other more sophisticated functions available for editing audio data that I'll describe in Chapter 7. There are, however, a few things that you should keep in mind while editing audio in the Track view.

AUDIO WAVEFORMS

When examining audio clips, you'll notice that they display the audio waveforms corresponding to the audio data inside them.

AUDIO WAVEFORMS: An *audio waveform* is a graphical representation of sound. Let me try to explain using the cup and string analogy. Remember when you were a kid, and you set up your own intercom system between your bedroom and your tree house using nothing but a couple of paper cups and a long piece of string? You poked a hole in the bottom of each cup and then tied one end of the string to one cup and the other end of the string to the other cup. Your friend would be in the tree house with one of the cups, and you would be in your bedroom with the other. As you talked into your cup, your friend could hear you by putting his cup to his ear and vice versa.

Why did it work? Well, when you talked into the cup, the sound of your voice vibrated the bottom of the cup, making it act like a microphone. This movement, in turn, vibrated the string up and down, and the string carried the vibrations to the other cup. This movement made the bottom of that cup vibrate so that it acted like a speaker, thus letting your friend hear what you said. If it were possible for you to freeze the string while it was in motion and then zoom in on it so you could see the vibrations, it would look similar to the audio waveform shown in Figure 6.13.

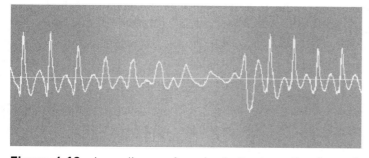

Figure 6.13 An audio waveform is similar to a vibrating string if you could freeze and zoom in on the string to observe the vibrations.
Source: Cakewalk®, Inc.

As you can see, a waveform shows up and down movements just like a vibrating string. A line, called the *zero axis*, runs horizontally through the center of the waveform. The zero axis represents the point in a waveform at which there are no vibrations or sound, so the value of the audio data at the zero axis is the number zero (also known as *zero amplitude*). When a waveform moves above or below the zero axis, vibrations occur, and thus there is sound. The amplitude value of a waveform in these places depends on how high above or how low below the zero axis the waveform is at a certain point in time (shown on the Time Ruler).

SNAP TO ZERO CROSSING

Another thing to keep in mind is that you need to make sure to edit your audio data at zero crossings in the waveform. You can do so by activating the Snap to Grid audio zero crossings feature. Press Shift+N. Then put a check mark next to the Snap to Nearest Audio Zero Crossings option in the Snap to Grid section of the Preferences dialog box. The Snap to Nearest Audio Zero Crossings option (when activated) makes sure that, when you make a selection or perform an edit, your selections or edits fall on zero crossings in the audio waveform.

> **ZERO CROSSING:** Remember the description of the zero axis? Well, any point in an audio waveform that lands on the zero axis is called a *zero crossing*. It's called that because as the waveform moves up and down, it crosses over the zero axis.

Why is it important that your selections and edits line up with zero crossings? A zero crossing is a point in the audio waveform at which no sound is being made, so it provides a perfect spot at which to edit the waveform—for example, when you're cutting and pasting pieces of audio. If you edit an audio waveform at a point where it's either above or below the zero axis, you might introduce glitches, which can come in the form of audible pops and clicks. You get these glitches because you cut at a moment when sound is being produced. You also get them because when you're pasting pieces of audio together, you cannot guarantee that the ends of each waveform will line up perfectly (unless they are both at zero crossings).

AUDIO SCALING

Lastly, SONAR provides some special zooming features when you are working with audio tracks. These are the audio scaling features, and they allow you to zoom in on the audio waveforms shown inside the clips in your audio tracks. Audio scaling measures the amplitude of your audio data, and it comes in handy for doing very precise audio editing.

When you are working with audio tracks, you'll notice some numbers displayed along the left side of the Clips pane in the Track view (see Figure 6.14). These numbers represent the Audio Scale, which displays a measurement of the amplitude of the audio data in your audio tracks.

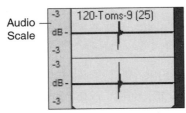

Figure 6.14 Use the Audio Scale to measure the amplitude of your audio.
Source: Cakewalk®, Inc.

The measurement can be shown in decibels, as a percentage or as a zoom factor. To change the measurement display, right-click anywhere in the Audio Scale area and choose an option.

To change the Audio Scale factor for a single audio track, just left-click and hold your mouse on the Audio Scale of the track. Then drag your mouse up or down to change the Audio Scale factor. You'll notice that the audio waveform display for the track changes as you move your mouse. So you can zoom in and out of the audio waveform, but it doesn't affect the Track view zooming. To return the Audio Scale factor to its default value, double-click inside the Audio Scale area.

You also can change the audio scaling factor for all audio tracks at once by using the Zoom Out Vertical, Zoom In Vertical, and Vertical Zoom Control functions. To use them for audio scaling, just hold down the Ctrl key while you manipulate the functions with your mouse.

Take Lanes and Comping

Back in Chapter 5, I discussed the Sound on Sound recording mode to record multiple takes into the same track. I also showed you that by right-clicking on that track and choosing Lanes > Show/Hide Takes, you could see those multiple takes displayed in separate lanes beneath the same track. This feature gives you easy access for editing those takes.

WORKING WITH TAKE LANES

You can work with Take Lanes similar to the way you work with separate tracks. Follow these steps to work with Take Lanes:

1. In addition to the method I mentioned earlier, you can show/hide lanes in a track by clicking the Take Lanes button (see Figure 6.15). You can also press Shift+T to show lanes for the active track. Once the lanes in a track are shown, you can apply a number of other functions.

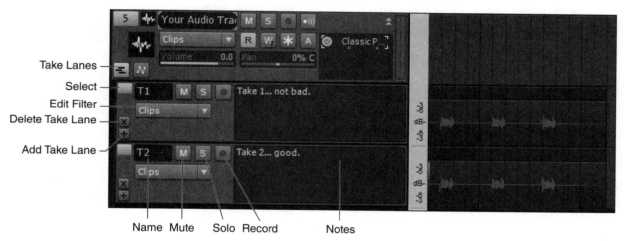

Figure 6.15 Use Take Lanes to access and edit overlapping clips in a track.
Source: Cakewalk®, Inc.

2. For playback control, there are Mute and Solo buttons for each lane. These buttons mute and solo each lane within a track independent of the Mute and Solo functions used for the entire track.
3. There is also an independent record button for each lane, which allows you to record new audio into a lane. The same input/output parameters are used for the lane(s) and the parent track.
4. Each lane also has an independent Edit Filter so that you can display and edit different types of data in each lane (Clips, Audio Transients, and Clip Automation - Envelopes).
5. The Notes area in each lane can be used to include text notes. Double-click the Notes area to activate it and then type in some text. Press Enter to finish.
6. The Name parameter of each lane can be changed by double-clicking it, typing some text, and pressing Enter. You can also drag the right edge of the Name parameter to display longer names.
7. Resize a lane by dragging the bottom of the lane (the same way you would resize a track). Unfortunately, individual lanes can't be resized independently. If you resize one lane in a track, all other lanes in that track are made the same size.
8. To insert a new lane into a track, click one of the Add Take Lane buttons. A new lane is added below the lane containing the button you clicked. You can copy clips into the new lane and arrange them just like clips in a track.

9. To delete a lane, click its Delete Take Lane button.
10. To select a lane for processing with any of SONAR's processing functions, click its Select button. Double-click any lane Select button to select all lanes.
11. You can rearrange lanes in the list by positioning your mouse just beneath the Select button until it turns into a double up/down arrow. Then click/drag the lane up/down, similar to the way you arrange tracks.

Besides normal editing tasks, layers are extremely useful for comping. Comping consists of recording multiple takes of the same performance and then piecing together the best parts of each take to get the best performance possible. In addition to multilane tracks, SONAR provides additional features to make comping a quick and easy process.

CLIP MUTING

In order to put together a composite track, you need to gather all the good parts of each take. You can do this in two ways. The first way is by muting selected parts of each take. Using muting, you can "turn off" any of the bad parts of each take and leave all the good parts alone. SONAR does this by using the Mute tool.

1. Activate the Mute tool, which is a sub-tool of the Erase tool (F10).
2. To mute part of a clip, position the mouse in the lower half of the clip. Then click and drag over the region of the clip you want to mute (see Figure 6.16). The part of the clip you've muted will show the audio waveform as an outline rather than a filled-in waveform.

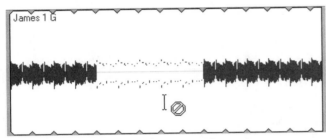

Figure 6.16 Click and drag inside the lower part of a clip to mute the data.
Source: Cakewalk®, Inc.

3. To unmute part of a clip, position the mouse in the upper half of the clip. Then click and drag over the region you want to unmute (see Figure 6.17).

Figure 6.17 Click and drag inside the upper part of a clip to unmute the data.
Source: Cakewalk®, Inc.

4. You can also mute/unmute an entire clip by clicking in the lower/upper half, respectively. A muted clip is displayed in a grayed-out color with a red, slashed circle shown in the upper-left corner.

> **MUTING ENTIRE CLIPS QUICKLY:** You can also mute/unmute entire clips in two additional ways. Right-click the clip and choose Clip Mute/Unmute, or select the clip and press K.

CLIP ISOLATING

The second way to create a composite track is to use clip isolating. This means that instead of muting all the bad parts in each take, you solo all the good parts. This method can be much easier and faster if you are working with a large number of clips. To isolate (solo) the good parts in a clip, do the following:

1. Activate the Mute tool, which is a sub-tool of the Erase tool (F10).
2. To isolate part of a clip, hold down the Ctrl key and drag through the part of the clip you would like to isolate. By doing so, this keeps the part of the clip you selected, and it mutes the same part of any clips that are in different take lanes but occupy the same time region.
3. You can de-isolate part of a clip by using the same method used to unmute part of a clip. Just click and drag the Mute tool in the upper part of the clip that you want to de-isolate (unmute).
4. You can also isolate an entire clip. Just hold down Ctrl and click a clip to isolate it. Click the muted clip to de-isolate (unmute) it.

Whichever method you choose, the comping tools in SONAR piece together the perfect composite track. And once you've muted or isolated all the parts you want, you can either leave the track as it is for future editing, or you can select the track and use the Bounce to Track(s) feature to mix all your edits down to a new, clean track. I recommend bouncing to a new track because when you hide lanes in a track, the last edited clips will be on top while some other clips will remain overlapped. This means that some of the muted parts may show in the track even though those are not the parts you want to keep. Bouncing to a new track ensures that all the good parts of the performance are combined into a single clip and displayed in the track properly.

Using the Piano Roll View

By manipulating the tracks and clips in your project, you can change the overall structure, but to fix single-note mistakes and make smaller changes, you need to do some precision editing. You do so by selecting individual or multiple tracks or clips in the Track view and then using the Views menu to open the data within one of the other available views. For editing MIDI data, that would be the Piano Roll view. You also can edit MIDI data as standard music notation in the Staff view. See Chapter 15 for more information about the Staff view.

Using the Piano Roll view, you can add, edit, and delete MIDI note and controller data within your MIDI tracks. Please refer to Figure 6.18 throughout this section as a reference to the different aspects of the Piano Roll view that I will be describing. Looking somewhat like a player-piano roll, the Piano Roll view represents notes as colored shapes on a grid display with the pitches of the notes designated by an on-screen music keyboard.

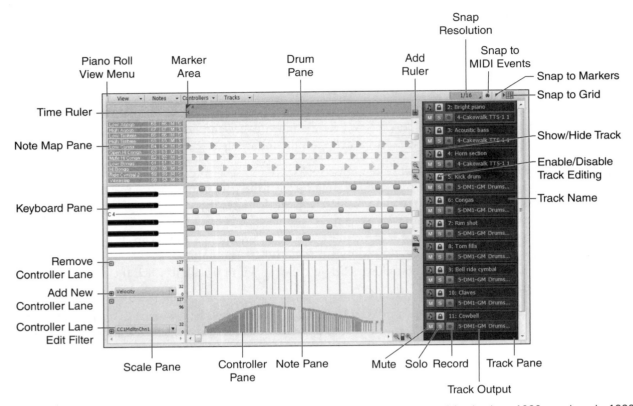

Figure 6.18 The Piano Roll view resembles the old player-piano rolls used in the late 1800s and early 1900s.
Source: Cakewalk®, Inc.

More precisely, the Piano Roll view consists of eight major sections: the menu (containing all the view's related functions), the Drum pane (displaying the drum notes in any selected drum tracks), the Note Map pane (displaying the drum instruments represented by the note shown in the Drum pane), the Note pane (displaying the melodic notes in the currently selected tracks), the Keyboard pane (displaying the pitch values of the notes shown in the Note pane), the Controller pane (displaying the MIDI controller data in the currently selected tracks), the Scale pane (displaying the number values of the controllers shown in the Controller pane), and the Track pane (showing a list of all the tracks currently being displayed—the Piano Roll view can display the data from more than one track at one time).

You'll also notice that the Piano Roll view has scroll bars and zoom tools just like the Track view. These tools work the same way as they do in the Track view. Other similarities are the Marker area and the Time Ruler, which are located just above the Drum pane. The Piano Roll view also has its own Snap to Grid function, which (when activated) overrides the global Snap to Grid function in the Control Bar. However, the Smart Grid feature still functions here and has to be toggled via the Snap Resolution in the Snap module of the Control Bar. Otherwise, the Snap to Grid function in the Piano Roll view provides its own Snap Resolution as well as Snap to MIDI Events and Snap to Markers options. If you turn off the Snap to Grid in the Piano Roll view (by clicking the Snap to Grid button), then editing in the Piano Roll view conforms to the global Snap to Grid function. If you turn off the global Snap to Grid function, then that turns off all Snap to Grid functions in SONAR.

Basically, you can use the Piano Roll view to edit and view the data in the MIDI tracks of your project in more detail. You can open the Piano Roll view in three different ways:

▷ In the Track view, select the tracks you want to edit and then choose Views > Piano Roll View (Alt+3).
▷ In the Track view, right-click a track or clip and choose Views > Piano Roll View.

▷ In the Track view, double-click a MIDI clip in the Clips pane. If the MIDI clip has its clip indicator set to a different view, then double-clicking will open that view instead. In this case, you can click the clip indicator and choose Piano Roll from the menu.

Whichever method you choose, SONAR will open the Piano Roll view and display the data from the track(s) you selected.

> **CHANGE DOUBLE-CLICK BEHAVIOR:** By default, when you double-click a MIDI clip or an audio clip, SONAR automatically opens the Piano Roll view or the Loop Construction view (see Chapter 9). You can change this behavior by choosing Options > Click Behavior > Double-Click in the Track view menu. For individual MIDI clips, you can also select a different default view by clicking the clip indicator and choosing a view from the menu.

Working with Multiple Tracks

If you select more than one track to be displayed at one time, the Piano Roll view will show the data from each track by using a unique color. For example, the notes and controllers from one track might be shown as yellow, and the data from another track might be shown as blue. You can change track colors by clicking a track in the Track view to make it active and then pressing Ctrl+Shift+I to open the Track Properties in the Inspector. Then change the Foreground parameter by clicking it and choosing a new color.

The Track Pane

When you open the Piano Roll view, the names and numbers of the tracks you selected are listed in the Track pane. For convenience, the associated Mute, Solo, and Record buttons for each track are provided as well. Plus, you'll notice two other controls available for each track in the list.

▷ **Enable/Disable Track Editing.** The button with the lock shown on it next to each track in the Track pane is the Enable/Disable Track Editing button. This button determines whether the notes for its associated track can be edited. When the button is white, the notes appear in color in the Drum and Note panes, and they can be edited. When the button is blue, the notes appear gray, and they cannot be edited. Clicking the button toggles it on and off.

▷ **Show/Hide Track.** The button to the left of the Track Editing button is the Show/Hide Track button. This button determines whether the notes for its associated track will be displayed in the Drum and Note panes. When the button shows a picture of notes on it, the notes are shown in the Drum and Note panes. When the button is blank, the notes are not shown. Clicking the button toggles it on and off.

The Track pane also allows you to change the order of the tracks by clicking and dragging them up or down in the list. However, this doesn't affect how the tracks are listed in the Track view.

The Track Functions

In addition to the Track pane controls, some other track-related functions are available via the Piano Roll view menu:

▷ **Tracks > Pick Tracks.** While you have the Piano Roll view open, you might want to add or remove some of the tracks in the Track pane. Instead of having to close the Piano Roll view, select other tracks in the Track view, and then open the Piano Roll view again, you can use the Pick Tracks function.

Choose Tracks > Pick Tracks to open the Pick Tracks dialog box. This box displays a list of all the tracks in your project. You can select one or more tracks from the list. (Hold down Ctrl or Shift to select multiple tracks.) After you click the OK button, the tracks that you selected will be listed in the Track pane.

▷ **View > Show/Hide Track Pane (H).** This menu item toggles the Track pane visibility.

▷ **View > Show/Hide Controller Pane.** This menu item toggles the Controller pane visibility.

▷ **View > Show/Hide Drum Pane.** This menu item toggles the Drum pane visibility.

▷ **Tracks > Hide All Tracks.** This menu item turns off the Show/Hide Track buttons for each track in the Track List pane. No matter what state each button is in (on or off), this function turns them all off.

▷ **Tracks > Show All Tracks.** This menu item is the exact opposite of Hide All Tracks. It turns on the Show/Hide Track buttons for each track in the Track List pane.

▷ **Tracks > Invert Tracks (V).** This menu item toggles the Show/Hide Track buttons. If one track has its Show/Hide Track button on and another track has its button off, the Invert Tracks function turns off the first track's Show/Hide button and turns on the second track's Show/Hide button.

Dealing with Notes

When you open a melodic MIDI track in the Piano Roll view, the notes in that track are displayed in the Note pane. Each note is represented by a colored rectangle. The horizontal location of a note designates its start time when you line up the left side of the rectangle with the numbers in the Time Ruler, and the vertical location of a note designates its pitch when you line up the whole rectangle with the keys in the Keyboard pane. The length of the rectangle designates the duration of the note (for instance, quarter note, eighth note, and so on). You can add new notes to a track or edit the existing ones by using SONAR's global tools. I personally recommend using the Smart tool whenever possible because it provides the most efficient workflow, which I'll talk about shortly.

Melodic Scales

Before you begin adding or editing notes into a track, you might want to set the melodic scale for that track. SONAR provides a Snap to Scale feature that when activated will automatically force all added or edited notes to conform to the melodic scale of your choice. This feature can make it much easier to add and edit notes in a track when you know you'll be composing using a certain melodic scale. To activate the Snap to Scale feature for a track, right-click the track in the Track pane and choose Enable/Disable Snap to Scale.

Setting the Scale

After you've enabled the Snap to Scale feature, you'll want to set the scale to be used for the track being edited. Follow these steps to set the scale:

1. Right-click the track in the Track pane and choose Root Note > [*name of musical note*] to set the root note for the scale. This allows you to choose the beginning note and musical key for the scale. For example, if your song is being composed in the key of C, choose C as the root note.

2. Right-click the track in the Track pane and choose Scales > [*type of scale*] > [*name of scale*] to set the scale for the track. For example, if your song is being composed in the key of C Major, choose Diatonic Scales > Ionian (Major) as the scale.

3. In addition to the root name and type of scale, you need to set the Snap Settings for the track. The Snap Settings determine how non-scale notes are handled. To set the Snap Settings, right-click the track in the Track pane and choose Snap Settings to open the Snap Scale Settings dialog box.

4. Choose one of the options in the dialog box. Choose Adjust to Next, Higher Note so that any non-scale notes are moved to the next higher note in the chosen scale. Choose Adjust to Previous, Lower Note so that any non-scale notes are moved to the previous lower note in the chosen scale. Choose Adjust to Nearest Note so that any non-scale notes are moved to the note closest in pitch in the chosen scale. Click OK.

INSPECTOR SNAP TO SCALE: You can also set up the Snap to Scale feature for a track by selecting the track in the Track view and then using the Snap to Scale section of the Inspector.

CREATE YOUR OWN SCALES

Even though SONAR ships with a large collection of scales from which you can choose, SONAR also allows you to create your own scales for use with the Snap to Scale feature. To create your own scale, do the following:

1. Right-click a track in the Track pane and choose Scale Manager to open the Scale Manager dialog box.
2. In the Scale Family section, select the scale category in which you would like your new scale to be listed.
3. In the Scale section, type a name for your new scale and then click the Create New Scale button (the one with the yellow star shown on it).
4. To add or remove degrees to or from the scale, either click the keys in the Keyboard display or click the buttons in the Scale Degrees section.
5. If you don't like your scale and want to delete it, just click the Delete Scale button (the one with the big red X shown on it).
6. If you edit one of the default scales included with SONAR, and you want to put it back to the way it was, click the Defaults button to open the Scale Defaults dialog box. Choose one of the options and click OK. The Restore Current Scale option restores the default scale with which you are currently working. The Restore Any Missing Scales option restores any default scales you may have deleted. The Restore All Factory Scales option restores all default scales to their original configurations.

When you close the Scale Manager dialog box, your new scale will be listed under your chosen category in the Scales menu.

QUICK SNAP TO SCALE OVERRIDE: In the following sections, I'll be talking about how to add and edit notes. If you have the Snap to Scale feature activated while adding or editing notes, your notes will be automatically moved to conform to your chosen scale. However, if you are working with a particular note that you do not want altered, you can temporarily bypass the Snap to Scale feature by holding down the right mouse button after you have already pressed and held the left mouse button as you move a note up/down to change its pitch.

Selecting Notes

Using the Smart and Select tools, you can select notes for further manipulation, such as deleting, copying, and so on. Essentially, you select notes the same way you select clips in the Track view. To select a single note, click the center of the note with the Smart tool or any part of the note with the Select tool. To select more than one note, hold down the Ctrl key while clicking the notes you want to select. To select a group of notes, right-click in a blank area and drag over the notes to create a lasso. When you let go of the mouse button, any notes touched by the lasso will be selected.

One additional selection method involves the Keyboard pane. To select all the notes of a certain pitch, you can click one of the keys in the Keyboard pane. You can also drag your mouse pointer across several keys to select the notes of a number of different pitches.

OVERLAPPING NOTES: If you have two or more tracks that contain the same notes, those notes overlap one another. The active track in the Track pane determines which track's notes are on top. To make a track the active track, simply click it in the Track pane.

In addition, to work on only one track at a time, click the Show/Hide Track button for the track to hide its notes. Then choose Tracks > Invert Tracks (or press V) from the Piano Roll view menu. This will hide the notes of all tracks except the one you want to work with. When you're finished, choose Tracks > Show All Tracks.

Basic Editing

After you've made a selection, you can copy, cut, paste, move, and delete the notes the same way you do with clips in the Track view. You can also edit notes individually by using the Smart tool (or a combination of the other tools).

AIM ASSIST: I discussed Aim Assist earlier in the "Selecting Clips" section of this chapter. In addition to working in the Track view, Aim Assist is also provided in the Piano Roll view. Press X to toggle it. In the Piano Roll view, Aim Assist not only provides the horizontal mouse position along the Time Ruler, but also the vertical mouse position along the Keyboard pane, which makes adding and editing notes much easier.

Using the Smart tool, change the start time of a note by dragging the left edge of its rectangle left or right. This action moves the beginning of the note to a different horizontal location along the Time Ruler. To change the pitch of a note, drag the middle of its rectangle up or down. This action moves it to a different vertical location along the Keyboard pane. To change the duration of a note, drag the right edge of its rectangle left or right. This action changes the length of the rectangle and thus the duration of the note. To move a note along the Time Ruler without changing its duration, drag the middle of its rectangle right or left. To change the velocity (loudness) of a note, click the top of its rectangle and drag your mouse up/down to raise/lower the value.

CONSTRAINING NOTE MOVEMENT: When you're moving a note up/down or left/right, you can first hold Shift and then move the note to constrain it to a single direction. So if you hold Shift and move up/down, the note will only move up/down (and not left/right) so that you don't accidentally change its position while changing its pitch. You can do the same thing with left/right movement.

Sometimes, you might want to make more precise changes to a note. There are two ways to do this. The first method is to select the note and then use the Time, Pitch, Vel (Velocity), Duration, and Channel parameters in the Event Inspector module of the Control Bar to change those characteristics of the note. You can also double-click a note to change the same parameters using the Note Properties dialog box.

EVENT INSPECTOR AND NOTE PROPERTIES: The Note Properties dialog box allows you to make precise changes to the start time, pitch, velocity, duration, and MIDI channel of an individual note by typing numerical values. However, it only works on one note at a time. But you can use the Event Inspector to change both single and multiple note selections. The Event Inspector is a global module in the Control Bar that can be accessed from any view. If it is not active, right-click the background of the Control Bar and choose Event Inspector Module to make it visible.

Now whenever you select a note, the note's properties are displayed in the Event Inspector. If you select a group of notes, some default values are shown instead. To change the note's properties, click a field in the Event Inspector and either type in a new value or use the spin controls to increase or decrease the value. In addition, you can use modifiers (+/−) to change values relative to their current values. For example, if you want to add 23 to a velocity value of 37, type **+23** for the Vel parameter, and SONAR will automatically change the value to 60. The plus and minus modifiers work for all parameters, but the Vel (velocity) and Duration parameters can also accept a percentage for scaling values. For example, with 100% representing the current value, if you want to lengthen a note by 20%, you would enter **120%** for the Duration value. If you wanted to shorten the same note by 20%, you would enter **80%**. To see the Event Inspector in action, go to **garrigus.com?SonarEventInspector** to watch my *Event Inspector Editing* video.

Drawing (or Adding) Notes

In addition to editing, the Smart and Draw tools add notes to a track by literally drawing them in. To do so, just follow these steps:

1. Choose the Smart (F5) or Draw (F9) tool.
2. If you want added notes to land exactly on the beat, activate the Snap to Grid.
3. You can also have a visible grid appear by choosing View > Show Vertical Gridlines in the Piano Roll view menu. Set the grid resolution by choosing View > Grid Resolution > [*note value*]. If you choose View > Grid Resolution > Follow Snap Settings, the resolution of the grid will be set to the same value as the current Snap to Grid resolution. I like to use this option because it's nice to see a visual representation of the snap grid while working in the Piano Roll view.
4. Select a duration for the new notes by choosing a value via the Event Draw Duration control in the Tools module of the Control Bar or via the Tools HUD (press T or the middle mouse button).
5. To add a single note, double-click with the Smart tool (single-click with the Draw tool) inside the Note pane at the point at which you want to place the new note. You can also Alt+click with the Smart tool. Remember, the horizontal position of the note determines its start time, and the vertical position of the note determines its pitch. You can also quickly add notes of any duration by clicking and dragging with the Smart tool. You can drag out the note to the desired duration and then let go of the mouse button.
6. To add multiple notes by "freehand painting," press and hold Ctrl+Alt with the Smart tool. Then click and drag the mouse anywhere in the Note pane. With the Draw tool, you can just click/drag.
7. To add multiple notes in a straight or diagonal line, press and hold Ctrl+Shift+Alt with the Smart tool. Click at the point where you want the line of notes to begin and then drag your mouse to where you want the line to end. The notes will be spaced according to the current Snap to Grid settings.

Erasing Notes

You can erase notes in a variety of different ways. Using the Smart and Select tools, click a single note or right-click to lasso multiple notes and press the Delete key. You can also use Edit > Delete after making a selection.

Using the Smart and Draw tools, right-click a note to delete it. SONAR also provides the Erase tool. With this tool, click a single note to delete it. For multiple notes, click and drag your mouse over the notes to highlight them; then let go of the mouse button to delete them.

Scrubbing

When you're editing the data in a track, the procedure usually involves making your edits and then playing back the project to hear how the changes sound. However, playing back very small sections can be a bit difficult, especially when you're working with a fast tempo. To remedy this situation, SONAR provides a Scrub tool.

Using the Scrub tool, you can drag your mouse pointer over the data in the Piano Roll view and hear what it sounds like. The Scrub tool can only be accessed by pressing J. It is not available via the Tools module or Tools HUD. After the Scrub tool is activated, click and drag your mouse pointer over the data in the Drum or Note pane. Dragging left to right plays the data forward (which would normally happen during playback), and dragging right to left enables you to hear the data played in reverse. This capability can be useful for testing very short (one or two measure) sections. The Scrub tool remains activated until you switch to a different tool. Press and hold J to use the Scrub tool temporarily; then let go of J to automatically switch back to the previous tool.

Special Editing Functions

In addition to the basic functions, SONAR provides Event Mute, Note Split, Note Glue, Drag Quantize, and MIDI Microscope for your MIDI editing pleasure.

EVENT MUTE

Event Mute allows you to remove notes from playback without actually deleting them. Using the Smart tool (F5), hold down the Alt key and right-click the top of a note to mute/unmute it. With the Mute tool (F10), just click a note. The note turns into an outline of a rectangle when muted. You can also mute multiple notes at the same time by selecting them first and then clicking one of the selected notes.

> **MUTED CLIPS:** As I mentioned earlier in this chapter, the Mute tool allows you to mute parts of a clip in the Track view. If you mute part of a MIDI clip, some of the notes in the clip are muted, and some are not. Notes that have been muted using the Mute tool look like solid gray rectangles rather than just outlines of a rectangle. So even though the results are the same, muted events (notes) and muted clips are actually different. As such, you can't use Event Mute to unmute part of a muted clip, and you can't use the Mute tool on notes modified with Event Mute. Also, to keep things more organized, SONAR allows you to hide muted clips in the Piano Roll view by choosing View > Hide Muted Clips from the Piano Roll view menu.

NOTE SPLIT

Using the Note Split function, you can divide a single note into multiple notes. First, press N to turn off Snap to Grid. (Otherwise, your split will occur at the Snap Resolution, rather than the exact mouse location.) With the Smart tool (F5), Alt+click the bottom or middle of a note, or with the Split tool (F8) click anywhere on a note. The note will be split at the exact point that you clicked. Press N again to turn on Snap to Grid, if needed.

NOTE GLUE

Using the Note Glue function, you can merge multiple notes. With the Smart tool, hold down Ctrl+Alt. Then click and hold the first note. While you continue holding Ctrl+Alt and the mouse button, drag your mouse and touch the note(s) you want to merge. Only notes of the same pitch (located on the same keyboard row) can be merged, but you can maneuver your mouse around to touch notes that are not next to each other in the same row to merge inconsecutive notes together. When you let go of Ctrl+Alt and the mouse button, the notes you touched will be merged into a single note. You can also use the Draw (F9) tool to merge notes just by clicking and dragging.

DRAG QUANTIZE

Using the Drag Quantize function, you can make corrections to the timing of your recorded MIDI data. When applied, the function will automatically move your notes to the closest specified Snap to Grid note value (resolution). If you don't have Snap to Grid enabled, SONAR will automatically choose a quantize resolution that it finds to be appropriate. I like to use Drag Quantize with Snap to Grid enabled because it gives me complete control of how the timing of my data is corrected.

To apply Drag Quantize, make a note selection (a single note or group of notes). Then activate the Timing tool (F8) and click/hold the mouse on a selected note. Now drag the mouse up/down to move the note(s) closer to/farther from the specified note resolution. This allows you to apply the amount of timing correction you would like so you can tighten up a performance, but not make it sound too mechanical. As you drag, you'll see the notes move, and you will also see the Drag Quantize Strength percentage shown next to the mouse cursor. The closer to 100%, the tighter the performance. The closer to –100%, the looser the performance. A value of 0% puts the notes at their original time locations.

MIDI MICROSCOPE

The farther you zoom out in the Piano Roll view, the more notes you can see at one time, but the smaller the notes become, making it more difficult to edit them precisely. To resolve this problem, SONAR provides the MIDI

Microscope function. To activate it, choose View > MIDI Microscope in the Piano Roll view menu. This creates a small, magnified area around the mouse cursor as you hover your mouse over notes in the Note pane, thus allowing you to edit the notes easily without having to zoom in.

You can adjust the MIDI Microscope settings by pressing P and choosing Customization – Editing in the Preferences dialog box. In the MIDI section, the Microscope option will turn the function on/off. The Diagonal Size parameter specifies how large the magnified area is in pixels—with 20 to 250 being the valid range of values. The Show When Note Height Less Than parameter designates how large a note has to be (2 to 20 pixels) for the function to be active. The Magnifying Time option determines whether notes will be magnified horizontally or not. This means that with the option off, even if you are zoomed out horizontally to a high degree, MIDI Microscope will not be active. Frankly, I can't think of a situation where you would want this to happen. I always keep the Magnifying Time option enabled.

Dealing with Drum Tracks

Because drum tracks are a bit different from regular MIDI tracks, SONAR provides some special features for dealing with them. Notes in a drum track usually represent a number of different percussion instruments grouped in the same track. Each note pitch in a drum track represents a different instrument. It used to be that if you wanted to work easily with each specific instrument, you had to split a drum track into many different tracks—one track for each note pitch. This allowed you to mute and solo different instruments, as well as do other things that you couldn't do when all the drum notes were grouped together on the same track.

With SONAR's drum-specific features, you no longer have to go through the trouble of creating separate tracks for each drum instrument. You also have the flexibility of specifying different MIDI channels and MIDI ports for each instrument (among other things) using drum maps.

Using Drum Maps

A drum map defines your drum instruments for SONAR, thus "telling" SONAR how each note pitch in a drum track should be handled. Each note pitch defined in a drum map can have its own instrument name, MIDI channel, MIDI port, velocity offset, and velocity scale.

ASSIGNING DRUM MAPS

The easiest way to explain drum maps is to show you how to assign a drum map to a MIDI track and explain the results. I'll use an example to help clarify things a bit, but keep in mind that you won't hear any sound. This example simply demonstrates how to assign a drum map.

1. Create a new project and insert a MIDI track.
2. Select the track and choose Views > Piano Roll View. Then double-click with the Smart tool (F5) to add some notes. This is what a drum track looks like without a drum map assigned to it. You can see the notes in the track, but you don't know what percussion instruments they represent. And you can't easily work with each individual instrument because there is no way to mute or solo a specific group of note pitches. In addition, all the notes in the track have to share the same MIDI port and channel specified by the track parameters. To get beyond these limitations, you need to assign a drum map to the track.
3. Close the Piano Roll view. Then in the Track view or the Inspector, click the track's Output control to display the Output menu.
4. Highlight the New Drum Map option and choose GM Drums (Complete Kit) from the extended menu. This assigns the GM Drums (Complete Kit) drum map to the track. SONAR ships with a number of predefined drum maps, as you can see from the list.
5. Select the track and choose Views > Piano Roll View to open the track in the Piano Roll view again. Also, choose Edit > Select > None (Ctrl+Shift+A) to get rid of the selection.

This time the track data looks a bit different, right? Instead of the Note pane, the Drum pane is shown, and instead of rectangles, there are triangles representing the notes, even though these are the same notes as before. If you don't see the Drum pane, choose View > Show/Hide Drum Pane from the Piano Roll view menu.

More important is what is shown in the Note Map pane. Each row in the Note Map pane represents a different percussion instrument. By lining up the notes in the Drum pane with the rows in the Note Map pane, you can see what instrument the notes represent. And even though all these note pitches (instruments) reside on the same MIDI track, each instrument can be muted or soloed individually using the M and S buttons next to each instrument name in the Note Map pane. This makes working with drum tracks much easier.

CREATING DRUM MAPS

However, there might be times when the predefined drum maps included with SONAR don't provide what you need. In that case, you'll need to create a drum map of your own. To do that, you need to use the Drum Map Manager, which you can access by clicking any MIDI track Output control and choosing Drum Map Manager or by accessing the MIDI – Drum Map Manager section of the Preferences (P) dialog box.

The Drum Map Manager is divided into three sections. The first section (Drum Maps Used in Current Project) lists all the drum maps being used in the current project. It allows you to delete existing drum maps or create new ones. The second section (Map Settings) shows all the parameter settings for the selected drum map. It also defines each instrument in the drum map by specifying note pitches, instrument names, MIDI channels, MIDI out ports, velocity offsets, and velocity scales. And the third section (Ports and Channels) lists all the MIDI output port and channel pairs that are used by the selected drum map. It also lets you specify a MIDI bank and patch for each port/channel combination.

To create a drum map of your own, follow these steps:

1. With a project already open in SONAR, open the Drum Map Manager.
2. Click the New button in the first section (Drum Maps Used in Current Project) to create a blank drum map. Don't worry about naming or saving it yet; you'll do that later.
3. Click the New button in the second section (Map Settings) of the window to create a new instrument mapping, complete with default parameter settings.
4. Double-click the In Note parameter for the new instrument mapping and enter a number (from 0 to 127) to specify the source pitch for this instrument. I'll explain what I mean by *source pitch* in a moment.

NOTE PITCHES: Note pitches in MIDI are represented by a range of numbers (0 to 127). These numbers represent the note pitches C0 (pitch/octave) to C8, with the number 60 (C5) being Middle C. Unfortunately, you have to enter numbers for note values in the Drum Map Manager. There is no way to enter the pitch/octave of a note directly. However, after you enter a number, the pitch/octave of the note is displayed.

Another thing to keep in mind is that there is no standard for representing MIDI note octaves. So although I mentioned 60 being equal to C5, that's just the way SONAR has the MIDI octaves set up by default. Most people agree that 60 is equal to C3 or C4. You can change the way SONAR handles MIDI octaves by pressing P and choosing Customization – Display. Then set a new number for the Base Octave For Pitches parameter. Type in –2 or –1 to make SONAR treat MIDI note 60 as C3 or C4, respectively. Or you can simply leave it at the default value, it's up to you.

---

5. Double-click the Out Note parameter for the new instrument mapping and enter a number (from 0 to 127) to specify the destination pitch for this instrument.

HOW DRUM MAPS WORK: A drum map is sort of like a MIDI data processor. After you assign a drum map to a MIDI track, SONAR passes all the data in that MIDI track through the drum map for processing during playback. As SONAR reads each note from the MIDI track, it compares the pitch of the note to all of the source pitches (In Note parameters) in the drum map. If it finds a match, it converts the incoming note to the destination pitch (Out Note parameter) of the matching source pitch. For example, if you set up an instrument mapping in your drum map with an In Note pitch of C4 and an Out Note pitch of D5, any incoming notes that have a pitch of C4 will be converted to a pitch of D5.

Why is this useful? Well, more often than not, the In Note and Out Note parameters for an instrument mapping will be the same. But there might be times when you have a MIDI drum track that was recorded using a MIDI percussion synth other than what you have in your studio. This means that the drum sounds in your MIDI percussion device will be different and are probably triggered with different pitches. Using a drum map, you can map the pitches from the MIDI track to the different pitches used by your MIDI percussion device. This saves you the work of having to rewrite all the note pitches in the MIDI track.

6. Double-click the Name parameter for the new instrument mapping and enter a name for the instrument. For example, if you are creating your own General MIDI drum map, and you enter 56 for both the In Note and Out Note parameters, that means you are creating an instrument mapping for a cowbell sound because the number 56 represents a cowbell in General MIDI. So for the name, you would enter something like *Cowbell*.

7. Double-click the Chn (channel) parameter and enter a MIDI channel for the instrument. This should be the same MIDI channel that your MIDI percussion synth is using to play the particular instrument sound.

8. Double-click the Out Port parameter and choose a MIDI output port for the instrument. This should be the same MIDI output port that your MIDI percussion synth is using to play the particular instrument sound.

9. If you find that this instrument sound in your MIDI track is too loud or soft, you can add an offset to the MIDI velocity of the notes for that instrument sound. Just double-click the Vel+ parameter and enter a number from –127 to +127. This number will be subtracted or added to the MIDI velocity value of each incoming note for that instrument sound.

10. You also can adjust the loudness of an instrument sound using the V Scale parameter. Instead of having to designate a set value to be added to or subtracted from the MIDI velocity values of the incoming notes, you can apply a velocity scale. Double-click the V Scale parameter and enter a value from 10% to 200%. A value of 100% means there is no change. A value less than 100% means the velocity values will be decreased. A value greater than 100% means the velocity values will be increased.

11. Repeat Steps 3 through 10 to create as many instrument mappings in the drum map as you need. If you make a mistake, you can use the Undo button to remove your last change. To delete an instrument mapping, click the Delete button.

12. In the third section (Ports and Channels) of the window, you can set the bank and patch parameters for each MIDI port/channel combination used in the drum map. Basically, this is where you designate the drum set sounds that each MIDI percussion synth connected to your computer system should use. Your MIDI percussion synths should allow you to choose from a number of different drum sets.

13. To save your drum map, type a name in the Presets field and click the Save button (located just to the right of the Presets field, showing a picture of a computer disk).

When you go to assign a drum map to a MIDI track, you'll see your new drum map listed there along with all the others.

Composing Drum Tracks

After you've assigned a drum map to a MIDI track, you can start composing the percussion parts for your project. By opening the track in the Piano Roll view, you can use the Note Map pane and the Drum pane to add, edit, and delete drum notes. Most of the procedures that I described earlier in the "Dealing with Notes" section can be applied here. But there are a few differences of which you need to be aware. Instead of just describing these differences, I'd like to walk you through the procedure I use to compose my own drum patterns. Here is how it goes:

1. Choose File > New to create a new project.
2. Insert a new MIDI track for the project.
3. Assign a drum map to the MIDI track. For this example, use the GM Drums (Complete Kit) drum map. You'll need to use a synth that has a General MIDI–compatible mode. Most modern synths have this capability.
4. If you need to set a bank and patch for your synth, open the Drum Map Manager. In the third section (Ports and Channels) of the window, set a bank and patch for single port/channel listing. Close the Drum Map Manager.

USE A SOFTWARE SYNTH: You can also use a software synth to play the sounds for your drum track. Follow these directions to set up one:

1. Choose Insert > Soft Synth > Cakewalk TTS-1.
2. In the Insert Soft Synth Options dialog box, activate the First Synth Audio Output option. Make sure that all other options are deactivated and click OK.
3. Open the Drum Map Manager.
4. While holding down the Ctrl+Shift keys, click one of the Out Port parameters in the Map Settings list and choose Cakewalk TTS-1 from the menu.
5. Close the Drum Map Manager.

Now the Cakewalk TTS-1 software synth will play any notes you add to your MIDI drum track. If you need to change the sound card output for the TTS-1, expand track 2 in the Track view and change its Output parameter.

---

5. I like to create my drum tracks by composing small sections at a time, and I also like to hear my music as I'm composing it. SONAR allows me to do this by using its playback looping features. Suppose that you want to create a one-measure drum pattern starting at the very beginning of the project and going to the beginning of measure 2. To set up a playback loop for this example, just use the Loop module in the Control Bar. Set the Loop Start parameter to 1:01:000 and the Loop End parameter to 2:01:000. Press L to activate looping.
6. Open the MIDI drum track in the Piano Roll view. You'll be presented with the Note Map pane filled with all the instruments available in the drum map, as well as a blank Drum pane. Scroll down the window vertically until you can see the last instrument (Acoustic Bass Drum) in the Note Map pane. You might also want to increase the horizontal zoom of the window a bit so the first measure of the track fills the window.
7. The best way to start composing a drum pattern is to lay down a solid beat foundation. That means creating a kick drum part. You'll see in the list that you've got two kick drum sounds available to you: Bass Drum 1 and Acoustic Bass Drum. To audition an instrument, just click its name in the list. Personally, I like the Acoustic Bass Drum, so I'll use that for this exercise. For the kick drum part of the pattern, lay down a basic four-quarter-note beat. To do that, activate the Smart tool (F5) and choose the quarter-note (1/4) Event Draw Duration. Then place a note at each of the four beats in the first measure of the track.

SNAP TO GRID: If you have a hard time placing the notes exactly on the beats, activate the Snap to Grid function. You can also have SONAR display a visual grid over the Drum Grid pane to help you place notes by choosing View > Show Vertical Gridlines from the Piano Roll view menu. Change the grid resolution by choosing View > Grid Resolution.

---

8. Start playback and listen to the drum pattern so far. It sounds good, but now you need to add accompanying instruments to emphasize the beat, like a snare drum part. There are two snare drum instruments available in the list: Electric Snare and Acoustic Snare. I think you should go with the Acoustic Snare sound for this example, so place a quarter note at beats 2 and 4 in the pattern for the Acoustic Snare instrument. You should hear both the kick and snare instruments playing.

FIX MISTAKES: Remember that if you make any mistakes, you can use the same editing techniques I talked about earlier to fix things. If you need to delete a note, right-click the tip of its triangle. If you place a note on the wrong beat, drag the middle of it right or left along the grid. Or if you place a note in the wrong instrument row, drag it up or down to the correct instrument row.

---

9. Now let's spice up the pattern a bit with a closed hi-hat rhythm. Instead of quarter notes, however, use sixteenth notes. Change the Event Draw Resolution to sixteenth-notes (1/16) and then place notes at every sixteenth note line on the grid using the Closed Hi-Hat instrument.

10. The closed hi-hat part is missing something. Usually, a part like this will emphasize each beat in a pattern by playing each sixteenth note that falls on a beat a little louder than the rest. To make this happen, you need to adjust the velocity of these four notes using the Show Velocity Tails feature. To turn it on or off, choose Notes > Show Velocity Tails in the Piano Roll view menu.

11. You'll notice some vertical lines attached to each of the notes in the pattern. These lines represent the MIDI velocity for each note. To adjust the velocity of a note, just hover your mouse over the lines of the note until your mouse turns into a pointer with some vertical lines attached to it. Then click and drag your mouse up to increase the note's velocity or down to decrease the note's velocity. For this example, increase the velocity of the four closed hi-hat notes that reside right on each beat of the pattern to 127.

EVENT INSPECTOR: Instead of using the Show Velocity Tails feature to change the velocity of each note graphically, you can make changes more precisely by selecting notes and then entering a new value in the Vel parameter of the Event Inspector toolbar or by double-clicking each note to access Note Properties. To see the Event Inspector in action, go to **garrigus.com?SonarEventInspector** to watch my *Event Inspector Editing* video.

---

12. Your new drum pattern sounds pretty good, no? I know it's basic (see Figure 6.19), but I mainly wanted to show you how to use all the tools at your disposal. To create more patterns, just repeat Steps 4 through 11. In Step 5 just change the loop points to cover the next measure in the track (or several measures if you want to create longer drum patterns).

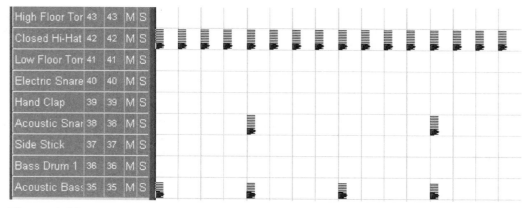

Figure 6.19 A basic drum pattern as seen in the Piano Roll view.
Source: Cakewalk®, Inc.

> **AUDITION DRUM INSTRUMENTS:** If you ever want to audition the entire drum track, you'll need to disable looping playback (press L) and then enable it again to continue working on your current drum pattern. Also, remember that as you're listening to your drum patterns, you can mute and solo individual instruments by using the M and S buttons next to each instrument in the Note Map pane. And for quick access to the drum map parameter settings for an individual instrument, just double-click the instrument name in the Note Map pane.

Dealing with Controllers

When you open a MIDI track in the Piano Roll view, in addition to the notes in the Drum Grid and Note panes, SONAR will display the MIDI controller data for that track in the Controller pane (refer to Figure 6.18). You can also have the MIDI controller data displayed as an overlay in the Note pane, if you'd rather work that way, by choosing View > Show/Hide Controller Pane in the Piano Roll view menu to close the Controller pane.

Because there are many different types of MIDI controller messages, SONAR allows you to control the type of data being displayed by choosing options under Controllers in the Piano Roll view menu. This scenario is for when the Controller pane is hidden. To show or hide individual MIDI controllers, choose the name of the controller from the Controllers menu. You can also show or hide notes or their velocities by choosing Notes > Show Notes or Notes > Show Velocity. The View > Show Clip Outlines option will display outlines of the clips that contain the MIDI notes you are editing. View > Hide Muted Clips toggles the display of notes contained in clips that have been muted in the Track view. Controllers > Show Controller Handles toggles the display of the small squares located at the top of individual controller lines. Notes > Show Velocity on Selected Notes only toggles whether or not to show velocity lines for selected notes, making editing velocities for stacked notes easier. Notes > Show Velocity on Active Track only toggles whether or not to show velocity lines for the currently active track (chosen in the Track pane) only.

Each controller is represented by a colored line that runs from the bottom of the Controller pane or Note pane toward the top. The height of the line designates the value of the controller, according to the scale on the left side of the Controller pane (called the *Scale pane*). Unfortunately, the Note pane doesn't provide a ruler, but controller values are shown beside the mouse as you edit. This scale gives you a reference for determining the value of a controller; it usually runs from 0 to 127, starting at the bottom of the Controller pane and going all the way to the top. The values can be different, according to the type of controller being edited. The horizontal location of a controller designates its start time, according to the Time Ruler at the top of the Piano Roll view.

> **PITCH WHEEL:** In one instance, the controllers in the Controller pane and the ruler values appear differently. If you select the pitch wheel event type for editing, you'll notice that, instead of originating at the bottom of the Controllers pane, the controllers start at the center and extend either up or down (see Figure 6.20). They do so because values for the pitch wheel range from –8192 to 0 to +8191, which you can see in the ruler values. Other than that, pitch wheel events are handled exactly the same as any other types.

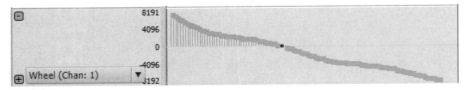

Figure 6.20 The pitch wheel is the one exception to the way controllers are displayed in the Controllers pane.
Source: Cakewalk®, Inc.

Working with Controllers

Adding, editing, and deleting controllers is similar to doing the same with notes, but with some exceptions. Here are the steps for working with controllers:

1. To designate a track as active and ready for editing, click the track in the Track List pane.

2. Initially, the Controller pane will display one lane for note velocities in that track (unless the track already contains additional controller data). However, you can have separate lanes for each different controller message displayed in the Controller pane. To add a new lane, click one of the Add New Controller Lane buttons. To delete a lane, click the Remove Controller Lane button for that lane. To make a lane the active lane, click the background of the lane.

3. After you have created a new lane and made it active, click the lane's Edit Filter control and choose New Value Type in the menu.

4. In the MIDI Event Type dialog box, choose the kind of MIDI controller you would like to add or edit, including the Type, Value, and MIDI Channel. For example, to edit modulation on MIDI channel 1, choose Type: Control, Value: Modulation, and Channel: Channel 1.

5. Use the Smart tool (F5) or Draw tool (F9) to add MIDI controller data to the Controller pane or Note pane. To add a single controller event, Alt+click once with the Smart tool or just click once with the Draw tool. To create a freehand series of controller events, just click/drag with the Smart or Draw tool. To create a straight line of controllers, click/drag with the Line tool (F9) or click/drag with the Smart tool while holding Ctrl+Alt +Shift. Keep in mind that if the Snap to Grid is activated, new controllers will only be created at the Snap Resolution intervals. For truly freehand drawing or smooth line drawing, press N to toggle the Snap to Grid.

6. If you want to erase any controller events, use the Smart (F5), Draw (F9), and Erase (F10) tools. To erase a single controller event, click the small square at the top of the event with the Erase tool or Alt+click with the Smart tool or right-click with the Draw tool. To erase multiple events at once, click and hold the left mouse button and then drag your mouse over the events you want to erase with the Erase tool or do the same thing with the right mouse button using the Draw tool. With the Smart tool, right-click/drag to select the notes and press Del(ete).

7. To edit controller events, use the Smart (F5) tool. To edit a single controller event, click the small square at the top of the event. While holding down your mouse button, move up or down to change the value of the controller. Move left or right to change the position of the controller. To edit multiple events, right-click and drag your mouse over the events to select them. Then click/drag one of the events to edit them all or use any of SONAR's editing functions to edit those events, just like you would with notes.

8. After making a selection, you can also copy or move controller events from one lane to another. Just right-click the name of the lane to which you want the controller events to be copied/moved and choose the appropriate option from the menu: Copy Selected Values To This Lane or Move Selected Values To This Lane.

9. To work with a different controller, go through Steps 1 through 8 again.

> **CONTROLLERS AS TRACK ENVELOPES:** You can also work with controllers as track envelopes in the Track view (see Chapter 12).

Inserting Controllers

SONAR provides one other way to add a smooth series of controller values to your tracks—the Insert Series of Controllers function. I find using the Smart tool much more intuitive, but if you need to add controllers over a very long span of time, the Insert Series of Controllers function can be useful. To use it, just follow these steps:

1. Select the track to which you want to add the controller values. You can do so in either the Piano Roll view or the Track view.

2. Choose Insert > Series of Controllers from SONAR's main menu to open the Insert Series of Controllers dialog box.

3. In the Insert section, choose the type of controller you want to add, the number of the controller (if appropriate), and the MIDI channel you want the controller to use.

4. In the Value Range section, type numbers for the Begin and End parameters. These numbers determine the values of the controller over the range of the series. For example, if you're using a volume controller type, you can have an instrument get louder over time by typing a smaller value for Begin and a larger value for End. If you want the instrument to get softer over time, you type a larger value for Begin and a smaller value for End.

5. In the Time Range section, type the measure, beat, and tick values for the location in the project where you want the series of controllers to be inserted.

TIME RANGE SELECTION: You can set the Time Range parameters before you open the Insert Series of Controllers dialog box by dragging your mouse pointer over the Time Ruler in either the Piano Roll view or the Track view. This action sets up a selection within the project that is used automatically to set the From and Thru values of the Time Range parameters.

BANK/PATCH CHANGE

The one type of data that the Piano Roll view doesn't allow you to manipulate is the bank/patch change. This type of event is useful when you want the sound of your MIDI instrument to change automatically during playback of your project. SONAR provides an Insert Bank/Patch Change function that you can use if you need it, as follows:

1. Click the number of the track into which you want to insert the bank/patch change.
2. Set the Now time to the measure, beat, and tick at which you want the bank/patch change to occur.
3. Choose Insert > Bank/Patch Change to open the Bank/Patch Change dialog box.
4. Choose a bank select method, bank, and patch from the appropriate lists. Click OK.

SONAR will insert a bank/patch change event in the track at the Now time you specified. By the way, you can insert (and also edit) bank/patch change events by using the Event List view, which I'll talk about later in this chapter.

The Inline Piano Roll View

In addition to the Piano Roll view, SONAR edits MIDI notes and controller data from within the Track view with the Inline Piano Roll view feature. Basically, this is like having the Piano Roll view integrated into the Track view. So why would you still need the Piano Roll view? Well, one reason is that the Piano Roll view allows you to edit data from multiple tracks simultaneously within the same display. In the Track view, the Inline Piano Roll view feature is limited to each individual track. Other than that, both the Piano Roll view and the Inline Piano Roll view work almost exactly the same way with only minor differences. Here are the steps needed to use the Inline Piano Roll view feature:

1. The same global tools work here the same way they do in the Piano Roll view. The Inline Piano Roll view uses the global Snap to Grid function in the Control Bar like the Track view. As usual, I recommend using the Smart (F5) tool whenever possible for the most efficient workflow.

2. To activate the Inline Piano Roll view feature for a single MIDI track, click the Event Filter control for the corresponding track and choose Notes from the menu. To activate the feature for all MIDI tracks (or a group of selected MIDI tracks), do the same thing while holding down Ctrl. You'll notice that the Clips pane turns into the Note pane or Drum pane, depending on the type of track you are editing.

3. The MIDI Scale (shown to the left of the Note pane) doubles as the Keyboard pane, Note Map pane, and Controller scale. Right-click inside the MIDI Scale and choose Notes (to edit melodic and drum tracks) or 7Bit Values (to edit controllers).

4. The MIDI Scale is also used for zooming. Right-click the MIDI Scale and choose Fit Content from the menu to fit that track's content into the current display. To fit the content for all tracks, choose View > Fit MIDI Content in the Track view menu. In addition, you can left-click and drag up or down within the MIDI Scale to change the zoom factor for the track.

5. To set a melodic scale for the current track, click the Scale Snap button in the Snap to Scale section of the Inspector. Then use the Root Note and Scale menus to choose a scale.

6. If you want to add or edit notes, click the Event Filter control for the corresponding track and choose Notes > Notes/Velocity from the menu. You can add, edit, and select notes using the same procedures as you would in the Piano Roll view. One exception is double-clicking to add a note doesn't work. You either need to click/drag or Alt+click. Another exception is when selecting notes using the MIDI Scale. Hold down the Shift key on your computer keyboard and then click a note in the MIDI Scale to select all notes of the same pitch. You can also drag your mouse to select a range of pitches.

7. If you want to add or edit controllers, click the Event Filter control for the corresponding track and choose Notes > New Value Type (or the name of an existing controller) to set the type of controller with which you would like to work. You can add, edit, and select controllers using the same procedures as you would in the Piano Roll view.

8. When working with both note and controller data or multiple controllers, use the MIDI category in the Track view menu to determine what types of events will be visible. This allows you to temporarily hide some events that may be overlapping and causing difficulty when editing.

Using the Step Sequencer View

For strict pattern-based composition, SONAR provides the Step Sequencer view (see Figure 6.21). Using this view, you can create both melodic and percussive patterns that can then be arranged in the Track view. Like the Piano Roll view (but with a different look), the Step Sequencer view uses a grid with rows (that represent pitch) and columns (that represent the timing of notes).

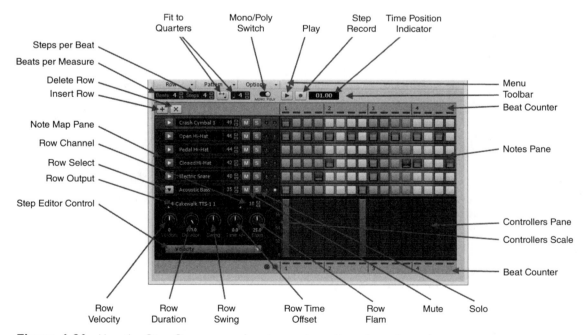

Figure 6.21 Use the Step Sequencer view to create pattern-based music.
Source: Cakewalk®, Inc.

The Step Sequencer view consists of four major sections: the menu and toolbar (containing all the view's global controls), the Notes pane (displaying the melodic or percussive notes in the current Step Sequencer clip), the Note Map pane (displaying the melodic pitches or the drum instruments represented by the notes shown in the Notes pane), and a Controllers pane for each row (displaying MIDI controller data). You'll also notice that this view has scroll bars, which work like they do in any other view. And there is a Beat Counter, which is similar to the Time Ruler in other views.

Opening the Step Sequencer View

You can use the Step Sequencer to create drum patterns or melodic patterns. These patterns are contained in special Step Sequencer clips, which reside on a normal MIDI track. Although the steps for accessing the view are the same, the initial steps for setting up your MIDI tracks are slightly different. If you want to create a drum pattern, you should first assign a drum map to that track. If you want to create a melodic pattern (like a bass part), you do not need to assign a drum map to the track—a default drum map consisting of pitches is automatically assigned. After you have set up your MIDI track, you can open the Step Sequencer view in a variety of ways:

▷ In the Track view, click a MIDI track to make it the active track. Then position the Now time to the point in the project where you want the new Step Sequencer clip created and choose Views > Step Sequencer (or press Alt+4).

▷ Position the Now time and then right-click in the MIDI track and choose View > Step Sequencer.

▷ In the Track view, double-click an existing Step Sequencer clip in the Clips pane.

Each Step Sequencer clip has its own unique instance of the Step Sequencer view. So when you open the view for an existing clip, only the notes from that clip are displayed and can be edited. When you open a new instance of the view, it is empty, and a new clip is created for that view as soon as you add the first note to the grid.

Setting Up the Step Sequencer View

Before you begin to create a new pattern in the Step Sequencer, there are a number of global parameters (that affect the entire pattern) you need to adjust. These include parameters that determine the length and style of the pattern.

Adjusting Pattern Length

There are three parameters that determine the length of a pattern: Beats per Pattern, Steps per Beat, and Fit to Quarters. The Beats per Pattern parameter determines how many beats are in a pattern. For example, in 4/4 time (the default time signature for a project), there are four beats per measure, and each beat is a quarter note in length. So if you set the Beats per Pattern to 4, the pattern will be 1 measure long. If you set it to 8, the pattern will be 2 measures long, and so on. This will change if you change the time signature of your project.

The Steps per Beat parameter determines the resolution of each beat—meaning how far each beat can be broken down into smaller note values. Using the previous example, in 4/4 time each beat is a quarter note. If you set the Steps per Beat to 4, this means that each beat can be broken down into four sixteenth notes. You will see the grid in the Notes pane change as you change the Beats per Pattern and Steps per Beat parameters. With each parameter set to 4, the Beat Counter will show a pattern of four beats in length with each beat getting four step squares. Thus, four multiplied by four equals sixteen, so each step square is equal to a sixteenth note.

The Fit to Quarters parameter forces a pattern to fit a specific number of quarter notes and correlates directly with the project time signature. In a time signature, you have two numbers—the first number specifies the beats per measure (similar to the previously mentioned Beats per Pattern parameter), and the second number specifies what type of note gets one beat. So essentially, Fit to Quarters lets you experiment with different time signatures. For example, if you have a project time signature of 4/4, and you want to create a pattern in 3/4 time that still occupies a full measure in the Track view Time Ruler, you can toggle the Fit to Quarters button and set the parameter to 4.

Then set the Beats per Pattern parameter to 3. This will give you a pattern that is only three beats long, but it fills an entire 4/4 measure in the Track view. This is a great way to experiment by having music with different time signatures play along with each other in different tracks.

> **CHANGING LENGTH OF EXISTING PATTERNS:** Keep in mind that if you already have some notes added to a pattern and you change any of the pattern length parameters, you will have to edit your pattern accordingly. Notes are not automatically shifted when you make a pattern longer. However, if you make a pattern shorter, notes at the end of the pattern will be erased.
>
> One exception to this is if you use the Preserve Pattern for Step Sizes option (which is activated by default). If you then add more steps to each beat, the relative position of the notes is preserved. However, if you remove steps, some notes can get deleted. You toggle the option by choosing Options > Preserve Pattern for Step Sizes in the Step Sequencer menu.

Adjusting Pattern Style: Mono or Poly

The Mono/Poly switch determines whether you can add single or multiple notes per step when creating/editing a pattern. In Mono mode, you can only add one note per step (column). This mode is best used when creating a single note melody or bass line patterns. In Poly mode, you can add multiple notes per step (column), so each row can contain a note in the same column if you'd like. This mode is best used when creating drum patterns because many times you'll have different drum instruments sounding at the same step—like a hi-hat and snare drum.

> **USING MONO WITH EXISTING PATTERNS:** If you are in the middle of editing a pattern that already contains notes that you added in Poly mode and you then switch to Mono mode, clicking a note in a column that contains multiple notes will erase all other notes in that column.

Working with Notes

When you open the Step Sequencer view, the notes in the associated clip are displayed in the Notes pane on a grid with rows (that designate pitch) and columns (that designate timing). Each note is represented by an illuminated square with lines showing approximate note velocity level (empty squares represent rests). The horizontal location of a note designates its start time when you line up the left edge of the square with the numbers in the Beat Counter. The vertical location of a note designates its pitch (and drum instrument) when you line up the square with the note names in the Note Map pane. The length of a square designates the duration of the note. You can merge squares together to create longer notes.

As you're working on a pattern, you can listen to it by clicking the Play button or pressing Ctrl+Shift+spacebar to toggle playback. The pattern will loop over and over, even while you add/edit notes and change parameters.

> **SIMULTANEOUS STEP SEQUENCER VIEWS:** Even though the Step Sequencer view only allows you to edit one pattern at a time, you can work on multiple patterns simultaneously by opening multiple instances of the view. To do this, open the first instance of the view. If the view is floating in its own window, click the upper-left corner of the view window and choose Lock Contents from the menu. If the view is in the Multi-Dock, right-click the Step Sequencer tab and choose Lock Contents. Then open another view to create/edit a different pattern.

Customizing the Note Map Pane

Each row in the Note Map pane represents a single pitch or drum instrument. Each row also has a number of adjustable parameters that affect the playback of all notes in the row. If you are working on a drum pattern and you assign a drum map to the associated MIDI track, the Note Map pane will display instrument names and note numbers. If you are working on a melodic pattern and do not assign a drum map, SONAR assigns a default drum map that contains note names and numbers.

Row Properties

Clicking on the name of a row auditions the pitch or drum instrument assigned to that row. Right-clicking and choosing Rename Row allows you to type a new name for the row. Double-clicking the note number to the right of the name allows you to remap the row to a new note. In addition, clicking a row's Select button opens that row to reveal more parameters, which affect playback of all notes in the row as follows:

▷ **Output (MIDI Output) and Channel (MIDI Channel).** You can assign each row to a different MIDI output and/or channel. This can be useful for sending the playback of a single pattern to multiple synths. For example, you may like the kick drum sound from one synth and the snare drum sound from another. Assign different rows to different synths to mix and match sounds in a single pattern. Double-click either parameter to change it.

▷ **Velocity.** Click/drag up/down this knob (and any of the others) to adjust the velocity (loudness) of all notes in the row with a range of –127 to 127, with 0 being the default. Double-click this knob (and any of the others) to quickly return it to the default value. In addition, you can click a row (to select it) and choose Row > Adjust Velocity Multiplier (from the Step Sequencer menu) to open the Adjust Velocity Multiplier dialog box. Entering a value below the default value of 1.000 compresses all velocities in the row and entering a higher value expands them.

▷ **Duration.** This parameter is mainly useful when creating melodic patterns and is used to adjust the length of all notes in a row. A default value of 100% means that all notes will play for their entire length and a lower value will shorten the playback.

▷ **Swing.** Add a swing feel to the notes in a row by setting this parameter above or below its default value of 50%. A setting above 50% makes the time between the first and second beats longer and the time between the second and third beats shorter. A setting below 50% does the opposite.

▷ **Time Offset.** Adjust the timing of all the notes in a row by setting this parameter above or below its default value of 50%. A setting above 50% makes the notes sound later than the beat and below 50% makes them sound earlier.

▷ **Flam.** This parameter adjusts the timing of flammed notes in a row. Flammed notes are single notes split into two hits (see Adding, Editing and Deleting Notes below). With a default setting of 25.5%, flammed notes sound with two equal hits. A lower setting decreases the space between the hits, making them sound more like a single note. A higher setting increases the spacing, making the hits sound more like two separate notes.

Manipulating Rows

Rows can also be inserted, deleted, and moved. All of these operations involve first selecting a row, and only one row can be selected at any given time. To select a row, either click its name or click its background (the blank space anywhere between or around the parameters and notes). When you do this, the row background is shown in a lighter color.

To delete the row, do one of the following: right-click its background and choose Delete Row from the menu, click the Delete Row button, or press the Delete key. To insert a new row above the active row, do one of the following: right-click the background of the selected row and choose Insert Row from the menu, click the Insert Row button, or press the Ins(ert) key. You can also move a row by clicking and dragging its background up/down in the list. Moving rows doesn't affect the notes in the row—it's for organizational purposes only.

MUTE AND SOLO

While working on a pattern, you can use the M and S buttons to mute or solo each row, which allows you to hear a pattern with different instrument arrangements. For example, you may want to hear what a drum pattern would sound like without the cowbell, but you don't actually want to delete that row. Instead, you can just mute the row to remove the cowbell but still have it available if you later decide you want it back.

Adding, Editing, Deleting Notes

Manipulating notes in a pattern is an extremely easy process, which is why the Step Sequencer provides a very quick way to create pattern-based music. Here is a list of all the procedures available for controlling notes in the Notes pane:

▷ **To add notes, click a step (square) to enable it.** You can also add multiple notes by clicking one note and then dragging over all the other notes you want to add. If you want to hear the notes play as you add them, choose Options > Trigger Note On Click in the Step Sequencer menu. In addition, you can quickly add multiple notes to a row by clicking its background and choosing Fill Every > [count]. The number you choose designates how steps are counted for note additions. For example, if you choose 2, every second step (after the first) is activated. The first step is always activated, and the count starts from the next step.

▷ **To delete notes, right-click a step to disable it.** You can also delete multiple notes by right-clicking one note and then dragging over all the other notes you want to remove. In addition, to delete all notes in a row, right-click the background of the row and choose Cut Row Steps from the menu.

▷ **The velocity of each note is shown as a bar graph on the step.** You can adjust the velocity of one or more steps by Shift+clicking and holding and then dragging your mouse up/down over a step. You can also click a note to give it focus and then move your mouse wheel up/down to adjust the value. (Press and hold the Shift key for small adjustments.) To change the velocity numerically, Ctrl+double-click a step and enter a new value. When you add a note, the default velocity is set to 100. You can change the default velocity for new notes by choosing Options > Set Default Velocity For Steps in the Step Sequencer menu.

▷ **To adjust the duration of notes, you can merge multiple steps together.** For example, in the default setup, the Step Sequencer provides four steps per beat. If you activate one step, that equals a sixteenth note. If you want to create an eighth note, you need to merge two steps together. You can do this by Ctrl+clicking and dragging over the steps (or multiple steps). To unmerge, Ctrl+right-click and drag.

▷ **To split a single note, you can add a flam to a step.** Double-click a step add/remove a flam for that step. This essentially splits the note in two, and the timing between the two pieces can be adjusted with the Flam parameter that I talked about earlier.

Copying and Moving Notes

The Step Sequencer lets you shift notes in the same row by right-clicking the background of the row and choosing Shift Steps Forward or Shift Step Backward. You can also copy, cut, paste, and even swap notes between rows.

COPY, CUT, AND PASTE NOTES

Copy, cut, and paste only work on whole rows, not on individual or selected groups of notes. To copy or cut notes from a row, right-click the background of the row and choose either Copy Row Steps (keeping the original notes) or Cut Row Steps (removing the original notes). Then right-click the background of the row in which you want to place the notes and choose Paste Row Steps.

SWAPPING NOTES BETWEEN ROWS

Let's say you have a cowbell part (represented by one of the rows in a pattern), but you would rather use that part to play the tambourine instrument (represented by a different row). This is different than copy, cut, and paste because you actually want to exchange the parts. To do this, just exchange the note numbers so that the cowbell row becomes the tambourine row and vice versa. For example, if the cowbell row has a note number of 56 and the tambourine row has a note number of 54, change the cowbell row note number to 54 and the tambourine row note number to 56. When you do this, the notes in each row remain the same, but the instruments played by each row change, which is effectively the same thing as moving the notes to different rows.

Working with Controllers

Like the Piano Roll view, the Step Sequencer view provides a Controllers pane for editing MIDI controller data. This pane works in a similar manner to the same pane in the Piano Roll view, but with a few differences as follows:

1. Each row has a dedicated Controllers pane. Click the row's Select button to reveal its parameters and pane.
2. Click the row's Step Editor control for a list of MIDI controllers that can be used. Some of the more common ones (like Pan and Volume) are listed by default, but if you want to work with something else, choose New Value Type. You'll also notice (at the top of the list) that the Controllers pane lets you edit three additional parameters for each step in the row. Velocity is the same as the step velocity described earlier. Time Offset is similar to the row Time Offset described earlier, except it can be set for each step. You can use this to make some steps sound before or after the beat to create more rushed or laidback rhythms. Finally, Step Play Probability lets you add some randomness to each step by setting the likelihood of whether or not a step will be played. The higher the probability, the more likely the step will be played and vice versa.
3. To draw in a single controller, align your mouse underneath a step and click once. The vertical position of your mouse when you click determines the value of the controller according to the Scale on the left side of the Controllers pane.
4. To draw in multiple controllers, click and drag in the Controllers pane.
5. To draw a perfect line of controllers, hold down the Shift key. Then click where you want the line to begin and drag to where you want the line to end. Then let go of the mouse button and Shift key.
6. To erase controllers, hold down the right mouse button and drag over the controllers.
7. To edit existing controllers, just redraw over those controllers.
8. Repeat Steps 1 through 7 for each different type of controller you would like to work with.
9. The Controllers pane only displays one type of controller at a time, but you can access any controllers you have added to the pattern by using the Step Editor control.

> **SAVING AND LOADING STEP SEQUENCER PATTERNS:** Once you've created a pattern, you can save it as a Step Sequencer Pattern file, even though the pattern already exists as a clip in the Track view. This allows you to save the pattern separately for future use in other projects or exchange patterns with other SONAR users. To save a pattern, choose Pattern > Save Pattern As from the Step Sequencer menu. You can also load patterns the same way by choosing Load Pattern.

Step Recording Patterns

In addition to manually creating a Step Sequencer pattern using a mouse, you can also step record a pattern using an external MIDI controller. Before you begin, you need to determine if you want to use the note velocities that you play using your controller or if you want to use a predetermined velocity value for all notes. By default, the Step Sequencer uses a fixed velocity value for all recorded notes. To change this, choose Options > Use Fixed/Default Velocity for Step Recording in the Step Sequencer menu. Now the velocity values you play will be recorded. If you keep the Fixed option activated, you can adjust the default velocity by choosing Options > Set Default Velocity for Steps. When you're ready, you can start step recording as follows:

1. Set the MIDI input of the MIDI track to the MIDI port you are using for your MIDI controller.
2. Set the Now time to the point in the track at which you want the Step Sequencer clip to start. Then make the Step Sequencer window the active window.

3. Enable step recording by clicking the Step Record button. You'll notice the button now turns red, indicating Step Recording mode.

4. Play one or more notes on your MIDI controller. As soon as you let go of the note(s), they will show up in the first beat of the pattern (recording always starts at the first beat). The beat indicator will automatically move to the next beat waiting for more note input. Keep in mind that if the notes that you press are not represented by a row in the pattern, then the notes will just be skipped. In addition, controllers are not recorded at all.

5. If you don't like what was recorded, you can go back and delete the previous beat by pressing Ctrl+Z to undo.

6. Repeat Steps 4 and 5 until you're finished recording the pattern. Then click the Step Record button to stop step recording.

Working with Step Sequencer Clips

When you have finished creating a pattern, you can further manipulate that pattern as you would a MIDI Groove clip (see Chapter 9), although Step Sequencer clips are slightly different.

Editing Step Sequencer Clips

When working with pattern-based music, it's normal to have multiple copies of the same pattern throughout sections of a track. You can make copies of Step Sequencer clips in a couple of ways. First, you can slip-edit a clip (drag the ends of the clip) to create multiple instances. This allows you to quickly fill up a large number of measures with the same pattern. In addition, if you double-click the clip and edit the pattern in the Step Sequencer view, those changes are reflected in every instance of the slip-edited clip.

You can also make copies of a clip using the Edit > Copy function or just by holding down the Ctrl key and clicking/dragging the clip to a new location. Like the slip-edited clip, these copies are linked, and if you edit the pattern in one, the pattern is changed in all the copies.

However, there may be times when you don't want changes to one clip to affect another clip. An example might occur when you've created a drum pattern and you would like to edit that pattern to create a variation of the same pattern. To do this, you could copy the clip, but any changes to the copy would also change the original. To prevent this from happening, just right-click the copied clip and choose Unlink Step Sequencer Clips. You can also unlink multiple clips at the same time if you select them first.

Converting Step Sequencer Clips

Step Sequencer clips are special and regular MIDI clips can't be edited in the Step Sequencer view. The reason for this is that patterns created in the Step Sequencer view are strictly quantized and can't contain any notes that are off beat or have loose timing. However, you can open and edit Step Sequencer clips in the Piano Roll view by clicking the Clip Header Indicator of a Step Sequencer clip and choosing Piano Roll from the menu. You no longer have to convert a Step Sequencer clip into a regular MIDI clip as was the case in previous versions of SONAR.

If you want to edit a regular MIDI clip in the Step Sequencer view, you can convert it to a Step Sequencer clip by right-clicking it and choose Convert MIDI Clip(s) to Step Sequencer. Then in the dialog box, choose the note value that represents the smallest note value in the clip. For example, if your clip contains sixteenth notes and nothing smaller than that, choose 1/16. In addition, if you want to keep the original timing of the MIDI clip, activate the Preserve original timing option. Then click OK.

Saving and Loading Step Sequencer Clips

In their default format, Step Sequencer clips can't be saved to a separate MIDI file. But you can still save them as MIDI Groove clips and then load them back up for use in different projects or share them with other users (even if they don't use SONAR).

To save a Step Sequencer clip to a separate MIDI file, select the clip. Then choose File > Export > MIDI Groove clip. In the dialog box, type in a name for the file and click Save.

To load the clip into a project, click a MIDI track to make it the active track. Then position the Now time to the point in the project you want the clip loaded. Choose File > Import > MIDI and double-click the file you want to load. Alternatively, you can position the Now time and then right-click in a MIDI track choose Import MIDI from the menu. You can also drag and drop MIDI clips into a project using the Media section of the Browser or directly from Windows Explorer or the Windows Desktop. After you've imported the clip, convert it to a Step Sequencer clip, as described earlier.

Using the Event List View

For the most precise data editing (meaning individual events and their properties), you have to use the Event List view. Using this view, you can add, edit, and delete any kind of event in any track within the entire project. The Event List view doesn't resemble any of the other views; instead of providing a graphical representation of your data, it provides a numerical representation, which you can edit and view. The Event List view displays events as one long list of columns and rows (similar to a spreadsheet). Each row holds the data for a single event, and columns separate the event's different properties.

You can use the first column in the list to select events. The second column (titled *Trk*) shows the track number in which an event is stored. The third column (titled *HMSF*) shows the start time of an event in hours, minutes, seconds, and frames. The fourth column (titled *MBT*) also shows the start time of an event, but as measures, beats, and ticks. If an event is a MIDI event, the fifth column (titled *Ch*) shows the MIDI channel to which that event is assigned. The sixth column (titled *Kind*) shows the type of data an event holds (for example, a MIDI note event). The seventh column (titled *Data*) actually spans the seventh, eighth, and ninth columns (the last three), and these columns hold the data values associated with each event. For instance, for a MIDI note event, the seventh column would hold the pitch, the eighth column would hold the velocity, and the ninth column would hold the duration for the note.

Because the Event List view doesn't have any graphical data to contend with, it doesn't provide any Snap to Grid, Zoom, Time Ruler, or Marker features. It does scroll the list up and down and left and right so you can access all the events shown. It also provides a menu with two buttons and two menu options, which I'll discuss shortly.

Opening the View

You can open the Event List view via the Track view by selecting one or more tracks and then selecting Views > Event List (Alt+8) or right-clicking one of the selected tracks and choosing View > Event List. Additionally, clicking the Clip Header Indicator of a MIDI clip and choosing Event List will open the associated track in the Event List view.

Filtering Events

There are many different types of events available in SONAR, and sometimes having to wade through them all in the Event List view can get a bit confusing, especially when you're displaying the data from multiple tracks. To help you deal with the problem, the Event List view filters each of the event types from being displayed. This filtering does not affect the data at all; it just helps unclutter the list display if that's what you need. You can show/hide event types by choosing View > [*type of event*] from the Event List view menu. Event types with check marks next to them are shown in the list.

To make filtering multiple event types easier, you can use the Event Manager by choosing View > Event Manager from the Event List view menu or pressing V. Initially, all the event types are activated so they will be displayed in the list. To filter out a certain type, just click it to remove its check mark. You can also use the All/None buttons to quickly activate or deactivate groups of event types. Click the Close button when you're done.

> **EVENT TYPE LIST:** You can also filter out event types by right-clicking anywhere in the Event List and selecting an event type from the list.

Editing Events

If you've ever used a spreadsheet application, you'll be right at home with editing events in the Event List view. To navigate through the list, you use the arrow keys on your PC keyboard. These keys move a small rectangular cursor through the list. This cursor represents the Now time. As you move the cursor up and down through the list, the Now time changes to reflect the time of the event upon which the cursor is positioned. You also can move the cursor (which I'll call the Now time cursor from this point on) left and right to access the different event parameters.

Changing Event Parameters

To change an event parameter, just position the Now time cursor over the parameter, press Enter, type a new value, and press Enter again to accept the new value.

> **MOUSE EDITING:** You also can increase or decrease the value of an event parameter by double-clicking it and then clicking the little plus or minus button, respectively.

You can change the start time in the HMSF or MBT column, the MIDI channel, the type of event, and most or all of the values in the data columns, depending on the type of event you're editing. The only thing you can't change is the track number of an event.

Changing the type of an event via the parameter in the Kind column is a bit different from changing the values of the other parameters. Instead of typing a new value, you must either press the Enter key or double-click the parameter. This action opens the Kind of Event dialog box, which displays a list of all the event types available. Select the type of event you want to use and click OK.

Selecting Events

If you ever need to copy, cut, or paste events in the Event List view, you have to select them first. To select a single event, click in the first column of the row representing the event. You also can select more than one event by dragging your mouse pointer in the first column of the list. If you want to remove a selection, click or drag a second time. You can also remove all selections by press Ctrl+Shift+A.

Inserting Events

You can add new events to the list by using the Insert Event function. It works as follows:

1. Position the Now time cursor at the point in the list at which you want to insert a new event.

> **POSITION THE NOW TIME CURSOR:** Setting the position of the Now time cursor in the Event List view isn't very intuitive. Because the list gives you such a specific close-up look at your data, it's sometimes hard to tell where in your project the Now time cursor is pointing. You might find it easier to use one of the other views (such as the Track view or the Piano Roll view) to position the Now time cursor. That way, you get a graphical representation of your project and a better feel for the placement of the cursor. Then you can switch to the Event List view, and the cursor will be positioned exactly at the point where you want to insert the new event (or at least very close to it).

2. Press the Ins(ert) key or click the Insert Event button in the menu (the one with the plus sign shown on it). SONAR will create a new event in the list, using the same parameter values as the event upon which the Now time cursor was positioned.

3. Edit the event parameters.

EVENT KIND HELP: When you're changing the type of event using the Kind parameter, the values in the Data columns change according to the type of event you choose. For a list of all the types of events available, along with all their associated parameters, look in the SONAR Help file under Editing MIDI Events and Continuous Controllers > The Event List View > Event List Buttons and Overview.

TEXT EVENTS

There are two types of events in SONAR that you can access only via the Event List view. You can't manipulate them in any of the other views. The first one, called a *text event*, adds notes to the data in your project. I'm not talking about musical notes; I'm talking about text notes. (You know, like those little sticky notes you have plastered all over your studio.) Text events can act as little reminders to yourself in case you need to keep track of some kind of special information in certain parts of your project. I haven't had a lot of use for text events, but it's nice to know they're available if I need them.

MCI COMMAND EVENTS

The other type of special event is called the *MCI Command event*, or the *Windows Media Control Interface (MCI) Command event*. You can use the MCI Command event to control the multimedia-related hardware and software in your computer system. For example, by setting the type of an event to MCI Command and setting the event's Data parameter to PLAY CDAUDIO, you can make the audio CD inside your CD drive start to play. You also can use MCI Command events to play audio files, video files, and more. But the problem is that you can't synchronize any of these files to the music in your project, so you can't really use these events for too many things. In addition, the subject of MCI commands can be complex and is well beyond the scope of this chapter. If you want to find more information, take a look at **http://msdn.microsoft.com** and do a search for the term *MCI*.

Deleting Events

Erasing events from the list is as easy as it gets. Just move the Now time cursor to the row of the event you want to remove and click the Delete Event button in the menu (the one with the minus sign on it). Alternatively, you can press the Del(ete) key. If you want to delete more than one event, select the events you want to remove and then choose Edit > Delete.

Playing

If you want to quickly preview the event you're currently editing, you can have SONAR play back that single event by holding down the Ctrl+Alt+Shift keys and then pressing the spacebar. If you continue holding the keys, each press of the spacebar will scroll down through the list and play each event. This capability is especially useful for testing MIDI note events.

PRINT THE EVENT LIST: You can print a hard copy reference of the Event List if you have a printer connected to your computer system. While the Event List view is open, just choose File > Print (from SONAR's main menu) to print a copy of the list. You also can preview the list before you print it by choosing File > Print Preview. If the Event List view is in the MultiDock, you'll need to undock it first before you can print. Right-click the Event List tab in the MultiDock and choose Undock. Once the Event List is displayed in its own window, click the upper-left corner of the Window and choose Disable Floating. Now you can print a copy of the view.

Using the Tempo View

You learned how to set the initial tempo for a project in Chapter 3. But in addition to the initial project tempo, you also can have the tempo change automatically during playback. To allow you to specify tempo changes in a project, SONAR provides the Tempo view. The Tempo view has some similarities to the Piano Roll view in that it displays a graphical representation of the data you need to manipulate—in this case, tempo. The Tempo view shows the tempo as a line graph with the horizontal axis denoting time (via the Time Ruler) and the vertical axis denoting tempo value.

More precisely, the Tempo view consists of three major sections: the toolbar (located at the top of the view, containing all the view's related controls), the Tempo pane (located in the main part of the view, displaying all the tempo changes in the project as a line graph), and the Tempo List pane (located at the right of the view, showing a list of all the tempo changes within the project). Because tempo affects the entire project, no track selection tools are available here.

Because the Tempo view shows tempo changes graphically, it has scroll bars and zoom tools just like in the Piano Roll view. And these tools work the same way here. In addition, this view is affected by the Snap to Grid function. The Tempo view also contains a marker area and a Time Ruler located just above the Tempo pane. Along the left of the Tempo pane are the tempo measurements, which show the value of the tempo changes displayed in the line graph.

Opening the View

To open the Tempo view, choose Views > Tempo (Alt+Shift+5). You don't need to select a track, clip, or anything else. For a new project (or a project that doesn't contain any tempo changes), the Tempo view will display a straight horizontal line located vertically on the graph at the tempo measurement value that corresponds to the current tempo setting for the project. For instance, if your project has a main tempo of 100, then the line is shown at a tempo measurement of 100 on the graph. In addition to the horizontal line, a single entry in the Tempo List pane shows the measure, beat, and tick at which the tempo event occurs, along with the tempo value itself. In this example, it is 1:01:000 for the measure, beat, and tick, and 100 for the tempo value.

Editing Tempo Changes

Just as you can edit controller messages graphically in the Piano Roll view, you can use the Tempo view to edit tempo changes. Also, the Tempo view works with the Select, Draw (Freehand), Draw (Line), and Erase tools. All these tools work the same way they do in the Piano Roll view. You can use the Select (F6) tool to select individual changes and groups of tempo changes by clicking and dragging. Using the Draw (Freehand – F9) tool, you can literally draw in tempo changes on the line graph in the Tempo pane. The Draw (Line – F9) tool enables you to create smooth tempo changes from one value to another by clicking and dragging. And using the Erase (F10) tool, you can erase single and multiple tempo changes by clicking and dragging. As you draw and erase within the Tempo pane, the line graph will change its shape accordingly to display how the tempo will change over time as the project plays. An increase in the tempo (*accelerando*, in musical terms) is shown as an incline in the line graph, and a decrease in tempo (*ritardando*, in musical terms) is shown as a decline in the line graph.

> **SMART TOOL TEMPO CHANGES:** You can also just use the Smart tool for most tempo editing tasks. Click to enter single tempo changes. Click and drag to freehand draw multiple tempo changes. Right-click and drag to select. And after selecting, you can choose Edit > Delete or press Del(ete) to erase. For drawing smooth changes, you'll still need to use the Draw (Line – F9) tool.

The Tempo List Pane

As I mentioned earlier, tempo changes also are listed numerically in the Tempo List pane. Luckily, you can edit them there, too. I find it easier and more accurate to add and edit tempo changes via the Tempo List pane than to draw them in.

INSERTING TEMPO CHANGES

To add a new tempo change to the list, follow these steps:

1. Set the Now time to the measure, beat, and tick at which you want the tempo change to occur.
2. Click the Insert Tempo button on the toolbar (the one with the plus sign on it) or press the Ins(ert) key to open the Tempo dialog box.
3. Enter a value for the Tempo parameter. You can also tap out a tempo by clicking the Click Here to Tap Tempo button. When you click repeatedly on the button, SONAR will measure the time between each click and calculate the tempo at which you're clicking. It will then enter the value into the Tempo parameter automatically.

> **TAP THE SPACEBAR:** Instead of using your mouse to click the Click Here to Tap Tempo button, you might find it easier (and more accurate) to use the spacebar. Click the button with your mouse once to highlight it, and then use your spacebar to tap out a tempo value.

4. Make sure the Insert a New Tempo option is activated.
5. You shouldn't have to enter a value for the Starting at Time parameter because you set the Now time earlier. However, you can change it here if you want.

After you click OK, SONAR will add the new tempo change and display it in the Tempo List pane, as well as on the graph in the Tempo pane.

DELETING AND EDITING TEMPO CHANGES

You can edit or remove a tempo change from the list by using the appropriate toolbar buttons. First, select the tempo change you want to edit or delete by clicking it in the list. If you want to delete the tempo change, click the Delete Tempo button on the toolbar (the one with the minus sign on it) or press the Del(ete) key. If you want to edit the tempo change, click the Tempo Properties button on the toolbar (the second-to-last button from left to right). This action will open the Tempo dialog box. Make any changes necessary, as per the same settings I described for inserting a new tempo change.

Using the Tempo Commands

In addition to the Tempo view, SONAR provides two other tempo-related functions. The Insert Tempo Change function works the same as adding a new tempo change in the Tempo List pane in the Tempo view. However, you can use this function from any of the other views. To access it, just choose Project > Insert Tempo Change to open the Tempo dialog box (which you learned about earlier).

SONAR also provides a function that inserts a series of tempos so you can have the tempo change smoothly from one value to another over time. Using it is similar to using the Draw (Line) tool in the Tempo view, but here you specify your values numerically. You use this function as follows:

1. Choose Project > Insert Series of Tempos to open the Insert Series of Tempos dialog box.

2. In the Tempo Range section, enter a beginning (Begin) and an ending (End) value for the range of tempos to be inserted.

3. In the Time Range section, enter a beginning (From) and an ending (Thru) value for the range of time in your project in which you want the tempo changes to occur.

> **TIME RANGE SELECTION:** If you make a selection by dragging your mouse pointer in the Time Ruler of the Track view, for instance, before you choose Project > Insert Series of Tempos, the Time Range values in the Insert Series of Tempos dialog box will be set according to your selection. This shortcut makes it easier to see where in your project the tempo changes will be inserted. You can also press F5 while editing the Time Range values to set the values to specific Marker locations.

4. For the Step parameter, enter a beat and tick value for how often you want a tempo change to be inserted within the Time Range you specified. For example, if you enter a value of 1.00, then the Insert Series of Tempos function will insert a new tempo change at every beat within the Time Range you specified.

After you click OK, SONAR will insert a smooth series of tempo changes, starting and ending with the Tempo Range values you specified within the time range you specified. Any existing tempo changes will be overwritten.

Advanced Audio and MIDI Editing

I N CHAPTER 6, you learned about some of the essential editing features found in SONAR, including all the views, as well as how to manipulate your data via copy, cut, paste, move, delete, and other functions. In addition to its fundamental tools, SONAR provides a full arsenal of sophisticated editing features. Some can be used to process audio data, some to process MIDI data, and some to process both kinds of data. One aspect they all have in common, however, is that they can be accessed in more than one view (similar to the copy, cut, and paste functions). As you learned previously, for MIDI data, you'll use the Track, Piano Roll, Staff, and Event views, and for audio data, you'll use the Track view.

Advanced Data Selection

You can select the data in your project in each of the views by using some basic clicking and dragging techniques. SONAR also provides some more sophisticated data selection features that enable you to use time, as well as individual event properties, for more precise editing.

Selecting a Range of Data by Time

If you ever need to select a range of data in a project that is based on time, rather than data that is neatly tucked away in individual clips, you can choose Edit > Select > By Time (Shift+F6) to do so. For example, suppose that you need to copy the data in track 8 that falls between the range of 4:2:010 (measure, beat, tick) and 13:3:050. But what if that data is stored in multiple clips within that range, and the clips don't neatly start and end at the beginning and ending times you specified? That's the kind of situation for which this feature is useful. It works like this:

1. Choose Edit > Select > By Time (Shift+F6) to open the Select by Time dialog box.
2. Type the beginning (From) and ending (Thru) measure, beat, and tick values to define the range of time you want to select. Then click OK. You use this dialog box to select a range of time within your project, but it doesn't select any actual data. For that, you need to select the tracks you want to edit.

> **RANGE SELECTION USING MARKERS:** While editing either the From or Thru parameter in the Select by Time dialog box, press the F5 key on your computer keyboard. This will open the Markers dialog box. Here you can select a predefined time to use for either of the parameters.

3. In the Track view, select the tracks that contain the data you want to edit.

> **USE THE TIME RULER:** You also can make time selections in any of the views by clicking and dragging over the numbers in the Time Ruler or within a clip with the Smart and Select tools (see Chapter 6). However, by choosing Edit > Select > By Time, you can make more precise selections because you can enter the exact numerical values for the measures, beats, and ticks that define the range.

Selecting a Range of Data by Filter

For really precise editing tasks, you can choose Edit > Select > By Filter (Ctrl+Alt+F6). Using this approach, you can refine a selection that you've already made with any of the other methods discussed previously. For instance, if you select some clips or tracks in the Track view, you can zero in (so to speak) to your selection even further on the individual events within those clips and tracks, based on their event properties.

Suppose that you have a MIDI track in which you want to change all the notes with a pitch of C4 to C5. You can easily select only those notes, and then you can change their pitch by using the Transpose feature. All the C4 pitches are then changed to C5, but none of the other notes in the track are affected. This feature works as follows:

1. Select the clips, tracks, or set of events you want to use as your initial selection. You can select clips and tracks in the Track view or a group of events in the Piano Roll view, Event view, or Staff view.
2. Choose Edit > Select > By Filter (Ctrl+Alt+F6) to open the Event Filter – Select Some dialog box.
3. Does this dialog box look familiar? The Event Filter – Select Some dialog box is the same as Chapter 4's Event Filter – Search dialog box. The same information about how to use all the options applies here, so go ahead and set the options as you want.

> **SAVE A SELECT PRESET:** As with the Event Filter – Search dialog box, the Event Filter – Select Some dialog box saves presets for instant access to your favorite settings. By the way, presets are also available in many of the features that you'll learn about later in this chapter.

After you click OK, SONAR will search through the data in your initial selection, find the events that fall under the filter parameters you specified, and then select those events while leaving any other events alone. If you want to refine your selection even further, just choose Edit > Select > By Filter again on the previous selection results.

Some Selection Applications

I've had many people ask me how to go about deleting specific notes or data within a MIDI track, while at the same time leaving other data in the track alone. Here's an example of how you can do that:

1. Select the clips, tracks, or set of events you want to use as your initial selection.
2. Choose Edit > Select > By Filter (Ctrl+Alt+F6) to open the Event Filter – Select Some dialog box.
3. Click the None button to deactivate all the available options.
4. Activate the options for the type of data you want to delete. For example, if you want to delete all notes with the value of C5 within a track, activate the Note option. Then set the Key Min and Key Max parameters to C5. Leave all the other parameters as they are.
5. Click OK. This selects all the notes with a value of C5 in your initial selection.
6. Choose Edit > Delete to delete the notes immediately or Edit > Delete Special to open the Delete dialog box.
7. Set the appropriate options. For this example, just make sure the Events in Tracks option is activated so the selected notes will be deleted.

After you click OK, SONAR will delete all the selected data from your initial selection. In this case, all the notes with a value of C5 have been deleted. You can use this procedure for any other kinds of specific data deletions as well. You also can use it to manipulate selected data in other ways. For example, instead of deleting all the C5 notes, maybe you want to transpose them. In that case, instead of using the Delete function, you would use the Transpose function by choosing Process > Transpose in Step 6 of the preceding steps.

Advanced Audio Editing

Using the cut, copy, paste, and slip-editing tools in the Track view, you can manipulate the data in your audio tracks in a variety of ways. SONAR also provides a number of advanced features you can use to adjust the volume, get rid of DC offset, and even reverse the data within audio clips. You access all these features by choosing Process > Apply Effect.

Removing DC Offset

Depending on the quality of your sound card, your audio may not get recorded as accurately as it should. Many times (especially with less expensive sound cards), an electrical mismatch may occur between a sound card and the input device. When this happens, an excess of current is added to the incoming signal, and the resulting audio waveform is offset from the zero axis. This is known as *DC offset*. To remove DC offset from existing audio data, do the following:

1. Select the audio data from which you want to remove the DC offset. If you want to process all the audio in your project, choose Edit > Select > All (Ctrl+A).
2. Choose Process > Apply Effect > Remove DC Offset to open the Remove DC Offset dialog box.
3. To have SONAR automatically detect and remove any DC offset in your audio data, leave the DC Offset Threshold parameter deactivated.
4. If you don't want SONAR to process the audio below a certain volume level, activate the DC Offset Threshold parameter and enter a value (in decibels). Anything below that value will not be processed.
5. If you are processing a lot of audio data, activate the Compute DC Offset from First 5 Seconds Only option. This instructs SONAR to look only at the first five seconds of audio data when determining how much DC offset it contains.

DC OFFSET STATS: To manually find out the amount of DC offset in your audio data, click the Audition button in the Remove DC Offset dialog box. Then click the Stop button. The Analyze section of the dialog box will display the amount of DC offset present.

ACCURATE OFFSET DETECTION: Activating the Compute DC Offset from First 5 Seconds Only option usually provides accurate results. However, if your audio data starts with a long period of silence or the volume of the data is gradually faded in, you should deactivate this option. In these circumstances, with the option activated, SONAR does not accurately detect the amount of DC offset.

After you click OK, the DC offset in your audio data is removed.

ALWAYS REMOVE DC OFFSET: If you have existing audio data and are not sure whether it contains DC offset, you should always process the data with the Remove DC Offset function before you do any other kind of editing or processing. If you don't, editing and processing can introduce noise and other anomalies into your data.

> **REMOVE DURING RECORDING:** In addition to removing DC offset from existing data, SONAR can remove DC offset during recording. Press P and choose Audio – Playback and Recording in the Preferences dialog box. Then activate the Remove DC Offset During Record option. Click OK. SONAR will now use the settings from the Remove DC Offset dialog box to remove DC offset from any audio data that you record.

Adjusting Audio Volume

If you ever need to adjust the volume of an audio clip, you can use a number of different SONAR features to increase or decrease the volume of your data.

The Gain Feature

Using the Gain feature, you can increase or decrease the volume of audio data by an amount that you specify. You can also use this feature to convert stereo audio into mono audio and even swap the channels of stereo audio. Here is how the Gain feature works:

1. Choose Process > Apply Effect > Gain to open the Gain dialog box.
2. In the New Left Channel section, adjust the From Left and From Right parameters. These parameters determine the amount of left/right original audio that will be added to the left channel processed audio. If you simply want to change the volume of the audio, adjust the From Left parameter to either boost or cut the volume and set the From Right parameter to 0.00 percent. If you want to convert stereo audio to mono, set both the From Left and From Right parameters to 100 percent. If you want to swap stereo channels, set the From Left parameter to 0.00 percent and the From Right parameter to 100 percent.
3. In the New Right Channel section, adjust the From Left and From Right parameters. These parameters determine the amount of left/right original audio that will be added to the right channel processed audio. If you simply want to change the volume of the audio, set the From Left parameter to 0.00 percent and adjust the From Right parameter to either boost or cut the volume. If you want to convert stereo audio to mono, set both the From Left and From Right parameters to 100 percent. If you want to swap stereo channels, set the From Left parameter to 100 percent and the From Right parameter to 0.00 percent.

> **CLIPPING AND DISTORTION:** When you're raising the volume of audio data, you have to be careful not to raise it too high because it can cause clipping. Clipping occurs when SONAR attempts to raise the amplitude of audio data higher than 100 percent. The top and bottom of the waveform become clipped, and the audio sounds distorted when you play it. So be careful when using the Gain feature. Be sure to keep an eye on the amplitude levels of your audio waveforms and remember to listen to your audio data right after you increase its volume to see whether it sounds okay. If you hear distortion, use Undo to remove the volume change.

4. Click the Audition button to hear how your audio will sound before you have SONAR make any actual changes to the data. If you don't like what you hear, click Stop and adjust the previous parameters again.
5. After adjusting the levels in the New Left Channel and New Right Channel sections, click the Audition button again. This time, listen to determine if the audio sounds "hollow." This usually happens due to phase cancellation, which occurs when one audio waveform increases in volume and the other decreases in volume at exactly the same time with the same amount. Because of this phenomenon, they cancel each other out, making the mixed audio sound hollow. If this occurs, try activating one of the Invert Left/Right Channel Phase options (the buttons located below the Channel sections)—don't activate both. These options invert the audio waveform and can usually fix the phase cancellation problem. Click OK.

The Normalize Feature

Like the Gain feature, the Normalize feature also raises the volume of audio, but in a different way. Instead of simply increasing the volume, Normalize first scans the audio waveform to find its highest amplitude level. It subtracts that amplitude level from the maximum level, which is 100 percent (or a maximum level that you set). Normalize then takes that value and uses it to increase the volume of the audio data. So when all is said and done, the highest amplitude in the waveform is 100 percent (or a maximum level that you set), and all the other amplitude values are increased.

In other words, if an audio waveform has its highest amplitude value at 80 percent, and you set a normalize level of 100 percent, Normalize subtracts that value from 100 percent to get 20 percent. It then increases the volume of the audio data by 20 percent, so the highest amplitude value is 100 percent, and all the other amplitude values are 20 percent higher. Basically, you can use Normalize to raise the volume of audio data to the highest it can be without causing any clipping.

To use Normalize, do the following:

1. Select the audio data that you want to normalize.
2. Choose Process > Apply Effect > Normalize to open the Normalize dialog box.
3. Adjust the Normalize Level parameter, which sets the highest amplitude level to where you want your audio to be normalized. More often than not, you want to set this to 100 percent, but if you plan to do any additional editing or processing to your data, you should set this parameter to a lower level, such as 50 percent or −6dB, because additional processing can raise the amplitude and cause clipping. Click OK.

The Fade Features

If you want to get a little more creative with your volume changes, you can build much more complex volume changes by using the Fade/Envelope feature as follows:

> **FADE-IN AND FADE-OUT:** A *fade-in* is a gradual and smooth increase from a low volume (loudness) to a higher volume. This increase in volume is also called a *crescendo* in musical terms. A *fade-out* is the exact opposite—a gradual and smooth decrease from a higher volume to a lower volume. In musical terms, this decrease in volume is called a *decrescendo*.

1. Select the audio data to which you want to apply the fade. Then choose Process > Apply Effect > Fade/Envelope to open the Fade/Envelope dialog box. The dialog box displays a graph. The left side of the graph displays amplitude values, 0 to 100 percent from bottom to top. Inside the graph is a line, which represents the fade that will be applied to your selected audio data. If you look at the line from left to right, the left end of the line represents the beginning of your audio data selection, and the right end of the line represents the end of your audio data selection. When you open the dialog box, the line runs from the bottom left to the top right of the graph. If you leave it this way, a straight linear fade-in will be applied to your audio data because, as you look at the graph, the left end of the line is set at 0 percent, and the right end of the line is set at 100 percent. Therefore, the volume of the audio data would begin at 0 percent and fade all the way up to 100 percent.
2. You can change the shape of the fade line in one of two ways. You can select one of the six available presets from the Name menu at the top of the dialog box. Alternatively, you can change the fade line graphically by clicking and dragging the small squares at the ends of the line. These squares are called *nodes*.
3. If you want to create some really complex fades, you can add more nodes by clicking anywhere on the fade line. The more nodes you add, the more flexibility you'll have in changing the shape of the line.
4. If you don't like the changes you've made, click Reset to start over. Otherwise, click OK.

In addition to the Fade/Envelope feature (which allows you to apply destructive fades to your data), SONAR applies nondestructive fades. To apply a fade nondestructively, follow these steps:

1. If you want to create a fade-in for an audio clip, choose the Smart tool (F5) and then position your mouse in the upper-left corner of the clip until the shape of the mouse changes to a triangle. Then click and drag the mouse toward the right end of the clip to define the fade, as shown in Figure 7.1.

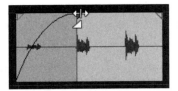

Figure 7.1 Apply a nondestructive fade-in to a clip by clicking in the upper-left corner of the clip and dragging toward the right.
Source: Cakewalk®, Inc.

2. If you want to create a fade-out for an audio clip, position your mouse in the upper-right corner of the clip until the shape of the mouse changes to a triangle. Then click and drag the mouse toward the left end of the clip to define the fade.

3. You also can define the shape of a fade if you would rather not use the straight linear process. SONAR provides three choices: Linear, Slow Curve, and Fast Curve. To change the type of fade, position your mouse on the fade line at the top of the clip so the shape of the mouse changes to a triangle. Then right-click and choose a fade type (see Figure 7.2).

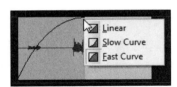

Figure 7.2 Change the fade type by right-clicking at the top of the fade line.
Source: Cakewalk®, Inc.

SET THE DEFAULT FADE TYPE: If you use a particular type of fade most often, you can set the default fade types. Choose Options > Crossfade Type in the Track view menu to select the default types for Fade-in, Fade-out, and Crossfades.

COMPLEX FADES WITH ENVELOPES: The nondestructive fade feature doesn't define complex fades by adding nodes as you can with the Fade/Envelope feature, but you can apply nondestructive complex fades or volume changes to a clip (or an entire track) by using envelopes (see Chapter 12).

You can also create nondestructive fades or edit existing nondestructive fades for multiple clips using the Fade Selected Clips feature. To use this feature, do the following:

1. Select the clips to which you want to apply fades. If the clips do not already contain fades, new ones will be created. If the clips already contain fades, the existing fades will be edited according to your specifications.

2. Choose Clips > Fade Clips in the Track view menu to open the Fade Selected Clips dialog box. Then choose the Fade option.

3. Set the Fade In parameter. This parameter determines the length of the fade-in in milliseconds. Most of the time, you'll probably want the fade to last for a certain number of seconds. In order to do this, just enter a multiple of **1,000** for each second. For example, for a two-second fade-in, type the value **2,000**.

4. Set the Fade Out parameter. This parameter determines the length of the fade-out in milliseconds.

5. Choose a Fade-In Curve and a Fade-Out Curve. You have three types of fades to choose from: Linear, Slow, or Fast.

6. If you are editing existing fades in your clips, you need to activate the Alter Existing Times and Alter Existing Curves options. If you are creating new fades for your clips, these options do not need to be activated.

7. You can use the same dialog box settings over again without having to open the dialog box. Simply activate the Only Show if Pressing Shift option. Now the dialog box will only open if you hold down the Shift key when you choose Clips > Fade Clips.

8. You might also want to process some of your clips multiple times if they overlap. In this case, you can create a quick fade-out/fade-in (a crossfade—see next section) between clips to fill gaps. Use the Fill Gaps, Xfade Between Audio Clips option. Set XFade (0–100ms) to set the length and set Max Gap (0–200ms) to choose which clips are processed. The overlaps must reside within the Max Gap setting in order to be processed. Click OK.

Crossfades

A crossfade is a special kind of fade that you can apply only to overlapping audio clips. This kind of fade can come in handy when you want to make a smooth transition from one style of music to another or from one instrument to another. It is especially useful when you're composing to video; you can change smoothly from one type of background music to another as the scene changes. It has many other types of creative uses as well.

When you apply a crossfade to two overlapping audio clips, it works like this: During playback, as the Now time reaches the point at which the two audio clips overlap, the first audio clip fades out, and the second audio clip fades in at the same time. You can apply a crossfade as follows:

1. Select the two overlapping audio clips to which you want to apply the crossfade. The two audio clips you select don't have to reside on the same track; they only have to overlap in time.

2. Choose Process > Apply Effect > Crossfade to open the Crossfade dialog box.

3. Notice that the Crossfade dialog box looks almost exactly the same as the Fade/Envelope dialog box. It works almost exactly the same, too. You can choose from three preset fades, and you can manipulate the fade line with your mouse by adding, clicking, and dragging nodes. The only difference here is that an additional line appears on the graph. The gray line represents the second selected audio clip, and you can't manipulate it directly. As you make changes to the purple line, the gray line mimics it. This feature ensures that the volumes of both audio clips are synchronized, and it provides a perfectly smooth crossfade. So go ahead and make your changes as discussed earlier and click OK.

In addition to the Crossfade feature (which allows you to apply destructive crossfades to your data), SONAR applies nondestructive crossfades. To apply a crossfade nondestructively, follow these steps:

1. Choose Options > Auto Crossfade in the Track view menu to activate the feature.

2. Choose Options > Drag and Drop Options. In the dialog box, choose the Blend Old and New option and click OK.

3. Click and drag one audio clip so it overlaps another audio clip. Both clips must reside on the same track.

4. If the Drag and Drop Options dialog box appears, just click OK.

5. SONAR will overlap the clips and automatically apply a perfect crossfade to the overlapping sections (see Figure 7.3). As with fades, you can define the shape of a crossfade, if you would rather not use the straight linear process. SONAR provides nine different choices. To change the type of crossfade, position your mouse in the crossfade area, and then right-click and choose a crossfade type.

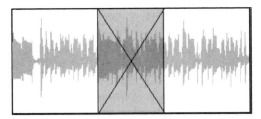

Figure 7.3 SONAR automatically applies a crossfade to the overlapping sections of the clips.
Source: Cakewalk®, Inc.

SET THE DEFAULT CROSSFADE: If you use a particular type of crossfade more often, you can set the default crossfade type. Choose Options > Crossfade Type > Default Crossfade Curves from the Track view menu.

Getting Rid of Silence

When you record an audio track in SONAR, even though there might be pauses in your performance (such as between musical phrases), your sound card still picks up a signal from your microphone or instrument, and that data is recorded. Although you might think that the data is just recorded silence, in actuality it contains a very minute amount of noise that might come from your sound card itself or the microphone or instrument connected there. More often than not, you can't really hear this noise because it's masked by the other music data in your project. And even during quiet passages, if you have only one or two audio tracks playing, the noise is probably still inaudible. With a large number of audio tracks, however, the noise can add up.

In addition, during playback, SONAR still processes those silent passages, even though they don't contain any actual music. These passages take up valuable computer processing power and disk space. To remedy this problem, SONAR provides the Remove Silence feature. This feature automatically detects sections of silence in audio clips, according to a loudness threshold that you set. Then, by first splitting long audio clips into shorter ones, it removes the resulting clips containing only silence. Thus, SONAR doesn't process that extra data during playback, and it doesn't save it to disk when you save your project.

To detect silent passages in audio, the Remove Silence feature uses a digital noise gate. Depending on the parameter settings you specify, this noise gate opens up when the Remove Silence feature comes upon a section in your audio that has an amplitude level greater than the one you set. It identifies this part of the audio as acceptable sound and lets it pass through. When the level of audio dips below a certain amplitude level that you set, the noise gate identifies that part of the audio as silence, and it closes to stop it from passing through. At that point, the Remove Silence feature splits the audio clip with one new clip containing just the music and another new clip containing just the noise. This process happens over and over until the entire initial audio clip is finished being scanned.

You use this feature by following these steps:

1. Select the audio data you want to scan for silence.
2. Choose Process > Apply Effect > Remove Silence to open the Remove Silence dialog box.
3. Type a value in the Open Level field. This parameter determines how loud the audio data has to be to make the noise gate open, thus identifying the data as acceptable sound.
4. Type a value in the Close Level field. This parameter determines how soft the data has to be to make the noise gate close, thus identifying the data as silence.

5. Type a value in the Attack Time field. This parameter determines how quickly (in milliseconds) the noise gate will open to the amplitude set in the Open Level parameter. If the beginning of your audio data starts off soft (such as with a fade-in) and its amplitude is below the Open Level setting, it could get cut off by the noise gate. For example, the beginnings of the words in a vocal part might be cut. To prevent this problem, you can set the Attack Time parameter so the noise gate takes this kind of situation into consideration.

6. Type a value in the Hold Time field. This parameter determines how long the noise gate will remain open, even when the amplitude level of the audio dips below the Close Level. This parameter is useful when the level of your audio goes up and down very quickly, which could make the noise gate react when it's not supposed to (such as during quick percussion parts). By setting a Hold Time, you can make sure that musical passages containing quick sounds don't get cut by mistake.

7. Type a value in the Release Time field. This parameter is the same as the Attack Time parameter, but in reverse. It determines how quickly the noise gate will close after the amplitude of the audio reaches the Close Level. This feature is useful if your audio data gradually gets softer at the end, such as with a fade-out.

8. Type a value in the Look Ahead field. This parameter determines how long (in milliseconds) the amplitude of the audio must stay above the Open Level before the noise gate will open. Basically, this setting lets you fine-tune the way the noise gate determines whether the audio being scanned is acceptable sound or silence.

9. If you want SONAR to delete the audio clips that contain only silence, activate the Split Clips option. Otherwise, the silent portions of the audio won't be deleted. They will be reduced to vacant space, but your clips will remain as they are.

10. You can save your settings as a preset, and you can use the Audition feature to hear the results of your settings if you want. Click OK.

> **SPLIT THE AUDIO CLIPS:** Unless the musical passages and silent passages of your audio are separated pretty neatly, it can be difficult to get the right settings for the Release Time. You might find it easier and more precise if you simply split the audio clips by hand using the Split function (see Chapter 6). The process is a bit more time-consuming, though.

Playing It Backward

Assuming you're old enough to remember vinyl recordings, did you ever take a record and play it backward to see whether your favorite band had left some satanic messages in their songs or perhaps a recipe for their favorite lentil soup? Well, guess what? You can do the same thing with your audio data. SONAR lets you flip the data in an audio clip so that it plays in reverse.

This feature doesn't have much practical use, but combined with some other processing, it can render some cool effects. To use it, simply select the audio clip you want to change and choose Process > Apply Effect > Reverse. Now the data in that clip will play backward.

> **REVERSE A TRACK:** If you want to reverse the data in an entire track, make sure to combine all the audio clips in the track into one large audio clip first by choosing Clips > Bounce to Clip(s) in the Track view menu (see Chapter 6). If you don't, the data in each separate clip will be reversed, which is not the same as reversing the entire track.

The Process Menu

Up until now, I've talked about editing features that pertain strictly to audio data. The rest of SONAR's editing features are more diverse in their uses, meaning some can be used with MIDI data, some with audio data, and some with both. The one aspect they all have in common is that they are accessed via the Process menu. Because of their diversity, I'll go through each feature, explaining what it does and how and why you would want to use it. I'll also let you know the kinds of data with which each feature works.

Deglitch

Occasionally, you might find that while you're playing your MIDI instrument, some unintended notes get recorded along with the legitimate musical material. This is especially true for people who play a MIDI guitar. The strings on a MIDI guitar can easily trigger notes when they're not supposed to. To help with this problem, SONAR provides the Deglitch feature. Using this feature, you can filter out any notes from your MIDI data that don't fall within the correct pitch, velocity, and duration range for the music you're recording. It works like this:

1. Select the MIDI data from which you want to filter any unwanted notes.
2. Choose Process > Deglitch to open the Deglitch dialog box.
3. If you want to filter out notes by pitch, activate the Pitch option. In the Notes Higher Than field, type the maximum note value allowed in your material. For example, if the highest note in your MIDI data should be C5, then you should set the Notes Higher Than parameter to C5. If the Deglitch feature finds any notes in the data that have a pitch higher than C5, it will delete them.
4. If you want to filter out notes by velocity, activate the Velocity option. In the Notes Softer Than field, type the minimum velocity value allowed in your material. For example, if the lowest velocity in your MIDI data should be 15, then you should set the Notes Softer Than parameter to 15. If the Deglitch feature finds any notes in the data that have a velocity lower than 15, it will delete them.
5. If you want to filter out notes by duration, activate the Duration option. In the Notes Shorter Than field, type the minimum duration value allowed in your material. Also, be sure to specify whether the duration should be measured in ticks or milliseconds by choosing either the Ticks option or the Milliseconds option for the Format parameter. For example, if the lowest duration in your MIDI data should be 20 ticks, then you should set the Notes Shorter Than parameter to 20 and the Format parameter to Ticks. If the Deglitch feature finds any notes in the data that have durations lower than 20 ticks, it will delete them. Click OK.

Slide

Remember back in Chapter 6 when I described how to move clips in the Track view by dragging and dropping them or by using the Clip section of the Inspector to change their start times? Well, the Slide feature performs the same function. You can use it to move clips backward or forward within a track. So why does SONAR provide the same functionality more than once? Because the Slide feature has a few differences. Instead of just working with clips, you can use it with any kind of selected data, from a group of MIDI notes to single events. And instead of having to specify an exact start time, you can move data by any number of measures, ticks, seconds, or frames. In addition, the Slide feature doesn't give you the option of blending with, replacing, or sliding over existing events in a track. It simply moves the selected data so that it overlaps with any existing data. You use it as follows:

1. Using the appropriate view, select the MIDI data or audio clips you want to move.
2. Choose Process > Slide to open the Slide dialog box.
3. If you want to move events, be sure the Events in Tracks option in the Slide section is activated. If you want to move any markers that happen to fall within the same time range as the selected data, activate the Markers option.

4. For the By parameter, type the number of units by which you want to move the selected data. If you want to move the data backward in time, enter a negative number. If you want to move the data forward in time, enter a positive number.

5. Choose the type of unit by which you want to move the selected data by activating the appropriate option. You can select Measures, Ticks, Seconds, or Frames. Click OK.

Nudge

In addition to the Slide feature, SONAR provides the Nudge feature. It works almost exactly the same as the Slide feature, except that the Nudge feature can be accessed with quick and simple keystrokes, and you can configure up to three different Nudge key bindings.

To use the Nudge feature, you select some data and choose Process > Nudge > Left 1 through 3 or Right 1 through 3. Or you can just press one of the appropriate numeric keypad numbers. (You can see the keypad numbers shown next to each Nudge option in the menu.)

> **NUM LOCK:** In order to access the Nudge feature using the numeric keypad, you must have the Num Lock key activated on your computer keyboard.

There is also a unique ability that the Nudge feature provides—it nudges data up or down into different tracks. The Slide feature can't do this. You select a clip in a track and choose Process > Nudge > Up or Down. This will move the clip up or down to the adjacent track.

In addition, you can configure each of the three left and right Nudge options by choosing Process > Nudge > Settings to open the Customization – Nudge section of the Preferences dialog box. In the dialog box, you'll see the three Nudge options listed, which correspond to Left 1/Right 1, Left 2/Right 2, and Left 3/Right 3. Each can be set to move data by a specific musical time, or an absolute time, or to follow the Snap to Grid settings. After you've finished configuring the options, click OK. Now you can nudge your data quickly with a click of the mouse or a press of a key.

Quantize

Even though you might be a great musician, you're bound to make mistakes occasionally when playing your instrument, especially when it comes to timing. No one I know can play in perfect time during every performance, and having to listen to a metronome while you play can be distracting. Instead of playing notes at the same time as the metronome sounds, you'll more than likely play some of them either a little ahead or a little behind the beat. You might even hold some notes a little longer than you're supposed to. Usually, if these timing errors are slight enough, they'll make your performance sound more human than anything else. But if the mistakes are obvious enough to stand out, they can make your performance sound sloppy. At this point, the Quantize feature comes in handy. It can help you correct some of the timing mistakes you make.

To understand how to use the Quantize feature, you first have to know how it works. The Quantize feature scans the MIDI events in your selected data one by one, and it changes the start time of each event so that it is equal to the nearest rhythmic value you specify (using the Resolution parameter). If you want all the events in your data to be moved to the nearest sixteenth note, you can set the Resolution parameter to Sixteenth. The Quantize feature uses this value to set up an imaginary (for lack of a better word) time grid over your data. In this case, the grid is divided into sixteenth notes.

During the scanning process, the Quantize feature moves an imaginary pointer along the grid, one division at a time. Centered on the pointer is an imaginary window, for which you can set the size using the Window parameter. As the Quantize feature moves its pointer and window along the grid, it looks to see whether any of your events are in the vicinity. Any events that fall within the window have their start times changed so they line up with the current position of the pointer. Any events that fall outside the window are left alone. This procedure continues until the Quantize feature comes to the end of the data you selected.

1. Select the data you want to quantize. It can be anything from all the data in your project to a single track or clip or a selected group of events.

2. Choose Process > Quantize (Q) to open the Quantize dialog box.

3. In the Resolution section, set the Duration parameter. This parameter determines the rhythmic value that will be used to set up the imaginary grid and the nearest rhythmic value to which the events in your data will be aligned. It's best to set this parameter to the smallest note value found in your data. For instance, your data might contain quarter notes, eighth notes, and sixteenth notes. Because the smallest note value in your data is the sixteenth note, set the parameter to Sixteenth.

4. In the Change section, activate the appropriate options for the types of events and the event properties you want to have quantized. You'll almost always want to activate the MIDI Event Start Times option. Along with the start times of events, you can also quantize the durations of MIDI note events by activating the Note Durations option. Usually, you'll activate this option as well. If you don't, the ends of some notes may overlap the beginnings of others, which might not sound good. You might not want to quantize the start times of events, but only the durations if you want to create a staccato (separated notes) feel to your music. When activated, the Only Notes and Lyrics option quantizes only MIDI note and lyric events and leaves any other events (such as MIDI controller events) alone. Usually, you'll want to keep this option activated; otherwise, the Quantize feature will move controller events to the nearest grid point, which can actually screw up their timing.

5. You can also quantize audio in two different ways. One way involves SONAR's AudioSnap feature (discussed later in this chapter) and the AudioSnap Beats option. The other way involves simply moving the start of entire audio clips. For this method, activate the Audio Clip Start Times option. Also, when quantizing the start time of audio clips, you may find that some audio clips become overlapped. To handle these clips more gracefully, you can apply a crossfade between the clips by activating the Auto XFade Audio Clips option and entering the number of milliseconds to control the crossfade time.

6. In the Options section, set the Strength parameter. Quantizing your data so that all the events are aligned in perfect time with the grid can make your performance sound mechanical (as if it is being played by a machine). So instead of having the Quantize feature move an event to the exact current pointer position on the grid during the scanning process, you can have it move the event only slightly toward the pointer, thus taking the sloppiness out of the performance but keeping the "human" feel. You can do so by setting a percentage for the Strength parameter. A value of 100 percent means that all events will be moved to the exact grid point. A value of 50 percent means that the events will be moved only halfway toward the grid point.

7. Set the Window parameter. This parameter tells SONAR how close to the current grid point an event has to be in order to be quantized. If the event falls inside the window, it is quantized. If it falls outside the window, it isn't. You set the Window parameter by using a percentage. A value of 100 percent means the window extends halfway before and halfway after the current pointer position on the grid. Basically, all events get moved; if they don't fall inside the window at the current pointer position, they will fall inside at the next position. A value of 50 percent means the window extends only one-quarter of the way before and after the current pointer position, meaning only half of the events in your selection will be processed.

8. Set the Offset parameter. This parameter is an extra setting thrown in to make the Quantize feature even more flexible (and complicated) than it already is. When the Quantize feature sets up its imaginary grid over your selected data, the grid is perfectly aligned to the measures and beats in your project. So if your data selection started at the beginning of your project, the grid would be set up starting at 1:01:000 (measure, beat, and tick).

If you enter a value for the Offset parameter (in ticks), the grid will be offset by the number of ticks you enter. For example, if you enter an Offset of +3, the grid will be set up starting at 1:01:003 instead of 1:01:000. This means that if the current event being scanned was initially supposed to be moved to 1:01:000, it would be moved to 1:01:003 instead. Basically, you can use this parameter to offset the selected data from the other data in your project, in case you want to create some slight timing variations, and so on. It works similarly to the Time Offset parameter in the Track view.

9. Set the Swing parameter. You might use this parameter to work on a song that has a "swing" feel to it, similar to a waltz, where the first in a pair of notes is played longer than the second. It's difficult to explain, but essentially the Swing parameter distorts the grid by making the space between the grid points uneven. If you leave the parameter set at 50 percent, it doesn't have any effect. If you set it to something like 66 percent, the space between the first two points in the grid becomes twice as much as the space between the second and third points. This pattern of long space, short space is repeated throughout the length of the grid, and your data is aligned according to the uneven grid points.

10. Click the Audition button to hear how the quantized data will sound. Go back and make any parameter changes you think might be necessary.

11. If you want to use the same settings again later, save them as a preset. Click OK.

The Groove Quantize Feature

Not only can you use quantizing to correct the timing of your performances, but you can also use it to add a bit of a creative flair. The Groove Quantize feature works almost the same as the Quantize feature, but it's slightly more sophisticated. Instead of using a fixed grid (meaning you can set the grid to use only straight rhythmic values, such as sixteenth notes), it uses a grid with rhythmic values that are based on an existing rhythmic pattern called a *groove pattern*. This groove pattern can contain any kind of musical rhythm, even one taken from an existing piece of music.

Basically, the Groove Quantize feature works by imposing the timing, duration, and velocity values of one set of events onto another set. For example, suppose that you record a melody that comes out sounding a bit too mechanical, but your friend slams out this really kickin' MIDI bass line that has the exact feel you want. You can copy the bass clip data and use it as a groove pattern to groove quantize the melody clip data. By doing so, you impose the timing, duration, and velocity values (depending on your parameter settings) from the bass line onto the melody. Thus, the melody will have the same rhythm as the bass line but keep its original pitches.

The preceding example is just one of the many uses for the Groove Quantize feature. Just like the Quantize feature, the Groove Quantize feature provides Strength parameters to give you control of how much influence a groove pattern has over the data you're quantizing. You can define via percentages how much the timing, duration, and velocity values of the events will be affected so that you can use this feature for all kinds of editing tasks. You can correct off-tempo tracks, add complex beat accents to each measure of a tune, synchronize rhythm and solo tracks, align tracks with bad timing to one with good timing, and steal the feeling from tracks. Naturally, you need to know how to use the Groove Quantize feature before you can use these groove pattern files, so let me tell you how:

1. If you want to grab the timing, duration, and velocity values from existing data, first select and copy that data so that it is placed onto the clipboard. Otherwise, you can use one of the groove patterns that comes included with SONAR.

2. Select the data you want to groove quantize.

3. Choose Process > Groove Quantize to open the Groove Quantize dialog box.

4. Set the Groove File parameter. If you're grabbing the values from existing data, as explained previously, then select Clipboard from the list and skip to Step 6. Otherwise, choose an existing groove file. SONAR ships with two groove files (Cakewalk DNA Grooves.grv and MPCake.grv), so unless you've created your own groove files, choose one of the included files. If you have other groove files available, you can load them by clicking

the ellipsis button to the right of the Groove File parameter to bring up the Open Groove File dialog box. Just select a file and click Open.

5. Set the Groove Pattern parameter. Each groove file can contain any number of groove patterns. For example, the Cakewalk DNA Grooves.grv file that comes with SONAR contains 12 different groove patterns. Choose the groove pattern you want to use.

6. The rest of the parameters for the Groove Quantize feature are the same as for the Quantize feature. You need to set the Resolution parameter, the AudioSnap Beats option, the Audio Clip Start Times and Auto XFade Audio Clips, the Only Notes, Lyrics, and Audio option, and the Window parameter. The Window Sensitivity parameter is the same as the Window parameter for the Quantize feature, but one additional Window parameter is available here. You can choose the If Outside Window parameter to have Groove Quantize change events, even if they fall outside the window. If you select Do Not Change, then events outside the window are left alone (just as with the Quantize feature). If you select Quantize to Resolution, any events outside the window are moved to the nearest grid point, as specified by the Resolution parameter. If you select Move to Nearest, then the Window Sensitivity parameter is ignored, and all events outside the window are moved to the nearest grid point, as defined by the groove pattern. If you select Scale Time, SONAR looks at the events located right before and after the current event being scanned (as long as they are within the window), and it sets their relative timing so that they're the same. The Scale Time parameter is very difficult to explain, so you should try it out to hear what kind of effect it has on your music.

7. You also need to set the Strength parameters. They work the same as with the Quantize feature, but instead of just having one parameter to affect the timing of events, three Strength parameters are provided to give you control over how the Groove Quantize feature will affect the time, duration, and velocity of each event. If you want the events to have the same timing, duration, and velocity as their counterparts in the groove pattern, then set all these parameters to 100 percent. Otherwise, you can make the events take on only some of the feel of the events in the groove pattern by adjusting the percentages of these parameters.

8. Click the Audition button to hear how the quantized data will sound. Go back and make any parameter changes you think might be necessary.

9. If you want to use the same settings again later, then save them as a preset.

After you click OK, SONAR will quantize the selected data so the timing, duration, and velocity of the events will sound exactly or somewhat like those in the groove pattern you used (depending on your parameter settings). By the way, if the groove pattern is shorter than the material you are quantizing, the Groove Quantize feature will loop through the groove pattern as many times as necessary to get to the end of your selected data. For example, if you use a groove pattern that is only one measure long, but your selected data is three measures, then the timing, duration, and velocity values of the groove pattern will be repeated over each of those three measures.

Saving Groove Patterns

If you create your own groove pattern by grabbing the timing, duration, and velocity values from existing data, you can save it for later use as follows:

1. After you've gone through Steps 1 through 4 in the preceding example, and you've set the Groove File parameter to Clipboard, click the Define button near the bottom-right of the dialog box to open the Define Groove dialog box.

2. In the Groove Library File section, select an existing groove file via the File parameter. You can also type a new name to create your own new groove file.

GROOVE FILE FORMATS: SONAR supports two types of groove files. One type is the DNA groove file, which contains only timing data but is compatible with other sequencing software. SONAR also has its own proprietary groove file format that stores timing, duration, and velocity data. Unless you really need to share your groove files with others who don't own SONAR, I suggest you save your files in the SONAR format because it provides more flexibility. To do so, be sure to activate the Cakewalk Groove File Format option.

3. If you want to replace an existing groove pattern in the current groove file, just select one from the Pattern list. If you want to save your groove pattern under a new name, type the name in the Pattern parameter.

DELETE EXISTING PATTERNS: You can delete existing groove patterns in the current groove file. Just select the groove pattern you want to delete from the Pattern list and click the Delete button. SONAR will ask you to confirm the deletion process.

4. Click OK. If you're replacing an existing groove pattern, SONAR will ask you to confirm the replacement process.

GROOVE QUANTIZE APPLICATIONS: For examples of some cool applications for the Groove Quantize feature, look at the SONAR Help in the Editing MIDI Events and Continuous Controllers > Changing the Time of a Recording > Quantizing section.

The Find/Change Feature

Throughout this book, I've mentioned the name SONAR quite a few times. What if I want to change all those instances of the phrase to SONAR X2 instead? Luckily, I'm using a word processing program on my computer, so all I would have to do is use the search and replace feature to have the program automatically make the changes for me. I mention this point because the Find/Change feature is similar to the search-and-replace feature you find in most word processing programs. The difference is that Find/Change works with event properties, and in addition to simply searching and replacing, it can scale entire ranges of event properties from one set of values to another. This means that you can easily transpose notes, change key signatures, convert one type of controller message into another, and so on. It works like this:

1. Select the data you want to change.
2. Choose Process > Find/Change to open the Event Filter – Search dialog box. You learned about this dialog box and its parameters in Chapter 4.
3. Set all the available parameters so that SONAR can select the exact events you want to process.
4. Click OK to open the Event Filter – Replace dialog box. This dialog box is almost the same as the Event Filter – Search dialog box. It has most of the same settings, except some of the settings are not available because here you need to enter only the values to which you want to change the original selected data. So enter the replacement values in the appropriate parameters.

After you click OK, SONAR will select all the events in your initial selection, according to the parameters you set in the Event Filter – Search dialog box. Then it will change the values of those events, according to the parameters you set in the Event Filter – Replace dialog box.

Find/Change Applications

You didn't think I was going to leave you high and dry, trying to figure out such a complicated feature, did you? The following sections describe some of the changes you can accomplish with this feature.

STRAIGHT REPLACEMENT

If all you want to do is replace one value with another, setting up the parameters in both dialog boxes is fairly easy. Suppose that you want to change all the notes with a pitch of C#2 to notes with a pitch of D#7. To do so, set up the Event Filter – Search dialog box so that only the Note option is activated in the Include section. Then type **C#2** for both the Key Min and Key Max parameters and click OK. In the Event Filter – Replace dialog box, type **D#7** for the Key Min and Key Max parameters and click OK. All the C#2 notes will be changed to D#7 notes. Pretty easy, no? And you can use this approach with any of the data. Earlier, I mentioned changing one type of controller message to another. Just use the Control option along with the Number Min and Number Max parameters, as you did with the Note option and the Key Min and Key Max parameters.

> **USING WILDCARDS:** You can also use wildcards when you're designating an octave number for the pitch of a note. With regard to the preceding example, suppose that you want to change all the C# notes to D notes, not just the ones in octave 2 to octave 7. Instead of using C#2, you can use C#?, and instead of using D#7, you can use D#?. The ? is the wildcard, which stands for any octave.

SCALING VALUES

When you're working with ranges of values, you can use the Find/Change feature to scale them from one range to another. This capability is useful for limiting certain values to keep them within a set of boundaries. For example, some of the note velocities in one of your MIDI tracks might be a bit high, and you might want to quiet them down a bit. Usually, quieting them would mean having to use the Piano Roll view to change them all one by one. Using the Find/Change feature, you can compress their range down in a couple of easy steps. To do so, set up the Event Filter – Search dialog box so that only the Note option is activated in the Include section. Then type **0** for Velocity Min and **127** for Velocity Max and click OK. In the Event Filter – Replace dialog box, type **0** for Velocity Min and **100** for Velocity Max and click OK. All the note velocities will be scaled down from a range of 0 to 127 to a range of 0 to 100. You can use this approach with any of the other value ranges, too.

INVERTING VALUES

You also can invert any of the value ranges by reversing the Min and Max parameters. For example, what if you want to make all the loud volume controller messages soft and the soft volume controller messages loud? To do so, set up the Event Filter – Search dialog box so that only the Control option is activated in the Include section. Then type **7** (the number for volume controller messages) for both the Number Min and Number Max parameters. Also, type **0** for Value Min and **127** for Value Max and click OK. In the Event Filter – Replace dialog box, type **7** for both the Number Min and Number Max parameters. Also, type **127** for Value Min and **0** for Value Max and click OK. All the loud sections of your selected data will become soft and vice versa. Again, you can use this technique for any of the other value ranges.

As a matter of fact, you can change a whole bunch of different parameters at once by activating the appropriate parameters in the Event Filter – Search dialog box. (You can even mix straight replacement, scaling, and inverting.) For instance, you could easily set up all three of the preceding examples so that you would have to use the Find/Change feature only one time to process the same data. This feature is very powerful. You should experiment with it as much as possible because it can save you a lot of editing time in the long run.

> **OTHER FIND/CHANGE APPLICATIONS:** You can find some other Find/Change ideas in the SONAR Help file under the Editing MIDI Events and Continuous Controllers > Searching for Events > Event Filters section.

The Length Feature

The Length feature is one of the very simple but also very useful features provided in SONAR. Using it, you can change the size of a clip or a group of selected data by specifying a percentage. It works like this:

1. Select the data you want to change.
2. Choose Process > Length to open the Length dialog box.
3. Activate the Start Times or Durations option. Activating the Start Times option makes the Length feature change the start times of the selected events so the entire selection will change in size. Activating the Durations option makes the Length feature change the durations of the selected events. If you activate the Durations option without the Start Times option, the Length feature will change only the durations of the selected events. This feature can be useful if you want to create a staccato effect for your notes.
4. If you want the length of your audio data to be changed, you can activate the Stretch Audio option. If your audio consists of a single musical voice, choose MPEX – Solo Instrument, Single Voice for the Type parameter. If your audio consists of a group of voices or instruments, choose MPEX – Mix, Polyphonic for the Type parameter. You can also experiment with the Radius choices for the Type parameter, depending on the material you are processing. If you choose Radius Mix – Advanced, you can also adjust the Radius Pitch and Phase Coherence parameters. Adjusting Pitch Coherence can help to preserve the natural sound of solo voices and instruments after they have been stretched. Adjust Phase Coherence can help to preserve the phase between stereo and surround sound channel audio. Both parameters default to 50 percent, and anything higher provides more preservation of the sound but can introduce artifacts.

> **FORMANT SCALING:** Changing the length of audio data with either of the MPEX settings for the Type parameter can also affect its timbre or musical characteristics. If this happens, you can use the Formant Scaling parameter to correct the problem. The Formant Scaling parameter can be set anywhere from −2.000 to +2.000 octaves. If the audio data sounds like it is tuned too low, try entering a positive value. If the audio data sounds like it is tuned too high, try entering a negative value.

5. Enter a value for the By Percent parameter. A value of 100 percent doesn't make any changes at all. A value of 50 percent changes the selection to half its original length. A value of 200 percent changes the selection to twice its original length. Click OK.

> **FIT TO TIME:** For a more intuitive way to change the length of your data (meaning you can enter a length using an actual time value instead of a percentage), use the Fit to Time feature (described later in this chapter).

The Retrograde Feature

The Retrograde feature works similarly to the Reverse feature. Instead of reversing the data in audio clips, the Retrograde feature reverses MIDI data. This means that you can have your MIDI data play backward if you apply this feature. Just select the data you want to reverse and then select Process > Retrograde. SONAR will reverse the order of the selected events. In other words, if you were looking at the data via the Event List view, the data would be changed so that the list essentially is flipped upside down.

The Transpose Feature

Transposition is a common occurrence when you're composing music, and SONAR's Transpose feature enables you to transpose quickly and easily. It works like this:

1. Select the data that you want to transpose.
2. Choose Process > Transpose to open the Transpose dialog box.
3. You can use the Transpose feature to transpose the pitches of your note events either chromatically (so they can be changed by half steps) or diatonically (so they remain in the current key signature of your project). If you want to transpose chromatically, leave the Diatonic Math option deactivated. If you want to transpose diatonically, activate the Diatonic Math option.
4. If you have selected any audio data, you can opt to have its pitch changed. To do so, activate the Transpose Audio option. Then choose a setting for the Type parameter, which works the same here as for the Length feature (refer to the "Length Feature" section earlier in this chapter for more information).
5. Enter a value for the Amount parameter. A positive value transposes up, and a negative value transposes down. If you are transposing chromatically, this value corresponds to half steps. If you are transposing diatonically, the Transpose feature changes the pitches of your notes according to the major scale of the current key signature. For example, if you enter a value of +1 and the key signature is D major, a D becomes an E, an E becomes an F#, and so on. Click OK.

The Scale Velocity Feature

You learned about scaling the velocity values of events earlier in the description of the Interpolate feature. Using the Scale Velocity feature, you can do the same thing, but this feature has an extra option that scales the velocities by a percentage, rather than entering exact values or a range of values. It works like this:

1. Select the data you want to change.
2. Choose Process > Scale Velocity to open the Scale Velocity dialog box.
3. If you want to scale the velocities by percentages, activate the Percentages option. Otherwise, the values that you enter will be exact velocity values.
4. Enter values for the Begin and End parameters. For example, you can use the Scale Velocity feature to create crescendos and decrescendos. To create a crescendo, enter a small value (such as **0** or **50** percent) for the Begin parameter and a larger value (such as **127** or **150** percent) for the End parameter. Do the opposite for a decrescendo. Click OK.

Fit to Time

The Fit to Time feature works similarly to the Length feature. Using it, you can change the size of clips and selected groups of data. But instead of having to use a percentage, you can specify an actual time (according to the Time Ruler) at which the data will end. For example, if you have a clip that begins at 1:01:000 and ends at 4:02:000, the start time of the clip will remain the same, but you can change the end time of the clip so that it stops playing at the exact moment you specify. This feature is great when you need to compose music to a precise length, such as for a radio commercial or a video. It works like this:

1. Select the data you want to change.
2. Choose Process > Fit to Time to open the Fit to Time dialog box.
3. The Original Time Span section shows the beginning and end times for the selected data. In the Adjust to End at New Time section, enter a new end time for the selected data. You can enter either hours, minutes, seconds, and frames, or measures, beats, and ticks. To change the format, click the Format button.
4. In the Modify by Changing section, activate either the Tempo Map option or the Event Times option. If you want the actual data to be changed (meaning the start times of every event in the selection will be adjusted to accommodate the new end time), activate the Event Times option. If you would rather leave the data as it is

and just have SONAR insert tempo changes into the project to accommodate the new end time, activate the Tempo Map option. The key difference here is that using the Tempo Map option affects the entire project, and all the data in all the tracks during the selected time will play at a different rate. If you want the data in only one track to be affected, you must use the Event Times option.

5. If you want to change the length of audio clips, you have to activate the Stretch Audio option. Then choose a setting for the Type parameter, which works the same here as for the Length feature (refer to the "Length Feature" section earlier in this chapter for more information). Click OK.

Fit Improvisation

Having to play along with a metronome while recording in SONAR can be a nuisance sometimes. Depending on the type of music you are performing, using the metronome might not be conducive to your mood during the performance, which means you might end up with a less than acceptable recording. Some people just can't stand using a metronome. The problem is that if you don't use the metronome while recording in SONAR, your data will not line up correctly to the measure, beat, and tick values along the Time Ruler. Therefore, editing your music can be a lot more difficult.

If you are one of those people who hates metronomes, then you're in luck. SONAR will record your MIDI tracks without using the metronome, but it still lines up your data correctly after the fact by using the Fit Improvisation feature. This feature works by adding tempo changes to your project according to an additional reference track that you must record. This reference track gives SONAR an idea of the tempo at which you were playing when you were recording your MIDI track without the metronome. Here is a more detailed version of how this feature works:

1. Record a MIDI track without using the metronome. For the most accurate results, try to play using as steady a tempo as possible.
2. Press P and choose MIDI – Playback and Recording in the Preferences dialog box. Be sure that only the Notes option in the Record section is activated. This filters out any extraneous events when you're recording your reference track so they don't mess up the timing. The more accurate your reference track, the better. After you're done recording your reference track, you can go back to the Global Options dialog box and change the options back to the way they were.
3. Record a reference MIDI track. To do so, simply tap out the tempo of your initial MIDI recording by hitting a key on your MIDI instrument for every beat. So, if you recorded a track in 4/4 time, you would have to hit the key four times for every measure of music you recorded. Also, be sure that the first note in your reference track has a start time of 1:01:000 so that it starts at the very beginning of the project. You can adjust it manually by using the Event view or Piano Roll view if you have to.
4. Select the reference track.
5. Choose Process > Fit Improvisation.

SONAR will scan your reference track, analyzing where the beats fall, and add tempo changes to your project so that the data in your recorded track lines up with the measure, beat, and tick values on the Time Ruler. Now you can edit your data just as you would any other data that was recorded along with the metronome.

Audio Snap

Expanding on the power provided by the previously mentioned time-based altering features, SONAR includes additional audio manipulation in the form of AudioSnap. A set of tools, AudioSnap changes the timing of audio data in a variety of ways. This includes changing tempo, groove, quantizing, and more.

Instead of rehashing the basic AudioSnap information included in the SONAR Help, I will walk you through a number of practical uses. As such, I advise that you first read the AudioSnap section of the Help before reading the rest of this chapter.

AudioSnap Preparation

To get started with AudioSnap, there are a number of things you can do to set up your working environment to make the process easier. First, make the AudioSnap palette (see Figure 7.4) visible by choosing Views > AudioSnap Palette (or pressing A).

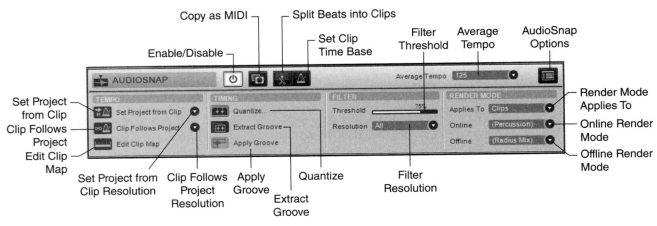

Figure 7.4 Use the AudioSnap palette to adjust AudioSnap settings for selected clips.
Source: Cakewalk®, Inc.

> **PALETTE OPACITY:** I like to position the AudioSnap palette at the bottom of the SONAR workspace and line up the bottom of the Track view with the top of the palette. That way I have complete access to the Track view and palette at the same time. You, however, might like to have the Track view fill the entire workspace. In that case, you can adjust the opacity of the palette so you can see through it but still access its functions. Use the X-Ray Windows feature discussed in Chapter 2 by hovering your mouse over the palette and pressing Shift+X.

Set the Default Stretch

AudioSnap provides a number of different options for stretching audio. Some options provide better quality than others but also take up more processing power, so they are only available when bouncing or exporting audio. You can set up the default stretching options by adjusting the parameters in the Render Mode section of the AudioSnap palette. Use the Applies To menu to choose the type of data for which you want to set the render modes. Clips, tracks, and the entire project (Global) can have their own render mode settings. In addition, using the Clip and Track sections of the Inspector, you can set a different render mode for each track or clip in the project.

You can set modes for Online and Offline rendering. Online represents the sound you hear during playback of a project in real time. If you are working with percussion material, choose the Percussion setting; otherwise, choose the Groove-Clip setting. For Offline Rendering, I've found the iZotope Radius Mix setting sounds quite nice, but this may be different depending on the material you are processing. The Offline Rendering option is used when you use the Bounce to Clip(s), Bounce to Track(s), and Export Audio features to create a permanent change in your processed audio.

Offline rendering also provides much better sound quality. As such, you may want to use Bounce to Clip(s) to test your AudioSnap results. You can quickly select all AudioSnap clips in a project by choosing Edit > Select > All AudioSnap/ SlipStretched (Ctrl+Alt+A). Then choose Clips > Bounce to Clip(s) in the Track view menu. This procedure can also be used to free up computer resources if you have a lot of AudioSnap processed clips in your project.

Align the Time Ruler

One of the most common scenarios for using AudioSnap is when working with a live performance recording. In this case, when you import the audio, the beats will more than likely not line up with the measure lines in the Track view Time Ruler. Lining up the measure lines makes working with your data and composing additional music (with the live performance track as a reference) much easier.

FIND THE DEFAULT TEMPO

If your audio recording already has accurate timing but just doesn't line up with the Time Ruler, you might be able to simply change the project tempo to the tempo of the recording. For example:

1. Import an audio file into SONAR.
2. You'll notice that the beats and the end of the clip do not line up with the Time Ruler. Double-click the clip to open it in the Loop Construction view (see Chapter 9).
3. In the toolbar of the Loop Construction view, you'll see a parameter called BPM, which displays the original tempo of the audio file as automatically determined by SONAR (see Figure 7.5).

Figure 7.5 Find the original audio tempo in the Loop Construction toolbar.
Source: Cakewalk®, Inc.

4. Use the Control Bar or the Tempo view to change the project tempo to the same value as the original tempo.

You'll notice that the audio beats now line up with the Time Ruler. Most of the time, you probably won't be this lucky, but for most accurate performances, it should work.

EXTRACT THE TIMING

Another way to line up accurate performances with the Time Ruler is to use the Set Project from Clip feature. For example:

1. Import an audio file into SONAR.
2. Select the imported clip and click the Enable/Disable button in the AudioSnap palette.
3. In the palette, use the Set Project from Clip Resolution menu to choose a tempo map resolution. This tells SONAR to copy the tempo map from the clip using a resolution of beats, measures, or the entire clip. If the clip has a steady tempo throughout, try using the Clip setting. If the clip spans multiple measures and its tempo changes, try the Measures setting. If the clip has many tempo changes, try the Beats setting.
4. Click the Set Project from Clip button in the palette. SONAR copies the tempo map from the clip into the project tempo map.
5. Choose Views > Tempo (Alt+Shift+5) to open the Tempo view and see what tempo changes were added.

As with the last example, you'll notice that the audio beats now line up with the Time Ruler.

SET THE MEASURE/BEAT: If you find that some of the beats still don't line up with the Time Ruler, you can enter changes manually. Set the Now time to the point in the clip where you know a specific beat is supposed to be and then choose Project > Set Measure/Beat at Now (Shift+M) to open the Measure Beat/

Meter dialog box. Enter the correct Measure and Beat numbers and click OK. This will add a new tempo change to the project tempo map to correct the Time Ruler. You'll probably need to do this in several places after you make changes because they'll affect the tempos that come afterward.

CLIP FOLLOWS PROJECT

After you've aligned the Time Ruler, you may want to import additional audio files into a project, but you can only align the Time Ruler to one file because there is only one tempo map per project. In order to make the additional clips line up correctly, you'll want to make them follow the current project tempo by using the Clip Follows Project feature. Once you've imported and selected the clip (as well as activated AudioSnap), choose a resolution from the Clip Follows Project Resolution menu in the palette. If you choose Measure or Clip, SONAR will adjust the length of the clip to conform to the tempo. If you choose Beat or Auto Stretch, SONAR adjusts the audio. I suggest you use Auto Stretch most of the time and then bounce the clip for the best quality. Your clip should now play in time with the project, although the timing of the performance may still not be exactly on the beat. To correct that, you can use quantizing.

Fix and Regroove (Quantize)

Using AudioSnap to actually change your data is where the real fun and usefulness begin. You can use the quantize features to fix sloppy performances, change the groove of a performance, and synchronize one track with another.

Quantize

No longer the exclusive domain of MIDI data, you can now use SONAR's Quantize feature to fix your audio performances. The basic steps for fixing a sloppy performance are as follows:

1. Select the audio clip(s) you want to quantize and click the Enable/Disable button in the AudioSnap palette.
2. You may want to adjust the Resolution and Threshold parameters in the Filter section of the palette to disable some of the transient markers so that some of the audio data is not quantized. This can be useful if you only want to alter the transients on each beat and leave the feel of the performance between each beat.

MANUAL TRANSIENT EDITING: If the Resolution and Threshold parameters are disabling too many transients or not the right ones, you can leave them alone and edit the transients manually. Simply right-click a transient and choose an option from the menu. Choose Disable to turn a marker off. Choose Promote to lock a marker so it can't be changed.

3. Click the Quantize button in the Timing section of the palette to open the Quantize dialog box.
4. Set the Duration parameter to the lowest rhythmic value in your audio.
5. Make sure the AudioSnap Beats option is activated.
6. Leave the Strength parameter set to 100, Swing to 50, Window to 100, and Offset to 0. These settings will give you exact quantization.

After you click OK, your audio is quantized so that the transients fall perfectly on the beat. If you want to experiment with the feel of the beat a bit, try setting the Swing parameter to 30 or 70 to have the performance fall before or after the beat.

Groove Quantize

You can experiment with the feel of the beat even more by using the Groove Quantize feature. The Groove Quantize feature applies pre-existing rhythmic grooves to your data. Here's an example:

1. Import an audio file into SONAR.
2. Select the imported clip and click the Enable/Disable button in the AudioSnap palette.

3. Either align the Time Ruler to the clip or have the clip follow the project tempo as described earlier.
4. Choose Process > Groove Quantize to open the Groove Quantize dialog box.
5. Choose Cakewalk DNA Grooves.grv for the groove file.
6. Choose a groove pattern.
7. For exact pattern matching, choose a Resolution set to the lowest rhythmic value in your audio. For this example, choose Eighth if the audio contains eighth notes. For lining up the beat at measure boundaries, but keeping the general feel between measures, try using the Whole setting.
8. For exact pattern matching, use a Window Sensitivity of 100 percent. For lining up the beat at measure boundaries, try a setting of 25 percent.
9. I usually use Do Not Change for the If Outside Window parameter, but when lining up the beat at measure boundaries, try using Scale Time.
10. Make sure the AudioSnap Beats option is activated.
11. Leave the Strength Time, Duration, and Velocity set to 100 percent. You can experiment with these (especially the Time parameter) by lowering them to keep more of the original rhythm, note durations, and note velocities intact.
12. Click the Audition button to preview the results while you experiment with the different groove patterns. Click OK.

The AudioSnap Pool

What do you do when you have multiple audio clips and you want to line them up to the same beat? The AudioSnap Pool feature will let you snap the groove of one audio clip to another as follows:

1. Select the audio clip from which you want to grab the "feel" and click the Enable/Disable button in the AudioSnap palette.
2. Click the Extract Groove button in the palette. SONAR extracts the rhythmic timing from the clip and adds it to the AudioSnap pool, which you can see when the transients in the clip are displayed as light blue.
3. Select the clip to which you want to apply the groove and click the Apply Groove button in the palette.

When you play the project, you'll hear that both clips are in sync with one another and playing with the same rhythmic groove. You can also see that all of the relevant transients are lined up.

Extract a Groove and MIDI

What we did in the previous example was to extract the groove from one clip and use it to align another clip to the same groove using the AudioSnap Pool feature. We can also use that groove for other things.

Extract a Groove

Using the AudioSnap Extract Groove feature, you can take a groove from selected audio data and save it as a groove pattern in a groove file for use with the Groove Quantize feature, as we did earlier. Here's how:

1. Select an audio clip.
2. Click the Enable/Disable button in the AudioSnap palette.
3. Set the track's Edit Filter to Audio Transients.
4. You may want to adjust the Resolution and Threshold parameters in the Filter section of the palette to disable some of the transient markers so that some of the clip's groove is not saved, but normally you'll want to extract it entirely.
5. Right-click the clip and choose Save As Groove to open the Define Groove dialog box.
6. In the Groove Library File section, select an existing groove file via the File parameter. You can also type a new name to create your own new groove file.
7. If you want to replace an existing groove pattern in the current groove file, just select one from the Pattern list. If you want to save your groove pattern under a new name, type the name in the Pattern parameter.

8. Click OK. If you're replacing an existing groove pattern, SONAR will ask you to confirm the replacement process.

After you save the groove using the Define Groove dialog box, the groove will be included in the Groove File and Groove Pattern parameters of the Groove Quantize dialog box and can be applied to any other audio or MIDI clip.

Extract as MIDI

In addition to extracting and applying grooves, you can also convert a groove into MIDI notes as follows:

1. Select an audio clip.
2. Click the Enable/Disable button in the AudioSnap palette.
3. Set the track's Edit Filter to Audio Transients.
4. You may want to adjust the Resolution and Threshold parameters in the Filter section of the palette to disable some of the transient markers so that some of the clip's groove is not saved, but normally you'll want to extract it entirely.
5. Click the AudioSnap Options button in the palette.
6. In the MIDI Extraction section of the dialog box, choose the MIDI note to be used during the conversion by setting a value for the Convert to MIDI Note parameter. Since we're only extracting rhythm, all notes will have the same pitch.
7. If you want to extract the velocity of each note, choose the Vary With Pulse Level option. This is a good choice if you plan to use the MIDI data with a percussion instrument. Otherwise, if you want all the notes to have the same velocity, choose the Set All To Same Value option and type in a value. Click OK.
8. Right-click the clip and choose Copy As MIDI.
9. Now use SONAR's Paste function to paste the MIDI data as a new MIDI clip in an existing or new MIDI track.

You can use the extracted MIDI groove to play a software synth (see Chapter 8), which can either enhance or replace the sound of the original audio clip.

Multitrack AudioSnap Alignment

Another very useful function of AudioSnap is lining up multiple tracks, such as when working with multitrack drums. Instead of stretching the audio, however, it can actually be better to just split all the tracks into multiple clips and then quantize the start times of the clips. That way you avoid all kinds of audio alignment problems. Here's an example of how to align multitrack drums with each instrument in the kit recorded on a separate track:

1. Select your reference track(s), which provide the timing on which the alignment will be based. In the case of drums, this will usually be the kick and snare tracks.
2. Choose Views > AudioSnap Palette (A) and click the Enable/Disable AudioSnap on Selected Clips button.
3. Adjust the Threshold and Resolution parameters in the Filter section of the Palette so that all the transients in the audio are accurately represented with markers. You may need to do some manual adjustment so that all the markers land right on the transients, but that's usually not the case.
4. Right-click on the background of one of the reference tracks and choose Pool > Add Clip to Pool to add both tracks the AudioSnap Pool.
5. Choose Edit > Select > None (Ctrl+Shift+A) to remove the selections from the reference tracks.
6. Select all the tracks you want to align.
7. Right-click the background of one of the tracks and choose Split Clip(s) at AudioSnap Pool. This will divide all the clips in all the selected tracks at the transient markers that were placed in the Pool, creating new clips at every marker in every track.
8. With all the tracks still selected, click the Enable/Disable AudioSnap on Selected Clips button in the Audio-Snap Palette to disable AudioSnap.

9. Choose Process > Quantize (Q) to open the Quantize dialog box. I talked about how to use the Quantize function earlier in the chapter, although there are a couple of different things you need to do when quantizing split clips on multiple tracks.

10. Set the Resolution, Strength, Swing, Window, and Offset as previously explained (see the "Quantize" section earlier in this chapter). Then in the Change section, activate the Audio Clip Start Times option and deactivate all the other options. This will allow you to align all the start times of the clips in the tracks, and since each clip now represents a single drum hit, you are effectively aligning all the hits.

11. The only caveat of this method is that when you move the clips around, some of them will end up overlapping each other. This can cause noticeable pops and clicks in the audio. To prevent this from happening, activate the Auto XFade Audio Clips option. This option will automatically create crossfades between any overlapping clips, thus eliminating any of the possible problems.

12. Adjust the XFade and Max Gap parameters. These parameters determine the length of the crossfades and the maximum allowed gap between clips, respectively. I've found that setting the XFade parameter to 1ms and the Max Gap parameter to 80ms usually work best, but you may need to experiment with these settings.

13. Click OK.

Your multiple tracks should now be quantized to the beat and nicely aligned without any kind of audio anomalies that can occur when stretching audio.

Using Soft Synths in Your Projects

$\mathbf{M}$IDI IS SIMPLY PERFORMANCE DATA. MIDI data alone does not produce any sound. In order to have sound produced from your MIDI data, you need a MIDI instrument. Usually, a MIDI instrument comes in the form of a MIDI synthesizer keyboard or module. These are hardware-based synthesizers. Today, however, personal computers have become so powerful that it is now possible to simulate a MIDI synthesizer via a computer software program. This process is known as *software synthesis*, and basically it has the power to turn your computer into a full-fledged MIDI synthesizer module. SONAR has built-in software synthesis features.

The technology for DX instruments (DXi for short) was developed by Cakewalk and based on Microsoft's DirectX technology. The VST instruments' (VSTi for short) technology was developed by Steinberg. Cakewalk refers to DXi and VSTi as *soft* (short for software) *synths*. Soft synths come in the form of plug-ins that can simulate any kind of hardware-based synthesizer module. As a matter of fact, many soft synths have interfaces that look like on-screen versions of a hardware-based synth, with all kinds of knobs and switches that you can tweak with your mouse. Because soft synths are plug-ins, you can use them interchangeably within SONAR, just like effects plug-ins.

WHAT IS A PLUG-IN? In basic terms, a *plug-in* is a small computer program that by itself does nothing, but when used with a larger application, it provides added functionality to the larger program. Therefore, you can use plug-ins to add new features easily to a program. In SONAR's case, plug-ins provide you with additional ways to produce music through the use of soft synths.

INTRODUCTION TO SOFTWARE SYNTHESIZERS: Before reading the rest of this chapter, you may want to learn a bit more about the background and basics of software synthesizers. Go to **www.digifreq. com/digifreq/article.asp?ID=28** to read the Introduction to Software Synthesizers. Also, go to **www.digifreq. com/digifreq/articles.asp** for more information on this and other music technology topics.

Using Soft Synths

Using a soft synth to generate music is just like using a hardware-based synth, except that because a soft synth is software-based, it is run on your computer as an application from within SONAR. You control the settings of a soft synth by tweaking on-screen parameters. You can generate sound with a soft synth either in real time, as you perform on your MIDI keyboard, or by using data from a pre-existing MIDI track.

There are a number of different ways to use a soft synth in a project. The one I am about to describe is how to add a synth manually, but most of the time you will want to use either the Insert > Soft Synth function or the Browser (described later in this chapter). Some synths need to be added manually, however, so it is still good to know the following procedure:

1. Create a new project or open a pre-existing project.
2. Right-click in the Track pane of the Track view and choose Insert Audio Track to create a new audio track. Then widen the track to display its parameters.
3. Set the Input parameter to None and set the Output parameter to one of your sound card outputs.
4. Right-click in the Fx bin of the audio track and choose Soft Synths > [*name of the soft synth you want to use*] to set up a soft synth for that track (see Figure 8.1). If you ever want to remove a soft synth, just right-click its name in the Fx bin and choose Delete.

Figure 8.1   One way to use a soft synth is to add it to the Fx bin of an audio track.
Source: Cakewalk®, Inc.

> **GENERATE SOUND:** Even though soft synths are software-based, they still need to use a sound card output (which is hardware) to generate sound. Adding a soft synth to an audio track allows the synth to use the output of the track to generate sound. You can also add soft synths to the audio bus Fx bins.

5. After you add a soft synth to the Fx bin of the audio track, the window for that soft synth will appear, showing the Property Page (or control interface) of the soft synth. Using those controls, you can set up the soft synth's parameters, such as the sounds it will produce, and so on. After you've finished setting the soft synth's parameters, you can close the window to get it out of the way (or drag it into the MultiDock). If you need to access the soft synth's controls again, double-click the name of the soft synth in the Fx bin of the audio track.
6. If you opened a pre-existing project that already contains MIDI tracks, you can skip this step. Otherwise, right-click in the Track pane of the Track view and choose Insert MIDI Track to create a new MIDI track. Then widen the track to display its parameters.
7. Set the Input parameter to the MIDI port and channel that are being used to receive data from your MIDI keyboard. Then click the Output parameter to display a list of available outputs. In addition to your MIDI interface outputs, the list will also show any soft synths you previously set up. Choose the soft synth you want to use.
8. Set the Channel, Bank, and Patch parameters for the MIDI track. The settings you choose for these parameters will depend on the soft synth you are using. For the Channel parameter, choose the same channel to which the soft synth is set. The Bank and Patch parameters automatically display different settings, depending on the soft synth. The parameters will show the sound presets available for the soft synth. Choose the bank and patch that correspond to the sound you want to use.

> **NO BANK AND PATCH INFO:** Some soft synths don't provide a bank and patch list that can be listed in the MIDI track parameters. In that case, use the soft synth's Property Page to choose the sound you want to use.

9. You can either start performing some music on your MIDI keyboard or start playback of the project. Whichever action you choose, you should hear sound coming from the soft synth.

> **REAL-TIME PERFORMANCE:** When you use a soft synth in real time by performing on your MIDI keyboard, you might hear a delay between the time you press a key on your keyboard and the time it takes for the soft synth to produce sound. This is caused by sound card latency. To prevent this delay, you need to use ASIO or WDM drivers for your sound card, and you also need to adjust the Buffer Size slider or the ASIO Panel via the Audio – Driver Settings section of the Preferences (P) dialog box. (See Chapter 2 for more information about latency.)

The Insert Soft Synth Function and the Browser

There is actually an easier way to add a soft synth to a project, but I wanted to be sure you knew everything that was needed to add one manually—and it allowed me to explain the process in more detail. The Insert > Soft Synths function, however, automatically adds a soft synth to a project, along with the accompanying instrument and MIDI tracks needed for the soft synth.

> **SOFT SYNTH TRACKS:** When using the Insert > Soft Synth function, special instrument tracks are created (instead of regular audio tracks), which serve as audio outputs for the soft synth. The difference between an audio track and an instrument track is that the instrument track simply provides fewer parameters and can't be used to record audio. The instrument track is simply an output track for the soft synth.

Using the Insert Soft Synth Function to Add Synths

Here is how the Insert > Soft Synth function works:

1. Create a new project or open a pre-existing project.
2. Choose Insert > Soft Synth > [*name of the soft synth you want to use*] to open the Insert Soft Synth Options dialog box.

> **SIMPLE INSTRUMENT TRACK:** As I explained earlier, SONAR needs at least two tracks (a MIDI track and an instrument track) to represent a soft synth in a project. In the Create These Tracks section of the dialog box, you have a choice of using either the Simple Instrument Track option or a combination of the MIDI Source and Audio Output options. Choosing the Simple Instrument Track option is basically the same as choosing the MIDI Source and First Synth Audio Output options. The Simple Instrument Track option creates a single track in the Track view that represents both the MIDI track and instrument track for a soft synth with a single stereo audio output. This option helps to keep things organized in the track view. In addition, it provides the flexibility of being able to be converted back to a pair of MIDI/instrument tracks by right-clicking it and choosing Split Instrument Track.
>
> You can also convert a MIDI/instrument track pair to a simple instrument track by right-clicking one of the tracks and choosing Make Instrument Track. Used in combination with the Inspector, I would recommend using Simple Instrument Tracks most of the time since they free up more space in the Track view. When you make an instrument track active, the Inspector provides two tabs at the bottom of its display, labeled Audio and MIDI. Clicking these tabs gives you access to all the track parameters, which are otherwise not available in the Track view. An exception to using Simple Instrument Tracks is when using a soft synth that provides multiple audio outputs, which I'll describe later. Another thing to keep in mind is that MIDI automation is not available via Simple Instrument Tracks (see "Automating Synth Parameters" later in this chapter).

3. In the Create These Tracks section of the Insert Soft Synth Options dialog box, activate the MIDI Source option if you want a MIDI track to be created automatically for your soft synth.

4. In the Create These Tracks section, activate either the First Synth Audio Output option or the All Synth Audio Outputs: Stereo/Mono options to create the instrument track(s) for your soft synth.

MULTIPLE AUDIO OUTPUTS: Some soft synths provide multiple audio outputs, similar to some hardware-based synthesizers. This gives you more control over how the sounds of the soft synth are processed and routed. For example, if a soft synth can produce 16 different instrument sounds at the same time and has four outputs (like the Cakewalk TTS-1), you can group those 16 instruments into 4 different sections and send them to their own outputs. This means you could send all drum sounds to one output, all guitar sounds to another output, and so on. You could then apply different effects to each output (or group of sounds).

Each output of a soft synth requires its own instrument track. If you choose the All Synth Audio Outputs: Stereo option in the Insert Soft Synth Options dialog box, and the soft synth provides four outputs, then four separate instrument tracks will be created. If you choose the All Synth Audio Outputs: Mono option, SONAR splits each stereo output/track to two mono tracks, and eight tracks will be created.

---

5. To keep things organized, you can have the MIDI and instrument tracks associated with a soft synth stored in their own track folder. To do this, activate the Synth Track Folder option.

6. In the Open These Windows section, activate the Synth Property Page option if you want the soft synth's Property Page (or control interface) to be opened after the soft synth is added to the project.

7. If you want to record the MIDI output from a soft synth, activate the Enable MIDI Output option.

SOFT SYNTH MIDI OUTPUT: While all soft synths must provide at least one audio output so that you can hear and record their sounds, some also provide MIDI output. This output can come from a built-in arpeggiator (melody generator) or some other feature provided by the soft synth. By activating the Enable MIDI Output option, you can record the MIDI data from the soft synth into SONAR for editing.

---

8. Use the Display Automation On menu to choose where the automation data for the soft synth will be recorded. By default, automation data is recorded into the soft synth's instrument track. To keep things organized, I usually leave this set to the default value.

SOFT SYNTH AUTOMATION: In addition to recording soft synth audio and MIDI output, you can also record soft synth parameter changes over time. This means that you can dynamically change the sound currently being played by the soft synth. As you change the parameters in the soft synth's Property Page, those changes are recorded as data in SONAR and then played back as your project plays. This gives you total tonal control over the sound of the soft synth (see "Automating Synth Parameters" later in this chapter).

---

9. The Synth Rack (located in the Browser) creates on-screen controls to represent the various parameters of a soft synth. If you will be using multiple instances (copies) of the same soft synth in your project and you want each instance to have the same on-screen controls, activate the Recall Assignable Controls option.

10. Click OK. The soft synth you chose will be added to the project along with the MIDI track and instrument track(s), depending on the options you activated in the dialog box.

11. If you chose to have a MIDI track automatically created for you, you still need to set the track parameters. Set the Channel, Bank, and Patch parameters for the MIDI track.

12. You can either start performing some music on your MIDI keyboard or start playback of the project. Whichever action you choose, you should hear sound coming from the soft synth.

Don't worry if the instructions in the last two sections seem a bit generic. I'll provide some more specific examples on how to use the soft synths that are included with SONAR a little later.

Using the Browser to Add Synths

Believe it or not, there is yet an even easier way to add soft synths to a project—dragging and dropping them from the Browser. You can drag and drop synths directly as plug-ins or as track templates by doing the following:

1. Press B to open the Browser.
2. To add a synth plug-in directly, click the PlugIns tab at the top of the Browser and then click the Instruments button below the tab (see Figure 8.2).

PlugIns Instruments
Tab Button

Synth Plug-In List

Figure 8.2 Drag-and-drop synth plug-ins from the Browser.
Source: Cakewalk®, Inc.

3. Drag and drop a synth from the list into the Track view. Then choose the options you want in the Insert Soft Synth Options dialog box and click OK.

> **(DON'T) ASK THIS EVERY TIME:** If you don't want the Insert Soft Synth Options dialog box opening every time you add a synth, remove the check from the Ask This Every Time option at the bottom of the box.

4. You can also add a synth using track templates, but even better is that you can add a group of synths simultaneously and have them all set up and ready to go exactly how you like them. Click the Media tab at the top of the Browser and then choose Track Templates from the Content location menu (see Figure 8.3).

Media Tab   Content Location Menu

Track Template List

Figure 8.3 Add synths to a project via track templates.
Source: Cakewalk®, Inc.

5. Double-click the Soft Synth Track Templates folder and then drag one of the templates that comes included with SONAR. In addition, you can create your own custom templates as I explained earlier in Chapter 6.

The Synth Rack

When you add a soft synth to a project, the soft synth is listed as an entry in SONAR's Synth Rack (see Figure 8.4). The Synth Rack manages all the soft synths in a project by letting you add, remove, and change soft synths, as well as manipulate their properties. The Synth Rack is located inside the Browser and can be accessed by clicking the Synth Rack tab.

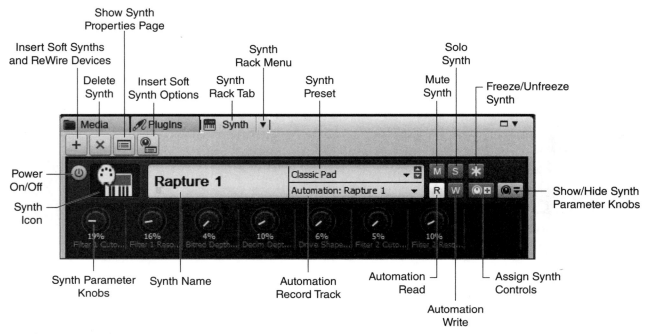

Figure 8.4 All soft synths in a project are listed in the Synth Rack view.
Source: Cakewalk®, Inc.

HIDDEN SYNTH RACK CONTROLS: Unfortunately, not all the Synth Rack controls can be shown when the Browser is docked at either side of the SONAR workspace. For access to all the controls (see Figure 8.4), either undock the Browser or dock it in the MultiDock.

Adding a Soft Synth

To add a soft synth to a project using the Synth Rack, click the Insert Soft Synths and ReWire Devices button. Then choose a soft synth from the menu. This will open the Insert Soft Synth Options dialog box. From there, you can follow the same steps as shown in the previous section.

Removing a Soft Synth

To remove a soft synth from a project using the Synth Rack, select the soft synth by clicking its icon. Then click the Delete button or press Del(ete).

> **DELETE ASSOCIATED TRACKS:** If there are any MIDI, audio, or software synth tracks associated with the soft synth, SONAR will ask you if you'd like to delete them. In the dialog box, keep the check mark next to the Delete Associated Tracks option and click OK to delete the tracks.

Replacing a Soft Synth

You also can replace an existing soft synth with a different synth by doing one of the following:

▷ In the Browser, click the Synth tab. Select the synth you want to replace by clicking its icon. Then from the Synth Rack menu (refer to Figure 8.4), choose Replace Synth and select a new synth.

▷ In the Browser, click the PlugIns tab and then click the Instruments button. Drag a synth onto the MIDI, audio, or Instrument track associated with the synth that you want to replace.

▷ In the Track view, right-click the MIDI, audio, or instrument track associated with the synth that you want to replace and choose Replace Synth from the menu.

When you use one of these three methods, the existing synth is replaced with the synth you chose and all track input/output routing is automatically configured as well.

Setting Soft Synth Properties

To access the Property Page (or control interface) of a soft synth via the Synth Rack, select the soft synth by clicking its icon and then click the Show Synth Properties Page button (which is only visible when the Browser is undocked or docked in the MultiDock). You can also just double-click the icon.

Synth Rack Parameters

When a soft synth is listed in the Synth Rack, it is shown using a graphical representation that has a number of control parameters you can use to manipulate certain aspects of the soft synth. These include turning the soft synth on or off, showing its name, displaying its current preset, muting or soloing the soft synth, and more.

POWER ON/OFF

Just like a hardware-based synth, you can turn a soft synth on or off. To do so, click the soft synth's Power On/Off button (which is only visible when the Browser is undocked or docked in the MultiDock) in the Synth Rack (refer to Figure 8.4). Internally, this changes the soft synth's connection to SONAR's audio engine. When the soft synth is on, it is connected to the audio engine, which means it produces sound and also takes up some of your computer's processing power. When the soft synth is off, it is not connected to the audio engine, which means it does not produce sound, and it doesn't use any of your computer's processing power. Using the Power On/Off button is an easy way to disable/enable a soft synth without having to keep adding it (and its associated tracks) to or removing it from a project. You can also choose Synth Connected from the Synth Rack menu to toggle a synth on/off.

> **CONNECTION METHODS:** Sometimes, you might notice that the Power On/Off button is not available. This is because soft synths are "connected" to a project in two different ways. When you add a soft synth manually to a project by inserting it into the Fx bin of an audio track, the soft synth is treated like an effect, and it can't be disconnected from the SONAR audio engine without being removed completely from the project. When you add a soft synth via the Insert Soft Synth function, it is inserted into the input of the instrument track, which means it can be disconnected from the SONAR audio engine without having to be removed from the project.
>
> Why two connection methods? Because while most soft synths are software synthesizers, there are some that can be used as effects (like z3ta+, included with SONAR). The soft synths that provide effects processing can be treated like effects. You'll need to refer to the documentation for your soft synth to determine whether it is a software synth, an effect, or both.

PRESETS

You can change the current synth preset (sound) of a soft synth in the Synth Rack by clicking the soft synth's Preset parameter, which is only visible when the Browser is undocked or docked in the MultiDock. This displays a menu that chooses the preset you want to use. Unfortunately, this only works with SONAR presets, meaning the presets listed in the Presets menu of the Property Page of a soft synth. Many soft synths have their own method of storing presets, and some soft synths are multitimbral. (This means that they can produce more than one sound at the same time.) For these soft synths, you need to access their Property Pages to change their presets. However, you can save your own presets using SONAR's Presets feature, and these presets will show up in the Synth Rack.

MUTE AND SOLO

You also can mute and solo soft synths in the Synth Rack by clicking their Mute and Solo buttons. This is just like muting and soloing tracks in the Track view. And just like muting a track, when you mute a soft synth, it no longer produces any sound, but it is still processed by your computer. Muting a soft synth doesn't disconnect it from the SONAR audio engine. If you want to mute and disconnect a soft synth, use the Power On/Off button instead.

SYNTH NAME AND ICONS

Each soft synth in the Synth Rack is provided with a synth name and icon. Of course, the name tells you which soft synth is loaded in the particular rack space. However, if you would rather use a more descriptive name, you can double-click the name and type something new. This new name will then show up in SONAR's track input/output menus.

Synth icons are similar to Track icons. Synth icons can be used to help organize your soft synths and help you quickly identify the current sound of a synth. For example, if your synth is set to a guitar sound, you could assign a picture of a guitar to the synth. To manipulate the icon for a soft synth, right-click the icon and choose one of the following options:

▷ **Load Synth Icon.** Use this option to load a new icon for the synth. Simply select a new icon in the Open dialog box and click Open.
▷ **Reset Synth Icon.** Use this option to reset the icon to the default synth icon.
▷ **Set Icon as Synth Default.** Use this option to set the current icon as the default synth icon. Now when you use the Reset Synth Icon option, it will use the current icon as the default synth icon.
▷ **Show Synth Icons.** This option is available from the Synth Rack menu. Remove/add the check mark from/to this option to hide/show all synth icons.

Freeze/Unfreeze a Soft Synth

Another feature provided by the Synth Rack is the Freeze/Unfreeze Synth function. Depending on the power of your computer, using many different soft synths at the same time can start to bog down playback and recording in SONAR. The more soft synths you use, the more computer power is consumed. This can cause SONAR's performance to be affected, and you may experience audio skips or stuttering. SONAR may even stop playback altogether. In order to help with this situation, SONAR "freezes" soft synth tracks, which basically turns them into audio tracks and deactivates their associated soft synths. This relieves the strain on your computer but still includes the soft synth performance in your project. Freezing tracks can also be helpful when you want to edit the audio of a MIDI track. For example, synth sounds usually evolve over time, and you may want to line up those changes with other audio in the project.

The Freeze/Unfreeze Synth function can be accessed in the Synth Rack by using a synth's Freeze/Unfreeze button or its Freeze Options menu. If you use a synth's Freeze/Unfreeze button, just click the button. To access a synth's Freeze Options menu, right-click its Freeze/Unfreeze button and choose one of the following options:

▷ **Freeze Synth.** Choose this option from the menu to freeze an active synth. The Freeze Synth option will automatically use SONAR's Bounce to Track function to take the audio output from the synth performance and place it in the synth's track. Then both the synth and its accompanying MIDI tracks are deactivated.

▷ **Unfreeze Synth.** After you have used the Freeze Synth function on a soft synth, you can "unfreeze" that synth by choosing this option. Choosing Unfreeze Synth will discard the bounced audio that was created with the Freeze Synth option, and it will reactivate both the synth and its accompanying MIDI tracks.

▷ **Quick Unfreeze Synth.** This option is similar to the Unfreeze Synth option, except that it doesn't discard the bounced audio.

FREEZE SYNTH FROM THE TRACK VIEW: In addition to using the Synth Rack, you can access the Freeze Synth function from the Track view. You can click the soft synth track's Freeze button or right-click the track and choose Freeze > [*one of the freeze options*].

FREEZE SYNTH OPTIONS

There are several things you can do to alter the way the Freeze Synth function works. To access these settings, right-click a synth's Freeze/Unfreeze button and choose Freeze Options to open the Freeze Options dialog box. The options in the Freeze Options dialog box work as follows:

▷ **Fast Bounce.** Having this option activated allows SONAR to bounce the audio output of a synth faster than real time, meaning it doesn't have to play through your entire project just to record the audio output of the synth. However, there are some soft synths on the market that require a real-time bounce. If you have trouble with a synth not having its audio output bounced correctly, then deactivating this option should solve the problem.

▷ **Audible Bounce.** If you deactivate the Fast Bounce option, SONAR will bounce the audio in real time (the same speed as playing back the project). If you would like to listen to the playback during the bounce, activate the Audible Bounce option.

▷ **Hide MIDI Tracks.** Normally, when you freeze a synth, the MIDI tracks stay visible in the Track view. However, if you would like them to be hidden when you freeze a synth, then activate this option. This can come in handy when you're working with a lot of tracks, and you want to keep things organized.

▷ **Single Bounce Per Track.** Having this option activated tells SONAR to bounce the synth's audio output into a single, long audio clip. If you would rather have the audio bounced to multiple clips (corresponding to the times in the synth performance when only audio output is present), then deactivate this option.

▷ **Remove Silence.** This option uses SONAR's Remove Silence function to remove the silent sections of the single, long audio clip created when using the Single Bounce Per Track option mentioned earlier. See the "Getting Rid of Silence" section in Chapter 7 for more information.

▷ **Freeze Tail Duration.** If you have applied any effects to a synth, you may have noticed that the sound of the effect can sometimes continue playing even after the audio output from the synth has stopped. This is called an *effect tail*. In order to compensate for the effect tail, you need to count how many seconds the effect tail continues to play and then enter that value into the Freeze Tail Duration parameter. The default value for this parameter is five seconds. This should be sufficient in most cases, but there may be times when it needs an adjustment. If you freeze a synth, and you hear its playback cut off at the end of its performance, then you may need to increase the value for this parameter.

▷ **Track FX.** If you've added any effects to the FX bin of the synth track, having this option activated will apply the effects to the audio and then disable the FX bin to save even more CPU power.

> **UNLOAD SYNTH AFTER FREEZE:** One last option provided by SONAR actually unloads a synth from your computer's memory when you freeze the synth. In a way, this can be a good thing because it will free up your computer's resources and may even give you a bit of a performance boost. However, if you decide to later unfreeze that same synth, it can take a lot longer because SONAR will then have to load that synth into memory again before unfreezing it. To access this option, use the Synth Rack menu and choose the Unload Synths on Disconnect option.

Controlling Synth Parameters

In addition to giving you quick access to some of the global parameters of a synth, the Synth Rack assigns on-screen knobs for easy access to specific synth parameters. Of course, you can simply open the Property Page of a synth to access all its parameters, but the control knobs in the Synth Rack give you easy access to multiple parameters for multiple synths all in one window. To begin using control knobs in the Synth Rack, first activate the Show/Hide Synth Parameter Knobs button (which is only visible when the Browser is undocked or docked in the MultiDock) for the synth you want to work with. From here, you can create knobs for various synth parameters. Simply follow these steps:

1. Click the Assign Synth Controls button for the synth you want to work with.
2. In the synth's Property Page, adjust each of the parameters for which you would like to create control knobs.
3. Close the synth's Property Page (this is optional).
4. Click the Assign Synth Controls button again.
5. SONAR asks you if you are sure you want to assign the controls you adjusted. Click Yes.

The control knobs you created appear below the synth in the Synth Rack. You can now adjust these knobs, and doing this will change the associated parameters in the synth.

> **ASSIGN CONTROLS MENU:** Instead of using the Assign Synth Controls button, you can simply right-click in the controls area beneath a synth and choose a parameter to create a control knob.

To edit a control knob, right-click the knob and choose one of the following options:

▷ **Grouping.** You can group more than one knob together so that they can be adjusted simultaneously. To group knobs, choose Group > *name of group* to add a knob to a group. Add multiple knobs to the same group to group them together.

▷ **Automation.** See the next section in this chapter, "Automating Synth Parameters."

▷ **Remote Control.** The Remote Control feature allows you to use an external MIDI device to control on-screen parameter knobs.

▷ **Delete Control.** To remove a control knob from the synth in the Synth Rack, choose this option.

▷ **Reassign Control.** To assign a different parameter to a control knob, choose Reassign Control > *name of the parameter* or choose Reassign Control > Assign Controls. If you use the Assign Controls method, adjust the parameter in the synths Property Page and click the Assign Synth Controls button for the synth, as described earlier.

Automating Synth Parameters

After you have created control knobs for a synth in the Synth Rack, you can automate the knobs so that a synth's parameters will change dynamically over time as a project plays. To automate a synth's control knobs in the Synth Rack, follow these steps:

1. In the Synth Rack, use the Automation Record Track parameter to specify in which track the automation data for the synth should be recorded. This defaults to the synth's own instrument track, and it's a good idea to leave it set this way for organizational purposes, but you can change it if you'd like.

2. Enable the synth's control knob(s) for automation recording. You can do this in two different ways. To enable only some of the control knobs, right-click each knob and choose Automation Write Enable from the menu. To enable all of a synth's control knobs, click the synth's Automation Write button.

3. Set the Now time to the point in the project at which you would like to start recording automation.

4. Start project recording or playback. Automation can be recorded during either situation.

5. Adjust the control knob(s) for the synth in the Synth Rack.

6. When you are finished, stop project recording or playback. Also, make sure the synth's Automation Read parameter is activated (it's on by default).

7. Set the Now time back to its original position and start project playback. If you don't like the automation that you recorded, go through Steps 3 through 6 again.

8. If you like the recorded automation, click the synth's Automation Write button to disable automation recording for all the control knobs.

After you've recorded some automation for a synth, you'll notice that SONAR creates automation envelopes in the synth's instrument track. The envelopes can be edited and adjusted in a variety of ways. See Chapter 12 for more detailed information on recording automation as well as envelopes.

> **THE DREAMSTATION SYNTH:** Because the DreamStation synth included with SONAR is a legacy plug-in and is not installed by default, I'm not including it here. Instead, I have created an online demo video that covers the basics of using the synth. Go to **garrigus.com?DreamStation** to view it.

The Cakewalk TTS-1

SONAR ships with a number of soft synths, one of which is the Cakewalk TTS-1. This soft synth is multitimbral (meaning it can play more than one different sound at a time and up to 16 different sounds), has a polyphony of 128 voices (meaning it can play up to 128 notes at a time), and comes with 256 built-in sounds, as well as nine different drum sets. You can also change the built-in sounds and save up to 512 user sounds and 128 user drum sets if you'd like.

TTS-1 Basics

If you examine the main interface for the TTS-1, you'll notice that it provides 16 parts—one part for each of the 16 available MIDI channels. Part 1 corresponds to MIDI channel 1, Part 2 to MIDI channel 2, and so on. Each part provides a number of adjustable parameters. These parameters include the instrument, volume, pan, reverb, and chorus.

Selecting Instruments

Instruments refers to the sounds, programs, or patches the TTS-1 provides. To assign an instrument to a part, click the name of the current patch located to the right of the volume fader for that part and choose an instrument (see Figure 8.5).

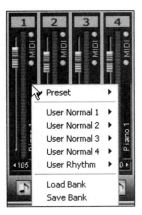

Figure 8.5 Click the name of the current patch to choose an instrument for a part.
Source: Cakewalk®, Inc.

To test the instrument and hear what it sounds like, click the Preview button for the part (see Figure 8.6). The button is located at the bottom of the Part column and displays a musical note symbol.

Figure 8.6 To test the sound of the instrument, click the part's Preview button.
Source: Cakewalk®, Inc.

Adjusting Volume and Pan

To adjust the Volume and Pan parameters for each part, follow these steps:

1. Each part has a volume fader (slider). In the Level section, click and drag the fader up or down to increase or decrease the volume. You can also double-click the numeric value, shown at the bottom of the fader, to type in a new volume level.
2. Each part also has a pan knob. Click and drag your mouse over the pan knob up or down to change the panning for that part (see Figure 8.7). Drag up to pan right and down to pan left. You can also double-click the numeric value located just below the pan knob to type in a new panning value.

Figure 8.7 Drag the part's pan knob up or down to change the panning for that part.
Source: Cakewalk®, Inc.

3. To set either the volume or pan for a part back to its default value, double-click the volume fader or pan knob, respectively.

Applying Effects

In addition, the TTS-1 provides effects that you can apply to each part individually. This gives you much more flexibility than if you were to apply SONAR's effects because, with the TTS-1 effects, you can apply a different amount of effect to each part. With SONAR's effects, you would have to apply them to all the parts in the same amount because you would be assigning the effects to the soft synth track to which the TTS-1 was assigned.

Assigning effects to parts works in exactly the same way as adjusting the Pan parameter. To add reverb to a part, just click and drag up or down on the part's reverb knob (located in the Reverb section) to increase or decrease the reverb value, respectively. To add chorus to a part, just click and drag up or down on the part's chorus knob (located in the Chorus section) to increase or decrease the chorus value, respectively.

The only difference when adding effects is that each effect provides a number of variations. Each part cannot have its own effect variation; all parts use the same effect variation. To change the variation of an effect, just click the Effect button, which is located on the right side of the TTS-1 window (see Figure 8.8).

Figure 8.8 Choose effect variations by clicking the Effect button.
Source: Cakewalk®, Inc.

Clicking the Effect button opens the Effects window, which chooses how the chorus and reverb effects will sound. You can choose a chorus and reverb type, as well as adjust various other parameters, to change the characteristics of the effects.

SAVE INSTRUMENTATION PRESETS: You can set some of the TTS-1 parameters by simply setting the corresponding MIDI track parameters. For instance, by changing the Volume, Pan, Bank, Patch, Chorus, and Reverb parameters of the MIDI track driving one of the TTS-1 parts, you can control the level, pan, instrument, chorus effect, and reverb effect parameters for that part. When you save your project, those parameters are stored along with it. But there is an advantage to adjusting parameters within the TTS-1 itself. You can save all the TTS-1 parameters as a preset using the Presets menu and Preset Save and Delete buttons located at the top of the TTS-1 window. By saving a number of parameter configurations as presets, you can switch quickly between configurations to test out different instrumentation for the project on which you are working.

Multiple Outputs

In the previous section, I mentioned that when you apply SONAR's effects to the TTS-1, you have to apply the same effect to all the parts because they share the same soft synth track. This isn't entirely true. The TTS-1 provides four separate audio outputs to which you can assign any of the 16 available parts. Each TTS-1 output gets its own soft synth track, so you could essentially separate the 16 parts into four different groups, each of which can use its own set of SONAR effects. This can come in handy if you want to apply one type of effect to your drum instruments, another type of effect to your guitar instruments, and so on.

Earlier, I talked about how to set up a soft synth to use multiple outputs in a project, but you still need to set up the internal parameters of the synth, and this procedure is different for each synth. To designate the parts that are assigned to the four available outputs in the TTS-1, follow these steps:

1. In the TTS-1, click the System button (located on the right side of the window) to open the System Settings dialog box. Then click the Option button to open the Options dialog box.
2. Under the Output Assign tab, you'll see the part numbers listed in two columns and the output numbers shown to the right of each part. To assign a part to a specific output, line up your mouse with the part number and the output, and then click at that grid point to make the assignment.
3. If you want to reset all part assignments to output 1, click the Reset button.
4. You can turn on or off multiple outputs by using the Use Multiple Outputs option. This keeps your grid assignments intact if you want to send all parts to output 1 temporarily. Click Close.

> **TTS-1 DEMO VIDEO:** To see a demonstration of the TTS-1 in action, go to **garrigus.com?TTS-1** to watch the video.

The Roland GrooveSynth

Similar to the Cakewalk TTS-1, the Roland GrooveSynth is a soft synth that provides a large collection of preprogrammed sounds and drum sets. You can also change the built-in sounds and save them as presets for future use. The Roland GrooveSynth, however, is single-timbral and can only play one synth sound or one drum set at a time. In this regard, it is similar to the DreamStation, where if you want to play more than one sound at the same time, you have to set up multiple instances of the synth.

Working with Synth Sounds

The Roland GrooveSynth can be set up to provide either a single synth sound or a single drum kit for playback. To set up the GrooveSynth to provide a single synth sound for playback, do the following:

1. Click the Sound Name display and choose a sound from the menu (see Figure 8.9). This sets the synth sound that will be played by the GrooveSynth.

Figure 8.9 Use the Sound Name display to choose a synth sound.
Source: Cakewalk®, Inc.

2. To adjust the volume and panning for the sound, use the Level and Pan parameters shown on the right side of the GrooveSynth window. To change these parameters, either click and drag the knobs up and down with your mouse or double-click the numeric displays and enter a new value.

3. To adjust the characteristics of the sound and create a unique sound of your own, adjust the other available parameters shown in the GrooveSynth window.

4. To save your sound, type a name for the sound in the Presets field (at the top of the window) and click the Save button (the one with a floppy disk shown on it).

5. Use the Presets list to load your sound any time you want to use it.

6. If you ever want to delete one of your sounds, just select it from the Presets menu and click the Delete button (the one with a red X shown on it).

The GrooveSynth is now ready to play the synth sound that you chose or created.

Working with Drum Kits

In addition to synth sounds, the GrooveSynth provides a number of drum kits. It can be used to play one kit at a time. You can adjust the overall sound of the entire kit, as well as the sound of each individual drum instrument in the kit. To set up the GrooveSynth to provide a single drum kit for playback, do the following:

1. Click the Sound Name display and choose a sound from the menu. In this case, move your mouse to the bottom of the menu and choose a kit from the Rhythm Set category. You'll notice that the GrooveSynth now displays its Rhythm Edit view.

2. To adjust the volume and panning for the entire drum kit, use the Level and Pan parameters shown on the right side of the window.

3. To adjust the characteristics of the entire drum kit, you can adjust the parameters in the Tone and Filter sections of the window.

4. To adjust the characteristics of a single drum sound in the kit, first choose the drum sound you would like to edit by clicking the Drum Name display in the center of the window and selecting a sound from the menu (see Figure 8.10). This menu will also show you the corresponding pitch for each of the drum sounds in the kit, so you will know what pitches to use when composing your drum tracks.

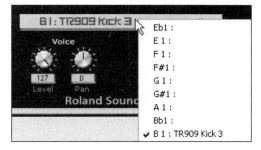

Figure 8.10 Use the Drum Name display to choose a drum sound from the selected drum kit.
Source: Cakewalk®, Inc.

5. To adjust the characteristics of the individual drum sound (such as volume, panning, and tuning), adjust the parameters in the Voice and Tune section shown in the center of the GrooveSynth window. You can make these adjustments for each of the individual drum sounds in the kit, which gives you a lot of flexibility over the sound of your drum tracks.

6. To save your drum kit, type a name for the kit in the Presets field and click the Save button (the one with a floppy disk shown on it).

7. Use the Presets menu to load your kit any time you want to use it.

8. If you ever want to delete a kit, just select it from the Presets menu and click the Delete button (the one with a red X shown on it).

The GrooveSynth is now ready to play the drum kit that you chose or created.

GROOVESYNTH DEMO VIDEO: To see a demonstration of the GrooveSynth in action, go to **garrigus. com?GrooveSynth** to watch the video.

The Pentagon I

Like the DreamStation, the Pentagon I simulates an analog modular synth. Also like the DreamStation, the Pentagon I can only play one sound at a time, which means that to use more than one sound, you need to load multiple instances of the synth.

The Pentagon I provides four oscillator modules; two amplifier modules; two filter modules; four LFO (*low-frequency oscillator*) modules; pitch and portamento features; built-in chorus, delay, and EQ effects; and controls pertaining to synth output, such as volume and panning. By adjusting the controls provided by each of the modules, you can create your own unique synthesizer sounds just like you would with a hardware-based analog synth.

Loading and Saving Programs

The Pentagon I sounds are called *programs*. You can save and load programs for your own use, and you also can share programs with others.

Loading Pentagon I Programs

To load programs for use in the Pentagon I, do the following:

1. To load a program, click one of the Bank buttons located at the top of the Pentagon I window. Programs are organized into six banks labeled A, B, C, D, E, and F (see Figure 8.11).

Figure 8.11 Use the Bank buttons to select a bank of programs from which to choose.
Source: Cakewalk®, Inc.

2. Click the up and down arrows in the Program area (located in the upper-right corner of the window) to cycle through the programs in the selected bank.

QUICK PROGRAM SELECTION: An easier way to select a program from a bank is to right-click anywhere in the Pentagon I window and choose a program from the menu.

---

3. Audition the program by dragging your mouse in the dark-colored strip located at the bottom of the Pentagon I window. Click and hold your left mouse button and drag your mouse within the strip to hear how the current program sounds. Click in the left half of the strip to hear low notes played and click in the right half of the strip to hear high notes played.

4. You can also load programs from files on disk. To do so, left-click over the Pentagon I name and choose Program > Load Program from the menu (see Figure 8.12).

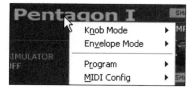

Figure 8.12 Use the Program menu to load programs from files on disk.
Source: Cakewalk®, Inc.

5. In the Load Program dialog box, choose a program file and click Open to load the program into the current program slot of the current bank.
6. You can also load entire banks of programs from files on disk. To do so, left-click the Pentagon I name and choose Program > Load Bank from the menu.
7. In the Load Program Bank dialog box, choose a bank file and click Open to load the bank file into the currently selected bank.

Saving Pentagon I Programs

To save programs for use in the Pentagon I, do the following:

1. Choose a bank into which you would like to save your new program.
2. Choose a program slot in the bank into which you would like to save your new program.
3. Create the new program by adjusting the synth parameters.
4. Name the new program by clicking in the Program area and typing a new name (see Figure 8.13). Press Enter to finish.

Figure 8.13 Name your new program by using the Program area in the Pentagon I window.
Source: Cakewalk®, Inc.

5. To save your new program as an individual file, left-click the Pentagon I name and choose Program > Save Program.
6. In the Save Program dialog box, type in a name for the program file and click Save.
7. To save your program as part of the currently selected bank, left-click the Pentagon I name and choose Program > Save Bank.
8. In the Save Program Bank dialog box, type a name for the bank file and click Save.

Using these procedures, you can create and save your own programs for future use, as well as share with other Pentagon I users.

The PSYN II

Like the DreamStation, the PSYN II simulates an analog modular synth. Also, like the DreamStation, the PSYN II can only play one sound at a time, which means that to use more than one sound, you need to load multiple instances of the synth.

The PSYN II provides four oscillator modules; a sub-oscillator; two filter modules; three LFO (*low-frequency oscillator*) modules; five Envelope Generators; pitch and portamento features; built-in drive, delay, and modulation effects; and controls pertaining to synth output, such as volume and panning. By adjusting the controls provided by each of the modules, you can create your own unique synthesizer sounds just like you would with a hardware-based analog synth.

Loading and Saving Programs

The PSYN II sounds are called *programs*. You can save and load programs for your own use, and you also can share programs with others.

Loading PSYN II Programs

To load programs for use in the PSYN II, do the following:

1. To load a program, click one of the Bank buttons located in the lower-left corner of the PSYN II window. Programs are organized into eight banks labeled A, B, C, D, E, F, G, and H (see Figure 8.14).

Figure 8.14 Use the Bank buttons to select a bank of programs from which to choose.
Source: Cakewalk®, Inc.

2. Left-click or right-click the Program Name display (located just below the Bank buttons) to cycle through the programs in the selected bank.
3. You can also load programs from files on disk. To do so, click the Disk button and choose Load Program from the menu (see Figure 8.15).

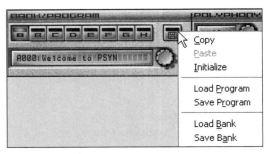

Figure 8.15 Use the Disk button menu to load programs from files on disk.
Source: Cakewalk®, Inc.

4. In the Load Program File dialog box, choose a program file and click Open to load the program into the current program slot of the current bank.
5. You can also load entire banks of programs from files on disk. To do so, click the Disk button and choose Load Bank.
6. In the Load Program Bank File dialog box, choose a bank file and click Open to load the bank file into the currently selected bank.

Saving PSYN II Programs

To save programs for use in the PSYN II, do the following:

1. Choose a bank in which you would like to save your new program.
2. Choose a program slot in the bank into which you would like to save your new program.
3. Create the new program by adjusting the synth parameters.
4. Name the new program by holding down the Shift key, clicking in the Program Name display, and typing a new name (see Figure 8.16). Press Tab to finish.

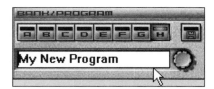

Figure 8.16 Name your new program by using the Program Name display in the PSYN II window.
Source: Cakewalk®, Inc.

5. To save your new program as an individual file, click the Disk button and choose Save Program.
6. In the Save Program File dialog box, type in a name for the program file and click Save.
7. To save your program as part of the currently selected bank, click the Disk button and choose Save Bank.
8. In the Save Program Bank File dialog box, type a name for the bank file and click Save.

Using these procedures, you can create and save your own programs for future use, as well as share with other PSYN II users.

> **MORE PSYN II INFORMATION:** For more information about the PSYN II, left-click once anywhere inside the PSYN II window and then press the F1 key to open the PSYN II Help file.

The Cyclone

The Cyclone is the equivalent of a very powerful MIDI sample playback device. Like the TTS-1, the Cyclone is multitimbral (meaning it can play more than one different sound at a time—up to 16), but instead of having built-in sounds, the Cyclone loads in your own sounds in the form of audio sample loops in the WAV file format.

Cyclone Basics

If you examine the main interface for the Cyclone, you'll notice that it provides 16 parts (called *Pad Groups*), with one Pad Group for each of the 16 available MIDI channels: Pad Group 1 for MIDI channel 1, Pad Group 2 for MIDI channel 2, and so on (although you can assign any MIDI channel to any Pad Group if you want).

Each Pad Group provides a number of adjustable parameters, which include Sample File Load, Volume, Pan, Sync, Loop, Mute, and Solo (see Figure 8.17).

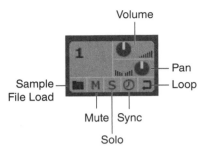

Figure 8.17 Each Pad Group provides some adjustable parameters.
Source: Cakewalk®, Inc.

Loading Sample Files

To load a sample file into a Pad Group, click the Load button. Then select a WAV file in the Open dialog box and click Open. If you want to remove a file from a Pad Group later, right-click the Pad Group and choose Clear Pad from the menu.

LOOP BIN LOADING

When you load a sample file into a Pad Group, the sample file is listed in the Loop Bin as well (see Figure 8.18).

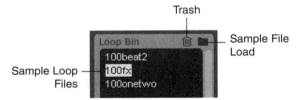

Figure 8.18 Sample files loaded into Pad Groups are also listed in the Loop Bin.
Source: Cakewalk®, Inc.

The Loop Bin lists all the sample files in the current Cyclone Sound Bank. You can load sample files into the Loop Bin separately and then apply them to Pad Groups later if you want. Just click the Loop Bin Load button, choose a sample file in the Open dialog box, and click Open. To apply a sample file from the Loop Bin to a Pad Group, drag and drop the file from the Loop Bin onto the Pad Group.

> **USE THE BROWSER OR TRACK VIEW:** You also can use the Browser to apply sample files to Pad Groups. Just drag and drop files from the Media section of the Browser onto the appropriate Pad Groups. In addition, you can drag and drop audio clips directly from the Track view.

If you want to delete a file from the Loop Bin, select the file and click the Trash button. If you delete a file that is being used by any of the Pad Groups from the Loop Bin, that file will be deleted from those Pad Groups as well.

PREVIEWING SAMPLE FILES

To preview a sample file listed in the Loop Bin, just select the file and click the Preview button on the Cyclone toolbar (see Figure 8.19).

Preview   Stop

Figure 8.19 Preview sample files using the Preview button on the Cyclone toolbar.
Source: Cakewalk®, Inc.

To stop the sample file preview, click the Stop button. You also can preview a sample file that's already loaded into a Pad Group by clicking the number of the Pad Group. Click the number of the Pad Group a second time to stop playback.

Adjusting Pad Group Parameters

To adjust the Volume, Pan, Mute, Solo, Sync, and Loop parameters for each Pad Group, do the following:

▷ **Volume and Pan.** Click and hold your mouse on the on-screen knob; then drag your mouse up or down to raise or lower the value. If you want to reset the parameter to its default value, just double-click it.

▷ **Mute and Solo.** To mute or solo a Pad Group, just click the Mute or Solo button.

▷ **Sync.** Activating the Sync parameter will synchronize the playback tempo of the sample file loaded into the Pad Group with the playback tempo of the current SONAR project.

▷ **Loop.** Activating the Loop parameter will loop the playback of the sample file loaded into the Pad Group so that the file keeps repeating.

The Pad Inspector

Each Pad Group also provides a number of other adjustable parameters, which are accessed via the Pad Inspector (located on the right side of the window). To see the Pad Inspector parameter values for a Pad Group, just click the number of the Pad Group.

OUTPUT

Like the TTS-1, the Cyclone provides multiple audio outputs (up to 17: 16 individual outputs and one mix output). Each Pad Group can be assigned to its own separate output using the Output parameter. If you choose the Mix Only option, the sound from the Pad Group will be sent only to the mix output, which contains a mix of all the sounds coming from all the Pad Groups in Cyclone.

MIDI IN

As I mentioned earlier, Cyclone can play up to 16 different sounds at once, with each one assigned to its own MIDI channel. Use the MIDI In parameter to assign a MIDI input channel to a Pad Group. Then any MIDI data coming into that channel will be used to trigger playback of that Pad Group. If you choose the MIDI Omni option, then the Pad Group will receive MIDI data from all 16 MIDI channels.

ROOT

The Root parameter determines the original pitch of the sample file loaded into a Pad Group. If you load an ACID-compatible WAV file or a SONAR Groove clip WAV file into a Pad Group, the Root parameter will be set for you automatically. If you load a regular WAV file into a Pad Group, you will have to determine the pitch of the file yourself and set the Root parameter manually.

Velocity and Key Map

When a Pad Group receives MIDI note messages via its assigned MIDI channel, those MIDI note messages trigger the playback of the sample file loaded into the Pad Group. You can limit the range of notes and their velocities that can be used to trigger the Pad Group by setting the Velocity and Key Map parameters as follows:

> ▷ **Velocity Low.** Set this to the lowest note velocity value that you want to trigger the Pad Group.
> ▷ **Velocity High.** Set this to the highest note velocity value that you want to trigger the Pad Group.
> ▷ **Key Map Unity.** Set this to the note value that will be used to play the sample file in the Pad Group at its Root pitch. Most of the time, you'll probably set this parameter to the same pitch value as the Root parameter.
> ▷ **Key Map Low.** Set this to the lowest note value that you want to trigger the Pad Group.
> ▷ **Key Map High.** Set this to the highest note value that you want to trigger the Pad Group.

Pitch Markers

I talked about pitch markers in Chapter 9. They are used to change the pitch of Groove clips in a project. You also can use them to change the pitch of Pad Groups throughout a project. If your project uses pitch markers, and you want your Pad Groups to change pitch along with the markers, activate the Pitch Markers option for the Pad Groups in the Pad Inspector.

The Loop View

When you select a sample file listed in the Loop Bin, its audio waveform is displayed in the Loop view section of the Cyclone main interface (located in the middle of the window).

If the selected sample file is an ACID-compatible loop or a SONAR Groove clip, then the Loop view will display any slices contained in the file as well; these slices are designated by vertical dotted lines shown on the audio waveform.

> **SLICES IN CYCLONE:** When you open a Groove clip in the Loop Construction view, you'll notice that SONAR breaks the clip down into small sections. These sections are called *slices*. Slices are based on the beat values and audio waveform spikes (transients) in a clip. They allow SONAR to accurately change the tempo and pitch of a Groove clip. In Cyclone, however, you can use slices to break sample files apart and create new sample files by combining the slices from several different files. This is where the Pad Editor comes into play.

The Pad Editor

When you load a sample file into a Pad Group, a track for that Pad Group is created in the Pad Editor (located in the bottom section of the window). This track contains green blocks, with each separate block representing a different slice in the sample file. At the end of the track is a white track handle that marks the point in the track at which the track will loop back to the beginning.

Using the Pad Editor, you can select, change, and edit slices to create entire compositions out of nothing but sample file slices if you want.

Selecting a Slice

To select a slice, just click its associated green block. If you want to select more than one slice, hold down the Shift key as you click the blocks. Also, to select all the slices in a track, double-click the track number.

THE SLICE INSPECTOR

You can edit the parameters of a slice using the Slice Inspector. Each slice has adjustable pitch, gain (volume), and panning. Just select the slice you want to change and then click and drag your mouse over the parameter knobs. You also can change the settings by double-clicking the numerical values and typing in new values.

CHANGING SLICES

You can change slices in a track by deleting them, moving them, or swapping them with slices from a different sample file. To delete a slice, just select it and press the Delete key.

You can move slices by clicking and dragging them with your mouse. To move a slice within the same track, click and drag the slice left or right. To move a slice to a different track, click and drag the slice up or down.

To swap a slice with another slice from a different file, first select a sample file in the Loop Bin so that its audio waveform is shown in the Loop view. Then click and drag a slice from the Loop view into the Pad Editor (see Figure 8.20).

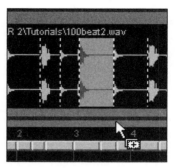

Figure 8.20 Click and drag slices from the Loop view into the Pad Editor to swap slices.
Source: Cakewalk®, Inc.

> **CYCLONE DEMO VIDEO:** To see a demonstration of the Cyclone in action, go to **garrigus.com?Cyclone-Synth** to watch the video.

RXP REX Player

Like the Cyclone, the RXP is a MIDI sample playback synth, but instead of loading ACID-compatible WAV files, it loads REX files. Another difference is that although the RXP can only load one file at a time, that doesn't mean it can only play one sound at a time. Instead of playing multiple files simultaneously, it plays multiple slices of a single file. In this capacity, it can be used as a drum machine, multiple-sound generator, sound editor, and more.

> **REX FILES:** REX files are similar to ACID-compatible sample loops or Cakewalk Groove clips in that they are divided into slices, which allows their timing and pitch to be changed without degrading the audio data. This means that REX files can be played as loops, which are synced to the tempo of your project. In addition to loop playback, however, REX files provide slice playback. This is where a REX file is loaded into a player, and the individual slices within the file are triggered by MIDI notes. Using sliced playback, REX files provide dynamic sample playback options, including being able to trigger different instrument sounds (such as those in a drum kit).

RXP Basics

If you examine the main interface for the RXP (see Figure 8.21), you'll notice that it is divided into three sections—the Waveform and Slice Display, the Filter (EQ) and Amp (Volume/Pan) section, and the Pad section.

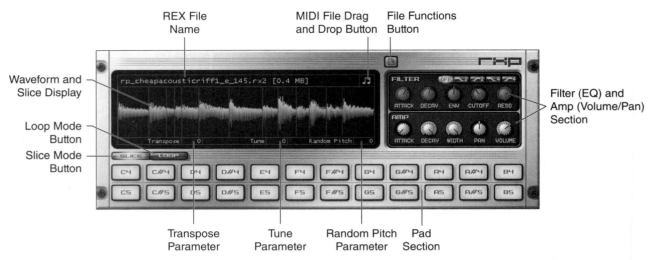

Figure 8.21 You can adjust the RXP parameters by using its main interface.
Source: Cakewalk®, Inc.

The Waveform and Slice Display shows the currently loaded REX file. The RXP can only load one file at a time, which means that in Loop mode, you would need to use multiple instances of the RXP to play more than one file at a time. In Slice mode, multiple slices from the one loaded file can be triggered simultaneously.

The Pad section allows you to play/preview the entire REX file in Loop mode or individual slices in Slice mode. I'll show you how this is done shortly.

Finally, the Filter and Amp section allows you to apply equalization and volume/pan changes to the entire REX file. You cannot make changes to individual slices.

Loading Sample Files

To load a sample file into RXP, click the File Functions button and choose Load from the menu. In the Load Multisample dialog box, select the file you want to load and click Open.

> **MULTIPLE FILE FORMATS:** You may have noticed in the Load Multisample dialog box that RXP supports many different audio file formats. REX files have a file extension of RX2. If you load something other than a REX file, it will be loaded and can be played as a loop in RXP, but slicing will not be supported. RXP will act as a simple audio loop player when loading files other than the REX format.

In addition to using the File Functions button, you can click the REX filename in the RXP window to open the Groove Browser. The Groove Browser allows you to view the files you have stored in the C:\Program Files\Cakewalk \Shared DXi\RXP\Contents folder on your hard drive. Click the plus sign next to a folder to open that folder. Double-click a file to load and preview that file in RXP automatically.

> **USE THE BROWSER OR TRACK VIEW:** You can also use the Browser to load files into RXP. Just drag and drop files from the Browser onto the Waveform and Slice Display in RXP. In addition, you can drag and drop audio clips from the Track view.

Previewing Sample Files

Once loaded, you can preview and play files in two different modes: Loop and Slice. To preview a file, do the following:

1. Click the Loop or the Slice button to activate the appropriate mode.
2. In Loop mode, you'll notice that the pads in the Pad area are labeled with numbers. These are pitch transposition numbers. To play the file at its normal pitch, click the 0 pad. To play the file at a lower or higher pitch, click one of the negative- or positive-numbered pads, respectively. If you left-click a pad, you can control partial playback by holding down your mouse button and then letting it go to stop playback. Right-click a pad to play the entire file.
3. In Slice mode, you'll notice that the pads are labeled with musical note values. Each pad corresponds to an individual slice in the file. Left-click or right-click a pad to hear its associated slice played. This also shows you which MIDI note each slice will respond to when using a MIDI file to trigger slices.
4. To hear the file played at a different tempo, change the tempo of your SONAR project because the RXP follows the project tempo for all playback.

> **EASY SLICE PREVIEW:** To preview a slice in either mode, just left-click the slice in the Waveform and Slice Display.

Editing, Saving, and Loading Programs

While the RXP doesn't allow you to edit and save REX files directly, you can edit and save the RXP settings, which are called *programs*. These settings include all of the Filter and Amp section parameters, as well as the slice positions and the Transpose, Tune, and Random Pitch parameters in the Waveform and Slice Display. All of these parameters affect the entire file rather than individual slices.

EDITING PROGRAMS

The Filter and Amp parameters apply EQ and volume/panning to the file. To adjust a parameter in one of these sections, click and drag your mouse up or down over the graphic knob. To return a parameter to its default setting, double-click the graphic knob.

To transpose, tune, or apply random pitch changes to the file, use the appropriate parameters located in the bottom of the Waveform and Slice Display. To adjust a parameter, click and drag your mouse up or down over the parameter value. To return a parameter to its default setting, double-click its value. The Transpose parameter transposes the file by +48 or –48 semitones. The Tune parameter fine-tunes the file by +100 or –100 cents. The Random Pitch parameter can be adjusted from 0 to 4800 cents and applies a random pitch change to each slice as the file is played.

In addition to editing the previously mentioned parameters, you can also change the position of slices in a file. Just click and drag a slice left or right to change its playback position in the file. This is also the way to change a slice's assigned MIDI note trigger. If you start making a mess of things and want to return to the original slice positions, right-click in the display and choose Reset from the pop-up menu. You can also reverse or randomize the slice positions by right-clicking in the display and choosing the appropriate option from the menu.

To clear the current file and return all parameters to their default values, click the File Functions button and choose Initialize Program.

SAVING AND LOADING PROGRAMS

Moving slices in a file or changing parameters doesn't actually change the file itself. This simply changes a pointer in the RXP program, and when saved, the program saves these pointers to the original REX file. This means that even when you save a program, you still need to keep the original REX file on hand in order for the program to be of any use. It also means that you can create and save multiple programs for the same REX file without taking up much disk space, which provides a lot of flexibility.

To save a program, click the File Functions button and choose Save Program As from the menu. In the Save Program dialog box, type a name for your new program and then click Save. Programs are saved with a Prog filename extension. After having saved a new program, you can quickly save it again (after making parameter changes) by clicking the File Functions button and choosing Save Program. In addition, you can set a default program (one that will be loaded every time you open the RXP) by clicking the File Functions button and choosing Save Program Default.

To load a previously saved program, click the File Functions button and choose Load. In the Load Multisample dialog box, select the program you want to load and click Open. This will load the program parameters, as well as its associated REX file.

> **RXP DEMO VIDEO:** To see a demonstration of the RXP in action, go to **garrigus.com?RXPSynth** to watch the video.

> **MORE RXP INFORMATION:** For more information about the RXP, left-click once anywhere inside the RXP window and then press the F1 key to open the RXP Help file.

TruePianos (Amber Module)

The TruePianos soft synth is a high-quality virtual instrument that simulates the sound of a real acoustic piano. Using TruePianos is as easy as inserting it into a project and starting to play; however, it does provides some settings so you can tweak the sound to your liking.

Basic Interface

When you add TruePianos to your project, you'll see the TruePianos window open with a picture representing a grand piano. You can click on the piano keys with your mouse to audition the sound, and the piano keys will animate when you play your MIDI controller.

The toolbar at the bottom of the window provides a number of settings you can adjust with your mouse, including Module and Preset. The Cakewalk Edition of TruePianos only provides the Amber module, but if you upgrade to the full version, you can access additional modules by clicking the name or arrows next to the Module label. Clicking the name or arrows next to the Preset label chooses the different piano characteristics available in the Amber module. For example, if you want a bright piano sound, choose the Bright preset, and so on.

Global Options

On the toolbar, click Options to display the Options dialog box. These TruePiano options are stored globally for the synth itself, rather than each individual SONAR project. So adjustments you make here will be used every time you insert the synth into any project. If you have a powerful PC, then the first three options should almost always remain activated.

The Increased Polyphony option allows you to have more notes sound simultaneously, so complex piano parts won't have their notes get cut off during playback. The Multi-CPU Engine option allows your PC to share the load between multiple processors for more efficiency and should be used if you have a dual-, quad- or any multiple-core processor. If you have problems with clicks in playback, however, you can try deactivating this option. The Sympathetic Resonance option simulates the vibration of piano strings when the sustain pedal is held down. The only time you might want to deactivate this option is if you need a really clean, sharp piano sound, as in electronic or techno music.

The Keyboard Dynamics option is an adjustable slider that conforms TruePianos to your style of playing and to your MIDI controller. If you have a very light touch when playing your keyboard, move the slider to the left to set a negative value, which will make TruePianos respond with a brighter and louder sound. If you have a heavy touch when playing your keyboard, move the slider to the right to set a positive value, which will make TruePianos respond with a softer sound. To save these settings, click Save Current Plug-in State as Default and click Close.

Advanced Interface

In the toolbar, click Advanced Interface to display the advanced settings provided by TruePianos.

The Module and Preset sections are equivalent to the toolbar settings, allowing you to choose modules and presets for the piano tone you need. The rest of the settings in the Advanced Interface are adjusted by dragging sliders with your mouse or by clicking on the numbers and typing in new values. You can also double-click any slider to return it to its default value. In addition, TruePianos provides a built-in reverb effect. In the Reverb section, you can adjust any amount of reverb you want with the Amount slider and the size of the environment with the Room Size slider. (See Chapter 11 for more information about reverberation and how it works.)

The settings in the Velocity Control section let you adjust how TruePianos reacts to your playing. The Keyboard Dynamics slider is the same as the one I described in the Options dialog box. However, this slider setting gets saved with the project, while the other slider setting is global. This allows you to have different settings for each project. The Velocity Floor and Velocity Threshold sliders work in conjunction with the Keyboard Dynamics slider to affect the shape of the Velocity Control graph. Moving the Velocity Floor slider up raises the velocity floor, which means that you can press the keys on your keyboard very lightly but get a louder sound out of them. Moving the Velocity Threshold to the right raises the velocity threshold, which means you have to press the keys on your keyboard harder in order to hear any sound out of True Pianos. Most of the time, I leave the Velocity Floor and Velocity Threshold values at their defaults and only adjust the Keyboard Dynamics slider.

The A4 Pitch sliders adjust the tuning of TruePianos, which by default is tuned to A440, but these settings allow you to use the synth in conjunction with other synths that may be tuned differently. The Release slider adjusts how long the notes continue to sound after you release them. Adjust the slider to the left for a shorter release and right for a longer release. And finally, the Output Level slider adjusts the volume output level of TruePianos.

MORE TRUEPIANOS INFO: Go to **www.truepianos.com/downloads.php** to download the PDF manual for more information about TruePianos.

ReWire

In addition to DX and VST instruments, there are software-based synthesizers that run as separate applications. This means that normally they cannot be connected in any way to a sequencing application such as SONAR. If, however, the software synth application supports a technology called *ReWire*, the synth can be used within SONAR, almost exactly like a soft synth.

ReWire is a virtual connection technology that allows two different music applications to connect to one another and share audio data, synchronize their internal clocks, and share transport control. For example, Cakewalk's Project5 software synthesizer studio (now discontinued) supports ReWire. Project5 provides built-in synthesis and sequencing features. When ReWired with SONAR, you can stream audio from Project5 to SONAR just like you would with a soft synth. In addition, the sequencer aspects in both Project5 and SONAR are completely synchronized, meaning that the Now time in SONAR would correspond to the same sequencer time in Project5. And both applications share common transport functions, meaning that using the Play, Stop, and Rewind functions in one application trigger those same functions in the other application. The ReWire technology is very powerful and allows you to use SONAR with any other ReWire-compatible application on the market.

As far as using the ReWire functions in SONAR—to be honest, there really isn't much more I can say that isn't already covered in the SONAR Help file. Instead of just rehashing the same information, I recommend that you read through the ReWire information in the file. If you have questions, go to **www.digifreq.com/digifreq/**, and don't be afraid to post them in the discussion area of my DigiFreq music technology website.

> **MORE REWIRE INFO:** For more information about the ReWire technology in general, be sure to visit **http://www.propellerheads.se/products/reason/index.cfm?fuseaction=get_article&article=rewire**.

SoundFonts

Most modern MIDI instruments and sound cards use sample playback to produce sounds. Sample playback can produce some very realistic sounds. The reason for this realism lies in the fact that a sample playback device plays samples, which are actually audio recordings of real-life instruments and sounds. When the sample playback device receives a MIDI Note On message, instead of creating a sound electronically from scratch, it plays a digital sample, which can be anything from the sound of a piano note to the sound of a coyote howling.

A SoundFont is a special type of digital sample format that works only with a SoundFont-compatible sound card. Creative Labs, the makers of the ever-popular Sound Blaster line of sound cards, developed the SoundFont format. For more information about Sound Blaster sound cards, check out **www.soundblaster.com**. For more information about SoundFonts, go to **www.digifreq.com/digifreq/article.asp?ID=32** to read the article entitled "Using SoundFonts in Your Computer Music Studio." And be sure to visit **www.digifreq.com/digifreq/articles.asp** for more great music technology articles.

Using the sfz SoundFont Player

SONAR allows you to use SoundFonts via the sfz SoundFont Player. To use the sfz, follow these steps:

1. Create a new project or open a pre-existing project and insert the SFZ soft synth. The sfz window opens (see Figure 8.22).

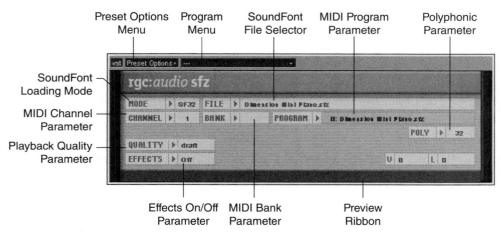

Figure 8.22 Use the sfz SoundFont Player to play SoundFonts within SONAR.
Source: Cakewalk®, Inc.

2. In the sfz window, click the arrow next to the SoundFont Loading Mode parameter and choose a loading mode from the menu.

SOUNDFONT LOADING MODES: For more information about SoundFont loading modes, go to **www. cakewalk.com/DevXchange/sfz.asp** to read the sfz FAQ (Frequently Asked Questions) page.

---

3. Click the SoundFont File Selector and choose the SoundFont you want to use. Click Open.
4. You can set up each of the MIDI channels with different bank, program, and polyphony settings. Use the MIDI Channel parameter to set the MIDI channel. Use the MIDI Bank parameter to set the bank for the channel. Use the MIDI Program parameter to set the program for the bank.
5. Use the Polyphonic parameter to set the polyphony for the MIDI channel. This parameter limits the number of voices that can be played simultaneously. The lowest setting is 1, and the highest setting is 256. If you experience playback problems, you might want to try lowering this parameter to take some of the strain off your computer processor.
6. You can use the internal chorus and reverb effects (if the SoundFont is programmed to use them) by setting the Effects parameter to either on or off.
7. Use the Playback Quality parameter to determine both the quality of the sound and the amount of computer processing power consumed during playback. Setting this parameter to Draft provides the lowest quality of playback but the least amount of strain on your computer processor.
8. Audition the SoundFont by dragging your mouse in the Preview Ribbon located at the bottom of the sfz window. Click and hold your left mouse button and drag your mouse within the strip to hear how the current program sounds. Click in the left half of the strip to hear low notes played, and click in the right half of the strip to hear high notes played.
9. If you opened a pre-existing project that already contains MIDI tracks, you can skip this step. Otherwise, right-click in the Track pane of the Track view and choose Insert MIDI Track to create a new MIDI track. Then widen the track to display its parameters.
10. Set the Input parameter to the MIDI channel that is being used to receive data from your MIDI keyboard and set the Output parameter to VST sfz.
11. Set the Channel parameter to the same MIDI channel as your MIDI keyboard. Set the Bank parameter to the same bank that contains the SoundFont you want to use for this MIDI track. Set the Patch parameter to one of the patches available in the SoundFont.
12. Repeat Steps 9 through 12 to set up any additional new or pre-existing MIDI tracks.

After you record some data in your MIDI tracks (or if the tracks already contained data), when you play the project, your MIDI tracks will drive the sfz, which, in turn, will play the appropriate sounds from the SoundFonts you have loaded.

Session Drummer 3

Like the Cyclone and RXP, Session Drummer 3 (SD3) is a MIDI sample playback synth, but it is geared toward the playback of percussion instruments. SD3 is multitimbral (meaning it can play more than one different sound at a time—up to 12), and instead of being limited to one-shot samples or sample loops, it can load multisamples, which provide very realistic playback.

Session Drummer 3 Basics

SD3 provides two interface modes, which can be switched via the Drumkit and Mixer buttons in the upper-right corner. In Drumkit mode, you can see an interactive picture of the drum kit, the File Functions, and the MIDI Pattern section.

The File Functions and MIDI Pattern section (see Figure 8.23) loads and saves programs/MIDI patterns, kits, and instruments. You also use this section to control MIDI playback. The drum kit section assigns different sounds to each instrument and previews instruments.

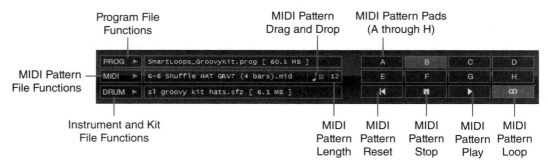

Figure 8.23 Load and save programs, patterns, kits, and instruments with these controls.
Source: Cakewalk®, Inc.

To begin working with SD3, you need to first load in some sounds, which come in the form of *instruments*. This is the name given to the sample files loaded into each instrument. A group of 12 instruments is called a *kit*. And a kit combined with Mixer settings and eight MIDI patterns (corresponding to the eight available MIDI Pattern Pads) is called a *program*. You can load/save programs, kits, and instruments.

Working with Programs

A program stores all of the SD3 parameter settings, including the currently loaded kit/instruments, the eight MIDI patterns associated with that kit, and all of the Mixer parameter values. The quickest way to start working with SD3 is simply to load an existing program. Click the Program File Functions button (PROG) to perform the following program-related tasks:

▷ **Initialize Program.** This option will clear all of SD3's parameter settings, including the currently loaded kit/ instruments and MIDI patterns.

▷ **Load Program.** Use this option to load an SD3 program. SONAR ships with a large number of predefined programs, which are located in the following hard drive folder: C:\Program Files\Cakewalk\Vstplugins\Session Drummer 3\Contents\Programs. After choosing a program, SD3 will load up a drum kit (along with the associated instruments), MIDI patterns, and Mixer settings.

▷ **Save Program or Save Program As.** If you make changes to a program (such as loading in different instruments or MIDI patterns, or changing Mixer settings), you can save your changes using these options. Use Save Program to save your changes into the same program file that you loaded. This will overwrite the existing program file. To keep the original program file and create a different file, use the Save Program As option and use a new name for the program.

▷ **Save Default Program.** Normally, when you load up SD3, it contains a blank program. If you would like a program to be automatically loaded every time you use SD3, then load a program and choose the Save Default Program option to save the current program as the default.

THE PROGRAM BROWSER: Click the program name (located to the right of the Program File Functions button) to open the Program Browser for a quick way to load an SD3 program.

Working with Kits

A kit keeps track of what instruments are loaded into each of the instrument pads. A kit does not contain any MIDI patterns or Mixer settings, so you can keep your existing MIDI patterns and Mixer settings loaded while experimenting with different drum kits. Click the Instrument and Kit File Functions button (DRUM) to perform the following kit-related tasks:

▷ **Load Instrument and Unload Instrument.** Click an instrument pad and then use one of these options to load an instrument into the selected pad or unload the current pad instrument.

▷ **Load Kit.** Use this option to load an SD3 kit. SONAR ships with a variety of drum kits, which are located in the following hard drive folder: C:\Program Files\Cakewalk\Vstplugins\Session Drummer 3\Contents\Kits. After choosing a kit, SD3 will load an instrument into each of the instrument pads. MIDI patterns and Mixer settings remain unchanged.

▷ **Save Kit or Save Kit As.** If you make changes to a kit (such as loading in different instruments), you can save your changes using these options. Use Save Kit to save your changes into the same kit file that you loaded. This will overwrite the existing kit file. To keep the original kit file and create a different file, use the Save Kit As option and use a new name for the kit.

Working with Instruments

SD3 can have up to 12 different instruments loaded at once. An instrument is actually the SD3 name for a sample file. An instrument can be any audio sample file in the following formats: WAV (Microsoft Windows Wave format), AIF or AIFF (Apple Interchange File Format), or OGG (Ogg-Vorbis format). In addition, instruments can be represented by SFZ files, which are not audio files but definition files that define how audio files should be loaded. SFZ files can be used to load multisamples into SD3.

SFZ AND MULTISAMPLES: Multisamples are special instruments that have more than one audio sample file associated with them. An SFZ file defines a multisample that tells SD3 the multiple sample files that need to be loaded for a single instrument and pad. Why use multiple sample files for a single instrument? When a real, live, acoustic drum is played, it sounds different at various loudness levels. If you hit the drum hard or soft, not only does the volume of the instrument change, but so does the timbre. In order to provide a more realistic sound, multisamples include audio recordings of the same instrument at various playing levels. These different samples are triggered at different MIDI velocity levels, so it sounds like you are

---

playing a real drum. SD3 ships with a number of multisample instruments, and you can even create your own, but you'll need to learn the SFZ file format. Go to **www.cakewalk.com/DevXchange/sfz.asp** for more information.

To use SD3 instruments, follow these steps:

1. Right-click an instrument on the drum kit display and choose Load Instrument to load a sample file or SFZ file. SONAR ships with a number of different instruments, which are located in the following hard drive folder: C:\Program Files\Cakewalk\Vstplugins\Session Drummer 3\Contents\Kits. In this folder, you'll find more folders for each of the various types of available instruments.

2. If you chose an SFZ file, you can skip this step. If you chose a regular audio file (like WAV, AIF, or OGG), you will also need to set a MIDI note number for the instrument. SFZ files contain all the information needed to set up an instrument, but regular audio sample files do not. After you have loaded a sample file, right-click the instrument again and choose a MIDI note number from the menu. This is the MIDI note number that must be used in your MIDI tracks to trigger/play the instrument.

3. To audition an instrument, click it in the drum kit display.

4. To clear an instrument, right-click it and choose Unload Instrument.

Using the Mixer

After you've loaded some instruments either individually or via a kit or program, you can manipulate them in various ways using the Mixer (via the Mixer button). The Mixer changes the volume, width, panning, and tuning of each instrument via on-screen controls, which can be adjusted by clicking and dragging up (to increase the value) or down (to decrease the value) with the mouse. Drag left/right to adjust panning. Double-click a control to return it to its default value. Here are descriptions of each of the Mixer controls:

▷ **Mute (M) and Solo (S).** Click the Mute and Solo buttons to mute or solo an instrument. Muting an instrument will silence it. Soloing an instrument will silence all other instruments while the soloed instrument continues to play. Use these options to audition different instrument combinations.

▷ **Volume.** Adjust the volume fader to increase or decrease the amplitude of an instrument. Volume is measured as decibels: −infdB (off) to +6dB (full volume).

▷ **Width.** Adjust the Width knob to alter the stereo spread of an instrument. The samples included with SD3 are in stereo. Using the Width knob, you can control the size of the stereo field of an instrument. Width is measured as follows: −100% to 0% to +100%. At −100%, an instrument sounds as if it is being played from an audience perspective. At +100%, an instrument sounds as if it is being played from the drummer's perspective. At 0%, a stereo instrument in converted into a mono instrument. The 0% setting can come in handy if you want to have full control over an instrument's position in the stereo field. Just set Width to 0% and use the Pan knob to control the exact position.

▷ **Pan.** Adjust the Pan horizontal slider (located below the Mute and Solo buttons) to alter the position of an instrument in the stereo field. Pan is measured as follows: −100% (full left) to 0% (centered) to +100% (full right).

▷ **Tune.** Adjust the Tune knob to alter the pitch of an instrument. Tuning is measured in semitones as follows: −24 st (lowered 2 octaves) to 0 st (original sound) to +24 st (raised 2 octaves). Some creative uses of the Tune knob can be to alter instruments to the point where a drum kit sounds entirely different.

▷ **Output.** You can also assign an audio output channel to each instrument. Click the Output menu (located at the bottom of each instrument channel in the Mixer) and choose an output number. Initially, each instrument is set to channel 1, which means all instruments will use the first SD3 track, but each instrument can have its own channel/track. To use multiple channels, you must have selected the All Synth Audio Outputs option in the Insert Soft Synth Options dialog box. This will create 12 different output tracks for SD3.

> **MULTIPLE OUTPUTS:** Using multiple outputs allows you to process each drum instrument separately with different effects. For example, the bass drum is usually presented dry in an audio mix, but the snare drum usually has some reverb added to it. In addition, you can apply EQ effects to each drum instrument and make your kit sound unique, rather than have it sound the same as every other SONAR user.

In addition to the individual instrument controls, the Mixer provides main controls, which can be used to adjust the volume, width, panning, and tuning of the entire drum kit.

Using MIDI Patterns

Along with instruments and Mixer settings, a program loads in eight associated MIDI patterns. These patterns are specifically matched to the program that is loaded. This means the patterns automatically work well with the instruments/kit in the program. This makes it very easy to create a drum part with a particular drum kit. To work with the SD3 MIDI pattern features, do the following:

1. After loading a program, the eight MIDI Pattern Pads (A through H) will each be loaded with a different MIDI pattern. Click a Pattern Pad to select it. When you select a Pad, the name of its MIDI pattern and the number of beats in that pattern is shown next to the MIDI Pattern File Functions button.
2. To play the Pad, click the MIDI Pattern Play button.
3. To stop Pad playback, click the MIDI Pattern Stop button.
4. To loop playback, activate the MIDI Pattern Loop button.
5. To reset playback of the Pad to the beginning of its pattern, click the MIDI Pattern Reset button.
6. To load a new pattern into the Pad independent of the current program, click the MIDI Pattern File Functions button and choose Load Pattern.
7. To clear the pattern in the Pad, click the MIDI Pattern File Functions button and choose Unload Pattern. You can also clear all patterns from all Pads by choosing Unload All Patterns.

Using those steps, you can quickly and easily audition the MIDI patterns in a program. To actually create a drum part for your project using the MIDI patterns, you can either drag and drop patterns into the SD3 MIDI track (by clicking and dragging the MIDI Pattern Drag-and-Drop button from the SD3 interface to the track) or trigger the SD3 MIDI Pattern Pads using individual MIDI notes in the MIDI track.

> **MIDI PATTERN TRIGGER NOTES:** Each of the MIDI Pattern Pads in SD3 has a designated MIDI trigger note. The notes are as follows: Pad A = D#2; Pad B = E2; Pad C = F2; Pad D = F#2; Pad E = G2; Pad F = G#2; Pad G = A2; Pad H = A#2. You'll need to keep this information handy if you want to build drum tracks with SD3 via MIDI Pattern triggering.

> **SESSION DRUMMER 3 DEMO VIDEO:** To see a demonstration of SD3 in action, go to **garrigus.com?SD3** to watch the video.

> **MORE SESSION DRUMMER 3 INFORMATION:** For more information about SD3, left-click once any-where inside the SD3 window and then press the F1 key to open the SD3 Help file.

Dimension Pro

Like SD3, Dimension Pro is a sample playback synth, but instead of being dedicated to percussion instruments, it is an all-around sample player that gives you access to both realistic and synthesized sounds. If you examine the Dimension Pro interface (see Figure 8.24), you'll notice that it is divided into three main sections: the Programs area, the Elements area, and the Mixer/Global Effects area.

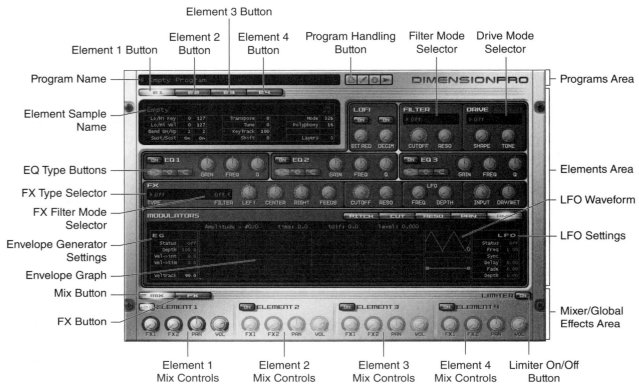

Figure 8.24 Adjust the Dimension Pro parameters using its main interface.
Source: Cakewalk®, Inc.

The sounds that Dimension Pro can produce are represented as *programs*. A program is represented by up to four elements and two global effects. Each element can hold a different sample file or multisample. The Programs area loads and saves programs. The Elements area loads in samples and adjusts various parameters to create programs. The Mixer/Global Effects area adjusts the volume, panning, and amount of global effects for each element.

Working with Programs

A program stores all of the Dimension Pro settings, including the currently loaded elements/samples, the element parameter settings, and the global effects values. The quickest way to start working with Dimension Pro is simply to load up an existing program. Click the Program Handling button to perform the following program-related tasks:

▷ **Initialize Program.** This option will clear all of Dimension Pro's parameter values, including the currently loaded elements and their settings.

▷ **Load Program.** Use this option to load a Dimension Pro program. SONAR ships with a large number of prede-fined programs, which are located in the following hard drive folder: C:\ProgramData\Cakewalk\Dimension Pro\

Programs. After choosing a program, Dimension Pro will load up a sound (made up of the combined elements/samples) you can use in your project.

▷ **Save Program or Save Program As.** If you make changes to a program (such as loading in different elements/samples or changing parameter settings), you can save your changes using these options. Use Save Program to save your changes into the same program file you loaded. This will overwrite the existing program file. To keep the original program file and create a different file, use the Save Program As option and use a new name for the program.

▷ **Save Default Program.** Normally, when you load up Dimension Pro, it contains a blank program. If you would like a program to be automatically loaded every time you use Dimension Pro, then load a program and choose the Save Default Program option to save the current program as the default.

THE PROGRAM BROWSER: Click the program name (located to the left of the Program Handling button) to open the Program Browser for a quick way to load a Dimension Pro program. Just double-click one of the programs in the list.

Using Elements to Create Programs

A program in Dimension Pro can have up to four different samples loaded at once, with each represented by an element. An element is a combination of a sample file along with some additional parameters. You can load any audio sample file (into an element) that is one of the following formats: WAV (Microsoft Windows Wave format), AIF or AIFF (Apple Interchange File Format), OGG (Ogg-Vorbis format), or REX/RX2 (ReCycle/REX loop file format). In addition, elements can load SFZ files, which are not audio files but definition files that define how audio files should be loaded. SFZ files can be used to load multisamples into elements.

To use Dimension Pro elements to create a program, follow these steps:

1. In the Elements area, click the Element button corresponding to the element with which you want to work. There are four element buttons available.
2. Click the Element Sample name to load a sample file into the element. SONAR ships with a number of different sample files, which are located in the following hard drive folder: C:\Program Files\Cakewalk\Dimension Pro\Multisamples. In this folder, you'll find more folders for each of the various types of available sample files.
3. The Lo Fi section provides a reduced sound quality effect. To use the Bit Reduction or Decimation option, click the associated buttons and adjust the corresponding knobs.
4. The Filter section provides a large array of EQ filtering options. Click the Filter Type selector to cycle through all of the available filter types. The Cutoff and Resonance knobs work differently, depending on the filter type you choose. Press F1 to access the Dimension Pro help and go to the Main Functions > Using the Filter section for more information on each of the available filter types.
5. The Drive section provides distortion/overdrive effects. Click the Drive Mode selector to cycle through all of the available modes. Then use the Shape and Tone knobs to adjust the overall sound of the effect.
6. There are three EQ sections: EQ1, EQ2, and EQ3. Each EQ section applies parametric equalization effects to the current element in three different modes (which are chosen using the EQ Type buttons): Lo Shelf, Band Pass, and Hi Shelf. For more information on equalization, see Chapter 11.
7. The FX section provides a multi-effects processor with 24 effects ranging from chorus and delay to auto-panning and reverb. To gain a better understanding of how to use effects, see Chapter 11.
8. Adjust the parameters in the Modulators section (see "Using the Modulators Section," later in this chapter, for more details).
9. Click the Mix button if it's not already activated. Then, in the Mixer/Global Effects area, you'll notice some additional controls for the element with which you are working.

10. Use the Pan and Vol knobs to adjust the stereo position and volume of the element, respectively.

11. Click the FX button, and the Mixer/Global Effects area will display the two global effects provided by Dimension Pro. These effects are the same for all four elements, except that you can adjust how much of the effects are applied to each element using the FX1 and FX2 knobs in the Mix display.

12. The Modulation effect provides chorus and phasing effects. The Reverb effect provides environment ambience effects. To activate an effect, click the corresponding Type parameter to cycle through the available effect types. Then adjust the associated parameters to fine-tune the effect.

13. Click the Mix button. Then use the FX1 and FX2 knobs to adjust how much of the global effects will be applied to the element. FX1 corresponds to the Modulation effect. FX2 corresponds to the Reverb effect.

14. Repeat Steps 1 through 13 to set up each of the elements you want to use in the program.

15. Use the Limiter On/Off button to toggle the Limiter, which prevents loud signals from overloading the Dimension Pro stereo output. I recommend keeping this activated as a safety precaution because some synth sounds can be very loud and can produce volume levels that may damage your monitors or your hearing (when using headphones).

16. Use the Program Handling button to save the program.

After you've created an element, you can save it, load it into another element, copy/paste it to another element, and more. To perform these actions, right-click on the corresponding Element button in the Elements area and choose one of the following from the menu:

▷ **Unload Element.** Use this option to remove the sample file from the element but keep all of the element's parameter settings.

▷ **Reset Element.** Use this option to initialize the element, removing the sample file and setting all parameter values to their defaults.

▷ **Load Element and Save Element As.** Use Load Element to load an existing element. Use Save Element As to save all element parameter settings in a new element file.

▷ **Copy Element.** Use this option to copy all of the element parameter settings.

▷ **Paste Element and Paste Element Fx.** After you have used Copy Element, right-click a different element and use Paste Element to duplicate all the parameter settings of the copied element. Use Paste Element Fx to only duplicate the effects parameter settings.

By loading up different sample files, mixing them together with various pan and volume values, and applying a variety of effects, you can use Dimension Pro to come up with some unique sounds. Remember that you can apply more effects to the Dimension Pro output by inserting plug-ins to the corresponding FX bin of the instrument track, too.

Using the Modulators Section

With the Modulators section, you can automate (automatically change over time) some of the parameters of an element. Using the corresponding buttons in the area, you can automate pitch (Pitch), the cutoff and resonance parameters (Cut and Reso), panning (Pan), and volume (Amp). Each of these parameters is automated using an Envelope Generator or a low-frequency oscillator (LFO), which work as follows:

1. In the Modulators section, first click the button representing the parameter you would like to automate. For example, if you want to automate the volume of an element, click the Amp button to activate it.

2. In the EG area of the Modulators section, there are a variety of parameters that need to be adjusted. The Status value turns the Envelope Generator on/off. To adjust this (and the other parameters here), either left/right-click to cycle through the values or click and drag your mouse up/down over the value. Double-click a value to return it to the default setting.

3. The Depth value determines the range of the values you can change in the Envelope Generator. This value is different, depending on what parameter you are automating. Lower values allow you to make more subtle changes, while higher values allow you to make more dramatic changes.

4. The Vel->int value determines how much MIDI note velocity affects the depth. This value is different, depending on what parameter you are automating.

5. The Vel->tim value determines how much MIDI note velocity affects the time of the Envelope Generator nodes (explained shortly). This value is different, depending on what parameter you are automating.

6. The Vel Track value determines how much MIDI note velocity affects the current envelope value. This value is different, depending on what parameter you are automating.

7. Once all the parameters in the EG section are set, you can start "drawing" in the Envelope Generator values. The Envelope Generator graphic display (envelope graph) shows a line graph where values are represented by a line with nodes. From bottom to top, the higher the line, the higher the value. During playback, the envelope values are generated and looped from left to right. To add/edit the envelope values (nodes), right-click in the graph.

8. You can move nodes by clicking and dragging them.

9. Delete nodes by right-clicking them a second time.

10. Line segments (between nodes) can be adjusted by clicking and dragging.

11. You can also modulate the different parameters using an LFO by setting the values in the LFO area of the Modulators section. Use the Status value to turn the LFO on/off.

12. Use the LFO Waveform display to choose a waveform for the LFO by clicking to cycle through the values or by clicking just above the display to choose a waveform from the menu.

13. The Freq (frequency) and Sync values determine the speed at which the LFO waveform cycles. If you set Sync to Off, the Freq value determines the step generator speed and can be set from 0 to 40Hz, which means the number of times the LFO waveform will loop every second. If you set the Sync to a specific beat value, the step generator will be synchronized to the same tempo as the SONAR project tempo and will loop once each time SONAR generates the specified beat value. For example, if you set Sync to 1, the step generator will loop once for every beat.

14. Use the Delay value to determine how long (in seconds) it takes the LFO to start cycling after a MIDI note sounds.

15. Use the Fade value to apply a fade-in (in seconds) to the LFO after it starts. This means the LFO will gradually affect the modulated parameter over time.

16. The Depth value determines how much the LFO will affect the modulated parameter.

Using the Modulators section of Dimension Pro, you can create many interesting sounds that evolve over time as they are played, which is the key to exciting and interesting music.

MORE DIMENSION PRO INFORMATION: Click once anywhere on the outer area of the Dimension Pro interface and then press F1 to access the Dimension Pro Help file for even more information.

Rapture

Operation of Rapture is similar to that of Dimension Pro, but although Rapture can load samples and multisamples, it uses them to provide wavetable synthesis rather than dedicated sample playback. What this means is that sample files are used as sound sources, which are mixed and processed to create new and unique synthesized sounds. Rapture is single-timbral, so it only plays one sound at a time, but it provides a lot of synthesis power.

If you examine the Rapture interface (see Figure 8.25), you'll notice that it is divided into nine sections: the Programs area, the Elements area, the DSP (Digital Signal Processing) area, the Envelope Generator area, the Step Generator area, the EQ area, the FX area, the Mixer area, and the Master area.

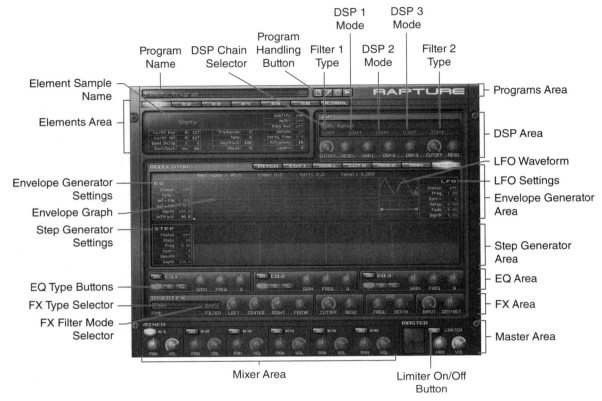

Figure 8.25 Adjust the Rapture parameters using its main interface.
Source: Cakewalk®, Inc.

The sounds that Rapture can produce are represented as programs. A program is represented by up to six elements. Each element can hold a different sample file or multisample. The Programs area loads and saves programs. The Elements area loads in samples. The DSP area applies effects to each element. The Envelope Generator and Step Generator areas adjust various element parameters over time. The EQ area provides parametric equalization effects. The FX area provides a multi-effects processor with 24 effects. The Mixer area adjusts volume and panning for each element. The Master area adjusts the overall volume and panning for Rapture's stereo output.

Working with Programs

A program stores all of the Rapture parameter settings, including the currently loaded elements/samples and all the settings for the various parameter areas. The quickest way to start working with Rapture is to load up an existing program. Click the Program Handling button to perform the following program-related tasks:

▷ **Initialize Program.** This option will clear all of Rapture's parameter values, including the currently loaded elements and their settings.

▷ **Load Program.** Use this option to load a Rapture program. SONAR ships with a large number of predefined programs. After choosing a program, Rapture will load up a sound (made up of the combined elements/samples) that you can use in your project.

▷ **Save Program or Save Program As.** If you make changes to a program (such as loading in different elements/samples or changing parameter settings), you can save your changes using these options. Use Save Program to save your changes into the same program file you loaded. This will overwrite the existing program file. To keep the original program file and create a different file, use the Save Program As option and use a new name for the program.

▷ **Save Default Program.** Normally, when you load up Rapture, it contains a blank program. If you would like a program to be loaded automatically every time you use Rapture, then load a program and choose the Save Default Program option to save the current program as the default.

THE PROGRAM BROWSER: Click the program name (located to the left of the Program Handling button) to open the Program Browser for a quick way to load a Rapture program. Just double-click one of the programs in the list.

Using Elements to Create Programs

A program in Rapture can have up to six different samples loaded at once, each represented by an element. An element is a combination of a sample file along with some additional parameters. You can load any audio sample file (into an element) that is one of the following formats: WAV (Microsoft Windows Wav format), AIF or AIFF (Apple Interchange File Format), or OGG (Ogg-Vorbis format). In addition, elements can load SFZ files, which are not audio files but definition files that define how audio files should be loaded. SFZ files can be used to load multisamples into elements.

To use Rapture elements to create a program, follow these steps:

1. In the Elements area, click the Element button corresponding to the element with which you want to work. There are six Element buttons available, labeled E1 through E6.
2. Click the Element Sample name to load a sample file into the element. SONAR ships with a number of different sample files, which are located in the following hard drive folder: C:\Program Files\Cakewalk\Rapture\Multisamples.
3. Adjust the parameters in the DSP area (see "Using the DSP Area," later in this chapter, for more details).
4. Adjust the parameters in the Envelope Generator area (see "Using the Envelope Generator Area," later in this chapter, for more details).
5. Adjust the parameters in the Step Generator area (see "Using the Step Generator Area," later in this chapter, for more details).
6. The EQ area provides three EQ sections: EQ1, EQ2, and EQ3. Each EQ section applies parametric equalization effects to the current element in three different modes (which are chosen using the EQ Type buttons): Lo Shelf, Band Pass, and Hi Shelf. For more information on equalization, see Chapter 11.
7. The FX area provides a multi-effects processor with 24 effects ranging from chorus and delay to auto-panning and reverb. To gain a better understanding of how to use effects, see Chapter 11.
8. In the Mixer area, find the corresponding element section and use the Pan and Vol knobs to adjust the stereo position and volume of the element, respectively.
9. Repeat Steps 1 through 8 to set up each of the elements you want to use in the program.
10. Click the Global button in the Elements area to access two more multi-effects processors and a step generator, as well as three master EQ sections and a master multi-effects processor. These parameters all work the same as the previously described EQ, FX, and Step Generator areas, except the Global Step Generator provides separate settings for left and right channels of Rapture's stereo output. The Global and Master effects are applied to all the elements so they affect the entire sound. Again, refer to Chapter 11 for more information about effects.

11. Use the Limiter On/Off button to toggle the Limiter, which prevents loud signals from overloading the Rapture stereo output. I recommend keeping this activated as a safety precaution because some synth sounds can be very loud and can produce volume levels that may damage your monitors or your hearing (when using headphones).

12. Adjust the Pan and Vol knobs in the Master area to set the overall panning and volume for the entire program.

13. Use the Program Handling button to save the program.

After you've created an element, you can save it, load it into another element, copy/paste it to another element, and more. To perform these actions, right-click the corresponding Element button in the Elements area and choose one of the following from the menu:

▷ **Unload Element.** Use this option to remove the sample file from the element but keep all of the element's parameter settings.

▷ **Reset Element.** Use this option to initialize the element, removing the sample file and setting all parameter values to their defaults.

▷ **Load Element and Save Element As.** Use Load Element to load an existing element. Use Save Element As to save all element parameter settings in a new element file.

▷ **Copy Element.** Use this option to copy all of the element parameter settings.

▷ **Paste Element and Paste Element Fx.** After you have used Copy Element, right-click a different element and use Paste Element to duplicate all the parameter settings of the copied element. Use Paste Element Fx only to duplicate the Effects parameter settings.

By loading up different sample files, mixing them together with various pan and volume values, and applying a variety of effects, you can use Rapture to come up with some unique sounds. Remember that you can apply more effects to the Rapture output by inserting plug-ins to the corresponding FX bin of the synth track, too.

Using the DSP Area

The DSP area allows you to apply effects to the current element. There are five effects available: Filter 1, DSP1, DSP2, DSP3, and Filter 2. You can use these effects as follows:

1. Click the DSP Chain selector to choose an effect signal routing. This selector determines how the audio signal from the element will be processed by the DSP effects. In the selector, the effects are represented as follows: Filter 1 (F 1), DSP1 (DSP 1), DSP2 (DSP 2), DSP3 (DSP 3), and Filter 2 (F 2). For example, if you choose chain 01 from the selector, the audio signal from the element will first pass through DSP 1 (DSP1), then DSP 2 (DSP2), then F 1 (Filter 1), then DSP 3 (DSP3), and finally F 2 (Filter 2). Different chains (routings) will affect the audio signal in different ways.

2. After choosing a chain, select different settings for each of the effects. You can even leave some effects turned off, which effectively bypasses the effects.

3. The Filter 1 and Filter 2 sections provide a large array of EQ filtering options. Click the Filter Type selectors to cycle through all of the available filter types. The Cutoff and Resonance knobs work differently, depending on the filter type you choose. Press F1 to access the Rapture help and go to the Main Functions > The DSP Section > Using the Filters section for more information on each of the available filter types.

4. The DSP (1 through 3) effects provide a variety of processing options to achieve a reduced sound quality effect. Use DSP Mode selectors to choose the type of effects you want and adjust the associated knobs to vary the strength of the effects.

Using the Envelope Generator Area

With the Envelope Generator area, you can automate (automatically change over time) some of the parameters of an element. Using the corresponding buttons (shown to the right of the word Modulators on the Rapture interface), you can automate pitch (Pitch), the cutoff and resonance parameters (Cut1 & 2 and Reso1 & 2), panning (Pan), and volume (Amp) of the currently selected element. Each of these parameters is automated using an Envelope Generator or a low frequency oscillator (LFO), which work as follows:

1. Shown to the right of the word Modulators on the Rapture interface, first click the button representing the parameter you would like to automate. For example, if you want to automate the volume of an element, click the Amp button to activate it.
2. In the Envelope Generator Settings section, there are a variety of parameters that need to be adjusted. The Status value turns the Envelope Generator on/off. To adjust this, left/right-click to cycle through the values. Set the Status to Shot if you want the step generator to play only once at the beginning of a note. Set it to On if you want the step generator to loop continuously.
3. If you set the Sync value to a specific beat, the envelope will be synchronized to the same tempo as the SONAR project tempo and will loop once each time SONAR generates the specified beat value. For example, if you set Sync to 1, the envelope will loop once for every beat. To adjust this, left/right-click to cycle through the values or click the word Sync to use the menu.

ADJUSTING NUMERIC PARAMETERS IN RAPTURE: To adjust numeric values, click and drag your mouse up/down over the chosen value. Double-click the value to type in a specific number.

---

4. The Depth value determines the range of the values you can change in the envelope. This value is different, depending on what parameter you are automating. Lower values allow you to make more subtle changes, while higher values allow you to make more dramatic changes.
5. The Vel->int value determines how much MIDI note velocity affects the depth. This value is different, depending on what parameter you are automating.
6. The Vel->tim value determines how much MIDI note velocity affects the time of the Envelope Generator nodes (explained shortly). This value is different, depending on what parameter you are automating.
7. The Vel Track value determines how much MIDI note velocity affects the current envelope value. This value is different, depending on what parameter you are automating.
8. Once all the parameters in the Envelope Generator Settings section are set, you can start "drawing" values in the Envelope Graph. The Envelope Graph shows a line graph where values are represented by a line with nodes. From bottom to top, the higher the line, the higher the value. During playback the envelope values are generated and looped from left to right. To add/edit the envelope values (nodes), right-click in the graph.
9. You can move nodes by clicking and dragging them.
10. Delete nodes by right-clicking them a second time.
11. Line segments (between nodes) can be adjusted by clicking and dragging.
12. You can also modulate the different parameters using an LFO by setting the values in the LFO Settings section. Use the Status value to turn the LFO on/off. Set the Status to Shot if you want the step generator to play only once at the beginning of a note. Set it to On if you want the step generator to loop continuously.
13. Use the LFO Waveform display to choose a waveform for the LFO by clicking to cycle through the values or by clicking just above the display to choose a waveform from the menu.
14. The Freq (frequency) and Sync values determine the speed at which the LFO waveform cycles. If you set Sync to Off, the Freq value determines the step generator speed and can be set from 0 to 40Hz, which means the number of times the LFO waveform will loop every second. If you set the Sync to a specific beat value, the LFO waveform will be synchronized to the same tempo as the SONAR project tempo and will loop once each time SONAR generates the specified beat value. For example, if you set Sync to 1, the LFO waveform will loop once for every beat.
15. Use the Delay value to determine how long (in seconds) it takes the LFO to start cycling after a MIDI note sounds.

16. Use the Fade value to apply a fade-in (in seconds) to the LFO after it starts. This means the LFO will gradually affect the modulated parameter over time.

17. The Depth value determines how much the LFO will affect the modulated parameter.

Using the Step Generator Area

Like the Envelope Generator area, with the Step Generator area, you can automate (automatically change over time) some of the parameters of an element. Using the corresponding buttons in the area, you can automate pitch (Pitch), the cutoff and resolution parameters (Cut1, Res1, Cut2, Res2) of Filters 1 and 2 in the DSP area, panning (Pan), and volume (Amp). Each of these parameters is automated using a step generator, which works as follows:

1. Shown to the right of the word Modulators on the Rapture interface, first click the button representing the parameter you would like to automate. For example, if you want to automate the volume of an element, click the Amp button to activate it.

2. In the Step Generator Settings area, various parameters need to be adjusted. The Status parameter turns the step generator on/off. To adjust this, left/right-click to cycle through the values. Set the Status to Shot if you want the step generator to play only once at the beginning of a note. Set it to On if you want the step generator to loop continuously.

3. Set the Steps parameter (click and drag your mouse up/down over the value or double-click to type in a value) for the number of steps you want to use for the automation. You can set this anywhere from 2 to 128. The larger the value, the more steps that will be shown in the step generator graphic display and the smoother the changes that can be applied.

4. The Freq (frequency) and Sync parameters determine the speed at which the step generator cycles through the values drawn in the step generator graphic display. If you set Sync to Off, the Freq parameter determines the step generator speed and can be set from 0 to 40Hz, which means the number of times the step generator will loop every second. If you set the Sync to a specific beat value, the step generator will be synchronized to the same tempo as the SONAR project tempo and will loop once each time SONAR generates the specified beat value. For example, if you set Sync to 1, the step generator will loop once for every beat.

5. The Smooth value sets the speed (in milliseconds) at which each step in the step generator moves to the next step. The lower the value, the quicker the change between steps.

6. The Depth value determines the range of the step values you can change in the step generator. This value is different, depending on what parameter you are automating. Lower values allow you to make more subtle changes, while higher values allow you to make more dramatic changes.

AUTOMATE THE STEP GENERATOR: By right-clicking on the Steps, Freq, Smooth, and Depth parameters, you can assign them to MIDI controller values. You can then manipulate these parameters in real time as the step generator automates the element parameters.

---

7. Once all the parameters in the Step Generator Settings section are set, you can start "drawing" in the step generator values. The step generator graphic display shows a bar graph where each value is represented by a single vertical bar. From bottom to top, the higher the bar, the higher the value. During playback, the step values are generated and looped from left to right. To add/edit the step values, click and drag your mouse in the display. This is similar to editing MIDI controller values in the Piano Roll view.

8. If you want to draw a smooth line of values, hold down the Shift key and then click at the beginning of the line and drag to the end of the line.

9. To set a single value back to its default, double-click it. To reset all values, right-click the display and choose Reset Steps from the menu.

10. You can also apply a number of different functions to the step values using the right-click menu, including randomizing, reversing, inverting, mirroring, normalizing, and even copying and pasting the steps between modulator parameters. For example, if you want the panning to follow the volume, copy the steps for the Amp parameter and then paste them in the display of the Pan parameter.

Using the Envelope Generator and Step Generator areas of Rapture, you can create many very interesting sounds that evolve over time as they are played, which is the key to exciting and interesting synthesizer music.

DropZone

Like Dimension Pro, DropZone is a sample playback synth that gives you access to both realistic and synthesized sounds. DropZone is single-timbral, but it can load multisamples. It is not as sophisticated as Dimension Pro, but DropZone is great for doing sample playback on a budget.

DropZone Basics

The DropZone interface (see Figure 8.26) provides a number of parameters that allow you to work with programs and elements, edit sample files, apply effects and modulators, and audition sounds.

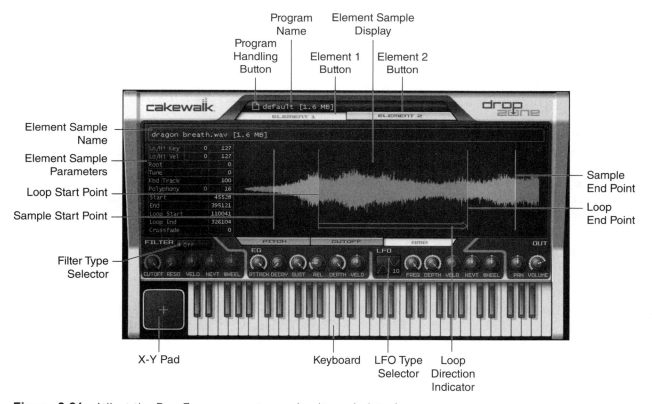

Figure 8.26 Adjust the DropZone parameters using its main interface.
Source: Cakewalk®, Inc.

The sounds that DropZone can produce are represented as *programs*. A program is represented by up to two elements and all the available parameters provided by DropZone. Each element can hold a different sample file or multisample. The Program Name and Handling button loads and saves programs. The Element buttons load in samples. The Element Sample display and parameters edit samples. The Filter, EG, and LFO areas apply effects and modulation to samples. The Out area adjusts the overall volume and panning for DropZone's stereo output.

Working with Programs

A program stores all of the DropZone parameter settings, including the currently loaded elements/samples and all the settings for the Element Sample parameters, and the Filter, EG, LFO, and Out areas. The quickest way to start working with DropZone is to load up an existing program. Click the Program Handling button to perform the following program-related tasks:

▷ **Initialize Program.** This option will clear all of DropZone's parameter values, including the currently loaded elements and their settings.

▷ **Load Program.** Use this option to load a DropZone program. SONAR ships with a large number of predefined programs. After choosing a program, DropZone will load up a sound (made up of the combined elements/samples) that you can use in your project.

▷ **Save Program or Save Program As.** If you make changes to a program (such as loading in different elements/samples or changing parameter settings), you can save your changes using these options. Use Save Program to save your changes into the same program file you loaded. This will overwrite the existing program file. To keep the original program file and create a different file, use the Save Program As option and use a new name for the program.

▷ **Save Default Program.** Normally, when you load up DropZone, it contains a default program. If you would like a program to be automatically loaded every time you use DropZone, then load a program and choose the Save Default Program option to save the current program as the default.

> **THE PROGRAM BROWSER:** Click the program name to open the Program Browser for a quick way to load a DropZone program. Just double-click one of the programs in the list.

Using Elements to Create Programs

A program in DropZone can have up to two different samples loaded at once, each represented by an element. An element is a combination of a sample file along with some additional parameters. You can load any audio sample file (into an element) that is in one of the following formats: WAV (Microsoft Windows WAV format), AIF or AIFF (Apple Interchange File Format), OGG (Ogg-Vorbis format), or REX/RX2 (ReCycle/REX loop file format). In addition, elements can load SFZ files, which are not audio files but definition files that define how audio files should be loaded. SFZ files can be used to load multisamples into elements.

To use DropZone elements to create a program, follow these steps:

1. Click the Element button corresponding to the element with which you want to work. There are two Element buttons available, labeled Element 1 and Element 2.
2. Click the Element Sample name to load a sample file into the element. SONAR ships with a number of different sample files, which are located in the following hard drive folder: C:\Program Files\Cakewalk\Vstplugins\DropZone\Programs\90-Multisamples. You can also drag and drop a sample file from Windows Explorer into the DropZone window for a quick way to load a sample file.
3. Adjust the Element Sample display and parameters (see "Editing Sample Files," later in this chapter, for more details).
4. Adjust the Filter, EG, and LFO parameters (see "Applying Effects and Modulators," later in this chapter, for more details).
5. Use the graphic keyboard to audition the sound. You can also apply pitch and vibrato changes as you play by dragging your mouse in the X-Y Pad. Left/right changes pitch, and up/down changes vibrato.
6. Repeat Steps 1 through 5 to set up each of the elements you want to use in the program.

7. Adjust the Pan and Volume knobs in the Out area to set the overall panning and volume for the entire program.
8. Use the Program Handling button to save the program.

After you've created an element, you can save it, load it into another element, copy/paste it to another element, and more. To perform these actions, right-click the corresponding Element button and choose one of the following from the menu:

▷ **Unload Element.** Use this option to remove the sample file from the element but keep all of the element's parameter settings.

▷ **Reset Element.** Use this option to initialize the element, removing the sample file and setting all parameter values to their defaults.

▷ **Load Element and Save Element As.** Use Load Element to load an existing element. Use Save Element As to save all element parameter settings in a new element file.

▷ **Copy Element.** Use this option to copy all of the element parameter settings.

▷ **Paste Element.** After you have used Copy Element, right-click a different element and use Paste Element to duplicate all the parameter settings of the copied element.

By loading up different sample files, mixing them together with various pan and volume values, and applying a variety of effects, you can use DropZone to come up with some unique sounds. Remember that you can apply more effects to the DropZone output by inserting plug-ins to the corresponding FX bin of the synth track, too.

Editing Sample Files

The Element Sample display and parameters define how a sample file will be played. You can edit a sample file using these parameters as follows (click and drag up/down over each parameter to change it):

1. Use the Lo/Hi Key parameters to designate the keyboard range for the current element. For example, if you want the sample to play only when the lower part of your MIDI keyboard is played, lower the Hi Key value to something like 65. That means that when DropZone receives MIDI note values from 0 to 65, the sample will play. But if it receives values from 66 to 127, the sample will not play. Using this feature, you can have a different sample play, depending on the note range you use on your MIDI keyboard. For example, you can play a bass sound in the lower range and a guitar sound in the upper range.

2. Use the Lo/Hi Vel(ocity) parameters to designate the velocity range for the current element. For example, if you want the sample to play only when you press a key softly, lower the Hi Key value to something like 65. That means that when the DropZone receives MIDI velocity values from 0 to 65, the sample will play. But if it receives values from 66 to 127, the sample will not play. Using this feature, you can have a different sample play, depending on how hard you press a key on your MIDI keyboard.

3. Using the Root and Tune parameters, you can change how notes are triggered in DropZone. For example, if DropZone receives a MIDI note message with a value of C4, it will normally play a C4 note. However, if you change the Root value to 2 st (semitones), a received note of C4 will actually be played as D4. Changing the Tune parameter lets you fine-tune this even more in cents. This functionality allows you to effectively transpose a performance without having to change your recorded MIDI data.

4. Using the Kbd (Keyboard) Track parameter, you can change the type of musical scale that DropZone uses to produce sound. The default value of 100 cents produces a scale with a half step (semitone) between each note. If you change the value to 50 cents, DropZone will play notes in a quarter tone scale. And a value of 200 cents produces a whole-tone scale. This can be used to experiment with making world music sounds.

5. To keep DropZone from consuming too much CPU power, you can limit the number of notes it can play simultaneously by setting the Polyphony parameter. The default value is 16.

6. If you load in a sample file and you don't want the entire file to play, you can adjust the playback start and end points using the Start and End parameters, which are measured in samples. You can also adjust these

points graphically by dragging (left to lower and right to raise) the Sample Start and Sample End points in the Element Sample display.

7. You can also loop part of a sample file using the Loop Start, Loop End, and Crossfade parameters. To activate looping, click anywhere in the Element Sample display and press the L key. You'll see an orange area appear over the sample waveform. This area designates the part of the sample that will loop over and over as you hold down a key on your MIDI keyboard.

8. Adjust the Loop Start and Loop End parameters or drag (left/right) the Loop Start and Loop End points to designate where the looping will begin/end, as well as the length of the loop region.

9. You can also designate how the loop will occur by pressing the D key to cycle between looping modes: Forward (from left to right), Reverse (from right to left), or Forward/Reverse (left to right and then right to left). As you cycle through these modes, the Loop Direction indicator will change in appearance.

10. As the sample loops, you may hear glitches or volume changes when playback reaches the Loop End point and transitions to the Loop Start point. To smooth out this transition, you can adjust the Crossfade parameter, which is designated in milliseconds from 0 to 1000 (1 second). The higher the value, the smoother the transition will be.

Applying Effects and Modulators

In addition to editing the loaded samples, you can apply effects and modulate (change automatically over time) some of the parameters.

The Filter area applies a wide variety of EQ filtering effects by doing the following:

1. Click the Filter Type selector to choose an available filter type. Press F1 to access the DropZone help and go to DropZone > Using the Filter section for more information on each of the available filter types.

2. Adjust the Cutoff and Reso(nance) knobs. These knobs work differently, depending on the filter type you choose.

3. You can control the Cutoff parameter in real time as you play your MIDI keyboard by adjusting the Velo(city) knob. If you set this knob to a value other than 0, how hard you press the keys on your MIDI keyboard will affect the Cutoff parameter value.

4. You can also control the Cutoff parameter by what notes you play. Set the Keyt(racking) knob to a value other than 0 to affect the Cutoff parameter value.

5. The Cutoff parameter can also be adjusted by moving the modulation wheel on your MIDI keyboard. Set the Wheel knob to a value other than 0 to affect the Cutoff parameter value.

The EG (Envelope Generator) and LFO (Low-Frequency Oscillator) areas modulate (change automatically over time during playback) the pitch (Pitch), filter cutoff (Cutoff), and volume (Amp) of the current element/sample file. To set the EG parameters, do the following:

1. Choose whether you want to modulate the pitch, filter cutoff, or volume by clicking the appropriate button: Pitch, Cutoff, or Amp.

2. Use the Attack knob to adjust how quickly the parameter will begin to change.

3. Use the Decay knob to adjust how quickly the parameter will reach a sustained (steady) level after the attack time has ended.

4. Use the Sust(ain) knob to adjust the level the parameter will stay at until the MIDI keyboard key being held is released.

5. Use the Rel(ease) knob to adjust how long it will take for the parameter changes to stop after the MIDI keyboard key is released.

6. Use the Depth knob to specify how much the Envelope Generator will affect the chosen parameter.

7. You can control the Depth parameter in real time as you play your MIDI keyboard by adjusting the Velo(city) knob. If you set this knob to a value other than 0, how hard you press the keys on your MIDI keyboard will affect the Depth parameter value.

To set the LFO parameters, do the following:

1. Choose whether you want to modulate the pitch, filter cutoff, or volume by clicking the appropriate button: Pitch, Cutoff, or Amp.
2. Use the LFO Type selector to choose the type of LFO waveform you want to use to modulate the chosen parameter. Click the selector to cycle through the available waveforms. For smooth parameter changes, use something like waveform 1, which shows a smooth curve. For more abrupt parameter changes, use something like waveform 2, which shows a square curve.
3. Use the Freq(uency) knob to adjust how quickly the LFO waveform cycles and thus how quickly the parameter being modulated changes.
4. Use the Depth knob to specify how much the LFO will affect the chosen parameter.
5. You can control the Depth parameter in real time as you play your MIDI keyboard by adjusting the Velo(city) knob. If you set this knob to a value other than 0, how hard you press the keys on your MIDI keyboard will affect the Depth parameter value.
6. You can control the Freq(uency) parameter in real time by what notes you play on your MIDI keyboard. Set the Keyt(racking) knob to a value other than 0 to affect the Freq(uency) parameter value.
7. The Depth parameter can also be adjusted by moving the modulation wheel on your MIDI keyboard. Set the Wheel knob to a value other than 0 to affect the Depth parameter value.

Using the EG and LFO areas in DropZone, you can create many very interesting sounds that evolve over time as they are played. DropZone may not be a full-featured sample player, but it provides plenty of power for many sample-based needs.

z3ta+

SONAR also includes z3ta+, which is a waveshaping synthesizer. This type of synthesizer allows you to take just about any kind of audio waveform and process it in a multitude of ways to create an infinite variety of synthesized sounds. The z3ta+ synth can only play one sound at a time, which means that to use more than one sound, you need to load multiple instances of the synth.

The z3ta+ synth provides six oscillators, two stereo filters, eight envelope generators, an arpeggiator, a modulation matrix, and a full complement of stereo audio effects. The effects include drive, modulation, compressor, delay, reverb, and EQ. An extra feature of the z3ta+ synth is that you can use the effects separately to process your audio tracks in SONAR.

Loading and Saving Programs

The z3ta+ sounds are called *programs*. You can save and load programs for your own use, and you can also share programs with others.

Loading z3ta+ Programs

To load programs for use in the z3ta+, do the following:

1. To load a program, click one of the Bank buttons located in the upper-right corner of the z3ta+ window. Programs are organized into six banks, labeled A, B, C, D, E, and F (see Figure 8.27).

Figure 8.27 Use the Bank buttons to select a bank of programs from which to choose.
Source: Cakewalk®, Inc.

2. Click the button located to the right of the Program Name display (it has the picture of a left arrow on it) to display a menu of programs in the currently selected bank. Click a program in the menu to load it.
3. You can also load programs from files on disk. To do so, click the Program button (located in the bottom-right corner of the z3ta+ window) and choose Load Program File from the menu.
4. In the Load Program File dialog box, choose a program file (.fxp extension) and click Open to load the program into the current program slot of the current bank.
5. You can also load entire banks of programs from files on disk. To do so, click the Bank button (located just above the Program button) and choose Load Bank File from the menu.
6. In the Load Program Bank dialog box, choose a bank file (.fxb extension) and click Open to load the bank file into the currently selected bank.

Saving z3ta+ Programs

To save programs for use in z3ta+, do the following:
1. Choose a bank into which you would like to save your new program.
2. Choose a program slot in the bank into which you would like to save your new program.
3. Create the new program by adjusting the synth parameters.
4. Name the new program by holding down the Shift key, clicking in the Program Name display, and typing a new name (see Figure 8.28). Press Ctrl+Tab to finish.

Figure 8.28 Name your new program by using the Program Name display in the z3ta+ window.
Source: Cakewalk®, Inc.

5. To save your new program as an individual file, click the Program button and choose Save Program File.
6. In the Save Program dialog box, type in a name for the program file and click Save.
7. To save your program as part of the currently selected Bank, click the Bank button and choose Save Bank File.
8. In the Save Program Bank File dialog box, type a name for the bank file and click Save.

Using these procedures, you can create and save your own programs for future use.

Using z3ta+ as an Effects Processor

In addition to synthesis features, z3ta+ provides a full arsenal of stereo audio effects. Normally, these effects are used to process the synthesizer sounds that you create inside of z3ta+. However, z3ta+ provides some special functionality that allows you to use the effects outside of the synth to process the audio tracks in your project.

To apply z3ta+ effects to an audio track, right-click in the FX bin of the track and choose Audio FX > z3ta+_fx. This will open the normal z3ta+ synth window. To access the Effects window, click the Effects button located in the lower-right corner. In the Effects window, you have access to a number of different effects processors including distortion, modulation, compression, three different delays, reverb, and an EQ/speaker emulator.

You can use these effects like you would any other audio effects (see Chapter 11), but for details on these specific z3ta+ effects, check the Effects section of the z3ta+ Help file.

> **MORE Z3TA+ INFORMATION:** For more information about the z3ta+ synth, left-click once anywhere inside the z3ta+ window and then press the F1 key to open the z3ta+ Help file.

Cakewalk Sound Center

The Cakewalk Sound Center (CSC) is a simple sound playback synth that gives you access to various instruments from Cakewalk's overall synth sound library. Instruments are categorized by type/subtype, and you can even search for them by name to quickly find the sound you need and start making music. It's simple to use and works as follows:

1. Insert the CSC into a project. The CSC is single-timbral so it can only play one instrument per instance. If you want to use more than one instrument from the CSC, you need to insert multiple instances.
2. In the Program list, you'll see sounds listed via four columns: Type, Subtype, Program, and Rating. Select a Type and then a Subtype to see a list of programs in those categories. Multiple types/subtypes can be selected via Ctrl+clicking or Shift+clicking in the list. If no types are selected, all available programs are listed.
3. You can also search for sounds by name by typing in the Search field located beneath the Program column of the Program list.
4. Once you've found a program you want to try, double-click it in the Program column to load it.
5. To the right of the Program list is the Program information, showing from what Cakewalk library the sound originated. At the bottom of the Program information section, click the MIDI Pattern Preview button (shown with a musical note) to audition the sound.
6. Depending on your opinion of the sound, you can rate it by clicking on the stars in the Rating column of the Program list.
7. You can also audition sounds more thoroughly by clicking on the notes in the on-screen keyboard. Once a sound is loaded, blue colored notes indicate playable notes and the range of the instrument.
8. The CSC also allows some basic tweaking of sounds via the Program controls (eight knobs and four buttons located above the keyboard). Unfortunately, these parameters are different for every sound so I can't describe what they do. In addition, some sounds only provide a few parameters while others provide more. To adjust the buttons, click them to toggle them on/off. To adjust the knobs, click and drag up/down to raise/lower their values. To set knobs back to default values, double-click them.
9. If you want to control the buttons/knobs via your MIDI controllers, right-click them and choose a MIDI controller option from the menu.
10. Finally, adjust the Master Pan and Volume parameters (located in the top-right of the CSC window) to adjust the panning and volume for the loaded sound.

> **MORE CAKEWALK SOUND CENTER INFORMATION:** For more information about the Cakewalk Sound Center, left-click once anywhere inside the CSC window and then press the F1 key to open the CSC Help file.

Studio Instruments

SONAR includes a suite of four synths all under the title of Studio Instruments. Included are Bass Guitar, Drum Kit, Electric Piano, and String Section. Each of these synths emulates the real-life sounds of their respective names, and they provide a quick and easy way for you to add good-quality versions of these instruments to your projects. To add these synths to a project, choose the following from the Soft Synth menu: SI-Bass Guitar, SI-Drum Kit, SI-Electric Piano, and SI-String Section.

Interface Basics

While each of the Studio Instruments provides a different sound (and thus some different interface parameters), if you look at the main interface of each synth, you'll notice that the left side of the window is exactly the same for all four. From top to bottom it provides Program functions, Transport buttons, a MIDI pattern list, and a Pattern Grid (containing four pattern pads). These aspects of the interface work exactly the same in all four synths.

Working with Programs

A program stores all of the synth parameter settings, and each synth has different settings available, which I'll discuss shortly. The quickest way to start working with a synth is simply to load an existing program. Click the Program File Functions button (PRG) to perform the following program-related tasks:

▷ **Load Program.** Use this option to load a synth program. SONAR ships with a large number of predefined programs, which are located in the following hard drive folder: C:\ProgramData\Cakewalk\Studio Instrument \[*name of instrument*]\Programs. You can also choose Browse Programs to automatically open Windows Explorer to the associated folder location.

▷ **Save Program or Save Program As.** If you make changes to a program (by changing parameter settings), you can save your changes using these options. Use Save Program to save your changes into the same program file that you loaded. This will overwrite the existing program file. To keep the original program file and create a different file, use the Save Program As option and use a new name for the program.

▷ **Save Default Program.** Normally, when you load up a synth, it contains a default program. If you would like a different program to be automatically loaded every time you use a synth, then load a program and choose the Save Default Program option to save the current program as the default.

> **THE PROGRAM BROWSER:** Click the program name (located to the right of the Program File Functions button) to open the Program Browser for a quick way to load a synth program.

Using MIDI Patterns

Along with programs, each synth includes a collection of MIDI patterns specifically matched to the represented instrument. This makes it easy to create a drum, bass, string, or electric piano part for your project. To work with MIDI patterns, do the following:

1. From left to right, the Transport contains buttons for Previous Pattern, Next Pattern, Stop, Play, and Loop Pattern. To play a pattern, select it in the pattern list and click the Play button. Alternatively, double-click a pattern to play it. Patterns always play at the current project tempo.

2. If you want playback to loop continuously, toggle the Loop Pattern button.

3. While a pattern is playing, you can click the Previous Pattern and Next Pattern buttons to quickly audition each pattern in the list.

4. To stop playback, click the Stop button.

5. Transpose a pattern by adjusting the Transpose parameter located to the right of the program name. Use the up/down arrows to transpose in semitones within a range of –12 to +12 (minus or plus one octave with zero being no transposition).

6. When you find a pattern you like, click and drag it into the synth track in the track view, where it will become a MIDI Groove clip that can be edited later (see Chapter 9 for more information on Groove clips). The copied pattern will also keep the transposition that you set.

> **THE PATTERN GRID:** You can also click and drag patterns into the Pattern Grid, but personally I never use it. While it's possible to trigger each pad in the grid via MIDI notes, only one pattern can play at a time and there are only four pads available. I find dragging patterns into the Track view much more flexible and useful.

Using those steps, you can quickly and easily create performances for each of the Studio Instruments.

SI-Bass Guitar

Simulating the sound of a real bass, SI-Bass Guitar presents an interactive on-screen representation of a bass guitar instrument. Click on the strings of the guitar to audition the current program. Additionally, you can click on the strings of the Fretboard section at the bottom of the interface. You can also adjust how the guitar works by manipulating the following controls shown on its graphic:

▷ **Pickup Selector switch.** The guitar provides a neck pickup (warm tone) and a bridge pickup (bright tone). Set the switch up/down to choose the neck/bridge pickup, respectively.

▷ **Mono Poly switch.** In Poly mode (switch down), the guitar can play multiple notes simultaneously. In Mono mode (switch up), the guitar can only play one note at a time.

▷ **Slide knob.** While in Mono mode only, the Slide knob can be adjusted to provide a portamento effect to the guitar playback. This means that instead of playing distinct notes when moving from one note to another, the sound will slide from one note to the next. The time it takes for the slide to occur is controlled by the Slide knob, which can be set from 0 to 3 seconds. Adjust it by clicking and dragging it up/down. Double-click it to return it to the default value of 1.5.

▷ **Tune knob.** Use this to change the tuning of the entire guitar in a range of –6 to +6 semitones. The default value of 0 means there is no change.

You can also adjust the sound of the guitar using the following on-screen controls located above the Fretboard:

▷ **Bass, Mid, and Treble.** These are EQ controls that adjust the overall tone of the guitar sound. You can learn more about EQ in Chapter 11. In the meantime, the Bass control applies a low-shelf filter affecting all frequencies below 80Hz. The Mid control applies a peak filter with a center frequency of 400Hz. The Treble control applies a high-shelf filter affecting all frequencies above 4kHz. All of the knobs can be set from –24dB to +12dB with 0dB as a default value.

▷ **Drive.** Adjust this control (0 to 100%) to add a distortion effect for a more dirty or gritty bass sound.

▷ **Compress.** This control adds a compression effect to the sound. As you raise the value (between 0 and 100%), the compression threshold drops from –6 to –24dB, the ratio ranges from 1:1 to 20:1, and the gain rises from 0 to +12dB. Basically, a higher Compress value gives you a louder, more in-your-face bass sound.

▷ **Pan.** Adjust this control to determine the position of the bass sound in the stereo sound field: –100% (full left) to 0% (centered) to +100% (full right).

▷ **Volume.** Adjust this control to determine the overall loudness of the synth: 0% (off) to 100% (full volume).

When you've finished adjusting parameters, you can save your new bass guitar sound as a program, as described earlier.

SI-Drum Kit

Simulating the sound of a real drum kit, SI-Drum Kit presents an interactive on-screen representation of a basic drum kit with eight percussion instruments. Click on the pictures of the instruments to audition the sounds in the current program. Additionally, you can click on the pictures in the drum pad section at the bottom of the interface.

You can also adjust how each instrument in the kit sounds by manipulating the following controls shown above the drum pad section:

▷ **Tune.** Adjust the Tune knob to alter the pitch of an instrument. Tuning is measured in semitones as follows: −24 st (lowered 2 octaves) to 0 st (original sound) to +24 st (raised 2 octaves). Some creative uses of the Tune knob can be used to alter instruments to the point where a drum kit sounds entirely different.

▷ **Pan.** Adjust the Pan knob to alter the position of an instrument in the stereo field. Pan is measured as follows: −100% (full left) to 0% (centered) to +100% (full right).

▷ **Volume.** Adjust the volume slider to increase or decrease the amplitude of an instrument. Volume is measured as a percentage: 0% (off) to 100% (full volume).

You can also adjust the sound of the entire drum kit using the controls located on the right side of the window:

▷ **Volume.** Adjust this control to set the overall loudness of the entire drum kit: 0% (off) to 100% (full volume).

▷ **Compress.** This control adds a compression effect to the entire drum kit sound. As you raise the value (between 0 and 100%), the compression threshold drops from −6 to −24dB, the ratio ranges from 1:1 to 20:1, and the gain rises from 0 to +12dB. Basically, a higher Compress value gives you a louder, more in-your-face sound.

▷ **Reverb.** This control adds a reverberation (echo) effect to the entire drum kit sound. It provides a room reverb sound, which means it simulates the sound of the drum kit being in a room. You can set it from 0% (no reverb) to 100% (full reverb). The higher the setting, the more room echo you will hear.

When you've finished adjusting parameters, you can save your new drum kit sound as a program, as described earlier.

SI-Electric Piano

Simulating the sound of a real electric piano, SI-Electric Piano presents an interactive on-screen representation of an electric piano instrument. Click on the keys in the piano keyboard section at the bottom of the interface to audition the current program. You can also add a number of effects to the piano by manipulating the following controls shown at the top of the interface:

▷ **Drive.** To activate the Drive effect, click its silver button. Then adjust its Depth control (0 to 100%) to add a distortion effect for a more dirty or gritty electric piano sound.

▷ **Chorus.** To activate the Chorus effect, click its silver button. Then adjust its Depth control (0 to 100%) to add a delay and detuning effect for a fatter or fuller sound.

▷ **Tremolo.** To activate the Tremolo effect, click its silver button. Then adjust its Depth control (0 to 100%) to add an amplitude modulation effect, which provides that familiar warbling sound you hear on an electric organ. Adjust its Rate control (0 to 100%) to control the speed of the modulation.

You can also adjust the sound of the piano using the following on-screen controls located above the keyboard:

▷ **Tune.** Use this to change the tuning of the entire piano in a range of −6 to +6 semitones. The default value of 0 means there is no change.

▷ **Tone.** This is an EQ control that applies a low-pass filter with the knob controlling the cutoff frequency. The range is 0% to 100% with a default of 50%. A lower setting gives you a duller piano sound, and a higher setting gives you a brighter sound.

▷ **Pan.** Adjust this control to determine the position of the piano sound in the stereo sound field: −100% (full left) to 0% (centered) to +100% (full right).

▷ **Volume.** Adjust this control to determine the overall loudness of the synth: 0% (off) to 100% (full volume).

When you've finished adjusting parameters, you can save your new piano sound as a program, as described earlier.

SI-String Section

Simulating the sound of a real orchestral string section, SI-String Section presents an interactive on-screen representation of a string section with three types of instruments represented: Bass, Cello, and Violin. Click on the keys in the piano keyboard section at the bottom of the interface to audition the current program (each instrument type has its own keyboard range). You can also adjust the loudness and stereo positioning of each instrument type in the section using the Vol (volume) and Pan controls shown above each instrument picture. Volume can be adjusted from 0% (off) to 100% (full volume) and panning can be adjusted from 100% (full left) to 0% (centered) to +100% (full right). This allows you to set up the string section however you like for your project.

You can also adjust the sound of the entire string section using the following on-screen controls located above the keyboard:

▷ **Attack.** Use this to control the time it takes for the sound to rise in volume when you trigger and hold a MIDI note. With a range of 0% (fast) to 100% (slow), a low setting gives you a hard string sound that is useful for staccato musical passages, and a high setting gives you a soft string sound that is useful for legato musical passages.

▷ **Release.** Use this to control the time it takes for the sound to fade away after a held MIDI note is released. The setting for this works similarly to Attack.

▷ **Tune.** Use this to change the tuning of the entire string section in a range of −6 to +6 semitones. The default value of 0 means there is no change.

▷ **Tone.** This is an EQ control that applies a low-pass filter with the knob controlling the cutoff frequency. The range is 0% to 100% with a default of 50%. A lower setting gives you a duller string sound and a higher setting gives you a brighter sound.

▷ **Chorus.** Adjust this control (0 to 100%) to add a delay and detuning effect for a fatter or fuller sound.

▷ **Reverb.** This control adds a reverberation (echo) effect to the entire string section sound. It provides a hall reverb sound, which means it simulates the sound of the string section in a concert hall. You can set it from 0% (no reverb) to 100% (full reverb). The higher the setting, the more hall echo you will hear.

▷ **Master.** Adjust this control to determine the overall loudness of the synth: 0% (off) to 100% (full volume).

When you've finished adjusting parameters, you can save your new string section sound as a program, as described earlier.

MORE STUDIO INSTRUMENT INFORMATION: For more information about each of the Studio Instruments synths, left-click once anywhere inside the synth windows and then press the F1 key to open the associated Help file.

Creating Music with Beats and Loops

IN ADDITION TO CREATING MUSIC BY RECORDING AND EDITING YOUR MIDI AND AUDIO PERFORMANCES, SONAR allows you to compose music with sample loops. Sample loops are usually (though not always) short audio recordings that you can piece together to create entire musical performances. Using them is a great way to add some acoustic audio tracks to your project without actually having to do any recording or knowing how to play an instrument. For example, you can buy a CD full of sample loops that contain nothing but acoustic drum beats. Not only can you buy drum loops, but you can also get real guitar solos, vocal chorus recordings, orchestral recordings, and more. You can create an entire project just by using sample loops, and SONAR even provides you with the tools to create your own loops.

Groove Clips

In SONAR, sample loops are known as *Groove clips*. If you're familiar with Sony's ACID software, you won't have any trouble with Groove clips because they are Cakewalk's equivalent to Sony's loops for ACID. Like loops for ACID, Groove clips automatically take care of the tedious chore of matching the playback tempo and pitch of each loop you use in a song. This is because Groove clips contain extra information that lets SONAR know their basic tempo, pitch, and playback properties. SONAR can accurately shift the tempo and pitch of the Groove clips so they match the tempo and pitch of the current project. Why is this important? Because not all sample loops are recorded at the same tempo and pitch, and in order to use them in the same song, they have to "groove" with one another, so to speak. Before loops for ACID or Groove clips came along, a musician would have to match the tempo and pitch of multiple loops manually.

Of course, not all sample loops contain the extra information I mentioned earlier. Plain sample loops need to be converted into Groove clips before you can use them in a SONAR project.

Creating Groove Clips

There are two types of Groove clips: audio Groove clips and MIDI Groove clips. For the most part, both types of Groove clips are handled in the same way, but there are some subtle differences.

Creating Audio Groove Clips

You can easily convert any audio clip in SONAR into a Groove clip by following these steps:

1. Select an audio clip in the Clips pane of the Track view and click the Clip tab (Shift+I) at the top of the Inspector (I) to open the Clip Properties pane.
2. Click the Groove Clip category to display the Groove clip parameters (see Figure 9.1).

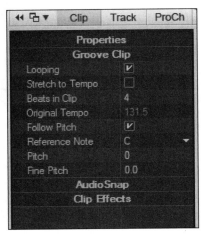

Figure 9.1 Find the Groove clip parameters in the Clip Properties pane of the Inspector.
Source: Cakewalk®, Inc.

3. Activate the Looping option. SONAR makes a guess as to how many rhythmic beats are in the clip, and it's usually correct. If the beats are inaccurate, you can change the number of beats for the clip by entering a new number in the Beats in Clip field. That's basically all you need to do, but there are some extra parameters that you need to deal with if you want some extra control over how SONAR will handle your new Groove clip.

> **QUICK GROOVE CLIP CREATION:** Instead of opening the Clip Properties to enable looping for an audio clip, you can right-click the clip and choose Groove-Clip Looping. You also can select the clip (or multiple clips) and press Ctrl+L. These methods are quicker, but they don't give you access to the extra parameters.

4. You can also have Groove clips that don't loop but still conform to the project tempo and pitch. When you activate the Stretch to Tempo parameter, SONAR makes a guess as to the original tempo of the clip. If the tempo is inaccurate, you can change it by entering a new number in the Original Tempo field.
5. In addition to changing the tempo of the clip, SONAR can change the pitch of the clip to follow the pitch of the project. This ensures that Groove clips stay in tune with one another in the same project. If you want SONAR to control the pitch of the clip, activate the Follow Pitch option.

> **PERCUSSION GROOVE CLIPS:** Not all Groove clips should follow the pitch of the project. Why? Well, if you have a Groove clip that contains percussive data like a drum instrument performance, you don't want the pitch of that clip to change because it will make the drum performance sound strange. The Follow Pitch option should be activated only for clips containing pitch-related performances such as guitar, bass, woodwinds, horns, strings, vocals, and the like.

6. When you activate the Follow Pitch option, you have to tell SONAR the original pitch of the material in the clip. SONAR doesn't determine the pitch automatically for you. Choose a pitch from the Reference Note list. For example, if the notes played in the clip are based on a C chord, choose C. How do you know the original pitch of the clip? You have to figure it out by listening to it. Either that or sometimes when you purchase sample loops, the CD will include information about each loop file, including the original pitch.
7. If you want to transpose the pitch of the clip so that it plays differently from the project pitch, you can enter a value (semitones) for the Pitch parameter. This parameter can come in handy if you are composing with orchestral instrument loops that need to be played in a different key.

8. If the pitch of the clip is slightly out of tune, you can adjust it by entering a value (cents) for the Fine Pitch parameter.

SONAR will now treat your original audio clip as a Groove clip. If the tempo or pitch of the project changes, the Groove clip will be stretched and transposed accordingly. In addition, you'll notice that in the Track view, a regular audio clip is shown as a rectangle, but when a clip is converted into a looping Groove clip, it is shown as a rectangle with rounded corners. Non-looping Groove clips look like regular audio clips.

Creating MIDI Groove Clips

To create a MIDI Groove clip, you can follow the same procedures for creating audio Groove clips. The only difference is that MIDI Groove clips provide fewer parameters in Clip Properties.

The Clip Properties for a MIDI Groove clip only provide the Looping option, the Beats in Clip parameter, the Follow Pitch option, and the Reference Note and Pitch parameters. These options and parameters work just like they do for audio Groove clips.

The Loop Construction View

There might be times when SONAR doesn't seem to stretch your audio Groove clips accurately. If this occurs, you'll hear slight anomalies in the audio when you change the tempo of your project. To correct this, you can try using the Loop Construction view to convert your audio clip by following these steps:

1. Right-click the audio clip in the Clips pane of the Track view and choose View > Loop Construction (Alt+7) or double-click the clip to open the Loop Construction view.

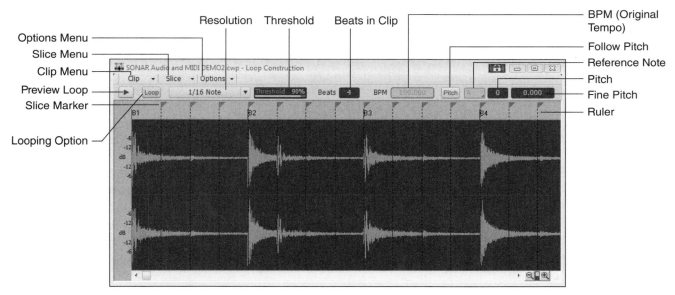

Figure 9.2 Use the Loop Construction view to create and edit Groove clips.
Source: Cakewalk®, Inc.

2. As you can see in Figure 9.2, all of the parameters found in Clip Properties are also found here either in the toolbar or the menus. You can set these parameters as I explained in the previous section.
3. Clicking the Preview loop button lets you listen to the loop currently displayed in the Loop Construction view. Choosing the Options > Preview Bus menu lets you choose which bus (audio channel or sound card output) will be used to play the loop.

4. You'll also see the audio waveform of the loop currently displayed in the Loop Construction view along with a Ruler on top of the waveform, which shows either beats or samples. Double-click in the Ruler to change its value. Notice that when you activate the Looping option, SONAR automatically adjusts the Resolution and Threshold parameters in the toolbar and adds vertical lines to the audio waveform. These lines are slicing markers, which designate a specific place in a loop where the timing data needs to be preserved when the timing of the loop is being stretched to fit the project tempo. The slicing markers make it possible for a loop to be stretched without having its pitch change at the same time.

> **EXPLANATION OF SLICING:** Normally, when you stretch (in other words, change the length of) audio data, the pitch is changed as well. Make the data shorter, and the pitch is raised. Make the data longer, and the pitch is lowered. By slicing the data into smaller pieces, you can stretch the data very accurately, preserving its original quality without changing its pitch. This slicing happens in real time during playback, and it is nondestructive (meaning the original data is not changed).

5. To control the way SONAR automatically adds slicing markers to your loop, you need to adjust the Resolution and Threshold parameters, which are located on the toolbar. The Resolution parameter places slicing markers at specific rhythmic locations in the loop according to the Beats in Clip parameter (which I mentioned earlier). For example, if you set the Resolution to 1/8 Note, slicing markers will be placed at every eighth note location in your loop. If your loop contains four beats, it will have seven slicing markers. You would think there should be eight slicing markers (since there are two eighth notes to every beat, and two multiplied by four is eight), but the beginning of a loop never needs a slicing marker, so there is one fewer than expected. When you adjust the Resolution parameter, it's usually best to go with a note value equal to the smallest rhythmic value in your audio data performance. For example, if your loop contains sixteenth notes, try setting Resolution to 1/16 Note. You also can try a setting that is one value lower, which in this case would be eighth notes. Just be aware that too few or too many slicing markers will introduce unwanted artifacts into the audio when your loops are being stretched.

6. When you adjust the Threshold parameter, slicing markers are placed at the beginning of detected transients in the audio data of the loop. Transients are large spikes (big changes in volume) in the audio waveform. Because of this, the Threshold parameter works best with percussive material. A setting of about 90 percent usually works well. Usually, you'll want to use a combination of the Resolution and Threshold parameters to get the optimum number of slicing markers set up in your loop.

7. If the Resolution and Threshold parameters don't provide enough slicing markers, or if they provide the wrong placement, you can use the Smart (F5), Select (F6), and Erase (F10) tools to create, erase, and adjust the slicing markers manually. Use the Smart or Select tool to move existing slicing markers by clicking and dragging the marker flags or marker lines in the audio waveform display (see Figure 9.3). You also can create your own slicing markers by simply double-clicking in the marker flag area. Manually created or changed markers are shown with a purple flag.

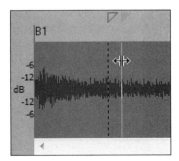

Figure 9.3 Use the Select tool (F6) to create or move slicing markers.
Source: Cakewalk®, Inc.

8. To erase a slicing marker, just choose the Erase tool (F10) and click the triangle or line of the slicing marker that you want to erase.

9. If you moved any of the automatically created slicing markers and you want to put them back in their original positions, just choose Slice > Reset Markers from the menu. If you created any slicing markers manually, those markers will remain untouched.

Usually, you can rely on the automatic settings that SONAR provides, but just in case, it's good to know that you have total control over how your Groove clips are handled.

Editing Individual Slices

In addition to manipulating the slicing markers themselves, SONAR lets you adjust the gain (volume), panning (stereo location), and pitch of the individual slices as follows:

1. Use the Smart (F5) or Select tool (F6) to click between any two slicing markers to select that slice.

2. To hear what that slice sounds like, choose Options > Auto Slice Preview On/Off (which is on by default) from the menu. If you would like to have the slice playback looped continuously, choose Options > Auto Slice Preview Loop On/Off and click the slice. To stop playback when looping, click the Preview loop button.

3. Using the options in the Slice menu, you can adjust the gain, panning, and pitch of each individual slice. To adjust the volume of slices, choose Slice > Show/Hide Gain Envelope. To adjust the panning of slices, choose Slice > Show/Hide Pan Envelope. To adjust the pitch of slices, choose Slice > Show/Hide Pitch Envelope.

4. When you choose any of the Show/Hide options, they toggle the Gain, Pan, and Pitch envelopes in the audio waveform. The envelopes adjust the gain, panning, and pitch of each slice graphically. The Slice > Previous Slice (PgUp) and Slice > Next Slice (PgDn) options move quickly to the previous or next slice from the currently selected slice.

5. To adjust an envelope segment for a slice, just drag the part of the envelope located inside the slice you want to change (see Figure 9.4). To increase the value, drag up. To decrease the value, drag down. If you want to return the segment to its default position, double-click it.

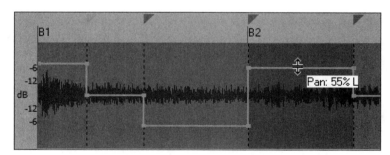

Figure 9.4 To adjust the Gain, Pan, or Pitch envelopes for a slice, drag the envelope segments up or down with your mouse.
Source: Cakewalk®, Inc.

6. Play the slice or the entire Groove clip to preview how it will sound.

With these new Groove clip parameters, you can get very creative with loop-based projects.

EDIT MIDI GROOVE CLIPS: MIDI Groove clips don't rely on slicing, so you can't edit them with the Loop Construction view. Instead, you edit the data in MIDI Groove clips in the Piano Roll view (see Chapter 6), just like a regular MIDI clip. However, there are a couple unique aspects to editing MIDI Groove clips. First, you can edit data in any of the clip repetitions without affecting other repetitions. For example, if

---

you delete a note in the first clip repetition, that note is not deleted in the other repetitions. Also, if you slip-edit a MIDI Groove clip to make it shorter, any edits you performed will be lost.

Saving Groove Clips

When you create Groove clips in a SONAR project, those clips are saved along with the project. But what if you want to use your Groove clips in another project? Or maybe you'd like to share the clips with your friends. This is where the Save Loop option comes in handy. The Save Loop option lets you save your Groove clips to disk as a special WAV file. Unlike most ordinary WAV files, which just contain audio data, the Groove clip WAV files contain all the special looping information I talked about earlier. Here's how it works:

1. With your Groove clip still open in the Loop Construction view, choose Clip > Save Loop from the menu to open the Save As dialog box.
2. Use the Save In list to navigate to the location on your disk drive to which you want to save the file.
3. Type a name for the file in the File Name field and click Save.

Your Groove clip will be saved to disk as a WAV file that contains the audio data for the clip, plus all the looping information that you set, such as the Beats in Clip, Root Note, Pitch, and slicing markers. The next time you open the clip, this information will be loaded automatically.

Exporting MIDI Groove Clips

In addition to saving audio Groove clips, you can save (or export) MIDI Groove clips for later use in other projects. MIDI Groove clips are exported as standard MIDI files that can be imported later. To export a MIDI Groove clip, follow these steps:

1. Select the MIDI Groove clip and choose File > Export > MIDI Groove Clip to open the Export MIDI Groove Clip dialog box. (You can export only one clip at a time.)
2. Use the Save In list to navigate to the location on your disk drive to which you want to save the file.
3. Type a name for the file in the File Name field and click Save.

Your MIDI Groove clip will be saved as a MIDI (MID) file that contains the MIDI data for the clip, plus all the looping information you set, such as the Beats in Clip, Follow Project Pitch, and Reference Note parameters.

Working with Groove Clips

After you've created your Groove clips, you can use them to compose music in a current project or to create an entirely new project. Composing with Groove clips involves a combination of dragging and dropping to add clips to a project and slip-editing to make the clips conform to the music you are trying to create.

Adding clips to a project involves using the Media Browser, which I've already covered. Please see "The Media Browser" section in Chapter 5. After you've added your Groove clips, you can slip-edit them to make them conform to the music you are trying to create. You can also add Groove clips to a project by using the File > Import > Audio or File > Import > MIDI features (also described in Chapter 5 in the "Importing" section).

Controlling Project Pitch

Controlling the pitch of the Groove clips in your project is extremely easy. The first thing you need to do is set the default pitch for the entire project. This is called the *project pitch*. To set the project pitch, choose Project > Set

Default Groove Clip Pitch in SONAR's main menu and choose a project pitch. For example, if you want the music in your project to start using a C chord, choose C.

Pitch Markers

After you've set the initial pitch for your project, all the Groove clips automatically will be transposed to play using that pitch until you change it. To change the project pitch at specified points in your project, you need to use pitch markers. Although pitch markers work almost the same as regular markers, they do have a slight difference.

Creating Pitch Markers

Creating pitch markers is essentially the same as creating regular markers. You simply set the Now time to the measure, beat, and tick at which you want to place the marker in the project, activate the Marker dialog box, and type in a name. But you also have to designate a pitch setting for that marker, which tells SONAR to change the project pitch at that point in the project. To create a pitch marker, follow these steps:

1. Set the Now time to the measure, beat, and tick or the SMPTE time at which you want to place the marker in the object.
2. Choose Project > Insert Marker to open the Marker dialog box. You can also open the Marker dialog box by pressing M; holding the Ctrl key and clicking just above the Time Ruler (the Marker section) in the Track, Staff, or Piano Roll view; right-clicking in a Time Ruler; clicking the Insert Marker button in the Markers module of the Control Bar; or clicking the Insert Marker button in the Markers view.
3. Type a name for the marker.
4. If you want the marker to be assigned to a measure/beat/tick value, you don't need to do anything more.
5. If you want the marker to be assigned to a SMPTE time, activate the Lock to SMPTE (Real World) Time option.
6. Assign a pitch to the marker using the Groove-Clip Pitch list.

After you click OK, your pitch marker (and its pitch) will be added to the marker section (just above the Time Ruler) in the Track, Staff, and Piano Roll views.

ADD MARKERS DURING PLAYBACK: Usually, you add markers to a project while no real-time activity is going on, but you also can add markers while a project is playing. Simply press the M key, and SONAR will create a marker at the current Now time. The new marker will be assigned a temporary name automatically, which you can change later. You also need to add a pitch to each marker after you stop playback because SONAR will not assign pitches to markers automatically.

Changing Pitch Marker Names

To change the name of a pitch marker, follow these steps:

1. Right-click the marker in the Marker section of the Time Ruler in one of the views to open the Marker dialog box (or double-click the marker in the Markers view).
2. Type a new name for the marker and click OK.

Changing Pitch Marker Time

Follow these steps to change the time value of a pitch marker numerically:

1. Right-click the marker in the Marker section of the Time Ruler in one of the views to open the Marker dialog box (or double-click the marker in the Markers view).

2. Type a new measure/beat/tick value for the marker. If you want to use a SMPTE value, activate the Lock to SMPTE (Real World) Time option and then type a new hour/minute/second/frame value for the marker. Click OK.

You also can change the time value of a pitch marker graphically by simply dragging the marker in the marker section of the Time Ruler in one of the views. Drag the marker to the left to decrease its time value, or drag it to the right to increase its time value.

Making a Copy of a Pitch Marker

To make a copy of a pitch marker, follow these steps:

1. Hold down the Ctrl key.
2. Click and drag a pitch marker to a new time location in the Marker section of the Time Ruler in one of the views.
3. Release the Ctrl key and mouse button. SONAR will display the Marker dialog box.
4. Enter a name for the marker. You can change the time by typing a new value if you want. The time value is initially set to the time corresponding to the location on the Time Ruler to which you dragged the marker. Click OK.

Deleting a Pitch Marker

You can delete a marker in one of two ways—either directly in the Track, Staff, or Piano Roll view or via the Markers view. Here's the exact procedure:

1. If you want to use the Track, Staff, or Piano Roll view, click and hold the left mouse button on the marker you want to delete.
2. If you want to use the Markers view, select Views > Markers (Alt+Shift+4) to open the Markers view. Then select the marker you want to delete from the list.
3. Press the Del(ete) key.

GROOVE CLIPS DEMO VIDEO: To see a demonstration of Groove clips in action, go to **garrigus.com? GrooveClips** to watch the video.

The Matrix View

While somewhat similar to the Cyclone soft synth discussed in Chapter 8, the Matrix view (see Figure 9.5) has a few major differences. First, it is not a soft synth, but a dedicated loop sequencing view that loads in your own sounds in the form of audio and MIDI files in the following formats: plain audio and Groove clips (WAV), REX audio loops (RX2), MIDI Groove clips (MID), Step Sequencer Patterns (SSP), and Project5 Patterns (PTN). Each of the loaded files is represented by a *cell* (of which there can be an unlimited number). These cells are arranged in a grid of columns and rows; there can be an unlimited number of both of these as well. A column represents a single performance made up of the playback of all the cells in that column. And because they are connected, each row in the Matrix view can represent a track in the Track view (although this is not always the case, as I'll explain later).

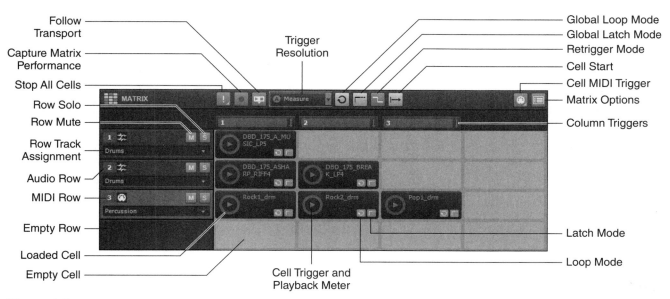

Figure 9.5 The Matrix view is a dedicated loop sequencing view.
Source: Cakewalk®, Inc.

Grabbing Files for the Grid

When you first open the Matrix view, all the cells are empty, and clicking a cell does nothing except make it the selected cell (shown by a yellow outline). You can load a cell with a file by importing or dragging and dropping. To import a file, right-click a cell and choose Import File. Then select a file in the Import Audio dialog box and click Open. Files can also be loaded by dragging and dropping them from SONAR's Browser or by dragging clips from the Track view.

> **LOADING MULTIPLE CELLS SIMULTANEOUSLY:** A quick way to load up cells in a column or row is by selecting multiple files or clips and dragging them all at once into the grid. To populate a column, drag the files into a cell in that column. The files will be automatically added to the column sequentially, starting with the cell to which you dragged. Use the same procedure to populate a row of cells, but hold down Shift while dragging and dropping.

Keep in mind that a row can only contain audio or MIDI files, not both. The first cell that you load in a row determines the data type for that row. So, if you load an audio file, a Groove clip, or a REX loop into a cell, the data type for that corresponding row will be audio. If you load a MIDI Groove clip, Step Sequencer pattern, or Project5 pattern, the data type for the row will be MIDI.

> **IMPORT AUDIO AS GROOVE CLIPS:** When you import a normal audio file, it will play back at its original tempo. If you want the Matrix view to automatically stretch normal audio files when loaded (so that they play at the project tempo), click the Matrix Options button. Then activate the Import all audio as Groove Clips option. You should also activate this option if you want your Matrix view performance to be recorded as Groove clips in the Track view. See "Record a Matrix View Performance" later in this chapter.

After loading one or more cells, you can manipulate them in the following ways (press Ctrl+Z to undo any mistakes):

▷ **Rename.** By default, a cell uses the same name as the file loaded into it. To change the name of a cell, right-click it and choose Rename Cell. Type a name and click OK.

▷ **Clear.** To unload (or clear) the file from a cell, right-click it and choose Clear Cell. To clear all cells in the entire grid, click (and hold for a second) the Stop All Cells button in the toolbar and choose Clear All Cells. Keep in mind that this will also remove all column and row settings.

▷ **Move.** To move a loaded cell (along with its settings) to an empty cell, click and drag it.

▷ **Copy.** To copy a loaded cell to an empty cell, Ctrl+click and drag it.

▷ **Replace.** You can also replace a loaded cell by Ctrl+clicking and dragging another loaded cell onto it.

Configuring Columns and Rows

With cells loaded and organized, there are a number of things you can do to change the configuration of both columns and rows. Columns can be changed by right-clicking a Column Trigger and choosing one of the following options:

▷ **Rename Column.** Choose this option to open the Rename Column dialog box. Type in a new name and click OK. This allows you to give a descriptive name to the performance represented by that column.

▷ **Insert Column.** Choose this option to insert an empty column to the left of the column you clicked (which is then shifted to the right in the grid and renumbered).

▷ **Duplicate Column.** Choose this option to create an exact copy to the left of the column you clicked. The only difference is the new column will not be named, and the clicked column is shifted to the right in the grid and renumbered.

There are also three row parameters that can be changed, which mainly pertain to how the cells in the row sound during playback.

Row Track Assignment

As I mentioned earlier, a row can only contain one type of file: audio or MIDI. The first file you drag into a row determines the type of row, as well as its track assignment in the Track view. Normally, rows are assigned to existing tracks. Audio rows are assigned to the first audio track in a project, and MIDI rows are assigned to the first MIDI track. You can change this by clicking on a row's Track Assignment parameter and choosing a track from the list.

AUTOMATIC MATRIX TRACK CREATION: If you'd like a new row to be automatically assigned to a new track, press and hold Alt while dragging files into the grid.

Having rows assigned (and connected) to tracks in the Track view means that you control the output of the rows using the assigned track parameters. So volume, pan, and other track parameters control how a row will sound. This also allows you to apply effects to a row's output. Keep in mind that MIDI rows are assigned to MIDI tracks, which need a synth for playback, so you need to assign the output of the MIDI track(s) to either a hardware synth or a soft synth. You can also assign MIDI rows to Simple Instrument Tracks as well as directly to a soft synth, which is really the most efficient workflow.

MULTIPLE ROWS TO ONE TRACK: Personally, I like to assign each row to its own track, which helps keep things organized. However, there's nothing to stop you from assigning multiple rows to the same track. One scenario where this might come in handy is if you have multiple rows of MIDI drum loops and you want to drive a single drum synth from all those rows.

Row Playback Control

Rows themselves can't be triggered—only cells and columns can be triggered for playback, which I'll talk about shortly. However, you do control the output of each row with its Mute and Solo buttons. These work in the same way as track Mute and Solo buttons in the Track view: click Mute to silence a row during playback, and click Solo to play only that row and silence all others. However, the row buttons are independent of the track buttons. So, if you mute or solo a row, its associated track still produces output because multiple rows can be assigned to the same track, as explained earlier.

Controlling Cells and Columns

To trigger a cell or column, click its Cell Trigger or Column Trigger, respectively. Triggering a cell starts playback of only that cell. Triggering a column starts playback of all cells in that column. Click a Cell Trigger or Column Trigger a second time to stop playback. If you have multiple cells/columns playing and want to stop them all, click the Stop All Cells button in the Matrix view toolbar.

EMPTY CELL OPTION: By default, if you click/trigger an empty cell in a row, it will stop any cell in that row that is currently playing. If you don't want that to happen, click the Matrix Options button and deactivate the Empty cells stop active cells when triggered option.

MIDI Triggering

Cell and column playback can also be started/stopped (triggered) via MIDI by doing the following:

1. Right-click a Cell or Column Trigger and choose MIDI Learn. Do the same for additional cells and columns if you want them to be triggered by the same MIDI message. A cell or column in MIDI Learn mode will show an orange outline.
2. Make sure the Cell MIDI Trigger Enable option is on (via the Cell MIDI Trigger button in the toolbar). By default, this turns on automatically whenever you put a cell or column into MIDI Learn mode. In addition, you can click (and hold for a second) the button to choose a MIDI channel for the Matrix view. By default, it is set to Omni, which means it will receive all incoming MIDI data on all channels. Normally, when you have only one MIDI controller, keeping this set to Omni works fine.
3. Press a key (if you're using a MIDI keyboard) or move a control to send the MIDI message you want to use as the trigger for the cell/columns that are currently in MIDI Learn mode. After you do this, the orange outlines disappear, and a small MIDI port icon shows in the corner of the cell(s)/column(s) to indicate they are out of MIDI Learn mode and have been assigned MIDI triggers.
4. If you make a mistake and want to remove a MIDI trigger, right-click the cell/column and choose Clear MIDI Learn. To remove MIDI triggers from all cells/columns, click (and hold for a second) the Stop All Cells button and choose Clear All MIDI Learn.

Now, when you press a key or move a control on your MIDI controller, the corresponding cell(s)/column(s) will start/stop just as if you were clicking them with the mouse.

Matrix Playback Control

Each cell provides a number of adjustable playback parameters, which are also influenced by a number of global parameters:

▷ **Loop Mode.** By default, a cell is set to loop playback continuously after it is triggered. If you don't want a cell's playback to loop, click its Loop Mode button. You can also stop/start looping for all loaded cells by clicking the Global Loop Mode button. In addition, by clicking a cell's Loop Mode button, you remove the link between it and the Global Loop Mode. A cell then has individual control over looping even when the

Global Loop Mode button is clicked. To restore the link between the cell and the Global Loop Mode, Ctrl +click the cell's Loop Mode button.

▷ **One-Shot.** Individual instrument hits (like a snare drum hit) or sound effects that are only meant to play once when triggered and never loop are called *one-shot samples*. If you load these into a cell, you can right-click the cell and choose One-Shot Trigger so the Matrix knows the cell contains a one-shot sample.

▷ **Latch Mode.** By default, a cell is set to continue playing even after you let go of the mouse button or MIDI key. If you would rather have the cell stop playing in that situation, click its Latch Mode button. You can also disable/enable Latch Mode for all loaded cells by clicking the Global Latch Mode button. In addition, by clicking a cell's Latch Mode button, you remove the link between it and the Global Latch Mode. A cell then has individual control over latching even when the Global Latch Mode button is clicked. To restore the link between the cell and the Global Latch Mode, Ctrl+click the cell's Latch Mode button.

▷ **Trigger Mode.** By default, when you trigger a cell/column, it doesn't start playing right away. Instead, it waits for a designated period of time (called the *trigger resolution*) so that its playback can synchronize with the other cells/columns in the grid. To change this value, use the Trigger Resolution menu in the toolbar. In addition, each cell can have its own trigger resolution. Right-click a cell and choose Trigger Resolution to set this option.

Some additional global parameters are available that provide even more control over playback:

▷ **Retrigger Mode.** By default, all cells/columns that are currently playing will stop playing when you trigger them a second time (also called *retriggering*). If you would rather have them start playback again (from the beginning) in this situation, click the Retrigger Mode button in the toolbar.

▷ **Follow Transport.** By default, playback in the Matrix view and project playback are separate from each other and can be controlled individually. However, you can make it so that the Matrix view will only play when the project is playing. In this case, playback in the Matrix view will be synchronized with the project's Now time. Click the Follow Transport button in the Matrix view toolbar to activate this feature.

▷ **Cell Start.** By default, all cells/columns are set to start playback at any point in their loaded files so that they may synchronize with the project's Now time. However, you can make it so that they will always start playback at the beginning of their loaded files. Click the Cell Start button in the toolbar to activate this feature.

Record a Matrix View Performance

Once you've loaded the cells/columns, configured their settings, and assigned rows to the proper tracks, you're ready to record a Matrix view performance, as follows:

1. Click the Follow Transport button to activate that option. This isn't mandatory, but it makes sure that your recorded clips line up correctly with the Track view Time Ruler.
2. Click the Capture Matrix Performance button to activate that option.
3. Set the Now time in the Track view to the point in the project that you'd like to start recording.
4. If you want the Matrix output to start being recorded immediately at the Now time, you can trigger cells/columns now, and they will wait until project playback begins.
5. Start project playback by clicking the Play button in the Control Bar or pressing the spacebar.
6. Trigger some cells/columns to create a performance. As you do this, you'll see audio clips being recorded in audio tracks and MIDI clips being recorded in MIDI and Instrument tracks.
7. When your performance is finished, stop project playback by clicking the Stop button or pressing the spacebar. Both the project and the Matrix view should stop, and the Matrix view is taken out of capture mode.

When you're finished, you'll see clips recorded where you started cell/column playback and blank space where you stopped playback to re-create an exact replica of your real-time Matrix performance.

MATRIX PERFORMANCE PITCH MARKERS: You'll recall that I talked about pitch markers earlier in this chapter. In addition to working with Groove clips, you can also use them with your recorded Matrix performance when the performance is recorded as Groove clips in the Track view.

The performance will only be recorded as Groove clips if you had the Import All Audio As Groove Clips option activated when you loaded the Matrix cells, as I mentioned earlier in the "Grabbing Files for the Grid" section of this chapter.

So, after you've finished recording, you can edit the performance using the same Groove clip techniques from earlier in the chapter. In addition, if you have pitch markers in a project while recording a Matrix performance, they will be applied in real time so you can hear the pitch of the cell playback change.

MATRIX VIEW DEMO VIDEO: To see a demonstration of the Matrix view in action, go to **garrigus.com? MatrixView** to watch the video.

MORE MATRIX VIEW INFORMATION: For more information about the Matrix view, left-click once anywhere inside its window and then press the F1 key to open the Matrix view Help.

Mixing Music in SONAR

AFTER YOU'VE RECORDED AND EDITED YOUR MIDI AND AUDIO DATA, it's time to mix down your project. This is called the *mixdown process* because you are taking all the MIDI and audio tracks in your project and mixing them together into a single stereo audio track. From there, you can put your music on CD, distribute it over the Internet, or record it onto tape. SONAR provides a number of different features that make the mixdown process as simple and intuitive as possible.

The Console View

For mixing down the MIDI and audio tracks in your project, you can use either the Console view or the Track view. I've already covered many of the Track view features in earlier chapters, so in this chapter I'll tell you about the Console view and also let you know how the Track view fits into the mixdown process.

The Console view adjusts the main parameters for each track in your project via on-screen buttons, knobs, sliders, and faders (vertical sliders). Similar in appearance to a hardware-based mixing board found in most recording studios, the Console view displays tracks as a collection of strips and modules, each with its own set of adjustable controls.

More precisely, the Console view consists of four major sections (starting from left to right): the MIDI and audio track strips (displaying modules containing controls for each MIDI and audio track in the project); the buses (containing additional mixing controls, which I'll explain later); the mains (also containing additional mixing controls, which I'll explain later); and the menu at the top of the view.

To open the Console view, simply choose Views > Console View (Alt+2). You can also right-click inside the Clips pane of the Track view and choose View > Console View. The Console view will open, displaying modules for every track and bus in the current project.

The MIDI Track Strips

Each MIDI track strip contains a number of different modules containing controls that manipulate many of its corresponding track parameters (see Figure 10.1).

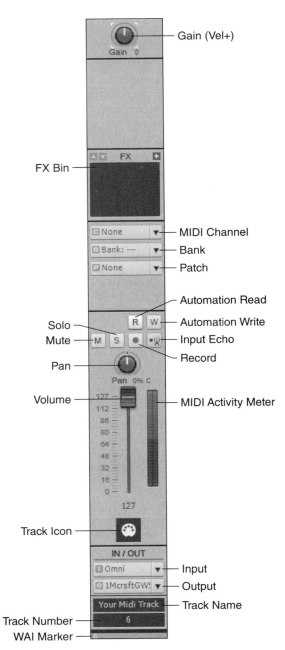

Figure 10.1 A MIDI track module contains controls for adjusting the parameters of its corresponding track.
Source: Cakewalk®, Inc.

As a matter of fact, all the controls are the equivalent of the track parameters shown in the Inspector. This means that if you change the value of a control in the Console view, the equivalent track parameter is also changed in the Track view. To adjust knobs and faders, click/drag them up/down and double-click them to return them to their default values.

> **SET DEFAULT VALUES:** To set your own default values for controls, adjust the control to the value you want to use. Then right-click the control and choose Value > Set Snap-To = Current. The next time you double-click the control, it will be set to this value.

From top to bottom, the controls in a MIDI track strip correspond to the controls described in the following sections.

Gain (Vel+)

The Gain (same as Vel+ in the Track view) parameter raises or lowers the MIDI velocity of each note in a track by adding or subtracting a number from −127 to +127.

FX Bin

You can use the FX bin to assign effects to the track. These effects are applied only in real time. The FX bin works exactly the same as the FX bin in the Track view. See Chapter 11 for more information about using effects.

MIDI Channel

The MIDI Channel parameter sets the MIDI channel of the track. It is the equivalent of the MIDI Channel parameter in the Track view. Click the parameter to choose a channel from the menu.

Bank

You can use the Bank parameter to set the MIDI patch bank of the track. It is the equivalent of the Bank parameter in the Track view. Click the parameter to choose a bank from the menu.

Patch

You can use the Patch parameter to set the MIDI patch of the track. It is the equivalent of the Patch parameter in the Track view. Click the parameter to choose a patch from the menu. Right-click the parameter to launch the Patch Browser.

> **THE PATCH BROWSER:** You also can choose patches for a track using the Patch Browser. In the dialog box, you will see a list of all the patches available for the MIDI track (this list is affected by Instrument Definitions, see Chapter 2). To search for a particular patch, type some text in the Show Patches Containing the Text field. To choose a patch, select it from the list and click OK.

Automation Read and Write

Click these buttons to toggle Automation Read and Automation Write on/off for the track (see Chapter 12).

Input Echo

You can use the Input Echo parameter to turn MIDI echo on or off for the track. It is the equivalent of the Input Echo parameter in the Track view (see Chapter 5).

Mute, Solo, and Record

The Mute, Solo, and Record parameters turn the mute, solo, and record options on or off for the track. They are the equivalents of the Mute, Solo, and Record options in the Track view. Click them to toggle them on/off. See Chapter 5 for more information about recording.

DIM SOLO

Normally, when you solo a track, all other tracks are silenced. However, SONAR has a special Dim Solo mode. Instead of silencing the other tracks, it only reduces their volume so you can still hear all the tracks in a project, but the soloed track is more pronounced. This is very useful if you want to focus on a particular track, but still want to hear it in context with the rest of the tracks in a project. You can toggle the Dim Solo mode by clicking the Dim Solo Mode button (labeled DIM) in the Mix module of the Control Bar. You can also assign a key binding by choosing Global Bindings for the Bind Context in the Key Bindings section of the Preferences dialog box and selecting Dim Solo Mode in the Function list. To configure the Dim Solo mode to adjust how much other tracks are reduced, press P and choose Audio – Driver Settings in the Preferences dialog box. Then select one of the Dim Solo Gain options (–6dB, –12dB, or –18dB).

SOLO OVERRIDE

When using the Solo feature, you may want to keep some tracks playing so that you can compare the soloed track to the other tracks, but not the entire project. For this situation, SONAR provides the Solo Override feature. To assign a track with solo override status, hold the Shift key and click the track's Solo button. Now, when you solo other tracks in the project, the track(s) with solo override status will not be silenced. Keep in mind, however, that if you have the Dim Solo feature activated, Solo Override has no effect.

EXCLUSIVE SOLO MODE

Another situation that may arise with SONAR's Solo feature is when you have a number of different tracks soloed, but now you want to solo only a single track. Normally, you would need to unsolo all the currently soloed tracks and then solo the track you want to hear. Instead, you can activate the Exclusive Solo Mode by clicking the Exclusive Solo button (labeled <S>) in the Mix module of the Control Bar. You can also assign a key binding by choosing Global Bindings for the Bind Context in the Key Bindings section of the Preferences dialog box and selecting Exclusive Solo in the Function list.

After activating the mode, click the single track you want to solo, and all other tracks are automatically unsoloed. Keep in mind that when you solo a track folder, soft synth, tracks, or buses in a group, or solo selected tracks using Quick Groups (hold Ctrl and click the Solo button of one of the selected tracks), multiple tracks are soloed and any others not belonging to one of those situations are unsoloed.

> **CONSOLE VIEW RECORDING:** The Record control is available in the Console view because you can actually use the view during recording instead of the Track view if you want. You can even create new tracks in the Console view. To do so, right-click in any blank space and choose Insert Audio Track or Insert MIDI Track (or choose Track > Insert in the Console view menu). A new MIDI or audio track module will be added to the Console and Track views.

Pan

You can use the Pan parameter to set the MIDI panning of the track. It is the equivalent of the Pan parameter in the Track view.

Volume

Using the Volume parameter, you can set the MIDI volume of the track. It is the equivalent of the Volume parameter in the Track view. You can change the volume by clicking and dragging the fader up or down. As you drag the fader, the number box located below it will display the current value of the parameter. The value can range from 0 (the lowest volume level) to 127 (the highest volume level). You can also set the volume by clicking on the number box. Then press Enter, type in a new value, and press Enter again.

Input

The Input parameter sets the MIDI input of the track. It is the equivalent of the Input parameter in the Track view. You can change the input by clicking the control and choosing a new input from the menu.

Output

Using the Output parameter, you can set the MIDI output of the track. It is the equivalent of the Output parameter in the Track view. You can change the output by clicking the control and choosing a new output from the menu.

Track Number

The track number is the equivalent of the same track number in the Track view. Click the number to select a single track. Click and drag over multiple numbers to select multiple tracks.

> **QUICK CONTROL CHANGES WITH QUICK GROUPS:** After selecting multiple tracks or selecting none at all (Ctrl+Shift+A), you can hold down the Ctrl key and click/drag a control to change all the same controls in all selected tracks. If no tracks are selected, then all tracks are affected. However, this only works in the same type of tracks, so if you adjust a control in a MIDI track, other MIDI tracks will be affected, but not audio tracks. This is SONAR's Quick Groups feature, and it allows you to change multiple controls in multiple tracks quickly. For more detailed information on grouping, see Chapter 12.

Name

The Name parameter displays the name of the track. It is the equivalent of the Name parameter in the Track view. You can change the name by double-clicking the parameter, typing some new text, and pressing the Enter key.

WAI Marker

The WAI markers indicate which tracks are currently being controlled by a control surface (see Chapter 12).

The Audio Track Strips

Like the MIDI track strips, the audio track strips contain a number of different controls you can use to manipulate their corresponding track parameters (see Figure 10.2).

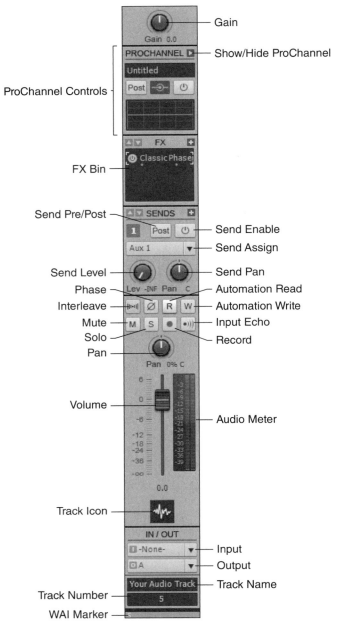

Figure 10.2 The audio track strips are similar to the MIDI track strips in terms of the controls they provide.
Source: Cakewalk®, Inc.

Many of the controls are the same as those on the MIDI track strips. Included are the Input, FX Bin, Mute, Solo, Record, Pan, Volume, Track Number and Name, Automation Read and Write, and WAI Marker parameters. They all work in exactly the same manner as they do on the MIDI track strips, except they are controlling audio data instead of MIDI data. The one difference is with the Volume control. Instead of displaying its value as a MIDI volume controller number, its value is shown in decibels (dB).

Some of the parameters, however, are unique to audio track strips.

Gain

The Gain parameter (which used to be called *Trim* in SONAR 8.5 and older versions) adjusts the volume of a track before the signal gets to the FX Bin, ProChannel, and the regular Volume parameter. This can be helpful for adjusting the volume of the signal coming from the track's clips into the FX Bin or into the ProChannel, as well as the relative volume of one track to another without having to change the final mix positions of your Volume parameters. It is the equivalent of the Gain parameter in the Track view.

ProChannel (SONAR Producer Edition)

This section of the audio track strip displays a scaled-down version of the ProChannel channel strip effect included with SONAR Producer Edition. The ProChannel provides EQ, compression, tape saturation (and more) built in to every audio track and bus in a project. To display the entire ProChannel interface, click the Show/Hide ProChannel button. For more information, see Chapter 11.

Phase

Sometimes, phase cancellation can occur between the audio data of two different tracks. Phase cancellation occurs when one audio waveform increases in volume, and the other decreases in volume at exactly the same time and by the same amount. Because of this phenomenon, they cancel each other out, making the mixed audio sound hollow. The Phase parameter inverts the audio waveform of the data in an audio track around the zero axis. Sometimes, this can help eliminate phase cancellation. To invert the data in an audio track, just click the Phase button in the Console view. The Phase parameter is the equivalent of the Phase parameter in the Inspector.

Interleave

There might be times when you want to hear a stereo track play in mono (via one channel) or a mono track play in stereo (if stereo effects are applied). Using the Interleave parameter in the Console view or the Inspector, you can determine how the data in a track will be played. To adjust the parameter, just click the Interleave button. A blue button means stereo, and a gray button means mono.

Input Echo

When you record an audio track, you usually want to listen to your performance as it's being recorded. In the past, due to the limitations of sound card drivers, you were able to listen only to the "dry" version of your performance. This meant that you had to listen to your performance without any effects applied. With the input monitoring feature, SONAR allows you to listen to your performance with effects applied as it's being recorded. This can be especially useful, for example, when you are recording vocals, when it's customary to let the singer hear a little echo or reverberation during the performance. Similar to MIDI tracks, audio tracks provide an Input Echo button. This button can be turned on or off, and it activates or deactivates the input monitoring feature.

Output

The Output parameter routes the data from the track represented by the audio track strip to one of the available buses or mains. This parameter is the equivalent of the Output parameter in the Track view. You can change the output by clicking the parameter and selecting a new bus or main.

Send Parameters

The Send parameters route (send) the audio data from the track represented by the audio track strip to one of the available buses or mains. You can have as many sends as you want for each audio track strip. Each send has a number, which corresponds to the number of the bus to which its data will be sent (although you can change this, too). Each send also has four controls within it: an on/off button (Send Enable), a level knob (Send Level), a pan knob (Send Pan), and a pre/post button (Send Pre/Post).

To toggle a send on or off, just click its Send Enable button. The Send Level knob controls the volume (or level) of the audio data that will be sent to the bus. You can adjust the send level from −INF (infinity, the lowest level setting) to +6dB (the highest level setting). The Send Pan knob controls the panning of the audio data that will be sent to the bus. The Send Pre/Post button determines from what point in the audio track strip the audio data will be taken and sent to the bus. You can toggle the Send Pre/Post button by clicking it. Initially, the button is set to Pre (its color is gray). When you click the button, it changes its color to blue, which means it is set to Post.

AUDIO SIGNAL FLOW: As SONAR plays a project, it reads the data for each audio track from your hard drive. It then routes the data through the appropriate sections of the Console view, until it is finally sent to your sound card and then to your speakers so you can hear it. The routing works as follows: The data for an audio track is read from your hard drive and routed through the corresponding audio track strip. Within the strip, the data first passes through the Gain parameter. The data then passes through either the ProChannel or the FX bin (depending on if the ProChannel is set to Pre or Post), where any assigned effects are applied. The data is then sent through the Volume parameter (where its level can be adjusted), then the Pan parameter, and finally to the Output parameter. From here, it is sent out of the strip and into the assigned bus or main.

During this routing process, the data can be sent to a bus either before or after it reaches the Volume parameter. If the Send Pre/Post button is set to Pre, the data is routed to the bus after it goes through the FX bin but before it reaches the Volume parameter. This means that the Volume parameter will have no effect on the level of the signal being sent to the bus. If the Send Pre/Post button is set to Post, the data is routed to the bus after it goes through the Volume parameter. This means that the Volume parameter does affect the level of the signal being sent to the bus. For a graphical view of how audio signals are routed in SONAR, take a look at the following topic in the SONAR Help: Mixing > Signal Flow.

The Buses

The buses provide additional mixing control for your audio signals (see Figure 10.3). Buses include most of the same parameters as the audio track strips, including Gain, ProChannel, FX Bin, Interleave, Mute, Solo, Pan, Volume, Output, and Name. A bus provides one parameter not found in an audio track strip: Input Pan. This parameter adjusts the panning of the signal coming into the bus.

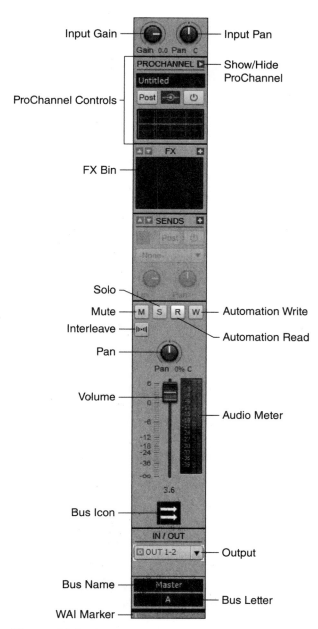

Figure 10.3 Shown here in the Console view, the buses provide some of the same controls as the audio track strips.
Source: Cakewalk®, Inc.

You can also access the buses in the Track view by clicking the Show/Hide Bus Pane button located at the bottom of the Track view (see Figure 10.4).

Figure 10.4 Access the buses in the Track view by clicking the Show/Hide Bus Pane button.
Source: Cakewalk®, Inc.

What Are the Buses Good For?

One good use for the buses is to add the same effects to a number of different tracks. For example, suppose that you have four audio tracks (1, 2, 3, and 4) containing the background vocals for your project, and you want to add some ambience to them. Without using a bus, you would have to set up a reverb effect (see Chapter 11) in the FX bin of each of the audio track strips for tracks 1, 2, 3, and 4 (each with identical parameter settings). Not only is this approach cumbersome and tedious, but it also puts extra strain on your computer because it has to process each of the four effects at the same time.

Using a bus, however, the process becomes much more streamlined. First, you create a send in track 1 by right-clicking the background of track 1 and choosing Insert Send > New Stereo Bus. This creates a new send in track 1 and also a new bus in the Bus pane (call it *Bus 1* for this example). Then you create new sends for tracks 2, 3, and 4. But this time, instead of choosing Insert Send > New Stereo Bus, you choose Insert Send > Bus 1. This ensures that each send in each track is set to Bus 1. Also make sure to click the Send Enable button for each send, although it should come on by default. Then you set the Send Level for each of the sends. In the FX bin for Bus 1, you set up the reverb effect. You only need to set up one effect because all four tracks are being sent to the bus. You then set the Input Gain, Input Pan, Volume, and Pan parameters for Bus 1. Finally, you set the Send Pre/Post buttons to Pre or Post. If you set the buttons to Pre, the data in each audio track strip is sent to the bus before it's routed through each Volume parameter. This means you can control the level of the effect (with the Send Levels) and the level of the original data (with the Volume parameter) independently. If you set the buttons to Post, the level of the effect goes up and down with the level of the original data via the Volume parameters.

> **SURROUND SOUND:** There is another special kind of bus provided by SONAR, which creates surround sound mixes for your projects. I will cover all surround sound-related information in Chapter 14; however, please finish reading this chapter to learn about mixing stereo projects first. You will need this knowledge in order to understand the additional information presented in Chapter 14.

The Insert Send Assistant

In addition to manually inserting and setting up buses, SONAR provides the Insert Send Assistant, which makes it easy to insert sends on single or multiple tracks, as follows:

1. In the Console or Track view, right-click a single track or select multiple tracks and right-click one of the selected tracks. Then choose Insert Send > Insert Send Assistant.
2. In the dialog box, click the Send to Existing Bus option if you want to create a new send to a bus that already exists. Then choose the existing bus from the menu and skip to step 7.

3. If you want to create a new bus, choose the New Bus option and then choose either the Stereo or Surround option.

4. In the New Bus Options section, choose an output for the bus using the Bus Output menu.

5. Type in a name for the new bus in the Bus Name field.

6. If you plan to use this as an effects bus (as described earlier in the "What Are the Buses Good For?" section), click the Choose Effect button and select an effect from the menu. Also, if you want the effect's property page to open automatically (after you click OK) so that you can make parameter adjustments, activate the Show Effect Property Page option.

7. Choose whether you want the send to be Pre or Post fader (as described earlier in the "What Are the Buses Good For?" section) by activating the Pre Fader option (for Pre) or leaving it deactivated (for Post).

8. If you want the send Gain and Pan parameters to be set to the same values as the track to which it is being added, activate the Match Track's Pan and Gain. Click OK.

If you chose to create a new bus, SONAR will insert a new send to the track(s) you chose and create a new bus. It will also automatically insert your chosen effect into the FX bin of the bus and open the window for the effect, depending on the options you chose. The Insert Send Assistant is a great tool for quickly setting up effects buses for groups of tracks (like drum tracks and background vocal tracks) that need to share the same type of effects.

The Mains

For every output on your sound card, a main will be displayed in the Console view (see Figure 10.5).

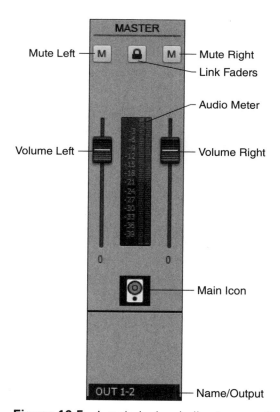

Figure 10.5 A main looks similar to an audio track strip.
Source: Cakewalk®, Inc.

If your sound card has only one output, only one main is displayed, and all the audio data from the audio track strips and buses is sent to it. If your sound card has more than one output, more than one main is shown, and you can choose to which main the data from each audio track strip and bus will be sent.

A main provides seven different parameters: Mute (Left and Right), Volume (Left and Right), Link Faders, and Name/Output. These parameters all work the same way as the same parameters in an audio track strip. The only differences are the Name/Output and Link Faders parameters. The Link Faders button links the two volume faders together so that you can change the volume of both the left and right sides of the stereo output simultaneously. The Name/Output parameter simply displays the name of the sound card output assigned to that main. It cannot be changed in the Console view.

FRIENDLY SOUND CARD DRIVER NAMES: Although the names of the mains cannot be changed directly in the Console view, you can change them via SONAR's Preferences dialog box. Press P and choose Audio – Devices. In the dialog box, activate the Use friendly names to represent audio drivers. Then double-click the name of an output (or input) and type in a new name. This change will be reflected in the Console view and all track Input/Output controls.

Configuring the Console and Track Views

Earlier, I mentioned that you could change the number of buses shown in the Console view. Along with these changes, you can customize how the Console view looks and works in many other ways. These methods are described in the following sections.

Strip Arrangement and Selection

To adjust the position of a track strip or bus strip in Console view, press and hold Alt. Then click the background of the strip and drag it left/right. This also changes the track/bus position in the Track view. In addition, you can select multiple, discontiguous track strips by Ctrl+clicking on the track numbers. To select multiple, contiguous track strips, just click and drag over the track numbers.

Number of Buses

To add a new bus, simply right-click a blank area of the Bus pane in the Console view and choose Insert Stereo Bus or Insert Surround Bus. You can also choose Insert Stereo Bus or Insert Surround Bus from the Bus menu. To delete a bus, right-click a blank part of the bus and choose Delete Bus. When you adjust the number of buses, it also affects the number of buses displayed in the Bus pane of the Track view.

The Track Managers

SONAR provides Track Managers for both the Console view and the Track view, which hide modules, buses, and mains. The Track Managers work as follows:

1. Make the Track or Console view the active window (by clicking its background), depending on which Track Manager you want to access.
2. Press H to open the Track Manager. The Track Managers for both views are identical, so the remaining instructions apply to both.
3. To hide an individual component, click to remove the check mark next to that component in the list and then click OK.

4. To hide a group of components (such as all the MIDI tracks, all the audio tracks, or all the buses), click the appropriate button in the Toggle section—Audio, MIDI, or Bus—to select the appropriate group and then press the spacebar to remove the check marks. There are also buttons for synth, muted, archived, and frozen tracks.

5. By default, the Track Managers are synchronized. This means that if you hide a track in the Console view, that same track will be hidden in the Track view. I recommend that you keep SONAR set to work this way. However, if you want to have independent Track Managers, you can remove the check mark from the Keep track/console visibility states in sync option. With this option deactivated, any changes you make in either view will *not* be reflected in the other. So if you hide a track in the Console view, that same track will *not* be hidden in the Track view. Click OK.

You also can make the components reappear by doing the opposite of the preceding procedures. These changes to the Console view and Track view are in appearance only; they don't affect what you hear during playback. For example, if you hide an audio track that outputs data during playback, you still hear that data even if you hide the track. Hiding components of the Console view or Track view can come in handy when you want to work only on a certain group of tracks, and you don't want to be distracted or overwhelmed by the number of controls displayed.

BEWARE OF HIDING TRACKS IN GROUPS: If you have any tracks that have grouped parameters or grouped clips, be careful when hiding some of the tracks in the groups (but not all of them). If you make any changes to the tracks that are still visible, the hidden tracks will be changed as well. For more on grouping clips, see Chapter 6. For more on grouping parameters, see Chapter 12.

Show/Hide Console Components

In addition to configuring the visibility of the tracks, buses, and mains in the Console view, you can also show/hide all tracks, buses, or mains, or the individual strip modules using the Console view menu. To show/hide the modules in each strip, use the Modules menu. To show/hide the different types of strips (tracks, buses, mains, etc.), use the Strips menu. The Strips menu also provides the Widen All Strips and Narrow All Strips options. By default, the Console view displays wide strips, which take up more space on the screen but allow you to see all available parameters. To gain more space in the view, choose Narrow All Strips, but you will lose access to some parameters.

In addition, you can use the Options menu to choose whether to show one or two sends in each audio strip. You can also adjust the ProChannel EQ plot resolution as well in order to show a compact EQ in the ProChannel interface (see Chapter 11). Finally, you can choose to show assignable controls for effects in the FX bin of the track strips. When you choose Options > Fx > Show Assignable Controls, you'll notice four sliders show below all the FX bins. These correspond to the first four parameters in the currently selected effect in the FX bin. This feature gives you quick access to some of the effect parameters without having to open the effect's property page.

Changing the Meters

You can also change how the volume meters in the Console and Track views behave. Choose Options > Meters in the Console view menu to turn groups of meters on and off using the Track Record Meters, Track Playback Meters, Bus Meters, and Mains Meters options. In the Track view, choose Options > Meter Options from the Track view menu.

METER INDEPENDENCE: Like the Track Managers, the meters in the Console view and Track view work independently. For instance, if you turn off the record meters in the Track view, the record meters in the Console view are *not* turned off, and vice versa.

METER PERFORMANCE: If you ever need to lighten the load on your computer during recording or playback, you might want to try turning off some or all of the meters. The meters can take up quite a bit of your computer's processing power and affect SONAR's performance.

In addition to being able to turn the meters on and off, you can set various options to determine how the meters will work. Using the same Options menus mentioned earlier, you'll see a menu with a number of options available. These options let you set the way the meters will display the audio signal, the audio signal measurement, the range of measurement, and various cosmetic options, such as whether or not the decibel markings are shown. For detailed descriptions of each option, take a look at the following section of the SONAR Help file: Mixing > Metering > Changing the Meters' Display.

Waveform Preview

In addition to the normal metering options, SONAR provides the Waveform Preview feature that allows you to see a real-time display of the audio waveform being produced by buses. Not only does this feature let you see the waveform, but it also provides a quick way to determine where your audio may be clipping. To turn the Waveform Preview feature on/off for a bus, click the Waveform Preview button, which is located next to the Solo button (see Figure 10.6) in the Track view.

Figure 10.6 Use the Waveform Preview feature to view a real-time waveform display for buses.
Source: Cakewalk®, Inc.

When you play back your project, SONAR displays the audio waveform in the Clips pane of the Track view. By default, the waveform is green, but when clipping occurs, the waveform is red.

Peak Markers

SONAR provides one more convenient feature for identifying clipping called *Peak Markers.* Each bus and audio/synth track has its own Peak Marker, which can be activated by simply right-clicking the bus or track and choosing Show Peak Marker. You can also activate Peak Markers for all buses or tracks by choosing Options > Meter Options in the Track view menu. When you activate the Peak Marker for a track or bus, SONAR will display a marker that follows the Now time cursor during playback. The marker briefly indicates the current audio level and is red when clipping occurs (see Figure 10.7).

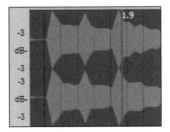

Figure 10.7 Use the Peak Markers feature to identify clipping during audio playback.
Source: Cakewalk®, Inc.

After you stop playback, you can also move the Now time cursor to the current Peak Marker by right-clicking the peak display of the track or bus and choosing Go to Peak (see Figure 10.8).

Figure 10.8 Quickly move the Now time cursor to the current Peak Marker by right-clicking the peak display.
Source: Cakewalk®, Inc.

MIXING AUDIO: There's still more to learn about the features that SONAR provides for mixing. In Chapters 11 and 12, I'll discuss how to use effects, automation, and control surfaces. In the meantime, I recommend you pick up a copy of *Mixing Audio* (Focal Press, 2011) by Roey Izhaki. It's currently one of the best books on the topic of mixing, and it teaches just about everything you need to know to create excellent music mixes. Go to **garrigus.com?IzhakiMixing** for more information.

Exploring Effects Plug-Ins

J UST AS ADDING SPICES TO A RECIPE MAKES IT TASTE BETTER, adding effects to your music data makes it sound better. Effects can make the difference between a dull, lifeless recording and a recording that really rocks. For example, you can apply echoes and background ambience to give the illusion that your song was recorded in a certain environment, such as a concert hall. You also can use effects to make your vocals sound rich and full. And the list goes on. SONAR provides a number of different effects features that you can use to spice up both your MIDI and audio tracks.

Offline or Real Time?

SONAR's effects features are very similar to its editing features, but there are a couple of differences. Although the effects features are included with SONAR, they are not actually part of the main application. Instead, they come in the form of plug-ins.

> **PLUG-INS:** In basic terms, a plug-in is a small computer program that by itself does nothing, but when used together with a larger application, it provides added functionality to the larger program. You can use plug-ins to add new features to a program easily. In SONAR's case, plug-ins provide you with additional ways to process your MIDI and audio data. As a matter of fact, Cakewalk (and other manufacturers) has additional plug-in products for sale so that you can add even more power to your copy of SONAR, which uses any plug-ins that are in the DirectX or VST format.

Because the effects features are plug-ins, not only do they add functionality to SONAR, but they also add more flexibility. Unlike the editing features, you can use the effects features to process your data in two different ways: offline and real-time.

Offline Processing

You already know what offline processing is because you used it when you learned about SONAR's editing features. With offline processing, the MIDI and audio data in your clips and tracks are permanently changed. Therefore, offline processing is also called *destructive processing* because it "destroys" the original data by modifying (or overwriting) it according to any processing you apply.

> **UNDO OFFLINE PROCESSING:** You can remove any offline processing done to your data by using SONAR's Undo feature. You also can load a saved copy of your project that contains the original data. But neither of these restoration methods is as convenient as using real-time processing.

The basic procedure for using effects in offline mode is essentially the same as when you use any of SONAR's editing features. You just follow these steps:

1. Select the data you want to change.
2. Choose the MIDI or audio effects feature you want to use by right-clicking the selected data and choosing either Process Effect > Audio Effects or Process Effect > MIDI Effects.
3. Make the appropriate parameter adjustments in the dialog box that appears.
4. Click the Audition button to test the current parameter settings. Make further adjustments, if necessary.
5. Click OK to close the dialog box.

SONAR will process the data by applying the effect, according to the parameter settings you specified.

Real-Time Processing

On the other hand, real-time processing doesn't change the actual data in your clips and tracks. Instead, the effects features are applied only during playback, which lets you hear the results while leaving your original data intact. Therefore, real-time processing is also called *nondestructive* because it doesn't apply any permanent changes to your data. By simply turning off the effects features, you can listen to your data as it was originally recorded.

The basic procedure for using effects in real-time mode isn't any more difficult than using them in offline mode, although it is a little different, as you can see here:

1. In the Track view, right-click in the FX bin of the track/bus to which you want to add an effect. A menu will appear. You can also apply effects via the track FX bin in the Inspector and the Console view.
2. Choose the effect you want to use from the menu. Depending on whether the track is for MIDI or audio, the list of effects will be different. Choose Audio FX for audio tracks/buses or MIDI Plugins for MIDI tracks. The effect you choose will be added to the list in the FX bin.

> **DRAG-AND-DROP EFFECTS:** An even quicker way to add an effect to an FX bin is to drag and drop it from the Browser. In the Browser, click the Plugins tab. Then drag and drop an effect from the Browser to any of the FX bins. In addition, you can drag and drop to individual clips (see "Clip-Based Effects" below).

3. The corresponding window for the effect will be opened automatically. You also can open an effect window by double-clicking it in the FX bin.

> **EFFECTS WINDOWS:** In real-time mode, the parameters of an effect are displayed in a window instead of a dialog box. Therefore, you can access any of the other features in SONAR while still having access to the effect parameters. You also can use more than one effect at the same time. In addition, you can drag effects windows to the MultiDock to organize them in one place on the screen.

4. Make the appropriate parameter adjustments.
5. Start playback of the project. You immediately will hear the results of the effect being applied to the data. While the project plays, you can make further parameter adjustments, if necessary.

BYPASSING EFFECTS: If you want to make a quick comparison between how the original data sounds and how it sounds with the effect applied, some of the effects provide a Bypass button.

When you activate the button, it bypasses (or turns off) the effect so you can hear how the original data sounds. When you deactivate the button, you can hear how the data sounds with the effect applied. You also can bypass an effect by clicking the blue button next to the name of the effect in the FX bin.

In addition, if you have many effects applied to an FX bin, you can bypass all the effects at once by right-clicking the FX bin and choosing Bypass Bin or Bypass Bins of This Type (to bypass only track FX bins, bus FX bins, or clip FX bins). Also, to bypass all FX bins in the entire project, click the FX button in Mix module of the Control Bar or press E.

6. If you want to add another effect to the same track (or add some effects to different tracks), go back to Step 1. You can leave the effects windows open, or you can close them; it doesn't matter. You also can let the project continue to play as you add new effects. As soon as you add an effect to the FX bin, you will hear the results, according to the current parameter settings.

7. If you want to remove an effect, right-click the effect you want to remove and select Delete, or click the effect to make it the active effect (its name is shown with a white outline) and press Del(ete).

ORDER OF EFFECTS: If you apply more than one effect to a track, the order in which the effects appear in the FX bin will determine the order in which they are applied to the data in the track. For example, if you have the Chorus and Reverb effects added (in that order) to the FX bin of an audio track, SONAR will apply the Chorus effect to the data and then take the result of that application and apply the Reverb effect to it. This means that the order in which you apply effects to a track matters. If you apply effects in a different order, you will get different results. This makes for some interesting experimentation. To change the order of the effects listed in the FX bin, drag the name of an effect up or down within the list.

COPY AND MOVE EFFECTS: In addition to changing the order of effects by dragging them in the FX bin, you can also copy and move effects from one FX bin. Move an effect by clicking and dragging it. Copy an effect by holding Ctrl and then clicking and dragging.

You can continue using SONAR with the real-time effects in place. Remember that you will be aware of the results only during playback. The original data looks the same, even if you examine it in various views. Also, editing your original data doesn't change how the effects are applied to it. For example, if you have a track set up with some effects applied, and you transpose the pitch of one of the clips within that track, during playback SONAR still will apply the effects to the track in the same way. When the Now time reaches the point in the track containing the transposed clip, you simply will hear the effect applied to the transposed data. This is one of the features that makes real-time effects so flexible.

APPLY EFFECTS DURING RECORDING: You also can hear real-time effects during recording. For example, you can add some reverberation to a vocal part to make it sound more appealing to the performer while his part is being recorded. This helps a performer get more "in the groove," so to speak. To hear real-time effects during recording, you have to activate input monitoring (see Chapter 5).

Clip-Based Effects

In addition to applying effects to entire tracks, you can apply effects to individual clips. Each clip in a SONAR project contains its own unique FX bin. This feature gives you the flexibility to apply different effects to different parts of the same track, rather than being limited to applying effects to all the clips in that track.

To apply an effect to a clip, right-click the clip and choose Insert Effect or drag and drop an effect onto a clip from the Browser. Once you apply an effect to a clip, a small FX button will appear in the upper-right corner of the clip. To access the FX bin for the clip, click the FX button. From here, you can use the same procedures outlined in the last section for applying effects in real time.

CLIP PROPERTIES FX BIN: You can also access the FX bin for a clip by selecting the clip, clicking the Clip tab at the top of the Inspector (or pressing Shift+I), and choosing Clip Effects.

FX Chains

While presets save parameter settings for individual effects, FX Chains save different combinations of entire effects. For example, if you add a number of effects to an FX bin and you use that same combination on a regular basis, you can save the contents of the FX bin as an FX Chain. You can then load that FX Chain in a single operation, rather than having to load all the individual effects. Keep in mind that FX Chains only work with audio effects, not MIDI effects.

FX CHAIN BASICS

The basic function of FX Chains is to act as containers for multiple effects, and for that purpose they work as follows:

1. After loading an FX bin and setting the effects parameters, right-click the FX bin and choose Convert Bin to FX Chain. You can also right-click an FX bin and choose FX Chain to create an empty FX Chain, which can then be edited (see Step 3).
2. To give the new FX Chain a unique name, right-click it and choose Rename. Then type in a new name and click OK.
3. To edit the FX Chain, double-click it (although if you create a new FX Chain, an empty FX Chain window will open automatically). As shown in Figure 11.1, any effects added to the FX Chain are displayed in the Plug-In List area of the window. The Plug-In List shows plug-ins from left to right, meaning the beginning of the FX Chain starts at the left side of the List and ends at the right. This also means that the audio signal flows through the effects from left to right.

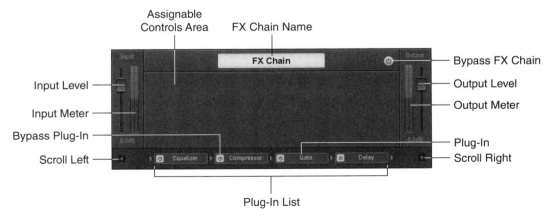

Figure 11.1 The FX Chain window allows you to create and edit FX Chains.
Source: Cakewalk®, Inc.

4. If more than four plug-ins are in the Plug-In List, use the Scroll Left and Scroll Right buttons to show the other plug-ins.

5. To add plug-ins, drag/drop a plug-in from the Browser to a point in between two existing plug-ins in the Plug-In List (or to the empty List, if you're creating a new FX Chain). You can also right-click between two plug-ins in the List and choose Audio FX from the menu.

6. To delete a plug-in, right-click the plug-in and choose Delete.

7. Adjust the Input Level to control the volume of the audio going into the FX Chain.

8. Adjust the Output Level to control the volume of the audio going out of the FX Chain.

9. To hear the audio without one of the plug-ins, toggle its Bypass Plug-In button.

10. To hear the audio without the entire FX Chain, toggle the Bypass FX Chain button.

11. You can change the name of the FX Chain in the window by double-clicking the FX Chain Name, typing in a new name, and pressing Enter.

12. To save the FX Chain for future use, right-click in the Plug-In List (or right-click the FX Chain in the FX bin) and choose Save FX Chain Preset. Type in a name (or keep the current name) and click Save. You can also drag the FX Chain from the FX bin of the track into the Browser to save it automatically using the current name.

13. To transform the FX Chain back to individual effects, right-click it in the FX bin and choose Extract FX Chain Plugins.

14. To load a previously saved FX Chain, right-click the FX bin and choose Load FX Chain Preset. You can also drag and drop FX Chains from the Plug-Ins section of the Browser, just like regular effects. And if you press Shift while dragging, the FX Chain will be loaded and automatically extracted into its individual effects (similar to the Extract FX Chain Plug-Ins command mentioned in Step 13).

Other than the aforementioned steps, FX Chains can be manipulated (deleted, moved, copied, and so on) just like regular effects in an FX bin.

FX Chain Assignable Controls

FX Chains also provide some advanced functionality in the form of assignable controls. You may have noticed the large blank space in the FX Chain window, which is the Assignable Controls area. With assignable controls, you can create up to six knobs and six buttons that can be used to control parameters from the different plug-ins inside an FX Chain. Assignable controls work as follows:

1. Right-click in the Assignable Controls area of the FX Chain window and choose either Learn Knob or Learn Button to create a knob or button.

2. Double-click one of the plug-ins in the Plug-In List to open the plug-ins' window.

3. Adjust anywhere from one to four parameters. (Each knob or button in an FX Chain can control up to four plug-in parameters simultaneously.) If creating a knob, adjust parameters that can manipulated by clicking and dragging with the mouse (like a knob or slider). If creating a button, adjust a clickable parameter (like a button).

4. If you adjust fewer than four parameters, right-click in the Assignable Controls area of the FX Chain window again and choose either Learn Knob or Learn Button. SONAR will then ask you if you want to assign these controls. Click Yes, and a new knob or button is created.

> **MANUAL FX CHAIN CONTROL CREATION:** You can also create knobs or buttons manually by right-clicking and choosing Add Knob or Add button, but it's much easier to use the Learn method and then edit the controls later, if need be.

5. To make changes to a control, right-click the control and choose Edit Control to open the Control Properties dialog box.

6. Change the name of the control by typing a new name into the Name parameter.

7. Change the position of the control in the Assignable Controls area by choosing a new position from the Position menu.

8. To change one of the assigned plug-in parameters, click one of the Destination menus and choose a new parameter from the list.

9. You can also set a range for each parameter by setting the Start and End values. For example, you could use an EQ plug-in to do a double filter sweep by assigning two different frequencies to one knob. Then set the Start and End for one frequency to 0% and 100%, respectively. And set the Start and End for the other frequency to 100% and 0%, respectively. When you turn the knob, one frequency parameter would rise in value and the other would fall in value, simultaneously. Click OK when you've finished editing the control.

RIGHT-CLICK TO SET CONTROL RANGE: In addition to setting the Start and End values in the Control Properties dialog box, you can right-click a control and choose Ranges. First, adjust the parameters in the plug-in window and then right-click the control and choose Ranges > All Parameters Set Start or All Parameters Set End. You can also choose to set the Start or End for individual parameters, but it's easier to do them all at once.

---

10. After you've created some buttons and knobs, you can manipulate them like other similar controls in SONAR. Click a button to toggle it on/off. Click/drag a knob up/down to adjust it. For finer control, hold Shift while adjusting a knob.

11. To set a knob to its default value, double-click it. You can also set the default value by first adjusting the knob and then right-clicking it and choosing Set Default Value.

12. Delete a knob or button by right-clicking it and choosing Remove Control. Be careful when deleting controls because this action can't be undone.

13. To create automation for any of the controls in an FX Chain, right-click inside the Assignable Controls area and choose Write Enable Automation. Choose the same option again when you're finished. For more information about automation, see Chapter 12.

FX Chain Custom UI

You can also change the look of an FX Chain interface by using your own custom graphics for knobs, buttons, etc. To access this feature, right-click the background of the Assignable Controls area of an FX Chain and choose Customize UI to open the Settings dialog box. Here you'll find a number of color and image parameters that can be changed, which correspond to the FX Chain interface as follows:

▷ **Background Image.** Changes the background of the entire FX Chain interface except the Plug-In List. File format: 600 × 187 PNG file. This graphic must include the divider lines and the words Input and Output.

▷ **Preset Background Image.** Changes the background of the FX Chain Name. File Format: 186 × 32 PNG file.

▷ **Fader Cap Image.** Changes the slider cap for the Input and Output parameters. File Format: 22 × 37 PNG file.

▷ **Button Image.** Changes the look of all buttons in the FX Chain. File Format: 195 × 27 PNG file. This graphic must include five different buttons showing different button states.

▷ **Rotary Image.** Changes the look of all knobs in the FX Chain. File Format: 6996 × 54 PNG file. This graphic must include all the different knob states.

▷ **Preset Text Color.** Changes the color of the FX Chain Name text.

▷ **Label Text Color.** Changes the color of the label text for all knobs and buttons.

To change any of the images, click the ellipse button to the right of the parameter and choose one of the graphics that comes included with SONAR. You can find those graphic files in your Cakewalk Content folder in the FX Chain Graphics subfolder. Use those files as templates when creating your own FX Chain interface graphics.

Real-Time Advantages and Disadvantages

You might be wondering, "Why don't I just use real-time processing all the time? It's so much more flexible?" Well, applying effects in real time is very flexible, but in a couple of instances you need to apply them offline. The first instance deals with your computer's processing power. Most of SONAR's effects need to perform complex mathematical calculations to achieve their results. Applying effects in real time means that not only does your computer have to deal with these calculations, but it also has to deal with SONAR playing back your MIDI and audio data. All these things going on at once can put a lot of strain on your computer's CPU. If you use too many effects in real time at once, your computer might not be able to keep up. You might hear skips in playback, or SONAR might stop playing altogether. If this ever happens, you need to apply some of the effects offline and keep only a few of them going in real time. You lose a bit of flexibility in terms of being able to make changes to your data, but there's no limit to the number of effects you can apply to your data offline.

Applying effects offline also comes in handy when you want to process some specifically selected data. For example, if you want to process a short segment of data within a track or clip, you have to do it offline. In real time, you can apply effects only to entire clips or tracks.

> **USE AUTOMATION:** Actually, you can apply real-time effects to specific parts of a track by using automation, but it's a bit more complicated than simply applying an effect offline (see Chapter 12).

The Freeze Tracks Function

To make working with real-time effects even easier, SONAR provides the Freeze Tracks function. Depending on the power of your computer, using many different real-time effects at the same time can start to bog down playback and recording in SONAR. In order to help with this situation, SONAR "freezes" the real-time effects in audio tracks, which basically bounces the audio in the track to new audio clips and applies the real-time effects to the data. It also temporarily disables the FX bin, which allows you to hear your effects but takes the strain off your computer.

The Freeze Tracks function can be accessed by right-clicking the number of an audio track and choosing Freeze. The Freeze Track, Unfreeze Track, Quick Unfreeze Track, and Freeze Options features all work the same as the Freeze Synth features described in the "Freeze/Unfreeze a Soft Synth" section of Chapter 8.

Audio Effects

SONAR provides a wide selection of audio effects, and you'll notice that some of these effects cover the same type of processing. Why would Cakewalk include multiple effects that accomplish the same task?

Well, some of the effects are designed to process audio with a lower level of quality, and they include fewer parameter settings. So why include them? Because they provide one advantage: They don't take up as much computer processing power. This means that you can apply more of the lower-quality effects to your tracks in real time, especially if you have a slow computer system.

You also might have noticed that some of the effects mimic some of SONAR's editing features. They mimic these editing features so you can process your data with these features in real time. You can't use SONAR's editing features in real time because they aren't plug-ins. The effects features, however, come with their own sets of parameters, so I'll go over them here step-by-step.

OFFLINE, REAL-TIME, AUDITION, AND PRESETS: Keep in mind that during each of the following step-by-step procedures, the previously discussed offline and real-time information also applies. In addition, you can use the Audition button to listen to how the effect is processing your audio data during offline applications. You also can save your parameter settings as presets. I won't be mentioning this again, so I just wanted to give you a quick reminder.

NOT INSTALLED BY DEFAULT: Please note that some of the plug-ins described in this chapter may not be installed on your system. There are a couple reasons for this: the plug-ins are not installed by default or you are running the 64-bit version of SONAR.

Some of the older legacy plug-ins are included with SONAR for compatibility with older projects, but they aren't part of the default installation. To install older plug-ins, do an advanced install. Go to **garrigus.com/?DreamStation** to see an example video of how this is done. In addition, the 64-bit version of SONAR doesn't support 32-bit DirectX plug-ins, so those will not be available for use at all.

Equalization

You have a radio in your car, right? Maybe even a cassette or a CD player, too? If so, then you've probably used equalization without even knowing it. Adjusting the bass and treble controls on your car radio is a form of equalization. Equalization (EQ) enables you to adjust the tonal characteristics of an audio signal by increasing (boosting) or decreasing (cutting) the amplitude of different frequencies in the audio spectrum.

THE AUDIO SPECTRUM: When a musical object (such as a string) vibrates, it emits a sound. The speed at which the object vibrates is called the *frequency*, which is measured in vibrations (or cycles) per second. This measurement is also called *Hertz* (Hz). If an object vibrates 60 times per second, the frequency would be 60Hz. The tricky point to remember here, though, is that most objects vibrate at a number of different frequencies at the same time. The combination of all these different vibrations makes up the distinct sound (or *timbre*) of a vibrating object. That's why a bell sounds like a bell, a horn sounds like a horn, and so on with all other types of sounds.

We humans can't perceive some very slow and very fast vibrations. Technically, the range of human hearing resides between the frequencies of 20Hz and 20kHz (1kHz is equal to 1,000Hz). This range is known as the *audio spectrum*.

Equalization enables you to manipulate the frequencies of the audio spectrum, and because sounds contain many of these frequencies, you can change their tonal characteristics (or timbre).

In other words, using EQ, you can bump up the bass, add more presence, reduce rumble, and sometimes eliminate noise in your audio material. Not only that, but you also can use EQ as an effect. You know how in some of the modern dance tunes, the vocals sound like they're coming out of a telephone receiver or an old radio? That's an effect done with EQ.

Cakewalk 2-Band EQ

The Cakewalk 2-Band EQ effect uses parametric equalization, which allows you to specify an exact frequency to adjust, and you can cut or boost that frequency. You also can process a range of frequencies at the same time, such as cutting all frequencies above 10kHz by 20dB (which would reduce all the frequencies between 10kHz and 20kHz, but leave the frequencies between 20Hz and 10kHz alone). I can explain the Cakewalk 2-Band EQ feature a little better by showing you how it works:

1. Choose 2-Band EQ, which opens the Cakewalk 2-Band EQ window.
2. Activate one or both of the Active options to turn on each type of EQ. The Cakewalk 2-Band EQ effect applies two different types of EQ at the same time if you would like.
3. Choose one of the options in the Filter Type section—High-Pass, Low-Pass, Band-Pass (Peak), or Band-Stop (Notch). Then set the appropriate parameters in the Filter Parameters section. You can use the F1 and F2 parameters to set the frequencies you want to adjust. They work differently, depending on the type of filter you choose.

   The Cut parameter enables you to reduce the volume of the frequencies. To change this setting, just enter a negative number (such as −20) to cut by that number of decibels. The Gain parameter boosts the volume of the frequencies. To change this setting, just enter a positive number (such as +20) to boost by that number of decibels.

   If you select the High-Pass filter type, all the frequencies below the frequency that you set in the F1 parameter will be cut, and all the frequencies above it will be boosted, depending on how you set the Cut and Gain parameters. If you select the Low-Pass filter type, all the frequencies above the frequency that you set in the F1 parameter will be cut, and all the frequencies below it will be boosted, depending on how you set the Cut and Gain parameters.

   If you select either the Band-Pass (Peak) or Band-Stop (Notch) filter types, you have to set up a range of frequencies using both the F1 and F2 parameters. Use the F1 parameter to mark the beginning of the range and the F2 parameter to mark the end of the range. For the Band-Pass (Peak) filter type, any frequencies outside the range are cut, and frequencies within the range are boosted, depending on how you set the Cut and Gain parameters. For the Band-Stop (Notch) filter type, any frequencies outside the range are boosted, and frequencies within the range are cut, depending on how you set the Cut and Gain parameters.

Cakewalk Para-Q

Another (more modern) version of a two-band EQ is the Cakewalk Para-Q, which works as follows:

1. Choose Para-Q, which opens the Cakewalk Para-Q window.
2. Like the Cakewalk 2-Band EQ effect, you have two separate bands of EQ, each with Frequency (f), Gain, and Bandwidth (BW) parameters (bandwidth is also known as Q). Click and drag up/down to adjust the knobs and double-click them to return them to their default values.
3. Adjust the Frequency (f) parameter (40Hz to 20.5kHz) for each band to set the center frequency that will be cut or boosted, depending on the Gain parameter.
4. Adjust the Gain parameter (−12 to +12dB) for each band to cut or boost the chosen frequency.
5. Adjust the Bandwidth (BW) parameter (0.1 to 5.0) to determine how many frequencies around the center frequency are affected. The lower the value, the narrower the band and the fewer frequencies affected. Using a lower value allows you to do more pinpoint EQ adjustments. The higher the value, the wider the band and the more frequencies affected. Using a higher value allows you to do broader EQ adjustments.
6. Adjust the Level parameter (−20 to 0dB) to set the overall output level of the Cakewalk Para-Q effect. When you boost frequencies, you also boost volume. To keep your track volume at the same level as it was before you added the Cakewalk Para-Q effect, lower the Level parameter when boosting frequencies.
7. Use the Power button to turn the Cakewalk Para-Q on/off in order to bypass the effect and do comparisons.

> **UNLIMITED CAKEWALK PARA-Q EQ BANDS:** Since the Cakewalk Para-Q takes up very little CPU power, you can easily add a large number of instances of the effect to an FX bin, giving you essentially an unlimited number of bands with which to work. You can even create your own multiband EQ configurations by adding multiple instances of the Cakewalk Para-Q to an FX Chain.

Sonitus:fx Equalizer

Like the Cakewalk Para-Q, the Sonitus:fx Equalizer provides multiple EQ bands for you to adjust; in this case, it's six bands. Here is how it works:

1. Choose Sonitus:fx Equalizer, which opens the Sonitus:fx Equalizer window.
2. In the lower section of the window, there are six EQ bands. You need to activate bands in order for their parameters to be adjusted. To activate a band, click its number button. You also can turn the entire Equalizer effect on or off by clicking the Bypass button in the upper section of the window.
3. To adjust the gain for a band, just drag its Gain slider left or right.

> **PRECISE ADJUSTMENTS:** To make precise parameter adjustments, double-click the parameter numerical value and enter a new value using your PC keyboard.

4. There are also Center Frequency (Freq) and Bandwidth (Q) parameters available for each band. These parameters work the same as they do for the Cakewalk Para-Q effect.
5. To set the type of equalization a band will use, click the Filter button. If you choose the Peak/Dip option, the exact frequency designated by the Freq parameter will be boosted or cut, depending on how you set the Gain parameter. If you choose the Shelving Low option, any frequencies below the Freq setting will be boosted or cut. If you choose the Shelving High option, any frequencies above the Freq setting will be boosted or cut. If you choose the Lowpass option, all the frequencies above the Freq setting will be cut, and all the frequencies below it will be boosted. If you choose the Highpass option, all the frequencies below the Freq setting will be cut, and all the frequencies above it will be boosted.
6. To reset a band to its default parameter values, right-click the band's number button and choose Set Band Defaults. You also can reset the parameters for all the bands by clicking the Reset button in the upper section of the window.
7. If you want to set up more than one EQ band, repeat Steps 2 through 6.

> **THE EQ GRAPH:** You've probably noticed that in addition to the parameter settings, the Equalizer window contains a graph display. This graph shows the current equalization settings for all six bands. Along the left, it shows the amplitudes (Gain), and along the bottom, it shows the frequencies. The shape of the line drawn on the graph shows you what frequencies in the audio spectrum are either boosted or cut. Six numbered points on the graph represent each EQ band. Click and drag a point left/right to change the corresponding band's Frequency. Click and drag a point up/down to change Gain. Shift+drag left/right to change Q.

8. To adjust the final output volume of the Equalizer effect, use the Output parameter in the lower section of the window.

> **SAVE YOUR SETTINGS:** You can save Equalizer presets using the standard method for all SONAR effects, or you can use a special method by clicking the Presets button in the upper section of the window. This will bring up a menu that will load and save presets to separate files that you can share with friends. Another advantage to saving presets this way is that if you use another program to access the Equalizer effect, your presets will be available in that program, too—not just in SONAR.

LP64 Linear EQ (Producer Edition)

A high quality EQ effect provided by SONAR is the LP64 Linear EQ, which is only available to SONAR Producer Edition users. The operation of the LP64 EQ is similar to that of the Sonitus:fx Equalizer because it also provides an editable EQ graph. I'll show you how to create a 60Hz hum removal notch filter as an example for how this EQ works:

1. Choose LP-64 EQ, which opens the LP-64 EQ window (see Figure 11.2).

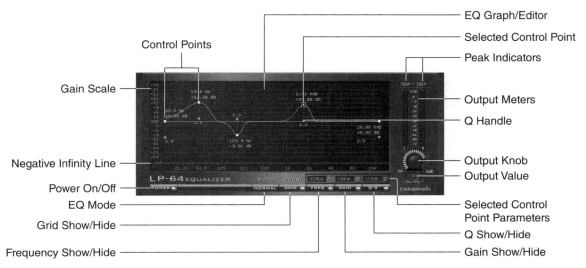

Figure 11.2 Create your own EQ filters by manipulating control points on an EQ graph.
Source: Cakewalk®, Inc.

2. Click the EQ Mode button to choose the EQ mode you want to use. The Normal mode shows a graphic representation of the EQ parameters. The Curve mode displays how the actual EQ frequency curve looks, according to the current parameter settings. You can use either mode to edit the EQ parameters; however, the Curve mode doesn't allow you to graphically edit Q. Because of this, I like to use Normal mode for editing and Curve mode to see how the audio frequencies will actually be processed. Choose Normal mode for this example.
3. The EQ Graph provides a number of options that make editing EQ parameters easy. These include a grid, as well as frequency, gain, and Q values for each control point. To toggle these options, click the appropriate show/hide buttons at the bottom of the window. For this example, toggle all of them to show.
4. The EQ Graph also shows the EQ line (or curve), which provides a graphic representation of the EQ parameters. On this line are control points that each represents a single EQ band. Attached to each point are frequency and gain values, as well as a Q handle. To change the frequency of a point, drag it left/right. To change the gain of a point, drag it up/down. To change the Q of a point, drag the point's Q handle up/down.
5. As you drag a control point within the EQ Graph, you'll notice the values change accordingly. These values line up with the horizontal frequency scale (located at the bottom of the graph) and the vertical gain scale

(located at the left of the graph). The frequency scale is permanently set, but the gain scale can be adjusted by clicking and dragging your mouse up/down over the scale.

6. When you first open the LP-64 EQ, the EQ Graph shows a line with two control points, but you can have up to 20 points. To add a point, double-click anywhere on the line. To delete a point, first click the point to select it and then press the Delete key. A selected point is shown with a square outline around it. For this example, we'll leave the first and last control points alone, but we want to add some more points to create the hum removal notch filter. So add a point to the line and edit it so that its frequency, gain, and Q are as follows: 60Hz, −24dB, and 20Q.

7. As you edit control points, you'll notice that it's not always easy to position them to get precise parameter values. To remedy this, you can first select a point and then use the Selected Control Point parameters to enter exact values. To the right of the word Show, the boxes represent frequency, gain, and Q, respectively. To edit a parameter, click/drag or Shift+click/drag (for finer adjustments) up/down with your mouse, or you can double-click and type in a value.

8. For this example, create five more points, all with the same −24dB gain and 20Q values, but each with a different frequency as follows: 120Hz, 180Hz, 240Hz, 300Hz, and 360Hz. The final EQ Graph should look like the one in Figure 11.3.

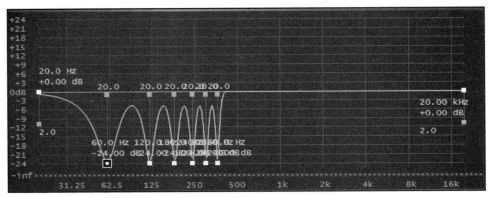

Figure 11.3 An EQ Graph for a 60Hz hum removal notch filter.
Source: Cakewalk®, Inc.

NEGATIVE INFINITY GAIN: When adjusting the gain of a control point, the lowest value you can enter in the Gain Selected Control Point parameter is −24dB. This is also the lowest value available on the main part of the EQ Graph. However, just below the graph is a special Negative Infinity Line. You can drag the control point to that line to set the gain of the point to −infdB, which is effectively a level of zero gain and completely cuts the point's related frequency from the audio spectrum. For this example, −24dB gain should be plenty for hum removal, but you could also try using −inf for each point in the filter.

---

9. Use the Output knob and value to adjust the processed audio signal output level. The Output meters display the level during playback, and the Peak indicators show the highest level hit.

10. Use the Power button to bypass the LP-64 EQ so that you can compare the original and processed audio signals.

Cakewalk HF Exciter

The Cakewalk HF Exciter is a special type of EQ effect that stimulates the high frequencies of an audio signal so that you can make it sound brighter. This effect is best used on single instruments and groups of instruments that already contain some high frequencies. For example, you could brighten a dull-sounding electric guitar recording. You can also use it on an entire project mix, but subtlety is the key when applying this effect. It works as follows:

1. Choose HF Exciter, which opens the Cakewalk HF Exciter window.
2. Adjust the Frequency (f) parameter (3kHz to 15kHz) to set the center frequency that will be stimulated in regards to the Drive parameter.
3. Adjust the Drive parameter (0 to 100%) to determine the amount of stimulation to the center frequency. The higher the value, the more stimulation is applied, but if you set it too high, you'll get a harsh sound.
4. Adjust the Spread parameter (0 to 100%) to determine the stereo width of the processed frequencies. The higher the value, the wider the stereo signal will sound.
5. Adjust the Mix parameter (0 to 100%) to determine how much of the HF Exciter effect is heard. Lower values mean more of the original signal is heard. Higher values mean more of the HF Exciter effect is heard. A setting of 0% means you'll only hear the original signal, which is the same as not applying the effect at all. A setting of 100% means that you'll hear only the Cakewalk HF Exciter effect.
6. Use the Power button to bypass the Cakewalk HF Exciter so that you can compare the original and processed audio signals.

DSP-FX EQ AND PARAMETRIC EQ VIDEO DEMOS: Because the DSP-FX EQ and Parametric EQ included with SONAR are legacy plug-ins (32-bit only) and are not installed by default, I'm not including them here. Instead, I have created online demo videos that cover the basics of using both effects. Go to **garrigus.com?DSPFxEQ** and **garrigus.com?SonarPEQ** to view them.

PROCHANNEL EQ: SONAR Producer Edition also provides a high-quality EQ built in to every track and bus in a project as part of the ProChannel channel strip effect. See the "Other Effects" section later in this chapter.

Delay

An echo is a repeating sound that mimics an initial sound. For example, if you yell the word *hello* in a large enclosed area (such as a concert hall or a canyon), you will hear that word repeated (or echoed) over and over until it fades away. This is exactly what the Delay effect does to your audio data. You can create echoes that vary in the number of repeats and the time between each repeat.

Sonitus:fx Delay

The Sonitus:fx Delay effect provides a single stereo delay with separate controls for both the left and right channels. It works like this:

1. Choose Sonitus:fx Delay, which opens the Sonitus:fx Delay window.
2. If you want to specify a delay using a time value, make sure the Tempo Sync option is Off and then set the Delay Time parameters for each channel. These parameters determine the time (in milliseconds) that occurs between each echo. You can set the Delay Time from 0.1 to 4,000 milliseconds (which is equal to 4 seconds) for the left and right stereo channels. A Link option is also available. Activating this option links the Delay Time parameters, so if you change the value of one, the other will be set to the same value.
3. If you want to specify a delay that will be synchronized to a specific musical tempo, activate the Tempo Sync option. If you choose Manual mode, you can type in a tempo. If you choose Host mode, the tempo of your current project will be used. Now, instead of using the Delay Time parameters, set the Factor parameters for

each channel. These parameters set the delay by using musical values based on the tempo. A Factor of 1 equals a quarter-note delay, a Factor of one-half equals an eighth-note delay, and so on.

4. Set the Mix parameters. A value of 0% equals a totally dry (original) signal, a value of 50% equals a 50/50 mix of the dry and wet (effect) signal, and a value of 100% equals a totally wet signal.

5. Set the Feedback parameters. With some effects, you can take their resulting signals and send them back through to have the effect applied multiple times. That's what the Feedback parameter does. The resulting sound can differ, depending on the effect. For delay effects, the Feedback controls the number of echoes that occur. You can set it anywhere from 0 to 100%. The lower the value, the fewer the number of echoes; the higher the value, the greater the number of echoes.

6. Set the Crossfeed parameters. Using the Crossfeed parameter, you can take the resulting signal from the left channel and send it back through the right channel, and you can take the resulting signal from the right channel and send it back through the left channel. Essentially, this means that this parameter provides control over the number of echoes that will occur and, at the same time, helps to make the stereo field sound "fuller."

7. The Diffusion parameter simulates environments more precisely. Instead of hearing distinct echoes, you hear a large number of echoes that sound together very quickly, giving you the illusion of your audio being played in an irregularly shaped environment. The higher the Time value, the farther apart the echoes will sound, simulating a larger environment. The higher the Amount value, the more pronounced the effect.

8. If you want to apply some low-pass and high-pass EQ to your delay effect, use the High Filter and Low Filter functions. You can set frequency and Q for both functions. There's no gain control because they both simply cut out frequencies. Use High Filter to cut frequencies above its Frequency setting; use Low Filter to cut frequencies below its Frequency setting. Check out some of the supplied presets to see how you can use these functions to simulate different effects.

LISTEN MODE: Click the Listen button to set it to either Mix or Delay. When it is set to Mix, you will hear both the original audio signal and the delay effect. When it is set to Delay, you will hear only the delay effect.

Cakewalk Tempo Delay

Like the Sonitus:fx Delay, the Cakewalk Tempo Delay effect provides a single stereo delay with separate controls for both the left and right channels. The difference between the two effects is that the Cakewalk Tempo Delay provides some additional delay and EQ modes. It works like this:

1. Choose Tempo Delay, which opens the Cakewalk Tempo Delay window.
2. Choose a Delay Mode value. The Stereo mode provides a basic stereo delay. The Ping mode provides a "ping-pong" delay where the signal bounces back and forth between the stereo channels. The Cross mode provides a cross feedback delay where the left and right channel signals are fed into each other. The LRC mode provides a "left-right-center" delay where the signal moves to the left, right, and then center of the stereo field.
3. If you want to specify a delay that will be synchronized to a specific musical tempo, activate the Tempo Sync option. Set the Tempo Sync value using musical values based on the tempo. A setting of 1 equals a quarter-note delay, a setting of 1/2 equals an eighth-note delay, and so on. Values with D or T next to them are the equivalent of dotted and triplet values as found in standard music notation.
4. If you want to specify a delay using a time value, make sure the Tempo Sync option is Off and then set the Time Left and Time Right parameters, which correspond to the left and right stereo channels. These parameters determine the time (in seconds) that occurs between each echo and can be set from 0.00 to 2.00 (two seconds).
5. If you want to apply some EQ to the Cakewalk Tempo Delay effect, adjust the EQ Mode parameter. There are six modes available, each providing different band frequencies, resonance, and Q. You can find an EQ information chart in the Cakewalk Tempo Delay help file by clicking the background of the window and pressing F1. Basically, the EQ controls cut various frequencies in the effect signal and also add resonance (brightness) to

the echoes. In a real environment, the sound of each echo degrades, and cutting frequencies with EQ can help simulate that and also provide some strange sounds, depending on the settings you use.

6. Adjust the Feedback parameter to control the number of echoes produced by the effect.

7. Adjust the Mix parameter (0 to 100%) to determine how much of the Stereo Delay effect is heard.

8. Adjust the Level parameter (−20 to 0dB) to set the overall output level of the effect.

9. Use the Power button to bypass the Cakewalk Tempo Delay so that you can compare the original and processed audio signals.

> **DSP-FX DELAY VIDEO DEMO:** Because the DSP-FX Delay included with SONAR is a legacy plug-in (32-bit only) and is not installed by default, I'm not including it here. Instead, I have created an online demo video that covers the basics of using the effect. Go to **garrigus.com?DSPFxDelay** to view it.

Chorus

SONAR's chorus effects have many of the same parameters as its delay effects. Why? Because technically, chorus is a form of delay. Chorus uses delay and detuning to achieve its results. You don't hear echoes when using chorus, though, because the delay is extremely short. Instead, chorus makes your audio data sound fatter or fuller. The name *chorus* comes from the fact that people singing in a chorus produce a fuller sound because each person sings slightly out of tune and out of time—not enough to make the music sound bad, but enough to actually make it sound better. You can use SONAR's chorus effects to achieve similar results with your audio data. The following sections describe how to use them.

Cakewalk Chorus (Mono)

The Cakewalk Chorus (Mono) effect is designed to work with monophonic audio, rather than stereo, as follows:

1. Choose Chorus (Mono), which opens the Cakewalk Chorus (Mono) window.

2. Set the Delay Time parameter. The only difference between this Delay Time parameter and the same parameter in the Sonitus:fx Delay is that this one has a range of only 20 to 80 milliseconds. If you set this parameter high enough, you actually can get some quick repeating echoes out of it. For adding chorus to your audio, though, you should keep it set somewhere between 20 and 35.

3. Set the Dry Mix and Wet Mix parameters. Dry Mix controls how much of the original signal is heard, and Wet Mix controls how much of the effect signal is heard.

4. Set the Feedback Mix parameter. Instead of setting the number of echoes to occur (as with delay effects), this parameter determines the thickness of the chorus. The higher the value, the thicker the chorus.

5. Set the Mod Rate and Mod Depth parameters. These parameters determine how detuning is added to the chorus. The Mod Rate determines how quickly the detuning occurs, and the Mod Depth determines the amount of detuning. A high Mod Depth setting makes your audio sound really out of tune (which isn't usually desirable), but a lower setting produces a nice chorusing.

Cakewalk Chorus

The Cakewalk Chorus effect is designed to work with stereo audio. To apply this effect, follow these steps:

1. Choose Chorus, which opens the Cakewalk Chorus window.

2. Set the Left Delay and Right Delay parameters. They provide the same chorusing results as the Delay Time parameter in the Cakewalk Chorus (Mono) effect, but for the separate left and right stereo channels. You also can link these parameters by activating the Link option.

3. Set the Dry Mix and Wet Mix parameters (see "Cakewalk Chorus (Mono)").

4. Set the Left Feedback and Right Feedback parameters. They provide the same chorusing results as the Feedback Mix parameter in the Cakewalk Chorus (Mono) effect, but for the separate left and right stereo channels. Also, just as the Cross Feedback parameter in the delay effects enhances the delay, this Cross Feedback parameter enhances the chorus.

5. Set the LFO Depth and LFO Rate parameters. They provide the same results as the Mod Depth and Mod Rate parameters in the Cakewalk Chorus (Mono) effect.

Cakewalk Multivoice Chorus/Flanger (Part 1)

The Cakewalk Multivoice Chorus/Flanger effect provides some more advanced chorus features (in addition to flanging), and it works as follows:

1. Choose Multivoice Chorus/Flanger, which opens the Cakewalk Multivoice Chorus/Flanger window.

2. Choose a Chorus Mode value. The Mono Chorus (Mon Ch) mode provides a chorus effect for mono audio. If used with stereo audio, the left/right channels are summed together. The Stereo Chorus (Ste Cho) mode provides a stereo chorus effect. The 6-Voice Chorus (6Vo Cho) mode also provides stereo chorus, but with three chorus effects for each stereo channel to provide a much fuller chorus sound. The Ensemble (Ensmbl) mode provides an additional stereo chorus effect, but the sound is thinner than the 6-Voice Chorus mode. The Mono Flanger (Mon Fla) and Stereo Flanger (Ste Fla) modes provide flanging effects (see the "Flanging and Phasing" section of this chapter).

3. Choose a Waveform value to determine the type of detuning that is added to the chorus. Sin uses a basic sine wave, Sin 3 uses a cubed sine wave, and Tri uses a triangle wave. The sine wave is the most common waveform used for chorus and will give you the typical results.

4. Set the Speed and Depth parameters, which work the same as the Mod Rate and Mod Depth parameters of the Cakewalk Chorus (Mono) effect.

5. Set the Delay parameter, which is similar to the Delay Time parameter of the Cakewalk Chorus (Mono) effect. It controls the thickness of the chorus effect.

6. If you want to apply some EQ to the Cakewalk Multivoice Chorus/Flanger effect, adjust the EQ Mode parameter. There are six modes available, each providing different band frequencies, resonance, and Q. You can find an EQ information chart in the Cakewalk Multivoice Chorus/Flanger help file by clicking the background of the window and pressing F1. Basically, the EQ controls cut various frequencies in the effect signal and also add resonance (brightness) to the chorus.

7. Adjust the Feedback parameter (in conjunction with the Delay parameter) to control the thickness of the chorus effect.

8. Adjust the Mix parameter (0 to 100%) to determine how much of the Cakewalk Multivoice Chorus/Flanger effect is heard.

9. Adjust the Level parameter (−20 to 0dB) to set the overall output level of the effect.

10. Use the Power button to bypass the Cakewalk Multivoice Chorus/Flanger so that you can compare the original and processed audio signals.

> **DSP-FX CHORUS VIDEO DEMO:** Because the DSP-FX Chorus included with SONAR is a legacy plug-in (32-bit only) and is not installed by default, I'm not including it here. Instead, I have created an online demo video that covers the basics of using the effect. Go to **garrigus.com?DSPFxChorus** to view it.

Flanging and Phasing

As with SONAR's chorus effects, you'll find that the program's flanger and phaser effects have many of the same parameters as its delay effects because flanging and phasing are also forms of delay. Flanging and phasing both produce a kind of spacey or whooshy type of sound by mixing a slightly delayed version of the original data with itself. As with the chorus, you don't hear echoes because the delay occurs so quickly. It's difficult to describe what these effects sound like, so you'll have to hear them for yourself. You can apply SONAR's flanging and phasing effects, as described in the following sections.

Cakewalk Flanger (Mono)

The Cakewalk Flanger (Mono) effect is designed to work with monophonic audio, rather than stereo. To apply the Cakewalk Flanger (Mono) effect, follow these steps:

1. Choose Flanger (Mono), which opens the Cakewalk Flanger (Mono) window.
2. Set the Delay Time parameter. The only difference between this Delay Time parameter and the same parameter in the Cakewalk Chorus (Mono) effect is that this one has a range of only 1 to 20 milliseconds. If you set this parameter high enough, you can actually get some chorusing out of it. To add flanging to your audio, you should keep it set somewhere between 1 and 11.
3. Set the Dry Mix and Wet Mix parameters (see "Cakewalk Chorus (Mono)").
4. Set the Feedback Mix parameter. Instead of setting the number of echoes to occur (as with delay effects), this parameter determines the thickness of the flanging. The higher the value, the thicker the flanging.
5. Set the Mod Rate and Mod Depth parameters. These parameters determine the speed and amount of the flanging. The Mod Rate determines the speed at which the flanging occurs, and the Mod Depth determines the amount of flanging.

Cakewalk Flanger

The Cakewalk Flanger effect is designed to work with stereo audio. To apply this effect, follow these steps:

1. Choose Flanger, which opens the Cakewalk Flanger window.
2. Set the Left Delay and Right Delay parameters. They provide the same flanging results as the Delay Time parameter in the Cakewalk Flanger (Mono) effect, but for the separate left and right stereo channels. You also can link these parameters by activating the Link option.
3. Set the Dry Mix and Wet Mix parameters (see Cakewalk Chorus (Mono)).
4. Set the Left Feedback and Right Feedback parameters. They provide the same flanging results as the Feedback Mix parameter in the Cakewalk Flanger (Mono) effect, but for the separate left and right stereo channels. Also, just like the Cross Feedback parameter in the delay effects enhances the delay, this Cross Feedback parameter enhances the flanging.
5. Set the LFO Depth and LFO Rate parameters. They provide the same results as the Mod Depth and Mod Rate parameters in the Cakewalk Flanger (Mono) effect.

Cakewalk Multivoice Chorus/Flanger (Part 2)

As I mentioned in the "Cakewalk Multivoice Chorus/Flanger (Part 1)" section, the Cakewalk Multivoice Chorus/Flanger effect can produce both chorus and flanging. Set the Chorus Mode parameter to Mono Flange (Mon Fla) or Stereo Flange (Ste Fla) to obtain a flanging effect for mono and stereo audio, respectively. When in one of the flanger modes, the Waveform, Delay, Speed, and Depth parameters control the type, thickness, rate, and amount of flanging. All the other parameters work the same as they do in the chorus modes.

Cakewalk Classic Phaser

The Cakewalk Classic Phaser effect provides that classic phasing sound heard on numerous guitar tracks, and it works as follows:

1. Choose Classic Phaser, which opens the Cakewalk Classic Phaser window.
2. Choose a Phaser Mode value. The Mono mode provides a phaser effect for mono audio. If used with stereo audio, the left/right channels are summed together. The Stereo mode provides a stereo phaser effect. The Quadra mode also provides stereo phasing, but it's a different type that gives a wider sound to the stereo field.

3. Choose a Waveform value to determine the characteristic of the phasing. Sin uses a basic sine wave, Sin 3 uses a cubed sine wave, and Tri uses a triangle wave. Each waveform gives the phasing a different sound that I can't really describe in words.

4. Set the LFO Rate and LFO Depth parameters to adjust the speed and amount of the phasing.

5. Adjust the Center f parameter to control the frequency to which the phasing is applied, which also alters the characteristic of the phasing.

6. Adjust the Feedback parameter to control the thickness of the phasing. Any value above 70 will give you some very far-out effects.

7. Adjust the Level parameter to set the overall output level of the effect.

8. Use the Power button to bypass the Cakewalk Classic Phaser so that you can compare the original and processed audio signals.

Sonitus:fx Modulator

The Modulator effect is actually a number of different effects rolled into one. It provides flanging, phasing, and chorus effects. I've already talked about all these effects in previous sections of this chapter, and you'll find most of the parameters for the Modulator effect to be familiar. Choose Sonitus:fx Modulator to access the effect.

The main differences are the Mode and Tape parameters. The Mode parameter sets the type of effect you want to use. The Flanger setting creates a flanging effect. The Ensemble setting creates a chorus effect. The String Phaser, Phaser 6, and Phaser 12 settings create phasing effects. Phasing effects let you change the phase of stereo data in real time for some very interesting sounds. The Tremolo setting creates warble effects by modulating the amplitude of your audio data, similar to the tremolo effect you hear on an electronic organ. Use the Tape parameter to create an effect similar to the old type of analog tape-recorder flanging. This effect ships with a large number of presets. Be sure to try them out for demonstrations of what they can do.

> **DSP-FX FLANGE VIDEO DEMO:** Because the DSP-FX Flange included with SONAR is a legacy plug-in (32-bit only) and is not installed by default, I'm not including it here. Instead, I have created an online demo video that covers the basics of using the effect. Go to **garrigus.com?DSPFxFlange** to view it.

Reverberation

Reverb (short for *reverberation*) is also a form of delay, but it's special because instead of distinct echoes, it adds a complex series of very small echoes that simulate artificial ambience. In other words, reverb produces a dense collection of echoes that are so close together that they create a wash of sound, making the original audio data sound like it's being played in another environment, such as a large concert hall. Using SONAR's reverb effects, you can make your music sound like it's being played in all kinds of different places, such as in an arena, in a club, or even on a live stage.

Cakewalk Reverb (Mono)

The Cakewalk Reverb (Mono) effect is designed to work with monophonic audio, rather than stereo. To apply the Cakewalk Reverb (Mono) effect to your data, follow these steps:

1. Choose Reverb (Mono), which opens the Cakewalk Reverb (Mono) window.

2. Set the Decay Time parameter. When you're applying reverb to your data, you should imagine the type of environment you want to create. Doing so will help you set the effect parameters. Technically, the Decay Time determines how long it takes for the reverberation to fade away, but you can think of it as controlling how

large the artificial environment will be. The lower the Decay Time, the smaller the environment; the higher the Decay Time, the larger the environment. You can set the Decay Time from 0.20 to 5 seconds. If you want to make your music sound like it's playing in a small room, a good Decay Time might be about 0.25. If you want to make your music sound like it's being played on a live stage, a good Decay Time might be about 1.50. Be sure to check out some of the included presets for more sample parameter settings.

3. Set the Dry Mix and Wet Mix parameters (see "Cakewalk Chorus (Mono)"). One point you should note is that in the case of reverb, the Dry Mix and Wet Mix parameters also make a difference in how the effect sounds. If you set the Dry Mix high and the Wet Mix low, your audio data will sound like it's positioned closer to the front of the imaginary environment. If you set the Dry Mix low and the Wet Mix high, your audio data will sound like it's positioned farther away. For example, if you want to simulate what it sounds like to be seated in the very back row of a music concert, you can set the Dry Mix low and the Wet Mix high. You need to experiment to get the exact parameter settings.

4. In the Early Reflections section, choose one of the following options: None, Dense, or Sparse. When you make a sound in any enclosed environment, some very quick echoes always occur because of the reflective surfaces (such as walls) that you are standing next to. These echoes are known as *early reflections*. To make your reverb simulations sound more authentic, SONAR provides this parameter so that you can control the density of the early reflections. If you select None, no early reflections are added to the effect. The Sparse option makes the reflections sound more like distinct echoes, and the Dense option makes the reverb effect sound thicker. Early reflections are more pronounced in larger spaces, so if you want to simulate a really large space, you'll probably want to use the Sparse option. If you want to simulate a moderately sized space, you'll probably want to use the Dense option. And if you want to simulate a small space (such as a room), you should use the None option.

5. In the Frequency Cutoff section, set the High Pass and Low Pass parameters. If you think these parameters look like equalization settings, you're right. Using these parameters also helps to create more authentic environment simulations because smaller, closed environments tend to stifle some frequencies of the audio spectrum, and larger environments usually sound brighter, meaning they promote more of the frequencies. The High Pass and Low Pass parameters work just like the previous EQ effect parameters. If you activate the High Pass parameter and set its frequency (in Hz), any frequencies above that frequency will be allowed to pass and will be included in the effect, and any frequencies below that frequency will be cut. If you activate the Low Pass parameter and set its frequency, any frequencies below that frequency will be allowed to pass, and any frequencies above that frequency will be cut. If you want to simulate a small room, you can leave the High Pass parameter deactivated, activate the Low Pass parameter, and set its frequency to around 8,000Hz. This setting would cut out any really high frequencies, making the room sound small and enclosed. For more examples on how to set these parameters, be sure to take a look at some of the included presets.

Cakewalk Reverb

The Cakewalk Reverb effect is designed to work with stereo audio. To apply this effect, follow these steps:

1. Choose Reverb, which opens the Cakewalk Reverb window.
2. Set the Decay parameter. It is exactly the same as the Decay Time parameter in the Cakewalk Reverb (Mono) effect, except that it controls both the left and right channels of the signal if your audio is in stereo.
3. Set the Dry Mix and Wet Mix parameters. They are exactly the same as the Dry Mix and Wet Mix parameters in the Cakewalk Reverb (Mono) effect, except that they control both the left and right channels of the signal if your audio is in stereo. A Link option is also available.
4. Choose an Early Reflections option. The No Echo, Dense Echo, and Sparse Echo options are exactly the same as the None, Dense, and Sparse options in the Cakewalk Reverb (Mono) effect, respectively.
5. Activate and set the frequency cutoff parameters. The LP Filter and HP Filter parameters are exactly the same as the Low Pass and High Pass filters in the Cakewalk Reverb (Mono) effect, respectively.

Sonitus:fx Reverb

The Sonitus:fx Reverb provides more powerful reverb processing than any of the previously mentioned reverb effects. Here is how it works:

1. Choose Sonitus:fx Reverb, which opens the Sonitus:fx Reverb window.
2. Set the Input parameter. This parameter lets you set the level of the signal coming into the Reverb effect.
3. Set the Low Cut and High Cut parameters. These are EQ parameters that define the frequencies for different types of environments. The Low Cut parameter cuts out low frequencies below the frequency you specify. The High Cut parameter cuts out frequencies above the frequency you specify.
4. Set the Predelay parameter. This parameter determines the time between when your audio is first heard and when the reverb effect begins. To simulate small spaces, use a low setting (such as 1 millisecond). For large spaces, use a higher setting (such as 45 to 70 milliseconds).
5. Set the Room Size parameter. This parameter determines the size of the environment you are trying to simulate. For small spaces, use a low value (such as 20). For large spaces, use a high value (such as 70).
6. Set the Diffusion parameter. This parameter determines the thickness of the reverberation. Experiment with it to hear what I mean.
7. Set the Decay Time parameter. When you're applying reverb to your data, you should imagine the type of environment you want to create. Doing so will help you set the parameters. Technically, the Decay Time determines how long it takes for the reverberation to fade away, but you can also think of it as controlling how large the environment will be. It works in conjunction with the Room Size parameter. The lower the Decay Time, the smaller the environment, and vice versa. You can also click the Tail button to add an extended decay to short sounds, although I have personally never had any use for it.
8. Set the Crossover and Bass Multiplier parameters. There may be times when you want to simulate an environment that has more or less bass sound to it. The Bass Multiplier parameter specifies how much longer or shorter the Decay Time of the bass frequencies (as compared to the other frequencies) will last in your environment. Setting the Bass Multiplier higher than 1.0 makes the bass decay longer; setting it lower than 1.0 makes the bass decay shorter. The Crossover parameter determines the frequency below which other frequencies will have a longer or shorter decay. For example, if you want to simulate a bright-sounding room, you would want the bass frequencies to decay faster. So you might set the Crossover parameter to something like 500Hz and the Bass Multiplier to something like 0.5.
9. Set the High Damping parameter. Using this parameter also helps to create a more authentic environment simulation because smaller, closed environments tend to stifle some frequencies, and larger environments usually sound brighter, meaning they promote more of the frequencies. When you set the High Damping parameter (in Hz), any frequencies above that frequency are slowly reduced (dampened) to simulate the same high-frequency reduction that happens as the reverb effect fades.
10. Set the Dry parameter. This parameter determines the level of the original nonaffected audio signal.
11. Set the E.R. parameter. This parameter determines the level of the early reflections in the reverb effect (see Cakewalk Reverb (Mono)).
12. Set the Reverb parameter. This parameter determines the level of the affected audio signal, also known as the *wet signal*. It works the same as the Wet Mix parameter (see Cakewalk Reverb (Mono)).
13. Set the Width parameter. This parameter adjusts the stereo width of the reverberation effect. Use a setting of 0 to create a monophonic signal, use a setting of 100 to create a regular stereo signal, and use a setting of more than 100 for a simulated wide stereo signal.

Cakewalk Studioverb2

Another high-quality reverb included with SONAR is the Cakewalk Studioverb2, which works as follows:

1. Choose Studioverb2, which opens the Cakewalk Studioverb2 window.

2. Set the Room Size parameter. This parameter determines the size of the environment you are trying to simulate.

3. Set the Mix parameter. It is similar to the Wet and Dry Mix parameters used in other effects. One point you should note is that in the case of reverb, the Mix parameter also makes a difference in how the effect sounds. If you set the Mix parameter low, your audio data will sound like it's positioned closer to the front of the imaginary environment. If you set the Mix parameter high, your audio data will sound like it's positioned farther away. For example, if you want to simulate what it sounds like to be seated in the very back row of a music concert, you can set the Mix parameter high. You need to experiment to get the exact parameter settings you desire.

4. Set the Decay Time parameter. When you're applying reverb to your data, you should imagine the type of environment you want to create. Doing so will help you set the parameters. Technically, the Decay Time determines how long it takes for the reverberation to fade away, but you can also think of it as controlling how large the artificial environment will be. It works in conjunction with the Room Size parameter. The lower the Decay Time, the smaller the environment, and vice versa. If you want to make your audio sound like it's playing in a small room, a good Decay Time might be about 0.5 seconds. If you want to make your audio sound like it's playing in a large area, a good Decay Time might be about 3 seconds.

5. Set the Pre Delay parameter. This parameter is similar to the Decay Time parameter, except that the Pre Delay determines the time between when your audio is first heard and when the reverb effect begins. This gives you even more control in determining your artificial environment. For small spaces, use a low setting (such as 1 millisecond). For large spaces, use a high setting (such as 70 milliseconds).

6. Set the High Frequency Rolloff and High Frequency Decay parameters. If you think these parameters look like equalization settings, you're right. Using these parameters also helps to create more authentic environment simulations because smaller, closed environments tend to stifle some frequencies of the audio spectrum, and larger environments usually sound brighter, meaning they promote more of the frequencies. When you set the High Frequency Rolloff parameter (in Hz), any frequencies below that frequency are allowed to pass, and any frequencies above that frequency are cut. Setting the High Frequency Decay parameter determines how quickly the high frequencies above the High Frequency Rolloff are cut as the reverberation sounds. For examples on how to set these parameters, be sure to take a look at some of the included presets.

7. Set the Density parameter. This parameter determines the thickness of the reverberation. Experiment with it to hear what I mean.

8. Set the Motion Depth and Motion Rate parameters. In a real environment, reverberation is constantly changing as it sounds; it isn't static at all. The reverberant echoes actually move around the environment, which is what gives the environment a distinct sound. You can simulate this movement using the Motion Depth and Motion Rate parameters. The Motion Depth parameter determines how much movement there is, and the Motion Rate parameter determines the speed of that movement. For examples on how to set these parameters, be sure to take a look at some of the included presets.

9. Set the Level parameter, which controls the overall volume level of the effect output.

10. Use the Power button to bypass the Cakewalk Studioverb2 so that you can compare the original and processed audio signals.

BREVERB 2 Cakewalk (SONAR Producer)

These final two reverb effects are the highest quality that SONAR provides. The BREVERB 2 Cakewalk effect provides professional reverberation based on algorithms, which mathematically model environments, and it works as follows:

1. Choose BREVERB 2 Cakewalk, which opens the BREVERB 2 Cakewalk window (see Figure 11.4).

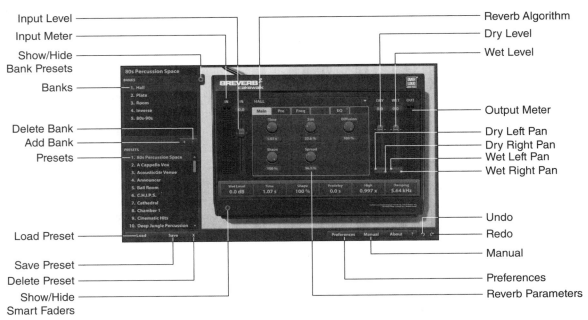

Figure 11.4 Use the BREVERB 2 Cakewalk effect to apply high-quality reverberation to your audio.
Source: Cakewalk®, Inc.

2. Click a bank to select it in the Banks area. BREVERB 2 includes five default banks with the first four (Hall, Plate, Room, and Inverse) representing the four reverb algorithms provided by the effect, and the last bank representing various presets simulating reverb effects from the 1980s and 1990s. Hall presets represent large environments; Plate represents a specific type of reverb called *plate reverb*; Room represents small environments; and Inverse represents a reverse reverb effect.

3. When you click a bank, a list of presets in that bank is shown in the Presets area. To load a preset, double-click it (or you can click the preset to select it and then click the Load Preset button).

4. Use the Input Level slider to adjust the volume of the signal coming into the BREVERB 2 effect.

5. Use the Dry Level and Wet Level sliders to adjust the volume of the original audio signal and the effect audio signal, respectively. Using the combination of these sliders, you can determine where the audio signal is placed in the virtual environment. If you set the Wet Level low and the Dry Level high, the audio signal will sound like it's positioned closer to the front of the environment. If you set the Wet Level high and the Dry Level low, the audio signal will sound like it's positioned farther away. For example, if you want to simulate what it sounds like to be seated in the very back row of a music concert, you can set the Wet Level high and the Dry Level low.

6. Use the Dry Left/Right Pan and Wet Left/Right Pan parameters to adjust the stereo image of the original audio signal and the effect audio signal, respectively. By default, the stereo image of both signals is spread out all the way between both speakers. You can narrow the stereo images by moving the Left parameters toward the right and the Right parameters toward the left. If you move all four parameters to the center, you'll effectively turn the stereo signal into a mono signal.

7. Most of the presets include the Time and Size parameters, which can be found under the Main tab of the Reverb Parameters section. Use the Time parameter to control the length of the reverb effect. The higher the Time value, the longer the reverb effect will sound. Use the Size parameter to control the size of the virtual environment. The higher the Size value, the larger the environment. If you'd like to create more sophisticated changes and build your own presets, click the Manual button to access the documentation that comes with BREVERB 2 and explains all the parameters in detail.

8. For quick access to some of the most used parameters in a preset, you can use the Smart Faders, which can be accessed by clicking the Show/Hide Smart Faders button.

9. Use the Undo and Redo buttons to undo or redo any parameter changes you make.

10. If you make changes to an existing preset and want to save it, click the Save Preset button. You can also delete a preset by clicking the Delete Preset button. Additionally, you can access more preset functions by right-clicking a preset to access the pop-up menu.

11. You can create/remove banks using the Add Bank and Delete Bank buttons, respectively. Additionally, you can right-click a bank to access more bank functions.

12. If you make changes to any of the factory presets and decide that you want to restore them, right-click the bank that contains the presets and choose Restore From Factory Bank.

Perfect Space Convolution Reverb (SONAR Producer)

The highest-quality reverb effect provided by SONAR is the Perfect Space Convolution Reverb, which is only available to SONAR Producer users. Like other reverb effects, Perfect Space simulates environments, but it is much more sophisticated because the simulations are based on real-life environments. Here is how it works:

1. Choose Perfect Space, which opens the Perfect Space window (see Figure 11.5).

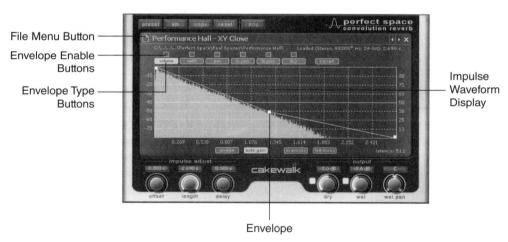

Figure 11.5 Use the Perfect Space effect to apply complex environment simulation effects to your audio data. *Source:* Cakewalk®, Inc.

2. Click the File Menu button to open the Select Wave File to Load dialog box and choose an Impulse file. Click Open. The Perfect Space effect bases its environment simulations on real-life environments by using what are called *Impulse* files. An Impulse file is similar to an actual recording of an acoustic space or signature. It models the characteristics of a real environment, such as a concert hall or even a kitchen in someone's home. SONAR ships with a large collection of Impulse files that you can use to make it seem as if your audio is playing in a variety of real environments. Perfect Space supports Impulse files in the WAV or AIF audio file format.

CREATIVE IMPULSES: In addition to environments, Impulse files can be used to model the characteristics of different audio equipment. This includes guitar amps. What this means is that you can make it sound as if your audio was played through a certain type of amp using Perfect Space, even if you don't own that particular amp. Perfect Space ships with a number of amp-based Impulse files that you can use. The effect is pretty cool.

The Perfect Space effect also lets you use any ordinary WAV or AIF file as the basis for its processing. You can get some really weird effects using the effect in this manner. Sound effects work really well here. For example, try using a quick car horn sound and process your audio data with it. Your audio takes on the characteristics of the car horn.

3. Located just below the Impulse waveform display are the In-Mono, Left-Mono, Auto Gain, and Reverse parameters. You can turn these parameters on or off by clicking on them. If your original audio is monophonic (one channel), activate the In-Mono parameter so that Perfect Space will process the original audio as mono rather than stereo. If your original audio is in stereo (two channels), but you only want to process the left channel, activate the Left-Mono parameter. The Auto Gain parameter automatically adjusts the volume of loaded Impulse files so that they are equal. This loads different Impulse files without having to continuously adjust the Dry and Wet parameters to compensate. You'll usually want to keep the Auto Gain parameter activated. The Reverse parameter simply reverses the Impulse file to allow you to hear what it is like to have your audio processed by the Impulse file in reverse. This can provide some interesting effects, depending on the Impulse file being used.

4. Set the Dry, Wet, and Wet Pan parameters in the Output section. The Dry parameter controls the volume of the original audio signal. The Wet parameter controls the volume of the processed audio signal. For example, if you are processing a guitar part, the higher you set the Dry parameter, the more of the guitar part you will hear. And the higher you adjust the Wet parameter, the more of the reverb effect you will hear. The Wet Pan parameter controls the panning for the processed audio. For example, if your guitar part is panned to the center, you could use the Wet Pan parameter to pan the reverb effect to the left or right for some interesting effects. Personally, I like to keep the Dry and Wet parameters set to 0dB and the Wet Pan parameter set to C (Center). This gives me a frame of reference when I'm adjusting the other parameters, and then afterward I can come back and adjust these parameters again if they need some final tweaking.

5. The Offset, Length, and Delay parameters in the Impulse Adjust section determine how the Impulse file is used to process your audio. Change the Offset parameter to the starting point within the Impulse file at which your audio will begin to be processed, which allows you to use only part of the Impulse file to process your audio. As you raise the Offset parameter, the beginning of the Impulse file is cropped so that less of the beginning of the file is used. You'll also notice that this changes the Length parameter. If you want to crop the end of the Impulse file rather than the beginning, you can set the Offset to 0 and lower the Length parameter. When using an environment-based Impulse file, either adjustment will make it sound like the environment is getting smaller. The Delay parameter is somewhat different, in that raising its value will cause you to hear the processed audio later than the original audio. It is sort of like introducing an echo into the effect, and it can be used to make an environment sound larger.

6. Like the parameters in the Impulse Adjust section, the Envelope Type buttons represent parameters that determine how the Impulse file is used to process your audio. These parameters adjust the volume, stereo width, panning, lo-pass EQ, hi-pass EQ, and overall EQ of the Impulse file over time using envelopes. To access and edit the envelope for each parameter, click the appropriate Envelope Type button. To enable or disable each parameter, click its associated Envelope Enable button. Adjust envelope nodes by clicking and dragging them. Parameter values are displayed on the right side of the Waveform display, with time values being shown at the bottom (except for EQ, when frequencies are shown). Add envelope nodes by double-clicking anywhere on the envelope line. Delete nodes by double-clicking them.

You can also adjust the Waveform display by holding down the Alt key on your computer keyboard and then clicking and dragging your mouse to zoom in on a section. To zoom out, hold down Alt and double-click the display. While zoomed in, you can scroll the display by holding down the Ctrl key and clicking and dragging your mouse left or right.

7. Adjust the Volume envelope. This parameter controls the volume of the Impulse file over time. When using an environment-based Impulse file, adjusting the Volume envelope essentially controls the start and stop points of the file, similar to the Offset and Length parameters. But using an envelope gives you much more control.

8. Adjust the Width envelope. This parameter controls the stereo width of the Impulse file over time. The lower you set the value, the narrower the stereo field will be. This means that the audio sounds more like it's being compressed between your two speakers. If you set the value to 0, you are basically converting the stereo signal to mono. Setting the value above 100 expands the stereo signal.

9. Adjust the Pan envelope. This parameter controls the panning of the Impulse file over time. It is essentially the same as the Wet Pan parameter (discussed earlier), except that it gives you much more control.

10. Set the Lo Pass, Hi Pass, and EQ envelopes. These parameters apply low pass, high pass, and overall equalization to the Impulse file over time.

MORE PERFECT SPACE INFO: In the Perfect Space window, click the Info button. Then click the Help button to access the Perfect Space help file for more information about this effect.

DSP-FX REVERB VIDEO DEMO: Because the DSP-FX Reverb included with SONAR is a legacy plug-in (32-bit only) and is not installed by default, I'm not including it here. Instead, I have created an online demo video that covers the basics of using the effect. Go to **garrigus.com?DSPFxReverb** to view it.

Dynamics

SONAR includes a number of effects that apply dynamic processing to your audio data, including compression and limiting. What does that mean? Well, one way to explain it would be to talk about taming vocal recordings. Suppose that you recorded this vocalist who can really belt out a tune but doesn't have very good microphone technique. When he sings, he just stays in one place in front of the mike. Professional singers know that during the quiet parts of the song, they need to sing up close to the mike, and during the loud parts, they need to back away so that an even amplitude level is recorded. If a singer doesn't do this, the amplitude of the recorded audio will be very uneven. That's where compression and limiting come in. Compression squashes the audio signal so that the amplitude levels are more even. Limiting stops the amplitude of the audio signal from rising past a certain level to prevent clipping. This can happen if the performer sings too loudly. I'll talk about each of the available effects one at a time.

Cakewalk FX Compressor/Gate

The Cakewalk FX Compressor/Gate effect applies compression to your audio data. Here is how it works:

1. Choose FX Compressor/Gate to open the Cakewalk FX Compressor/Gate window. The window displays a graph. The right side of the graph shows output amplitude, and the bottom of the graph shows input amplitude. Inside the graph is a line representing the input amplitude and output amplitude as they relate to one another. Initially, the line is drawn diagonally, and you read it from left to right. This shows a 1:1 ratio between input and output amplitudes, meaning as the input level goes up 1dB, the output level also goes up 1dB.

2. Set the Compressor Thr (threshold) parameter. The Cakewalk FX Compressor/Gate effect uses a digital noise gate to identify the parts of your audio data that should be processed. The Compressor Thr parameter

determines at what amplitude level your audio data will start being compressed. When the amplitude of your audio data reaches the Threshold level, processing will begin.

3. Set the Compressor Ratio parameter. This parameter determines how much processing is done to your audio data. A ratio of 1:1 means no processing is done. A ratio of 2:1 means that for every 2dB increase in input amplitude, there is only a 1dB increase in output amplitude. Thus, the amplitude is being compressed. If you set the Ratio parameter to its highest value (Inf:1), that causes limiting, so no matter how loud the input amplitude gets, it is limited to the level set by the Threshold parameter.

4. Set the Attack Time parameter. This parameter determines how quickly after the input level has reached the threshold that processing is applied. For example, if the input level reaches the threshold, it doesn't have to be compressed right away. A slow attack means the signal won't be compressed unless it lasts for a while. This is a good way to make sure fast, percussive parts are left alone, but long, drawn-out parts are compressed.

5. Set the Release Time parameter. This parameter determines how quickly after the input level goes below the threshold that processing is stopped (or the digital noise gate is closed). If you set the Release Time parameter too low, your audio could be cut off. A longer release allows processing to sound more natural. You'll have to experiment to get the right setting.

6. In addition to being able to compress audio data, the Cakewalk FX Compressor/Gate effect can cut out noises using a special noise gate (hence the name Compressor/Gate). By setting the Gate Thr (threshold) parameter, you can remove any unwanted noises that have an amplitude level that falls below the threshold. This is great for removing bad notes or string noise on guitar parts, for instance. Setting the Expander Ratio determines how soft the amplitudes below the Gate Thr will be made. For example, if you set the Expander Ratio to 100:1, then any sounds that fall below the Gate Thr will be cut out completely.

7. Set the Detection Algorithm parameter. This parameter establishes how the Cakewalk FX Compressor/Gate effect will determine the amplitude level of the incoming audio signal. Choosing the Average option tells the effect to determine the average value of the input signal and use that to apply compression appropriately. Choosing the RMS (root mean square) option tells the effect to determine the perceived loudness (as a listener would hear it over a period of time) of the input signal and use that to apply compression appropriately. The best method to use depends on the material being processed. You'll need to experiment to see which one works best.

8. Set the Stereo Interaction parameter. Choose the Maximum option to apply compression to both stereo channels equally. Choose the Side Chain option to apply compression only to the right channel of the stereo signal, while using the left channel signal to activate the threshold. You can use this option as a *ducking* effect, which can come in handy if you have music playing in the right channel and a voiceover playing in the left channel. As the voice comes in, the music will be lowered so that listeners can hear the voice over the background music. For most applications, you'll want to use the Maximum option.

9. Activate the Soft Knee option to give a smoother transition as the input signal starts to be compressed.

10. Set the Output Gain parameter. This parameter adjusts the overall amplitude of your audio after it is processed.

Cakewalk Compressor/Gate

SONAR also includes the Cakewalk Compressor/Gate effect, which works almost exactly the same as the Cakewalk FX Compressor/Gate effect, but with a few parameter differences, as follows:

1. Choose Compressor/Gate to open the Cakewalk Compressor/Gate window.

2. Set the Attack, Release, Compressor Threshold, and Compressor Ratio parameters, which work the same as the Attack Time, Release Time, Compressor Thr, and Compressor Ratio parameters for the Cakewalk FX Compressor/Gate.

3. Set the Compressor Input Gain, which gives you some additional control over when the compressor starts working. The Input Gain lets you boost the incoming signal so that its level will rise above the threshold sooner, thus compressing the signal more than normal.

4. If you want to automatically cut out unwanted noises, set the Gate Mode to Normal and then set the Gate Threshold. Any audio below the threshold will be cut out completely. Keep in mind that the Attack and Release parameters also work with the gate, and they control how quickly the gate opens and closes, respectively.

5. If you want to manually cut out audio, set the Gate Mode to Manual. In this mode, the only parameter that controls how the gate opens/closes is the Manual Trigger. Click the button once to close the gate and click it again to open the gate. Of course, the Manual Trigger can be automated (see Chapter 12 for more information on automation), which lets you control it via a track envelope.

6. Set the Level parameter, which controls the overall volume level of the effect output.

7. Use the Power button to bypass the Cakewalk Compressor/Gate so that you can compare the original and processed audio signals.

Cakewalk FX Expander/Gate

Like the special noise gate option in the Cakewalk FX Compressor/Gate effect, the Cakewalk FX Expander/Gate effect cuts out unwanted noises below a certain amplitude threshold. This effect takes less CPU processing power for those times when you don't need compression. Here is how it works:

1. Choose FX Expander/Gate to open the Cakewalk FX Expander/Gate window, which displays a graph that is the same as the one in the Cakewalk FX Compressor/Gate effect.

2. Set the Expander Thr (threshold) parameter. This parameter works the same as the Gate Thr parameter in the Cakewalk FX Compressor/Gate effect.

3. Set the Expander Ratio parameter. This parameter works the same as the Expander Ratio parameter in the Cakewalk FX Compressor/Gate effect.

4. Set the Attack Time parameter. This parameter works the same as the Attack Time parameter in the Cakewalk FX Compressor/Gate effect.

5. Set the Release Time parameter. This parameter works the same as the Release Time parameter in the Cakewalk FX Compressor/Gate effect.

6. Set the Detection Algorithm parameter. This parameter works the same as the Detection Algorithm parameter in the Cakewalk FX Compressor/Gate effect, except that there is one additional option. Choosing the Peak option tells the effect to determine the peak value of the input signal and use that to apply processing appropriately.

7. Set the Stereo Interaction parameter. This parameter works the same as the Stereo Interaction parameter in the Cakewalk FX Compressor/Gate effect.

8. Activate the Soft Knee option to give a smoother transition as the input signal starts to be processed.

9. Set the Output Gain parameter. This parameter adjusts the overall amplitude of your audio after it is processed.

Cakewalk FX Limiter

The Cakewalk FX Limiter effect stops an audio signal from getting any louder than a specified amplitude level. You can put this effect to good use during recording to prevent your input signal from getting too high and causing distortion or clipping. Here is how the effect works:

1. Choose FX Limiter to open the Cakewalk FX Limiter window.

2. Set the Limiter Thr (threshold) parameter. This is the level above which you don't want your audio signal level to go. This means the amplitude of the audio won't be able to get any higher than this value.

3. Set the Stereo Interaction parameter. This parameter works the same as the Stereo Interaction parameter in the Cakewalk FX Compressor/Gate effect.

4. Set the Output Gain parameter. This parameter adjusts the overall amplitude of your audio after it is processed.

Cakewalk FX Dynamics Processor

The Cakewalk FX Dynamics Processor effect combines all of the features of the previous dynamics effects into one. This means that this one effect can perform all of the functions of the Cakewalk FX Compressor/Gate, FX Expander/ Gate, and Cakewalk FX Limiter effects. It also has the same parameter settings, which were previously described. Choose FX Dynamics Processor to open the Cakewalk FX Dynamics Processor window.

Sonitus:fx Compressor

There are three additional high-quality dynamics effects at your disposal. The first is the Sonitus:fx Compressor, which provides pretty much the same functionality as Cakewalk FX Compressor/Gate effect. Here is how it works:

1. Choose Sonitus:fx Compressor to open the Sonitus:fx Compressor window.
2. To adjust the input signal level, just drag the Input slider up or down.
3. Set the Threshold parameter. This parameter works the same as the Threshold parameter for the Cakewalk FX Compressor/Gate effect.
4. Set the Ratio parameter. This parameter works the same as the Ratio parameter for the Cakewalk FX Compressor/Gate effect.
5. Set the Attack parameter. This parameter works the same as the Attack parameter for the Cakewalk FX Compressor/Gate effect.
6. Set the Release parameter. This parameter works the same as the Release parameter for the Cakewalk FX Compressor/Gate effect, with one exception. Just to the right of the Release parameter is a button labeled *TCR*. Activating this button tells the Compressor effect to try to determine the release time automatically during processing. This may or may not work well, depending on the material you are processing.
7. In addition to being able to compress audio data, the Compressor effect can apply limiting to your data. To turn limiting on or off, use the Limiter button located to the right of the Attack parameter.
8. Set the Type parameter by clicking the Type button. A setting of Normal provides the operation of a normal compressor effect. A setting of Vintage emulates the compression characteristics of a classic analog-based compressor like the Teletronix LA2A. This might give your audio data more warmth and punch.
9. Set the Knee parameter. Choosing a soft setting (10dB or greater) will give you a warmer quality to the compression. Choosing a hard setting (below 10dB) will give you a harsher quality to the compression.
10. Set the Gain parameter. This parameter works the same as the Output Gain parameter in the Cakewalk FX Compressor/Gate effect.

Sonitus:fx Gate

I've talked about digital noise gates before as they pertain to other functions, but you also can use digital noise gates independently to remove (or reduce the level of) parts of your audio data. For example, if you want the quiet sections in a vocal dialogue recording to be turned to silence, you can use a noise gate. The Sonitus:fx Gate effect can do this, and here is how it works:

1. Choose Sonitus:fx Gate to open the Sonitus:fx Gate window.
2. To adjust the input signal level, just drag the Input slider up or down.
3. Set the Threshold parameter. This parameter determines at what amplitude audio passes through the gate unaffected. Anything below the threshold will have its level reduced.
4. Set the Depth parameter. This parameter determines how soft the input signal level will be made after the gate is closed. Most of the time, this parameter is set to −Inf, making the signal completely silent.
5. Set the Low Cut and High Cut parameters. These are EQ parameters that allow you to gate an audio signal according to frequency. Any frequencies below the Low Cut frequency are reduced; any frequencies above the High Cut frequency are reduced.
6. Set the Gate Mode parameter using the Gate Mode button (which is located below the High Cut parameter). Initially, the button displays a Normal setting. Click the button to toggle it to Duck mode and vice versa. In

Duck mode, the gate is inverted so that signals below the threshold are allowed to pass, and signals above the threshold are attenuated.

7. Set the Punch Mode, Punch Level, and Punch Tune parameters (which are located next to the Gate Mode button). The Punch feature adds gain to the signal as it starts to pass through the gate. This can be useful to add punch to percussion sounds. Setting the mode to Wide adds punch to a wide signal range. Setting the mode to Tuned adds punch to a specific frequency. The Level and Tune parameters specify the amount of gain added and the frequency used.

8. Set the Attack parameter. This parameter determines how quickly after the input level has reached the threshold that the noise gate opens and allows audio through. A low setting keeps any quick, percussive sound intact.

9. Set the Hold parameter. This parameter determines how long the gate stays open after the input signal has gone below the threshold.

10. Set the Release parameter. This parameter determines how quickly after the input level goes below the threshold and the hold time ends that the noise gate is closed. A low setting makes the noise gate close quickly. Again, this is good for percussive sounds.

11. Set the Lookahead parameter. Increasing this parameter allows the Gate effect to scan the input signal ahead of time. This can be useful if you have percussive sounds, but you want to use a longer attack time and not chop off part of the signal.

12. Set the Gain parameter. This parameter adjusts the overall amplitude of your audio after it is processed.

Sonitus:fx Multiband

Like the Sonitus:fx Compressor effect, the Multiband effect applies compression to your audio data. This effect has one important difference, though: It allows you to process different frequency ranges in your audio independently. Why is that important? Well, one way to explain it is to talk about *de-essing*. You might have noticed while doing vocal recordings that some singers produce a sort of hissing sound whenever they pronounce words with the letter "s" in them. That hissing sound is called *sibilance*, and you usually don't want it in your audio. The process of removing sibilance is called de-essing, and it is done by compressing certain frequencies in the audio spectrum. To use the Multiband effect, follow these steps:

1. Choose Sonitus:fx Multiband to open the Sonitus:fx Multiband window.

2. The Multiband effect actually provides five compression effects in one. It's basically like having five of the Sonitus:fx Compressor effects together in one effect. You'll find five sets of controls called *bands* in the upper-left section of the dialog box. You can turn each band on or off using the Byp (bypass) buttons, and you can solo a band using the Solo buttons. All the bands are identical.

3. To set the Threshold parameter for each band, use the vertical sliders or type in a value. The Threshold parameters work the same as for the Sonitus:fx Compressor effect.

4. In the lower-right section of the dialog box, you'll find a tabbed area. Clicking a numbered tab displays the compression settings for each band.

5. Set the Ratio, Knee, Type, Gain, Attack, and Release parameters for each band. All of these parameters work the same as the corresponding parameters for the Sonitus:fx Compressor effect.

6. Clicking the Common tab displays all the band settings in a grid, as well as some global effect settings.

7. Set the TCR, Limit, and Out parameters. These parameters also work the same as they do for the Sonitus:fx Compressor effect.

8. The lower-left portion of the dialog box contains the frequency graph. This graph displays the frequency ranges for each band. You can adjust the ranges by clicking and dragging the four separators on the graph, or you can type in new values for the Low, LowMid, HighMid, and High parameters. These parameters determine the range of frequencies that will be affected by each band.

9. There is also a global Q parameter that affects all the bands located in the Common panel. The Q parameter works the same as the previously mentioned Q parameter in the "Equalization" section of this chapter.

LP64 Multiband Linear Compressor (SONAR Producer)

The highest-quality compressor effect provided by SONAR is the LP64 Multiband Linear Compressor, which is only available to SONAR Producer Edition users. The operation of the Linear Compressor is similar to that of the Sonitus: fx Multiband because it also provides five bands of compression. It is also similar to the LP64 Linear EQ because it provides an editable EQ Graph. To use the Linear Compressor, do the following:

1. Choose LP-64 Multiband to open the LP-64 Multiband window (see Figure 11.6).

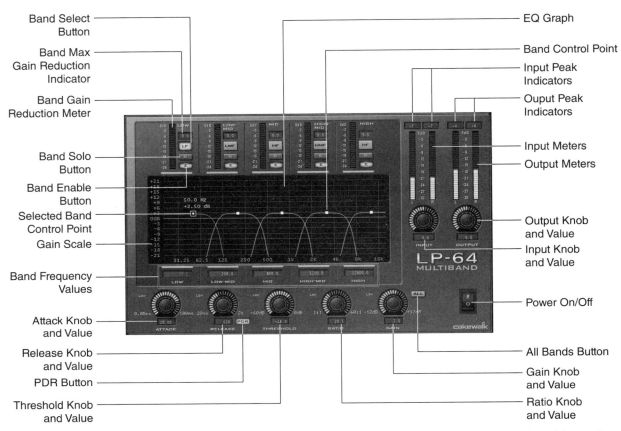

Figure 11.6 Create your own compression filters by manipulating the band parameters of the Linear Compressor.
Source: Cakewalk®, Inc.

2. The Linear Compressor provides five bands of compression, each with an identical set of adjustable parameters. The difference between the bands is that they each must have a different center frequency value, which allows you to apply different compression filters to five separate frequency ranges of the audio spectrum. To enable a band, click its Band Enable button.
3. To listen to a single band processing, click its Solo button.
4. To choose a band for parameter editing, click its Band Select button.
5. To change the center frequency for a band, you can use either the EQ Graph or the Band Frequency value. On the graph, click/drag the band's control point left/right. To adjust the value directly, click/drag or Shift+click/drag your mouse up/down over the value. You can also double-click the value, type in a new number, and then press Enter.
6. To change the gain for a band, you can use either the EQ Graph or the Gain Knob/Value. On the graph, click/drag the band's control point up/down. You can also adjust the Gain Scale of the graph by clicking and

dragging up/down over the scale. To use the Gain Knob, click/drag or Shift+click/drag your mouse up/down over the knob.

7. Adjust the Attack for the band using the Attack Knob/Value.

8. Adjust the Release for the band using the Release Knob/Value. You can also have the release time adjusted automatically by clicking the PDR (Program Dependent Release) button. An inappropriate release time can cause anomalies such as a "pumping" sound. This is where you can hear the compressor trying to compress the audio, but it is out of time with the music, and it sounds strange. Using the PDR feature, the Linear Compressor will automatically set the release time, according to the material being processed.

9. Adjust the Threshold for the band using the Threshold Knob/Value.

10. Adjust the Ratio for the band using the Ratio Knob/Value.

11. Repeat Steps 3 to 11 for each band you want to use.

12. If you ever need to adjust all of the band Attack, Release, Threshold, Ratio, and Gain parameters at once so they are identical, click the All button and then make the adjustments.

13. Use the Input Knob/Value to adjust the volume level of the audio signal coming into the Linear Compressor.

14. Use the Output Knob/Value to adjust the volume level going out.

15. Use the Power button to bypass the Linear Compressor so you can compare the original and processed audio signals.

Boost 11 Peak Limiter

During the mixing stage of your project, you may have some tracks that are a bit too low in volume, but can't be boosted because doing so would cause the peaks to go over the 0dB level and cause clipping. A limiter like Boost 11 can be used to remedy this situation, as well as to bring up the level of an entire mix. To use Boost 11, do the following:

1. Choose Boost11 to open the Boost 11 Peak Limiter window (see Figure 11.7).

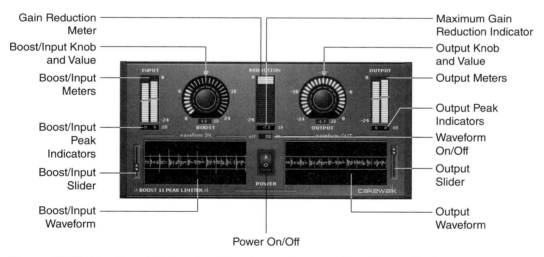

Figure 11.7 Use Boost 11 to raise the volume of your audio without clipping.
Source: Cakewalk®, Inc.

2. If it's not set already, set the Power On/Off switch to On. Turning this switch off allows you to bypass Boost 11 for comparison of the processed/unprocessed audio.

3. If it's not set already, set the Waveform On/Off switch to On. Turning this switch off can save CPU resources, but you'll only need to do so if your PC starts getting bogged down and you hear skipping during playback.

4. Use the Boost Knob or Slider to increase the volume of the audio being processed by clicking/dragging (up/down) or Shift+clicking/dragging (for finer value adjustments) with your mouse. You want this to be a subtle increase because setting the input too high can make the audio sound flat or squashed. I recommend that you don't set this any higher than 6dB.

5. Use the Output Knob or Slider to set the final output level of the audio. Because Boost 11 is a limiter, it will stop (or limit) the audio level from going any higher than the output value. This allows you to boost the volume without going over 0dB, which would cause clipping. I recommending setting this between −1dB and −2dB or lower.

6. As you adjust the parameters, you'll notice the waveform displays being updated. What you want to see in the Boost/Input Waveform is a small number of red lines above and below the waveform boundaries. This indicates you have a good boost in level without damaging the sound of the audio. If you have a lot of red lines showing, you should lower the Boost/Input Knob/Slider. Also, as a side note, you can double-click the waveform displays to reset them at any time.

7. The input meters and indicators will show you the input level as well. And the output meters and indicators will show you the output level. The gain reduction meter and indicator shows how much Boost 11 is lowering the peaks of the audio to keep it from clipping. Double-click any of the indicators to reset them at any time.

MASTERING: In addition to regular compression/limiting tasks, the high quality of the Sonitus:fx Multiband, LP64 Multiband Linear Compressor, and Boost 11 Limiter effects allows you to use them for mastering. *Mastering* is the procedure during which the final mixed-down stereo audio for a song is processed with various effects (such as EQ, compression, and limiting) to give the song that final professional touch before being released via the Web or burned to CD. There have been entire books written on the topic of mastering, but check out the following articles for some good information:

▷ *Audio Mastering Basics—An Introduction to Mastering*—**www.digifreq.com/digifreq/article.asp?ID=33**
▷ *Audio Mastering Advice from Professional Engineers*—**www.digifreq.com/digifreq/article.asp?ID=34**
▷ *Audio Mastering—A Step-by-Step Guide to Mastering Your Recordings*—**www.digifreq.com/digifreq /article.asp?ID=35**

Also, go to **www.digifreq.com/digifreq/articles.asp** for more information on these and other music technology topics.

And be sure to get my free DigiFreq music technology newsletter so you don't miss the mastering information I will be providing in future issues. Go to **www.digifreq.com/digifreq/** to sign up.

TS-64 Transient Shaper

Another useful effect that can be used during the mixing and mastering stages of a project is the TS-64 Transient Shaper. This tool allows you to shape the sound of percussive tracks that have distinct transients (hits), like drum tracks. For example, you may have a track containing hi-hat and snare, but the snare just doesn't have enough presence or punch. You can use the TS-64 Transient Shaper to alter the sound of the snare without affecting the hi-hat, as well as do much more. To use the TS-64 Transient Shaper, do the following:

1. Choose TS-64 Transient Shaper to open the TS64 Transient Shaper window (see Figure 11.8).

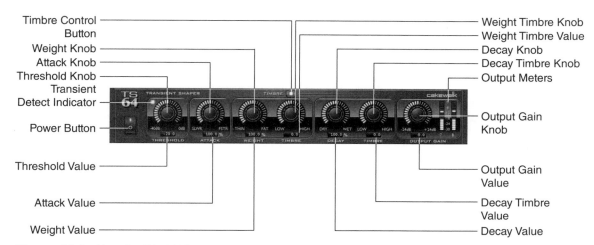

Figure 11.8 Use the TS-64 Transient Shaper to shape the sound of percussive tracks.
Source: Cakewalk®, Inc.

2. If it's not set already, set the Power button to I (or on). Turning this button off allows you to bypass the TS-64 for comparison of the processed/unprocessed audio.
3. Taking the example of a hi-hat and snare drum track, you can use the Threshold parameter to determine what transients (or hits) are processed. Let's say you only want to change the sound of the snare. Since the snare is louder than the hi-hat, you can raise the Threshold so that only the snare is affected. The Threshold can be set from −40dB to 0dB. Raising the Threshold means moving it closer to 0dB. As you raise the Threshold, notice the Transient Detect Indicator and make sure it only lights up when the snare drum sounds.

SETTING THE TS-64 PARAMETERS: You can set the TS-64 parameters in a few ways. Use the mouse by clicking and dragging up/down on any of the knobs. Use the keyboard by first mouse-clicking on a knob or value to give it focus and then using the arrow keys to make adjustments. You can also set a parameter directly by double-clicking its value, typing in a new value, and pressing Enter.

---

4. With the snare drum isolated, you can now change the initial sound of the snare hit using the Attack parameter. By default, Attack is set to 100%, which means it has no effect. To give the snare hit a softer quality, set the Attack below 100%. To give the snare hit a harder edge, set the Attack above 100%.
5. Use the Weight parameter to give the snare a thinner or fatter sound. By default, Weight is set to 100%, which means it has no effect. To make the snare sound thinner/fatter, set the Weight to less than or greater than 100%, respectively.
6. The Weight Timbre parameter works in conjunction with the Weight parameter and allows you to add/subtract weight to a certain frequency range, rather than the entire sound. For example, if you want to give the snare a bit of boom in the bass, you would set the Weight to something above 100% and set the Weight Timbre to something below 0.0. The default value for Weight Timbre is 0.0, which means it has no effect and all frequencies are affected by the Weight parameter. Also, be sure to activate the Timbre Control button. Turning this button off bypasses both Timbre parameters, allowing you to quickly compare the sound with/without timbre changes.
7. The Decay parameter allows you to control the tail end of the snare hit, meaning you can make the end of the hit short (giving it a dry sound) or long (giving it a wet, ambient sound). By default, the Decay parameter is

set to 100%, which means it has no effect. To give the snare a dry sound, set the Decay below 100%. To give the snare a wetter sound, set the Decay above 100%.

8. The Decay Timbre parameter works in conjunction with the Decay parameter and allows you to add/subtract decay to a certain frequency range, rather than the entire sound. For example, if you want to hear more of the snares and have them ring out a bit with each hit, you would set the Decay to something above 100% and set the Decay Timbre to something above 0.0 so that only the high frequencies are affected. The default value for the Decay Timbre is 0.0, which means it has no effect and all frequencies are affected by the Decay parameter. The Timbre Control button also turns the Decay Timbre on/off.

9. Adjust the Output Gain to make sure the signal isn't too hot (high). You can see the output level on the Output Meters.

Keep in mind that the TS-64 isn't just for drums. It can be used on any material that has percussive transients, like quick guitar chord hits or brass stabs, and so on.

Changing Time and Pitch

In addition to the Length and Transpose editing features, SONAR provides the Pitch Shifter and Time/Pitch Stretch effects, which you also can use to change the length and pitch of your audio data. The effects, however, are more powerful and flexible. This is especially true of the Time/Pitch Stretch effect. SONAR Producer and Studio users also get a very powerful vocal processing effect called *V-Vocal*.

Cakewalk Pitch Shifter

The Cakewalk Pitch Shifter effect provides low quality, but it doesn't take up as much CPU processing power. If you want to try out the Cakewalk Pitch Shifter, here's how it works:

1. Choose Pitch Shifter to open the Cakewalk Pitch Shifter window.
2. Set the Pitch Shift parameter. It is exactly the same as the Amount parameter in the Transpose editing function. You can use it to transpose the pitch of your audio data from −12 to +12 semitones (an entire octave down or up).

UNWANTED ARTIFACTS: Normally, when you change the pitch of audio data, the length is altered, too. Raise the pitch, and the data gets shorter; lower the pitch, and the data gets longer. When this happens, the processed audio no longer plays in sync with the other data in your project. Luckily, you can use SONAR's pitch-shifting effects to change pitch without changing the length of the audio data. The only problem to be leery of is that pitch shifting can produce unwanted artifacts if you use too great an interval. Alvin & the Chipmunks were a product of this phenomenon. It's best to stay within an interval of a major third (four semitones) up or down, if possible.

---

3. Set the Dry Mix and Wet Mix parameters. You should almost always keep the Dry Mix set to 0% and the Wet Mix set to 100%.
4. As far as the Feedback Mix, Delay Time, and Mod Depth parameters are concerned, they don't seem to have anything to do with the Cakewalk Pitch Shifter effect. Changing these parameters only introduces unwanted artifacts into the sound. My advice is simply to leave them set at their default values: Feedback Mix = 0, Delay Time = 0, and Mod Depth = 35.

Time/Pitch Stretch 2

The Time/Pitch Stretch 2 effect is much more advanced and flexible, and it provides better quality than the Pitch Shifter effect. However, that doesn't mean it's difficult to use. Some of the more advanced parameters can be a bit confusing, but I'll go over them one at a time. The major disadvantage to the Time/Pitch Stretch 2 effect is that it can't be used in real-time, only offline. The effect works like this:

1. Choose Time/Pitch Stretch 2 to open the Time/Pitch Stretch 2 window.
2. Set the Time parameter. Using the Time parameter, you can change the length of your audio data as a percentage. If you want to make the data shorter, set the Time parameter to a percentage less than 100. For example, to make the data half of its original length, use a setting of 50%. If you want to make the data longer, set the Time parameter to a percentage greater than 100. If you want to make the data twice its original length, use a setting of 200%. To change the Time parameter, just type a value or use the horizontal slider.

STAY WITHIN 10 PERCENT: When you're transposing audio, it's best to stay within a major third (four semitones) up or down, if possible, because audio doesn't react well to higher values. The same concept applies when you're changing the length of audio data. You should try to stay within 10% longer or shorter, if possible; otherwise, the results might not sound very good.

---

3. Set the Pitch parameter. Using the Pitch parameter, you can transpose your audio data up or down one octave (in semitones). To change the Pitch parameter, just type a value or use the vertical slider.

TIME/PITCH GRAPH: Notice that a graph is shown in the Time/Pitch Stretch dialog box. Using this graph, you can change the Time and Pitch parameters by dragging the small blue square. Drag the square up or down to change the Pitch parameter. Drag the square left or right to change the Time parameter. If you hold down the Shift key on your computer keyboard at the same time, the square automatically will snap to the exact grid points on the graph.

---

4. To get the best quality, make sure the MPEX option under the Advanced tab is activated. Processing will probably be a bit slower, but the audio will sound better. Also, choose a setting for the Quality parameter. If you are processing a single instrument, choose one of the single instrument options.

V-Vocal Voice Processor (SONAR Producer and Studio)

V-Vocal is an accurate and powerful vocal processing effect that adjusts the pitch, timing, loudness, and timbre of monophonic vocal audio recordings.

V-Vocal Basics

V-Vocal is not applied in the same way as all the other audio effects in SONAR. When you apply V-Vocal to a selected region of audio data or a selected clip, a new V-Vocal clip is created. This new clip overlaps the original audio data, which still exists below the V-Vocal data, but is muted. The steps to start using V-Vocal to process your audio are as follows:

1. Select a region of audio and either choose V-Vocal > Create V-Vocal Clip from the Track view menu or right-click the audio and choose V-Vocal > Create V-Vocal Clip. You can also press Shift+V on your PC keyboard. A new V-Vocal clip is created (displaying the V-Vocal logo in the upper-right corner), and the V-Vocal window is automatically opened (see Figure 11.9).

V-VOCAL CLIP MENU: The V-Vocal logo displayed in the upper-right corner of the clip can be clicked to access a menu that provides a number of functions. Bypass/Unbypass toggles the V-Vocal effect on the clip off/on so that you can compare the original to the processed audio. Remove V-Vocal completely removes

V-Vocal and leaves you with the original audio unchanged. V-Vocal Editor opens the V-Vocal window. Bypass All V-Vocal Clips is the same as Bypass/Unbypass but it functions on all V-Vocal clips in a project.

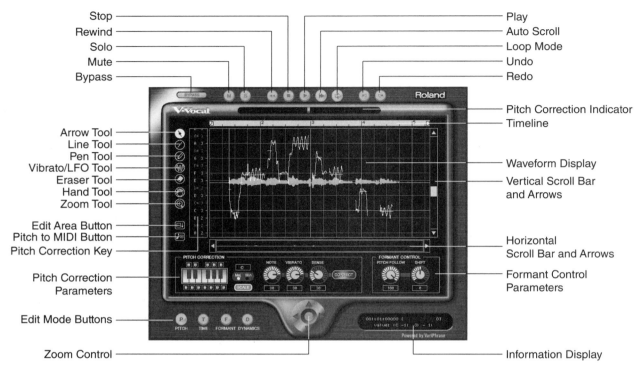

Figure 11.9 Use the V-Vocal window to access the V-Vocal effect parameters.
Source: Cakewalk®, Inc.

2. The V-Vocal window displays the V-Vocal clip in its entirety within a Waveform display. Along the top of the Waveform display is the Timeline (which is the same as the Time Ruler in the Track view). Along the left of the Waveform display are values, which differ, depending on the editing mode you are using. Along the bottom and right of the Waveform display are the horizontal and vertical scroll bars and arrows. Use these controls to scroll the Waveform display. You can also click and drag with the Hand tool directly within the display to scroll.

> **WAVEFORM DISPLAY SIZE:** To make the Waveform display larger or smaller, click the Edit Area button to hide or show some of the V-Vocal parameters. You can also change the size of the V-Vocal window itself to create a larger display.

3. For zooming, use the Zoom control and Zoom tool. Click the up and down arrows on the Zoom control to zoom out and in vertically. Click the left and right arrows on the Zoom control to zoom out and in horizontally. To zoom out all the way both vertically and horizontally (thus fitting the entire clip within the display), double-click the center of the Zoom control. To zoom in on a specific area, use the Zoom tool to make a rectangular selection in the Waveform display.

4. Without a data selection, V-Vocal parameters make changes to the entire audio waveform. To edit only a portion of the waveform, use the Arrow tool and click and drag within the Waveform display to make a selection.

5. Use the Line, Pen, Vibrato/LFO, and Eraser tools to edit your data.

6. Use the Undo and Redo buttons to remove mistakes that you've made during editing. You can also right-click the Waveform display and choose Undo or Redo from the pop-up menu, or you can press Ctrl+Z (Undo) or Ctrl+Shift+Z (Redo).

7. Use the Rewind, Stop, and Play buttons to control playback of the clip. These buttons are the same as the regular transport buttons in SONAR. During playback, you'll notice a cursor moving across the Waveform display. This cursor is the same as the Now time cursor in the Track view.

8. If you are zoomed in, you can have the Waveform display automatically scroll during playback by clicking the Auto Scroll button.

9. You can also loop playback (just like in the Track view) by clicking the Loop Mode button. If you've made a data selection, only that selection will be played and looped; otherwise, the entire clip is played and looped.

10. Click the Bypass button to temporarily turn off all V-Vocal processing and allow you to compare the original audio to the V-Vocal processed audio.

11. Use the Mute and Solo buttons to mute or solo the track upon which the V-Vocal clip resides. This enables you to hear the clip alone or along with the other audio in your project.

12. When you're finished, close the V-Vocal window. When you play your project, the V-Vocal processing will be played as well.

13. To open the V-Vocal window and make additional changes, just double-click the clip.

14. To permanently remove any V-Vocal changes, right-click the clip and choose V-Vocal > Remove V-Vocal (or choose V-Vocal in the Track view menu).

Automatically Adjusting Vocal Pitch

When adjusting the pitch of a vocal part, the first thing you'll want to do is let V-Vocal try to make the corrections automatically. The results can be very accurate if the vocal part isn't too far off pitch to begin with. Here are the steps for using V-Vocal's automatic pitch correction features:

1. With the V-Vocal clip created and the window open, click the Pitch Edit Mode button.

2. To have the audio waveform shown under the V-Vocal waveform markings, right-click the Waveform display and choose View > Waveform. This will give you a better idea of the vocal part section you are editing.

3. Make sure that the Pitch Follow parameter in the Formant Control section is set to 0. This ensures that the timbral characteristics of your vocal will not change when you change the pitch. If you set the Pitch Follow parameter above zero, it will give you a Munchkin-sounding type of vocal. If you set the Pitch Follow parameter below zero, it will give you a strange low-voice type of vocal.

4. To correct only the pitch of one section of the clip, choose the Arrow tool and make a data selection. Otherwise, V-Vocal will pitch-correct the entire clip.

5. In the Pitch Correction section, adjust the Note, Vibrato, and Sense parameters. The Note parameter controls how close the notes in your audio will be moved to the correct pitches. You would think you'd want them moved all the way, but depending on how far off your notes are to begin with, moving them too much can cause artifacts to be introduced into the audio. I've found that the best setting for the Note parameter is between 70 and 90, but if your original audio isn't too far off, a setting of 100 could work. The Vibrato parameter controls how much of the original vibrato you want to keep. Most of the time, I keep this set to 100 because when I start lowering it too much to remove vibrato, the vocal ends up sounding artificial. The Sense parameter controls the amount of pitch correction applied. The higher the value, the closer your audio is changed to fit an exact pitch. I've found the default value of 30 to work nicely most of the time. If you set the Sense parameter too high, it will make the vocal sound very artificial.

6. Click the Correct button to apply the pitch correction. If you don't like the results, undo them and try again.

> **ARTIFICIAL VOCALS EFFECT:** Remember that Cher song called "Believe" where she had those strange sounding vocals? Well, you can get the same effect with V-Vocal. Just set the Note parameter to 100, the

Vibrato parameter to 0, and the Sense parameter to 100. Click the Correct button. Voilà! Instant artificial vocals.

7. V-Vocal can also automatically conform your audio to a musical scale. Click the Scale button to activate the Scale feature. Choose either the Maj or Min option to choose a major or minor musical scale. Then click a key on the tiny keyboard display to choose the root note for the scale. If you want to define your own scale, you can click the B buttons above/below the keyboard to include (blue) or bypass (red) notes. Click the Correct button. To set the Scale feature back to its default values, double-click the Scale button.

> **NOTE SELECTION:** Click the note names in the Pitch Correction Key (shown on the left of the Waveform display) to include (blue), exclude (gray), or bypass (red) notes.

MANUALLY ADJUSTING VOCAL PITCH

Instead of relying on the automatic adjustments provided by V-Vocal, you can make pitch adjustments manually by doing the following:

1. With the V-Vocal clip created and the window open, click the Pitch Edit Mode button.
2. To have the audio waveform shown under the V-Vocal waveform markings, right-click the Waveform display and choose View > Waveform. This will give you a better idea of the vocal part section you are editing.
3. Make sure that the Pitch Follow parameter in the Formant Control section is set to zero. This ensures that the timbral characteristics of your vocal will not change when you change the pitch. If you set the Pitch Follow parameter above zero, it will give you a Munchkin-sounding type of vocal. If you set the Pitch Follow parameter below zero, it will give you a strange low-voice type of vocal.
4. Looking at the Waveform display, you'll notice the yellow curved lines representing the different pitches in your audio. These are called *Pitch Curves*. To edit a Pitch Curve, select the Arrow tool. Then hover the Arrow tool over the center line of the Pitch Curve and click and drag the curve up or down to change its pitch (see Figure 11.10). After you move a Pitch Curve, you'll notice the original Pitch Curve is also displayed in red. This gives you a reference for your edits. You can also change multiple Pitch Curves at once by first making a selection with the Arrow tool.

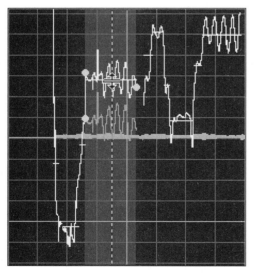

Figure 11.10 Drag the yellow Pitch Curves up or down to change the pitch of your audio data.
Source: Cakewalk®, Inc.

> **SNAP TO PITCH:** While dragging a curve up or down, hold down the Ctrl key to snap the curve to the nearest pitch value. Hold down the Shift key to snap to the nearest 100-cent increment.

5. You can also change multiple Pitch Curves at once or parts of a single curve by first making a selection with the Arrow tool. You'll notice a number of green nodes that appear on the curve. Click and drag the nodes up or down to make changes to the curve.
6. In addition to changing the curves, you can draw your own curve by using the Line and Pen tools. To draw straight lines, use the Line tool. To draw freehand (any shape of curve you would like), use the Pen tool.
7. To remove specific edits that you've done, select the Eraser tool and draw your mouse over the edits to return the curves to their original values.
8. Finally, using the Vibrato/LFO tool, you can adjust the vibrato of the vocal parts. To add vibrato, place your mouse at the point on the curve where you want to start drawing. The mouse will turn into a pen with a vibrato icon attached to it. Click and drag to draw vibrato. To edit vibrato, place your mouse over the vibrato portion of the curve. The mouse will turn into a double-arrow icon. Click and drag up and down to edit amplitude, or left and right to edit frequency. To fade in a vibrato section, move your mouse to the beginning of the vibrato to see another double-arrow icon. Then click and drag to the right to create a vibrato fade-in.

Converting Pitch to MIDI

Once you have the pitch corrected, you can convert the pitches in your vocal to MIDI notes. This can be useful if you want to double your vocal track with a synth track, or you could use it as a melody converter. Sing the tune you have in your head into SONAR, correct the pitch with V-Vocal, and then convert the pitches to MIDI notes. This essentially allows you to create musical instrument parts just by singing them. To convert V-Vocal pitches to MIDI notes, do the following:

1. Right-click in the V-Vocal Waveform display and choose Pitch to MIDI Settings from the menu to open the Pitch to MIDI dialog box.
2. If you want the Pitch to MIDI conversion to include MIDI pitch bend data, activate the Include Pitch Bend Data option. This can come in handy if your singing includes a lot of bent notes, pitch slides, or vibrato. If you want a straight note conversion, don't use this option.
3. Choose a pitch bend range from 1 to 24 semitones. I usually set this to 24 so that V-Vocal can include any and all pitch bends necessary.
4. Choose a Time Resolution, which determines how many ticks are included between each pitch bend event that is generated. I usually set this to 20 to capture the finest pitch bend resolution.
5. Click OK.
6. From the V-Vocal window, click and drag the Pitch to MIDI button into the Clips pane of the Track view. You can drag into an existing MIDI track or into a blank area of the pane. A new MIDI clip will be created in the existing MIDI track or an entirely new MIDI track, along with the clip will be created.
7. Double-click the clip to open it in the Piano Roll view and make any necessary edits.

As long as your vocal is clean and you have properly corrected the pitch, V-Vocal does a good job of converting the pitches to MIDI. But the conversion isn't usually perfect, especially when the vocal contains embellishments, which show up as extra MIDI notes between the main pitches.

Adjusting Vocal Timing

To adjust the timing of your vocal parts, do the following:

1. With the V-Vocal clip created and the window open, click the Time Edit Mode button. You'll notice that the Waveform display now shows only your audio data waveform.

2. Select the Arrow tool.

3. Move your mouse to the center of the display over a point in the waveform that you would like to edit. Your mouse will turn into a double-pointed arrow icon.

4. Double-click to add a green line to the display.

5. Click and drag the green line left or right to change the timing of the audio data. You can also click and drag over the audio data between the green lines to change the timing.

6. Add more green lines and edit them. While editing, hold down the Ctrl key to move all the green lines the same distance simultaneously.

7. To remove any edit lines, choose the Eraser tool and drag your mouse over the lines.

What I like to do is separate the words in my vocal part by placing edit lines between each word (see Figure 11.11). Then I can easily adjust the timing of each word in the vocal.

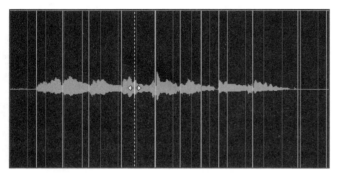

Figure 11.11 Separate each word in the vocal part for more efficient editing.
Source: Cakewalk®, Inc.

ADJUSTING VOCAL DYNAMICS (LOUDNESS)

To adjust the dynamics (loudness) of your vocal parts, do the following:

1. With the V-Vocal clip created and the window open, click the Dynamics Mode button. You'll notice that the Waveform display now shows only your audio data waveform. You'll also notice a yellow line across the center of the waveform and the display. This is the amplitude envelope. You can adjust the envelope in a number of ways.

2. Using the Arrow tool, you can grab the envelope and move it up or down to increase or decrease the amplitude of the audio. You can also double-click the envelope to add nodes. You can then drag these nodes up and down to create your own envelope shape, thus changing the amplitude of the audio (see Figure 11.12).

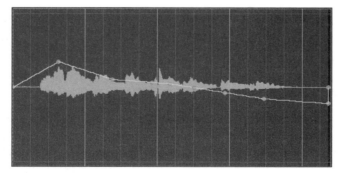

Figure 11.12 Use the Arrow tool to adjust the amplitude envelope.
Source: Cakewalk®, Inc.

> **INVISIBLE NODES:** To see all the nodes on the envelope, you must have the entire waveform selected. Right-click the Waveform display and choose Select All.

3. If you want to get really creative, you can use the Line and Pen tools to draw your own unique envelope. Just select a tool and click and drag your mouse over the display to draw an envelope.

4. You can also use the Vibrato/LFO tool to draw an amplitude modulation envelope. This is where the waveform moves up and down in a pattern. In this case, it can be a sine wave or a square wave. Right-click the Waveform display and choose LFO Type > [*type of wave you want to use*].

5. To remove any envelope nodes, choose the Eraser tool and drag your mouse over the nodes.

I like to use the Arrow tool to select a single word and then drag the envelope segment inside the selection up or down to change the amplitude of the word (see Figure 11.13). This way I can easily adjust the amplitude of each word in the vocal without affecting the others at the same time.

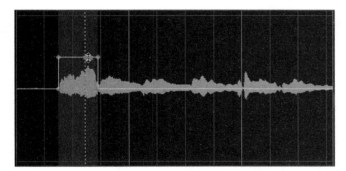

Figure 11.13 Use the Arrow tool to select a word and drag the envelope segment to change the amplitude of only that word.
Source: Cakewalk®, Inc.

ADJUSTING VOCAL FORMANTS (TIMBRE)

Last, but not least, V-Vocal edits the timbre of your vocal data using its Formant features. You can do this either automatically for an entire clip or manually for individual parts of a clip.

To adjust the timbre of an entire clip, adjust the Shift parameter in the Formant Control section. If you adjust it too high, you'll get a Munchkin-type of vocal sound. If you adjust it too low, you'll get a really creepy low vocal sound. Useful settings are anywhere from −10 to +10. I've found that anything beyond that just doesn't sound right.

Adjust the timbre manually just like you adjusted the amplitude back in the "Adjusting Vocal Dynamics (Loudness)" section. You can follow those same steps. Just keep the envelope values between −10 and +10, and you should get some good results.

Amplifier Simulation

For all you electric guitar players out there, SONAR provides a couple of amplifier simulation effects. Using these effects, you can simulate the sound of real-life guitar amplifiers, making your recorded guitar audio data sound like it's being played through different kinds of amps. To achieve this sound, the effect uses technology called *physical modeling*. In this technology, the characteristics of a real instrument or device are converted into a mathematical algorithm (called a *model*). You can use the model to apply those same characteristics to your audio data to achieve more authentic-sounding recordings. This explanation of the process is simplified, but that's the gist of it.

Cakewalk Amp Sim

The first amplifier simulation effect provided by SONAR is the Cakewalk Amp Sim effect, which works like this:

1. Choose Amp Sim to open the Cakewalk Amp Sim window.

USEFUL FOR VOCALS: Even though the Cakewalk Amp Sim effect was designed for guitar amplifiers, that doesn't mean you can't use it on other types of data. The distorted sounds the effect produces also work well on vocals, especially if you're looking for that hard rock sound. Check out some of the music by Kid Rock to hear what I mean.

---

2. In the Amp Model section, select the type of guitar amplifier you want to simulate. An additional parameter called *Bright* also is available in this section. It is similar to the Brightness switch found on many guitar amplifiers. It makes the effect sound brighter by boosting the high frequencies (everything above 500Hz) of the audio spectrum.

3. In the Cabinet Enclosure section, select the type of cabinet you want to use for your virtual guitar amplifier. By setting this parameter, you can simulate different types of speaker enclosures. You have five options to choose from—No Speaker, 1 × 12, 2 × 12, 4 × 10, and 4 × 12. If you choose the No Speaker option, the effect will sound as though you plugged your guitar directly into the output of the amplifier and recorded the sound without using a microphone or the amplifier speakers. If you choose any of the other options, the effect will sound as though you played your guitar through an amplifier that has a certain number of speakers of a certain size and recorded the output by placing a microphone in front of the amp. For example, if you choose 4 × 12, the simulated amp will contain four speakers, each at 12 inches in size. Also, when you select the other options, two other parameters become available—Open Back and Off-Axis. Activating the Open Back parameter makes the effect simulate a guitar amplifier that has a cabinet enclosure with an open (rather than closed) back. Activating the Off-Axis parameter makes the effect sound as though you placed the virtual microphone off to the side of the amplifier speaker, rather than directly in front of it.

4. In the Tremolo section, set the Rate and Depth parameters. Setting these parameters adds a warble type of sound to the effect. The Rate parameter controls the speed of the tremolo, and the Depth parameter controls the amount of tremolo added. There is also a bias control (like that found on most guitar amps) that lets you determine whether the tremolo will add to or subtract from the volume level of the effect. In addition, by activating the Mono option, the tremolo will produce a mono output rather than stereo.

5. Set the Bass, Mid, and Treb parameters in the EQ section. These parameters act similarly to the parameters in SONAR's Graphic EQ editing feature. Each parameter cuts or boosts a specific frequency by −10 or +10dB. The Bass parameter is set to 60Hz, the Mid parameter is set to 600kHz, and the Treb parameter is set to 6,000kHz.

6. Set the Drive parameter. This parameter basically controls the amount of distortion added to the audio data being processed.

7. Set the Presence parameter. This parameter acts like a high-pass EQ with a permanent frequency of 750Hz. You can use it to boost some of the higher frequencies of the effect, giving it more presence.

8. Set the Volume parameter. This parameter controls the overall volume of the effect. No Dry Mix or Wet Mix parameters are available for this effect, so you hear only the totally processed signal through this one.

TH2 Producer

SONAR also includes a lite edition of the Overloud TH2 for amp simulation, which I won't be covering here because it already includes comprehensive documentation. For in-depth information about how TH2 works and how to adjust the parameters of each individual module, check out the TH2 manual by clicking the Manual button located at the bottom of the TH2 window.

Analog Tape Simulation – Cakewalk FX2 Tape Sim

Similar to the Cakewalk Amp Sim effect, the Cakewalk FX2 Tape Sim effect uses physical modeling to simulate a realistic audio situation. But instead of simulating the sound of a guitar amplifier, the Cakewalk FX2 Tape Sim effect simulates the sound of your audio data being played off an analog tape deck. Why would you want to simulate old recording technology, especially when you have the clean and crisp sound of digital recording? Well, analog tape recording provides a sort of warm sound that can't be produced with digital recording, and you can use that sound to create authentic jazz or blues recordings. And some musicians just prefer the warm sound of analog, as opposed to the crisp sound of digital. The Cakewalk FX2 Tape Sim effect lets you achieve that warm sound, and here is how it works:

1. Choose FX2 Tape Sim to open the Cakewalk FX2 Tape Sim window.
2. Choose the type of tape machine you want to simulate by setting the Tape Speed and EQ Curve parameters. An additional parameter called *LF Boost* adds a small increase to the lower frequencies of the audio data, giving it an even warmer sound.
3. Set the Input Gain parameter. This parameter controls the volume of the input signal into the effect. Usually, you'll just want to keep it set at 0dB.
4. Set the Rec (short for Record) Level parameter. This parameter controls the level of the audio that would be recorded in an actual tape-recording situation. Setting this parameter too high will cause distortion.
5. Set the Warmth parameter. This parameter controls that warm sound.
6. Set the Hiss parameter. As in an actual tape-recording situation, you usually get tape hiss. If you want to be totally authentic in your simulation, you can use this parameter to add hiss to your audio data. A setting of 0 will turn off the Hiss parameter.
7. Set the Output Gain parameter. This parameter controls the overall volume of the effect. No Dry Mix or Wet Mix parameters are available for this effect, so you hear only the totally processed signal through this one.

Analog Vacuum-Tube Simulation – TL-64 Tube Leveler

Like the Cakewalk FX2 Tape Sim effect, the TL-64 Tube Leveler gives you another way to add analog warmth to your crisp digital tracks by providing advanced analog vacuum-tube circuit modeling. Vacuum-tube circuits are found in various effects processors and amplifiers and are used to warm the sound of individual tracks (like guitar and bass) or even entire mixes. The TL-64 Tube Leveler works as follows:

1. Choose TL-64 Tube Leveler to open the TL-64 Tube Leveler window (see Figure 11.14).

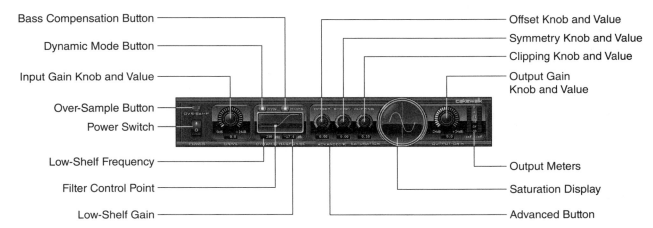

Figure 11.14 Use the TL-64 Tube Leveler to add analog "warmth" to audio tracks.
Source: Cakewalk®, Inc.

2. Adjust the Input Gain in the Drive section. This parameter controls how much of the signal is going to be processed by the virtual vacuum-tube circuit. By default, Input Gain is set to 0dB, which means you'll hear little or no change to the audio (unless you raise or lower the Output Gain, which I'll talk about shortly). Raise the Input Gain to drive the virtual circuit. For subtle processing, use values in the range of 7 to 10dB. For more noticeable processing, use values in the range of 15 to 20dB.

SETTING THE TL-64 PARAMETERS: You can set the TL-64 parameters in a few ways. Use the mouse by clicking and dragging up/down on any of the knobs. Use the keyboard by first mouse-clicking on a knob or value to give it focus and then using the arrow keys to make adjustments. You can also set a parameter directly by double-clicking its value, typing in a new value, and pressing Enter.

---

3. The Dynamic Response section controls the type of virtual circuit used for processing. When the Dynamic Mode button is off, the TL-64 uses a static circuit, which is more artificial-sounding, but it can be useful if you're looking for a more distorted sound. When the Dynamic Mode button is on, you get a more authentic vacuum-tube sound.

4. Activating the Dynamic Mode button also enables a low-shelf filter and a bass compensation filter. The low-shelf filter allows you to remove bass frequencies, which can sometimes overdrive the circuit and make the result sound dirty. You can hear how this sounds by applying the TL-64 to a guitar track, choosing the Tubular Guitar preset, and then listening to the sound with the Dynamic Mode button on/off. To adjust the low-shelf filter, you can either click and drag the Filter Control point or type in new values for the Low-Shelf Frequency and Low-Shelf Gain parameters. When you remove bass frequencies using the low-shelf filter, it can make the audio sound very thin. To compensate for that, activate the Bass Compensation button. Again, to hear the difference, check out the Tubular Guitar preset.

5. The Saturation section provides two modes: basic and advanced. To access the advanced parameters, click the Advanced button. The Offset, Symmetry, and Clipping parameters all work together and affect the shape of the waveform in the Saturation display, which shows how the audio signal is affected as the parameters are changed.

6. By default, the Offset parameter is set to 0.00, which means it has no effect. If you set the Offset below 0.00, more of the positive part of the audio signal is affected. If you set the Offset above 0.00, more of the negative part of the audio signal is affected. Taking the Tubular Guitar example, you'll notice that setting the Offset above 0.00 gives the signal a sort of hollow but smooth sound. (You'll need to raise the Output Gain parameter because the Offset will also affect the signal volume.) Setting the Offset below 0.00 gives the signal a sort of hard and gritty sound.

7. By default, the Symmetry parameter is set to 0.00, which means it has no effect. The Symmetry parameter controls how much clipping is applied to either the negative or positive part of the audio signal. When Symmetry is set below 0.00, more clipping is applied to the negative part and less to the positive part. When Symmetry is set above 0.00, more clipping is applied to the positive part and less to the negative part. In musical terms (using the Tubular Guitar example), setting Symmetry above 0.00 gives the signal a clean, hard sound. Setting the Symmetry below 0.00 gives the signal a more distorted sound.

8. By default, the Clipping parameter is set to 0.50, which means it has no effect. The Clipping parameter works in conjunction with the Symmetry parameter and determines how much clipping is applied to the entire signal. If Clipping is set below 0.50, then it allows Symmetry to have more control over how clipping is applied to the positive and negative parts of the signal. If Clipping is set above 0.50, Symmetry has less control. To see what I mean, try setting Clipping to its maximum value (1.00). Now, no matter what value you use for Symmetry, it has no effect on the signal. If you set Clipping to 0.00, you now see that changing Symmetry has much more of an effect.

9. Adjust the Output Gain to make sure the signal isn't too hot (high), which can distort the signal. You can see the output level on the Output Meters. You'll also use the Output Gain to control the sound of the effect. The higher you set the Input Gain, the lower you'll need to set the Output Gain, and vice versa, so that you get a good signal level coming out of the TL-64.

10. When you've got your sound set, click the Over-Sample button to enable the TL-64's high-quality sound processing. If you have enough CPU power, you can keep this setting enabled, but if not, keep it off until you're ready to mix the project.

Other Effects

SONAR users also have some additional effects—Cakewalk AliasFactor, Cakewalk Modfilter, Sonitus:fx Phase, Sonitus:fx Wahwah, Sonitus:fx Surround, Vintage Channel, Pro Channel, VX-64 Vocal Strip, PX-64 Percussion Strip, and Cakewalk Analyst. These effects didn't fit entirely into the previously mentioned categories, so I will cover them separately here.

Cakewalk AliasFactor

If you're looking to emulate the sound of a cheap audio device (like music playing out of a cell phone or pocket radio), then Cakewalk AliasFactor is for you. It works as follows:

1. Choose AliasFactor to open the Cakewalk AliasFactor window.
2. Set the Sampling Freq (frequency) parameter (100Hz to 32kHz) to adjust the digital audio sampling rate you want to emulate. The lower the value, the lower the quality of the sound will be. This parameter also adjusts the Nyquist frequency, which is half of the sampling rate. The Nyquist frequency comes into play when you set the Cutoff Mode.
3. Set the Cutoff Mode. Cakewalk AliasFactor provides a low-pass EQ filter. When the Cutoff Mode is set to Free, you can adjust the Filter Cutoff parameter (50Hz to 16kHz), and then any audio above the Filter Cutoff value is lowered in volume. This allows you to degrade the audio by filtering out the high frequencies. When the Cutoff Mode is set to Under, At, or Over, the cutoff frequency is automatically set below, at, or above the Nyquist frequency (which is half of the Sampling Freq parameter value). Each mode (Under, At, and Over—in that order) leads to successively lower-quality sound.
4. Set the Filter Reso (resonance) parameter (0 to 100%) to adjust the brightness of the sound. The higher the value, the brighter the sound.
5. Set the Bit depth parameter (1 to 24) to adjust the digital audio bit depth you want to emulate. The lower the value, the lower the quality of the sound.
6. Adjust the Mix parameter (0 to 100%) to determine how much of the Cakewalk AliasFactor effect is heard.
7. Set the Level parameter, which controls the overall volume level of the effect output.
8. Use the Power button to bypass the Cakewalk AliasFactor effect so you can compare the original and processed audio signals.

Cakewalk Modfilter

The Cakewalk Modfilter effect is a sophisticated low-pass EQ filter, but instead of being used for equalization, it is more for creating various effects, as follows:

1. Choose Modfilter to open the Cakewalk Modfilter window.
2. Set the Filter Mode to Manual to use the Cakewalk Modfilter as a basic low-pass filter. Then set the Cutoff parameter (which sets the filter cutoff frequency—16Hz to 18.378kHz), and any frequencies above that value are lowered in volume or cut out completely.
3. Set the Filter Mode to EG to have the filter cutoff frequency modulated (automatically changed over time) via the built-in Envelope Generator. Then set the Attack and Release parameters to control the attack and release times (and thus the shape) of the envelope.

4. Set the Filter Mode to LFO to have the filter cutoff frequency modulated via the built-in low-frequency oscillator. Set the Waveform parameter to control the shape of the LFO – Sin (sine), Tri (triangle), Sqr (square), or S&H (sample and hold – random). To control how quickly the center frequency is changed via the LFO, set the LFO Rate (0.01 to 20Hz) or set the Tempo Sync so that the change is synchronized to the project tempo. A Tempo Sync setting of 1 equals a quarter-note. A setting of one-half equals an eighth-note, and so on. Values with D or T next to them are the equivalent of dotted and triplet values as found in standard music notation.

5. For all three Filter Mode settings, you can adjust the Reso (resonance) parameter to control the brightness of the sound.

6. For the Filter Mode settings EG and LFO, adjust the Mod Depth parameter to control how much of the Cakewalk Mod Filter effect is applied to the sound.

7. For all three Filter Mode settings, adjust the Overdrive parameter to add some distortion to the sound.

8. Adjust the Level parameter (−20 to 0dB) to set the overall output level of the effect.

9. Use the Power button to bypass the Cakewalk Modfilter so that you can compare the original and processed audio signals.

Sonitus:fx Phase

When you mix certain sound files together, phase cancellation can occur. Phase cancellation occurs when one audio waveform increases in volume and the other decreases in volume at exactly the same time and by the same amount. Because of this phenomenon, they cancel each other out, making the mixed audio sound hollow. You can use the Sonitus:fx Phase effect to change the phase of audio data either for correction or for many different kinds of effects. Here is how it works:

1. Choose Sonitus:fx Phase to open the Sonitus:fx Phase window.

2. Set the Filter parameter. Use the IIR (*Infinite Impulse Response*) filter type for more accurate phase shift of low-frequency material. Use the FIR (*Finite Impulse Response*) filter type for more accurate phase shift of high-frequency material.

3. Set the Mode parameter. The LR Phase mode adjusts the phase of the left and right channels of a stereo signal. The MS Phase mode adjusts the phase of the middle (mono) and side (stereo difference) signals. The CS Encode mode adjusts the phase of a stereo signal by placing the center part of the signal in the left channel and the surrounding material in the right channel. The SC Encode mode adjusts the phase of a stereo signal by placing the center part of the signal in the right channel and the surrounding material in the left channel.

4. Set the Phase parameter. This parameter specifies the amount of phase shift that will occur. A value of 0 means no phase shift. To make the left and right channels of a stereo signal completely out of phase with one another, you can use a value of −180 degrees or +180 degrees.

5. Set the Width parameter. This parameter controls the width of the stereo signal. A value of 100% means no change to the incoming stereo signal. A value of 0% converts the stereo signal into a mono signal. A value of 200% makes it sound like the stereo signal is spread beyond the positions of your stereo speakers.

6. Set the Output parameter. This parameter adjusts the overall amplitude of your audio after it is processed.

Be sure to check out the presets supplied with the Phase effect. This effect has many uses, including converting a mono signal to a stereo signal, widening a stereo signal, and even removing vocals from a song.

Sonitus:fx Wahwah

The Sonitus:fx Wahwah effect simulates the classic guitar wahwah stomp box effect. Here is how it works:

1. Choose Sonitus:fx Wahwah to open the Sonitus:fx Wahwah window.

2. Set the Mode parameter. The Wahwah effect uses the up-and-down movement of an envelope to apply itself to your audio data. The Mode parameter determines how that envelope is controlled. Use the Auto mode to control the up-and-down speed of the envelope using a tempo setting. Use the Triggered mode to control the

envelope using a threshold setting. Use the Manual mode to control the envelope manually using the Wah slider.

3. Set the Wah parameter. If you choose the Auto mode, the Wah parameter will determine the starting point of the envelope as it is applied to the audio. If you choose the Triggered mode, the Wah parameter will determine the range of the envelope and thus how much of the effect will be applied to the audio after the amplitude of the audio goes above the threshold. If you choose the Manual mode, you can use the Wah parameter slider to control the up-and-down motion of the envelope.

4. If you choose the Auto mode, set the Tempo parameter. This parameter determines the cycling speed (meaning the speed of one up-and-down motion) of the envelope and thus the wah effect.

5. If you choose the Triggered mode, set the Threshold parameter. If the level of your audio stays below the threshold, the Wah effect will not be applied. If the level of your audio goes above the threshold, the Wah effect will be applied, and the amount above the threshold determines the amount of the effect applied.

6. If you choose the Triggered mode, also set the Attack and Release parameters. These parameters determine the up and down speeds of the envelope, respectively.

7. You also can apply some EQ to the effect using the High and Low Freq, Q, and Gain parameters. These parameters work just like all the other similarly named EQ parameters I've described.

8. Set the Mix parameter to determine how much of the original audio signal and how much of the affected signal will be heard.

9. Set the Output parameter to determine the overall volume level of the effect output.

Sonitus:fx Surround

The Sonitus:fx Surround effect creates surround sound panning for your audio data. To get the full effect, you need to have a surround sound decoder and speaker system, but even with only a pair of stereo speakers, you can hear some of the effect. Here is how it works:

1. Choose Sonitus:fx Surround to open the Sonitus:fx Surround window.

2. In the left portion of the dialog box, you will see a graph with four speaker icons and a crosshair icon. The four speakers represent the locations of the Left, Center, Right, and Surround speakers, thus designating the listening field. The crosshair icon represents the position of your audio data being played in the listening field. You can click and drag the crosshair to move the playing position of your audio data.

3. If you want to move your audio data position outside of the listening field (so it sounds like the audio is being played from a point beyond the speaker positions), use the Zoom parameter. A setting of 1 designates a normal listening field. Settings of 3 or 5 designate larger listening fields outside of the speaker range.

4. Set the Input parameter. Choose Mono to process your audio as a mono signal. Choose stereo to process your audio as a stereo signal. Choose Left to process the left channel of a stereo signal. Choose Right to process the right channel of a stereo signal.

5. Set the Focal Point parameter to On or Off. If you turn the parameter on, a yellow cross will appear on the graph, designating the position of a virtual listener in the listening field. You can click and drag the cross to change the position of the virtual listener. This creates attenuation and Doppler shift effects.

6. If you turn the Focal Point parameter on, you also need to set the Attenuation and Doppler parameters. The Attenuation parameter determines how soft your audio data will get when its position is moved away from the virtual listener. This creates more realistic surround effects because as audio moves away from a listener in real life, its volume gets lower. The Doppler parameter determines how much of a pitch change will be applied to your audio data as it gets closer or farther away from the virtual listener. In real life, a sound seems to get higher in pitch as it moves toward you and lower in pitch as it moves away from you. The Doppler parameter lets you simulate that effect.

7. In addition to manually setting the playing position of your audio data in the listening field, you can have the playing position move in real time, according to a path that you draw on the listening field. To create this automatic panning effect, set the Path parameter to On. When you do this, the crosshair icon will turn into a

white square, designating the starting position of the path. Click the white square and drag your mouse to a new position. This will drag the first line in the path. To create additional lines, double-click anywhere on the path to create a node. You can drag this node to another position. You can keep creating nodes and dragging them to new positions to create a complex path.

8. With the Path parameter on, you also can determine whether the path will be open or closed by setting the Closed Path parameter.

9. With the Path parameter on, use the Path Time parameter to determine how long it will take for the audio position to move along the path.

10. If you have the Path parameter off, you can control the audio position using a joystick. Set the Joystick parameter to On to use the joystick to control the audio panning position.

Channel Tools

The Channel Tools effect provides a host of functions that can be used to fix or process stereo tracks. These include fixing track phase and timing problems, adjusting panning and width of the individual left and right channels, and swapping the channels—all the things you can't normally do with the regular parameters that SONAR provides for stereo audio tracks. In addition, the Channel Tools effect allows you to work easily with Mid-Side recordings.

MID-SIDE RECORDING: A Mid-Side recording is a special type of recording in which one microphone is pointed directly at the performer to record the middle channel (stored in the left side of a stereo track), and another microphone is pointed 90 degrees away from the performer to record the side channel (stored in the right side of a stereo track). These signals must then be decoded to achieve a normal stereo signal. The Channel Tools effect provides Mid-Side decoding. For more details on Mid-Side recording, click anywhere inside the Channel Tools window, press F1 to access the Channel Tools help, and read the Mid-Side section.

The Channel Tools effect works as follows:

1. Choose Channel Tools to open the Channel Tools window (see Figure 11.15).

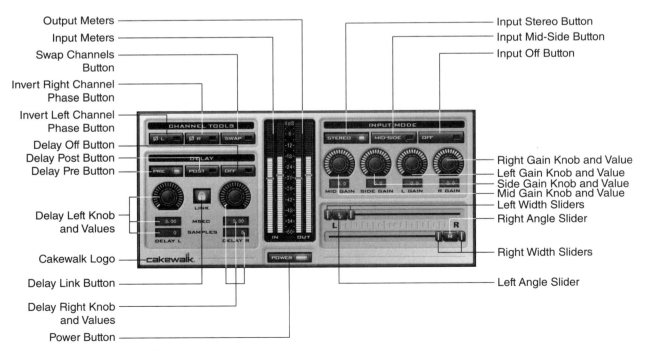

Figure 11.15 Use the Channel Tools effect to change various aspects of a stereo audio track or bus.
Source: Cakewalk®, Inc.

SETTING THE CHANNEL TOOLS PARAMETERS: You can set the Channel Tools parameters in a few ways. Use the mouse by clicking and dragging up/down on any of the knobs. Use the keyboard by first mouse-clicking on a knob or value to give it focus and then using the arrow keys to make adjustments. You can also set a parameter directly by double-clicking its value, typing in a new value, and pressing Enter. Sliders must be dragged with the mouse.

2. The Channels Tools section of the Channel Tools window contains buttons that allow you to change the phase of the left and right channels of a stereo track and also to swap the channels. Click the Invert Left/Right Channel phase buttons to invert the phase of the left/right channels. These buttons make corrections in case of phase cancellation. Click the Swap Channels button to move the audio in the left channel to the right channel and vice versa. This can come in handy for correcting stereo recordings where the microphones were plugged into the wrong channels.

PHASE CANCELLATION: Phase cancellation occurs when one audio waveform rises above the zero-axis while the other descends below the zero-axis at exactly the same rate. Because of this phenomenon, they cancel each other out, making the mixed audio sound hollow. Using the Invert Channel buttons can help eliminate this problem. If you invert the phase of one channel in a normal stereo track, you will hear what phase cancellation sounds like.

3. The Delay section of Channel Tools is not the same as a typical delay effect, as described earlier in this chapter. Instead, it allows you to make small corrections to the timing of the individual stereo channels. The Off button turns the Delay section on/off and allows you to compare the sound of the original and delayed signals. The Pre and Post buttons determine where in the signal chain the signal is delayed. Click Pre/Post to apply the delay before/after the signal is routed through the rest of the Channel Tools processing. Click the Cakewalk Logo to see a flowchart of how the audio signal flows through the Channel Tools effect.

4. The Delay Left/Right knobs and values control how much the left/right channels of the stereo signals are delayed. By default, they are set to 0, which means no delay is applied. They can be set up to 1,000 milliseconds (1 second). These values can be used to correct the timing of the stereo channels in relation to one another by leaving one parameter set to 0 and setting the other to a smaller value (whatever it takes to make the correction). If you do this with a normal stereo track, and set the value to around 0.20, you can use it to create a stereo widening effect. You can also use the delay settings to correct the timing of one track to another. If the timing of a stereo track is off in a project, you can set both Delay values to zero, click the Delay Link button, and then adjust one value (which adjusts them both because of the link). This will change the timing of the track in relation to others in the project.

5. The Input Mode section allows you to control the type of track you are processing—either stereo or Mid-Side using the appropriate buttons. The section also provides a number of adjustable parameters: Mid Gain, Side Gain, Left Gain, and Right Gain. The knobs work differently when processing stereo or Mid-Side, but for this example, let's say we're processing a regular stereo track. The Mid Gain controls the volume of the signal center from the combined stereo channels. The default value is 0.0 (no effect). Lower/raise the value to lower/raise the volume of the center of the stereo signal. The Side Gain controls the volume of the signal sides. Lower/raise the value to lower/raise the value of the sides of the stereo signal. If you lower the Side Gain to $-\infty$, you are effectively left with a mono signal centered in the stereo image. The Left/Right Gain parameters control the volume of each side of the stereo signal. These can be useful for fixing an unbalanced stereo signal where one channel is louder/softer than the other.

6. Below the Input Mode section are the Panner controls. They control the angle and width of each of the stereo channels, which effectively lets you pan (position) them in the stereo image. Use the Left/Right Angle sliders to

move the left/right channels left/right in the stereo image. Use the Left/Right Width sliders to control the width of the channels. You may notice that when changing the angle or width, the other is automatically adjusted, depending on how far you move the sliders. You can lock whatever parameter you are not adjusting in place while adjusting the other by holding down the Shift key. The most common use for the Panner controls is for narrowing the image of a stereo track to make it fit better in the mix. For example, if you have a piano track that is throwing the mix out of balance because its sound is just too big, you can fix that by moving the Left/Right Angle sliders slightly toward the center and decreasing the distance of the Left/Right Width sliders from one another. This will constrain the track to a distinct space in the stereo field and open up more room in the mix for other tracks.

7. Use the Input/Ouput Meters to monitor the signal level and use the Power button to turn the Channel Tools effect on/off so you can compare the original and processed signals.

Vintage Channel (SONAR Producer)

Vintage Channel is a multi-effects channel strip plug-in (exclusive to SONAR Producer) that can be used to process individual tracks or entire mixes. You can even use it for mastering. Vintage Channel provides dual-EQs, dual-compressors, gating, and de-essing. Other than the fact that all these processes are provided in one plug-in, Vintage Channel is special because it provides high-end processing. More importantly, it allows you to route an audio signal internally through the different effects in a variety of ways to provide superior output. Choose Vintage Channel to open the Vintage Channel window.

MASTER, DE-ESSER, AND GATE

Vintage Channel is divided into three vertical sections. The Master, De-Esser, and Gate controls are located in the left area of the interface (see Figure 11.16). To utilize these controls, do the following:

Figure 11.16 Utilize the Master, De-Esser, and Gate controls to begin working with the Vintage Channel.
Source: Cakewalk®, Inc.

1. Activate the Master Power button. This button toggles the entire Vintage Channel on/off. You can use the Master Power button as a Bypass button to quickly test your audio with or without the Vintage Channel processing.
2. Right-click inside the Routings area and choose an effect routing from the menu. Choosing a routing allows you to determine how your audio signal will be sent through each of the effects in the Vintage Channel. In the Routings area, you'll see a small graphic representing the effects routing. The audio signal (represented by a line) flows left to right in the graphic, and each box represents a different effect. The effect abbreviations are as

follows: NG (Gate), DE (De-Esser), E1 (Equalizer 1), E2 (Equalizer 2), C1 (Compressor 1), and C2 (Compressor 2). For example, if you choose the Instrument Setup routing, your audio signal will flow through the effects in the following order: Gate, De-Esser, Equalizer 1, Compressor 1, Equalizer 2, and Compressor 2.

ROUTING, NOT PROCESSING: Just because you choose a specific routing that shows your audio signal will flow through all the effects in the Vintage Channel does not mean your audio will definitely be processed by all the effects. You can choose whether or not an effect will be used by toggling its individual Power button.

---

3. Adjust the Master Gain. The Master Gain parameter determines the final amplitude level of the audio signal coming out of the Vintage Channel. At this point, you can leave it set to the default value, but you will probably have to adjust it after you have finished adjusting the other effect parameters because they will change the signal level.

4. Toggle the Master Phase Invert button. Use this button to invert the phase of the final audio signal output. When you mix certain sound files together, phase cancellation can occur. Phase cancellation occurs when one audio waveform increases in volume and the other decreases in volume at exactly the same time and by the same amount. Because of this phenomenon, they cancel each other out, making the mixed audio sound hollow. You can use the Phase parameter to change the phase of the audio data, for correction or even for different kinds of processing.

5. If you want to use the Gate effect, activate the Gate Power button.

6. Adjust the Gate Threshold. The Gate effect uses a digital noise gate to identify the parts of your audio data that should be processed. The Gate Threshold parameter determines at what amplitude level your audio data will start being compressed. When the amplitude of your audio data reaches the Threshold level, processing will begin. Gating is usually used to remove noise. Start by setting the Threshold to its lowest value (−80dB) and gradually raise it to the point where you hear the noise being reduced but your audio quality isn't being compromised.

7. Adjust the Gate Release. This parameter determines how quickly after the input level goes below the threshold that processing is stopped (or the digital noise gate is closed). If you set the Gate Release parameter too low, your audio could be cut off. A longer release allows processing to sound more natural. Start off with a value of around 900ms. If your audio is being cut off, try slowly increasing the Release value, or if you hear noise, try slowly decreasing the value.

8. If you want to use the De-Esser effect, activate the De-Esser Power button.

DE-ESSING WITH VINTAGE CHANNEL: You may have noticed while doing vocal recordings that some singers produce a sort of "hissing" sound whenever they pronounce words with the letter "s" in them. That "hissing" sound is called *sibilance*, and you usually don't want it in your audio. The process of removing sibilance is called *de-essing*, which is done by compressing certain audio frequencies. When de-essing with the Vintage Channel, it's best to process a single track (with the vocal on its own), rather than a mix that has both the music and vocal mixed together already.

---

9. Adjust the De-Esser Threshold. The Threshold parameter determines at what amplitude level de-essing will begin. Start with a high setting and gradually decrease the value until you hear "hissing" sounds being reduced.

10. Adjust the De-Esser Freq (Frequency). Any audio frequencies above this setting will be processed. A good starting point is 5kHz. At and above this frequency is where most "hissing" noises occur.

COMPRESSORS

The Vintage Channel provides two Compressor effects with identical parameters. The controls for both compressors are located in the center of the interface (see Figure 11.17). To utilize the Compressor effects, do the following:

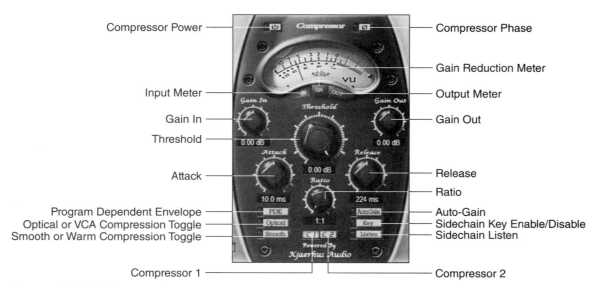

Figure 11.17 Adjust the Compressor effects with the controls located in the center of the Vintage Channel interface.
Source: Cakewalk®, Inc.

1. To adjust the parameters for Compressor 1 or 2, click the C1 or C2 button, respectively.
2. Turn the Compressor on using the Compressor Power button.
3. You can adjust the phase of the audio signal using the Compressor Phase button.
4. Use the Input Meter, Output Meter, and Gain Reduction Meter buttons to change how the signal of the VU Meter will display. Click IN to show the level of the signal entering the Compressor. Click OUT to show the level of the signal leaving the Compressor. Click GR to show how much the Compressor is reducing the signal level.
5. Set the Gain In parameter. This controls the level of the audio signal entering the Compressor. You'll usually want to keep this set at 0dB, which keeps the audio at its original level.
6. Set the Threshold. The Threshold determines at what amplitude level your audio data will start being compressed. When the amplitude of your audio data reaches the Threshold level, processing will begin.
7. Set the Ratio parameter. This parameter determines how much processing is done to your audio data. A ratio of 1:1 means no processing is done. A ratio of 2:1 means that for every 2dB increase in input amplitude, there is only a 1dB increase in output amplitude. Thus, the amplitude is being compressed. If you set the Ratio parameter to its highest value (Inf:1), that causes limiting, so no matter how loud the input amplitude gets, it is limited to the level set by the Threshold parameter.
8. Set the Attack parameter. This parameter determines how quickly after the input level has reached the threshold that processing is applied. For example, if the input level reaches the threshold, it doesn't have to be compressed right away. A slow attack means the signal won't be compressed unless it lasts for a while. This is a good way to make sure fast, percussive parts are left alone, but long, drawn-out parts are compressed.
9. Set the Release parameter. This parameter determines how quickly after the input level goes below the threshold that processing is stopped. A longer release allows processing to sound more natural.
10. When you set a medium-to-long release time, you can sometimes get what is called a "pumping" sound in your audio. This is where you can hear the compressor trying to compress the audio, but it is out of time with

the music, and it sounds strange. Activating the Program Dependent Envelope feature while using a medium-to-long release time can help minimize pumping. Click the PDE button to toggle this feature on/off.

11. Click the Optical button to choose between Optical compression and VCA compression. Basically, Optical compression simulates an older type of compression that relied on imprecise optical components to produce a distinct sound of its own. In part, this means that the parameter settings are not taken to be exact (such as the Threshold). VCA compression provides a more precise means of processing; for example, you can rely on the Threshold values that you set.

12. Click the Smooth button to choose between a smooth (clean) sound and a warm sound. This parameter is a matter of taste, and you'll need to try it to hear which setting works best with the material you are processing.

13. After compressing the audio signal, the level will obviously be lower. To bring the overall level back up, you can activate the Auto-Gain option and adjust the Gain Out parameter.

For information on the Sidechain Key and Sidechain Listen options, see "Sidechaining Effects," later in this chapter.

EQUALIZERS

The Vintage Channel provides two Equalizer effects with identical parameters. The controls for both EQs are located in the right area of the interface (see Figure 11.18). To utilize the EQ effects, do the following:

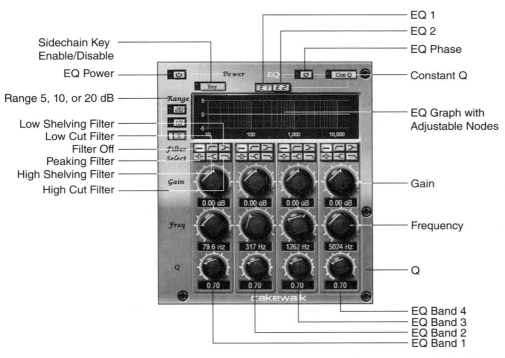

Figure 11.18 Adjust the EQ effects with the controls located on the right in the Vintage Channel interface.
Source: Cakewalk®, Inc.

1. To adjust the parameters for EQ 1 or 2, click the E1 or E2 buttons, respectively.
2. Turn the EQ on using the EQ Power button.
3. You can adjust the phase of the audio signal using the EQ Phase button.

4. Each EQ in the Vintage Channel provides up to four bands, which means you can have up to four different types of simultaneous EQ processing for each EQ. Use the Filter Select area to choose the type of EQ you want to use for each band. Click the Filter Off button to turn a band off. Click one of the other Filter buttons to turn a band on and select an EQ type. If you choose Peaking, the exact frequency designated by the Freq parameter will be boosted or cut, depending on how you set the Gain parameter. If you choose Low Shelving, any frequencies below the Freq setting will be boosted or cut, depending on how you set the Gain parameter. If you choose High Shelving, any frequencies above the Freq setting will be boosted or cut, depending on how you set the Gain parameter. If you choose High Cut, all the frequencies above the Freq setting will be cut. If you choose Low Cut, all the frequencies below the Freq setting will be cut.

5. Adjust the Freq (frequency) parameter for each EQ band. This parameter works a bit differently, depending on what type of equalization you choose. Essentially, it determines the frequency below which other frequencies will be cut or boosted, above which other frequencies will be cut or boosted, or exactly where boosting or cutting will occur.

6. Adjust the Gain parameter for each EQ band. This parameter boosts or cuts the amplitude of the frequencies you set with the EQ type and Freq parameters.

7. Adjust the Q parameter for each EQ band. Also known as *bandwidth*, this parameter influences how many other frequencies around the Freq you set will be affected. A low value means few frequencies will be affected. A high value means more frequencies will be affected. For example, if you are trying to get rid of a precise frequency (like the 60Hz hum you sometimes get from electrical interference), you should set the Q to a low value in order to cut that one frequency and no others. In addition to Q, there is the Constant Q option. For a more musical sounding EQ, turn the Constant Q option off. For surgical equalization tasks, turn the Constant Q option on.

EQ GRAPH DISPLAY: You've probably noticed that in addition to the parameter settings, the EQ area contains a graph display. This graph shows all the current equalization settings for all four types (bands). Along the left, it shows the amplitudes (gain), and along the bottom, it shows the frequencies. The amplitude range of the graph can be adjusted using the Range buttons. (This setting only affects the display and not actual Gain range.) The shape of the line drawn on the graph shows you what frequencies in the audio spectrum are either boosted or cut, but that's not all. Four colored points on the graph represent each EQ band. Red is for band 1, yellow is for band 2, green is for band 3, and blue is for band 4. By clicking and dragging these points, you can change the Gain and Freq settings graphically for each of the EQ types (bands), essentially "drawing" the EQ settings. You still have to set the EQ type and Q settings manually, though.

The Vintage Channel is an extremely powerful effect that can be used for a multitude of tasks on single tracks and entire mixes. Be sure to check out some of the presets for starting points. For information on the Sidechain Key option, see "Sidechaining Effects," later in this chapter. And for more general info, click the word *Manual* on the Vintage Channel interface to access the Vintage Channel help file.

VX-64 Vocal Strip (SONAR Producer)

Like the Vintage Channel, the VX-64 (exclusive to SONAR Producer) is a multi-effects channel strip, but it is dedicated to processing vocals and provides compression, expansion, equalization, de-essing, doubling, delay, and tube saturation in one plug-in. It provides high-quality sound with sophisticated routing and works as follows:

1. Choose VX-64 Vocal Strip to open the VX-64 window (see Figure 11.19).

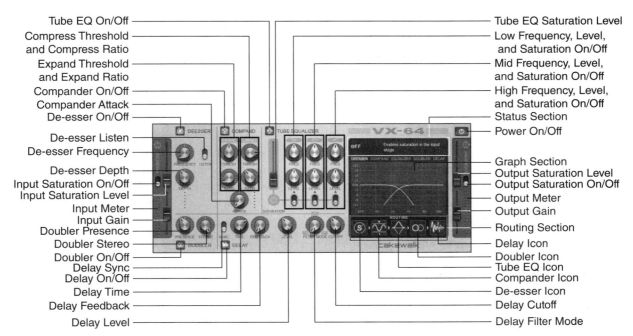

Tube EQ On/Off — Tube EQ Saturation Level
Compress Threshold and Compress Ratio — Low Frequency, Level, and Saturation On/Off
Expand Threshold and Expand Ratio — Mid Frequency, Level, and Saturation On/Off
Compander On/Off — High Frequency, Level, and Saturation On/Off
Compander Attack — Status Section
De-esser On/Off — Power On/Off
De-esser Listen
De-esser Frequency — Graph Section
De-esser Depth — Output Saturation Level
Input Saturation On/Off — Output Saturation On/Off
Input Saturation Level — Output Meter
Input Meter — Output Gain
Input Gain
Doubler Presence — Routing Section
Doubler Stereo — Delay Icon
Doubler On/Off — Doubler Icon
Delay Sync — Tube EQ Icon
Delay On/Off — Compander Icon
Delay Time — De-esser Icon
Delay Feedback — Delay Cutoff
Delay Level — Delay Filter Mode

Figure 11.19 The VX-64 Vocal Strip provides sophisticated vocal processing.
Source: Cakewalk®, Inc.

2. Click and drag (left/right) the module icons in the Routing section to adjust how the signal is routed through the VX-64. The Input and Output sections always remain in their places, but you can move any of the other sections around. By default, audio passes through the modules in the following order: De-esser, Compander, Tube EQ, Doubler, and Delay. However, there may be times when you want to apply the modules in a different order to obtain different effects.

3. As you work with the various controls, keep an eye on volume levels via the Input and Output meters. Adjust the Input Gain and Output Gain to avoid distortion. You can also apply tube saturation to either input or output via the Saturation On/Off and Level controls. Also keep in mind that as you adjust any controls, you can see the values and descriptions for those controls in the Status section. Plus, each of the five modules provides a graphical value display in the Graph section.

4. Click the De-esser On/Off control to toggle the De-esser, which can be used to reduce sibilance in a vocal performance. Click the De-esser Listen control so that you only hear the sibilance. Adjust the De-esser Frequency to find the offending noise. Then use the De-esser Depth to adjust how much sibilance is removed. I recommend starting at a frequency of 5kHz and a depth of 40%, and then adjusting to find the best settings for your vocal.

5. Click the Compander On/Off control to toggle the Compander, which can be used to level out volume changes (compression) and remove low-level noise (expansion) in the vocal. For a natural vocal sound, I recommend starting with the following settings and then adjusting to taste—Attack: 1ms; Compress Ratio: anywhere from 2.0:1 to 4.0:1; Expand Ratio: 1:10.0; and Compress Threshold: 15dB, but will need to be adjusted, depending on the volume level of the vocal. For the Expand Threshold, listen to the space between the vocal phrases and adjust the parameter to the value where you no longer hear low-level noises, such as hand-held microphone movements, out-of-place breaths, and so on.

6. Click the Tube EQ On/Off control to toggle the Tube Equalizer, which provides a three-band parametric EQ plus saturation. Use the low-band controls to either cut out unwanted low rumble noise or add some bass to a thin-sounding vocal. Use the mid-band controls to give a boost to the mid-range of the vocal—maybe a frequency of around 3kHz with a level of +4dB as a starting point. Use the high-band controls to either cut out

harshness or add a bit of presence. Then turn saturation on for the high-band and adjust the saturation level to add a subtle "shine" to the vocal.

7. Click the Doubler On/Off control to toggle the Doubler, which doubles the vocal, making it sound like two people singing the same thing at the same time, but combined to provide a fuller vocal. Adjust the Doubler Presence control to determine the volume of the doubled parts. Adjust the Doubler Stereo control to determine the stereo width of the doubled parts. Try –19dB for the Presence and 80% for the Stereo to obtain a subtle doubling effect.

8. Click the Delay On/Off control to toggle the Delay, which (as its name implies) lets you add delay (echo) to the vocal. If you want the echoes to sound in time with the project tempo, adjust the Delay Sync and Delay Time controls. When Delay Sync is off, the Delay Time controls the amount of delay in milliseconds. To set how many echoes occur, adjust the Delay Feedback control. To set the volume level of the echoes, adjust the Delay Level control. If you would like to add echo to only part of the frequency range of the vocal, adjust the Delay Filter Mode and Delay Cutoff. These controls provide a basic EQ feature with the Filter Mode adjusting the type of EQ (low-pass, band-pass, or high-pass), depending on where the knob is set (0, 50, or 100% with varying types of EQ in-between). If you want to echo the entire vocal, set the Filter Mode to 0% and the Cutoff to 22kHz.

9. Use the Power On/Off control to bypass the VX-64 so you can compare the original and processed audio signals.

For more information on the VX-64, click the background of the VX-64 window and press F1 to open the VX-64 help file.

PX-64 Percussion Strip (SONAR Producer)

Very similar to the VX-64, the PX-64 Percussion Strip (also exclusive to SONAR Producer) is a multi-effects channel strip, but it is dedicated to processing drums and provides transient shaping, compression, expansion, equalization, delay, and tube saturation in one plug-in. The PX-64 provides high-quality sound with sophisticated routing and works as follows:

1. Choose PX-64 Percussion Strip to open the PX-64 window (see Figure 11.20).

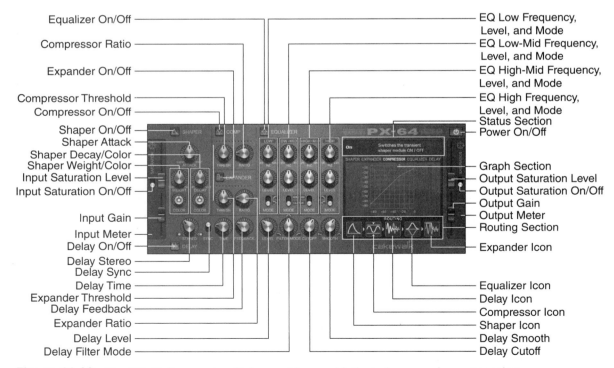

Figure 11.20 The PX-64 Percussion Strip provides sophisticated percussion processing.
Source: Cakewalk®, Inc.

2. Click and drag (left/right) the module icons in the Routing section to adjust how the signal is routed through the PX-64. The Input and Output sections always remain in their places, but you can move any of the other sections around. By default, audio passes through the modules in the following order: Equalizer, Compressor, Expander, Shaper (transient shaper), and Delay. However, there may be times when you want to apply the modules in a different order to obtain different effects.

3. As you work with the various controls, keep an eye on volume levels via the Input and Output meters. Adjust the Input Gain and Output Gain to avoid distortion. You can also apply tube saturation to either input or output via the Saturation On/Off and Level controls. Also keep in mind that as you adjust any controls, you can see the values and descriptions for those controls in the Status section. Plus, each of the five modules provides a graphical value display in the Graph section.

4. Click the Shaper On/Off control to toggle the transient shaper, which lets you shape the sound of percussive hits in a drum track. Set the Attack below/above 100% to soften/harden the initial hit (attack) of an instrument. Set the Weight below/above 100% to thin/fatten the hit, and then set the Weight Color below/above 0.0 to darken/brighten the hit. Set the Decay below/above 100% to reduce/increase the sound of the tail end of the hit. For example, on a snare track, you can make each snare hit sound short (giving it a dry sound) or long (giving it a wet sound) by setting the Decay below/above 100%, respectively. Then set the Decay Color below/above 0.0 to darken/brighten the sound of the tail end of the hit.

5. Click the Compressor On/Off control to toggle the compressor, which can be used to level out volume changes in the drum performance. Set the Ratio to determine how much compression is applied, with 4.0:1 being a good place to start, but it really depends on the style of music and how big of a drum sound you want. Set the Thresh (threshold) to determine the volume level at which compression will start, with a good initial value being about −12dB or higher if you want a more natural drum sound.

COMPRESSOR AS LIMITER FOR BIG DRUM SOUNDS: If you're after a really big drum sound, set the Ratio very high and lower the Threshold. You can even use the compressor as a limiter by setting the Ratio to its highest value (Inf:1). Adjust the Threshold to −12dB or lower, and then adjust the Output Gain to get a really big sound. Just keep in mind that this will squash most of the dynamics out of the drum performance, which isn't what you want if you're looking for a more natural sound.

---

6. Click the Expander On/Off control to toggle the Expander, which can be used to remove low-level noise in the drum performance, such as room noise or bleed from other drum microphones. Set the Ratio to determine how much of the sound is cut. The higher the Ratio value, the more sound it will cut. Set the Threshold to determine what parts of the sound are cut. The higher the Threshold value, the more of the quiet parts or transient tail of the sound will be cut. You'll need to adjust both parameters so that the noise you're trying to remove is cut without cutting any parts of the actual drum instruments.

EXPANDER AS GATE: Set the Ratio to 1:Inf for a gate effect. This can be used to get that popular gated tom effect used in many songs, such as "In the Air Tonight" by Phil Collins.

---

7. Click the Equalizer On/Off control to toggle the Equalizer, which provides a four-band parametric EQ. Each band has controls for frequency and level. Each band also has a Mode control, which provides Vintage and Classic modes for the Low-Mid and High-Mid bands. These modes give you different Q settings, with Vintage affecting a wider range of frequencies and Classic a narrower range. The Mode controls for the Low and High bands switch those bands between shelf and roll-off filter types. When set to shelf, the low and high frequencies can be smoothly boosted or cut. When set to roll-off, the low and high frequencies are always cut, no matter what the Level setting is.

8. Click the Delay On/Off control to toggle the Delay, which lets you add delay (echo) to the drum sound. If you want the echoes to sound in time with the project tempo, adjust the Delay Sync and Delay Time controls. When Delay Sync is off, the Delay Time controls the amount of delay in milliseconds. To set how many echoes occur, adjust the Delay Feedback control. To set the volume level of the echoes, adjust the Delay Level control. If you would like to add echo to only part of the frequency range of the drum sound, adjust the Delay Filter Mode and Delay Cutoff. These controls provide a basic EQ feature, with the Filter Mode adjusting the type of EQ (low-pass, band-pass, or high-pass), depending on where the knob is set (0, 50, or 100%, with varying types of EQ in-between). If you want to echo the entire drum sound, set the Filter Mode to 0% and the Cutoff to 22kHz. Adjust the Smooth control to sharpen or smooth (with lower and higher values, respectively) the initial hit of the drum sounds.

9. Use the Power On/Off control to bypass the PX-64 so you can compare the original and processed audio signals.

For more information on the PX-64, click the background of the PX-64 window and press F1 to open the PX-64 help file.

ProChannel (SONAR Producer)

Another SONAR Producer exclusive is the ProChannel, which is also a multi-effects channel strip with one important difference from all the others mentioned previously—it is not a plug-in. Instead, the ProChannel is actually built in to every audio track and bus in a project, so it's always there and always available without the need for inserting it into an FX bin. ProChannel is actually an advanced FX bin with its own proprietary plug-ins (called *modules*) that can be added or removed. By default, each ProChannel includes one EQ module that can't be removed (but it can be disabled). SONAR also includes default modules for compression and tube saturation, and only one instance of these modules can be used. In addition, SONAR includes add-on modules for console emulation, reverb, and tube saturation, and FX Chains. Cakewalk also sells a number of add-on modules.

PROCHANNEL OPERATION

To access ProChannel for a track/bus, either make the track/bus active in the Track view and then click the ProCh tab at the top of the Inspector (or press Ctrl+I), or click the Show/Hide ProChannel button for the appropriate track/bus strip in the Console view.

At the very top of the ProChannel you'll find a group of controls (see Figure 11.21). Displayed is the name of the current ProChannel preset. Hover your mouse over the preset name to make the Load Preset and Save Preset buttons, which let you load and save ProChannel presets, respectively. Click the Add Module button to load additional modules into the ProChannel. Click the Global On/Off button to turn the ProChannel on/off, which allows you to bypass all the modules to compare the original and processed audio.

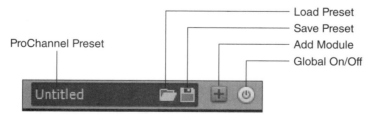

Figure 11.21 Use the group of controls at the top of the ProChannel to manipulate its settings.
Source: Cakewalk®, Inc.

You can also right-click in the ProChannel background or on the name of a module to access a menu that will allow you to Insert, Replace, and Remove modules. If you have a certain group of modules that you like to use all the time and want to set as the default for all new tracks, choose Set Modules as Default for Tracks from the menu. In addition, you can use the ProChannel in conjunction with the FX bin. By default, the ProChannel comes before the FX bin in the signal chain. This means that the track's audio is first processed by the modules in the ProChannel and then processed by the plug-ins in the FX bin. If you would rather have the audio processed by the FX bin first, choose Post FX Bin from the menu.

Another way you can control how the audio is processed is by moving modules within the ProChannel. The audio signal moves from top to bottom through the ProChannel, so it goes through the module at the top of the ProChannel first and through the module at the bottom last. To change this, you can drag modules to change their order. Click and hold over the name of a module and then drag up/down to change its location. If you have more modules loaded than can be displayed, click the name or background of any module and then use your mouse wheel to scroll the ProChannel up/down. You can also collapse/expand and bypass individual modules using the Collapse and Enable controls in the header at the top of every module (see Figure 11.22).

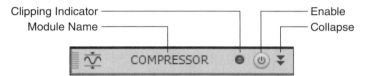

Figure 11.22 The top of every module provides controls to enable/disable and collapse/expand a module.
Source: Cakewalk®, Inc.

PC76 U-TYPE CHANNEL COMPRESSOR

The ProChannel provides two compressor effects with different parameters—the PC76 for track compression and the PC4K for bus compression, although there's nothing stopping you from using either compressor on tracks or buses. One oddity about these modules is that although they are listed in the Add Module menu as two separate modules, they are actually one module. If you insert one, then the other is no longer listed in the menu. Also, both the PC76 and PC4K are default modules, so only one instance can be added. To utilize the PC76 (see Figure 11.23), do the following:

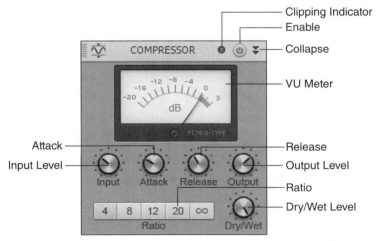

Figure 11.23 The PC76 U-Type Channel Compressor provides track compression.
Source: Cakewalk®, Inc.

1. Click the Enable control to toggle the PC76. This can also be used as a bypass switch to compare the original and processed audio signals.

2. Because the PC76 works a bit differently from other compressors by not providing a threshold control, it's best to start off by setting all controls to their default values. Do that by double-clicking the Input, Attack, Release, Output, and Dry/Wet controls.

3. Set the Ratio to control the amount of compression. The five buttons represent the following fixed ratio values: 4:1, 8:1, 12:1, 20:1, and Inf:1. The higher the first number, the more compression will be applied.

4. Adjust the Attack to determine how much of the initial part of the sound is compressed. A low value compresses everything (including fast transients like drum hits), while a high value applies less compression.

5. Adjust the Release to determine how much of the tail part of the sound is compressed. A low value applies less compression, allowing more room ambience to come through, while a high value applies more compression and gives a tighter sound.

6. Adjust the Input to determine both the input signal level and the threshold. The higher the input, the lower the threshold will be and the more compression that will be applied.

7. Adjust the Output to determine the final output signal level. The Output also allows you to get a higher level when the Input is set low so you can get less compression but still have a good volume level.

8. Adjust the Dry/Wet control to determine how much of the original signal and how much of the compressed signal are heard. Normally, you would keep this set to the default value of 100%, where only the compressed signal is heard. However, by using a lower value, you can apply what is known as *parallel compression*.

PARALLEL COMPRESSION: Parallel compression is a technique where both the original audio signal and compressed audio signal are heard at the same time. They are mixed together to create a smoother-sounding type of compression. Using this technique, you get the benefits of compression without making the signal actually sound like it is compressed.

PC4K S-Type Bus Compressor

The PC4K S-Type Bus Compressor provides a somewhat different set of controls (see Figure 11.24), and it also provides sidechaining. To utilize the PC4K, do the following:

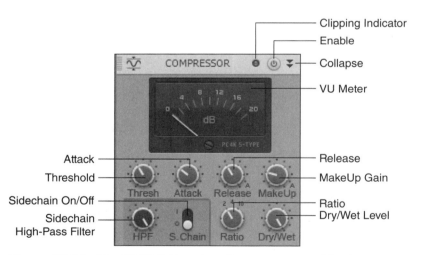

Figure 11.24 The PC4K S-Type Bus Compressor provides bus compression.
Source: Cakewalk®, Inc.

1. Click the Enable control to toggle the PC4K. This can also be used as a bypass switch to compare the original and processed audio signals.

2. Set the Threshold. The Threshold determines at what amplitude level your audio data will start being compressed. When the amplitude of your audio data reaches the Threshold level, processing will begin. More of

the audio signal is compressed when the Threshold is set low, and less is compressed when the Threshold value is high.

3. Set the Ratio to determine how much compression is applied. You have three value choices: 2:1, 4:1, and 10:1.

4. Set the Attack parameter. This parameter determines how quickly after the input level has reached the threshold that processing is applied. For example, if the input level reaches the threshold, it doesn't have to be compressed right away. A slow attack means the signal won't be compressed unless it lasts for a while. This is a good way to make sure fast, percussive parts are left alone, but long, drawn-out parts are compressed.

5. Set the Release parameter. This parameter determines how quickly after the input level goes below the threshold that processing is stopped. A longer release allows processing to sound more natural.

6. After compressing the audio signal, the level will obviously be lower. To bring the overall level back up, you can adjust the MakeUp Gain parameter.

7. Adjust the Dry/Wet control to determine how much of the original signal and how much of the compressed signal are heard. Normally, you would keep this set to the default value of 100%, where only the compressed signal is heard. However, by using a lower value, you can apply what is known as *parallel compression* (see Step 8 in the previous section).

To activate sidechaining for the PC4K, click the Sidechain On/Off control. Then use the Sidechain High-Pass Filter control to determine what frequencies can be used as a trigger. If you set it to 0.0Hz, then all frequencies will trigger the compressor. If you set the control to a higher value, then only those frequencies above the value will trigger the compressor. For information on sidechaining, see "Sidechaining Effects," later in this chapter.

QuadCurve Equalizer

The ProChannel provides a high-quality parametric equalizer with six bands: Low, Low-Mid, High-Mid, High, High-Pass, and Low-Pass (see Figure 11.25). The QuadCurve Equalizer is a default module, so only one instance can be used. To utilize the QuadCurve Equalizer, do the following:

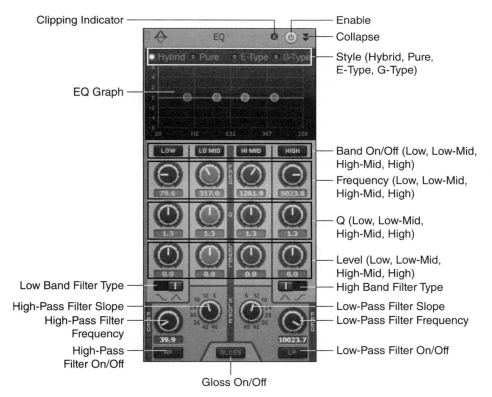

Figure 11.25 Apply EQ to any track or bus in a project with the ProChannel.
Source: Cakewalk®, Inc.

1. Click the Enable control to toggle the QuadCurve Equalizer.
2. Choose a Style by clicking on it. Pure provides a transparent EQ that doesn't impose any distinct characteristics on the audio. E-Type provides an emulation of a vintage hardware EQ. G-Type provides an emulation of a modern hardware EQ. Hybrid is sort of a combination of E-Type and Pure. It provides a similar sound to E-Type when boosting frequencies and a similar sound to Pure when cutting frequencies.
3. You can adjust the parameters for all four EQ bands either via the individual controls or by using the EQ Graph. The controls work in a self-explanatory way; click/drag up/down on a knob or double-click a numerical value. Using the EQ Graph to turn a band on/off, click on the corresponding colored dot. To adjust the frequency and level for a band, click and hold the mouse on the corresponding colored dot and then drag left/right to adjust frequency and up/down to adjust level. To adjust Q, press and hold Alt while dragging up/down. To make more precise adjustments, press and hold Shift while dragging. You can also change the resolution of the graph by right-clicking the associated strip's EQ plot in the Console view and choosing Plot Resolution.
4. The type of EQ can be set for the Low and High bands using the Low Band Filter Type and High Band Filter Type controls. Clicking these controls toggles each band between bell-and-shelf type equalization. When using the bell type of EQ, the band will boost/cut frequencies around the center frequency set by the band's Frequency control. When using the shelf type of EQ, the band will boost/cut frequencies either below (Low band) or above (High band) the Frequency value.
5. If you want to cut a wide range of low frequencies, click the High-Pass Filter On/Off control to activate the High-Pass Filter. Adjust the High-Pass Filter Frequency to determine the range of low frequencies to cut. The higher the value, the more low frequencies that will be cut. Then adjust the High-Pass Filter Slope to determine the level of the cut. The higher the value, the more drastic the cut will be.
6. If you want to cut a wide range of high frequencies, click the Low-Pass Filter On/Off control to activate the Low-Pass Filter. Adjust the Low-Pass Filter Frequency to determine the range of high frequencies to cut. The higher the value, the more high frequencies will be cut. Then adjust the Low-Pass Filter Slope to determine the level of the cut. The higher the value, the more drastic the cut will be.
7. To apply a finishing touch to the EQ, click the Gloss On/Off control to toggle the Gloss feature, which adds a unique filter to the high frequencies, giving them more presence in the mix.

TUBE SATURATION

The ProChannel Tube Saturation module (see Figure 11.26) lets you add some warmth to the audio signal. The Tube Saturation module is a default module, so only one instance can be used. To utilize the tube saturation, do the following:

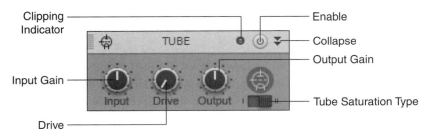

Figure 11.26 Add some warmth to the audio with the ProChannel Tube Saturation module.
Source: Cakewalk®, Inc.

1. Click the Enable control to toggle the Tube Saturation module.
2. Set the Tube Saturation Type to I or II. Type I applies pure tube saturation to the entire range of frequencies. Type II provides a dual-tube emulation where the high frequencies are not saturated as much, preventing them from sounding harsh or metallic. Use Type II on instruments with a lot of high-frequency content, like drum cymbals, etc.
3. If you want to cut/boost the audio signal before it is saturated, use the Input Gain. Leave it at its default value of 0.0dB to use the original audio signal level.
4. Adjust the Drive control to determine the amount of saturation. If you set the value too high, you can get distortion, depending on the Input Gain value.
5. If you want to cut/boost the audio signal after it has been saturated, use the Output Gain.

SOFTTUBE SATURATION KNOB

The ProChannel provides an additional tube saturation module called the Softube Saturation Knob (see Figure 11.27). Why use this instead of the Tube Saturation module? Two reasons: it provides a different kind of saturation, and it's an add-on module, so you can use as many instances of it as you'd like. To utilize the Softube Saturation Knob, do the following:

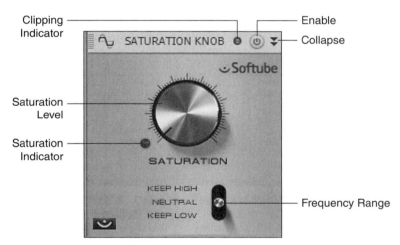

Figure 11.27 Add a different type of saturation to audio with the Softube Saturation Knob.
Source: Cakewalk®, Inc.

1. Click the Enable control to toggle the Softube Saturation Knob.
2. Click/drag the Frequency Range switch up/down to set which frequencies will be processed. Choose Neutral to process all frequencies, which is ideal for processing an entire stereo mix. Choose Keep High to process only high frequencies, which is ideal for emphasizing the "bite" of a synth lead or similar track. Choose Keep Low to process only low frequencies, which is ideal for processing kick drum, bass guitar, and other low frequency instruments.
3. Click/drag the Saturation Level knob up/down to set the amount of saturation applied. This should be set to taste, but a setting between eleven and twelve o'clock will give a nice subtle and not oversaturated sound.

BREVERB 2

In addition to the BREVERB 2 Cakewalk effect (discussed earlier in this chapter), SONAR Producer includes a BREVERB 2 ProChannel module (see Figure 11.28), which provides the same reverb processing and similar controls, but with a slightly different workflow. The BREVERB 2 module works as follows:

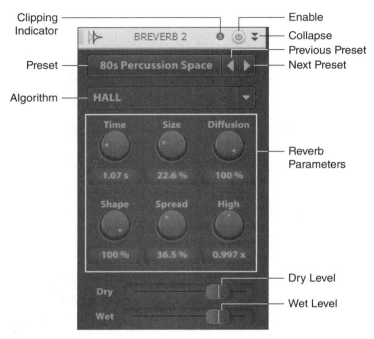

Figure 11.28 BREVERB 2 is also provided as a ProChannel module in SONAR Producer.
Source: Cakewalk®, Inc.

1. Click the Enable control to toggle the BREVERB 2 module.
2. Choose a reverb preset by clicking the Previous Preset or Next Preset buttons. You can also click the Preset name field to access a menu of presets. Click on a preset in the menu to select it and then click the Preset name field again to close the menu.
3. If you'd like to create your own reverb effect, choose a reverb algorithm from the Algorithm menu and then adjust the Reverb Parameters.
4. Use the Dry Level slider to control the volume of the original audio.
5. Use the Wet Level slider to control the volume of the reverb effect.
6. You can save your settings, but only as a part of a ProChannel preset. You can't save a preset for the module itself.

For more information on using BREVERB 2, refer to the *BREVERB 2 Cakewalk* section found earlier in this chapter.

FX CHAIN

I talked about FX Chains in detail in the *FX Chains* section earlier in this chapter. In addition to being able to use FX Chains in the FX bin of a track/bus, you can also use them in the ProChannel. This is an extremely powerful option because it allows you to use any VST plug-in inside the ProChannel. So you can process the audio signal with plug-ins between ProChannel modules by inserting an FX Chain module (see Figure 11.29). The FX Chain module provides most of the same features as a regular FX Chain, but with some differences in the workflow, as follows:

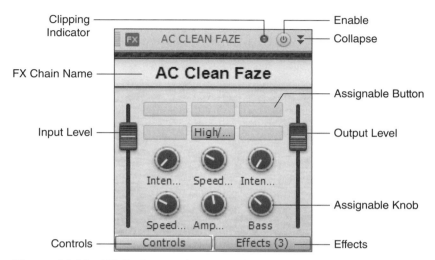

Figure 11.29 FX Chains can be used within the ProChannel by utilizing the FX Chain module.
Source: Cakewalk®, Inc.

1. An FX Chain module can be added in two ways: by right-clicking in the ProChannel and choosing Insert Module > FX Chain, or by dragging a plug-in from the Browser into the ProChannel. If you use the Insert Module method, an empty FX Chain will be added to the ProChannel. If you drag a plug-in from the Browser, SONAR will automatically add a new FX Chain module to the ProChannel and load it with the plug-in. You can also drag FX Chain presets from the Browser.

2. Add plug-ins to an existing FX Chain module by clicking the Effects button and then right-clicking in the FX Chain and choosing Audio FX. You can also load and save FX Chains from the same menu, as well as delete plug-ins in the FX Chain by right-clicking the plug-in and choosing Delete.

3. The plug-in list in the FX Chain module works just like an FX bin. The audio flows through the plug-ins from top to bottom, and you can change the order by clicking and dragging a plug-in up/down in the list. You can toggle a plug-in on/off by clicking the Bypass button, and you can double-click a plug-in to access the plug-in interface.

4. Click the Controls button to access the FX Chain parameters (refer to Figure 11.29).

5. Double-click the FX Chain Name to rename the FX Chain.

6. Right-click a knob or button and choose Edit Control to customize the controls. You can also customize the interface.

7. Use the Input Level and Output Level sliders to adjust the input and output volume, respectively.

For more details on FX Chains, refer to the *FX Chains* section earlier in this chapter.

CONSOLE EMULATOR

Most of today's music is recorded and mixed "inside-the-box," meaning the audio gets recorded directly into an audio interface, converted to digital, and stored on a PC without being routed through a mixing console. Because of this, some people say that the sound lacks a certain pleasing characteristic that would be added by going through the electronic components of a mixing console. SONAR's Console Emulator (see Figure 11.30) module simulates the "sound" of three classic mixing consoles and allows you to add those characteristics to your audio. You can, of course, use the Console Emulator to your liking, but to get the most out of it, I've found the following procedures to work nicely:

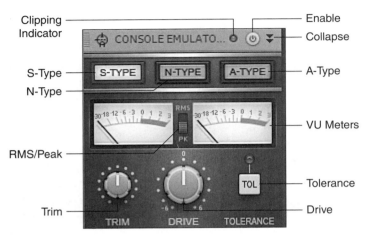

Figure 11.30 The Console Emulator simulates the "sound" of three classic mixing consoles.
Source: Cakewalk®, Inc.

1. Before you start mixing your project, add the Console Emulator Channel module to every track and add the Console Emulator Bus module to every bus. The reason you want to use the modules this way (instead of just adding it to the final master bus of your project) is because the Console Emulator provides a cumulative effect. This means that each instance of the module processes each track and bus independently, but the combined sound is what gives it a unique characteristic. Plus, this emulates the same situation as using a real mixing console—each track and bus will be processed through a separate channel on the console.

2. You'll also want to move the module to the bottom of the ProChannel so that it is the last module in the list. Also, right-click in the ProChannel and make sure that the Post FX Bin option is activated. The reason for this is the signal will pass through the FX Bin first and then any ProChannel modules, and finally the Console Emulator, which is what would happen to the signal flow if you were using a mixing console to mix a project.

QUICK GROUP PROCHANNEL PRESET: In order to avoid having to go through each track and bus in the project by adding the Console Emulator manually, first set up the ProChannel with the default modules you would like to use (including the Console Emulator at the top of the list). Then save a ProChannel preset. Create one preset for tracks (using the Console Emulator Channel module) and one preset for buses (using the Console Emulator Bus module).

Now select all tracks (by clicking on a track and then pressing Ctrl+A) and then hold Ctrl and click the Load Preset button at the top of the ProChannel. Select the preset you want to use and click Open. That preset will be automatically loaded into every selected audio track. Do the same thing for buses.

---

3. Choose an emulation mode by clicking the S-Type, N-Type, or A-Type buttons. Be sure to set every track and bus to the same emulation mode to get the correct effect. If you use different emulation modes, the results probably won't sound very good, but you can experiment, if you'd like. You can use the Quick Group function to set all tracks/buses at once. The S-Type mode provides a clean, transparent sound. The N-Type mode provides a warm sound. The A-Type provides a bright sound.

4. Use the Trim knob to adjust the input level. You may not need to use this, although I've found that a setting around 2dB provides a subtle effect. Also, you only need to set this for tracks because the Console Emulator Bus module doesn't include a Trim knob.

5. Use the Drive knob to adjust the level of console emulation. Again, a setting of about 2dB provides a nice, subtle effect. This should be set to the same value for all tracks and buses.

6. Click on the Tolerance parameter to activate it. You may or may not want to use this option, depending on the sound you need, but I tend to activate it most of the time. Adding tolerance to the emulation simulates the minute differences found in the electronic circuitry of a mixing console. Not all electronic components are exactly alike, so the sound can be subtly altered. As to whether you'll be able to hear the difference with or without this option, I can't say. You'll have to try it and see if it makes a difference for your project.

7. Use the RMS/Peak switch to set the VU Meters to RMS or Peak mode. RMS provides an average volume measurement, and Peak displays the highest volume measurement in each frequency cycle.

8. Group all the Console Emulator module Enable buttons so that you can turn all the modules on/off with a single click. This will allow you to quickly compare the sound of an emulated and non-emulated mix. Do this for tracks and then for buses, adding all the buttons to the same group. First, select all tracks. Then hold Ctrl and click the Enable button on one of the Console Emulator Channel modules. While still holding Ctrl, right-click the button and choose Group > *name of group*. Do the same thing for buses and assign them to the same group as the tracks.

In addition to saving a ProChannel preset, you may want to set up a default ProChannel configuration with the Console Emulator already set up so that when you create a new track or bus, you'll have the Console Emulator ready to go. Just set up the ProChannel with the modules you want to use and then right-click on the name of a module and choose Set Modules as Default for Tracks or Set Modules as Default for Buses. You will still need to group the Enable buttons for each project, because grouping isn't saved in the ProChannel configuration.

The ProChannel is an extremely powerful feature that can be used for a multitude of tasks on single tracks and entire mixes. Be sure to check out some of the presets for starting points.

Cakewalk Analyst—Spectrum Analyzer

In Chapter 7, I talked about frequencies, the audio spectrum, and how different sounds are created via multiple, simultaneous vibrations at different frequencies. I also talked about how you can alter the tonal characteristics (or timbre) of a sound by using equalization. But in order to know what frequencies should be boosted or cut to get the changes you want, you have to know which frequencies (and their amplitudes) are present within a sound. That's where spectrum analysis comes in.

If you happen to have a boom box or a stereo component that has an animated graph feature, which changes as music is played, then you've had some experience with spectrum analysis. That animated graph shows the amplitudes of different frequencies within the music as it is being played. It can tell you if there is too much bass or too much treble and allow you to make the appropriate adjustments so that the music sounds better. SONAR's Cakewalk Analyst lets you do this, too, but with a much higher degree of accuracy.

You can use Cakewalk Analyst to analyze the frequency content in your audio and determine which frequencies are loud or soft. Then you can use the equalization features to make changes. The best way to use Cakewalk Analyst is in real time. Here is how Cakewalk Analyst works:

1. Choose Analyst to open the Cakewalk Analyst window (see Figure 11.31). The window displays a graph showing frequency values along the bottom and amplitude values along the left side. This lets you look at the graph, pick out a frequency, and find the amplitude of that frequency within your audio data.

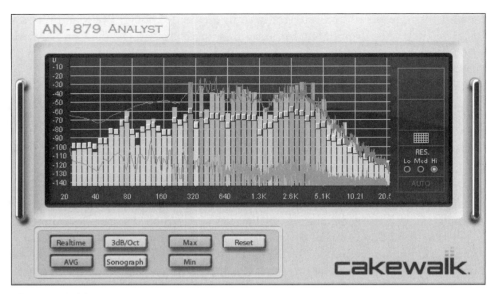

Figure 11.31 Use Cakewalk Analyst to analyze the frequency content in your audio.
Source: Cakewalk®, Inc.

2. When you first open the window, the amplitude scale will show 0 to −70dB, and the frequency scale will show 20Hz to 20kHz, but these scales can be changed. To change the range of the amplitude scale, hover your mouse over the bottom edge of the graph until it turns into a double-arrow. Then click and drag up or down. To change the range of the frequency scale, click and drag over the right edge of the graph.

3. You can also zoom in or out on the graph vertically (for more detailed amplitude readings) or horizontally (for more detailed frequency readings). To zoom vertically, click and drag over the top edge of the graph. To zoom horizontally, click and drag over the left edge of the graph.

4. To return the range or zoom of any part of the graph to its default value, double-click the appropriate edge of the graph.

5. To the right of the graph is a small area separated into five sections. The first two sections provide specific amplitude and frequency information. As you move your mouse within the graph, you'll see the amplitude of the current mouse position shown in the first section. The second section displays the frequency and pitch. By aligning the cursor to the top of a frequency bar in the graph, you can get a reading of the amplitude and pitch of that frequency.

6. The third section controls the grid display. Click this to toggle the graph background grid on/off.

7. The fourth section controls the accuracy (or Resolution) of the analysis. The Lo setting provides faster graph updates while Cakewalk Analyst is analyzing your data in real time, but it is the least accurate. If your computer can handle it, you will get the best results using the Hi setting.

8. When you start project playback, Analyst displays its data in real time. In addition to the individual frequency bars, you can choose to have an average value shown as a small square at the top of each bar. Click the AVG button to toggle this on/off.

9. You can also have the minimum and maximum values of each frequency shown as line graphs by clicking the Min and Max buttons to toggle these options. To have the values re-evaluated at a specific time during playback, click the Reset button.

10. Initially, Cakewalk Analyst runs in Spectrum mode, but it also provides the Sonograph mode. Click the Sonograph button to activate this mode (see Figure 11.32).

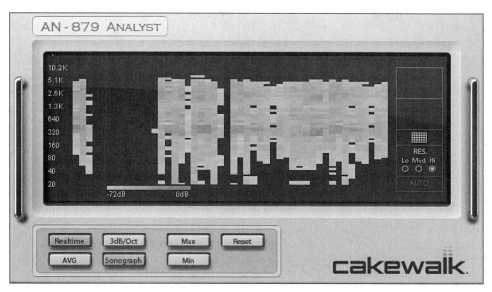

Figure 11.32 In addition to Spectrum mode, Cakewalk Analyst provides the Sonograph mode.
Source: Cakewalk®, Inc.

11. In the Sonograph mode, Cakewalk Analyst provides a color-coded display of your audio data over time. During playback, the display scrolls from right to left, with the right edge of the graph representing the current Now time. The left side of the graph shows the frequency scale. The bottom of the graph shows the color key so you can get a basic idea of the amplitude of each frequency. Like Spectrum mode, you can adjust the accuracy of the graph using the Resolution options to the right of the graph. None of the other options is available in this mode.
12. As in the Spectrum mode, you can move your mouse over the graph, but here you only get frequency and pitch information.

CAKEWALK ANALYST AUTOMATION

As I mentioned earlier, Cakewalk Analyst provides an automation function. This function splits up the audio spectrum into four bands and records the amplitude of these bands over time as four automation envelopes. (A fifth envelope records the overall amplitude of the entire spectrum.) You can then assign these envelopes to other functions (such as EQ) to achieve some interesting effects, based on the spectrum information of your audio. Here is how the Cakewalk Analyst automation function works:

1. With Cakewalk Analyst already set up in the Fx bin of an audio track or bus, click the Auto option located to the right of the graph.
2. In the upper-right corner of the Analyst window, click the W button to activate the Automation Write option for Analyst.

3. Right-click Cakewalk Analyst in the Fx bin and choose Write Enable Parameter to open the Cakewalk Analyst dialog box (see Figure 11.33).

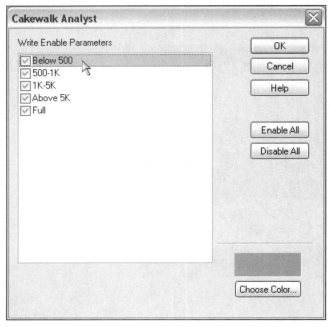

Figure 11.33 Use the Cakewalk Analyst dialog box to set up automation parameters for Cakewalk Analyst.
Source: Cakewalk®, Inc.

4. Activate the Cakewalk Analyst frequency bands for which you would like to record automation. Click Enable All or Disable All to activate or deactivate all bands. You can also select each band one at a time and assign an envelope color using the Choose Color button. Click OK.
5. Set the Now time to the point in the project where you would like to begin recording automation and start playback.
6. Stop project playback when you're done. SONAR will display the automation in the track as envelopes representing each band: Below 500Hz, 500Hz to 1kHz, 1kHz to 5kHz; Above 5kHz, and Full (the entire spectrum).
7. In the Cakewalk Analyst window, click the W button to deactivate the Automation Write option.
8. Add another effect plug-in to the Fx bin.
9. Right-click each envelope and choose Assign Envelope > [*parameter you would like to automate*].

By reassigning the envelopes to control other effect parameters, you can control various effects using the audio spectrum analysis output from Cakewalk Analyst.

R-MIX SONAR (SONAR Producer)

Taking spectrum analysis a step further, R-MIX SONAR allows you to do spectral editing. Similar to Cakewalk Analyst, R-MIX SONAR displays a graphic representation of the audio spectrum (see Figure 11.34), but it then allows you to manipulate that graphic to change specific parts of the audio. For example, you can select the vocal portion of a stereo mix and then adjust the volume and panning of the vocal (even though it's already been mixed with other instruments). You can also add effects and even reduce different types of noise in the audio. R-MIX SONAR works as follows:

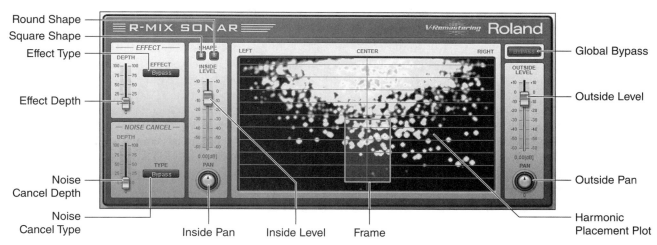

Figure 11.34 Perform spectral editing on your audio with R-MIX SONAR.
Source: Cakewalk®, Inc.

1. Choose RMixSONAR_32 to open the R-MIX SONAR window. The window displays a graph called the Harmonic Placement Plot. As audio plays, the Harmonic Placement Plot displays that audio as colored blobs with the vertical location of the blob representing its frequency (22,050Hz to 15Hz from top to bottom), and the horizontal location representing its position in the stereo field Left, Center, and Right). Right-click on the Plot to check the frequency of a specific location.

2. Located inside the Plot is the Frame, inside of which represents the portion of the audio spectrum that will be processed. Use the Square Shape and Round Shape buttons to choose the type of Frame. Drag the sizes (or corners) of the Frame to change its shape and size. Click/drag inside the Frame to move it around the Plot. For most operations, you'll want to place the Frame over the portion of the audio that you want to process. To reset the frame to its default shape and location, double-click anywhere in the Plot.

3. Use the Inside Level and Inside Pan parameters to change the volume and stereo position of the audio within the Frame, respectively. Ctrl+click the parameters to set them back to their default values, which works on all the R-MIX SONAR parameters.

4. Use the Outside Level and Outside Pan parameters to change the volume and stereo position of the audio outside the Frame, respectively.

5. To apply one of the built-in effects to the audio inside the Frame, click the Effect Type menu and choose an effect. Use the Effect Depth fader to determine the amount of the affect to be applied. The higher the amount, the more the effect is applied. R-MIX SONAR provides eight built-in effects in three categories (compression, delay, and reverb). Type 1 C provides low-frequency compression. Balanced C provides both low- and high-frequency compression. Short D, Medium D, and Long D provide short, medium, and long delay effects, respectively. Room Rev, Hall Rev, and Plate Rev provide room, hall, and plate reverb simulations. Choose Bypass to disable the built-in effects.

APPLY ANY EFFECT TO R-MIX SONAR: You can also apply any effect to the R-MIX SONAR output by cloning the track and placing R-MIX SONAR at the top of the FX bin in one of the tracks. Then lower the Outside Level to −60dB, and any effects placed in the FX bin after R-MIX SONAR will be applied to the audio inside the Frame.

---

6. R-MIX SONAR also allows you to perform two types of noise reduction: specific and global. Specific noise reducing is performed by simply placing the Frame over the offending noise in the Plot and then using the Inside Level parameter to lower the volume of the noise.

7. Additionally, R-MIX SONAR provides noise cancellation features, which are applied to the entire audio signal, regardless of where the Frame is located in the Plot. Click the Noise Cancel Type menu to choose the type of noise you would like to remove. Hiss, hum, wind, and air conditioning are the available options. Then use the Noise Cancel Depth parameter to determine how much of the noise is removed. Raise the value to remove more noise, but the higher the value, the more processing artifacts can be heard.

8. Click the Global Bypass button to toggle R-MIX SONAR on/off.

By allowing the selection of specific parts of the audio spectrum, R-MIX SONAR provides a wide variety of audio processing possibilities. One of my favorite uses is being able to apply effects to different frequency ranges anywhere in the stereo field.

SPECTRAFX VIDEO DEMO: Because the SpectraFX included with SONAR is a legacy plug-in (32-bit only) and is not installed by default, I'm not including it here. Instead, I have created an online demo video that covers the basics of using the effect. Go to **garrigus.com?SpectraFX** to view it.

Sidechaining Effects

Sidechaining is another method of automating effects using audio output. Essentially, sidechaining allows you to use the output of an audio track to control the effects being used on another audio track. SONAR provides four effects that can be used for sidechaining: Sonitus:fx Compressor, Sonitus:fx Gate, Vintage Channel, and ProChannel. Other plug-ins that provide sidechaining capabilities can be used as well. Two common uses for sidechaining are *ducking* and *keying*.

Ducking in SONAR

The most common example of ducking is used with voiceovers. You have one audio track with a voice recording on it. You have another track with background music, and you apply a compressor effect to the music track. You take the output from the voice track and feed it into the sidechain input of the compressor effect. Now when the voice track is producing a signal, it tells the compressor effect to lower the volume of the music track so that the voice can be heard more clearly. And when the voice is not present, the volume of the music track comes back up to its previous level. In musical terms, one example of ducking might be bringing out a lead guitar part or vocal part above the mix. To apply ducking in SONAR, do the following:

1. Right-click in the FX bin of the audio track or bus (to which you would like to apply compression—this would be the background music track from the previous example) and choose Audio FX > Sonitus:fx Compressor. Leave the Sonitus:fx Compressor window open for now.

2. Right-click the track number of the audio track or bus (the output of which you want to use to control the compressor effect—this would be the vocal track from the previous example) and choose Insert Send > Sonitus:fx Compress (Side Input) from the menu. If you were using the Vintage Channel, you would choose Insert Send > Vintage_Channel_VC64 (Input2). If you were using the ProChannel, you would choose Insert Send > Built In Channel Fx (Input2). A new send will be added to the track—clicking the Send Enable button toggles the send on/off but it's on by default (see Chapter 10 for more information about buses and sends). You can also assign the actual output of the track to the sidechain input of the effect, but if you do that, the track can no longer be heard. By using a send, you can continue to hear the track (the voice from the previous example), as well as send its output to control the effect on the other track.

3. As an example, in the Sonitus:fx Compressor window, choose the Complete Mix preset to use as a starting point, although you can use any settings you'd like. Then start playback.

4. As you listen to both tracks, per the example, you should hear the music track get softer whenever the voice track comes in. To determine how soft the music will get, adjust the Threshold parameter in the Sonitus:fx Compressor window. The lower the Threshold, the softer the music.

5. Adjust the Attack parameter to determine how quickly the music will get softer. The lower the Attack value, the quicker the music will get softer. However, if you use too low of a value, you may get a "chopping" or "pumping" sound. The higher the Attack value, the smoother the transition. What you want is a value that lowers the music smoothly, but quickly enough for the voice to be heard. A value of 50ms (milliseconds) is a good starting point.

6. Adjust the Release parameter to determine how quickly the music will return to its normal volume level after the voice ends. The lower the Release value, the quicker the music will get louder. But again, if the level is too low, you can introduce unwanted sounds. What you want is a value that brings the music back in smoothly and keeps it low long enough to cover any short gaps in the voice track. A value of 440ms is a good starting point.

7. If you were using the Vintage Channel, the parameter settings would be the same, but one additional step would be to activate the Key option for the compressor.

So, if we take the voiceover example, what is happening in the previous procedure is that the same audio from the voice track is being routed through both a send and the track output simultaneously. The regular track output allows us to hear the voice. The send allows the voice track to control the amount of compression (volume reduction) applied by the compression effect to the music track. As such, when the voice comes in, the music is lowered, and when the voice goes out, the music is raised back up to its previous level.

Keying in SONAR

The most common example of keying is used with track triggering, which is the opposite of ducking. Using the previous example, instead of lowering the music track when the voice track was playing, keying makes it so the music will only play when the voice plays. In musical terms, one example of keying might be having a sustained string part in one audio track that only played when the guitar part played in another track. When the guitar played quick, separated chords, the string part came through in short segments as well. To apply keying in SONAR, do the following:

1. Right-click in the FX bin of the audio track or bus (to which you would like to apply keying—this would be the background music track from the previous example) and choose Audio FX > Sonitus:fx Gate. Leave the Sonitus: fx Gate window open for now.

2. Right-click the track number of the audio track or bus (the output of which you want to use to control the gate effect—this would be the vocal track from the previous example) and choose Insert Send > Sonitus:fx Gate (Side Input) from the menu. Clicking the Send Enable button toggles the send on/off, but it's on by default (see Chapter 10 for more information about buses and sends).

3. As an example, in the Sonitus:fx Gate window, choose the Standard Noise Gate preset to use as a starting point. Then start playback.

4. As you listen to both tracks, per the example, you should hear the music track play only when the voice track plays. Adjust the Threshold so that the value is below the input signal level. For example, if the input signal level is −12dB, you must set the Threshold below that level in order to hear the music track play when the voice track plays.

5. Adjust the Attack parameter to determine how quickly the music track will start to play after the voice track starts playing.

6. Adjust the Release parameter to determine how quickly the music track will stop playing after the voice track stops playing.

So, if we take the example, what is happening in the previous procedure is that the same audio from the voice track is being routed as it was in the previous section describing ducking. But this time, the voice track is triggering or keying the music track so that the music track only plays when the voice track plays.

External Hardware Effects

Even with the high cost of hardware, there are still many people who enjoy using external effects. The problem with external hardware is the delay that is introduced to the audio signal as it travels out of the computer, through the external hardware, and then back into the computer again. In past versions of SONAR, this delay had to be calculated manually, but SONAR provides a special External Insert plug-in that compensates for the delay automatically. To use external hardware with SONAR, do the following:

1. The sound card you are using must have a set of inputs/outputs that is not being used in order to work with the External Insert plug-in. Connect the outputs to the inputs of your external hardware device and then connect the device's outputs to the inputs of your sound card.
2. In SONAR, right-click the FX bin of an audio track/bus and choose External Insert from the menu to open the External Insert window (see Figure 11.35).

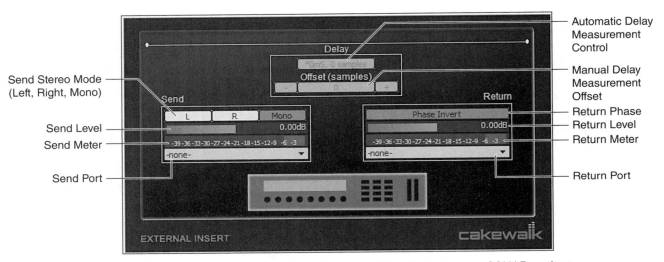

Figure 11.35 Use the External Insert plug-in to include external hardware in your SONAR project.
Source: Cakewalk®, Inc.

3. Use the Send Port menu to choose the sound card output port that is connected to the input of your hardware device.
4. Use the Return Port menu to choose the sound card input port that is connected to the output of your hardware device.
5. Turn on your hardware device and then click the Automatic Delay Measurement Control to tell SONAR to measure the delay and compensate for it. If your hardware device is a Delay or Reverb effect, you should activate the Bypass button (if your hardware device has one) so that SONAR won't get a false delay reading.
6. Play the SONAR project. Then adjust the Send Level and Return Level to the desired volume levels you want to use.
7. If you hear a delay problem with the audio, stop project playback and adjust the Manual Delay Measurement Offset. You'll have to experiment with this setting to find the right value.
8. If you hear a phase problem with the audio, click the Return Phase (Phase Invert) button to reverse the phase of the signal coming back from the hardware device.

One other thing you need to know when using external hardware is that when you are ready to mix your project, you will probably want to convert any tracks that have the External Insert plug-in applied by bouncing those tracks with the Bounce to Track function. When doing so, you will need to turn off the Fast Bounce option (in the Bounce to Track dialog box) because audio from hardware must be bounced in real time (meaning the same time it would take to play through the entire SONAR project). You can listen to the bounce by activating the Audible Bounce option.

MIDI Effects

SONAR provides a set of seven MIDI effects, one of which (Chord Analyzer) is not really an effect. Like the audio effects, some of the MIDI effects mimic some of SONAR's editing features. Again, they have this capability so that you can process your data with these features in real time. You cannot use SONAR's editing features in real time because they aren't plug-ins. In addition, the effects provide more power and flexibility, and they include additional parameters not found in the editing features, so I'll go over them here step-by-step.

Automatic Arpeggios

In music, you can play the notes of a chord in a number of different ways. Most often, the notes are played all at once. You also can play them one at a time in sequence; this is called an *arpeggio*. SONAR's Arpeggiator effect automatically creates arpeggios for each note or chord in your selected MIDI data. Depending on how you set the parameters, you can achieve some very strange and interesting "melodies." This feature works as follows:

1. Choose MIDI Plugins > Cakewalk FX > Arpeggiator to open the Arpeggiator window.
2. Set the Swing parameter. This parameter works the same as the Swing parameter in the Quantize editing feature. The only difference is that 50% is the normal setting (meaning no swing is applied); in this case, 0% is the normal setting. And you can set this Swing parameter from −100 to +100%. More often than not, you'll want to keep it set to 0%.
3. Set the Rate and Units parameters. These two parameters work together. The Rate parameter determines the amount of time between each note in the arpeggio, and the Units parameter determines what units you want to use to set the Rate parameter. You can set the Rate parameter in notes, ticks, or milliseconds. By setting the Units parameter to Notes, you can easily synchronize the notes in the arpeggio to a certain note value so that you know they will play in sync with the rest of the music in your project.
4. Set the Legato parameter. This parameter determines the duration of the notes in the arpeggio. If you set the Legato parameter to 1% (the lowest value), the notes in the arpeggio will be played with a very short duration (as in a staccato fashion, in which the note is played and let go very quickly). If you set the Legato parameter to 99% (the highest value), the notes in the arpeggio will be played with a very long duration. To be exact, each note plays until the start of the next note in the arpeggio.
5. Set the Path parameter. This parameter determines the direction in which the notes in the arpeggio will be played. If you select Up, Up, the notes in the arpeggio will go up consecutively in pitch. If you select Up, Down, the notes in the arpeggio will go up in pitch first and then come back down. If you select Down, Down, the notes in the arpeggio will go down consecutively in pitch. If you select Down, Up, the notes in the arpeggio will go down in pitch first and then come back up.
6. Set the Play Through option. If you activate the Play Through option, your original data will remain intact and play along with the new arpeggio data. If you deactivate the Play Through option, only the arpeggio data will remain, and your original data will be removed.
7. Set the Output option and parameters. If you activate the Output option, additional notes will be added so the arpeggio will play smoothly over each octave in the range you specify. Otherwise, only your original notes will be used to create the arpeggio. The Lowest Note parameter (located near the bottom of the Output option)

determines the lowest note that will be included in the arpeggio. The Highest Note parameter (located near the top of the Output option) determines the highest note that will be included in the arpeggio.

8. Set the Chord option and parameters. If you activate the Chord option, the Arpeggiator effect will analyze the original data that falls in the range you specify and then guess at what chord is being played. If you use the effect in real-time mode, the name of the chord that is guessed will be shown in the Recognized Chord field. The effect uses the recognized chord to create the notes for the arpeggio (meaning the notes in the arpeggio are based on the recognized chord).

I know the parameter settings for the Arpeggiator effect can be a bit confusing. Sometimes, it's difficult to tell what the results will be after you apply the effect. Basically, they'll be different, depending on the data you process. This effect usually works best on slow, chord-based data.

ARPEGGIATOR AS MIDI NOTES: If you apply the Arpeggiator effect to a MIDI track in real time (by adding it to the FX bin of the track) and you'd like to edit the output as MIDI notes in the track, select the track and choose Process > Apply Effect > MIDI Effects from SONAR's main menu. This will permanently apply the effect to the track by converting the Arpeggiator notes to MIDI notes and adding them to the track. You can then edit the notes, just like you would any other MIDI notes in the track.

Chord Analysis

As I mentioned earlier, the Chord Analyzer isn't really an effect. It doesn't do anything to your data, meaning it doesn't make any changes. The Chord Analyzer simply looks at your data and guesses what kind of chord is being played. Here is how it works:

BEST IN REAL TIME: Although you can use the Chord Analyzer effect offline, it works best in real time as your project is playing. Therefore, I'll go through the real-time procedure here.

---

1. In the Track view, right-click in the FX bin of the MIDI track to which you want to add an effect.
2. Choose MIDI Plugins > Cakewalk FX > Chord Analyzer to add the Chord Analyzer to the list.
3. The Chord Analyzer window will open.
4. Set the Analysis Window parameter. Using this parameter, you can control how often the Chord Analyzer effect analyzes your data. The lower the number, the more accurate it is at guessing the names of the chords being played. This feature also requires more processing power from your computer, but I've never had any problems keeping this parameter set at 1 (the lowest setting). Unless you have trouble with playback, I recommend that you just leave this setting at its default value.
5. Start playback of the project. As the project plays, the effect will analyze your data and display the name of the chord it thinks is being played, along with how the chord looks in music notation and on a piano keyboard.

This effect can be useful as a learning tool because it displays the chords being played on a piano keyboard and as music notation. Plus, it lists (in the Chord Recognized section) some possible alternatives you might want to try in place of the chord you are using currently.

Echo Delay

Just as delay effects add echoes to your audio data, the Echo Delay effect adds echoes to your MIDI data. But because this effect works on MIDI data, some of the parameters are different, and some additional parameters are available as well. This feature works as follows:

1. Choose MIDI Plugins > Cakewalk FX > Echo Delay to open the Echo Delay window.
2. Set the Delay and Delay Units parameters. These two parameters work together. The Delay parameter determines the amount of time between each echo. The Delay Units parameter (located below the Delay parameter) determines the units you want to use to set the Delay parameter. You can set the Delay parameter in notes, ticks, and milliseconds. By setting the Delay Units parameter to Notes, you can easily synchronize the echoes to a certain note value so you know they will play in sync with the rest of the music in your project.

> **THE TAP BUTTON:** You also can set the Delay parameter by clicking the Tap button in the Echo Delay dialog box. Clicking the button at a certain tempo sets the Delay parameter to that tempo.

3. Set the Decay parameter by double-clicking the numerical value or moving the crosshair in the graphic display. This parameter determines whether the echoes get softer or louder (and by how much). If you set the Decay parameter to a value below 100%, the echoes will get softer. If you set the Decay parameter to a value above 100%, the echoes will get louder.
4. Set the Echoes parameter by double-clicking the numerical value or moving the crosshair in the graphic display. This parameter determines how many echoes you will have.
5. Set the Swing parameter. This parameter works the same way as the Swing parameter in the Quantize editing feature. The only difference is that 50% is the normal setting (meaning no swing is applied); 0% is the normal setting. And you can set this Swing parameter from −100 to +100%. More often than not, you'll want to keep it set to 0%.
6. Set the Pitch parameter. If you want, you can have each echo transposed to a different pitch value, which creates some interesting sounds. You can set the Pitch parameter from −12 to +12 steps. You determine the types of steps by choosing either the Diatonic (the pitches follow the diatonic musical scale) or Chromatic (the pitches follow the chromatic musical scale) option.

MIDI Event Filter

The MIDI Event Filter effect works almost the same as the Select by Filter editing feature. The only difference is that instead of simply selecting the specified events, it deletes (offline) or filters (real time) them. This feature gives you a quick way to remove specific kinds of MIDI data from your clips or tracks. It works like this:

1. Choose MIDI Plugins > Cakewalk FX > MIDI Event Filter to open the MIDI Event Filter window.
2. Set the appropriate parameters for the types of MIDI data you want to remove. These settings are the same as the settings for the Event Filter - Select Some dialog box (see Chapter 7).
3. If you want to use the current settings at a later time, save them as a preset.

Quantize

The Quantize effect works almost exactly the same as the Quantize editing feature. The only difference is that the effect provides a couple of additional parameters. It works like this:

1. Choose MIDI Plugins > Cakewalk FX > Quantize to open the Quantize window.
2. Set the Quantize parameter by activating/deactivating the Start Times and Durations options. These settings simply tell SONAR whether you want to quantize the start times or durations of each selected MIDI event.
3. Set the Resolution parameter. This parameter works exactly the same as the Resolution parameter in the Quantize editing feature (see Chapter 8).
4. Set the Tuplet option. Using this option, you can further define the Resolution parameter. For example, if you want to quantize your data according to an odd note value, activate the Tuplet option and set its related

parameters to 5 and 4 (which would mean you want to quantize your data to the value of five notes occurring in the time of four notes).

5. Set the Strength, Swing, Window, and Offset parameters. These parameters work exactly the same as the Strength, Swing, Window, and Offset parameters in the Quantize editing feature.

6. Set the Random option. If you activate this option, a random time offset will be applied to the timing of each quantized event. You can use this option to achieve some very strange sounds. Do a little experimenting to hear what I mean.

Transpose

Like the Transpose editing feature, the Transpose effect transposes your MIDI note data up or down by a number of half-steps, either chromatically or diatonically. However, the Transpose effect also provides some more advanced transposition methods. It works like this:

1. Choose MIDI Plugins > Cakewalk FX > Transpose to open the Transpose window.

2. If you want to transpose your data by a simple musical interval, choose the Interval option for the Transposition Method parameter. Then enter the number of half steps (−127 to +127) into the Offset parameter by which you want to transpose the data.

3. If you want to transpose your data diatonically so that the notes are changed according to degrees of a certain musical scale, choose the Diatonic option for the Transposition Method parameter. Then enter the number of scale degrees (−24 to +24) into the Offset parameter by which you want to transpose the data. Also, choose the musical scale you want to use by setting the To parameter.

CONSTRAIN TO SCALE: If you want any of the notes in your data that don't fit within the chosen musical scale to be transposed so they will fit, activate the Constrain to Scale option. This feature works well for pop music. For something like jazz, though, in which many different nonscale notes are used in the music, it's best to keep this option deactivated. This option works for both the Diatonic and Key/Scale Transposition Methods.

---

4. If you want to transpose your data from one musical key and scale to another, choose the Key/Scale option for the Transposition Method parameter. In the From and To parameters, choose the musical keys and scales by which you want to transpose your data. You also can transpose the data up or down by a number of octaves at the same time by setting the Offset parameter.

5. To specify exactly how each note in the musical scale will be transposed, choose the Custom Map option for the Transposition Method parameter. Using this option, you can define your own transposition map. This means you can set the note to each note in the musical scale that will be transposed. To change the transposition value of a note in the musical scale, double-click the note in the From column of the Transposition Map and then type in a new note value to transpose that note up or down. This option is pretty tedious, but it gives you precise control over every musical note.

PITCH OR NOTE NUMBER: You can view notes in the Transposition Map either by note name or by MIDI note number. Simply select the appropriate option (Pitch or Notes).

Velocity

I'm tempted to compare the Velocity effect to the Scale Velocity editing feature, but the effect not only enables you to scale MIDI velocity data, but it also enables you to change it in many more advanced ways. As a matter of fact, you'll probably stop using the Scale Velocity editing feature when you get the hang of the Velocity effect because you can use this effect as an editing tool as well. It works like this:

1. Choose MIDI Plugins > Cakewalk FX > Velocity to open the Velocity window.
2. To change all MIDI velocity values to an exact number, choose the Set To option and then designate the value (1 to 127) you want to use.
3. To add or subtract a certain amount to or from each MIDI velocity in your selected data, choose the Change option and designate the value (−127 to +127) you want to use.
4. To scale all MIDI velocity values by a certain percentage, choose the Scale option and designate the value (1 to 900%) that you want to use.
5. If you choose the Limit option, all the MIDI velocities in your selected data will be changed to fit within the range of velocity values (1 to 127) you specify.
6. The next two options also scale MIDI velocities, but from one value to another. If you choose the first Change Gradually option, you can scale MIDI velocities by exact values (1 to 127). If you choose the second Change Gradually option, you can scale MIDI velocities by a percentage (1 to 900%).
7. In addition to choosing one of the previous options, you can choose the Velocity effect's Randomize option, which works in tandem with the others. By activating this option, you can add or subtract a random offset to or from each MIDI velocity in your selected data. You can enter a maximum value (1 to 127) to be used (by adjusting the Amount parameter), and you can give priority over whether the random offset will be lower or higher (−10 to +10) than the maximum value that you specify (by adjusting the Tendency parameter).

And that will do it for this chapter. You should now have a good working knowledge of all the effects that SONAR provides. Remember to have fun and don't be afraid to experiment!

Automation and Control Surfaces

I N ADDITION TO LETTING YOU ADJUST PARAMETERS MANUALLY WITH A MOUSE, SONAR provides a number of other features that help with the mixing process, including automation and control surface support. Automation lets you record parameter changes over time so that during playback those changes will occur automatically, allowing you to add more depth to your music mixes. Control surfaces let you control SONAR via hardware-based buttons, knobs, and faders, giving you more realism with your automation recordings (compared to what you might get when manipulating on-screen controls with a mouse).

Taking Snapshots

SONAR automates parameters in a number of ways, one of which is called *Snapshots*. Using Snapshots, you can take a "picture" of all the current control values in the Console and Track views and then store those values in your project at a specified Now time. For example, if your project is a pop song with a number of different sections (such as the intro, verse, chorus, and so on), you might want to change the mix each time a new section is reached by the Now time during playback. You can do so by creating a different Snapshot at the beginning of each section of the song. During playback, as the Now time passes a point in the project where a Snapshot is stored, the values for all the recorded controls are changed to reflect the Snapshot automatically.

> **LINKED AUTOMATION:** For automation purposes, the controls in the Console view and the Track view work together, rather than independently. This means that if you automate a control in the Console view, its corresponding control in the Track view will be automated as well and vice versa.

To create a Snapshot, just follow these steps:

1. Set the Now time to the point in the project where you want the Snapshot to be stored.
2. Adjust the control(s) in the Console or Track view to the value(s) at which you want them to be set during that part of the project. To take a Snapshot of a single control, right-click the control and choose Automation Snapshot.
3. If you want to take a Snapshot of multiple controls, right-click each control you adjusted and choose Automation Write Enable.

> **MULTIPLE ARMING:** Instead of arming each control one-by-one, you can arm all the controls in a track by clicking its Automation Write button (labeled with a W). You also can arm the controls in multiple tracks at once. Just select all the tracks whose controls you want to arm (use Ctrl+click or Shift+click to select more than one track) and then Ctrl+click the Automation Write button of one of the selected tracks.

> **ARMING UNAVAILABLE:** You'll notice that not all the controls can be automated. If a control cannot be automated, the Automation Write Enable option in the menu will be grayed out. Also, after a parameter in the Track view is armed for automation, it will have a red outline displayed around it.

4. Set up a key binding (see Chapter 2) to trigger the Snapshot. Since some of the existing automation key bindings center around F12, I have my key binding set for Alt+F12. Set it to Automation Snapshot in the Function list of the Preferences – Keyboard Shortcuts dialog box. Type *Automation Snapshot* in the Search field to quickly find the function.
5. Press Alt+F11 to take a Snapshot of all controls that are enabled.
6. Repeat Steps 1 through 5 (skipping Step 4) until you've created all the Snapshots you need for your project.
7. When you're finished, press F12 to disarm all of the previously armed parameters.

When you play your project, you'll notice that the Snapshots take effect as the Now time passes each Snapshot point.

> **ENABLE/DISABLE AUTOMATION:** If you want to disable automation playback temporarily without changing or deleting any of the Snapshots in your project, press Ctrl+F12 to toggle Enable/Bypass Read Automation. You can also click the Enable/Bypass Read Automation button in the Mix module of the Control Bar.

Snapshot control values for each of the tracks and buses are stored as nodes on individual envelopes in the individual tracks. These envelope nodes can be edited, allowing you to change your recorded Snapshot data. See "Working with Envelopes" later in this chapter.

Automating the Mix

Snapshots are great if you need quick control for changing values at certain points in your project, but most of the time, you'll want the controls to change smoothly over time as the project plays. To achieve this effect, you need to use SONAR's Write Automation feature. Using Write Automation, you can record the movements of the controls in the Console or Track view. You can do so in real time during project playback or when recording.

Automation Write Modes

Before recording automation, you'll need to decide how the data is recorded by choosing an Automation Write mode. SONAR provides three modes: Overwrite, Touch, and Latch.

Overwrite Automation Write Mode

The Overwrite mode overwrites (erases) any automation data that already exists for the armed parameter(s). This mode is useful for recording new automation data or replacing existing automation data. Using the Overwrite mode, data is constantly recorded, whether or not you change the parameter value(s). This means that as soon as you start, data is recorded to the track/bus, and recording continues until you stop.

Touch Automation Write Mode

The Touch mode also overwrites existing automation data, but only when you change the parameter value(s). For example, if you previously recorded volume automation to a track/bus, and you use Touch mode to record volume automation to the same track/bus again, only the value changes will be recorded and the previous data will remain intact. This mode is useful for replacing sections of automation data rather than all the data in a track. The Touch mode is especially useful if you have a touch-sensitive control surface. In that case, automation data is only written when you touch a control.

Latch Automation Write Mode

The Latch mode is sort of a combination of the Overwrite and Touch modes. When you start recording, previous automation data remains intact, but as soon as you change the parameter value(s), the data is overwritten (which is similar to Touch mode). However, from that point on, the data continues to be overwritten until you stop recording (which is similar to Overwrite mode). The Latch mode is useful for replacing all automation data after a chosen point in a project.

Setting the Automation Write Mode

You can set the Automation Write mode by doing the following:

1. Select the track(s) or bus(es) to which you want to record automation.
2. Press Ctrl+Shift+I, which opens the Track or Bus tab of the Inspector.
3. In the Automation section, choose a value for the Write Mode option. If you want to change the mode for multiple selected tracks/buses, hold Ctrl while you change the Write Mode option.

When you change the Automation Write mode of a track/bus, the Automation Write button for that track/bus will indicate the current mode as shown in Figure 12.1.

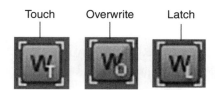

Figure 12.1 The Automation Write button reflects the current Automation Write mode.
Source: Cakewalk®, Inc.

Automation Time Base

In addition to the Write mode, you need to choose an automation time base. This feature determines what happens to recorded automation data when you change the project tempo. The two time base values available are Musical and Absolute. If you choose Musical, the position of the automation data is locked to the measure, beat, and tick values. This means that when you change the project tempo, the automation envelope nodes (see "Working with Envelopes" later in this chapter) will remain lined up to the same measure, beat, and tick values at which they were recorded. This time base is useful when you're creating most music projects.

If you choose Absolute, the position of the automation data is locked to the hour, minute, second, and frame values. This means that when you change the project tempo, the automation envelope nodes will remained lined up to the same hour, minute, second, and frame values at which they were recorded. However, their measure, beat, and tick values will change. This time base is useful when you're creating music for video and you need to have automation occur at exact time values throughout the project, even if the tempo changes.

You can set the automation time base by doing the following:

1. Select the track(s) or bus(es) to which you want to record automation.
2. Press Ctrl+Shift+I, which opens the Track or Bus tab of the Inspector.
3. In the Automation section, choose a value for the Time Base option. If you want to change the time base for multiple selected tracks/buses, hold Ctrl while you change the Time Base option.

Recording Automation

Once you've set the Write mode and time base you want to use, you can record automation by doing the following:

1. Right-click each track and bus parameter you want to automate and choose Automation Write Enable. You can arm all parameters for a track/bus at the same time by clicking its Automation Write control. Hold Ctrl while clicking the Automation Write control to arm all parameters on all selected tracks/buses.
2. Set the Now time to just before the point in the project where you want to start recording control changes.
3. Start project playback or recording to start recording automation data.
4. When the Now time gets to the point in the project at which you want to begin recording control changes, adjust the controls with your mouse.
5. When you're finished, stop playback.
6. Because you're manipulating on-screen controls with your mouse, you can make only one change at a time. What if you want to have two different controls change at the same time? For every control that you want to change in the same time frame, repeat Steps 2 through 5.

LOOP RECORDING: Instead of starting and stopping playback each time you want to record additional control changes, try setting up a loop so that SONAR will play the project (or the section of the project) over and over again.

---

7. After you've finished recording all the control changes you need for your mix, click the Clear All Automation Write Enables button in the Mix module of the Control Bar to disarm all of the previously armed controls/parameters.

When you play your project, you'll notice the automation taking effect as the Now time passes the sections in which you recorded data. Just as with Snapshots, the control values for each of the MIDI and audio tracks (as well as the buses) are stored as envelopes in the individual tracks. These envelopes can be edited, allowing you to change your recorded automation data (see "Working with Envelopes").

Grouping

As I mentioned earlier, to change more than one parameter at the same time while you're recording automation data, you have to play through your project several times. To make things easier, you can connect a number of parameters together so if you move one, the others will move with it. You do so by using SONAR's Grouping feature. With the Grouping feature, you can create groups of controls whose changes are linked to one another.

Quick Groups

The easiest way to group parameters in SONAR is to use the Quick Groups feature. A Quick Group is a temporary group where all the controls on a track (or bus) become linked to the same controls on one or more tracks (or buses). In other words, when multiple tracks are part of a Quick Group, all of their Volume parameters are grouped, all of their Pan parameters are grouped, and so on.

To create a Quick Group, you simply hold down the Ctrl key and adjust a track control. If no tracks are selected, then that control will change in all tracks of the same type. If you have some selected tracks and you Ctrl+adjust a control in one of the selected tracks, that same control will change in only the selected tracks of the same type. You can do the same thing with buses. Select a bus by clicking its letter. Select multiple buses with Ctrl+click or Shift +click. In addition, you can group tracks and buses together.

So, to sum up…Ctrl+click/hold a control in a selected or non-selected track/bus (in the Inspector, Track view, or Console view), and that same control will be adjusted in all selected or non-selected tracks/buses of the same type (audio or MIDI).

Creating Permanent Groups

In addition to Quick Groups, SONAR creates Permanent Groups that can be saved. Permanent Groups also have the advantage of being able to group controls from different track types. The number of controls that can belong to a group is unlimited, and you can group different types of controls to one another instead of having to group like controls, as with Quick Groups. Permanent Groups use names and colors to differentiate themselves from one another. SONAR provides 24 default group names and colors, but you can also define your own. To create a Permanent Group, follow these steps:

1. Right-click a control in the Console view or the Track view and choose Group > A-X or choose Group > New. If you choose one of the default groups, that control is assigned to the group, and it will take on the associated color. If you choose to create a new group, the Group Attributes dialog box will appear.
2. Type in a name for the new group. Then click the Choose Color button to choose a color for the group from the Color dialog box.
3. Click OK to close the Color dialog box. Click OK to close the Group Attributes dialog box. The control is assigned to the new group and takes on the chosen color.
4. Right-click another control and assign it to a group. This time, choose the same group for this control as you did for the previous control. This other control will take on the same color.
5. Continue to add as many other controls to the group as you want. You can even create other groups. However, the same control cannot belong to more than one group.

Now, if you change the first control, the second control will change as well and vice versa. The values of both of these controls will be recorded if you have them grouped while you are recording automation data.

> **QUICK PERMANENT GROUPS FOR MULTIPLE TRACKS/BUSES:** You can create a Permanent Group quickly for multiple tracks/buses by first selecting the tracks/buses. This makes it easy to group all selected track/bus Volume controls, for example. After selecting the tracks/buses, right-click one of the control types you would like to permanently group (such as the Volume controls) and choose Group > New. Choose a name and color for the group and click OK.

Ungrouping and Deleting Groups

To remove a parameter from a group, right-click the parameter and select Remove from Group. The color of the parameter will return to normal.

If you want to remove all parameters from a group while keeping the group itself intact for future use, just right-click one of the parameters in the group and choose Clear Group.

To delete a group, right-click one of the group parameters and choose Group Manager. Select the group you want to delete from the menu at the top of the dialog box. Then click the Delete button located to the right of the menu (shown with a big red X). Click OK.

Group Properties

In addition to simple groups, in which you link different controls so they change identically, you can create some advanced groups by manipulating the properties of a group. To change the properties of a group, right-click one of the controls in the group and choose Group Manager to open the Group Manager dialog box.

By changing the properties of a group, you can change the way the controls in the group are related to one another in terms of their values. Controls in groups can be related absolutely, relatively, or via a custom definition.

Absolute

To make the controls in a group related absolutely, select the Absolute option (which is the default setting when you create a new group) in the Group Manager dialog box and click OK. Controls in a group that are related absolutely have the same range of change. This means that if you change one control in the group, the others will change by the same amount. This is true even if one control starts at one value and another control starts at a different value. For example, suppose that you have two Volume controls on two different MIDI tracks linked together, and one of the Volume controls has a value of 10, and the other has a value of 20. If you increase the value of the first control by 10, the other control value will increase by 10, too. Now the first control has a value of 20, and the second control has a value of 30.

Relative

To link the controls in a group relatively, select the Relative option in the Group Manager dialog box and click OK. Controls in a group that are linked relatively do not have the same range of change. This means that if you change one control in the group, the others can change by different amounts. For example, suppose that you have two Pan controls linked, and one has a value of 100% Left and the other has a value of C (centered in the middle). If you change the first control so it has a value of C (centered in the middle), the other will change so that it has a value of 100% Right. Now if you change the first control to a value of 100% Right, the second parameter will remain at 100% Right. The second control can't go any higher, so it stays at that value, while the first control continues to increase in value.

Custom

To relate the controls in a group according to your own custom definition, select the Custom option in the Group Manager dialog box. All the controls in the group will be listed in the dialog box (see Figure 12.2).

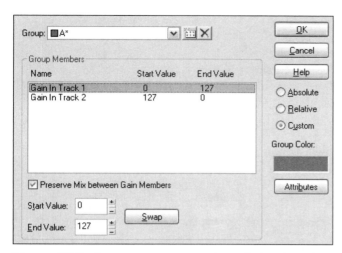

Figure 12.2 You can create complex relationships between parameters in a group by using the Custom option. *Source:* Cakewalk®, Inc.

Along with the names of each control, the Start and End values are listed. By changing the Start and End values for each control, you can define some complex value changes. For example, one good use of the Custom option is to create a crossfade between two Volume controls. Suppose that you have one Volume control in a group with a Start value of 0 and an End value of 127, and another Volume control in the same group with a Start value of 127 and an End value of 0. As you increase the value of the first control, the second control value will decrease and vice versa. You also can set up more complex relationships simply by assigning different Start and End values to each control in a group.

To change the Start or End value of a control in the list in the Group Manager dialog box, select the control and then type a value for either the Start Value or End Value located at the bottom of the box. If you want to exchange the current Start and End values, click the Swap button. After you've finished creating your custom definition, click OK.

> **QUICKLY SET START AND END:** You also can change the Start and End values of a control without opening the Group Manager dialog box. Just set the control to the value you want to set as the start or end, right-click the control, and choose either Value > Set Start = Current or Value > Set End = Current.

Remote Control

Even with grouping, you still might find it cumbersome to adjust on-screen controls with your mouse. To remedy this situation, SONAR provides a Remote Control feature. With the Remote Control feature, you can use an external MIDI device to make changes to the on-screen controls in the Console view or Track view. For example, if you have a MIDI keyboard, you can use a key on the keyboard to manipulate one of the buttons. Or if you have a pitch bend wheel on your keyboard, you can use it to manipulate one of the knobs or sliders.

By assigning different types of MIDI controller messages to the controls in the Console view or Track view, you no longer have to use your mouse to change the values; you can use the actual buttons and keys or levers and sliders on your MIDI instrument or device. To activate the Remote Control feature for a control, follow these steps:

1. Right-click the control and choose Remote Control to open the Remote Control dialog box.
2. If you want to use a key on your MIDI keyboard to manipulate this control, choose either the Note On option or the Note On/Off option and then enter the pitch of the key that you want to use. If you choose Note On,

the value of the control will be toggled on or off (for a button) or set to a minimum or maximum value (for knobs and sliders) each time you press the key. If you select the Note On/Off option, the value of the control will be toggled on when you press the key and off when you release the key.

3. If you want to use a lever or slider on your MIDI keyboard to manipulate this control, choose the Controller option and then enter the value of the MIDI controller you want to use. You can use this option only to manipulate knobs and sliders.

4. If you want to use the pitch bend wheel on your MIDI keyboard to manipulate this control, choose the Wheel option.

5. If you want to use the special registered parameter number or nonregistered parameter number MIDI messages to manipulate this control, choose either the RPN or NRPN option and then enter the number of the RPN or NRPN that you want to use.

6. If you want to use a Sysx message to manipulate this control, choose a byte option. If the message contains a single byte of data that changes while the rest of bytes in the message remain static, choose the Single Byte option. If the changing data contains two bytes, with the first being the high byte, choose the High Byte First option. If the changing data contains two bytes with the first being the low byte, choose the Low Byte First option. Then enter into the Starts With field the bytes in the Sysx message that come before the changing data, and enter into the Ends With field the bytes in the Sysx message that come after the changing data.

7. Set the MIDI Channel parameter to the same channel your MIDI keyboard or device is using to transmit data and click OK.

THE LEARN FEATURE: Instead of having to figure out how you need to set the options for Remote Control, you can use the Learn feature to have it done for you automatically. First, move a control on your external MIDI device. Right-click the control in SONAR that you want to manipulate and choose Remote Control; then click the Learn button. The Remote Control options will be set up for you automatically.

Now you can manipulate the control from your MIDI keyboard or device even while you are recording automation. To stop using Remote Control for a control, right-click the control and choose Disable Remote Control.

Global Remote Control Support

The Remote Control feature is fine for quick uses, but even though your Remote Control settings are saved with a project, they can't be transferred to other projects. This means you have to set up Remote Control for controls with each new project. To remedy this, SONAR provides global remote control features that can be used with any project. These features come in the form of support for dedicated control surface devices. These devices provide hardware-based knobs, sliders, and buttons, which transmit MIDI messages that can be used to adjust on-screen controls. Some MIDI keyboards also provide built-in control surface hardware.

Control Surface Setup

SONAR provides special support for many of the control surfaces available today. To find out if your control surface is supported and to set it up, do the following:

1. Press P and choose MIDI – Control Surfaces in the Preferences dialog box.
2. Click the Add New Controller/Surface button (shown with the yellow star) to open the Controller/Surface Settings dialog box.
3. Choose the name/model of the control surface that you have from the Controller/Surface list.

4. Choose the MIDI In port to which your control surface is connected from the Input Port list.

5. Choose the MIDI Out port to which your control surface is connected from the Output Port list.

After you click OK, you can access the Properties window for your control surface by choosing it from the bottom of SONAR's Utilities menu. From here, you are on your own in configuring the surface because each device is different. Please refer to the documentation that came with your device.

Edirol PCR-800 MIDI Controller

I myself have one of the Roland Edirol PCR-800 MIDI controller keyboards, although they are no longer available. You won't see this keyboard listed in the Controller/Surface Settings dialog box, but that is because all the PCR keyboards use the same control surface configuration.

To set up the Edirol PCR-800 (or one of the other PCR keyboards), follow the same steps as outlined in the last section but choose Edirol PCR-300 from the Controller/Surface list. If you have one of the older PCR-M series keyboards, choose Edirol PCR-M30 from the list. You can then choose the control surface from the SONAR Utilities menu and see how all the buttons, knobs, and sliders are currently configured. This control surface works in a similar manner to the ACT MIDI Controller (see the next section), so you can use the same procedures to make new control definitions.

CAKEWALK V-STUDIO SYSTEMS: Cakewalk and Roland have also worked together to create the V-Studio series of control surfaces that are specifically designed to work with SONAR. I have their V-Studio 700 system. Go to **garrigus.com?VStudio700** to find more information about my setup, as well as to grab a copy of my free V-Studio eBook.

The Active Controller Technology (ACT) MIDI Controller

What about those of us who have an older or unsupported control surface? For this situation, SONAR provides the ACT MIDI Controller, which can be set up to work with just about any control surface you may have. For example, I have an old Kenton Control Freak Live that still works. What's also great about the ACT MIDI Controller is that not only can you control track, bus, and SONAR transport functions, but you can also control effect and soft synth plug-in parameters. In addition, as you switch from one plug-in to another, the ACT MIDI Controller remembers your parameter configurations so that your control surface is automatically set up to control the different plug-in parameters.

Set Up the ACT MIDI Controller

As with all control surfaces, you must first set up the ACT MIDI Controller as follows:

1. Press P and choose MIDI – Control Surfaces in the Preferences dialog box.
2. Click the Add new Controller/Surface button to open the Controller/Surface Settings dialog box.
3. Choose ACT MIDI Controller in the Controller/Surface list.
4. Use the Input and Output Port lists to set the MIDI input and output ports for your surface. Click OK twice.

Create an ACT Preset

After setting up the ACT MIDI Controller, you need to create an ACT preset for your control surface. This procedure involves "telling" SONAR the MIDI messages that are transmitted by all of the buttons, knobs, and sliders on your control surface. SONAR can then translate these messages into on-screen control changes. To set up an ACT preset, do the following:

1. Set up your control surface to use one of the factory presets that came with the device. Most control surfaces are programmable and provide factory presets so that you can start using them right away. You should base your ACT preset on one of the factory presets to prevent problems in case you reprogram your control surface in the future.

2. Choose Utilities > ACT MIDI Controller to open the ACT MIDI Controller properties window (see Figure 12.3). The ACT MIDI Controller provides support for up to four banks of eight knobs, sliders, and buttons. Each bank shares the same knob, slider, and button MIDI messages, but can be assigned to different SONAR functions. Displayed are four rows of control assignments, with the first row representing knobs (or rotaries), the second row representing sliders, and the third and fourth rows representing buttons. Each row has eight cells representing the eight knobs, eight sliders, and eight buttons (with an extra row for shifted buttons).

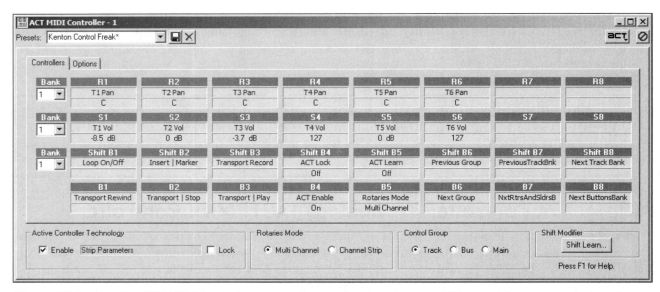

Figure 12.3 Use the ACT MIDI Controller properties window to set up an ACT preset for your control surface.
Source: Cakewalk®, Inc.

3. You can change the name of each cell by clicking the cell label and typing a new name into the Edit Label dialog box (see Figure 12.4).

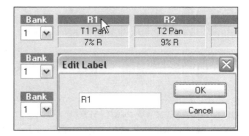

Figure 12.4 Use the Edit Label dialog box to edit the name of a control cell.
Source: Cakewalk®, Inc.

4. To assign a MIDI message to a cell, click the green area of the cell so that it displays the words "MIDI Learn" and then move the associated knob, slider, or button on your control surface (see Figure 12.5). Do this for every knob, slider, and button on your surface (up to eight each). For example, click in cell R1 in the ACT window and then move knob 1 on your control surface. Do this for all eight knobs. Then click in cell S1 and move slider 1 on your control surface. Do this for all eight sliders. Then click in cell B1 or Shift B1 (they share the same button) and push button 1 on your control surface. Do this for all eight buttons.

> **KNOBS AND SLIDERS:** Because knobs and sliders transmit the same type of MIDI messages, they look the same to SONAR. So, if your control surface has all knobs and no sliders, you can assign control surface knobs to the slider cells in the ACT window, and they will work just fine.

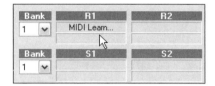

Figure 12.5 Click each cell in the ACT window to assign MIDI messages.
Source: Cakewalk®, Inc.

5. Because there are two rows representing buttons in the ACT window, you need to set up a Shift key that when pressed will access the shifted row of buttons. Even though you only have eight regular buttons on your control surface, there is usually a Shift key (button) provided that allows you to use the buttons for two different tasks. When the Shift key is not pressed, the buttons each access one program function. When the Shift key is pressed, the buttons each access a different program function. To assign a Shift key MIDI message, click the Shift Learn button in the Shift Modifier section of the ACT window and then press the Shift key (button) on your control surface.

6. In the Active Controller Technology section of the ACT window, make sure the Enable option is activated. This turns ACT on so that it will work with effect and soft synth plug-ins. If ACT is off, the ACT MIDI Controller will only work on regular SONAR functions.

7. In the Rotaries mode section, make sure the Multi Channel option is activated. This controls multiple track and parameter controls, whereas the Channel Strip mode only works on one track at a time (the currently active or selected track).

8. Click the Options tab to access the Options area of the ACT window (see Figure 12.6). Here is where you can assign different SONAR functions to the knob, slider, and button cells shown in the Controllers area of the window. Each bank of knobs and sliders must share the same function. For example, if you choose Bank 1 and Pan for the Rotaries parameters, then all knobs in Bank 1 will control track panning.

9. As you use ACT to control different parameters in different parts of SONAR, the knobs and sliders can change values suddenly. For example, if you move the same knob on your keyboard controller to adjust a parameter in one plug-in window and then a different parameter in another plug-in window, the values of those parameters will not be the same. When you jump from one to the other, the position of the knob on your controller will be different, and adjusting the knob will make the parameter value jump to match the knob value. You can change this behavior with the Capture Mode settings. Jump mode will work as I just described. However, if you use Match mode (which is what I recommend), the parameter value won't change until the knob value matches it. This will keep parameter values from jumping.

10. Although all knobs and sliders must share the same function, each button in each bank can be assigned a unique function. You can do this by using the Button parameters—first choose a bank, then a button, and finally a function from each of the lists.

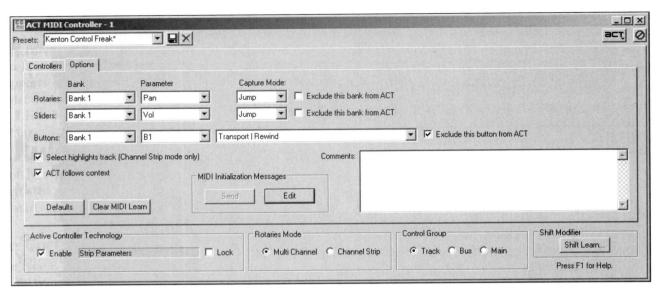

Figure 12.6 Use the Options area of the ACT window to assign knob, slider, and button functions.
Source: Cakewalk®, Inc.

11. When ACT is enabled, it allows you to control parameters in effect and soft synth windows. When one of these windows has focus, the ACT cells take on different functions. Normally, this means you would no longer be able to control SONAR functions like Stop, Play, and so on. But you can exclude buttons from being "taken over" while working in an effect or soft synth window. When assigning button functions, activate the Exclude This Button from ACT option so that the button will retain its original function assignment.

12. If you want a track to be highlighted in Channel Strip mode so that you know what track you're working with, activate the Select Highlights Track option.

13. Make sure the ACT Follow Context option is activated. Having this option turned on allows SONAR to automatically change knob, slider, and button assignments when you switch between different effect and soft synth windows.

14. Type some notes for this preset in the Comments section. It's a good idea to include info about what control surface and factory preset you used here.

15. Use the Presets parameters at the top of the window to type a new name for the preset and save it. (Click the Save button—the one showing a floppy disk icon.)

You can now close the ACT window and move on to creating knob, slider, and button assignments for the effects and soft synths with which you want to work.

Create an ACT Map

Although you have already created basic SONAR function assignments for the knobs, sliders, and buttons on your control surface in the ACT properties window, you still need to create assignments for each of the parameters in each of the effect and soft synth windows that you use. Do the following:

1. Make sure the ACT module in the Control Bar is visible.
2. In the module, make sure the ACT MIDI Controller is selected in the Controller/Surface list (see Figure 12.7).

Figure 12.7 Activate the ACT MIDI Controller to prepare for effect and soft synth parameter control assignments.
Source: Cakewalk®, Inc.

3. Open the window for the effect or soft synth whose parameters to which you want to assign controls. To open an effect window, double-click the name of the effect in one of the FX bins. To open a soft synth window, double-click the synth in the Synth Rack.
4. Click the ACT Learn mode button in the ACT module of the Control Bar to activate ACT Learn mode. You can also activate ACT Learn from the effect or synth window with the button located in the upper right area.
5. Change one of the on-screen controls with your mouse.
6. Move the first slider on your control surface.
7. Click the ACT Learn button again. SONAR will tell you how many parameters and controls were touched and ask you if you want to keep the assignments. Click Yes to save the assignments.
8. Repeat Steps 4 through 7 to assign all controls.

MULTIPLE ASSIGNMENTS: Instead of clicking the ACT Learn button for each single control you want to assign, simply click the button and then adjust each of the on-screen controls you want to assign in the order you want to assign them. Then move the control surface knobs, sliders, and buttons in the same order. Click the ACT Learn button again, and all assignments will be made in the order that you chose.

Make parameter assignments for all of the effects and soft synths you want to use with your control surface. When you're finished, you can simply switch from one window to the other, and SONAR will automatically remember your parameter assignments. For example, if you are controlling the Band 1 Gain slider in the Sonitus:fx Equalizer with slider 1 on your surface and then you click in the Track view to make that the focus, slider 1 will now control track volume 1 instead (or whatever track parameter you assigned).

Where Am I?

As you use your control surface, SONAR provides you with feedback as to which tracks and buses are being controlled by your surface using the WAI (Where Am I) feature. WAI displays a set of colored markers for each control surface you are using. These markers are shown to the left of the track numbers in the Track view (see Figure 12.8) and the bottom of the strips in the Console view.

Figure 12.8 WAI markers show you which tracks and buses are being controlled by your surface.
Source: Cakewalk®, Inc.

To use the WAI feature with your control surface, do the following:

1. Press P and choose MIDI – Control Surfaces in the Preferences dialog box.
2. Put a check mark in the WAI column for your control surface.
3. Select a color for your surface in the WAI Color column.
4. To display WAI markers in the Track or Console view, activate the Track View and Console View options in the WAI Display section of the box. Click OK.
5. Once the WAI markers are visible, you can click and drag them to change which tracks are being controlled by your surface. You can also right-click the markers and choose Move-[*name of control surface*] from the menu.
6. Double-click the markers to open the Properties window for the associated control surface.

Working with Envelopes

In addition to the Snapshot and Record Automation features, SONAR provides one more method of automating its controls: the Envelope feature. Using this feature, you can "draw" control changes into individual clips or entire tracks in the Track view.

Automation Lanes

SONAR provides two ways for working with envelopes—in the clips area of a track or in separate lanes displayed below a track. When working in the clips area, all envelopes are displayed together and overlap the clip waveforms. In addition, you can only manipulate one envelope at a time when working this way. When working with Automation Lanes, each envelope is displayed in its own separate lane and multiple envelopes can be manipulated simultaneously (see Figure 12.9). Individual clip envelopes are accessed in the clips area or via Take Lanes (see Chapter 6).

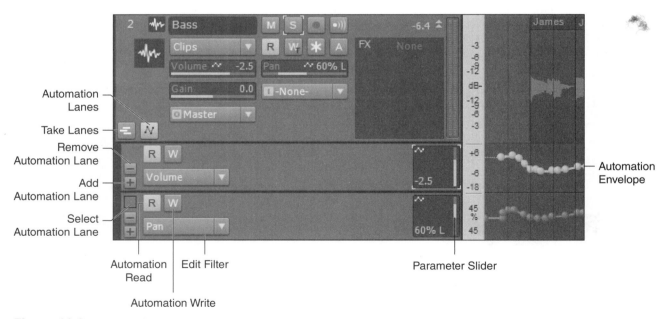

Figure 12.9 Automation Lanes provide access to multiple envelope manipulation.
Source: Cakewalk®, Inc.

To access the automation lanes of a track/bus, click its Automation Lanes button. If you already have existing automation envelopes in the track/bus, they will be moved into their own individual lanes. If automation doesn't exist, a single new lane is created and assigned a default automation value. Clicking the Automation Lanes button again will collapse the lanes and move the envelopes back into the clips area of the track/bus. This gives you the flexibility to work with envelopes using either method.

When displayed, you'll notice that automation lanes provide a number of controls. You can add new lanes and remove existing lanes using the Add Automation Lane and Remove Automation Lane buttons, respectively. Adding a lane creates a new lane with a default value. Removing a lane hides the lane, but it doesn't delete the automation envelope. Instead, the envelope is moved back into the clips area of the track/bus. If you'd like to display that envelope (or any other envelopes in the clips area) in automation lanes again, hold Shift and click the track's Automation Lanes button.

You can assign a new value to a lane using the lane's Edit Filter control. When you assign a new value, the existing automation envelope is moved back into the clips area of the track/bus.

In addition, you can record automation directly into a lane by clicking the lane's Automation Write button. Then position the Now time to the location in the project to begin recording. Start playback (or recording) in SONAR, and adjust the lane's Parameter Slider with your mouse (or using your control surface to manipulate the corresponding track/bus value). The Parameter Slider represents the track/bus value currently assigned to the lane. The lane's Automation Read button determines whether or not the automation envelope is active during playback.

You can select a lane by clicking the space located just to the left of the Automation Read button. There are no markings to indicate that space can be clicked, so you'll just have to trust me. When you select a lane, it selects the entire automation envelope in that lane. You can select multiple lanes by Ctrl+clicking or Shift+clicking on the aforementioned space of additional lanes.

Finally, you can rearrange and resize lanes. Click and drag the upper half of a lane's background up/down to move it to a new location. Resize lanes by hovering your mouse over the black divider at the bottom of a lane and then click/drag up/down. Resizing one lane resizes them all. Currently, there is no way to have individual lanes of different sizes.

Creating and Editing Envelopes

Earlier, I mentioned that whenever you use the Snapshot or Record Automation feature, SONAR stores the automation data as envelopes in the Track view. Well, you can also create (as well as edit) envelopes manually using the Smart and Draw tools, and your mouse.

Audio Envelopes

SONAR creates envelopes for both audio and MIDI tracks, as well as the buses in the Track view. Since the buses deal with audio data, you automate them by using audio envelopes. MIDI and audio envelopes are basically the same, but they have enough differences to require separate step-by-step procedures. To create or edit an audio envelope, follow these steps:

1. Activate the Smart tool (press F5).
2. If you want to create an envelope for an individual clip, click the associated track's Edit Filter control (see Chapter 6) and choose Clip Automation. For individual clips, you can automate the gain (volume) or panning. SONAR automatically creates a default envelope for each clip or track the first time you select that envelope.
3. If you want to create an envelope for an entire track (including the buses), click the Edit Filter control for the track (or bus) and choose Automation. If you'd like to display the envelope in an automation lane, hold Shift

while choosing the type of automation from the Edit Filter control. A new automation lane will be automatically created. For tracks, you can automate the Mute, Volume, Pan, Bus Send Level/Pan, and EQ controls. If you have SONAR Producer, you can also automate the ProChannel controls. The buses provide different controls for automation: Input Gain, Input Pan, Output Gain, Output Pan, and ProChannel (Producer) or EQ (Studio/Essential).

ENVELOPE OVERRIDE: If you have clip-based Gain or Pan envelopes in a track, and you later create track-based envelopes for Volume or Pan, the track envelopes will override the clip envelopes during playback. The clip envelopes will still exist, but SONAR will ignore them.

---

4. Initially, the envelope is shown as a straight line that runs from left to right in the clip, track, or lane. If it's a clip envelope, it will stop at the end of the clip. If it's a track envelope, it will continue past the right side of the Track view. The vertical position of the envelope indicates the current value for its associated control. For example, if you're automating the Volume control and its current value is –INF, the envelope will be shown at the very bottom of the clip, track, or lane. If the Volume control value is +6dB, the envelope will be shown at the very top of the clip, track, or lane. Other values will be shown somewhere between the top and bottom.

SHOW/HIDE ENVELOPES: If you're displaying envelopes in the clips area of the track (rather than in automation lanes), only one envelope can be edited at a time. The envelope currently being edited is shown in color. All others are shown as dark lines in the background, called *ghosted data*. You can show/hide ghosted data by choosing View > Display > Display Ghosted Data in the Track view menu.

---

5. At the beginning of the envelope is a small circle (called a *node*). To change the value of the node, click/drag it up/down. As you drag the node, you will see the value of the control represented by an envelope displayed alongside your mouse cursor.

6. In addition to dragging them up or down, you can also drag nodes left or right (to change their time/location within the project), so you can create any envelope shape you want. You also can change the time and value of a node more precisely by right-clicking it, choosing Properties, and entering the new values in the Edit Node dialog box.

RESTRICTING NODE MOVEMENT: While dragging a node left/right, you'll notice that its movement conforms to SONAR's snap grid (see "Snap to Grid" in Chapter 6). You can also "snap" a node's vertical movement by holding Ctrl while dragging the node up/down. This allows you to easily line up the node with other nodes in the envelope.

In addition, while dragging a node up/down, you may accidentally drag it left/right (thus changing its start time). Click and hold the mouse button on a node and then hold down Shift to prevent it from moving left/right while dragging it up/down.

---

7. You can add more nodes to the envelope by clicking anywhere on the envelope with the Smart tool (F5). You can add as many nodes as you need, which enables you to create some very complex control value changes. To "draw" new nodes, hold Alt while clicking/dragging over the envelope.

8. Multiple nodes can be selected either by selecting an entire lane, clicking/dragging horizontally in the background of a clip, track, or lane, or by clicking/holding the right mouse button and lassoing the nodes (see Figure 12.10). Multiple nodes from multiple clips, tracks, or lanes can be selected simultaneously.

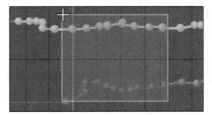

Figure 12.10 Right-click and drag to select nodes by lassoing them.
Source: Cakewalk®, Inc.

9. By holding Ctrl, you can click/drag (up/down) the line segments between two nodes, and you can also change their shape. Right-click a line segment and choose one of the following options: Jump, Linear, Fast Curve, or Slow Curve. You can also change the shape of a line segment by switching to the Edit tool (press F8) and then holding Ctrl while you click/drag the segment up/down. I prefer the right-click method so I don't have to change tools. If you want abrupt changes in the parameter values, choose Jump. For straight changes in the values, choose Linear. For fast but smooth changes in the values, choose Fast Curve. For slow and smooth changes in the values, choose Slow Curve. Depending on the option you choose, the shape of the line segment will change accordingly.

> **ADD NODES AT SELECTION:** Using the Smart tool, hover your mouse inside a clip or lane so that it looks like a capital I. Click and drag horizontally to create a selection. Now position your mouse near the top of the clip or lane so that it looks like a horizontal line with up/down arrows. Click and hold to create nodes at the selection boundaries, and then drag up/down to move the new envelope line segment. This feature provides a quick way to make envelope changes for selected data. Go to **digifreq.com?DFVI6** to see a video demonstration of this technique.

10. To create new line segments, press F9 to choose the Line tool. (It looks like the Draw tool with a line above it.) Then click/hold to create a start point, drag to create the segment, and then let go of the mouse button to create an end point (see Figure 12.11).

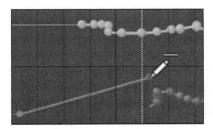

Figure 12.11 Use the Line tool to create new line segments.
Source: Cakewalk®, Inc.

11. To move an entire track envelope using the Smart tool (F5), make sure there are no selections by pressing Ctrl+Shift+A. Then select the entire envelope by selecting its automation lane. Now click/drag any node up/down or left/right. To move all track envelopes in all lanes at once, first select the track, which automatically selects all lanes. To conform your movement, first hold Shift and then click/drag in the direction you want to move. If you move horizontally, you won't be able to move vertically and vice versa.

12. If you need to delete a node, right-click it and choose Delete Node. To delete all nodes, right-click the envelope and choose Clear All.

13. If you need to reset a node to its original position, right-click it and choose Reset Node (or just double-click the node).

14. If you want to delete an entire envelope, right-click it and choose Delete Envelope.

15. If you want to change an envelope assignment to a different control value, right-click the envelope and choose Assign Envelope > [*name of the new control to automate*].

QUICK ENVELOPE SELECTION: When editing multiple envelopes in the clips area of a track, you can change the track's Edit Filter control via SONAR's Tools HUD (press T). Even easier is to simply Shift+click the envelope you want to edit with the Smart tool. Also, Shift+right-click will quickly switch between the last two envelopes.

MIDI Envelopes

To create or edit a MIDI envelope, follow these steps:

1. Activate the Smart tool (press F5).

2. If you want to create an envelope for an individual clip, click the associated track's Edit Filter control and choose Clip Automation. For individual MIDI clips, you can automate the velocity.

3. If you want to create an envelope for an entire track, click the Edit Filter control for the track and choose Automation. If you'd like to display the envelope in an automation lane, hold Shift while choosing the type of automation from the Edit Filter control. A new automation lane will be automatically created. For MIDI tracks, you can automate the Mute, Volume, Pan, Chorus, and Reverb controls, as well as the track's Arpeggiator controls. In addition, you can automate any other MIDI controller messages by choosing Automation > MIDI, which opens the MIDI Envelope dialog box. In the dialog box, choose the type of controller, the value of that controller, and the MIDI channel you want to use for the controller. Then click OK to create the new envelope.

CONVERT MIDI TO SHAPES: If you think the parameters in the MIDI Envelope dialog box look familiar, you're right. They are the same parameters found in the MIDI Event Type dialog box, which is accessed in the Piano Roll view when editing MIDI controllers in the Controller pane. If a track contains MIDI controller messages and you create an envelope for that track with the same controller, they will contradict one another. In this case, you should select the track and choose Clips > Convert MIDI Controllers to Envelopes from the Track view menu. You'll see the Convert MIDI to Shapes dialog box, which is exactly the same as the MIDI Envelope dialog box. Choose the controller you want to convert and click OK. The controller messages in that track will be converted to envelopes.

---

4. Follow Steps 4 through 15 in the previous "Audio Envelopes" section, as the actions are the same when working with MIDI envelopes.

ENABLE/DISABLE ENVELOPES: If you want to temporarily turn off all envelopes in your tracks to hear how your project sounds without the automation, click the Enable/Bypass Read Automation button in the Mix module of the Control Bar.

ENVELOPE/OFFSET MODE: Normally, during playback, if you have an envelope assigned to a track control, you cannot change that control because the envelope is controlling it. But SONAR provides a special mode in which you can add an offset to envelope values by changing controls during playback. This is called *Offset mode*, and you can toggle it on/off by pressing O (the letter, not the number) on your PC keyboard. When you enter Offset mode, you'll see a plus sign (+) displayed next to track controls. Also be aware that when you turn the mode off, your last control offset settings are still in effect. A good use for this feature is when you have an envelope that's just about perfect, but you want to make a precise adjustment to the entire envelope without having to change all the nodes in it.

Additional Envelope Editing

Even though I've covered most of the editing procedures for envelopes in the previous sections, there are some additional ways in which you can edit envelopes.

The Draw Tool

In addition to the Smart tool, SONAR provides the Draw tool. You can use the Draw tool to alter the shape of the envelope by simply drawing on the screen with your mouse. Here is how the Draw tool works:

1. Activate the Draw tool (press F9). The Draw tool provides a number of different modes, which you can cycle through by repeatedly pressing F9. You can also activate the tool and choose the mode by right-clicking its button (either in the Tools module of the Control Bar or via the Tools HUD). Freehand allows you to simply draw any type of envelope shape you would like. (This is the same as holding Alt and "drawing" nodes with the Smart tool.) Sine, Triangle, Square, and Saw mimic basic audio waveform shapes. Random creates a totally random envelope shape. The Line mode allows you to create new line segments, as I explained in the previous section entitled "Audio Envelopes."
2. Create a new envelope or choose an existing envelope to edit.
3. Hover your mouse over the point at which you would like to start "drawing." Then click and hold the left mouse button. If you chose the Freehand shape, you can simply move your mouse anywhere over the track or clip and draw in any envelope shape. If you chose one of the waveform shapes, drag your mouse from left to right (as well as up and down, depending on how much parameter value change you want to occur) to create that waveform shape. Keep in mind that when drawing with one of the waveform shapes, the cycle of the waveform is controlled by SONAR's Snap Grid. For example, if you set the Snap to Grid resolution to Measure and draw with the Sine mode, one cycle of the sine wave will cover the length of one measure.

QUICK WAVEFORM CYCLE CHANGE: Even though the Snap to Grid resolution determines the frequency of the waveform cycle, you can quickly double or halve the frequency by holding down Alt or Ctrl, respectively.

4. If you don't like the new envelope shape, simply draw over it. You can also choose Edit > Undo (or press Ctrl+Z) to change the envelope back to its original shape.

Deleting Envelopes

Earlier, I mentioned that to delete an envelope, you just need to right-click it and choose Delete Envelope. But if you want to delete more than one envelope or only part of an envelope, the procedure is a bit different.

1. Activate the Smart tool (F5) or Select tool (F6).
2. Select the data containing the envelope data you want to delete. This can be a single clip, an entire track, multiple tracks, part of a clip or track, as well as automation lanes and buses.

3. Choose Edit > Delete (or press Delete) when working in automation lanes. Choose Edit > Delete Special when working in tracks/buses to open the Delete dialog box.
4. Depending on the data you selected in Step 2, either the Track/Bus Automation option or the Clip Automation option will be available (or maybe both). Activate one or both options.

DELETE ENVELOPES ONLY: If you don't want to delete any other data along with the envelope data, make sure to deactivate all other options in the Delete dialog box. For example, remove the check mark next to Events in Tracks if you want to delete clip automation, but not the clip(s).

Copying and Pasting Envelopes

You can also copy and paste an envelope (or part of an envelope) from one track/lane to another. Why would you want to do that? Well, you might want the volume of one instrument in your project to follow the volume of another instrument. You can do this by copying and pasting the volume envelope from the first instrument track to the other. Here is how it works:

1. Activate the Smart tool (F5) or Select tool (F6).
2. Select the data containing the envelope data you want to copy. This can be a single clip, an entire track, multiple tracks, part of a clip or track, as well as automation lanes and buses.

SELECT TRACK ENVELOPES OPTION: If you are selecting clips in the Clips pane and you want to select the track envelope data for the track in which the clips reside, be sure to choose Options > Select Track Envelopes with Clips in the Track view menu. This option is activated by default.

---

3. Choose Edit > Copy (or press Ctrl+C) when working in automation lanes. Choose Edit > Copy Special when working in tracks/buses to open the Copy dialog box.
4. Depending on the data you selected in Step 2, either the Track/Bus Automation option or the Clip Automation option will be available (or maybe both). Activate one or both options.

COPY ENVELOPES ONLY: If you don't want to copy any other data along with the envelope data, make sure to deactivate all other options in the Copy dialog box. Keep in mind that clip automation can't be copied without the clip itself, so you can't choose the Clip Automation option by itself.

---

5. Click OK.
6. Select the tracks and change the Now time to the position in the project at which you want to paste the envelope data.
7. Choose Edit > Paste Special to open the Paste dialog box. Then click the Advanced button to expand the Paste dialog box to its full size. If you're pasting to a bus, choose the Bus option in the Destination section and choose the bus from the menu.
8. Make sure the Blend Old and New option is activated in the "What to Do with Existing Material" section.
9. Make sure the Track/Bus Automation or Clip Automation option is activated in the "What to Paste" section. Click OK.

Automating Effects and Soft Synths

In addition to automating track parameters, SONAR automates individual audio effect and software synthesizer parameters. The procedures for automating audio effects and soft synths are essentially the same as for track parameters, but arming the parameters is a bit different.

Automating Effects Parameters

To automate effects parameters, you can follow the same procedures outlined in the "Taking Snapshots" and "Automating the Mix" sections of this chapter. But when you get to the part of the procedure where you need to arm the parameter that you want to automate, follow these steps instead:

1. Right-click the FX bin of the audio track to which you want to apply the real-time effect and choose Audio FX > [*the name of the effect you want to use*]. You can also drag and drop the effect from the Plug-In section of the Browser.
2. After the window for the effect appears, right-click the name of the effect in the FX bin and choose Write Enable Parameter. Or if you want to automate all the parameters, click the W button located in the upper-right corner of the effect window.
3. If you use the right-click method, a dialog box appears. Put a check mark next to each of the parameters you want to automate in the Write Enable Parameter list and click OK.

Now just follow the procedures in the "Taking Snapshots" or "Automating the Mix" section of this chapter to record automation for your effect parameters.

As with track parameters, you can use envelopes to automate effects parameters. The procedure is the same as outlined in the "Audio Envelopes" section of the chapter. After you add an effect to a track, you'll see the parameters listed in the Edit Filter control menu.

Automating Soft Synth Parameters

Unlike effects, some soft synths can be automated only by using envelopes. It depends on the soft synth. In addition, the procedure for recording soft synth parameter movements is different from what I described earlier, so I'll go through each procedure step by step.

Recording Parameter Movements

If you want to record automation for a soft synth by directly manipulating its on-screen controls, follow these steps:

1. If you haven't done so already, set up a soft synth in the Track view of your project. Be sure to keep the soft synth's window open. Also, if you are using an older soft synth like the Cakewalk TTS-1, make sure to activate the Enable MIDI Output option in the Insert Soft Synth Options dialog box.
2. If you are using an older soft synth, arm the MIDI track you want to use for recording the automation data. If you are using a new soft synth like the PSYN II, you can record automation during either recording or playback.
3. If you're using an older soft synth, right-click the Record button in the Transport module of the Control Bar to set the recording mode. I explained this feature in Chapter 5; it works the same way here. More than likely, you'll want to keep the recording mode set to Sound on Sound. This will record new data to the track without overwriting any of the existing data.
4. Set up the soft synth to enable automation recording. This procedure is different for every soft synth, so you will have to refer to the soft synth's documentation for instructions. Most synths don't need any preparation because their controls already have automation values assigned to them.

5. For newer soft synths, be sure to activate the W (Automation Write) button in the upper-right corner of the synth's Property Page window. You can also do this in the Synth Rack.

6. Set the Now time to the point in the project at which you want to start recording automation.

7. If you're using an older soft synth, press the R key to start recording. For newer soft synths, you can just start project playback.

8. Move the soft synth's controls to record their movements.

9. Press the spacebar to stop recording.

10. If you want to record more automation, repeat Steps 6 through 9. Also remember that the MIDI controller data that you record from older synths can be converted to envelopes, as explained earlier in the tip labeled "Convert MIDI to Shapes."

Using Envelopes

You'll find that using envelopes to automate soft synth parameters is more accurate since you can actually draw the control movements. To use envelopes to automate soft synth parameters, follow these steps:

1. Set up a soft synth in the Track view of your project.

2. If you're using an older soft synth and you inserted it via a Simple Instrument Track, you'll need to separate that track into two tracks: one MIDI track and one audio track. Right-click the instrument track and choose Split Instrument Track.

3. If you're using an older soft synth, click the Edit Filter control of the MIDI track that drives the soft synth and choose Automation > MIDI to open the MIDI Envelope dialog box. If you're using a newer soft synth, click the Edit Filter control of the instrument track and choose Automation > [name of the soft synth]. Then choose a parameter to automate.

4. If you're using an older soft synth, in the MIDI Envelope dialog box use the Type list to choose from the Control, RPN, and NRPN options. The Value list will show all of the parameters that the soft synth offers for automation. Choose a parameter from the list. Use the Channel list to choose the MIDI channel of the current patch (program) being used in the soft synth.

After you finish Step 3 or Step 4 (depending on the type of soft synth you're using), an envelope is created for the selected parameter. Now follow the procedures in the "MIDI Envelopes" section of this chapter to automate the soft synth parameters.

The Next Steps

After you've finished mixing all the data in your tracks at just the right settings, it's time to create a final stereo track, which you can use to burn your project onto CD or get it ready for distribution in a multimedia project or on the Internet. Of course, if you're working on a surround sound project, there's still more to learn. Check out the Chapter 14 for surround sound information.

13

Export Audio and Burn CDs

ONGRATULATIONS! Your project has been recorded, edited, and mixed, and now you can share it with the rest of the world. To be able to share it, you need to create your very own CD.

Preparing a Project for CD Audio

A project can't be laid down as audio tracks on a CD as-is. Instead, you have to convert all your hardware synth MIDI tracks in a project to audio tracks. Then you have to export those audio tracks to a WAV file, so that your CD recording software can write the file to your CD. To do so, you need to follow a number of steps, which the following sections will detail.

Converting Your MIDI Tracks

If you happen to have a consumer-level sound card that provides a built-in synthesizer, and you used that sound card synth for some of your MIDI tracks, the first step is to convert any MIDI tracks that use your sound card's built-in synthesizer for playback to audio tracks as follows:

1. Insert a new audio track and assign the input for the track to your sound card's stereo input. For instance, if you have a Sound Blaster card, set the track to the Stereo SB Wave Device input. Also, activate the Record control for the track.
2. Solo the new audio track, as well as the MIDI tracks you're going to convert.
3. Open your sound card's mixer controls (see Figure 13.1) by double-clicking the small speaker icon in the Windows Taskbar.

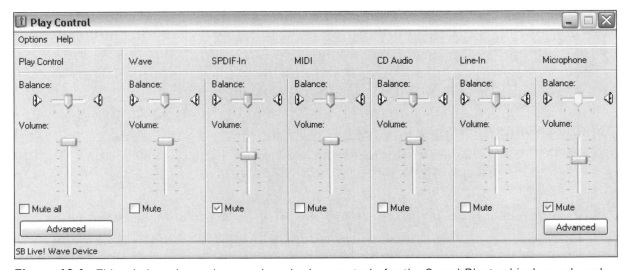

Figure 13.1 This window shows the sound card mixer controls for the Sound Blaster Live! sound card.
Source: Creative Technology Ltd., All Rights Reserved.

4. Choose Options > Properties and click Recording in the Adjust Volume For section of the resulting Properties dialog box. Then click OK to bring up the recording mixer controls, as shown in Figure 13.2.

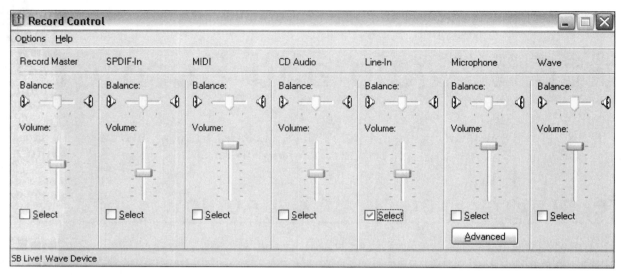

Figure 13.2 This window shows the recording mixer controls for the Sound Blaster Live! sound card.
Source: Creative Technology, Ltd., All Rights Reserved.

5. Activate the recording source for your sound card's synth by clicking the appropriate Select option (see Figure 13.3).

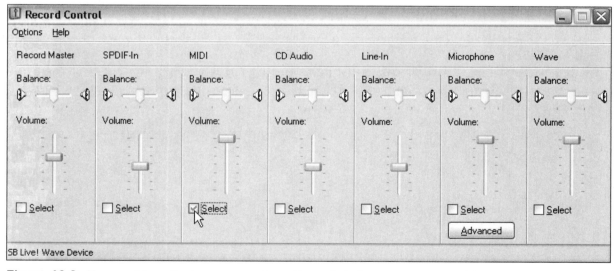

Figure 13.3 You need to activate your sound card's synth before you can record its output.
Source: Creative Technology, Ltd., All Rights Reserved.

6. Press R to start recording in SONAR, and your MIDI tracks will be recorded to the stereo audio track.

Next, you need to convert any MIDI tracks that use external MIDI instruments for playback to audio tracks, as shown in the following steps. If you don't have any MIDI tracks of this kind, you can skip this section.

1. Insert a new audio track and assign the input for the track to your sound card's stereo input. For instance, if you have a Sound Blaster Live! card, set the track to the Stereo SB Live Wave Device input. Also, activate the Record control for the track.
2. Solo the new audio track, as well as the MIDI tracks you're going to convert.
3. Open your sound card's mixer controls by double-clicking the small speaker icon in the Windows Taskbar.
4. Choose Options > Properties and then click Recording in the Adjust Volume For section of the resulting Properties dialog box. Then click OK to bring up the recording mixer controls.
5. Activate the recording source for your sound card's line input(s) by clicking the appropriate Select option (see Figure 13.4).

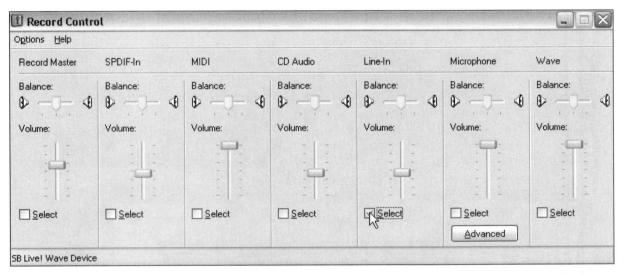

Figure 13.4 You need to activate your sound card's line input(s) before you can record any external MIDI instruments.
Source: Creative Technology, Ltd., All Rights Reserved.

6. Be sure the audio outputs from your external MIDI instrument are connected to the line inputs of your sound card. If you have more than one MIDI instrument, and you're using a mixing board, connect the stereo outputs of your mixing board to the line inputs of your sound card.
7. Press W to set the Now time so that recording will start at the beginning of the song. Then press R, and your MIDI tracks will be recorded to the stereo audio track.

After you're finished, you should have two new audio tracks representing your sound card's built-in synthesizer and your external MIDI instruments.

CONVERTING SOFTWARE SYNTH TRACKS: If you have any MIDI tracks in your project that use software synths, you do not need to do anything with these tracks when exporting. They will be exported just like regular audio tracks.

Exporting Your Audio Tracks

After all your sound card and external MIDI tracks are converted to audio tracks, you need to mix and export all your audio tracks down to a WAV file. SONAR provides a very convenient feature expressly for this purpose, called *Export Audio*. This feature takes any number of original audio tracks (preserving their volume, pan, and effects settings) and mixes them into a single stereo WAV file. Here's how to use it:

1. Mute any of the MIDI tracks in your project and any audio tracks that you don't want included in the exported WAV file. Then choose Edit > Select > None (or press Ctrl+Shift+A) to remove any data selections. If you have only a part of the project selected, then only that part will be exported. This can come in handy if you want to create a short demo of the project to be used as an excerpt, if you plan to sell the song on the Internet.
2. Choose File > Export > Audio to open the Export Audio dialog box, as shown in Figure 13.5.

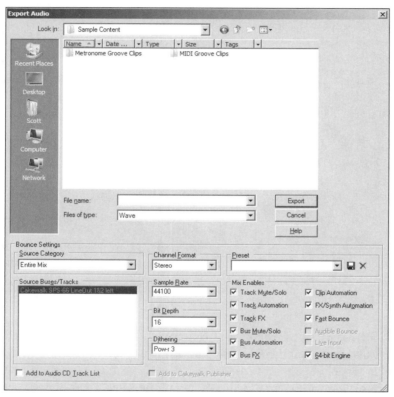

Figure 13.5 You use the Export Audio dialog box to mix and export your tracks.
Source: Cakewalk®, Inc.

3. From the Look In list, select the folder into which you want to save the WAV file. Then type a name for the file in the File Name field.
4. Choose the file type from the Files of Type list. In this case, use the Wave option. For information on the other file options available, check out Chapter 18, "Audio for Video with SONAR."
5. Select the Channel Format you want to use. You can mix your audio tracks to a single stereo file, two mono files (that, when combined, create a stereo file), or a single mono file. You can also set the bit depth and sampling rate by using the Bit Depth and Sample Rate parameters.

BURNING TO CD: If you plan to burn your project to CD, then choose the Stereo option for the Channel Format parameter, the 16-Bit option for the Bit Depth parameter, and the 44100 option for the Sample Rate parameter. This will give you a single stereo WAV file with a bit depth of 16 and a sampling rate of 44.1kHz, which is what you need for audio CD burning.

6. For the Source Category parameter, choose the Entire Mix option. You can also choose the Main Outputs option and then select the appropriate audio interface output (the one connected to your monitors/speakers) in the Source Buses/Tracks area. Either option should export the same audio that you hear when playing the project, but if Entire Mix doesn't produce the desired results, try Main Outputs.

SOURCE CATEGORY – TRACKS OR BUSES: In addition to exporting an entire mix, SONAR allows for exporting of individual tracks and buses by choosing either Tracks or Buses for the Source Category. You can then select which tracks or buses you want to export via the Source Buses/Tracks area. When you do this, SONAR will create a separate audio file for each track or bus, depending on your selection(s). These options can come in handy for a variety of situations. Individual tracks are useful for sending tracks to a studio for mixing, or for sharing tracks when collaborating with other musicians. Individual buses (also called *stems*) are useful for creating audio files for each major part of a project, such as drums, vocals, guitars, etc. The stems can then be used for remixes, minus-one accompaniment mixes, or music licensing.

7. If the original bit depth of your project is 16-bit, then set the Dithering parameter to None. If the original bit depth is higher than 16-bit, you need to choose a dithering method. Why? Because converting audio from a high bit depth down to a lower bit depth can introduce harmonic distortion, making the sound less desirable. Dithering applies special mathematical processes to the data and smoothes out this noise so that it can't be heard. In this case, I would choose the Pow-r 3 option because it provides the most accurate processing. Pow-r 3 also requires the most computing power, so if it overtaxes your PC, try using Pow-r 2 or Pow-r 1.

8. Leave all the Mix Enables options activated to ensure that your new WAV file will sound exactly the same when played back as the original audio tracks. One exception might be the 64-bit Engine option. If your PC can handle it, I recommend activating the option because it will provide the most accurate processing, but if your PC gets overtaxed, deactivate the option.

MIX ENABLES FOR ALTERNATE EXPORTING: In conjunction with the Source Category, the Mix Enables options allow you to export different configurations of tracks/buses. While the Source Category lets you choose which tracks/buses to export, the Mix Enables let you choose whether or not those tracks will include automation or effects. One situation where this can be useful is for exporting raw tracks (without effects or automation) when you want to share or license the originally recorded tracks. Put a check mark next to a Mix Enable option to include it in the export.

The Mix Enables options provide the following functionality:

▷ **Track Mute/Solo:** When activated, muted tracks are not included in the export. If any tracks are soloed, then only those tracks are included in the export. You'll normally want this option activated, unless you're exporting individual tracks and need to include those that are muted.

▷ **Bus Mute/Solo:** This option works the same as Track Mute/Solo, but with buses.

▷ **Track Automation:** When activated, track volume and pan parameters, as well as automation, are included in the export. You'll normally want this option activated, unless you're exporting individual tracks and you want only the raw tracks with no volume/pan settings or changes.

> **Clip Automation:** This option works similarly to Track Automation, except that it controls whether or not the clip gain and pan envelope automation is included with the export.

> **Bus Automation** This option works the same as Track Automation, but with buses.

> **FX/Synth Automation:** This option provides control over just effects and synth automation. So, if you have other types of automation in tracks and you want to keep that, but you don't want effects and synth automation, you can keep the other Automation options activated while deactivating this option. Normally, however, you'll want to keep this option activated.

> **Track FX and Bus FX:** These two options control whether or not effects added to the FX bins in tracks/ buses are included in the export. Normally, you'll want these options activated, unless you're exporting raw tracks/buses.

> **Fast Bounce:** If you have trouble exporting, you can try deactivating this option to do a real-time export (needed for some software synths).

> **Audible Bounce:** Activate this option when doing a real-time export to listen to the project as it's being exported. Because the project may sound louder than expected, depending on your other export options, it's a good idea to turn down your monitor volume before you begin the export.

> **Live Input:** If you choose to do a real-time export, you can also include any live performance input by activating this option. Personally, I haven't found any use for this option, so I always keep it turned off.

9. If you plan to use SONAR's built-in CD burning function (explained later in this chapter), you can have your exported WAV file automatically added to the burning list by activating the Add to Audio CD Track List option.

10. If you want to save your current Export Audio dialog settings, you can do so via the Preset area. Just type in a name in the Preset field and click the Save button (shown with a floppy disk icon). Cakewalk has also included a number of export presets that you can choose by clicking the down arrow to the right of the Preset field.

11. Click the Export button, and SONAR will mix all your audio tracks down to a new WAV file.

When you're done, you should have a WAV file that you can use along with your CD recording software to create an audio CD.

Burning CDs with SONAR

Even though SONAR provides its own CD burning capabilities, I recommend using some other burning software if you need to create an audio CD that is compatible with most CD players. The reason is because SONAR only provides Track-at-Once burning, rather than Disc-at-Once burning. Track-at-Once burning can be useful if you just want to create a demo CD to test your mix in different environments, but it's not good for creating a final master disc of your album.

TAO VERSUS DAO: If you plan to have your CD duplicated professionally, you should have all your audio files together and burned to CD all in one session using Disk-at-Once (DAO) burning. This method of burning writes and closes a CD in one operation without turning the CD burning laser on and off between CD tracks. If you use Track-at-Once (TAO) burning, the CD burning laser is turned on and off between tracks to create 'links' between them. These 'links' will show up as errors when the disc manufacturer tries to create a master disc from your CD-R disc.

If you would still like to use SONAR's CD burning feature, follow these steps:

1. In SONAR, choose Utilities > Burn Audio CD to open the Audio CD Burner window (see Figure 13.6).
2. Use the Target Drive menu to select your CD burner.

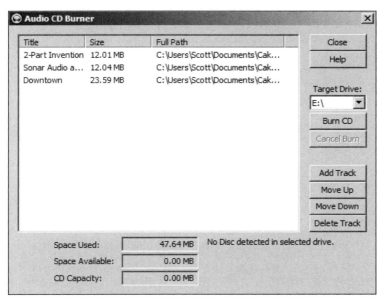

Figure 13.6 Use SONAR's Audio CD Burner to create your own audio CD.
Source: Cakewalk®, Inc.

3. Insert a blank CD-R disc into your CD burner. The Audio CD Burner will recognize the blank disc and display CD Capacity at the bottom of the window.
4. Click the Add Track button, and in the Open dialog box, choose a WAV file to add to the CD track list. You can also choose multiple files at once by holding down the Ctrl key. Click Open. Your files will be displayed in the CD track list.
5. To change the order of the tracks, select a track and click the Move Up or Move Down button.
6. To delete one or more tracks, select the track(s) and click the Delete Track button. As you manipulate the track list, you will see the Space Used and Space Available shown at the bottom of the window, which gives you an idea of how many more tracks you can include on the disc.
7. When your track list is complete, click the Burn CD button to create your new audio disc. As the disc is created, the Audio CD Burner will display its progress at the bottom of the window.
8. When your disc is finished, it will automatically be ejected from your CD burner. From here, you can create another copy of the same CD by inserting another blank CD-R and clicking Burn CD again, or you can click Close.

CD ARCHITECT: For burning professional, Disc-at-Once audio CDs, I personally like to use CD Architect from Sony. It provides perfect Red Book audio CDs, which is the specification needed when creating discs for duplication. In addition, it allows you to add UPC (Universal Product Code) and ISRC (International Standard Recording Code) codes to your discs (if your CD burner supports those options). UPC and ISRC codes are required if you plan to sell your CDs via retail, such as through Amazon or CD Baby. Go to **garrigus.com/?CDArchitect** for more information on CD Architect.

14

Surround Sound with SONAR

I N ADDITION TO CREATING A STEREO MIX OF YOUR PROJECT, you may also want to create a surround sound mix. Surround sound is extensively used in movie soundtracks, as well as soundtracks for games. And these days, it is being used more and more for audio-only projects. You can create your own surround sound music with the special surround mixing tools provided by SONAR. From there, you can burn your music to CD or DVD and share it with others for playback on any home theater system.

SURROUND SOUND BACKGROUND: Before reading the rest of this chapter, you may want to read some background and overview information about surround sound. Check out the following resources:

Introduction to Surround Sound

www.digifreq.com/digifreq/article.asp?ID=21

Setting Up Your Studio for Surround Sound

www.digifreq.com/digifreq/article.asp?ID=22

Surround Sound Mixing Techniques

www.digifreq.com/digifreq/article.asp?ID=23

More Audio and Surround Articles

www.digifreq.com/digifreq/articles.asp

Setting Up Your Studio

Working with surround sound isn't just a simple matter of changing a few settings in SONAR and, like magic, having a surround sound mix of your project. There are certain steps you need to take in order to start working with surround sound. The first step will be to invest your money in some new studio equipment, including a new sound card and new monitors (speakers).

Surround Sound Cards

I'm going to assume you'll be working with a format of surround sound known as *5.1 Surround Sound*. There are many different surround sound formats, but 5.1 is the most common and is used in audio for DVDs and video games, as well as DVD-A (DVD Audio) discs (special music-only DVDs). As such, you will need a sound card that provides six separate mono audio outputs (or three stereo outputs). If your card already provides this number of outputs or more, then you're all set in the sound card department.

If your card doesn't provide at least six outputs, you'll need to invest in a new card. For demonstration purposes, I'm using an older M-Audio Revolution 7.1, but you can get both professional and prosumer cards from a number of different manufacturers.

Surround Sound Monitors

In addition to a multi-output sound card, you'll need five matched monitors and a subwoofer (a special monitor for playing low-frequency audio, often called the *Low-Frequency Effects monitor*) to work in the 5.1 surround format. By matched monitors, I mean they should all be identical. For example, I have two KRK V4 monitors for creating stereo mixes in my studio. In order to expand that for 5.1 surround, I would have to purchase three more V4 monitors. This is the best way to go for a professional setup, but it can get very expensive.

You may want to ease your way into surround and get a prosumer monitor setup instead. I'm currently using the Z-5500 Digital 5.1 5-Piece Speaker System from Logitech. The cost of the system is about $250, but it provides everything you need to monitor in 5.1 surround. By everything, I mean five monitors plus a subwoofer, six analog inputs, two digital inputs, a computerized controller, and even a nifty remote control. On top of all that, it provides built-in Dolby and DTS decoding. Go to www.digifreq.com/digifreq/newsinfo.asp?NewsID=2567 for more information about the Logitech system.

Surround Monitor Setup

Once you have your monitoring equipment, you'll need to set it up. If you're thinking you can simply plop the speakers around your studio and get a good surround listening image, think again. The five monitors need to be placed in a certain pattern around the room, with equal distance from your listening position; otherwise, you won't get a clear indication of where the musical elements are located in your mix during playback. Here's how to do it:

1. Place the center channel monitor dead center behind your mixing console or on top of your computer monitor. When you sit down to mix your tracks, you should see the center channel monitor centered right in front of you.
2. Get a microphone stand and place it in the same position where you will be sitting when mixing your audio.
3. Use a tape measure to measure the distance from the microphone stand to the center channel monitor.
4. Get a roll of string and tie the free end of the string to the microphone stand. Unroll the string, starting at the microphone stand and ending at the location of the center channel monitor. Then cut the string. This marks the distance you will use to position all of the other monitors.
5. Get a compass (one that includes degree markings). At the microphone stand position, point the compass at the center channel monitor. Then turn left so that the compass reading changes 30 degrees.
6. Extend the string in that 30-degree direction. Now you have the location for your left channel monitor.
7. Reposition the compass so that it points at the center channel monitor again. Then turn 30 degrees to the right and find the location for your right channel monitor.
8. To find the locations for the right and left surround monitors, follow the same procedure with the compass and the string. This time, however, move 120 degrees to the left and right to find the left and right surround monitor locations, respectively.

When you're done positioning the monitors, they should be placed at precise locations along an imaginary circle, as shown in Figure 14.1. This is the standard 5.1 monitor positioning, according to the SMPTE (Society of Motion Picture and Television Engineers) and ITU (International Telecommunication Union) organizations. Since low frequencies are not directional, you can place the LFE monitor anywhere on the floor. Mine is placed on the floor to one side of my DAW (Digital Audio Workstation) desk.

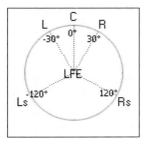

Figure 14.1 This is the standard 5.1 surround monitor positioning, according to the SMPTE and ITU.
Source: Cakewalk®, Inc.

Surround Monitor Calibration

Even after you've placed your monitors correctly, you're still not quite finished with setting them up. You also have to calibrate them. This means that you need to make sure they are all set to the same volume level so that when you are mixing, you don't get misled by how loud an audio track may be playing when you pan it around the surround sound field.

You'll need two things to calibrate your monitors: a pink noise source and an SPL (Sound Pressure Level) meter. For pink noise, you can use a test tone CD, a tone generator, or even an audio editor that includes a built-in noise generator. If you don't have any of these, you can download a pink noise audio file from www.whitenoisemp3s.com/free-white-noise. For the SPL meter, you'll have to spend a few bucks, but you don't need anything expensive. Many audio engineers use basic meters that can be bought for about $50. Go to www.digifreq.com/?CM140 to check out the Galaxy Audio CM140 Checkmate Sound Level SPL Meter. Once you have these two items, you can calibrate your monitors by doing the following:

> **MONITOR CONNECTIONS:** Before you can calibrate your monitors, you need to connect them to your sound card. Since there are many different sound cards and monitoring systems on the market, I cannot walk you through this process. Read the documentation that came with your sound card and monitors. These documents should provide you with all the information you need to properly connect your monitors to your sound card.

1. Set your sound card output levels to 0dB. For example, if you are using the M-Audio Revolution, open its control panel. Then, in the Output Mixer section of the panel, set all the outputs to a volume level of 0dB (see Figure 14.2). In addition, if your sound card has a surround sound configuration option, be sure to set that as well. For this example, set up your card for 5.1 surround sound.

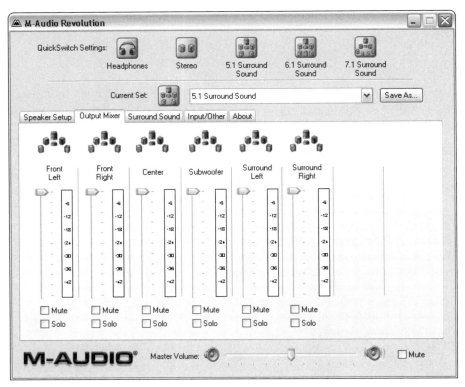

Figure 14.2 Set your sound card output levels to 0dB.
Source: M-Audio®, Inc.

2. Change the settings on your SPL meter to Slow Scale and C weighting. Refer to the documentation that came with your meter for explanations of these settings if you need them.
3. Play pink noise through the left-front monitor.

> **LOGITECH TEST TONE:** If you're using the Logitech Z-5500 Digital 5.1 5-Piece Speaker System I mentioned earlier, you can use the built-in noise generator. Just press the Test button on your remote control. The Logitech system will cycle noise through each of the monitors automatically.

4. While sitting at your mix position, raise the SPL meter to ear level and point it at the left-front monitor.
5. Adjust the monitor volume so that the SPL meter reads 85dB.
6. Repeat Steps 3 through 5 for each of the remaining monitors, except for the LFE monitor.
7. Point the SPL meter at the LFE monitor and adjust the volume of the monitor so that the meter reads 90dB. The reading needs to be slightly higher because most SPL meters don't register low frequencies very well. The higher adjustment compensates for this shortcoming.

Setting Up SONAR for Surround

When your studio configuration is complete, you're ready to start working with surround sound in SONAR. The first step in creating a surround sound project is to either open an existing project file or create a new project. SONAR's surround sound settings need to be configured for each individual project that you create, but you can save your settings for use in multiple projects if you'd like.

Surround Project Options

After you've either created a new project or opened an existing one, choose Edit > Preferences. In the Preferences dialog box, click the Advanced option and then choose Surround in the Project section to access the surround sound preferences (see Figure 14.3).

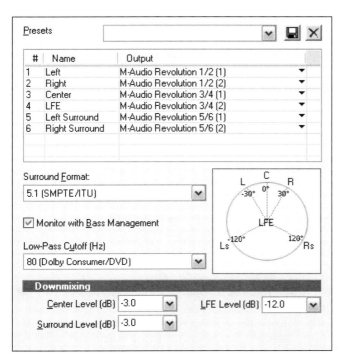

Figure 14.3 Use the Preferences – Surround dialog box to adjust your project's surround settings.
Source: Cakewalk®, Inc.

This dialog box is used to adjust the initial surround settings for your project. These settings include the surround format, sound card outputs, bass management, and downmixing.

Surround Format

Even though I've been primarily talking about the 5.1 surround sound format, there are actually many different formats available—even different 5.1 formats. SONAR provides support for these multiple formats and includes preset options from which you can choose. When you choose a surround format, what you are actually doing is specifying the number of monitors that are in use, the position of those monitors, and how they are connected to your sound card. With the Preferences – Surround dialog box already open, use the Surround Format list to choose a format (see Figure 14.4).

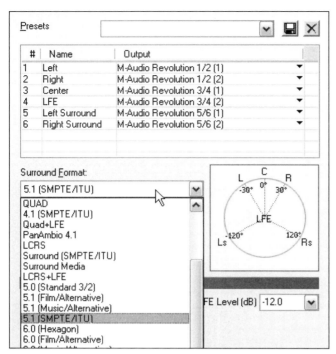

Figure 14.4 Use the Surround Format drop-down list to choose a surround format for your project.
Source: Cakewalk®, Inc.

Notice that as you choose different formats, the diagram (shown to the right of the Surround Format drop-down list) changes as well. This diagram displays the number of monitors required for the chosen format. It also shows how those monitors should be positioned around your mixing location. For demonstration purposes, I'll be using the default format: 5.1 (SMPTE/ITU).

Surround Sound Card Outputs

After you've chosen a format, you also need to configure your sound card outputs so that SONAR knows where to send the appropriate audio data to the monitors in your surround setup. You do this by using the sound card output list in the top half of the Preferences – Surround dialog box. This section of the box will list all of the monitors required to support the surround format that you have chosen. For example, with the 5.1 (SMPTE/ITU) format chosen, you'll see six monitors listed by number (#) and name. To the right of each monitor is shown a sound card output. To change the output for a monitor, click the down arrow to the right of the output and choose a new one from the list (see Figure 14.5).

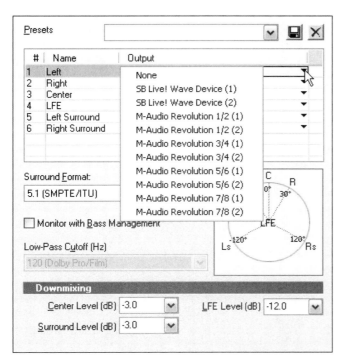

Figure 14.5 Configure your sound card outputs in the Preferences – Surround dialog box.
Source: Cakewalk®, Inc.

When using a sound card such as the M-Audio Revolution (which provides multiple stereo outputs with individual left/right settings), you'll see the same sound card output listed twice, but each will have a different number in parentheses next to it. For example, M-Audio Revolution 1/2 (1) means that you are choosing the left channel of the first stereo output of the sound card. The number in parentheses tells you if you're choosing the left (1) or right (2) channel.

Bass Management

When your surround sound project is played on a home theater system, all the frequencies below a certain point are routed to the LFE monitor (subwoofer). This is because the smaller monitors that take care of the rest of the surround field are not large enough to reproduce very low frequencies. Because of this, you need to listen to your project in the same way. The bass management option provided by SONAR emulates the low-frequency playback of a home theater system.

To activate bass management for your project, put a check mark next to the Monitor with Bass Management option in the Preferences – Surround dialog box. Then choose a cutoff point (the point below which frequencies will be routed to the LFE sound card channel) from the Low-Pass Cutoff drop-down list. The standard for playback on a home theater system is 80Hz, but there are other options available if you need them, as shown in Figure 14.6.

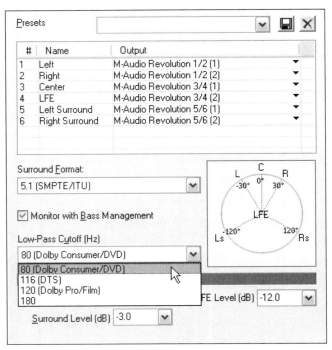

Figure 14.6 You should monitor your project with bass management so you can hear what it will sound like when played by consumers.
Source: Cakewalk®, Inc.

Surround Sound Bussing

One last thing you need to do before you can start mixing your project in surround sound is to add at least one surround bus to your project. There are a number of different ways to add a surround bus.

The Insert Menu

To add a surround bus to your project using the Insert menu, choose Insert > Surround Bus (see Figure 14.7).

Figure 14.7 You can use the Insert menu to add a surround bus.
Source: Cakewalk®, Inc.

The Bus Pane

You can also use the Bus pane in the Track view to add a new surround bus to your project. In the Bus pane, right-click and choose Insert Surround Bus (see Figure 14.8).

Figure 14.8 You can also add a surround bus via the Bus pane in the Track view.
Source: Cakewalk®, Inc.

Insert Send

An indirect way of adding a new surround bus to a project is to do it at the same time you are inserting a new send into an existing track. Right-click an existing audio track and choose Insert Send > New Surround Bus.

Track Output

Another way to add a new surround bus to a project is simply to assign the output of an audio track to a new bus. SONAR creates the new bus automatically. Just click the Output parameter of the audio track and choose New Surround Bus.

Console View

One last way to add a new surround bus is by using the Bus menu in the Console view. Just choose Bus > Insert Surround Bus. You can also right-click over the background of Bus area in the Console view and choose Insert Surround Bus.

> **TRACK ASSIGNMENT:** If you don't use the track output method of creating a new surround bus, then you will have to manually assign the output of your audio tracks to the new bus or create a new bus for each track. You can also assign the output of your tracks to the Surround Main, which is a virtual main output dedicated to surround sound in SONAR. The Surround Main simply routes your audio directly to your sound card outputs as they were assigned in the Preferences – Surround dialog box. The drawback to this method is that you won't be able to assign any surround effects to your tracks. You need to use a surround bus to utilize surround effects.

Surround Sound Mixing

After you've created one or more surround buses for your project, you need to assign the outputs of your audio tracks to those buses, if you haven't done so already. When you assign the output of an audio track to a surround bus, you'll notice a number of changes made to the track. One change is the display of the output meters. Instead of two channel meters, you'll see multiple channel meters. The number of meters depends on the surround format you've chosen and how many channels exist in that format. For example, for the 5.1 (SMPTE/ITU) format, you will have a six-channel meter, as shown in Figure 14.9.

Figure 14.9 SONAR provides multichannel output meters for audio tracks when mixing in surround.
Source: Cakewalk®, Inc.

Surround Sound Panning

Another change made to the audio track is the replacement of the usual Pan parameter with the Surround Panner. Instead of simply panning between two stereo speakers, you can now pan your audio track around a circular sound field between multiple speakers (the number of which depends on the surround format you are using). The Surround Panner comes in a variety of sizes, depending on where it is being accessed within SONAR.

The Micro Surround Panner

When working in surround, the normal Pan parameter of an audio track becomes the Micro Surround Panner (see Figure 14.10).

Figure 14.10 The normal Pan parameter of an audio track transforms into the Micro Surround Panner.
Source: Cakewalk®, Inc.

By clicking and dragging within the Micro Surround Panner, you can change the surround panning location of your audio track. As you drag your mouse, you'll notice the Surround Pan Angle and Focus parameters being displayed and changed.

To the right of the Micro Surround Panner, you'll see the LFE Send parameter. This parameter determines how much of the signal from the current audio track you would like to send to the LFE channel. This can come in handy if you want to dedicate an audio track for effects that contain low-frequency content like thunder claps and such.

The Small Surround Panner

If you add an aux send to an audio track that is routed to a surround bus, the send will provide a Small Surround Panner, as shown in Figure 14.11. This works in a similar fashion to the Micro Surround Panner and provides an LFE send, as well as a bus send level and pre/post parameter like normal aux sends.

Figure 14.11 The Small Surround Panner is displayed on an aux send that is routed to a surround bus.
Source: Cakewalk®, Inc.

The Medium Surround Panner

As with the Micro Surround Panner, the Medium Surround Panner also replaces the normal Pan parameter on an audio track, but in this case, the Medium Surround Panner is displayed in the Inspector and the audio channel strip for that track in the Console view (see Figure 14.12).

Figure 14.12 The Medium Surround Panner is displayed in the Track and Console views.
Source: Cakewalk®, Inc.

The Medium Surround Panner works the same way as the previous Panners. Click and drag within the Panner to pan your audio track in the surround field. One additional feature of the Medium Surround Panner is its capability to mute individual monitors (speakers) in the surround field. You will see these monitors represented within the Panner as small white boxes. Just click a box to mute that monitor. Click the box again to unmute the monitor.

MUTING MONITORS: You can also mute monitors by right-clicking in the Panner and choosing Mute [*name of monitor*]. This technique will work with all the other Panners mentioned as well.

The Large Surround Panner

To give you the most detailed access to the surround parameters for an audio track, SONAR provides the Large Surround Panner (see Figure 14.13). To access the Large Surround Panner, just right-click one of the other Panners and choose Open Surround Panner.

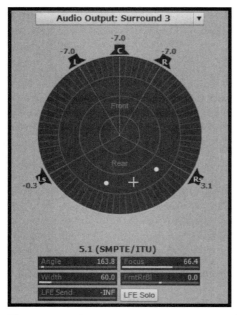

Figure 14.13 Use the Large Surround Panner for more detailed changes to surround parameters.
Source: Cakewalk®, Inc.

CHANGING TRACKS: Once open, you can change the track assignment for the Large Surround Panner by clicking the track name bar located at the top of the window.

In the top portion of the Large Surround Panner window, you will see a circular graphic representation of the surround sound field. Around this field, all the monitors are shown as small speaker symbols and positioned according to the surround format you have chosen. You can click the speaker symbols to mute and unmute the appropriate monitors just like you did with the Medium Surround Panner.

Inside the surround field, a small crosshair icon represents the pan position of the current track in the surround sound field. As with the other Panners, you can simply click and drag your mouse within the field to change the pan position. As you do this, you will see the crosshair move, and you will also see the numerical values change next to each monitor. These values represent the volume (in dB) of the audio track within each of the monitors.

In addition to the volume changes, you'll notice some other parameters changing in the bottom portion of the Large Surround Panner window. To change any of these parameters, just click and drag your mouse over the appropriate slider. Drag left or right to make a change. Double-click a parameter to return it to its default value. You can also type a new value by selecting the parameter and pressing the Enter key.

These parameters represent the pan position of your audio track in the surround field, the stereo width of your track, and the volume balance between the front and rear monitors of the surround field. You'll also find an LFE send parameter (just like with the other Panners) and an LFE solo button so you can quickly check only the sound coming from the LFE monitor.

Angle and Focus

The Angle and Focus parameters work together to designate the pan position of the audio track in the surround field. This is the reason both parameters change when you drag the crosshair around in the surround field. The Angle parameter designates the circular position of the audio track panning within the surround field. You can set the Angle parameter from −180 to 0 to +180 degrees. Notice that when you change the Angle parameter, the crosshair moves around in a circle within the surround field.

The Focus parameter designates how close the pan position of the audio track will be to the center of the surround field. You can set the Focus parameter from 0 to 100. A setting of 0 will put the pan position at the exact center of the surround field. A setting of 100 will put the pan position at the outer edge of the surround field (closest to the surrounding monitors).

Width

The Width parameter designates the width of the stereo audio track within the surround field. In the surround field graphic, the width is represented by two dots—one for the left channel and one for the right channel of the stereo track. You can set the Width parameter from 0 to 360 degrees. The larger the value, the farther apart the stereo channels sound from one another. The smaller the value, the closer they sound. For example, a value of 0 will essentially make the track sound like a mono track because the stereo channels are right next to each other. Using a value of 0, you can make the pan position of the track sound like it's coming from a single focused point in the surround field.

Front/Rear Balance (FrntRrBl)

There may be times when you've found just the right pan position for an audio track in the surround field, but you would like to change its overall volume as it pertains to the front and rear monitors. This is where the Front/Rear Balance parameter (abbreviated as FrntRrBl in the Panner window) can be used. The value for this parameter ranges from −100 to 0 to +100. The lower the value, the lower the volume of the front monitors. The higher the value, the lower the value of the rear monitors. A value of 0 makes the front/rear volumes equal.

Surround Panning Scenarios

Just to give you a few examples of how you can position an audio track within the surround field, I'll go through a few scenarios and show you what settings you need to achieve them.

Exact Center

To place your audio track in the exact center of the surround field, set the Angle, Focus, Width, and FrntRrBl parameters to 0.

Pinpoint Location

To place your audio track at an exact pinpoint location in the surround field, set the Width and FrntRrBl parameters to 0. Now adjust the pan position by either changing the Angle and Focus parameters manually or clicking and dragging your mouse in the surround field graphic. This scenario also lets you make your audio track sound like it is coming directly from one of the monitors in the surround field. To do this, set the Focus parameter to 100 and then adjust the Angle parameter so that the pan position is exactly in front of the monitor from which you want the audio track to be heard.

Front and Rear Stereo

To make your audio track sound like an ordinary stereo track coming from the front monitors, set the Angle parameter to 0, the Focus parameter to 100, and the FrntRrBl parameter to 0. Then adjust the Width parameter so that the two dots line up with the front left and right monitors. To do this with the rear monitors, just change the Angle parameter to 180. Then adjust the Width so that the green dots line up with the rear left and right monitors.

Side Stereo

To make a stereo audio track sound like it is being played in stereo on the side of the surround field, set the Angle parameter to 90 to place the track on the right of the field or set the parameter to −90 to place the track on the left side of the field. Set the Focus parameter to 100 and the FrntRrBl parameter to 0. Then adjust the Width parameter to your liking (a good setting is about 60).

> **SURROUND AUTOMATION AND GROUPING** Automation and grouping for surround parameters work the same as for any other parameter. Just right-click the parameter and choose Automation Write Enable to designate the movements of that parameter for recording. Then follow the steps outlined in Chapter 12 for recording automation. In addition, you can arm all parameters for the Surround Panner at the same time by right-clicking the surround field graphic.
>
> For grouping, right-click the parameter and choose Group > [*group letter*] to group that parameter. Then follow the instructions provided in Chapter 12 covering how to use SONAR's grouping features.

Surround Sound Effects

Working with effects in surround is similar to that of stereo, except that in surround you're dealing with multiple channels rather than just two. You can apply effects evenly to all surround channels, or you can apply an effect to a single surround channel. The only caveat is that you must apply surround effects to a surround bus. Surround effects cannot be applied to an audio track without using a surround bus. Because of this, there will probably be many times where you will want to assign a new surround bus to each of your audio tracks so that you can apply different effects to each track.

To apply an effect to a surround bus, you simply follow the same procedure as applying an effect to a stereo bus. Just right-click in the Fx bin of the surround bus and choose the effect you would like to apply or drag-and-drop an effect from SONAR's Browser.

Dedicated Surround Effects

SONAR provides one dedicated surround effect for use in your projects: the Sonitus Surround Compressor, which is based on its stereo version. Be sure to read through that material (Chapter 11) in order to learn how to use this effect. There are a few basic differences, though, and I will explain those here.

The Sonitus Surround Compressor provides four separate compressor effects in one. Each effect provides the same parameters. The difference between the surround and the stereo versions comes into play when you are assigning the surround channels to each of the four compressor effects provided. When you open the Surround Compressor, you will see four compressor select buttons located at the top of the dialog box (see Figure 14.14). Initially, all the surround channels are assigned to the same compressor. You can leave them this way if you want. This will let you apply the same compression effect to all the surround channels.

Figure 14.14 The Sonitus Surround Compressor provides four compression effects.
Source: Cakewalk®, Inc.

To assign a surround channel to a different compressor effect, click the down arrow next to one of the effects and choose the surround channel(s) you want to use (see Figure 14.15).

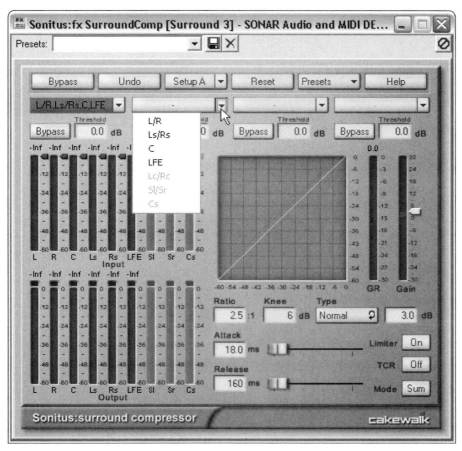

Figure 14.15 Use the down arrow next to an effect to assign its surround channels.
Source: Cakewalk®, Inc.

You'll notice that each effect is given its own color. From left to right. you'll see red, blue, green, and orange. When you assign a surround channel to a different effect, its input controls and its compression graph take on those colors, which lets you tell at a glance which effect matches which surround channel.

Other than those differences, the Sonitus Surround Compressor works the same way as the stereo version. The surround version provides some presets from which you can learn. Just click the Presets button at the top of the dialog box and choose a preset from the list.

Using Stereo Effects in Surround

If SONAR simply provided one surround effect out of its entire arsenal, it wouldn't provide much power, would it? Even though there is only one dedicated surround effect included with SONAR, you can actually use all of SONAR's effects in your surround projects using some special built-in features.

When you assign a stereo effect (mono effects work, too) to a surround bus, SONAR automatically creates multiple instances of that effect for each of the surround channels you are using. For example, when using the 5.1 surround format, SONAR will assign the front left and right channels to the left and right channels of the first stereo effect, the rear left and right channels to the left and right channels of the second stereo effect, the center channel to the left channel of the third stereo effect, and the LFE channel to the left channel of the fourth stereo effect. All of these controls are available in a single effect window, as shown in Figure 14.16.

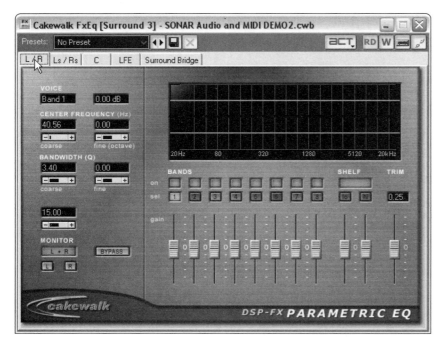

Figure 14.16 One effect window holds multiple instances of the effect to provide for all the surround channels.
Source: Cakewalk®, Inc.

Each effect instance can be accessed by clicking the appropriate tab at the top of the effect window. All the controls for each instance are identical, and the effect works just like its stereo version. In addition, all of the parameters for each instance are linked by default. This means that if you change a parameter on one instance, that same parameter will change on all the other instances. Having the parameters linked makes it easy to be sure the effect sounds the same on all the surround channels.

If you want to have the effect sound different on certain surround channels, you can unlink the parameters for each instance. First, click the tab for the effect instance you would like to change; then click the Unlink Automation Controls button at the top-right of the effect window (see Figure 14.17). Now the parameters for that instance can be changed, and the equivalent parameters in the other instances will remain the same.

Figure 14.17 Click the Unlink Automation Controls button to change the parameters for one instance and not the others.
Source: Cakewalk®, Inc.

As far as the effect parameters themselves, they work exactly the same as their stereo versions.

The Surround Bridge

One other thing that makes using stereo effects in a surround project unique is SONAR's Surround Bridge feature. This is actually the feature that uses stereo effects in surround and automatically creates the multiple effects instances when you apply an effect to a surround bus. But there may be times when you want to change the order of the effect instances and assign the instances to different surround channels. You can do this by clicking the Surround Bridge tab in the effect window (see Figure 14.18).

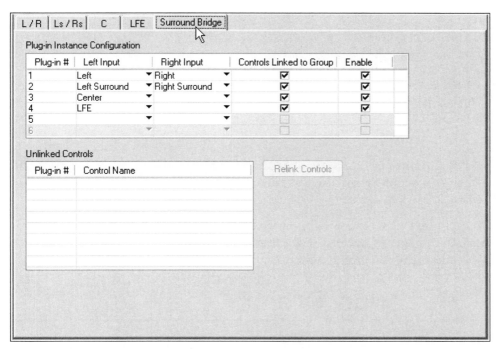

Figure 14.18 Click the Surround Bridge tab to access the Surround Bridge settings.
Source: Cakewalk®, Inc.

Under the Surround Bridge tab, you'll see the Plug-in Instance Configuration section showing how each of the effect instances is configured. The number of the instance is shown in the first column. The second column shows which surround channel is assigned to the left input of the instance. The third column shows which surround channel is assigned to the right input of the instance. To change a channel assignment, just click the down arrow next to the channel and make a new choice (see Figure 14.19). For example, you may want each surround channel to have its own effect instance. You would simply click the left channel input of a blank effect instance and assign it to a surround channel. This would remove the surround channel's current instance assignment and create a new instance tab at the top of the window for the new surround channel assignment.

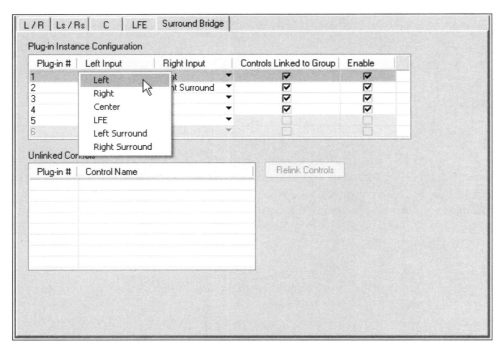

Figure 14.19 Change surround channel effect instance assignments with a simple click.
Source: Cakewalk®, Inc.

You can also quickly link or unlink all the controls in an effect instance by adding or removing its check mark in the column labeled Controls Linked to Group. In addition, if you want to disable an effect instance, just remove its check mark in the Enable column. Add the check mark to enable the instance again.

One last feature of the Surround Bridge is the Unlinked Controls section. When you select an effect instance in the Plug-in Instance Configuration section, the Unlinked Controls section lists all unlinked controls for that instance. You can relink any of the listed controls by clicking the control to select it and then clicking the Relink Controls button.

Exporting Your Surround Project

After you've added effects and mixed your tracks into a superb, surround masterpiece, you can use SONAR's export features to save your project as a multichannel audio file, which can then be burned to CD or DVD. Before exporting, however, be sure to check the downmix of your project.

Downmixing

When mixing a project in surround sound, you should always keep in the back of your mind the fact that your surround mix might be heard in stereo at one time or another. The reason for this is that listeners could select the stereo mode on their home theater system when playing your music. If they do this, the home theater system automatically mixes the six surround channels (in a 5.1 surround mix) down to the two stereo channels. The center surround channel is added to the left and right stereo channels equally. The left and right surround channels are also added to the left and right stereo channels. And the LFE channel is either added or, in some instances, just removed. Because of this, you should always listen to your surround mix in stereo when you're finished. Here's how to check the downmix of your surround project:

1. If you don't have one, insert a stereo bus into your project by right-clicking in the Bus pane and choosing Insert Stereo Bus.
2. For every surround bus that you have in your project, assign its output to the new stereo bus.
3. Choose Edit > Preferences. Choose the Advanced option. Then click Surround under the Project heading.
4. In the Downmixing section, choose the volume levels (in dB) at which you want the center channel, surround channels, and LFE channel mixed into the left and right stereo channels. The default settings usually work well, but every project is different, so you'll have to try the different settings to see which ones work with your project.

> **CONFIGURABLE DOWNMIXING SETTINGS:** Even though SONAR provides a number of default downmixing values from which to choose, you can actually type any dB level into the downmixing parameters that you would like. Just click inside a parameter and type in a new value.

5. Click OK.
6. Listen to your project through the new stereo bus. If it doesn't sound quite right, either adjust your mix or adjust the downmixing settings.
7. When you've got the right mix, you can export your project to a stereo file if you'd like, and SONAR will take into account your downmixing settings.

After you've finished downmixing, you can set your surround bus outputs back to their original values.

Exporting to Multichannel WAV or WMA

To let others hear your surround project, SONAR exports your project to a multichannel WAV file or Windows Media File. Here is how it's done:

1. Choose Edit > Select > None to make sure no tracks are selected if you want to export the entire project. Choose File > Export > Audio to open the Export Audio dialog box.
2. Set the Look In parameter to the folder on your hard drive in which you would like to save your file.
3. Type in a File Name for the file.
4. Select a Files of Type for your file. If you plan on burning your project to DVD in the DVD-Audio or DVD-Video format, export it as a WAV file by choosing the Wave format. If your project will be played using the Windows Media Player, you can export it as a Windows Media File by choosing the Windows Media Advanced Streaming Format.
5. More than likely, you have your surround buses all being output to the Surround Main (otherwise you wouldn't be able to mix in surround). So set the Source Category to Main Outputs.
6. Select Surround Main in the Source Buses/Tracks list.
7. Choose Multichannel for the Channel Format.

8. Depending on what you used for your project sampling rate, set the Sampling Rate to that same value here. You can use a sampling rate up to 96,000 for 5.1 surround in the DVD-Audio format.

9. Depending on what you used for your project bit depth, set the Bit Depth to that same value here. You can use a bit depth up to 24-bit for 5.1 surround in the DVD-Audio format.

10. In order to make sure all your automation and effects get included in your exported file, be sure to put check marks next to all the options in the Mix Enables section.

11. Click Export. If you chose the Wave format for your file, then SONAR will export the file, and you are now finished. If you chose the Windows Media Advanced Streaming Format file, there are some additional steps.

12. After you click Export, SONAR will display the Windows Media Format Encode Options dialog box.

13. Enter the information for your project in the Title, Author, Rating, Copyright, and Description fields. The Windows Media Player will display this information for your listeners.

14. Add or remove the check mark next to the Variable Bit Rate option. Activating this option tells SONAR to vary the bit rate during the encoding process. Sometimes this can yield a higher-quality sound and a smaller file size, but it depends on the material you are encoding. In addition, activating this option affects the selections available from the Codec and Format parameters.

15. With the Variable Bit Rate option activated, choose Windows Media Audio 10 Professional for the Codec parameter.

16. With the Variable Bit Rate option activated, you can choose a number of different options for the Format parameter. Each option begins with the text VBR Quality. The higher the quality number, the higher the quality of your encoded audio, but the larger the file. With the Variable Bit Rate option deactivated, you can choose from a larger variety of options for the Format parameter. The higher the kbps rating you choose, the higher the quality of your encoded audio, but the larger the file.

17. Click OK.

After SONAR encodes your file, you can take it and burn it to CD or DVD for sharing with others.

Encoding and Burning

The two most common forms of distributing a 5.1 surround mix are on DVD in either the DVD-A (DVD-Audio) format or the DVD-V (DVD-Video) format. Unfortunately, SONAR doesn't provide the features for creating DVD-A or DVD-V discs. There's a reason for this—it would add a lot of extra cost to the software, and with so many different choices on the market, users are better off being able to make their own choice as to what they need for DVD-A or DVD-V software.

I'm not going to go into the encoding process because each product is different, and there's no way to cover them all. However, you can find more information about creating DVD-A and DVD-V discs at the following resources:

▷ *Encoding and Recording Your Surround Sound Mix to Disc*—www.digifreq.com/digifreq/article.asp?ID=24

▷ More audio and surround sound articles—www.digifreq.com/digifreq/articles.asp

▷ *Dolby Digital Guidelines*—www.minnetonkaaudio.com/info/PDFs/DolbyDigital_Guidelines.pdf

Good luck in creating your very own surround sound projects using SONAR! Remember to experiment, since mixing in surround gives you so much more flexibility than mixing in plain old stereo.

Standard Music Notation via the Staff View

I N ADDITION TO PREVIOUSLY DESCRIBED EDITING FEATURES, SONAR allows you to edit your MIDI data as standard music notation and guitar tablature. As a matter of fact, you can compose new music while working with notation by graphically adding, editing, and deleting notes. You can also add many of the symbols used in music notation, such as chord symbols, expression markings, and lyrics. When you're ready, you can print your music as sheet music, complete with title, copyright notice, page numbers, and more by using the printer attached to your computer.

The Staff View

SONAR provides three different tools for editing MIDI data: the Event view, the Piano Roll view, and the Staff view. For really precise numerical editing, the Event view can't be beat. For precise graphical editing of both MIDI note and controller data, the Piano Roll view is the tool you'll want to use. Many musicians, however, are used to composing and editing in standard music notation. The Staff view comes into play at this point.

Using the Staff view (see Figure 15.1), you can add, edit, and delete MIDI note data within your MIDI tracks. The Staff view looks similar to sheet music on a piece of paper and represents notes as standard music notation and guitar tablature on musical staves with clefs, key signatures, time signatures, and many of the other symbols you might expect to see on a sheet of music.

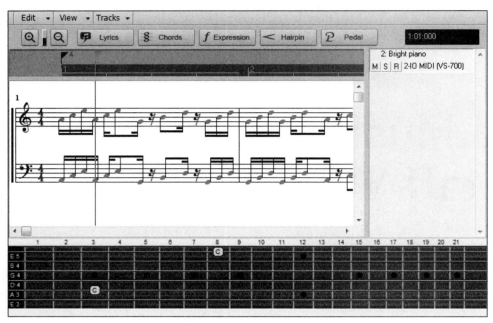

Figure 15.1 Working in the Staff view is just like composing music on paper, but a lot easier.
Source: Cakewalk®, Inc.

More precisely, the Staff view consists of three major sections: the Staff pane (located in the center of the view, displaying the notes in the currently selected tracks), the Track pane (located at the right of the view, listing the tracks currently shown in the view), and the Fretboard pane (located at the bottom of the view, displaying the notes currently being played as they would appear on a six-string guitar neck that uses standard tuning). There are also a menu and toolbar you can use to access the various functions provided by the Staff view, but I'll be referencing the equivalent keyboard shortcuts instead. You'll also notice that the Staff view has scroll bars. They work just as they do in the other views. Other similarities are the Marker area and the Time Ruler, which are located just above the Staff pane.

You can open the Staff view in two different ways:

▷ In the Track view, select the MIDI track(s) you want to edit and then choose Views > Staff (or press Alt+6).
▷ In the Track view, right-click a clip and choose View > Staff View.

OPEN THE STAFF VIEW WITH A DOUBLE-CLICK: By default, double-clicking a MIDI clip opens the Piano Roll view. But you can change that by clicking Options in the Track view menu and choosing Click Behavior > Double-Click > MIDI Clips > [*the view you want to use*]. If you choose Staff View from the menu, the Staff view will open any time you double-click a MIDI clip. In addition, you can click on the upper-right corner of a MIDI clip to choose a view for that individual clip.

Whichever method you choose, SONAR will open the Staff view and display the data from the track(s) you selected.

Changing the Layout

If you select more than one track to be displayed, the Staff view will show the data from each track on a separate stave.

> **PICK TRACKS:** Just like the other views, the Staff view provides a Pick Tracks feature, which you can access by using the Staff view Tracks menu or by pressing Shift+T. You can use Pick Tracks to change the tracks that are displayed.

SONAR picks the clef (treble or bass) for each stave automatically by looking at the range of notes contained in the data. If a track has notes that fall into both clefs, it shows the data on two connected staves: one with a treble clef and one with a bass clef.

> **UP TO 24 STAVES:** You can display up to 24 staves of notation in the Staff view at once. This does not necessarily mean you can display 24 tracks, though. If the data from each track is shown on a single stave, then you can display 24 tracks at once. If, however, the data from each track is shown on a pair of staves (as previously mentioned), you can display only 12 tracks at once. Of course, you can show some tracks with one stave and some with two, so the number of tracks will vary.

If you want, you can override these automatic stave settings by adjusting the Staff View Layout parameters. To adjust the way the data from your MIDI tracks is displayed in the Staff view, just follow these steps:

1. Choose Edit > Layout from the Staff view menu or right-click anywhere in the Staff pane and choose Layout to open the Staff View Layout dialog box (see Figure 15.2).

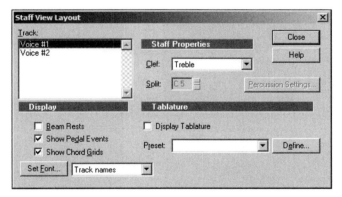

Figure 15.2 You can use the Staff View Layout dialog box to change the way your data is displayed in the Staff view.
Source: Cakewalk®, Inc.

2. From the Track list, select the name of the track that you want to change.
3. In the Staff Properties section, set the Clef parameter to the type of clef you want to use for that track. If you choose the Treble/Bass option, the track will be displayed on two staves. To determine the notes that will be shown on each stave, enter a note value for the Split parameter. Notes that are equal to or higher than the

pitch you enter are shown on the treble clef staff, and notes that are lower than the pitch you enter are shown on the bass clef staff.

4. Click Close.

The track will be shown with the stave settings you specified.

Percussion Tracks

If you open in the Staff view a MIDI track that has its Channel parameter set to 10, and you had previously set up your sound card ports to use the General MIDI instrument definitions (which you learned about in Chapter 2), the Staff view will display that track automatically as percussion notation in a percussion staff. It displays the track this way because when you're using General MIDI, it is standard practice to put all percussion instruments on MIDI channel 10. If you want to override this automatic setting, you can do so as explained previously.

You can also change a number of other settings to customize the way your percussion staves appear. If you select your percussion track in the Staff View Layout dialog box, a new button (called *Percussion Settings*) will become active. If you click this button, the Percussion Notation Key dialog box will appear (see Figure 15.3).

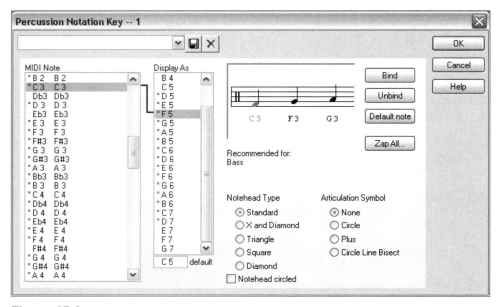

Figure 15.3 You can use the Percussion Notation Key dialog box to further adjust how your percussion tracks appear.
Source: Cakewalk®, Inc.

By manipulating the parameters in this dialog box, you can change the noteheads and articulation symbols used to display your percussion notes. You can also change the percussion sounds that correspond to the different positions on the percussion staff.

1. In the MIDI Note section, select the name of the instrument you want to change.
2. If you want to change the position on the percussion staff where that instrument will be shown, select the appropriate pitch in the Display As section. Then click the Bind button to assign that staff position to the selected instrument.

3. If you don't want an instrument to have a specific staff position assignment, select the instrument and click either the Unbind button or the Default Note button. To remove all instrument assignments, click the Zap All button.

DEFAULT PITCH POSITION: Any instruments that don't have a specifically assigned staff position automatically use the default position, shown at the bottom of the Display As section. This means that those instruments are shown at that pitch position on the percussion staff. You can change the default position by typing in a new pitch value.

---

4. After you've bound an instrument to a position on the staff, you can designate the notehead type and articulation symbol it will use. Just select the appropriate options in those sections of the dialog box. When you set the notehead type, you can also opt to have the notehead circled or not by setting the Notehead Circled parameter.
5. If you want to use these settings again later, save them as a preset.
6. Click OK to close the Percussion Notation Key dialog box.
7. Click Close to close the Staff View Layout dialog box.

Now the data in your percussion tracks will be shown using the settings you specified.

GHOST STROKES: SONAR displays *ghost strokes* (percussion notes played very softly for ornamentation) using the standard method of parentheses around the percussion notehead. It determines ghost strokes by testing to see whether the note velocity is lower than 32. This number is a fixed value that can't be changed. You can change the note velocities of your data and then use the Velocity Trim track parameter to trick SONAR into using a different determining value. For example, to stop notes from being shown as ghost notes, simply raise their velocity values. Then, so the sound of the data isn't changed, set the Velocity Trim parameter so that it lowers the velocities to their original values during playback. Do the opposite to have notes shown as ghost notes.

Showing Pedal Events and Chord Grids

You also can control whether or not the Staff view will display pedal events or guitar chord grids. To do so, in the Display section of the Staff View Layout dialog box, set the Show Pedal Events and Show Chord Grids options.

Changing Text Fonts

You can also change how any of the text used in your data will be displayed. For example, you can change track names and measure numbers, lyric text, expression text, chord text, triplet numbers, and tablature fret numbers by following these steps:

1. Choose Edit > Layout from the Staff view menu or right-click anywhere in the Staff pane and choose Layout to open the Staff View Layout dialog box.
2. In the Display section, choose the type of text you want to change by picking its designation from the Set Font list. For example, if you want to change how the track names look in your sheet music, select Track Names from the list.

3. Click the Set Font button to open the Font dialog box (see Figure 15.4).

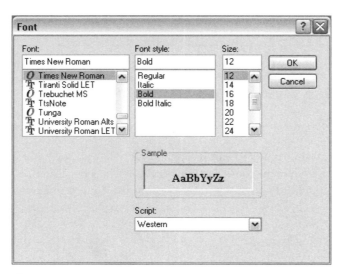

Figure 15.4 Using the Font dialog box, you can set how you want the text in your sheet music to appear.
Source: Cakewalk®, Inc.

4. In the Font section, choose the font you want to use.
5. In the Font Style section, choose a style for your text, such as Bold or Italic.
6. In the Size section, choose the size of the text you want to use. You can see your changes in the Sample section. Click OK.

Rhythmic Appearance

When converting your MIDI data into music notation, SONAR has to make some educated guesses about how to display the rhythmic values of the notes. It does so because when you record your musical performance in real time, instead of playing notes with perfect timing, you'll more than likely play some of them either a little ahead or a little behind the beat. You might also hold some notes a little longer than they should be held. Most often, these slight timing errors are desirable because they give your music a more human feel.

SONAR doesn't understand these slight rhythmic variations; it knows only exact note timing and duration. So, when SONAR displays your data in the Staff view, the data might not always look like it should. That's why SONAR provides a number of parameters you can adjust to give it a better idea of how the music should be displayed.

Using Beam Rests

When you're notating music with very complex rhythms, it is standard practice to lengthen the beams on beamed groups of notes to also include rests. Lengthening the beams makes it much easier for the person reading the music to pick out the correct rhythms. For rhythmically simple music, it's usually best not to beam rests. If you need this feature, you can turn it on and off by opening the Staff View Layout dialog box and setting the Beam Rests option in the Display section.

Setting the Display Resolution

For SONAR to make an educated guess about how the rhythms in your music should be displayed, you have to give it a point of reference, which is called the *display resolution*. By setting this parameter, you are telling SONAR the smallest rhythmic note value used in your music. For example, if the smallest rhythmic value in your music is a sixteenth note, you would set a sixteenth-note value to be used for the display resolution. SONAR would then round any start times and note durations to the nearest sixteenth note so that your music would look more like it should. This setting changes only the appearance of the music, not how it sounds. To set the display resolution, select a rhythmic value from the View > Display Resolution menu (see Figure 15.5).

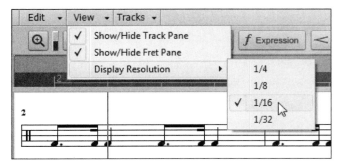

Figure 15.5 You can set the display resolution so that SONAR can make a better guess as to how your data should be displayed.
Source: Cakewalk®, Inc.

Filling and Trimming Durations

In addition to the Display Resolution parameter, SONAR provides two other options you can set to help it better understand how to display your music. The Fill Durations option rounds note durations up to the next beat or note (whichever comes first). For example, instead of showing two quarter notes tied together in the same measure, SONAR simply shows a single half note.

The Trim Durations option rounds note durations down so they do not overlap. For example, if you have a note with a duration that extends past the start of the next note, the first note's duration will be shortened so that you don't end up with something like a half note tied to a quarter note with an eighth note sitting between the two.

Neither of these options changes the music in any way—just how it's displayed. The results will vary, depending on the music you are trying to display as notation, so you'll have to try either one or both of these options to see whether they help clean up the rhythmic notation values. To turn the options on or off, choose View > Fill Durations and View > Trim Durations in the Staff view menu (or press Alt+D and Alt+Shift+D, respectively).

Dealing with Notes

As you know, when you open a MIDI track in the Staff view, the notes in that track are displayed in the Staff pane as standard music notation. In addition to simply displaying the notes, the Staff view edits and deletes them, as well as adding new ones.

You can add new notes to a track or edit the existing ones by using the Select, Draw, Erase, and/or Smart tools. These tools can be activated via SONAR's Control Bar or via keyboard shortcuts.

Selecting

Press F6 to activate the Select tool. Using this tool, you can select the notes for further manipulation, such as deleting, copying, moving, and so on. Essentially, you select notes the same way you would in the Piano Roll view. To select a single note, click it. To select more than one note, hold down the Ctrl key while you click the notes you want to select. You can also click and drag to lasso a group of notes.

> **TIED NOTES:** When you select a note that is tied to another note, both notes are selected automatically because they are essentially the same MIDI note with its duration shown as two tied notes, rather than as one note with a larger rhythmic value.

Editing

After you've made a selection, you can copy, cut, paste, move, and delete the notes the same way you would in the Piano Roll view. You can also edit notes individually using the Draw tool or the Smart tool. Press F9 or F5 to activate the Draw tool or Smart tool, respectively. Using either tool, you can add and edit the notes in the Staff pane.

To move a note to a different location within a staff, simply click its notehead and drag it left or right. This action moves the note to a different horizontal location on the staff and along the Time Ruler. If you have the Snap to Grid feature activated, the note will snap to the nearest Musical Time Snap value set in the Snap module of the Control Bar.

To change the pitch of a note, simply click its notehead and drag it up or down in the same staff or drag it into another staff. As you move the note, SONAR will play the different pitches so you can hear what they sound like.

> **CHROMATIC NOTE CHANGES:** By default, SONAR uses note pitches that match the current diatonic key signature of the music. This means that as you drag a note to a new pitch, it automatically remains in the correct musical key. If you don't want the note to stay within the key, press the right mouse button after you've begun to drag the note to a new pitch. This changes the pitch of the note chromatically in half steps.

Sometimes you might want to make more precise changes to a note or change its duration. You can do so by using the Note Properties dialog box. Right-click a note to open the Note Properties dialog box (see Figure 15.6).

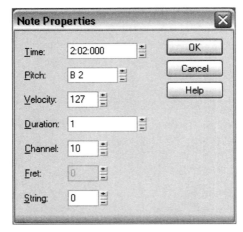

Figure 15.6 Using the Note Properties dialog box, you can make precise changes to a note in the Staff view.
Source: Cakewalk®, Inc.

In the Note Properties dialog box, you can make precise changes to the time, pitch, velocity, duration, and MIDI channel of an individual note by typing in numerical values. You can also specify the fret and string upon which the note will be played in the Fretboard pane.

THE EVENT INSPECTOR: You can get quicker access to the properties of a note by using the Event Inspector module in the Control Bar. Right-click the Control Bar and choose Event Inspector Module to toggle it on/off. Now whenever you use the Select tool to select a note in the Staff view, the note's properties will be displayed in the Event Inspector module. You can also change the note's properties. Just click a property in the module and either type in a new value or use the spin controls to increase or decrease the value. In addition, you can use modifiers (+/-) to change values relative to their current values. For example, if you want to add 23 to a velocity value of 37, type **+23** for the Vel parameter and SONAR will automatically change the value to 60. The plus and minus modifiers work for all parameters, but the Vel (velocity) and Duration parameters can also accept a percentage for scaling values. For example, with 100% representing the current value, if you want to lengthen a note by 20%, you would enter 120% for the Duration value. If you wanted to shorten the same note by 20%, you would enter 80% for the Duration value.

Drawing (or Adding)

In addition to editing, the Draw and Smart tools enable you to add notes to a staff by literally drawing them. To do so, follow these steps:

1. Activate either the Draw or Smart tool by pressing F9 or F5, respectively.
2. Select a duration for the new note(s). If you look in the Tools module of SONAR's Control Bar, you'll notice a Draw Resolution (note value) menu located below the Draw tool button. Clicking this menu allows you to determine the duration of your new notes. For example, if you choose 1/4, the duration will be set to a quarter note.

QUICK DURATION SELECTION: To choose duration values quickly, use your computer keyboard. Hold Ctrl+Shift and then press 1 for a whole note, 2 for a half note, 4 for a quarter note, 8 for an eighth note, 6 for a sixteenth note, and 3 for a thirty-second note. Press Alt+D for a dotted note and Alt+T for a triplet.

3. Click anywhere on a staff in the Staff pane to place the new notes at the start times and pitches you want.

DISABLE FILL AND TRIM: It's a good idea to turn off the Fill Durations and Trim Durations options when you're entering new notes in the Staff pane. When you add notes, SONAR will try to change the way they are displayed, and you might find this confusing when you're trying to read the music.

Erasing

Even though you can select and delete notes as described earlier, the Staff view includes an Erase tool for added convenience. To use it, press F10 and click any notes in the Staff pane that you want to delete. You can also click and drag the Erase tool over a number of notes to erase them all at once.

Scrub and Step Play

When you're editing the data in a track, the procedure usually involves making your edits and then playing back the project to hear how the changes sound. But playing back very small sections can be a bit difficult, especially when you're working with a fast tempo. To remedy this situation, you can use the Scrub tool and the Step Play feature in the Staff view.

Scrub

Using the Scrub tool, you can drag over the notes in the Staff view to hear what they sound like. To use it, press J; then click and drag over the notes in the Staff pane. Dragging left to right plays the data forward (what would normally happen during playback), and dragging right to left enables you to hear the data played in reverse. This feature can be useful for testing very short (one- or two-measure) sections.

Step Play

The Step Play feature steps through (plays) the notes in the Staff view note by note. To use it, follow these steps:

1. Set the Now time to the point in the music where you want to begin stepping through the notes. You can do so by clicking the Time Ruler.
2. To step forward through the notes, press Ctrl plus the right arrow key.
3. To step backward through the notes, press Ctrl plus the left arrow key.

SONAR will move the Now time cursor one set of notes at a time, either to the right or left, and play the notes on which it lands.

USE LOOPING FOR EDITING: Instead of using the Scrub tool or the Step Play feature, you might want to try another useful technique for hearing what your changes sound like. Did you know that you could edit the data in your project as it's being played back? Of course, it's a bit difficult to edit anything while SONAR is scrolling the display as the project plays. What I like to do is work on a small section of a project. I set up a section of the project to loop over and over, and as SONAR is playing the data, I make any changes I think might be needed. Because the data is being played back while I edit, I can hear instantly what the changes sound like. Using this approach is much easier than going back and forth, making changes, and starting and stopping playback manually. I described looping in Chapter 5.

Dealing with Symbols and Lyrics

In addition to notes, SONAR lets you add other markings to your notated music, including chord symbols, guitar chord grids, expression marks, and pedal marks. These markings are ornamental in nature; they have nothing to do with the data in your MIDI tracks. They also do not affect your music in any way (although there is one exception, which I'll explain later).

Essentially, SONAR provides these features so you can create sheet music with a more professional look, but you have to enter the marks manually. The procedures are basically the same as when you're working with notes. You use the Draw tool or Smart tool to add the markings, and you can select, copy, cut, paste, delete, and move them. To give you an idea of how to utilize the markings, I'll go through them one at a time.

Chord Symbols and Grids

Most sheet music sold to the public includes chord symbols with simple chord names or with both names and guitar grids. SONAR gives you the flexibility to enter one or both.

Adding and Editing

To add a chord symbol to your music, follow these steps:

1. Activate either the Draw or Smart tool by pressing F9 or F5, respectively.
2. Activate the Chord mode by clicking the Chords button or pressing Alt+C.
3. Position your mouse pointer above the staff to which you want to add the symbol.

CHORD SYMBOL POSITIONING: You can add chord symbols only in certain positions in your music. If a track is displayed as a single staff, you can place symbols above that staff. If a track is shown using a pair of staves (treble and bass clefs), you can place symbols above the top (treble clef) staff only.

Also, chord symbols in music are usually lined up with the notes in the staff. SONAR places chord symbols in the same horizontal location above a note, only along the staff (although there is an exception, which I'll explain later). SONAR highlights the area where you can place chord symbols when you activate Chord mode.

4. Click to place the symbol above the staff. SONAR will add a copy of the most recently added chord (the default is C).
5. To change the name of the chord symbol, right-click it to open the Chord Properties dialog box (see Figure 15.7).

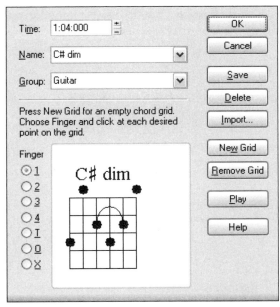

Figure 15.7 You can change the name (and other assets) of a chord symbol by using the Chord Properties dialog box.
Source: Cakewalk®, Inc.

6. Select the types of chords from which you want to choose by selecting a group from the Group list. SONAR includes only a single group of chords, called *Guitar*. You can, however, create your own groups and chord symbols.
7. For the Name parameter, select a new name from the list. You'll notice that multiple chords in the list have the same name. They're named the same because some chords have guitar chord grids associated with them and some don't. If a chord includes a grid, the grid is shown in the Grid section of the dialog box. You'll also find multiple chords with grids that have the same name. This is to accommodate the different fingerings that you can use to play each chord on a guitar.

QUICK CHORD SELECTION: The list of chords is very long, and it can be tedious to scroll through it all just to find the chord you want. For a quicker way to navigate through the list, type the name of the chord you want to find in the Name field. Then press the up or down arrow key (depending on which way you want to move through the list).

---

8. Earlier I mentioned that SONAR places chords only at certain horizontal locations along the top of a staff. Although this is true when you are initially adding a chord, you can change the position of the chord by changing its start time. Just enter a new time (in measures, beats, and ticks) in the Time field of the Chord Properties dialog box. This way, you can place chord symbols anywhere along the top of a staff—they don't have to line up with the notes.

After you click OK, SONAR will change the name and position of the chord symbol and add a grid to it, according to the new properties you specified.

The Chord Library

SONAR includes a large number of predefined chord symbols, which it stores as a Chord Library in a file named *CHORDS.LIW*. You can edit these chords or add your own by using the Chord Properties dialog box.

To add a chord into a new or existing group, follow these steps:

1. Right-click a chord symbol to open the Chord Properties dialog box.
2. To add a chord to an existing group, select the group from the Group list. To add a chord to a new group, type the name of the new group in the Group field.
3. Type the name of the new chord in the Name field.
4. To add a grid to the new chord, click the New Grid button. An empty grid will be displayed in the Grid area (see Figure 15.8).

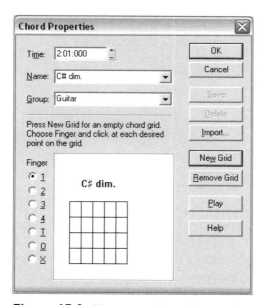

Figure 15.8 You can add a grid to a chord symbol by clicking the New Grid button.
Source: Cakewalk®, Inc.

5. To place a dot on the grid, first choose a finger number from the Finger options and then click the appropriate string and fret location on the grid. To assign an open string, select O for the finger number. To assign a muted string, select X for the finger number.

6. To insert a fret designation for the grid, click just to the right of the grid in the Grid section to open the Chord Fret Number dialog box. Then type a fret number and click OK.

7. To hear what the chord sounds like, click the Play button.

8. When you're satisfied with the new chord, click the Save button to save it to the Chord Library.

To edit a chord or group in the Chord Library, follow these steps:

1. Right-click a chord symbol to open the Chord Properties dialog box.
2. To delete a group, select it from the Group list and click the Delete button.
3. To edit a chord in an existing group, select the group from the Group list.
4. To delete a chord, select the chord from the Name list and click the Delete button.
5. To edit a chord, select the chord from the Name list and type a new name.
6. If the chord has an accompanying chord grid, you can either delete it or edit it. To delete it, click the Remove Grid button.
7. To edit the grid, change the finger assignment for a dot by clicking the dot repeatedly to cycle through the finger options.
8. To hear what the chord sounds like, click the Play button.
9. When you're satisfied with the edited chord, click the Save button to save it to the Chord Library.

IMPORTING CHORD DEFINITIONS: You can also import new chord definitions into the Chord Library by clicking the Import button and selecting an .LIW file.

Expression Marks

Expression marks in music designate any kind of text that provides instructions on how the music should be played during different passages. These marks include tempo designations (such as *allegro*), musical characteristics (such as *play with feeling*), and dynamic instructions (such as *cresc.*, *ppp*, or *fff*). Essentially, expression marks are just simple text added to the sheet music.

Adding an Expression Mark

To add an expression mark to your music, follow these steps:

1. Activate either the Draw or Smart tool by pressing F9 or F5, respectively.
2. Activate Expression mode by clicking the Expression button or pressing Alt+X.
3. Position your mouse pointer below the staff to which you want to add the mark.

EXPRESSION MARKS POSITIONING: As with chord symbols, you can place expression marks only at certain positions in your music. If a track is displayed as a single staff, you can place a mark below that staff. If a track is shown using a pair of staves (treble and bass clefs), you can place marks below the top (treble clef) staff only.

Also, as with chord symbols, marks are initially lined up with the notes in the staff (although you can change the way they're lined up by editing the marks and altering their start times).

---

4. Click to place the mark below the staff. SONAR will open an insertion box.

5. Type the text you want to use for the mark (see Figure 15.9) and then press Enter.

Figure 15.9 Expression marks are just simple text that you type into the Staff pane.
Source: Cakewalk®, Inc.

DANGLING HYPHENS: To leave a dangling hyphen at the end of an expression mark, type a space and a single hyphen after the text in the insertion box. Dangling hyphens are often used with expression marks in sheet music to show that the expression should be continued over a range of notes or measures until the next expression mark appears.

Editing an Expression Mark

To edit an expression mark, follow these steps:

1. Right-click the expression mark to open the Expression Text Properties dialog box (see Figure 15.10).

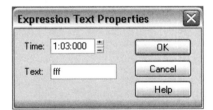

Figure 15.10 Using the Expression Text Properties dialog box, you can edit expression marks.
Source: Cakewalk®, Inc.

2. To change the position of the expression mark, enter a new start time (in measures, beats, and ticks) in the Time field.
3. To change the text of the expression mark, enter the new text in the Text field. Click OK.

EDIT WITH THE DRAW TOOL: You can also edit the text of an expression mark by clicking it with the Draw or Smart tool to reopen the insertion box.

Hairpin Symbols

In addition to showing crescendos and decrescendos as text via expression marks, you can show them graphically via hairpin symbols. These symbols look like large greater-than and less-than signs (see Figure 15.11).

Figure 15.11 You can designate crescendos and decrescendos via hairpin symbols.
Source: Cakewalk®, Inc.

Adding a Hairpin Symbol

To add a hairpin symbol to your music, follow these steps:

1. Activate either the Draw or Smart tool by pressing F9 or F5, respectively.
2. Activate Hairpin mode by clicking the Hairpin button or pressing Alt+H.
3. Position your mouse pointer below the staff to which you want to add the symbol.

> **SYMBOL PLACEMENT:** As with expression marks, if a track is displayed as a single staff, you can place the symbol below that staff. If a track is shown using a pair of staves (treble and bass clefs), you can place the symbol below the top (treble clef) staff only.

4. Click to place the symbol below the staff.

SONAR will add a copy of the most recently added hairpin symbol. To change the symbol, you can edit it by using the Hairpin Properties dialog box.

Editing a Hairpin Symbol

To edit a hairpin symbol, follow these steps:

1. Right-click the hairpin symbol to open the Hairpin Properties dialog box (see Figure 15.12).

Figure 15.12 Using the Hairpin Properties dialog box, you can edit hairpin symbols.
Source: Cakewalk®, Inc.

2. To change the position of the hairpin symbol, enter a new start time (in measures, beats, and ticks) in the Time field.

DRAG TO A NEW POSITION: You can also change the position of the hairpin symbol by dragging it.

---

3. To change the type of the hairpin symbol, choose either the Crescendo option or the Diminuendo (same as decrescendo) option.
4. To change the length of the hairpin symbol, enter a new value (in beats and ticks) in the Duration field. Click OK.

Pedal Marks

Earlier, I mentioned that there was one exception to the rule that markings do not affect the data in your MIDI tracks; that exception is pedal marks. On a sheet of music, pedal marks usually designate when the performer is supposed to press and release the sustain pedal on a piano. In SONAR, they mean essentially the same thing, but they refer to the sustain pedal attached to your MIDI keyboard (if it has one). More precisely, pedal marks in the Staff view designate MIDI controller number 64 (pedal-sustain) messages in your MIDI tracks (which you can also edit in the Controller pane of the Piano Roll view). So whenever you add or edit pedal marks in the Staff view, you are also editing the MIDI controller number 64 messages in that track.

Adding a Pedal Mark

To add a pedal mark to your music, follow these steps:

1. Activate either the Draw or Smart tool by pressing F9 or F5, respectively.
2. Activate Pedal Mark mode by clicking the Pedal button or Alt+A.
3. Position your mouse pointer below the staff to which you want to add the mark.

PEDAL SYMBOL PLACEMENT: Similar to expression marks, if a track is displayed as a single staff, you can place the symbol below that staff. If a track is shown using a pair of staves (treble and bass clefs), you can place the symbol below the bottom (bass clef) staff only.

---

4. Click to place the mark below the staff.

SONAR will add a pair of pedal marks (pedal down, which looks like an asterisk, and pedal up, which looks like a *P*) to your music. To edit the marks, you can use the Pedal Properties dialog box.

Editing a Pedal Mark

To edit a pedal mark, follow these steps:

1. Right-click the pedal mark (either a pedal down mark or a pedal up mark; you can't edit them both at once) to open the Pedal Properties dialog box (see Figure 15.13).

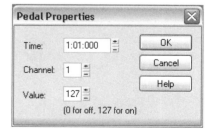

Figure 15.13 You can use the Pedal Properties dialog box to edit pedal marks.
Source: Cakewalk®, Inc.

2. To change the position of the pedal mark, enter a new start time (in measures, beats, and ticks) in the Time field.

DRAG TO A NEW POSITION: You can also change the position of the pedal mark by dragging it.

---

3. To change the MIDI channel for the pedal mark, type a new channel number in the Channel field.
4. To change the type of pedal mark, enter a new number in the Value field. Enter **0** to make it a pedal up mark; enter **127** to make it a pedal down mark. Entering any number between that range produces no effect. Click OK.

Lyrics

Just like any good notation software, SONAR enables you to add lyrics to your sheet music. Lyrics (like expression marks) are represented by simple text displayed below a staff. You can add lyrics to a track by using the Lyrics mode in the Staff view or the Lyrics view.

The Lyrics Mode

Follow these steps to add lyrics to your music using the Lyrics mode:

1. In the Staff view, activate either the Draw or Smart tool by pressing F9 or F5, respectively.
2. Activate Lyrics mode by clicking the Lyrics button or Alt+Y.
3. Position your mouse pointer below the staff, underneath the first note to which you want to add lyrics.

LYRIC PLACEMENT: If a track is displayed as a single staff, you can place the lyrics below that staff. If a track is shown using a pair of staves (treble and bass clefs), you can place lyrics below the top (treble clef) staff only.

Also, each word or syllable in the lyrics must be aligned with a note. SONAR automatically aligns the lyrics to the notes in the staff.

---

4. Click to place the lyric below the staff. SONAR will open an insertion box, just like when you add expression marks.
5. Type a word or syllable to be aligned with the current note.
6. To move forward and add a lyric to the next note, enter a space, type a hyphen, or press the Tab key. The insertion box will move to the next note and wait for you to enter text.
7. To skip over a note, don't type any text in the insertion box. Enter a space or type a hyphen.
8. When you're finished entering lyrics, press the Enter key.
9. To edit lyrics, click the word you want to change. Then edit the word and press Enter.

The Lyrics View

After you've entered some lyrics in the Staff view, you can display them in a separate window called the *Lyrics view*. This view is useful for providing a cue for performers who are recording vocal tracks because you can make the lyrics appear in any size font you like (see Figure 15.14).

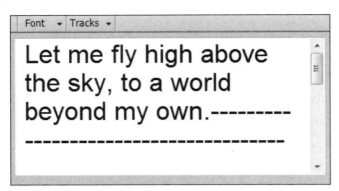

Figure 15.14 The Lyrics view is useful as a cue for vocal performers.
Source: Cakewalk®, Inc.

To open the Lyrics view, select a track in the Track view and then choose Views > Lyrics (or press Alt+Shift+1). To change the size of the text, use the Font menu, which provides two different preset font sizes (Font A and Font B). You can use more specific font settings by choosing Font > Fonts to open the Font dialog box. In this dialog box, you can change the font, style, and size of the text. The Lyrics view also has a Tracks menu that works just as in the other views.

You can also add and edit lyrics in the Lyrics view, but I wouldn't recommend it. The process is not very intuitive because you can't see the notes to which the words and syllables are being aligned. If you want to use the Lyrics view for adding and editing, you can do so just as you would enter and edit text in Windows Notepad. Each word you type is aligned automatically to a note in the current track.

> **COPY AND PASTE LYRICS:** In addition to typing and editing lyrics in the Lyrics view, you can also select, cut, copy, paste, and delete text. Again, this procedure works just like Windows Notepad with a right-click of your mouse. What's nice about the Lyrics view is that if you already have some text saved in a text file, you can copy and paste it into this view to add lyrics quickly to a track. When you look at the lyrics in the Staff view, the words are aligned automatically to the notes in the staff.

The Fretboard and Tablature

For all the guitar players out there, SONAR provides a couple of nice notation-related features just for you. The first one I'll describe is the Fret pane.

The Fret Pane

The Fret pane, located at the bottom of the Staff view, is both a visual aid and an editing tool. During playback, the Fretboard displays the notes at the current Now time in a selected track as they would be played on a six-string guitar using standard tuning. This makes the Fretboard a cool learning tool when you're trying to learn to play a new piece of music. It also displays notes when you use the Scrub tool or Step Play feature, which makes it even easier to pick out the fingerings.

Fretboard Properties

You can configure certain aspects of the Fretboard, such as its background style and the orientation of the strings. You can also turn it on or off. To toggle the Fretboard on and off, use the View menu or press Alt+V.

To change the background style, right-click the Fretboard and choose Wood Grain and one of the following from the list: Rosewood Hi, Rosewood Lo, Ebony Hi, Ebony Lo, Maple Hi, or Maple Lo. The Hi and Lo designations deal with the screen resolution you are using on your computer monitor. If you're using a high screen resolution, use one of the styles marked Hi. If you're using a low screen resolution, use one of the styles marked Lo. To be honest, the resolution you choose really doesn't make that much of a difference.

To change the orientation of the strings, right-click the Fretboard and select Mirror Fretboard to invert the Fretboard so that the highest sounding string appears at the bottom. To change it back, just select Mirror Fretboard again.

Adding Notes

In addition to using the Fretboard to display notes, you can add new notes to a track (staff) by clicking the Fretboard. Just follow these steps:

1. Set the Now time so that the cursor rests at the point in the staff where you want to add the note(s). You can do so by clicking in the Time Ruler.
2. Activate either the Draw or Smart tool by pressing F9 or F5, respectively.
3. Select a note duration.
4. Click the guitar strings in the Fretboard to enter notes on the staff. You can enter up to six notes (one per string).
5. Make the Now time cursor move forward by the same amount as the current note duration setting by pressing the Shift and right arrow keys.
6. Repeat Steps 3 through 5 to continue adding more notes.

Editing Notes

You can also edit existing notes in a track (staff) by using the Fretboard. You can change only the pitch of the notes, though. To do so, just follow these steps:

1. Set the Now time so the cursor rests on top of the note(s) that you want to edit. You can do so by clicking the Time Ruler. You can also use the Step Play feature.
2. Activate either the Draw or Smart tool by pressing F9 or F5, respectively.
3. Drag the notes along the strings to a new fret (thus changing the pitch).

After you release the mouse button, SONAR will change the pitch of the notes in the staff.

Tablature

As a guitar or bass player, you might be more comfortable reading and working with tablature than standard notation. If that's the case, you're in luck because SONAR includes a number of features that display and edit your music as tablature.

Displaying Tablature

To display tablature for a track (staff), follow these steps:

1. Right-click in the Staff pane and select Layout to open the Staff View Layout dialog box.
2. Select from the list the name of the track for which you want to display tablature.
3. In the Tablature section, activate the Display Tablature option.
4. Select a tablature style from the Preset list and click OK.

SONAR will display a tablature staff below the current staff, complete with tablature for each note in the track (see Figure 15.15).

Figure 15.15 Adding tablature to a track in the Staff view is easy.
Source: Cakewalk®, Inc.

Defining a Tablature Style

When you're setting up a track to display tablature, you might not find a preset style that fits your needs. If that's the case, you can always create your own tablature style by following these steps:

1. Right-click the Staff pane and select Layout to open the Staff View Layout dialog box.
2. Select from the list the name of the track for which you want to display tablature.
3. In the Tablature section, activate the Display Tablature option.
4. Click the Define button to open the Tablature Settings dialog box (see Figure 15.16).

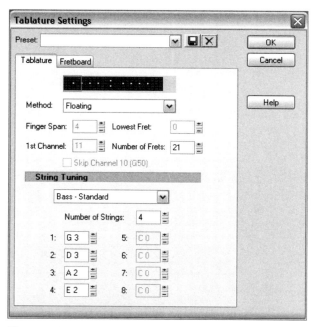

Figure 15.16 You can create your own tablature styles by using the Tablature Settings dialog box.
Source: Cakewalk®, Inc.

5. Under the Tablature tab, set the Method parameter. This parameter determines how the tablature will be displayed. If you select Floating, the notes can be shown anywhere on the Fretboard. If you select Fixed, notes are limited to a specific area on the neck of the guitar. To determine the size and position of that area, you must set the Finger Span and Lowest Fret parameters. The Finger Span parameter sets the size of the area in a number of frets. The Lowest Fret parameter sets the position of the area on the neck of the guitar by specifying the first fret upon which the area is based. The last tablature method (MIDI Channel) is useful if you record your guitar parts using a MIDI guitar and you use Mono mode so that each string is recorded using its own MIDI channel. If this is your situation, then select the MIDI Channel method and set the 1st Channel parameter to the lowest number channel used by your MIDI guitar.

6. In the Number of Frets field, enter the number of frets on which the tablature should be based.

7. In the String Tuning section, choose an instrument/tuning upon which to base the tablature.

8. Set the Number of Strings parameter to the number of strings the instrument provides.

9. The pitches of each string for the instrument appear in the parameters below the Number of Strings field. You can either leave them as-is, or you can customize the pitches to your liking.

10. Save your settings as a preset and click OK to close the Tablature Settings dialog box.

Your new tablature style should appear in the Preset list in the Tablature section of the Staff View Layout dialog box.

Regenerating Tablature

You can use different tablature styles for different sections of the same tablature staff by following these steps:

1. In the Staff pane, select the notes or tablature numbers for which you want to use a different tablature style.

2. Right-click anywhere in the Staff pane and select Regenerate Tablature to open the Regenerate Tablature dialog box (see Figure 15.17).

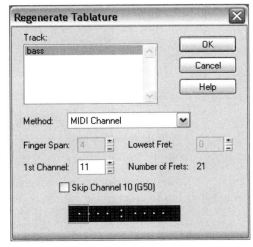

Figure 15.17 You can define different tablature styles for selected notes by using the Regenerate Tablature feature.
Source: Cakewalk®, Inc.

3. Set the Method, Finger Span, Lowest Fret, and 1st Channel parameters, if applicable. These parameters work the same way as described previously. Click OK.

Adding Notes via Tablature

In addition to displaying tablature, you can use a tablature staff to add notes to a track by following these steps:

1. Activate either the Draw or Smart tool by pressing F9 or F5, respectively.

2. Choose a note duration.

3. Move the mouse pointer over the tablature staff. It will change its shape to a crosshair.

4. Position the crosshair within any measure and over a line in the tablature staff.

5. Click and hold the left mouse button and then drag your mouse pointer up and down to select a fret number.

6. Release the mouse button to enter the note.

Editing Notes via Tablature

You can also edit notes via a tablature staff. To do so, just follow these steps:

1. Activate either the Draw or Smart tool by pressing F9 or F5, respectively.

2. To change the fret number of a note, right-click it and select a new number.

3. To move a note to a different string (line) on the tablature staff, click and drag the note while pressing the Alt key. Drag the note up or down to move it. If the note is not supposed to play on a certain string, it will not be allowed to move there.

Exporting Tablature to a Text File

One last tablature feature that you might find useful is being able to save the tablature as a text file for either printing or distribution over the Internet. By saving the tablature this way, you can share it with other guitarists—even if they don't own SONAR. You use this feature as follows:

1. Select a MIDI track.

2. In the Staff view, right-click anywhere in the Staff pane and select Export to ASCII TAB. The Save As dialog box will open.

3. Type a name for the file and click Save.

QUANTIZE FOR ACCURACY: You might want to try quantizing the track before you save it as tablature. Doing so usually produces more accurate results.

Printing Your Music

After all is notated and done, you can print your music to paper if you have a printer connected to your computer. SONAR automatically sets up your music on separate pages, including the song title, composer, and other information, along with the notation. You can print your musical score by following these steps:

1. Choose Project > Info to open the File Info window and then fill out all the information you want to include on your sheet music. You can use the Title, Subtitle, Instructions, Author, and Copyright parameters. For more information about the File Info window, refer to Chapter 3.

2. In the Staff view menu, choose Print > Print Preview. SONAR will go into Print Preview mode (see Figure 15.18) and display your music on virtual pages, letting you see how it will look before you print it.

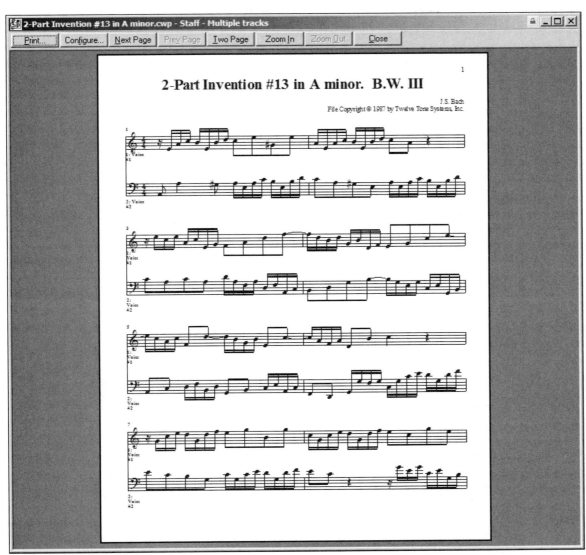

Figure 15.18 You can use Print Preview mode to see how your music will look on paper before you print it.
Source: Cakewalk®, Inc.

3. To zoom the display in or out, click the Zoom In or Zoom Out button.

4. Depending on the length of your song, SONAR usually shows two pages at once on the screen. If you would rather view only one page at a time, click the One Page button.

5. If your song takes up more than two pages, you can navigate through them by using the Next Page and Prev Page buttons.

6. Before you print your music, you need to select a size for your score. To do so, click the Configure button to open the Staff View Print Configure dialog box.

7. From the single list, choose the size you want to use. SONAR provides nine different standard music-engraving sizes used by professional music publishers. Each size is used for a different purpose. Size 0 (Commercial or Public) usually is used for wire-bound manuscripts. Size 1 (Giant or English) usually is used for school band music books or instructional books. Sizes 2 and 3 (Regular, Common, or Ordinary) usually are

used for printing classical music. Size 4 (Peter) usually is used for folios or organ music. Size 5 (Large Middle) usually is used for ensemble music. Size 6 (Small Middle) usually is used for condensed sheet music. Size 7 (Cadenza) usually is used for pocket music editions. And Size 8 (Pearl) usually is used for thematic advertisement.

8. Click OK. The music will be redrawn using the new size.
9. Click the Print button.

When the standard Windows Print dialog box opens, you can set up your printer and print your music.

Studio Control with StudioWare and Sysx

MOST OF TODAY'S MODERN APPLIANCES ARE computer-controlled. Need to cook a meal? Push a few buttons on the stove, and it automatically sets the right time and temperature for your recipe. Need to wash your clothes? Yada, yada, yada… It's the same thing with modern recording-studio gear—almost everything is computer-controlled, and the gear supports MIDI, too. I'm not just talking about MIDI instruments (such as synthesizer keyboards), but also about audio-processing equipment and mixing boards.

Why would these products include support for MIDI? Because like MIDI instruments, they have internal parameters that you can change and store. Because these products provide support for MIDI, their parameters become accessible to other MIDI devices, such as your computer. This means that it is now possible to control almost every piece of equipment in your studio via your computer, provided the equipment supports MIDI and you have the right software. Luckily for you, you don't need to buy any additional software because SONAR has some built-in features for controlling and storing the parameters for any outboard MIDI gear. All you have to do is connect your MIDI devices to your computer (just as you would any MIDI instrument), and they can "talk" to each other.

System Exclusive

MIDI devices (other than MIDI instruments) usually don't provide standard musical functions, so their internal parameters are not compatible with standard MIDI messages, such as Note On messages. Instead, they have to communicate using special MIDI messages called *system exclusive* messages. They give you access to any special functions that a manufacturer includes in a MIDI instrument or device.

Not only do you have access to these functions, but also by utilizing system exclusive messages, you can send all the data from the MIDI instruments and devices in your studio to SONAR to be stored in your projects. Why is this capability important? Because you can set up all your equipment with specific settings for a project, store the data in the project, and then send the data back to the devices at the beginning of your next recording session. This means that the next time you open the project, you can have all the equipment in your studio set up automatically, and you won't have to touch a single knob.

The Sysx View

SONAR gives you access to system exclusive data via the Sysx view (see Figure 16.1). Using the Sysx view, you can store up to 8,191 banks, each of which can contain any number of system exclusive messages (limited only by the amount of memory in your computer system). For example, you could dedicate a different bank to store the data for each separate piece of equipment in your studio. You could also store different sets of patch data for a single MIDI instrument in separate banks. Then, at different times in your project, you could send specific patch data to change the sounds in the instrument for that part of the song.

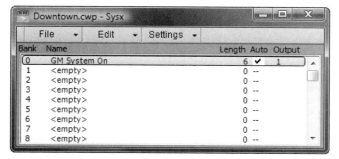

Figure 16.1 The Sysx view lets you store system exclusive data within the current project.
Source: Cakewalk®, Inc.

Receiving System Exclusive Data

To store system exclusive data in a bank in the Sysx view, you need to do a data dump. Essentially, the MIDI device from which you want to grab data dumps (or sends) it to your computer to be stored in one of the Sysx view banks.

> **THE RECORD SYSTEM EXCLUSIVE SETTING:** Be sure to check SONAR's global MIDI options to see whether the Record System Exclusive Data setting is activated. To do so, choose Edit > Preferences and then select the MIDI - Playback and Recording category. In the Record section, click System Exclusive to place a check mark next to it. If this setting isn't turned on, SONAR will block all incoming system exclusive data. By default, SONAR has this option activated.

To do a data dump, follow these steps:

1. Choose Views > Sysx (or press Alt+Shift+7) to open the Sysx view and then click a bank to highlight it for incoming system exclusive data.
2. Choose File > Receive (or press C) to open the Receive System Exclusive dialog box (see Figure 16.2).

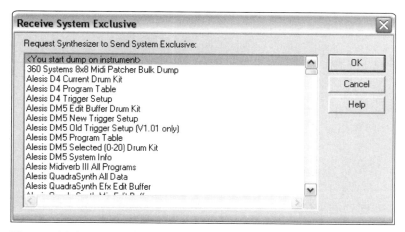

Figure 16.2 You use the Receive System Exclusive dialog box to request a data dump from your MIDI device.
Source: Cakewalk®, Inc.

3. Choose a DRM (*Dump Request Macro*) from the list. If you don't see your MIDI device listed, select the very first option: <You start dump on instrument>. Click OK. Then start the data dump using the control panel on your device. (See the device's user manual for more information on how to use the control panel.)

WHAT ARE DUMP REQUEST MACROS?: DRMs are special system exclusive messages. Some MIDI devices support them, and some don't. If you have a MIDI device that supports DRMs, SONAR can send a DRM to the device, asking it to send back its parameter data. If you have a MIDI device that doesn't support DRMs, you have to initiate the data dump manually from the control panel on the device.

ADDING NEW DUMP REQUEST MACROS: If your MIDI device isn't listed in the Receive System Exclusive dialog box, it doesn't necessarily mean the device doesn't support DRMs. You need to look in the device's user manual to see whether it has DRMs available. If it does, you can set them up to be used within SONAR. To do so, open the file C:\Documents and Settings\<*Username*>\Application Data\Cakewalk \SONAR X2 Producer Edition\Cakewalk.ini (in Windows XP) or C:\Users\<*Username*>\AppData\Roaming \Cakewalk\SONAR X2 Producer Edition\Cakewalk.ini (in Windows Vista/7) using Windows Notepad. Inside that file, you'll find instructions for how to add new DRMs to the list in the Receive System Exclusive dialog box.

---

4. If you see your device listed, select the appropriate DRM and click OK. The DRM might ask you for additional information. For instance, if the DRM requests that the device send the data for a single sound patch, you need to input the patch number you want it to send. This process is pretty straightforward; you can simply follow the prompts.
5. Whichever method you use to initiate the data dump, SONAR ultimately displays the Sysx Receive dialog box when it's ready to receive the data (see Figure 16.3). The dialog box shows the number of bytes of data being received as the dump takes place.

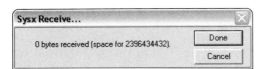

Figure 16.3 The Sysx Receive dialog box displays a count of the system exclusive data.
Source: Cakewalk®, Inc.

6. When the count stops, click Done.

TRANSFER TROUBLESHOOTING: If the number of bytes stays at zero for more than a few seconds, most likely something is wrong. Your MIDI device might not be hooked up properly, or you could have given the wrong answers for the additional DRM questions. Those answers differ, depending on the MIDI device, so you'll need to consult its user manual. In any event, if you have this problem, click Cancel and then check your connections and try the procedure again.

After the dump is complete, the Sysx view will show the bank you selected with a new name and length (in bytes).

Changing the Name of a Bank

If you want to change the name of a bank, follow these steps:

1. Select the bank.
2. Choose Edit > Name (or press N) to open the Sysx Bank Name dialog box.
3. Type a new name in the Sysx Bank Name field.
4. Click OK.

RECORDING SYSTEM EXCLUSIVE DATA: You can also record system exclusive data directly to a track, just as you would any other MIDI data. To do so, just set up your track parameters, start SONAR recording, and then manually initiate a data dump from your MIDI device. You should be aware of some limitations, though. When you're recording directly to a track, SONAR stores the data in Sysx Data Events instead of banks. Each Sysx Data Event can hold a single system exclusive message of only 255 bytes in length. This means that if your MIDI device sends a message longer than 255 bytes, the message will be cut off, and it won't work when you try to send back the data. Plus, you won't get any warning that this has happened—it just won't work. Essentially, you're better off using the Sysx view and banks to handle system exclusive data. It's much easier and more efficient, and you can still send data back to a device during playback.

Sending System Exclusive Data

After you set up your banks in a project, you can send the data back to your MIDI devices. Before you do, though, you should be sure that each bank being sent is first set to the appropriate MIDI output. Just as you can set each track in the Track view to send data to a particular MIDI output on your MIDI interface, you can set each bank in the Sysx view to a specific output as follows:

1. Select the bank.
2. Choose Settings > Output (or press P) to open the Sysx Bank Output dialog box (see Figure 16.4).

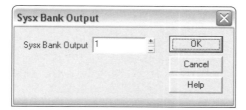

Figure 16.4 In the Sysx Bank Output dialog box, you can change the MIDI output assigned to a bank.
Source: Cakewalk®, Inc.

3. Type a new output number. Remember that the data in this bank will be sent only to this MIDI output, so be sure the number is the same as the output number to which your device is connected.
4. Click OK.

After you assign the right output numbers to each of your banks, you can easily transmit the data to the appropriate MIDI devices in one of three ways.

Sending Data Manually

To send the data in a bank manually, just select the bank and choose File > Send (or press S). You also can send all the data in every bank at once. You don't need to make any selections; just choose File > Send All (or press L).

Sending Data Automatically

Each bank in the Sysx view has an option called *Auto*. If you activate this option for a bank, that bank will be sent automatically every time you open the project. For example, if you store all the parameter data from all your MIDI devices in a number of banks using the Sysx view, and you set the Auto option on each of those banks, the next time you open your project, SONAR will send the system exclusive data to your MIDI devices automatically. Your studio will then be ready to go with all the correct settings for your project, without your having to do anything manually. To set the Auto option for a bank, just select the bank and choose Settings > Auto Send On/Off (or press A).

Sending Data During Playback

Although using the Auto option is a very convenient way to send system exclusive data, sometimes you might want to send a bank at a specific time during the playback of your project. For this purpose, SONAR provides a special Sysx Bank Event that you can place in any MIDI track in your project. Whenever SONAR encounters a Sysx Bank Event, it looks up the event's associated bank number in the Sysx view and then sends that bank.

You have to add a Sysx Bank Event to a MIDI track manually by using the Event List view. Here's how:

1. Select a MIDI track in your project and choose View > Event List to open the Event List view for that track (see Figure 16.5).

Trk	HMSF	MBT	Ch	Kind	Data		
1	00:00:00:00	1:01:000	10	Note	49	83	1
1	00:00:00:00	1:01:000	10	Note	35	127	2
1	00:00:00:07	1:01:320	10	Note	40	31	2
1	00:00:00:10	1:02:000	10	Note	42	66	1
1	00:00:00:17	1:02:320	10	Note	35	127	2
1	00:00:00:20	1:03:000	10	Note	42	127	1
1	00:00:00:20	1:03:000	10	Note	40	127	2
1	00:00:00:27	1:03:320	10	Note	42	12	1
1	00:00:01:00	1:04:000	10	Note	42	63	1

Figure 16.5 Using the Event List view, you can add Sysx Bank Events to your MIDI tracks.
Source: Cakewalk®, Inc.

2. Move the Now time cursor (the red outline) to the point within the list where you want to insert the new Sysx Bank Event. You can either click with the mouse or use the arrow keys on your PC keyboard to move the Now time cursor.
3. Click the plus sign (+) menu button (or press Insert) to insert a new event. Initially, the event will take on the characteristics of the event at which the Now time cursor was placed.
4. To change the event to a Sysx Bank Event, move the Now time cursor over to the Kind column and press Enter to open the Kind of Event dialog box (see Figure 16.6).

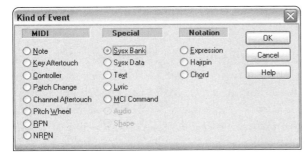

Figure 16.6 In the Kind of Event dialog box, you can change the type of the current event.
Source: Cakewalk®, Inc.

5. Select the Sysx Bank option in the Special section and click OK.

6. Move the Now time cursor over to the Data column and press Enter. The number in the Data column will be highlighted. Here, you enter the number of the bank you want to send.

7. Type a bank number and press Enter.

Now, when SONAR encounters that Sysx Bank Event during playback, it will send the appropriate system exclusive data to your MIDI device.

TOO MUCH INFORMATION: MIDI is meant to transmit only one piece of data at a time. Of course, it transmits the data so fast that it sounds as if all the data in the tracks is playing simultaneously. But MIDI does have its limits, and if you try to transmit huge amounts of data in a short amount of time, playback will be interrupted. This happens quite often with system exclusive data, so if you're going to send banks of data during playback, try to send only one bank at a time throughout your project and also try to keep each bank short. You'll have to do a little experimenting, but if you keep each bank between 100 and 255 bytes, you shouldn't have any problems.

Editing Bank Data

The Sysx view provides a feature that edits the data in a bank. To edit this data, select a bank and choose Edit > Edit Data (or press E), thus opening the Edit System Exclusive Bytes dialog box (see Figure 16.7).

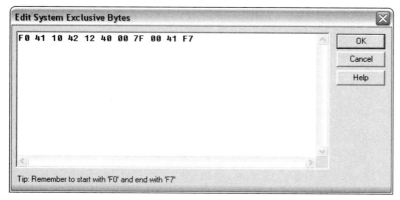

Figure 16.7 In the Edit System Exclusive Bytes dialog box, you can edit the data in a bank.
Source: Cakewalk®, Inc.

In the dialog box, you'll see a list of numbers. Each number represents one byte of system exclusive data in hexadecimal format. You can change the numbers just as you would change text in a word processor. If the bank contains more than one system exclusive message, the beginning of each message is designated by the number F0, and the end of each message is designated by the number F7. This way, system exclusive data stays compatible with standard data in the MIDI language.

Whenever a MIDI device sees the number F0, it automatically knows that this number designates the beginning of a system exclusive message. But that's as far as it goes in terms of identifying the data. All the bytes in a system exclusive message that fall between F0 and F7 are different, depending on which MIDI device they are associated with, so there's really not much else I can explain about this feature. If you want to learn more about the system exclusive messages your MIDI device supports, consult the user manual for the device.

If you want to delete a bank in the Sysx view, just select the bank and choose File > Clear (or press Delete). SONAR will ask whether you really want to delete. Be careful, because you cannot undo this procedure. When a bank is deleted, you cannot get it back without doing a data dump all over again.

Sharing with Friends

Even though all the data in the banks of the Sysx view is stored along with the data in your current project, you also can load and save banks individually in a special system exclusive data file format. This file format is the same one used by the public domain system exclusive data dump software utility called *MIDIEX*. MIDIEX is such a popular program that its file format has become a standard for storing system exclusive data on disk. What's great about the file format is that SONAR and many other sequencers support it, so you can easily share your system exclusive data with your friends. Of course, being able to share won't matter much if you don't own the same MIDI devices, but if you do, you can easily share sound data for your MIDI instruments and so on.

Saving

To save the data in a bank, follow these steps:

1. Select the bank.
2. Choose File > Save (or press V) to open the Save As dialog box.
3. Type a name for the file. The file should have an .SYX extension; SONAR should append this extension to the name automatically.
4. Click Save.

Loading

To load data into a bank, follow these steps:

1. Select a bank.
2. Choose File > Open (or press O) on your computer keyboard.
3. If the bank you selected already has some data in it, SONAR will ask whether you want to append the data from the file to the existing data. Click Yes to append the data or click No to replace the data. SONAR will display the Open dialog box.
4. Select an .SYX file to load and click Open.

The data from the file will be loaded into the bank you selected, and the bank will be named after the file. You can change the name of the bank, as you learned earlier.

> **COPYING A BANK:** There's no easy method for copying a bank, either within the same project or from one project to another, but you can copy using the Save Bank and Load Bank features. Just save a bank to an .SYX file from the current project. If you want to have a copy of that bank in the current project, just load it into another bank. If you want to have a copy of that bank in another project, open the other project and then load the bank into the Sysx view of that project.

Introducing StudioWare

Being able to store all the parameter settings for your MIDI gear within a project is great. You can have your entire studio set up in a matter of seconds. But to set those parameters initially, you still have to fiddle with the knobs and controls on the MIDI gear. Because some MIDI devices have a limited number of controls, the only way to change their parameters is to wade through an endless maze of menus on a small (and sometimes cryptic) LCD screen.

SONAR provides a feature called *StudioWare* that lets you adjust all the parameters in your MIDI devices without ever leaving your computer. More important, it lets you access those less-than-accessible parameters in a very intuitive and easy manner.

Using StudioWare, you can adjust the parameters for any of your MIDI devices remotely from your computer. Basically, you can have virtual buttons, knobs, and faders on your computer screen that represent each of the adjustable parameters in your MIDI devices. When you move a knob or fader on your computer screen, it changes the value of an assigned parameter in a MIDI device. Not only can you store MIDI device parameters, but you also can adjust them. Using the Sysx view and StudioWare, you may never have to touch your MIDI gear again (except maybe to turn it on). Plus, you can record the adjustments you make to any on-screen controls and then play them back in real time, which means you can automate parameter changes for a MIDI device as well.

The StudioWare View

StudioWare uses what are known as *panels* to represent your external MIDI devices. A panel can contain any number of controls (such as buttons, knobs, and faders), depending on the number of parameters your MIDI device provides. To start using StudioWare, you need to open a StudioWare panel file, which is displayed in the StudioWare view.

Opening a StudioWare Panel

A StudioWare panel is stored either as part of a project file or as a separate StudioWare file with the extension .CakewalkStudioWare. If a project file contains a panel, the panel is automatically opened when you open the project. To open a StudioWare file, just follow these steps:

1. Choose File > Open to display the Open dialog box.
2. Select StudioWare from the Files of Type list to display only StudioWare files.
3. Choose a file.
4. Click Open.

SONAR will display the StudioWare view containing the panel from the file you just opened (see Figure 16.8).

STUDIOWARE HIDE AND SEEK: The StudioWare view opens as a non-floating window in the background. To make it visible, minimize the Track view. Then click the upper-left corner of the StudioWare window and choose Enable Floating. You can then restore the Track view and the StudioWare view will stay in the foreground.

Figure 16.8 The StudioWare view displays your chosen panel.
Source: Cakewalk®, Inc.

Because all panels are different, I can't really explain how each one works. Usually, a panel mimics the controls of a MIDI device, so if you own the corresponding MIDI device, you shouldn't have any trouble figuring out how to use its StudioWare panel.

After you've opened a panel, you can adjust the controls, take a Snapshot, record your control movements, and so on. Adjusting the controls is straightforward. The buttons, knobs, and faders in a StudioWare panel work the same way they do in the Console view.

Unfortunately, SONAR no longer allows you to create your own StudioWare panels, but SONAR does include a number of predesigned panels that you can use in your own projects.

> **DESIGNING STUDIOWARE PANELS:** If you upgraded from SONAR 1 or 2 and you still want to design your own StudioWare panels, be sure to keep your previous version of the software. Using SONAR 1 or 2 is the only way you can access the StudioWare design mode, which has been removed from SONAR 3 and higher.

If you can't find a panel for your MIDI device, Cakewalk also provides a nice library of additional StudioWare panels in the Downloads area on its website; you can download them for free.

Taking a Snapshot

The Snapshot function works almost the same as with the Console view, but there are a few differences. Instead of recording the control data in separate tracks, the control data from a StudioWare panel is recorded into a single track. Most StudioWare panels include a knob control that sets the track into which the control data will be recorded. As an example, take a look at the General MIDI.CakewalkStudioWare panel, shown in Figure 16.9.

Figure 16.9 The General MIDI.CakewalkStudioWare panel provides a track control.
Source: Cakewalk®, Inc.

You'll see a knob labeled *Track*. Adjusting that knob changes the track number for the panel. If you open some of the other sample panels, you'll notice the same type of track control. It might look a little different, but it functions in the same way. By the way, if a panel doesn't have a track control knob, either the panel wasn't designed to record data to a track (some of them don't), or the panel will automatically record its data to track 1. When you're working with this kind of panel, it's a good idea to leave track 1 dedicated to recording MIDI control data.

To take a Snapshot of the controls in a StudioWare panel, follow these steps:

1. Set the Now time to the point in the project where you want the Snapshot to be stored.
2. Adjust the controls in the StudioWare panel to the desired values for that part of the project.
3. Click the Snapshot button (the one with the picture of a camera on it) in the toolbar at the top of the Studio-Ware view (see Figure 16.10).

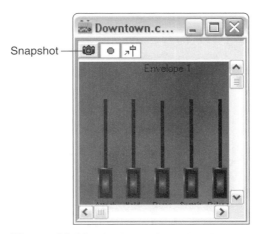

Figure 16.10 Click the Snapshot button to take a Snapshot in the StudioWare view.
Source: Cakewalk®, Inc.

4. Repeat Steps 1 through 3 until you've created all the Snapshots you need for your project.

Recording Control Movements

Recording the movements of the controls on a StudioWare panel is also similar to the same procedure in the Console view, but as with taking a Snapshot, there are a few differences.

The first difference is the track number procedure that was described in the preceding section. The second difference is in grouping controls together. Just as you can do in the Console view, you can group multiple controls together in a StudioWare panel so that you can easily change more than one control simultaneously. The differences here are in how controls are grouped and how single controls in a group are adjusted.

For grouping controls, instead of right-clicking on a control and assigning it to a colored group, you simply select an initial control, hold down the Ctrl key on your computer keyboard, and click one or more additional controls in the panel. Those controls are then grouped. Grouping controls in a StudioWare panel is much less sophisticated. StudioWare controls don't have any grouping properties like those that exist in the Console view. To adjust a single control that belongs to a group, just hold down the Shift key and then adjust the control.

All these techniques work with any StudioWare panel. However, there are also differences in the actual recording of the control movements. The procedure for recording control movements in the StudioWare view is as follows:

1. Turn on the Record Widget Movements function by clicking the Record Widget Movements button (the button with the big red dot on it), located just to the right of the Snapshot button at the top of the StudioWare view (see Figure 16.11). In addition, turn Automation Write to On for the track to which you are recording (see Chapter 12).

Record Widget Movements

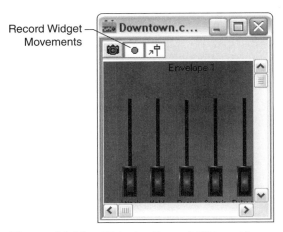

Figure 16.11 Click the Record Widget Movements button to activate the Record Widget Movements function.
Source: Cakewalk®, Inc.

2. Set the Now time to just before the point in the project where you want to start recording control changes.
3. Start the project playing.
4. When the Now time gets to the point in the project where you want to begin recording control changes, adjust the controls in the StudioWare panel with your mouse.
5. When you're finished, stop the playback of the project.
6. Because you're manipulating on-screen controls with your mouse, you can make only one change at a time. What if you want to have two different controls change at the same time? For every control that you want to change in the same timeframe, you must repeat Steps 2 through 5.

TRY LOOPING INSTEAD: Instead of starting and stopping playback each time you want to record additional control changes, try setting up a loop so that SONAR will just play the project (or section of the project) over and over again.

7. After you've finished recording all the control changes that you need, be sure to turn off the Record Widget Movements function and the Automation Write parameter.

UPDATING WIDGET VALUES: If you want the controls in your StudioWare panel to move according to the changes you recorded, activate the Update Widget Values function by clicking the Update Widget Values button (the button with the picture of a slider on it), located just to the right of the Record Widget Movements button at the top of the StudioWare view.

The Cakewalk Application Language (CAL)

One advantage that SONAR has over many other music-sequencing products I've worked with is that it enables you to extend its functionality. If you find yourself in a situation in which you need to edit your MIDI or audio data in some way that is not possible with any of the current SONAR features (which is not a common occurrence, but it can happen), you can create a new editing function to take care of the task by using CAL.

What Is CAL?

CAL (*Cakewalk Application Language*) is a computer-programming language that exists within the SONAR environment. You can extend the functionality of SONAR by creating your own custom MIDI and audio data editing commands using CAL programs (also called *scripts*). A CAL program is a set of instructions written in the Cakewalk Application Language that tells SONAR how to perform a certain task. For example, if you want to change the volume of every other MIDI note in track 1 to a certain value automatically, you can write a CAL program to do just that. And for future use, you can save CAL programs to disk as files with a .CAL extension.

> **PROGRAMMING LANGUAGES:** A *programming language* is a set of commands, symbols, and rules that are used to "teach" a computer how to perform tasks. By combining these language elements in different ways, you can teach a computer to perform any number of tasks, such as recording and playing music. The combination of elements for a certain task or set of tasks is called a *computer program*. For example, SONAR is a computer program, albeit a very complex one.
>
> A number of different kinds of programming languages exist, including BASIC, FORTRAN, C, LISP, and many others. Each has unique characteristics. If you are familiar with C and LISP, you'll feel right at home with CAL; it derives many of its characteristics from these two languages.

You might be saying to yourself, "Um, well, that's nice, but I know nothing about computer programming, so what good is CAL going to do for me?" Not to worry. Yes, CAL is a very complex feature of SONAR. If you really want to take full advantage of it, you have to learn how to use the language, but that doesn't mean CAL isn't accessible if you're a beginning user.

There are a number of prewritten CAL programs included with SONAR that you can use in your own projects, and you can find more by searching the Internet.

Running a CAL Program

Because all CAL programs are different, I can't explain how to use them in one all-encompassing way. When you run a CAL program, it usually asks you for some kind of input, depending on what the program is supposed to do and how it is supposed to manipulate your music data. But you can still follow this basic procedure to run a CAL program:

1. Select the track(s) (or data within the tracks) in the Track view (or other views) that you want the CAL program to edit. This first step is not always necessary; it depends on the task the CAL program is supposed to perform. It also depends on whether the CAL program was written to process only selected data in a project or all the tracks in a project. The only way to determine the function of a CAL program is to view it with Windows Notepad, which you'll learn about later in this chapter.
2. Choose Process > Run CAL (or press Ctrl+F1) to display the Open dialog box.
3. Choose the CAL program you want to run and click Open.

That's all there is to it. Some CAL programs carry out their tasks immediately, whereas others first display additional dialog boxes if you need to input any values. The best way to begin using CAL (and to see how it works) is to try out some of the sample programs included with SONAR.

RUN CAL PROGRAMS DURING PLAYBACK: You can run CAL programs while a project is being played back. This means that you can hear the results of how editing the CAL program applies to your data at the same time that your music is being played. If you don't like what the CAL program does, just choose Edit > Undo (or press Ctrl+Z) to remove any changes the program makes to your data. If you then decide that you actually like the changes, instead of running the CAL program again, just choose Edit > Redo (or press Ctrl+Shift+Z) to put the changes back in place.

The CAL Files

To give you a better understanding of how CAL works and how you can benefit from it, I'll describe some of the prewritten CAL programs included with SONAR in the following sections. I'll give you a brief description of what each program does and how to use it.

Dominant 7th Chord.CAL

The Dominant 7th Chord.CAL program builds dominant seventh chords by adding three notes with the same time, velocity, and duration to each selected MIDI note in a track. In other words, if you select a note within a track and run Dominant 7th Chord.CAL, the program treats the selected note as the root of a dominant seventh chord and adds a minor third, a perfect fifth, and a minor seventh on top of it, thus creating a dominant seventh chord automatically.

Of course, if you know how to compose music, you probably won't get much use out of this CAL program. However, you might find it useful while working in the Staff view. While you're editing a MIDI data track in the Staff view, try highlighting a note and then running Dominant 7th Chord.CAL. It's cool to see those additional notes just appear as if by magic. This program can save you some time while you're inputting notes by hand, too.

Other Chord.CAL Programs

SONAR includes a number of other chord-building CAL programs that work the same way as Dominant 7th Chord.CAL, except they build different kinds of chords:

▷ **Major 7th Chord.CAL.** This builds major seventh chords by adding the major third, perfect fifth, and major seventh intervals to the selected root note or notes.

▷ **Major Chord.CAL.** This builds major chords by adding the major third and perfect fifth intervals to the selected root note or notes.

▷ **Minor 7th Chord.CAL.** This builds minor seventh chords by adding the minor third, perfect fifth, and minor seventh intervals to the selected root note or notes.

▷ **Minor Chord.CAL.** This builds minor chords by adding the minor third and perfect fifth intervals to the selected root note or notes.

Random Time.CAL

If you overindulge yourself while using SONAR's quantizing features, your music can sometimes sound like computer music, with a robotic or machinelike feel to it. In some cases, this sound is desirable, but when you're working on a jazz or rhythm-and-blues piece, you don't want any of the instruments to sound like a robot played them. In this case, Random Time.CAL may be of some help.

This CAL program takes the start times of each selected event in a track and adds a random number of ticks to them. To give you some control over this randomization, the program first asks you for a number of ticks on which to base its changes. It then adds a random number to each event time that is between plus or minus one-half the number of ticks that you input. For instance, if you tell the program to use six ticks, each event time will have one of the following numbers (chosen at random) added to it: −3, −2, −1, 0, 1, 2, or 3. Using this program is a great way to add a little bit of "human" feel back into those robotic-sounding tracks. To use Random Time.CAL, just follow these steps:

1. Select the track(s) in the Track view that you want to process. Alternatively, you can select a single clip within a track or a specific range of events in one of the other views, such as the Piano Roll view or the Staff view.
2. Choose Process > Run CAL (or press Ctrl+F1) to display the Open dialog box.
3. Choose the Random Time.CAL file and click Open. The Random Time.CAL program will display a CAL dialog box (see Figure 17.1).

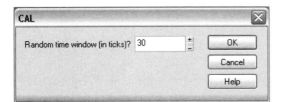

Figure 17.1 The Random Time.CAL program asks for the number of ticks upon which to base its event-time processing.
Source: Cakewalk®, Inc.

4. Enter the number of ticks you want to use and click OK.

You'll probably need to experiment a little bit with the number of ticks that you use, because a number that is too large can make your music sound sloppy or too far off the beat.

Scale Velocity.CAL

The Scale Velocity.CAL program is included with SONAR just to serve as a programming example; other than that, you don't really need it. SONAR already includes a Scale Velocity editing function, which provides even more features than Scale Velocity.CAL.

Split Channel to Tracks.CAL

If you ever need to share your music data with someone who owns a sequencing program other than SONAR, you can save your project as an .SMF (*Standard MIDI File*) file. Most computer music software products on the market support Standard MIDI Files; thus, they allow musicians to work together on the same song without having to own the same software.

However, not all Standard MIDI Files are created equally. Actually, several types of files are available; one in particular is called *Type 0*. A Type 0 MIDI file stores all its data—which is all the MIDI data from all 16 MIDI channels—on one track. Type 0 files are used often for video game composing, but they are hardly ever used when composing for any other medium. Still, you might run across a Type 0 MIDI file, and if you open the file in SONAR, all the data shows up on one track in the Track view. Editing the data is rather difficult, so Split Channel to Tracks.CAL is a useful tool in this situation.

Split Channel to Tracks.CAL takes the selected track and separates the data from it by MIDI channel into 16 new tracks. For example, if the track contains data on MIDI channels 1, 4, 5, and 6, Split Channel to Tracks.CAL creates 16 new tracks (from the initial track), with the first track containing data from channel 1, the fourth track containing data from channel 4, and so on. The remaining tracks that don't have corresponding channel data are just blank. You use Split Channel to Tracks.CAL like this:

1. Select a track in the Track view.
2. If you want to split only a portion of the track, set the From and Thru markers to the appropriate time values.
3. Choose Process > Run CAL (or press Ctrl+F1) to open the Open dialog box.
4. Choose the Split Channel to Tracks.CAL file and click Open. The Split Channel to Tracks.CAL program will display a CAL dialog box (see Figure 17.2).

Figure 17.2 The Split Channel to Tracks.CAL program asks for the number of the track to start with when you're creating the new tracks.
Source: Cakewalk®, Inc.

5. Enter the number of the first track that you want Split Channel to Tracks.CAL to use when it creates the new tracks. Be sure to enter the number of the last track in your project plus one and click OK.

After it's finished processing the original track, Split Channel to Tracks.CAL will create 16 new tracks, starting with the track number you selected, with each containing data from one of the 16 corresponding MIDI channels. Now you can access and edit the music data more easily.

Split Note to Tracks.CAL

The Split Note to Tracks.CAL program is similar to Split Channel to Tracks.CAL, except that instead of separating the MIDI data from a selected track by channel, it separates the data by note. For example, if you select a track that contains notes with values of C4, A2, and G3, Split Note to Tracks.CAL separates that track into three new tracks, each containing all notes with only one of the available note values. In this example, a new track containing only notes with a value of C4 would be created, another new track containing only A2 notes would be created, and another new track containing only G3 notes would be created.

This CAL program can be useful if you're working with a single drum track that contains the data for a number of different drum instruments. In MIDI, different drum instruments are represented by different note values because drums can't play melodies. So, if you want to edit a single drum instrument at a time, having each instrument on its own track would be easier. In that case, Split Note to Tracks.CAL can be put to good use. To apply Split Note to Tracks.CAL to your music data, follow these steps:

1. Choose Process > Run CAL (or press Ctrl+F1) to open the Open dialog box.
2. Choose the Split Note to Tracks.CAL file and click Open.
3. The Split Note to Tracks.CAL program will ask for the number of your Source Track (see Figure 17.3). This is the track you want to split into new tracks. Enter a track number and click OK.

Figure 17.3 Here you can enter the Source Track for the Split Note to Tracks.CAL program.
Source: Cakewalk®, Inc.

4. The program will ask you for the number of the First Destination Track (see Figure 17.4). This is the number of the first new track that will be created. Be sure to enter the number of the last track in your project plus one and click OK.

Figure 17.4 Here you can enter the First Destination Track for the Split Note to Tracks.CAL program.
Source: Cakewalk®, Inc.

5. The program will ask you for the number of the Destination Channel (see Figure 17.5). This is the MIDI channel to which you want all the new tracks to be set. Unless you want to change the channel, you should simply select the same channel that the source track is using. Enter a number from 1 to 16 and click OK.

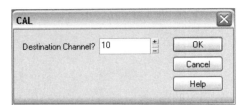

Figure 17.5 Here you can enter the Destination Channel for the Split Note to Tracks.CAL program.
Source: Cakewalk®, Inc.

6.   Finally, the program will ask you for the number of the Destination Port (see Figure 17.6). This is the MIDI output to which you want all the new tracks to be set. Again, you should simply select the same output that the source track is using. Enter a number from 1 to 16 and click OK.

Figure 17.6 Here you can enter the Destination Port for the Split Note to Tracks.CAL program.
Source: Cakewalk®, Inc.

After you answer the last question, Split Note to Tracks.CAL will process the original track and create a number of new tracks (depending on how many different note values are present in the original track), with each containing all the notes for each corresponding note value.

Thin Controller Data.CAL

You use MIDI controller data to add expressive qualities to your MIDI music tracks. For example, you can make a certain passage of music get gradually louder or softer (crescendo or decrescendo) by adding MIDI controller number 7 (Volume) to your MIDI tracks. Sometimes, though, an overabundance of MIDI data can overload your MIDI instruments and cause anomalies, such as stuck notes and delays in playback. If you have this problem, you can try thinning out the MIDI controller data in your tracks by using Thin Controller Data.CAL. This program decreases the amount of data being sent to your MIDI instruments by deleting only a select number of controller events—enough to reduce the amount of data without adversely affecting the music performance. It works like this:

1.   Select the track(s) in the Track view that you want to process. You also can select a single clip within a track, or you can select a specific range of events within one of the other views, such as the Piano Roll view or the Staff view.
2.   Choose Process > Run CAL (or press Ctrl+F1) to display the Open dialog box.
3.   Choose the Thin Controller Data.CAL file and click Open.
4.   The Thin Controller Data.CAL program will ask you for the number of the MIDI controller you want to process (see Figure 17.7). For example, if you want to remove some of the volume data from a track, use MIDI controller number 7. Enter a number from 0 to 127 and click OK.

Figure 17.7 Here you can enter the Controller number for the Thin Controller Data.CAL program.
Source: Cakewalk®, Inc.

5. The program will ask you for the thinning factor (see Figure 17.8). For example, if you enter a value of 4, the program will delete every fourth volume event it finds in the selected track or tracks. Enter a number from 1 to 100 and click OK.

Figure 17.8 Here you can enter the thinning factor for the Thin Controller Data.CAL program.
Source: Cakewalk®, Inc.

After you answer the last question, Thin Controller Data.CAL will process the selected track or tracks and delete all the MIDI controller events that correspond to the MIDI controller number and the thinning factor you entered. If this procedure doesn't clear up your MIDI playback problems, you can try thinning the data some more, but be careful not to thin it too much; otherwise, your crescendos and decrescendos (or other controller-influenced music passages) will start to sound choppy rather than smooth.

Other Thin.CAL Programs

SONAR also includes two other controller-thinning CAL programs. These programs work almost the same way as Thin Controller Data.CAL, but each is targeted toward one specific type of controller. Thin Channel Aftertouch.CAL thins out channel aftertouch MIDI controller data, and Thin Pitch Wheel.CAL thins out pitch wheel (or pitch bend) MIDI controller data. To run these programs, you use the same procedure as you do with Thin Controller Data.CAL, but with one exception. The programs don't ask you to input the number of a MIDI controller because each of them is already targeted toward a specific controller. Other than that, they work in the same manner.

Viewing CAL Programs

Unless a CAL program comes with some written instructions, you won't know what it is designed to do to the data in your project. This is especially true if you download CAL programs from the Internet. Many programs come with documentation, but many others don't. However, most programs do come with a brief description (as well as instructions for use) within their source code.

> **WHAT IS SOURCE CODE?:** *Source code* (or *program code*) is the text of the programming language commands used for a particular program. You create a program by first writing its source code. Then a computer can run the program by reading the source code and executing the commands in the appropriate manner, thus carrying out the intended task.

To read the source code of a CAL program, you need to use Windows Notepad (or some other plain text editor). As an example, take a look at the source code for Major Chord.CAL:

1. In Windows, choose Start > All Programs > Accessories > Notepad to open Windows Notepad.
2. Choose File > Open and select the Major Chord.CAL file from the SONAR directory on your hard drive (or some other directory where your CAL files are stored). Click Open. Windows Notepad will open Major Chord.CAL and display its source code (see Figure 17.9).

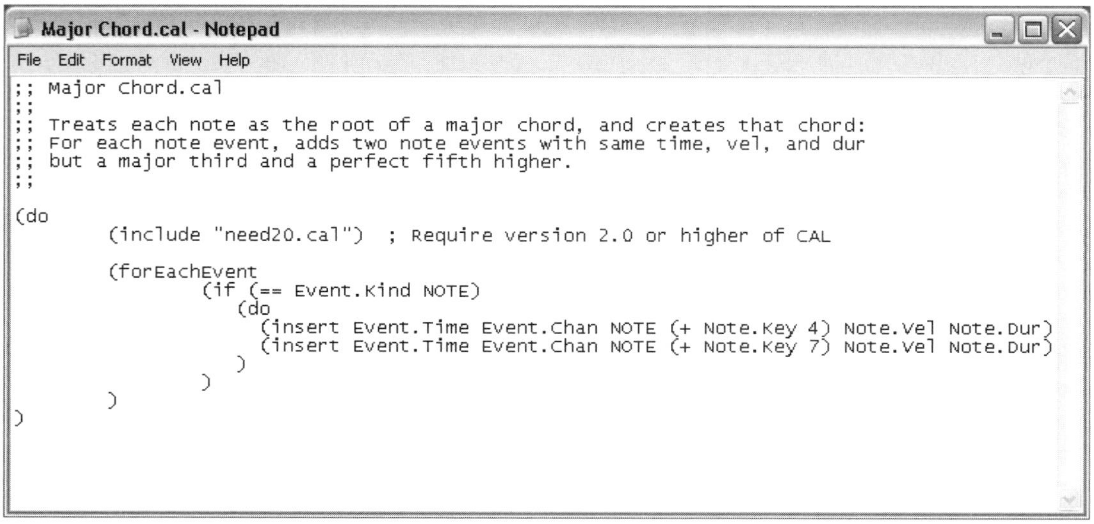

Figure 17.9 You can use Windows Notepad to examine and edit the source code of a CAL program.
Source: Cakewalk®, Inc.

As you can see in Figure 17.9, Windows Notepad allows you to see the source code of Major Chord.CAL and also to read the brief description included there. You can do the same thing with any other CAL program to find out how you can use it and what task it's supposed to perform. But that's not all! Using Windows Notepad, you can edit the source code for a CAL program, as well as create a CAL program from scratch. Because CAL programs are just plain text, you can use the same editing techniques you do with any other text, such as cut, copy, and paste.

Introduction to CAL Programming

Unfortunately, there is no easy way to create your own CAL programs. To tap the full power of its functionality, you need to learn how to create programs from scratch using the Cakewalk Application Language. The problem is that teaching a course in CAL programming would take up an entire book. So instead, I'll just get you started by providing a brief introduction to the language. The best way to do that is to walk you through the code of one of the CAL programs that comes included with SONAR.

To get started, open the Scale Velocity.CAL program (see Figure 17.10). The first thing you'll see is a bunch of lines that start with semicolons and contain some text describing the CAL program. These lines are called *comments*. Whenever you insert a semicolon into the code of a CAL program, SONAR ignores that part of the code when you run the program. This way, you can mark the code with descriptive notes. When you come back to the program at a later date, you will understand what certain parts of the program are supposed to accomplish.

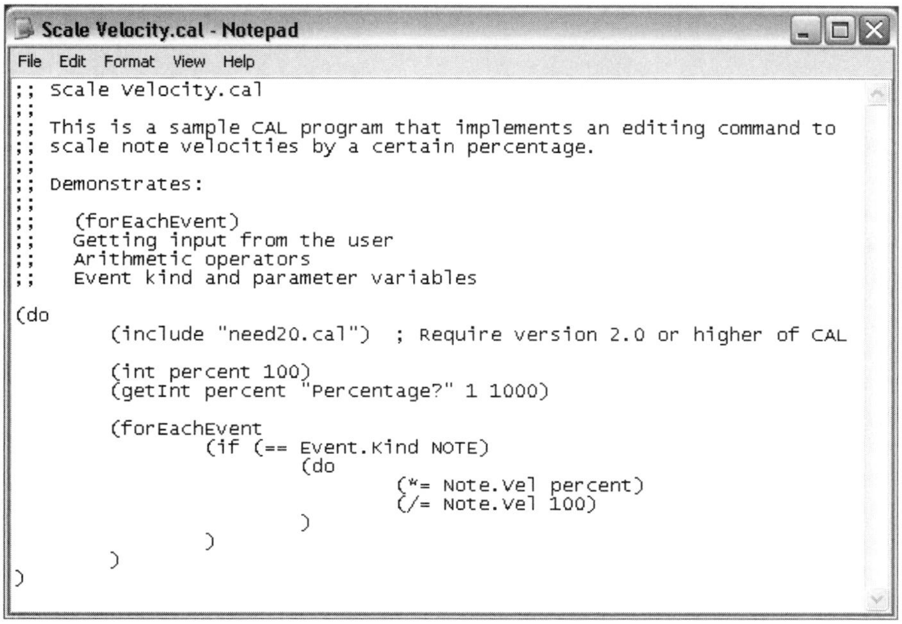

Figure 17.10 The code for the Scale Velocity.CAL program provides a nice example for an explanation of the Cakewalk Application Language.
Source: Cakewalk®, Inc.

A little farther down, you'll notice the first line of the actual code used when the program is run. The line reads (do. All CAL programs start with this code. The parenthesis designates the start of a function, and the do code designates the start of a group of code. As a matter of fact, a CAL program is just one big function with a number of other functions in it. You'll notice that for every left parenthesis, you'll have a corresponding right parenthesis. CAL programs use parentheses to show where a function begins and ends.

The include **Function**

The next line in Scale Velocity.CAL reads (include "need20.cal"). This is the include function, and it allows you to run a CAL program within a CAL program. You might want to do this for a number of reasons. For instance, if you're creating a very large program, you might want to break it down into different parts to make it easier to use. Then you could have one master program that runs all the different parts. You can also combine CAL programs. For example, you could combine the Thin Channel Aftertouch.CAL, Thin Controller Data.CAL, and Thin Pitch Wheel.CAL programs that come with SONAR by using the include function in a new CAL program. Then, when you run the new program, it will run each of the included programs, one right after another, so you can thin all the types of MIDI controller data from your project in one fell swoop.

In Scale Velocity.CAL, the include function is used to run the need20.CAL program. This program simply checks the version of CAL and makes sure it is version 2.0 or higher. Some CAL programs check the version to avoid an error, in case a very old version of CAL is being used.

Variables

After the `include` function, the code for Scale Velocity.CAL shows (`int percent 100`). This is a *variable* function. In CAL programs, you can define variables to hold any values you might need while the program is running. In this instance, the variable `percent` is defined as an integer and given a value of 100. You can use variables to store both number and text information. After you define a variable, you can refer to its value later in your code by simply using the variable name. That's what you see in the next line of code in Scale Velocity.CAL.

User Input

This next line reads (`getInt percent "Percentage?" 1 1000`). Here, the program asks for input from the user. In plain English, this line of code translates to, "Get an integer between 1 and 1,000 from the user by having the user type a value into the displayed dialog box. Then store the value in the variable named `percent`." Basically, when SONAR reaches this line of code in the program, it pauses and displays a dialog box (see Figure 17.11) and waits for the user to input a value and click the OK button. It then assigns the input value to the variable `percent` and continues running the rest of the program.

Figure 17.11 A CAL program gets input from the user by displaying dialog boxes.
Source: Cakewalk®, Inc.

The `forEachEvent` Function

The main part of the Scale Velocity.CAL program begins with the line of code that reads (`forEachEvent`. This is known as an *iterating* function. In this type of function, a certain portion of code is run (or cycled through) a specific number of times. In this case, for every event in the selected track(s), the code enclosed within the `forEachEvent` function is cycled through one time. So, in Scale Velocity.CAL, the following block of code is run through once for every event in the selected track(s):

```
(if (== Event.Kind NOTE)
  (do
    (*= Note.Vel percent)
    (/= Note.Vel 100)
  )
)
```

What does this code do? I'll talk about it in the following sections.

Conditions

Within the `forEachEvent` function in Scale Velocity.CAL, every event in the selected track is tested using the `if` function. This function is known as a *conditional* function. Depending on whether or not certain conditions are met, the code enclosed within the `if` function may or may not run. In Scale Velocity.CAL, every event is tested to see whether it is a MIDI note event. This test is performed with the line of code that reads (`== Event.Kind NOTE`).

In plain English, this line translates to, "Check to see whether the current event being tested is a MIDI note event." If the current event is a MIDI note event, then the next block of code is run. If the current event is not a MIDI note event, then the next block of code is skipped, and the forEachEvent function moves on to the next event in the selected track until it reaches the last selected event; then the CAL program stops running.

Arithmetic

The final part of Scale Velocity.CAL is just some simple arithmetic code. If the current event is a MIDI note event, the velocity value of the note is multiplied by the value of the percent variable, and the resulting value is assigned as the note velocity. Then the new velocity value of the note is divided by 100, and the resulting value is assigned to be the final value of the note velocity. This way, the program scales the velocities of the notes in the selected track(s).

Master Presets

One of the most effective uses I've found for CAL is in creating what I like to call *Master Presets*. SONAR lets you save the settings for some of its editing functions as presets. This way, you can use the same editing parameters you created simply by calling them up by name, instead of having to figure out the settings every time you use a function.

Presets are a real timesaver, but unfortunately, you can save presets only for each of the individual functions. What if you want to combine a few of the functions to create a certain editing process? For example, suppose that you like to shorten your MIDI tracks before you quantize them. To do so, you need to select the tracks, use the Length function, and then use the Quantize function to process your tracks. For each of the editing functions, you have to make the appropriate setting adjustments. If you create a CAL program to automatically run through the process for you, though, all you need to do is select your tracks and run the CAL program.

To show you what I mean, I've cooked up a sample Master Preset you can run as a CAL program and use in your projects. You need to complete the following steps:

1. Open Windows Notepad.
2. Type in the first few lines of code, as shown in Figure 17.12.

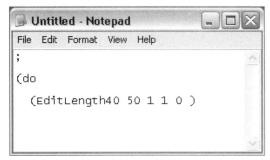

Figure 17.12 These are the first few lines of code in your new Master Preset.
Source: Cakewalk®, Inc.

3. Examine the code. The first line is just a blank comment. The second line designates the beginning of the program. The third line tells SONAR to activate the Length function using the parameters shown in Figure 17.13. In the source code, the command EditLength40 tells SONAR to activate the Length function. The number 50 corresponds to the Percent parameter in the Length dialog box. The numbers 1, 1, and 0 correspond to

the Start Times, Durations, and Stretch Audio options, respectively. A 1 indicates that the option is activated; a 0 indicates that it is not.

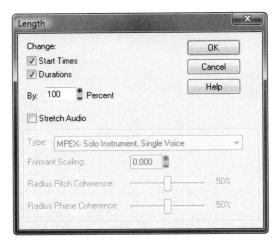

Figure 17.13 The first part of the CAL program shortens the selected MIDI tracks by 50% with the Length editing function.
Source: Cakewalk®, Inc.

4. Now type in the last two lines of code, as shown in Figure 17.14.

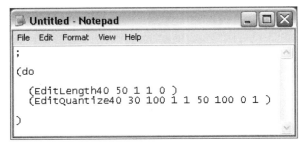

Figure 17.14 The final source code should look like this after you edit it.
Source: Cakewalk®, Inc.

5. Examine the code. The command EditQuantize40 tells SONAR to activate the Quantize function using the parameters shown in Figure 17.15. The numbers following that command designate the following parameter settings: Resolution, Strength Percent, Start Times (on/off), Note Durations (on/off), Swing Percent, Window Percent, Offset, and Notes/Lyrics/Audio (on/off).

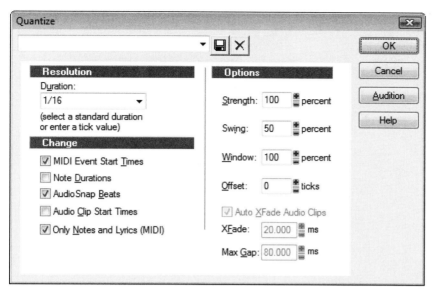

Figure 17.15 The second part of the CAL program quantizes the notes in the selected MIDI tracks with the Quantize editing function.
Source: Cakewalk®, Inc.

6. Save the new program with a file extension of .CAL.

Now when you run this CAL program, it performs all the editing functions for you automatically with the same settings you used.

CAL Conclusion

So are you totally confused yet? If you've had some previous programming experience, you should have no trouble picking up the Cakewalk Application Language. If you're familiar with the C or LISP computer programming languages, CAL is just a stone's throw away in terms of functionality.

Really, the best way to learn about CAL is to study the code of existing CAL programs. If you still find yourself lost in all this technical jargon, you can utilize CAL by using prewritten programs. As I mentioned previously, this part of SONAR has a lot of power, and it would be a shame if you let it go to waste. CAL can save you time and even let you manipulate your music data in ways you might never have considered. Don't be afraid to experiment. Just be sure to back up your projects in case things get a bit messed up in the process.

Audio for Video with SONAR

I N ADDITION TO ENABLING REGULAR MUSIC PRODUCTION, SONAR includes a number of features to help you create music for multimedia and the Internet. You can import a video file into a SONAR project and then compose music for it. You can also export video files along with your synchronized music. And you can export your music files to a number of popular Internet audio file formats, including Windows Media Format and MP3. In essence, these capabilities round out SONAR's full set of features, allowing you to use the program for most (if not all) of your music production needs.

Importing Video Files

If you're ever asked to compose music for film, video games, or some other visually based task, SONAR's File > Import > Video command will come in very handy. Using this command, you can include an AVI, MPEG, Windows Media, or QuickTime video in your project and edit the existing audio tracks or add new ones.

> **VIDEO FILE FORMATS:** AVI, MPEG, Windows Media, and QuickTime are special digital video file formats specifically designed for working with video on computers. Each format uses its own unique compression scheme to achieve the highest possible video quality in the smallest possible file size. Audio Video Interleaved (AVI) is a Windows-based format, which means that any computer running Windows can play AVI files. Windows Media is also a Windows-based format, but it is used more for posting video on the Internet. QuickTime is a Mac-based format, which means that any Macintosh computer can play QuickTime files. With special player software, a computer running Windows can play QuickTime files, too, which is why SONAR supports the format. Motion Pictures Expert Group (MPEG) is an advanced format that is used for DVD video as well as Internet video.

To add a video file to your project, follow these steps:

1. Choose File > Import > Video to open the Import Video dialog box (see Figure 18.1).

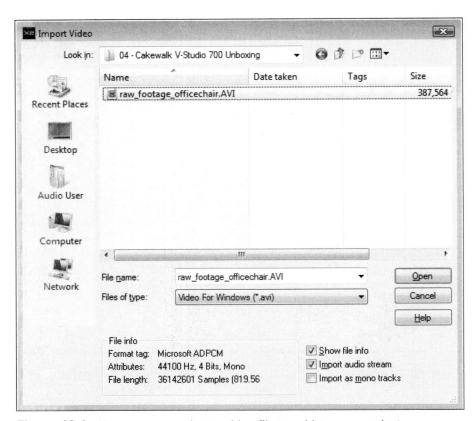

Figure 18.1 Here you can select a video file to add to your project.
Source: Cakewalk®, Inc.

2. Choose the type of video file (AVI, MPEG, Windows Media, or QuickTime) that you want to add from the Files of Type list and then select a file.

IMPORTING PROBLEMS: If you have trouble importing a video file, it may be that your computer doesn't have the proper video *codec* installed. A codec (coder/decoder) is a special piece of software that allows Windows to code and decode different types of video data. Each different type of video data requires a different codec. Most often, you can solve this problem by simply downloading and installing the latest version of the Windows Media Player (WMP). The WMP is a free download, and it includes many different types of codecs in its installation. Get the latest WMP at: www.microsoft.com/windows/windowsmedia/.

3. If the video file contains audio data, you can import that data by activating the Import Audio Stream option at the bottom of the dialog box. If the audio is in stereo, you can import it as a single stereo audio track or a pair of audio tracks containing the left and right channels of the stereo signal by deactivating or activating the Import as Mono Tracks option, respectively.
4. Click Open.

SONAR will load the video file and display the first video frame, along with the current Now time in the Video view. You'll also see a new section added to the Track view called the *Video Thumbnails pane*, which displays small frames of the video data, letting you see what is happening in the video at different points in time. If you imported audio along with the video, the new audio track(s) will be inserted into the project below any existing tracks so that you can see how the video and audio data are synchronized (see Figure 18.2).

Figure 18.2 SONAR displays the video using both the Video view and the Video Thumbnails pane.
Source: Cakewalk®, Inc.

> **DRAG-AND-DROP IMPORT:** You can also use SONAR's Browser to import video files. First, choose View > Video Thumbnail Show/Hide (or press V) in the Track view. In the Browser, click the Media tab and locate the video you'd like to import. Then simply drag and drop the video file into the Video Thumbnails pane.

When you initially play the project, the video will start playing back at the beginning, but you can change where the video starts by adjusting the start time, as well as the trim-in and trim-out times. Using these parameters, you can adjust when the video will start and end playback. To change the parameters, follow these steps:

1. Right-click in the Video view or Video Thumbnails pane and select Video Properties to open the Video Properties dialog box.
2. On the Video Settings tab, input the new values for the start time, trim-in time, and trim-out time. The start time uses measures, beats, and frames for its value. The trim-in and trim-out times use hours, minutes, seconds, and frames, just as with SMPTE time code.
3. Click OK.

The video will start and stop playing back within the project at the times you specified. You can adjust a number of other parameters for the Video view, and you can access all of them via the right-click menu. For instance, if you want to remove the video from your project, just select the Delete command. If you want to temporarily disable video playback, select the Animate command. You can even change the size of the video display by using the Stretch Options command.

EXITING FROM FULL-SCREEN MODE: If you choose Full Screen under the Stretch Options command, the video display will cover the entire computer screen, and you will not be able to access SONAR with the mouse (although the keyboard commands will still work). To get back to the normal display, press the Esc (Escape) key.

SONAR provides some additional settings on the Render Quality tab of the Video Properties dialog box. These include Preview Mode, Frame Rate, and Video Size. Basically, these parameters determine how you will view the video during playback in SONAR; they do not alter the video data itself. If you activate the Preview Mode option, SONAR will display the video using slightly lower quality. This lets SONAR use more processing power for audio playback and less for video playback, and it comes in handy if your PC is having a hard time playing both data formats at once. The Frame Rate parameter provides a similar functionality. Enter a lower frame rate for lower-quality video and to ease the strain on your PC. Using the Video Size parameters, you can adjust the size of the video during playback in SONAR. This essentially lets you preview how your video will look at a different size, but it doesn't actually change the size of the video when you export it.

Exporting Video Files

After you've imported a video file into your project and either edited its existing audio or added new audio tracks to it, you can export the file so other people can see and hear your work. Follow these steps to export the file:

1. Choose File > Export > Video to open the Export Video dialog box (see Figure 18.3).

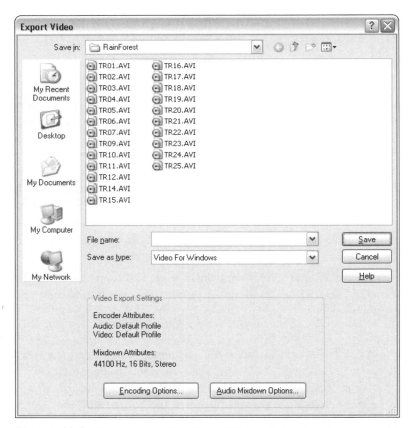

Figure 18.3 You can use the Export Video dialog box to export video files.
Source: Cakewalk®, Inc.

2. Type a name for the file in the File Name field. Then choose a file type, depending on what kind of video file you would like to save: AVI (Video for Windows), Windows Media, or QuickTime.

3. Click Save, and the video file will be saved with its original parameter settings. If you want to dabble with the method of compression used for the file or with other video-related parameters, you can set them by clicking the Encoding Options and Audio Mixdown Options buttons in the lower half of the dialog box.

> **HOW VIDEO WORKS:** For more information about multimedia and video-related parameters, you should consult a book dedicated to the subject. Don't let the title fool you; *How Video Works, Second Edition* (Focal Press, 2007) is very informative: garrigus.com?HowVideoWorks.

When you save your video file, any audio tracks in your project will be mixed down and saved along with the video.

Exporting Audio Files

In addition to exporting your audio tracks as WAV files for the purpose of burning to CD, you can also export them in a variety of other formats, including Windows Media and MP3 files, for distribution over the Internet or for other purposes.

> **SURROUND SOUND:** This section of the book discusses the exporting of stereo music projects. If you are working on a surround sound project, please refer to Chapter 14 for more information on working with and exporting surround sound audio.

> **CONVERTING YOUR MIDI TRACKS:** If you want to include the music from the MIDI tracks of your project in your exported audio files, read the "Converting Your MIDI Tracks" section of Chapter 13.

Audio File Formats

Just as different physical methods of storing audio were developed over time for different applications and reasons (vinyl records, tapes, compact discs, and now DVDs, etc.), different computerized methods for storing audio data have been developed as well. These methods come in the form of audio file formats. An audio file format is simply a specification stating the structure of how audio data in a file should be stored. For example, one audio file format may specify that the bits and bytes of audio data should be ordered in a certain manner, and another format may specify that the data be ordered in an entirely different manner. Of course, this is a very simplified explanation, but what it boils down to is that the same audio data can be stored in a variety of different ways.

Why do you need more than one audio file format? Because you may want to use your audio data for different tasks, such as playback on a CD, music or sound effects in a video game, a film or video soundtrack, or even for downloading over the Internet. Each task may require that your audio data be saved in a different way. For example, audio for a CD is usually saved in the WAV format and must be stored using a bit depth of 16 and a 44.1kHz sampling rate. But for downloading over the Internet, you would use a different format because with an uncompressed WAV file at 16-bit, 44.1kHz, every minute of stereo audio consumes about 10MB of disk space. Factor in that most songs average around four minutes, and that's a lot of data to download.

In addition to providing different bit depths and sampling rates, some audio file formats also offer data compression. This means that by saving to certain file formats, you can shrink the size of your audio files for use in low-bandwidth situations, as mentioned earlier with the Internet. Sometimes the compression doesn't affect the quality of your audio, but most of the time it does. With compression, you have to find a good compromise between the quality of your audio data and the size of the file you want to end up with.

Different audio file formats also exist because of the many different computer platforms that have been created over the years, such as Amiga, Macintosh, NeXT, and Windows PC. To provide you with as much flexibility as possible, SONAR allows you to import/export a large number of the existing audio file formats.

MP3 Audio (.MP3)

More than likely, you've heard of the MP3 audio file format. It's the most popular music format on the Internet. News about the format has even made it into the mainstream media because the format is being used to post illegal copies of music all over the Web. Why is the format so popular? Because it compresses your audio data with about a ratio of 12:1, and the quality of the audio is very close to CD quality. If you plan on posting your music on the Web, use the MP3 format for maximum audio player compatibility.

> **HOW MP3 WORKS:** For more information about the MP3 format, check out the HowStuffWorks site at: www.howstuffworks.com/mp3.htm.

Microsoft Wave and RIFF Wave (.WAV)

Like MP3, Wave is another very popular audio file format that you've probably heard about. Wave is a Windows-based format, which means that any computer running Windows can play Wave files. The format supports a lot of different types of audio data, including 8-bit, 16-bit, 32-bit, and even 64-bit monophonic and stereo audio. The Wave format also provides support for a huge number of different compression schemes, including many of the different ADPCM variants via the Microsoft ACM (Audio Compression Manager). The ACM is a part of Windows that works transparently, providing access to any compression schemes that are installed on your computer. Windows ships with a number of different schemes, and you probably also have a number of others from audio product manufacturers. If you're working with Windows, then you probably use the Wave format for about 90% of your audio work. Most sound and music software on the Windows platform supports this format. Wave files have a .WAV file extension.

You'll notice, however, that SONAR provides two Wave selections: WAV (Microsoft) and Wave (RIFF). Use Wave (RIFF) if you're exporting your audio to be used on an audio CD. Use WAV (Microsoft) if you would like to use a compression scheme. When you choose WAV (Microsoft) as your export format, SONAR provides an Extra Encoding Options dialog box. From the drop-down list, you can choose the encoding scheme you would like to use.

Broadcast Wave (.WAV)

You probably noticed one additional Wave file format in the SONAR export list: Broadcast Wave. This file format is similar to the other Wave formats, but in addition to the audio data, the file contains the following embedded information: Description (256 max. text characters), Originator (author of the file), Originator Reference (unique identifier created by SONAR), Origination Date (date file was created), Origination Time (time file was created), and Time Reference (SMPTE timestamp for the start of the file). The Description and Originator can be set by you in SONAR's Project > Info window using the Title and Author fields, respectively. The other information is added automatically to the file by SONAR. The Time Reference is the most important parameter because it tells you exactly when the file starts, thus aligning the beginning of the audio at the proper time in a project. A common use for Broadcast Wave files is remote recording. Most remote recording devices save to Broadcast Wave. This feature uses a portable device to do your location recording and then brings the Broadcast Wave files back into SONAR for assembling at the proper time codes. Broadcast Wave files also have a .WAV extension. SONAR's Import Audio dialog box will tell you what type of Wave file you are bringing into a project.

Windows Media Advanced Streaming Format (.WMA)

Windows Media is a special audio file format that creates streaming audio files for transmission over the Internet. The format is a Windows-based format, which means that any computer running Windows (with the Windows Media Player installed) can play Windows Media files. Windows Media supplies sophisticated proprietary compression features for making it possible to transmit audio data over the Internet in real time. This means that you can start listening to the data as it downloads, rather than having to wait for the whole file to be stored on your computer's hard drive. And the compression does affect the quality of your audio data. Windows Media files have a .WMA extension. Surf on over to www.microsoft.com/windowsmedia to find out more about this format.

Audio Interchange File Format AIFF (.AIF)

This is the standard file format for saving audio data on the Macintosh. If you ever need to transfer audio files between the PC and the Mac, this is the format you should use. Files in this format may or may not also contain a Mac-Binary header. If a file of this type doesn't contain a Mac-Binary header, it probably has .AIF for a file extension, which is the type that is supported by SONAR.

> **MAC-BINARY HEADER:** Files on the Macintosh are stored with what is called a Mac-Binary header. This is a small section of information stored in the beginning of a file that identifies the type of file to the Mac OS (operating system) and other applications. This is how the Mac can tell whether a file contains text, graphic, or audio data, and so on. If you want to learn more about how files work on the Mac, go to www.apple.com and check out all the technical information available there.

AU Sun/NeXT (.AU)

Like the Macintosh AIFF, the Sun/NeXT audio file format is also a standard format, but it's for the NeXT and Sun Sparc station computer systems, rather than the Mac or PC. This format supports many types of audio data, including 8-bit and 16-bit, monophonic, and stereo. It also provides support for a variety of compression schemes. If you download a lot of audio files from the Internet, you'll file many of them with the .AU file extension. Most of these files are 16-bit audio that have been compressed to 8-bit u-Law data for transferring over the Net or for use in Java applications.

Free Lossless Audio Codec (.FLAC)

Similar to MP3, FLAC uses compression to create small file sizes, but unlike MP3, the quality of the audio is not affected. FLAC is known as a lossless audio file format, which means there is no loss of quality when audio is saved to this format, even though the file size is smaller than if you had saved the same audio data to the WAV file format. This is a nice way to store audio data in a limited amount of space without having to worry about affecting the quality, but keep in mind that not all applications support this format. So you still need to store your data in another format if you want it to be accessible from within some other audio applications. In addition, because it is a lossless format, FLAC can't create the same small file sizes as the MP3 format. So either way, there is a trade-off between file size and audio quality. Go to http://en.wikipedia.org/wiki/Flac for more information about FLAC.

RAW File (.RAW)

RAW audio format files (as the name states) contain plain PCM audio data. The data is not saved in a specific format (like those mentioned earlier). When you save a RAW file, the audio data is saved in a "plain brown wrapper," so to speak. It's pure audio data. However, SONAR does allow you to choose the PCM format.

Sound Designer 2 (.SD2)

SD2 is a product-specific audio format for use with the Sound Designer 2 software application on the Macintosh. It only supports PCM audio, and the files have an .SD2 extension. Like AIFF, this format can be useful when you need to transfer your audio to the Mac.

Sony Wave64 (.W64)

If you work with very large projects in SONAR, you may have run into the 4GB file size limit imposed by the Microsoft Wave and RIFF Wave formats. The Sony Wave64 format does away with this limit and saves audio files of any length. In addition, SONAR now supports this format internally when recording audio tracks so that if your project starts to reach the 4GB limit, SONAR will automatically use the Sonar Wave64 format instead of RIFF Wave.

Apple Core Audio File (.CAF)

This file type is Apple's answer to the 4GB file size limit imposed by other audio file formats, but instead of being specific to Windows, this one is for the Macintosh operating system. You can use this file format when exchanging large audio files with another studio that uses Mac computers.

AUDIO FILE FORMAT FAQ: If you want to dig even deeper and find more in-depth information about these (and other) audio file formats, go to http://sox.sourceforge.net/AudioFormats.html to check out the Audio File Formats FAQ (Frequently Asked Questions).

Exporting to Windows Media

To mix and save your audio tracks as a Windows Media file, just follow these steps:

1. Select the track(s) you want to export in the Track view.
2. Choose File > Export > Audio to open the Export Audio dialog box.
3. From the Look In list, select the folder in which you want to save the Windows Media file. Then type a name for the file in the File Name text box.
4. Choose the type of file from the Files of Type list. In this case, use the Windows Media option.
5. Select the Channel Format you want to use. You can mix your audio tracks to a single stereo file, two mono files (that, when combined, create a stereo file), or a single mono file.
6. For the Source Category parameter, choose the Entire Mix option.
7. Leave all the Mix Enables options activated to ensure that your new Windows Media file will include the same effects and mix automation as you used on the original audio tracks. I also recommend activating the 64-bit Engine option if you want to use the best processing that SONAR provides.
8. Choose the Sample Rate. If you're exporting for the Internet, you'll probably want to use 44.1kHz (44100), but that is just an example.
9. Choose the Bit Depth. Again, for the Internet, you'll probably want to use 16-bit, but that's not a strict rule.
10. Set the Dithering. You usually want to set this to None, unless your project is recorded in 24-bit (or higher) and you are exporting to a lower bit depth (like 16-bit). In that case, you want to use dither, and the Pow-r 3 setting usually gives the best results.

11. Click Export to open the Windows Media Format Encode Options dialog box (see Figure 18.4).

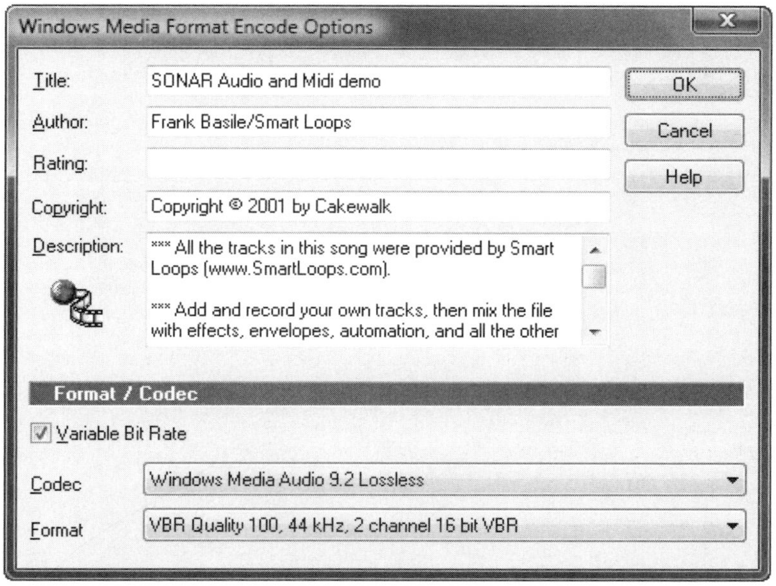

Figure 18.4 In the Windows Media Format Encode Options dialog box, you can adjust specific parameters for the Windows Media file.
Source: Cakewalk®, Inc.

12. Enter title, author, rating, copyright, and description information for the Windows Media file.
13. Choose a codec for the encoding process. A *codec* is a special piece of coder/decoder software code that specifies what type of audio file will be created. In this example, we are encoding a Windows Media Audio 9.1 file, but there are other versions of the Windows Media format available. If you have more than one Windows Media codec installed on your computer, you will have a choice here. Most of the time, you will want to use the latest version.
14. Choose a format for your Windows Media file. The Format parameter chooses the audio quality for your file. The higher the quality, the better the file will sound, but the bigger the file size will be. The standard for online audio is 128kbps. This produces a near-CD-quality audio file.
15. Click OK, and your audio will be saved as a Windows Media file with a .WMA extension.

Exporting to MP3

To mix and save your audio tracks as an MP3 file, follow these steps:

1. Select the track(s) you want to export in the Track view.
2. Choose File > Export > Audio to open the Export Audio dialog box.
3. From the Look In list, select the folder in which you want to save the MP3 file. Then type a name for the file in the File Name text box.
4. Choose the type of file from the Files of Type list. In this case, use the MP3 option.
5. Select the Channel Format you want to use. You can mix your audio tracks to a single stereo file, two mono files (that, when combined, create a stereo file), or a single mono file.
6. For the Source Category parameter, choose the Entire Mix option.
7. Leave all the Mix Enables options activated to ensure that your new MP3 file will include the same effects and mix automation as you used on the original audio tracks. I also recommend activating the 64-bit Engine option if you want to use the best processing that SONAR provides.

8. Choose the Sample Rate. If you're exporting for the Internet, you'll probably want to use 44.1kHz (44100), but that is just an example.

9. Choose the Bit Depth. Again, for the Internet, you'll probably want to use 16-bit, but that's not a strict rule.

10. Set the Dithering. You usually want to set this to None, unless your project is recorded in 24-bit (or higher) and you are exporting to a lower bit depth (like 16-bit). In that case, you want to use dither, and the Pow-r 3 setting usually gives the best results.

11. Click Export to open the MP3 Export Options dialog box (see Figure 18.5).

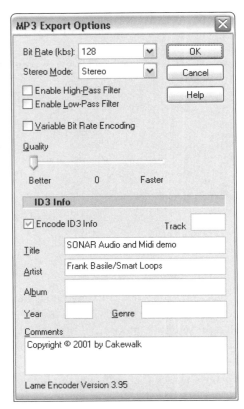

Figure 18.5 In the MP3 Export Options dialog box, you can adjust specific parameters for the MP3 file.
Source: Cakewalk®, Inc.

12. Here, you can select a bit rate and stereo mode for your file. Bit rate chooses the audio quality for your file. The higher the quality, the better the file will sound, but the bigger the file size will be. The standard for online audio is 128kbps. This produces a near-CD-quality audio file. The Stereo Mode parameter is pretty straightforward. Choose Stereo to produce a stereo file; choose Mono to produce a mono file. There is also a Joint Stereo mode, which lets you create smaller MP3 files by comparing the left and right audio signals and eliminating any material that is the same in both channels. Using this option usually degrades the audio quality, though, so I advise against it unless you really need smaller MP3 files.

13. The Enable High-Pass Filter and Enable Low-Pass Filter options apply some last-minute EQ to your MP3 file. You'll probably want to leave these options deactivated to avoid altering the sound of your project.

14. Set the Variable Bit Rate Encoding option. Activating this option tells SONAR to vary the bit rate during the encoding process. Sometimes this can yield a higher-quality sound and a smaller file size, but it depends on the material you are encoding. You'll have to experiment with this setting to see if it is worth using. Personally, I usually leave this option deactivated.

15. Use the Quality parameter to adjust the time it takes to encode your MP3 file. If you set the slider toward the left, encoding will go slower; set it to the right, and encoding will go faster. But the more time you spend on encoding, the better the quality of the file. I recommend you leave the slider set all the way to the left. Encoding a file (depending on its size) doesn't usually take very long anyway.

16. If you want to include some information about the file, activate the Encode ID3 Info option. Then you can enter title, artist, album, year, track number, comments, and genre information.

17. Click OK, and your audio will be saved as an MP3 file with an .MP3 extension.

OTHER FILE FORMATS: Exporting to MP3 or Windows Media requires additional steps. All other formats either export directly or simply allow you to choose a compression format.

Index

A4 Pitch sliders (TruePianos), 189
absolute grouping, 332
accelerando, 133
ACM (Audio Compression Manager), 432
ACT MIDI Controller
    ACT map, 338–339
    ACT preset, 335–338
active monitor, 7
AIF (Audio Interchange File Format), 433
Aim Assist function, 94, 112
AlphaTrack (Frontier Design Group), 6
Amber Module, 188–189
amplifier simulation effects, 287–288
analog tape simulation, 289
analog-vacuum tube simulation effect, 289
Angle and Focus parameter (Large Surround
    Panner), 369
anytime recording, 67
A-PRO keyboard, 6
archiving tracks, 66
arithmetic code, 423
Arpeggiator effect, 321–322
ASIO (Audio Stream Input Output), 4, 28
AU (AU Sun/NeXT) format, 433
audio clip conversion, 219–221
Audio Compression Manager (ACM), 432
audio editing, 103–104
audio effects. See effects
audio envelopes, 341–344
audio file
    exporting, 431–437
    formats, 431–434
    importing, 73
audio folder, 10
audio Groove clip, 218–219
audio hardware guide (Cakewalk), 4
Audio Interchange File Format (AIF), 433
audio metronome, 55–57
audio scaling, 104–105
audio settings
    buffer size slider adjustment, 27
    customization, 27–29
    panning laws, 29
    queue buffer and I/O buffer size, 28–29
    read and write caching, 29
audio signal flow, 238
audio spectrum, 254
Audio Stream Input Output (ASIO), 4, 28
audio track, exporting, 352–354
audio track strips (Console view), 235–238
Audio Video Interleaved (AVI) format, 427
audio waveform, 103
AudioSnap feature
    basic description of, 155–156
    default stretch, setting, 156–157
    Extract Groove feature, 159
    multitrack alignment, 160–161
    palette, 156

palette opacity, 156
    Time Ruler alignment, 157–158
auditioning
    drum tracks, 120
    effects, 254
Auto Zoom feature, 85–86
automation
    Automation Write mode, 329–330
    Cakewalk Analyst, 315–316
    effect, 347
    envelope, 347–348
    Latch mode, 329
    linked, 327
    mix, 328–330
    Overwrite mode, 328–329
    real-time effects, 253
    recording, 330
    Snapshots, 327–328
    soft synth, 166
    soft synth parameters, 172–173
    surround sound, 370
    time base, 329–330
    Touch mode, 329
automation lanes, 340–341
Automation Read button, 233
Automation Write on/off button, 233
Auto-Preview option, 72
Auto-Save feature, 42
AVI (Audio Video Interleaved) format, 427

backward play, 145
Bank parameter
    Console view, 233
    Track view, 36
Bank/Patch Change function, 122
banks, 23
bass guitar, 213
bass management, surround sound, 363–364
beam rests, 382
beat, splitting on the, 98
Beats per Pattern parameter, 124–125
Big Time view, 46
bit depth, 60
bit resolution, 5
Boost 11 Peak Limiter effect, 277–278
Bounce to Track(s) function, 96–97
BREVERB 2 Cakewalk (SONAR Producer)
    effect, 268–269
BREVERB 2 ProChannel module, 310
Broadcast Wave (WAV) format, 432
Browser
    adding soft synth using, 167–168
    description of, 3
buffer size slider, 27
bundle file, 1, 42
burning CDs, 353–355
bus
    adding, 242

Console view, 238–241
    controls, 238, 240
    deleting, 242
    Insert Send Assistant, 240–241
    number of, 242
    surround sound, 240, 364–365
    uses for, 240
Bus pane, 365
bypassing effects, 249

Cakewalk
    audio hardware guide, 4
    Plug-in Manager, 15
    Technical Support, 8
    V-Studio 700, 5–6, 335
    website, 7
Cakewalk 2-Band EQ effect, 255
Cakewalk AliasFactor effect, 291
Cakewalk Amp Sim effect, 288
Cakewalk Analyst-Spectrum Analyzer effect, 313–316
Cakewalk Application Language. See CAL program
Cakewalk Chorus effect, 261–262
Cakewalk Chorus (Mono) effect, 261
Cakewalk Classic Phaser effect, 263–264
Cakewalk Compressor/Gate effect, 272–273
Cakewalk Flanger effect, 263
Cakewalk Flanger (Mono) effect, 263
Cakewalk FX Compressor/Gate effect, 271–272
Cakewalk FX Dynamics Processor effect, 274
Cakewalk FX Expander/Gate effect, 273
Cakewalk FX Limiter effect, 273
Cakewalk FX2 Tape Sim effect, 289
Cakewalk HF Exciter effect, 258–259
Cakewalk Modfilter effect, 291–292
Cakewalk Multivoice Chorus/Flanger effect, 262–263
Cakewalk Para-Q effect, 255–256
Cakewalk Pitch Shifter effect, 280
Cakewalk Reverb effect, 265
Cakewalk Reverb (Mono) effect, 264–265
Cakewalk Sound Center (CSC), 211
Cakewalk Studioverb2 effect, 267
Cakewalk Tempo Delay effect, 261–262
Cakewalk TTS-1
    basics, 173
    demo video, 176
    effects, 175
    multiple outputs, 176
    pan and volume adjustment, 174–175
    saving instrumentation presets, 175
    selecting instruments, 173–174
CAL (Cakewalk Application Language) program
    arithmetic code, 423
    conditional function, 422–423
    description, 413
    Dominant 7th Chord.CAL, 414
    forEachEvent function, 422
    include function, 421
    Major 7th Chord.CAL, 415"

CAL (Cakewalk Application Language) program
(*Continued*)
    Major Chord.CAL, 415
    master presets, 423–425
    Minor 7th Chord.CAL, 415
    Minor Chord.CAL, 415
    Random Time.CAL, 415
    running a, 414
    Scale Velocity.CAL, 416
    Split Channel to Tracks.CAL, 416
    Split Note to Tracks.CAL, 417–418
    Thin Controller Data.CAL, 418–419
    Thin.CAL programs, 419
    user input, 422
    variable function, 422
    viewing, 419–420
calibration, monitor, 359–360
CDs
    burning, 353–355
    exporting audio tracks, 352–354
    MIDI track conversion, 349–351
    preparing project for, 349–354
Channel Tools effect, 294–296
Chord Analyzer, 322
chord grids, 381
Chord Library, 388–389
chord symbols
    adding and editing, 386–388
    positioning, 387
    quick chord selection, 388
chorus effects, 261–262
chromatic note changes, 384
clicking and dragging, 87
Clip Follow Project feature, 158
Clip Header Indicator, 93
clip-based effects, 250
clipping, 140
clips. *See also* Groove clip
    color, 92
    combining, 96–97
    copying, 98–99
    cropping, 101
    defined, 1
    deleting, 100
    erasing, 100
    groups, 61–62, 94–96
    header, 93
    hidden, 95
    inserting space in, 100–101
    isolating, 107
    linked, 99–100
    locking, 92–93
    moving, 98–99
    muted, 114
    muting, 92, 106–107
    name, 92
    overlapping, 61–62
    properties, 92–93
    repositioning, 102
    selection, 94
    shift-cropping, 102
    shifting, 102
    silent parts, 100–101
    slip-editing, 101–102
    splitting, 97–98
    start time, 92
    Step Sequencer, 129–130
    view options, 93
clock tick, 38
cloning tracks, 91
codec (coder/decoder), 428
color
    clip, 92
    customization, 11
columns and rows, configuring in Matrix view,
    226–227
combining clips, 96–97
comments, new project, 38

comping, 105–106
composing drum tracks, 117–119
compression, 306
compressors
    PC4K S-Type Bus Compressor, 306–307
    PC76 U-Type Channel Compressor, 305–306
    Sonitus Surround, 370–372
    Vintage Channel effect, 298–299
computer optimization, 4
computer program, 413
conditional function, 422–423
connection methods, soft synth, 169
Console Emulator, 311–313
Console view
    audio track strips, 235–238
    basic description of, 231
    buses, 238–242
    description of, 2–3
    hidden tracks in groups, 243
    MIDI track strips, 232–235
    opening, 231
    recording, 234
    show/hide console components, 243
    strip arrangement and selection, 242
    surround sound bussing, 365
Control Bar
    customization, 11–12
    description of, 3
    modules, changing, 12
    position of, changing, 11–12
    resizing, 12
    showing/hiding, 12
    Tools module, 79–80
control surface, 6
controllers
    adding, editing, and deleting, 121
    Bank/Patch Change function, 122
    colored line representation, 120
    inserting, 121–122
    pitch wheel, 120
    Scale pane, 120
    showing/hiding, 120
    in Step Sequencer view, 128
    time range parameters, 122
    as track envelope, 121
conversion
    groove to MIDI, 160
    sampling rate, 73
    SMPTE, 76
    Step Sequencer clips, 129
copying
    clips, 98–99
    effects, 249
    envelopes, 346
    imported audio file, 10
    importing files by, 72
    lyrics, 394
    notes, 127
corrupt bundle file, 42
count-in, 56
Creation Station DAW, 4
crescendo, 141
cropping clips, 101
crossfade, 143–144
CSC (Cakewalk Sound Center), 211
custom grouping, 332–333
customization
    audio folder, 10
    audio settings, 27–29
    color, 11
    Control Bar, 11–12
    file organization, 9–10
    key bindings, 18–19
    MIDI settings, 21–26
    plug-in menus, 12–14
    program and plug-in menus, 12–14
    screenset, 15–17
    Track view, 19–21

    workspace, 11–21
    X-Ray Windows, 17–18
.CWB file, 1, 42
.CWP file, 1, 41
Cyclone
    basics, 181
    demo video, 185
    Loop Bin loading, 182
    Loop view, 184
    Pad Editor, 184–185
    Pad Groups, 181, 183
    Pad Inspector, 183–184
    previewing sample files, 182–183
    slices in, 184–185

DAO (Disk-at-Once) burning, 354
DAT (Digital Audio Tape), 5, 75
data selection. *See* selection
DAW (Digital Audio Workstation), 4
DC offset
    accurate offset detection, 139
    removing, 139
    removing during recording, 140
    status, 139
decibel, 63
decrescendo, 141
De-Esser control (Vintage Channel effect), 296–297
Deglitch feature, 146
delay effects, 259–261
deleting
    buses, 242
    clip groups, 95
    clips, 100
    controllers, 121
    envelopes, 345–346
    event, 132
    groove patterns, 151
    groups, 332
    markers, 52
    notes, 113, 127, 385
    pitch marker, 224
    rows, 126
    soft synth from project, 168–169
    tempo changes, 134
demo video
    Cakewalk TTS-1, 176
    Cyclone, 185
    DSP-FX Chorus, 262
    DSP-FX Delay, 261
    DSP-FX EQ and Parametric EQ, 259
    DSP-FX Flange, 264
    DSP-FX REVERB, 271
    Groove clip, 224
    Matrix view, 229
    Roland GrooveSynth, 178
    RXP REX Player, 188
    Session Drummer 3, 195
    SPECTRAFX, 318
destructive processing, 101, 247
DigiFreq, 7–8
Digital Audio Tape (DAT), 5, 75
Dim Solo parameter, 234
Dimension Pro
    creating programs, 197–198
    elements, 197–198
    Elements area, 198
    interface, 196–197
    Modulators section, 198–199
    program related tasks, 196–197
disk caching, 29
display resolution, 382–383
distortion, 140
dithering, 97
docking
    Inspector, 55
    windows, 16
Dominant 7th Chord.CAL program, 414

downmixing, 375
Drag Quantize function, 114
dragging and dropping
  clips, 98–99
  effects, 248
  importing video files, 429
  track templates, 91
Draw tool
  activating, 79
  drawing notes, 113
  envelope editing, 345
drawing notes, 113, 385
Dreamstation synth, 173
driver mode, 27–28
DRM (Dump Request Macro), 403
DropZone
  basics, 205
  effects, 208–209
  elements, 206–208
  filters, 208
  interface, 205
  modulators, 208–209
  program-related tasks, 206
drum kit
  Roland GrooveSynth, 177–178
  Session Drummer 3, 192
  Studio Instruments, 213–214
drum machine, 74–75
drum maps
  assigning, 115–116
  creation, 116–117
  functionality, 117
drum tracks
  auditioning, 120
  composing, 117–119
  drum maps, 115–117
  mistakes, 119
DSP area (Rapture), 202
DSP-FX Chorus video demo, 262
DSP-FX Delay video demo, 261
DSP-FX EQ, 259
DSP-FX Flange video demo, 264
DSP-FX REVERB video demo, 271
ducking, 318–319
Dump Request Macro (DRM), 403
duration
  filling and trimming, 383
  note, 127
DVD-A, 376
DVD-V, 376
Dxi (DX instrument), 163
dynamic effects, 271–280. *See also* effects

echo
  applications, 58–59
  layering multiple synths, 58–59
  MIDI echo, 57
  recording multiple performances, 58
Echo Delay effect, 322–323
Edirol PCR-800 MIDI controller, 335
Edit Filter, 80–81
Edit menu, 12
Edit tool, 79
editing
  arranging with Track view, 4, 82–93, 95–107
  audio, 103–104
  chord symbols, 386–388
  clip selection groups, 95
  controllers, 121
  envelopes, 345–346
  in Event List view, 130–132
  events, 131–132
  expression marks, 390
  global editing tools, 79–82
  hairpin symbols, 391–392
  markers, 51–52
  MIDI data, 64

MIDI Groove clip, 221
notes, 112, 127, 384
notes via tablature, 398
pedal marks, 392–393
in Piano Roll view, 107–123
slip-editing, 101–102
Step Sequencer clips, 129
in Step Sequencer view, 123–130
system exclusive bank data, 406–407
tempo changes, 133–134
in Tempo view, 133–135
Track Folder, 88–89
effects
  amplifier simulation, 287–288
  analog tape simulation, 289
  analog-vacuum tube simulation, 289
  applying during recording, 249
  Arpeggiator, 321–322
  auditioning, 254
  automating, 347
  Boost 11 Peak Limiter, 277–278
  BREVERB 2 Cakewalk, 268–269
  bypassing, 249
  Cakewalk 2-Band EQ, 255
  Cakewalk AliasFactor, 291
  Cakewalk Amp Sim, 288
  Cakewalk Analyst-Spectrum Analyzer, 313–316
  Cakewalk Chorus, 261–262
  Cakewalk Chorus (Mono), 261
  Cakewalk Classic Phaser, 263–264
  Cakewalk Compressor/Gate, 272–273
  Cakewalk Flanger, 263
  Cakewalk Flanger (Mono), 263
  Cakewalk FX Compressor/Gate, 271–272
  Cakewalk FX Dynamics Processor, 274
  Cakewalk FX Expander/Gate, 273
  Cakewalk FX Limiter, 273
  Cakewalk FX2 Tape Sim, 289
  Cakewalk HF Exciter, 258–259
  Cakewalk Modfilter, 291–292
  Cakewalk Multivoice Chorus/Flanger, 262–263
  Cakewalk Para-Q effects, 255–256
  Cakewalk Pitch Shifter, 280
  Cakewalk Reverb, 265
  Cakewalk Reverb (Mono), 264–265
  Cakewalk Studioverb2, 267
  Cakewalk Tempo Delay, 261–262
  Cakewalk TTS-1, 175
  Channel Tools, 294–296
  Chord Analyzer, 322
  chorus, 261–262
  clip-based, 250
  copying, 249
  delay, 259–261
  dragging-and-dropping, 248
  DropZone, 208–209
  DSP-FX EQ and Parametric EQ video demo, 259
  dynamic processing, 271–280
  Echo Delay, 322–323
  EQ, 254–259
  external hardware, 320–321
  flanger, 262–264
  Freeze Tracks function, 253
  FX Chain, 250–253
  LP64 Linear EQ, 257–258
  LP64 Multiband Linear Compressor (SONAR
    Producer), 276–277
  MIDI Event Filter, 323
  modulator, 264
  moving, 249
  offline processing, 247–248
  order of, 249
  Perfect Space Convolution Reverb, 269–271
  phaser, 262–264
  pitch, 280–285
  presets, 254
  ProChannel
    BREVERB 2 ProChannel module, 310

Console Emulator, 311–313
functionality, 304–305
FX Chains, 310–311
PC4K S-Type Bus Compressor, 306–307
PC76 U-Type Channel Compressor, 305–306
QuadCurve Equalizer, 307–308
Tube Saturation module, 308–309
PX-64 Percussion Strip, 300–302
Quantize, 323–324
real-time processing, 247–248, 253
reverb, 264–271
R-MIX SONAR (SONAR Producer), 316–318
sidechaining, 318–320
Sonitus:fx Compressor, 274
Sonitus:fx Equalizer, 256
Sonitus:fx Gate, 274–275
Sonitus:fx Modulator, 264
Sonitus:fx Multiband, 275
Sonitus:fx Phase, 292
Sonitus:fx Reverb, 266
Sonitus:fx Surround, 293–294
Sonitus:fx Wahwah, 292–293
surround sound, 293–294, 370–374
TH2 Producer, 288
Time/Pitch Stretch 2, 280–281
timing, 285–287
TL-64 Tube Leveler, 289–291
Transpose, 324
TS-64 Transient Shaper, 278–280
Velocity, 324–325
Vintage Channel (SONAR Producer), 296–300
vocal timing, 285–287
V-Vocal, 281–287
VX-64 Vocal Strip, 300–302
window, 248
z3ta+, 210
electric piano, 214
elements
  Dimension Pro, 197–198
  DropZone, 206–208
  Rapture, 201–202
Elements area (Dimension Pro), 198
**E-mu PROformance Plus MIDI implementation
  chart**, 25–26
encoding, 376
Envelope Generator area (Rapture), 202–204
envelopes
  adding nodes at selection, 343
  audio, 341–344
  automation lanes, 340–341
  copying and pasting, 346
  deleting, 345–346
  editing, 345–346
  enable/disable, 344
  MIDI, 344
  Offset mode, 345
  override, 342
  quick envelope selection, 344
  quick waveform cycle change, 345
  restricting node movement, 342
  show/hide, 342
EQ (equalization)
  as effects, 254–259
  graph display, 300
  Vintage Channel effect, 299–300
equalization. *See* EQ
Erase tool, 79
erasing
  clips, 100
  notes, 113, 385
  tracks, 91
Essential edition, 3
event
  defined, 1
  deleting, 132
  editing, 131–132
  event type list, 131
  filtering, 130–131"

event (Continued)
   Go-Search function, 53
   inserting, 131–132
   MIDI command, 132
   parameters, 131
   preview, 132
   selecting, 131
   text, 132
Event Inspector
   note properties, 112, 385
   note velocity, 119
Event List view
   description of, 2
   editing events, 131–132
   editing in, 130–132
   filtering events, 130
   opening, 130
Event Mute function, 114
Exclusive Solo Mode parameter, 234
exporting
   audio file, 431–437
   audio tracks, 352–354
   to MP3, 435–437
   surround sound project, 374–376
   tablature to text file, 398
   video files, 430–431
   to Windows Media file, 434–435
expression marks, 389–390
external hardware effects, 320–321
Extract Groove feature, 159

fade
   crossfade, 143–144
   fade-in, 141–142
   fade-out, 141–142
   type settings, 141
Fade/Envelope feature, 141–143
Fast Zoom feature, 84–85
feedback, 61
file
   audio folder customization, 10
   copying imported, 10
   importing with Media Browser, 70–73
   locations, changing, 9–10
   missing audio file, 32–34
   organization, 9–10
File Info window, 39
file information, 38
File menu, 12
File Recovery Mode, 32
file types, 9–10
filling and trimming durations, 383
filter
   DropZone, 208
   Edit, 80–81
   selecting range of data by, 138
Filter and Amp section (RXP REX Player), 186
filtering events, 130–131
Find/Change feature, 151–152
Fit Improvisation feature, 155
Fit to Quarters parameter, 124
Fit to Time feature, 153–155
FLAC (Free Lossless Audio Codec) format, 433
flanger effects, 262–264
floating
   menu, 15
   MultiDock, 3
Focusrite Saffire PRO 40, 5–6
folder, audio, 10
font, 381–382
forEachEvent function, 422
formant scaling, 153
formats
   audio file, 431–434
   FAQs, 434
   surround, 361–362
   video file, 427

frame rate, 76
Free Lossless Audio Codec (FLAC) format, 433
Freeze Tracks function, 253
Freeze/Unfreeze Synth function (Synth Rack), 170–172
frequency
   audio spectrum, 254
   frequency response, 5
fretboard properties, 394–395
Frontier Design Group (AlphaTrack), 6
Front/Rear Balance parameter (Large Surround Panner), 369
FX bin
   adding soft synth to, 164
   MIDI track strip, 233
FX Chain
   assignable controls, 251–252
   basics, 250–251
   control range, 252
   custom interface, 252–253
   manual FX control creation, 251
   ProChannel effect, 310–311

gain
   Gain feature, 140
   negative infinity gain, 258
Gain parameter (Console view)
   audio track strip, 237
   MIDI track strip, 233
Gate control (Vintage Channel effect), 296–297
General MIDI standard, 22–23
ghost stroke, 381
global MIDI option settings, 22–26
global remote control support, 334–340
Go-Beginning function, 49
Go-End function, 49
Go-From function, 49
Go-Next Marker function, 50
Go-Next Measure function, 50
Go-Previous Marker function, 50
Go-Previous Measure function, 50
Go-Search function, 53
Go-Thru function, 49
Go-Time function, 49
groove
   converting to MIDI, 160
   extracting and applying, 159–160
Groove clip
   audio, 218–219
   creating, 217–219
   demo video, 224
   Loop Construction view, 219–222
   looping, 218
   MIDI, 219, 221
   percussion, 218
   pitch markers, 223–224
   project pitch, 222–223
   saving, 222
   slicing marker, 220–221
groove file formats, 150
groove patterns, 150–151
Groove Quantize feature, 149–150, 158–159
GrooveSynth
   demo video, 178
   drum kit, 177–178
   setting up for single synth sound, 176–177
grouping
   absolute, 332
   custom, 332–333
   description, 330
   Permanent Groups, 331
   Quick Groups, 331
   relative, 332
   surround automation and, 370
   ungrouping and deleting groups, 332
groups, clip, 94–96
guitar, Studio Instruments, 213

hairpin symbols, 391–392
hardware effects, 320–321
header, clip, 93
help
   Cakewalk Sound Center (CSC), 211
   Cakewalk Technical Support, 8
   Cakewalk website for, 7
   DigiFreq forum, 7–8
   Matrix view, 229
   offline, 7
   ProAudioTutor website, 8
   PSYN II, 181
   SONAR help file, 7
   user guide for, 7
Help menu, 12
Hertz (Hz), 254
hidden clips, 95
hidden controls, in Synth Rack, 168
hidden tracks in groups, 243
hiding
   Control Bar, 12
   controller, 120
   Track Folder, 92
   Track Icons, 89
   tracks, 91–92
horizontal zoom, 85
Hz (Hertz), 254

icon, soft synth, 170
implementation chart, MIDI instrument, 24–25
importing
   audio files, 73
   by copying and pasting, 72
   dragging and dropping, 429
   MIDI file, 73
   by ripping, 74
   screenset, 17
   from SONAR project files, 72
   using Media Browser, 70–73
   video file, 427–430
Impulse files, 269–270
include function, 421
Increased Polyphony option (TruePianos), 189
Inline Piano Roll view, 122–123
Input Echo button, 57–58, 60–61
Input Echo parameter (Console view)
   audio track strip, 237
   MIDI track strip, 233
input monitoring
   activating/deactivating, 61
   feedback, 61
   preliminary recording parameters, 60–61
Input parameter
   Console view, 235
   Track view, 37
Input Quantize button, 59
Insert menu
   changes to, 12
   surround sound bus, 364
Insert Send Assistant, 240–241
Insert Series of Controllers function, 121–122
Insert Soft Synth function, 165–167
Insert Tempo Change function, 134–135
Inspector
   description of, 3
   docking, 55
   preliminary recording parameters, 55
instrument
   Cakewalk TTS-1, 173–174
   MIDI
      banks, 23
      creation, 24–26
      General MIDI standard, 22–23
      implementation chart, 24–25
      NRPNs, 23
      patches, 23
      predefined definitions, 24

RPNs, 23
saving changes for next session, 24
setup, 23–24
Session Drummer 3, 193–194
instrumentation presets, 175
Interleave parameter (Console view), 237
internal synchronization, 74
International Standard Recording Code (ISRC), 356
I/O buffer size, 28–29
isolating clips, 107
ISRC (International Standard Recording Code), 356
Izhaki, Roey
Mixing Audio, 245

key bindings
assigning, 18
creation, 18–19
customization, 18–19
MIDI, 19
quick key finding, 18
saving changes for next session, 18
unbinding default, 18
key map, Pad Groups, 184
key signature, 39
keyboard
A-PRO, 6
MIDI keyboard controller, 6
TruePianos, 189
Keyboard Dynamics option (TruePianos), 189
keying, 318–320
Kind of Event dialog box, 405
kit-related tasks, Session Drummer 3, 193

Landmark, 82
Large Surround Panner, 368–369
lassoing, 94
Latch automation mode, 329
latency
MIDI playback optimization, 22
optimal audio settings, 27–29
sound card, 165
layout
plug-in menu, 13
Staff view, 379–383
Learn feature, 334
left-click scrolling, 86
Length feature, 153
LFO (low-frequency oscillator)
Pentagon I, 178
PSYN II, 180
linked automation, 327
linked clips, 99–100
Load Bank feature, 407
loading
programs
Dimension Pro, 196–197
DropZone, 206
Pentagon I, 178–179
PSYN II, 180
Rapture, 200
RXP REX Player, 188
Session Drummer 3, 193
Studio Instruments, 212
z3ta+, 209–210
sample files
in Cycle, 182
RXP REX Player, 186
Step Sequencer clips, 129–130
Track Icons, 90
loading modes, SoundFont, 191
Lock to SMPTE Time value, 51
locking
clips, 92–93
windows/views, 16
loop, 218
Loop Construction view
audio clip conversion, 219–221

description of, 2
loop recording, 64–66, 330
Loop view (Cyclone), 184
loudness (vocal dynamics) adjustment, 286–287
Low-Frequency Effects monitor, 358
LP64 Linear EQ effect, 257–258
LP64 Multiband Linear Compressor (SONAR
Producer) effect, 276–277
Lyrics mode, 393
Lyrics view, 393–394

Mac-Binary header, 433
mains (Console view), 241–242
Major 7th Chord.CAL program, 415
Major Chord.CAL program, 415
manual punch recording, 67
marker
creation, 50–51
deleting, 52
editing, 51–52
Go-Next Marker function, 50
Go-Previous Marker function, 50
jumping to specific, 52–53
Lock to SMPTE Time value, 51
making copy of, 51
name, 51
navigation with, 52
Now time, 48–49
quick marker list, 53
real-time, 51
rewind to Now time marker, 49
searching for data, 53–54
selecting range of data using, 137
slicing, 220–221
time value, 51
WAI, 235
Markers module, 52
Markers view, 52
Marks button, 82
Master control (Vintage Channel effect), 296–297
master device, 75
master presets, 423–425
mastering, 278
Matrix view
automatic matrix track creation, 226
basic description of, 224
columns and rows, configuring, 226–227
demo video, 229
Help file, 229
importing files, 225
loading cells, 225–226
recording performances, 228–229
row playback control, 227
triggering cell and column, 227–228
Media Browser
file management features, 72
importing files with, 70–73
Medium Surround Panner, 367
melodic scale, 110–111
menu
changes to, 12
floating, 15
meter
changing display range of, 63
meter independence, 243
Peak Markers, 244–245
performance, 244
setting the, 39
Waveform Preview feature, 244
zoom, 84
metronome
preliminary recording parameters, 55–56
sounds, 57
toggling on/off, 56
Micro Surround Panner, 366
microphone, 6–7
Microsoft Wave format, 432

MIDI
command events, 132
data
editing, 64
SMPTE/MIDI Time Code, 75–77
echo, 57
envelopes, 344
file, importing, 73
global option settings, 22–26
input preset, 38
instrument
banks, 23
creation, 24–26
General MIDI standard, 22–23
implementation chart, 24–25
NRPNs, 23
patches, 23
predefined definitions, 24
RPNs, 23
saving changes for next session, 24
setup, 23–24
interface, 6, 21
key bindings, 19
keyboard controller, 6
message, 22
note, 57, 322
patterns
Session Drummer 3, 195
Studio Instruments, 212–213
trigger notes, 195
playback, 22
port, 21–22
settings, 21–26
MIDI Channel parameter
Console view, 233
Track view, 36
MIDI effects. *See* effects
MIDI Event Filter effect, 323
MIDI Groove clip
creating, 219
editing, 221–222
MIDI In parameter (Pad Groups), 183
MIDI Input Quantize, 59–60
MIDI Microscope function, 114–115
MIDI Sync, 75
MIDI track strips (Console view), 232–235
MIDI/instrument track pair, 165
Minor 7th Chord.CAL program, 415
Minor Chord.CAL program, 415
missing audio file, 32–34
mistake, drum track, 119
Mix Enables option, 353–354
mixdown process. *See also* mixing
Console view
audio track strips, 235–238
basic description of, 231
bus, number of, 242
buses, 238–241
mains, 241–242
meters, changing, 243–245
MIDI track strips, 232–235
opening, 231
recording, 234
show/hide console components, 243
strip arrangement and selection, 242
Track Manager, 242–243
Track View configuration, 242–245
Mixer, Session Drummer 3, 194–195
mixing. *See also* mixdown process
automation, 328–330
downmixing, 375
surround sound, 365–370
Mixing Audio (Izhaki), 245
modulators
DropZone, 208–209
effects, 264
Modulators section (Dimension Pro), 198–199
modules, TruePianos, 189

monitor
    active, 7
    basic studio setup, 7
    connections, 359
    muting, 368
    nearfield, 7
    resources for, 7
    selection consideration, 7
    surround sound, 358–360
Mono/Poly switch, 125
Motion Picture Expert Group (MPEG) format, 427
Move tool, 79
moving
    clips, 98–99
    effects, 249
    moving, 127–128
    notes, 127–128
    rows, 126
MP3
    exporting to, 435–437
    format description, 432
MPEG (Motion Picture Expert Group) format, 427
MTC (MIDI Time Code), 75–77
Multi-CPU Engine option (TruePianos), 189
MultiDock
    description of, 3
    floating the, 3
    window positioning, 15–16
multiple track recording, 64
multitrack loop recording, 65
mute
    clips, 92, 106–107
    monitor, 368
    soft synth, 170
Mute button (Synth Rack), 170
Mute parameter (Console view), 234
Mute tool, 106

name
    clip, 92
    marker, 51
    pitch marker, 223
    soft synth, 170
    track, 36
Name parameter
    Console view, 235
    Track view, 36
nearfield monitor, 7
negative infinity gain, 258
newsletter, DigiFreq music technology, 8
nondestructive fade-in, 141
nondestructive processing, 248
nonregistered parameter numbers (NRPNs), 23
Normalize feature, 141
Note Glue function, 114
Note Map pane
    mute and solo options, 127
    row manipulation, 126
    row properties, 126
Note Split function, 114
notes
    adding, 127
    adding via tablature, 397–398
    constraining note movement, 112
    copying, 127
    deleting, 113, 127, 385
    Drag Quantize function, 114
    drawing, 385
    drawing (adding), 113
    duration, 127
    editing, 112, 127, 384
    editing via tablature, 398
    erasing, 113, 385
    Event Mute function, 114
    MIDI Microscope function, 114–115
    Note Glue function, 114
    Note Split function, 114
    overlapping, 111

    pitch, 116
    properties, 112
    scrubbing, 113, 385–386
    selection, 111, 383
    Snap to Scale feature, 110–111
    splitting, 127
    in Step Sequencer view, 125–128
    swapping between rows, 127
    Track Folder, 89
    velocity, 119–120, 127
Now time
    Big Time view, 46
    cursor, positioning, 132
    formats, 46
    location, 45–46
    marker, 48–49
    setting graphically, 48
    setting to precise numerical value, 47–48
    shortcut, 48
    stopping automatic playback, 47
    Time Ruler format, 47
NRPNs (nonregistered parameter numbers), 23
Nudge feature, 147
Num Pad key, 69
numerical value adjustment, Rapture, 203

offline processing, 247–248
Offline rendering, 156–157
Offset mode, 345
.OMF file, 41
Online rendering, 156–157
opening
    Console view, 231
    Event List view, 130
    projects, 31–34
    Staff view, 378
    Step Sequencer view, 124
    Tempo view, 133
optimization
    computer, 4
    MIDI playback, 22
oscillator modules
    Pentagon I, 178
    PSYN II, 180
output
    Cakewalk TTS-1, 176
    Pad Groups, 183
    surround sound card, 362–363
Output parameter
    Console view, 235, 237
    Track view, 37
overlapping
    clips, 61–62
    notes, 111
Overwrite mode, 61, 328–329

Pad Groups (Cyclone)
    adjustable parameters, 181
    MIDI In parameter, 183
    Output parameter, 183
    Pad Inspector, 183–184
    pitch markers, 184
    Root parameter, 183
    Velocity and Key Map parameters, 184
Pad section (RXP REX Player), 186
Pan parameter
    Console view, 235
    Track view, 37
panels, StudioWare, 408–409
panning, 37
    adjustment, 174–175
    optimal audio settings, 29
    surround sound, 366–370
parallel compression, 306
Parametric EQ, 259
pasting
    copying and pasting clips, 99

    copying and pasting notes, 127
    envelopes, 346
    importing files by, 72
    lyrics, 394
Patch Browser, 233
Patch parameter
    Console view, 233
    Track view, 37
patches, 23
Pattern Grid (Studio Instruments), 213
patterns
    importing, 73
    length, 124–125
    recording repeating, 69–70
    step recording, 128–129
    Step Sequencer view, 123–124
PC4K S-Type Bus Compressor, 306–307
PC76 U-Type Channel Compressor, 305–306
Peak Markers, 244–245
pedal events, 381
pedal marks, 392–393
Pentagon I
    loading programs, 178–179
    oscillator modules, 178
    quick program selection, 178
    saving programs, 178
percussion Groove clip, 218
percussion tracks, 380–381
Perfect Space Convolution Reverb (SONAR Producer) effect, 269–271
Perfect Space window, 271
performance, Matrix view, 228–229
Permanent Groups, 331
per-project audio folder, 10
phase cancellation, 237, 295
Phase parameter (Console view), 237
phaser effects, 262–264
physical modeling, 287
Piano Roll view
    basic description of, 107–109
    controllers, 120–122
    description of, 2
    drum tracks, 115–119
    editing in, 107–123
    Inline Piano Roll view, 122–123
    multiple track use, 109–110
    opening the, 108–109
    Track pane, 109
    track-related functions, 109–110
    working with notes in, 110–115
piano, Studio Instruments, 214
Pick Tracks feature, 379
picture folder, 10
pitch
    effects, 280–285
    note, 116
    project pitch, 222–223
pitch markers
    copy of, 224
    deleting, 224
    Matrix performance, 229
    name, 223
    Pad Groups, 184
    time value, 223–224
pitch wheel, 120
playback
    multiple track recording and, 64
    running CAL programs during, 414
    sending system exclusive data during, 405–406
plug-in
    basic description of, 247
    defined, 163
    menus
        accessing, 12–13
        customization, 12–14
        layout, 13
        organizing by category, 13–14
        presets, 13

Plug-in Layouts menu, 13
Plug-in Manager (Cakewalk), 15
Position slider, 48
Power On/Off button (Synth Rack), 169
PPQ (pulses per quarter note), 38
Preset parameter (Synth Rack), 170
presets
    ACT, 335–338
    effect, 254
    MIDI input, 38
    plug-in, 13
    saving, 54
    selection, 138
    soft synth, 170
    TruePianos, 189
previewing
    Auto-Preview option, 72
    event, 132
    personal settings, 72
    Preview at Host Tempo option, 72
    sample files
        Cyclone, 182–183
        RXP REX Player, 187
printing
    event list, 132
    music, 398–400
ProAudioTutor website, 8
Process menu
    changes to, 12
    Deglitch feature, 146
    Find/Change feature, 151–152
    Fit Improvisation feature, 155
    Fit to Time feature, 154–155
    Groove Quantize feature, 147–149
    Length feature, 153
    Nudge feature, 147
    Quantize feature, 147–149
    Retrograde feature, 153
    Scale Velocity feature, 154
    Slide feature, 146–147
    Transpose feature, 154
ProChannel effect (SONAR Producer)
    BREVERB 2, 310–311
    Console Emulator, 311–313
    functionality, 304–305
    FX Chains, 310–311
    PC4K S-Type Bus Compressor, 306–307
    PC76 U-Type Channel Compressor, 306
    QuadCurve Equalizer, 307–308
    Tube Saturation module, 308–309
ProChannel parameter (Console view), 237
Producer edition versus Studio and Essential, 3
program
    creation, 197–198
    customization, 12–14
    editing, 187–188
    loading
        Dimension Pro, 196–197
        DropZone, 206
        Pentagon I, 178–179
        PSYN II, 180
        Rapture, 200
        RXP REX Player, 188
        Session Drummer 3, 193
        Studio Instruments, 212
        z3ta+, 209–210
    saving
        Dimension Pro, 197
        DropZone, 206
        Pentagon I, 178
        PSYN II, 181
        Rapture, 201
        RXP REX Player, 188
        Session Drummer 3, 193
        Studio Instruments, 212
        z3ta+, 209–210
Program Browser
    loading Dimension Pro program, 197

loading DropZone program, 206
loading Rapture program, 201
loading Session Drummer 3 program, 193
loading Studio Instruments program, 212
program code, 420
project
    creating new, 34–40
    file information and comments, 38
    MIDI input presets, 38
    new project template, 35–37
    opening, 31–34
    reverting back to previous state, 43
    saving, 64
        Auto-Save feature, 42
        as .CWB file, 42
        as .CWP file, 41
        file versioning, 42–43
        as .MID file, 40–41
        as .OMF file, 41
        as project file, 41
    SONAR functionality, 1
    system exclusive banks, 38
    temp, meter, and key, 39
    timebase, 38
Project menu, 12
Project Navigator, 86
project pitch, 222–223
Project5, 73
PSYN II
    basics, 179–180
    Help file, 181
    loading programs, 180
    saving programs, 181
pulses per quarter note (PPQ), 38
Punch In and Out Times, 66
punch recording, 66–67
PX-64 Percussion Strip effect (SONAR Producer),
    302–304

QuadCurve Equalizer, 307–308
quantize
    Drag Quantize function, 114
    Groove Quantize feature, 149–150, 158–159
    MIDI Input Quantize, 59–60
    Quantize effect, 323–324
Quantize feature, 147–149, 158
queue buffer, 28–29
Quick Groups feature, 89, 235, 331
Quick Start dialog box, 31–32
QuickTime files, 427

Radio Frequency Interference (RFI), 5
Random Time.CAL program, 415
Rapture
    basics, 199–200
    DSP area, 202
    elements, 201–202
    Envelope Generator area, 202–204
    interface, 200
    numeric value adjustment, 203
    program-related tasks, 200–201
    Step Generator area, 204–205
RAW format, 434
read and write caching, 29
real-time marker, 51
real-time performance, 165
real-time processing, 247–248, 253
Record parameter (Console view), 234
Record Widget Movements function, 411
recording
    anytime, 67
    applying effects during, 249
    automation, 330
    Console view, 234
    editing MIDI data, 64
    loop, 64–66, 330

multiple tracks, 64
parameter movements, 347–348
preliminary parameters for, 55–62
punch, 66–67
removing DC offset during, 140
repeating patterns, 69–70
saving project after, 64
step, 67–70
step recording patterns, 128–129
step-by-step instructions, 62–64
synchronization basics, 74–77
Undo History feature, 63
Recording Mode, 61–62
registered parameter numbers (RPNs), 23
relative grouping, 332
remote control
    ACT MIDI Controller, 335–339
    control surface setup, 334–335
    Edirol PCR-800 MIDI controller, 335
    global remote control support, 334–340
    Learn feature, 334
    Remote Control feature, 333–334
    WAI (Where Am I) feature, 339–340
Remove DC Offset function, 139
Remove Silence feature, 144–145
rendering, 156–157
repeating patterns, 69–70
repositioning clips, 102
retriggering, 228
Retrograde feature, 153
reverb effects. See effects
reversing tracks, 145
reverting project, 43
rewind to Now time marker, 49
Rewire, 190
REX files, 185
RFI (Radio Frequency Interference), 5
RIFF format, 432
ripping, 74
ritardando, 133
R-MIX SONAR (SONAR Producer), 316–318
Roland GrooveSynth
    demo video, 178
    drum kit, 177–178
    setting up for single synth sound, 176–177
Root parameter (Pad Groups), 183
row
    deleting, 126
    inserting new, 126
    Matrix view, 226–227
    moving, 126
    properties, 126
    row track assignment, 226–227
    swapping notes between, 127
RPNs (registered parameter numbers), 23
RXP REX Player
    advanced interface, 189
    basics, 185
    controls, 186
    demo video, 188
    editing programs, 187–188
    loading sample files, 186
    multiple file formats, 186
    previewing samples files, 187
    REX files, 185
    saving and loading programs, 188

Safe Mode, 32
Saffire PRO 40 (Focusrite), 5–6
sampling rate, 5
    conversion, 73
    preliminary recording parameters, 60
    settings, 60
Save Bank feature, 407
saving
    Groove clip, 222
    groove patterns, 150–151

saving (*Continued*)
  presets, 54
  program
    Dimension Pro, 197
    DropZone, 206
    Pentagon I, 178
    PSYN II, 181
    Rapture, 201
    RXP REX Player, 188
    Session Drummer 3, 193
    Studio Instruments, 212
    z3ta+, 209–210
  projects, 64
    Auto-Save feature, 42
    as .CWB file, 42
    as .CWP file, 41
    file versioning, 42–43
    as .MID file, 40–41
    as .OMF file, 41
    as project file, 41
  Step Sequencer clips, 129–130
Scale Manager feature, 111
Scale Velocity feature, 154
Scale Velocity.CAL program, 416
scaling values, Find/Change feature, 152
screenset
  docking options, 15–16
  full screen, 17
screenshot
  creating and selecting, 17
  customization, 15–17
  importing, 17
Scroll Lock feature, 83
scrollbar, Track view, 83
scrolling
  left-click, 86
  in Project Navigator, 86
Scrub tool, 113
scrubbing notes, 113, 385–386
SD2 (Sound Designer 2) format, 434
SD3. *See* Session Drummer 3
Select tool
  activating, 79
  clip selection, 94
  creating or moving slicing markers, 220
selection
  applications, 138–139
  clips, 94
  event, 131
  MIDI port, 21–22
  note, 111
  preset, 138
  range of data by filter, 138
  range of data by time, 137
  track, 87
Selection Audition feature, 94
Send parameters (Console view), 237–238
sending system exclusive data, 404–406
Session Drummer 3
  basics, 192
  demo video, 195
  instruments, 193–194
  kit-related tasks, 193
  MIDI patterns, 195
  Mixer, 194–195
  program related tasks, 192–193
sfz SoundFont Player, 190–192
sharing data, 407
shift-cropping clips, 102
shifting clips, 102
shortcut
  Now time, 48
  zoom, 87
show/hide console components (Console view), 243
sibilance, 297
sidechaining effects
  ducking, 318–319
  keying, 318–320

signal-to-noise ratio, 5
silence, getting rid of, 144–145
Simple Instrument Track option, 165
simulation effects, 287–291
Skylight, 1–3
slave device, 75
slices, 184–185
slicing marker, 220–221
Slide feature, 146–147
slip-editing, 101–102
Small Surround Panner, 366–367
Smart Grid feature, 82
Smart tool
  activating, 79
  clip selection, 94
  splitting clips, 98
  switching between tools, 80
  tempo changes, 133
SMF (Standard MIDI File), 416
SMPTE converter, 76
SMPTE offset, 76
SMPTE (Society of Motion Picture and Television
    Engineers), 46
SMPTE/MIDI Time Code, 75–77
Snap Intensity feature, 82
Snap module, 81–82
Snap to Grid feature
  activating, 81
  alternate snap value, 82
  placing notes on beats, 118
  toggling on/off, 81
  zero crossings feature, 104
Snap to Scale feature, 110–111
Snapshot function, 409–410
Snapshots, 327–328
Society of Motion Picture and Television Engineers
    (SMPTE), 46
soft synth. *See also* Synth Rack
  adding, 168
  adding manually, 164–165
  automation, 166, 347–348
  automation synth parameters, 172–173
  Cakewalk Sound Center, 211
  Cakewalk TTS-1, 173–176
  connection methods, 169
  control knobs, 172
  controlling synth parameters, 172
  Cyclone, 181–185
  Dimension Pro, 196–199
  Dreamstation, 173
  DropZone, 205–209
  freezing/unfreezing, 170–172
  functionality, 163–164
  icon, 170
  Insert Soft Synth function, 165–167
  introduction to, 163
  MIDI output, 166
  multiple audio outputs, 166
  mute, 170
  name, 170
  Pentagon I, 178–179
  preset, 170
  properties, 169
  PSYN II, 179–181
  Rapture, 199–205
  real-time performance, 165
  removing, 168–169
  replacing, 169
  ReWire, 190
  Roland GrooveSynth, 176–178
  RXP REX Player, 185–188
  Session Drummer 3, 192–195
  solo, 170
  SoundFonts, 190–192
  Studio Instruments, 211–215
  TruePianos (Amber Module), 188–189
  unloading synth after freeze, 172
  using Browser to add, 167–168

z3ta+, 209–211
solo
  soft synth, 170
  Solo button (Synth Rack), 170
  Solo Override parameter, 234
  Solo parameter (Console view), 234
Sonitus Surround Compressor, 370–372
Sonitus:fx Compressor effect, 274
Sonitus:fx Delay effect, 259–260
Sonitus:fx Equalizer effect, 256
Sonitus:fx Gate effect, 274–275
Sonitus:fx Modulator effect, 264
Sonitus:fx Multiband effect, 275
Sonitus:fx Phase effect, 292
Sonitus:fx Reverb effect, 266
Sonitus:fx Surround effect, 293–294
Sonitus:fx Wahwah effect, 292–293
Sony Wave64 (W64) format, 434
sorting
  Track Sort function, 88
  tracks, 87–88
Sound Blaster sound card, 190
sound card
  ASIO technology, 4
  basic studio setup, 4–6
  bit resolution, 5
  digital inputs and outputs, 5
  latency, 165
  multiple audio connection capability, 5
  optimal audio settings, 28
  sampling rate, 5
  selection considerations, 4–5
  signal-to-noise ratio and frequency response, 5
  Sound Blaster, 190
  WDM technology, 4
Sound Designer 2 (SD2) format, 434
Sound on Sound mode, 61
SoundFonts, 190–192
sounds, metronome, 57
source code, 420
speaker. *See* monitor
SPECTRAFX demo video, 318
Split Channel to Tracks.CAL program, 416
Split function, 97–98
Split Note to Tracks.CAL program, 417–418
splitting clips, 97–98
splitting notes, 114, 127
Staff view
  adding/drawing notes, 385
  beam rests, 382
  description of, 2, 377–378
  display resolution, 382–383
  durations, filling and trimming, 383
  editing notes, 384
  erasing notes, 385
  fonts, 381–382
  fretboard properties, 394–395
  layout, changing, 379–383
  MIDI track display adjustment, 379–380
  note selection, 383
  opening the, 378
  pedal events and chord grids, showing, 381
  percussion tracks, 380–381
  Pick Tracks feature, 379
  printing music, 398–400
  rhythmic appearance, 382–383
  scrubbing notes, 385–386
  Step Play feature, 385–386
  step recording alternative, 70
  symbols and lyrics, 386–394
  tablature, 395–398
Standard MIDI File (SMF), 416
start time, clip, 92
Step Generator area (Rapture), 204–205
Step Play feature, 385–386
Step Record window, 68–70
step recording, 67–70, 128–129
Step Sequencer view

basic description, 123–124
clips, 129–130
controllers, 128
editing in, 123–130
importing patterns, 73
notes in, 125, 127–128, 1265
opening, 124
setting up, 124–125
simultaneous, 125
step recording alternative, 70
step recording patterns, 128–129
Steps per Beat parameter, 124
stereo to mono, 74
straight replacement, Find/Change feature, 152
strings, Studio Instruments, 215
strip arrangement and selection (Console and Track view), 242
striping, 76
Studio edition *versus* Producer and Essential, 3
Studio Instruments
bass guitar, 213
drum kit, 213–214
electric piano, 214
interface basics, 211–212
MIDI patterns, 212–213
Pattern Grid, 213
program-related tasks, 212
strings, 215
studio setup
audio interface (sound card), 4–6
computer system requirements, 4
control surface, 6
description, 3
microphone, 6–7
MIDI interface, 6
MIDI keyboard controller, 6
speakers (monitors), 7
StudioWare
description, 407–408
panels, 408–409
Record Widget Movements function, 411
recording control movements, 411–412
Snapshot function, 409–410
surround sound, 240
automation, 370
bass management, 363–364
bussing, 364–365
effects, 293–294, 370–374
encoding process, 376
exporting project, 374–376
Large Surround Panner, 368–369
Medium Surround Panner, 367
Micro Sound Panner, 366
mixing, 365–370
monitor calibration, 359–360
monitor setup, 358
panning scenarios, 369–370
preferences, 361
Small Surround Panner, 366–367
studio setup, 357–360
Surround Bridge feature, 373–374
surround format, 361–362
surround sound card output, 362–363
surround sound cards, 357–358
track assignment, 365
Sympathetic Resonance option (TruePianos), 189
synchronization
basics of, 74–75
to drum machine, 74–75
internal, 74
MIDI Sync, 75
SMPTE/MIDI Time Code, 75–77
to tape deck, 75
synth. *See* soft synth
Synth Rack. *See also* soft synth
Freeze/Unfreeze Synth function, 170–172
hidden controls, 168
Mute button, 170

Power On/Off button, 169
Preset parameter, 170
Property Page, 169
Show/Hide Synth Parameter Knobs button, 172
Solo button, 170
synth name and icons, 170
Unload Synths on Disconnect option, 172
system exclusive banks, 38
editing, 406–407
Load Bank feature, 407
Save Bank feature, 407
system exclusive data
receiving, 402–404
record system setting, 402
sending, 404–406
sharing, 407
Sysx view, 401–402
transfer troubleshooting, 403
Sysx view, 401–402

tablature
adding notes via, 397–398
displaying, 395
exporting to text file, 398
regenerating, 397
style, defining, 396–397
Take Lanes feature, 62, 65, 105–106
TAO (Track-at-Once) burning, 354
Tap Tempo button, 134
tape deck, sync to, 75
template, new project
Bank parameter, 36
Input parameter, 37
MIDI Channel parameter, 36
Name parameter, 36
Output parameter, 37
Pan parameter, 37
Patch parameter, 37
track configuration, 35–36
ultimate template setup, 40
Volume parameter, 37
template, track, 90
tempo
changes, editing, 133–134
commands, 134–135
setting the, 39
time range selection, 135
Tempo view
editing in, 133–135
opening the, 133
tempo changes, editing, 133–134
tempo commands, 134–135
Tempo List pane, 134
text event, 132
TH2 Producer effect, 288
Thin Controller Data.CAL program, 418–419
timbre
audio spectrum, 254
vocal formants adjustment, 287
time base, automation, 329–330
time code, 75–77
time range
parameters, 122
tempo, 135
Time Ruler
alignment, 157–158
Clip Follow Project feature, 158
default tempo, finding the, 157
extracting the timing, 157
format, 21, 47
zoom, 85
time, selecting range of data by, 137
time signature, 39
time value
marker, 51
pitch marker, 223–224
timebase, 38

Time/Pitch graph, 281
Time/Pitch Stretch 2 effect, 280–281
timestamp, 45–49
timing effects, 285–287
TL-64 Tube Leveler effect, 289–291
tools
activating, 79–80
switching between, 80
Tools HUD (Heads Up Display), 79–80
Tools module (Control Bar), 79–80
Touch automation mode, 329
track
adding and removing to/from Track Folder, 88
archive, 66
clicking and dragging, 87
cloning, 91
configuration, new project template, 35–36
defined, 1
erasing, 91
hidden tracks in groups, 243
hiding, 91–92
inserting multiple, 90
lanes, 61–62
melodic scale, 110
name, 36
recording multiple, 64
reversing, 145
selection, 87
sorting, 87–88
template, 90
Track Control menu
accessing, 19–20
moving controls, 20–21
uses for, 19
track envelope, 121
Track Folder
adding and removing tracks to and from, 88
creating, 88
editing, 88–89
grouping track parameters in, 89
hiding, 92
notes, 89
Track Icons
creating, 90
loading, 90
settings, 89
showing/hiding, 89
Track Manager, 242–243
track number (Console view), 235
Track pane (Piano Roll view), 109
Track Sort function, 88
Track view
Bank parameter, 36
basic description of, 82
buses, 242
customization, 19–21
description of, 2
editing basics, 82–107
freezing soft synths, 171
hidden tracks in groups, 243
Input parameter, 37
MIDI Channel parameter, 36
Name parameter, 36
Output parameter, 37
Pan parameter, 37
Patch parameter, 37
Project Navigator, 86–87
scrolling in, 83
selecting tracks, 87
sorting tracks, 87–88
strip arrangement and selection, 242
Track Folders, 88–89
Track Icons feature, 89–90
Track Manager, 242–243
Volume parameter, 37
zooming functions, 84–86
transparency, window, 17
Transpose feature, 154, 324

trigger resolution, 227–228
triggering cells and columns, 227–228
trimming durations, 383
TruePianos (Amber Module), 188–189
TS-64 Transient Shaper effect, 278–280
TTS-1. *See* Cakewalk TTS-1
Tube Saturation module, 308–309
tuning, TruePianos, 189
tuplets, 68

Undo function, 101
Undo History feature, 63
UPC (Universal Product Code), 356
user guide, 7
user input, 422
Utilities menu, 12

variable function, 422
velocity
    notes, 119–120, 127
    Pad Groups, 184
    TruePianos, 189
Velocity effect, 324–325
vertical zoom, 85
video file
    exporting, 430–431
    formats, 427
    importing, 427–430
Video Thumbnails pane, 428–429
view
    Console
        audio track strips, 235–238
        basic description of, 231
        bus, number of, 242
        buses, 238–242
        description of, 2–3
        hidden tracks in groups, 243
        mains, 241–242
        meters, changing, 243–245
        MIDI track strips, 232–235
        opening, 231
        recording, 234
        show/hide console components, 243
        strip arrangement and selection, 242
        surround sound bussing, 365
        Track Manager, 242
    docking multiple, 3
    Event List
        description of, 2
        editing events, 131–132
        filtering events, 130
        opening, 130
    Inline Piano, 122–123
    locking, 16
    Loop Construction, 2
    Markers, 52
    Matrix
        automatic matrix track creation, 226
        basic description of, 224
        demo video, 229
        Help file, 229
        importing files, 225
        loading cells, 225–226
        recording performances, 228–229
        row playback control, 227
        triggering cell and column, 227–228
    menu changes, 12
    Piano Roll
        basic description, 107–109
        controllers, 120–122
        description of, 2
        drum tracks, 115–119
        Inline Piano Roll view, 122–123
        multiple track use, 109–110
        opening the, 108–109
        Track pane, 109

track-related functions, 109–110
    working with notes in, 110–115
Staff
    adding/drawing notes, 385
    beam rests, 382
    description of, 2, 377–378
    display resolution, 382–383
    durations, filling and trimming, 383
    editing notes, 384
    erasing notes, 385
    fonts, 381–382
    fretboard properties, 394–395
    layout, changing, 379–383
    MIDI track display adjustment, 379–380
    note selection, 383
    opening the, 378
    pedal events and chord grids, showing, 381
    percussion tracks, 380–381
    Pick Tracks feature, 379
    printing music, 398–400
    rhythmic appearance, 382–383
    scrubbing notes, 385–386
    Step Play feature, 385–386
    symbols and lyrics, 386–394
    tablature, 395–398
Step Sequencer
    basic description, 123–124
    clips, 129–130
    controllers, 128
    editing in, 123–130
    importing patterns, 73
    notes in, 125, 127–128, 1265
    opening, 124
    setting up, 124–125
    simultaneous, 125
    step recording alternative, 70
    step recording patterns, 128–129
strip arrangement and selection, 242
Sysx, 401–402
Tempo
    opening the, 133
    tempo changes, editing, 133–134
    tempo commands, 134–135
    Tempo List pane, 134
Track
    Bank parameter, 36
    basic description of, 82
    buses, 242
    customization, 19–21
    description, 2
    freezing soft synths, 171
    hidden tracks in groups, 243
    Input parameter, 37
    MIDI Channel parameter, 36
    Name parameter, 36
    Output parameter, 37
    Pan parameter, 37
    Patch parameter, 37
    Project Navigator, 86–87
    scrolling in, 83
    selecting tracks, 87
    sorting tracks, 87–88
    strip arrangement and selection, 242
    Track Folders, 88–89
    Track Icons feature, 89–90
    Track Manager, 242–243
    Volume parameter, 37
    zooming functions, 84–86
viewing CAL programs, 419–420
Views menu, 12
Vintage Channel effect (SONAR Producer)
    compressors, 298–299
    De-Esser control, 296–297
    equalizers, 299–300
    Gate control, 296–297
    Master control, 296–297
vocal formants (timbre) adjustment, 287

vocal timing effects, 285–287
volume
    adjusting, 140–144
    Cakewalk TTS-1, 174–175
    silence, getting rid of, 144–145
Volume parameter
    Console view, 235
    Track view, 37
Volume parameter (Console view), 235
VSTi (VST instrument), 163
V-Studio 700 (Cakewalk), 5–6
V-Vocal effects
    artificial vocal effects, 283–284
    automatic vocal pitch adjustment, 283–284
    basics of, 281–283
    clip menu, 281–282
    converting pitch to MIDI, 285
    manual vocal pitch adjustment, 284
    note selection, 284
    snap to pitch, 285
    vocal dynamics (loudness) adjustment,
        286–287
    vocal formants (timbre) adjustment, 287
    vocal timing adjustment, 285–286
    waveform display size, 282
VX-64 Vocal Strip effect (SONAR Producer),
    300–302

W64 (Sony Wave64) format, 434
WAI marker, 235
WAI (Where Am I) feature, 339–340
WAV file, 375–376, 432
waveform, 103
Waveform and Slice Display (RXP REX Player), 186
Waveform Preview feature, 244
WDM (Windows Drivers Model), 4
website
    Cakewalk, 7
    ProAudioTutor, 8
Where Am I (WAI) feature, 339–340
Width parameter (Large Surround Panner), 369
window
    docking, 16
    effects, 248
    locking, 16
    positioning, 15–16
    transparency, 17
    X-Ray Windows feature, 17–18
Window menu, 12
Windows Driver Model (WDM), 4
WMA (Windows Media File), 375–376, 433–435
WMP (Windows Media Player), 428
workspace customization, 11–21
write caching, 29

X-Ray Windows, 17–18

z3ta+
    effects, 210
    program-related tasks, 209–210
zero amplitude, 103
zero axis, 103
zero crossing, 104
zoom
    Auto Zoom feature, 85–86
    Fast Zoom feature, 84–85
    horizontal, 85
    keyboard shortcuts, 87
    level, changing, 84
    meter, 84
    Project Navigator, 86
    redoing zoom action, 84
    Time Ruler zoom, 85
    vertical, 85
    Zoom In button, 84
    Zoom Out button, 84